PIMLICO

66

MEANS OF ASCENT

Robert A. Caro is the author of *The Path to Power*
– the first volume of *The Years of Lyndon Johnson*
and also available in Pimlico – and of *The Power
Broker: Robert Moses and the Fall of New York*. He
has won the Pulitzer Prize, the Francis Parkman
Prize (awarded by the Society of American Historians to the book that 'best represents the
union of the historian and the artist'), the H.L.
Mencken Award, the National Book Critics
Circle Award (for the best non-fiction book
published in 1982), and a number of other
prizes. He is a native of New York City, where
he and his wife now live.

The Years of Lyndon Johnson
Volume 2

MEANS OF ASCENT

ROBERT A. CARO

PIMLICO

PIMLICO

20 Vauxhall Bridge Road, London SW1V 2SA

London Melbourne Sydney Auckland Johannesburg
and agencies throughout the world

First published in Great Britain by The Bodley Head Ltd
1990
Pimlico edition 1992
Reprinted 2003

Printed and bound in Great Britain by
Bookcraft, Bath

ISBN 0-7126-9889-2

For Ina

and

For Katherine Hourigan

Contents

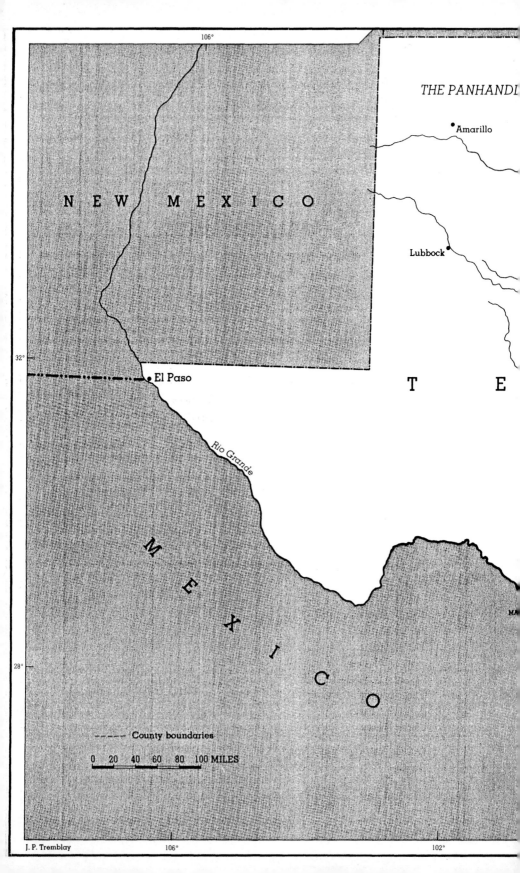

THE PANHANDI

• Amarillo

Lubbock •

N E W   M E X I C O

106°

32°

• El Paso

Rio Grande

T   E

M
E
X
I
C
O

MA

28°

---- County boundaries

0   20   40   60   80 100 MILES

J. P. Tremblay

106°   102°

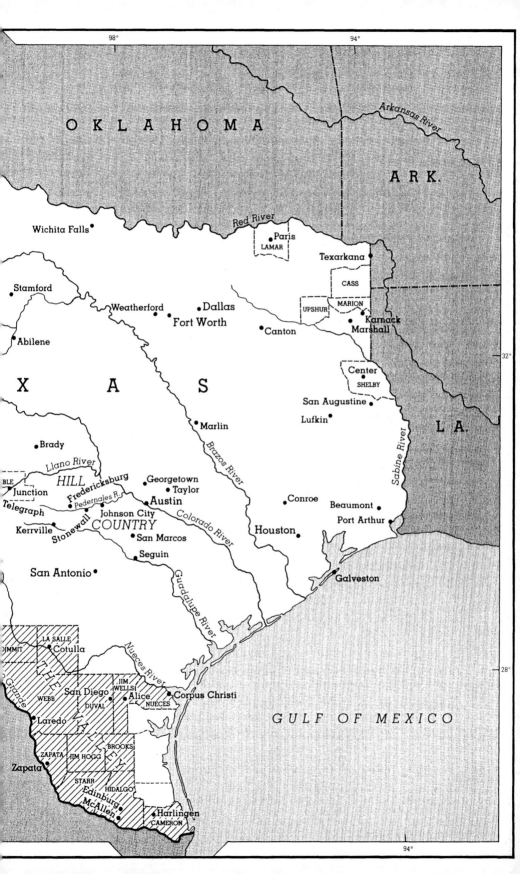

INTRODUCTION

Ends and Means

As THE LONG LINE of limousines began to pull away from the White House in the darkness, the protesters were there, outside the gates, as they had been for weeks. Over their radios they had been listening to the latest bulletins from Selma, and they were singing "We Shall Overcome."

It was a song of defiance—even as a hymn sung in black churches a century earlier it had contained the line "I do not yield"—and of demand: it had emerged from the churches into a broader sphere in October, 1945, during a strike in South Carolina by black women tobacco workers against a company that seemed too strong to be beaten; one day, after months of futile picketing, some of the women, surrendering, dropped off the picket line during a storm and went back to work; the others, to keep their courage up, began to sing in the rain, and suddenly one of them started singing the church song, adding two new lines—"We will win our rights" and "We will overcome." After the strike ended—in victory—the hymn was kept alive (with "will" changed to "shall") because two of the pickets attended a "folk school" in the mountains of Tennessee that had been founded to train labor and civil rights organizers, and taught the students its theme: "We shall overcome / We shall overcome / We shall overcome some day. / Oh, deep in my heart / I do believe / WE SHALL OVERCOME some day." (It was in that school that a new verse was added—during a raid in which local deputy sheriffs forced the students to sit on the floor in the dark for hours while they smashed furniture and windows in a search for "subversive" materials. Sitting in the dark, one of the students, a terrified black high school girl, began to sing: "We are not afraid / We are not afraid / We are not afraid today. . . .") In 1959, a white folk singer from the school taught it to the founding conference of the black Student Nonviolent Coordinating Committee, and led audiences in singing it at other civil rights rallies. Over the years, its tempo had been speeded up, but now the folk singer could feel the black audiences instinctively "tugging at the rhythm," and "I thought I'd better stop playing my banjo and just let them sing"—and as they sang it, they slowed it back down to its original stately, solemn, powerful meter, appropriate to its mighty words.

Nineteen sixty was the year of the first sit-ins to desegregate department store lunch counters in Southern cities. The young, neatly dressed blacks, sworn to nonviolence, sitting on the counter stools were taunted in attempts to make them relinquish their seats. When the taunts failed, mustard and ketchup were poured on them, to mingle with the spit. Then they were pulled off the stools, and knocked to the floor, and kicked and beaten as they lay there. Police arrived, arrested them and flung them into paddy wagons. But they got their breath back, and as the wagons drove off, from their barred windows could be heard: "Deep in my heart / I do believe / We shall overcome some day."

During the next years the hymn was sung at a thousand sit-ins, during a thousand "freedom rides." A new verse, "We'll walk hand in hand," had been added, and that verse inspired a ritual: civil rights workers would cross their arms, and with each hand clasp the hand of the person standing next to them, and sway rhythmically as they sang. As the movement caught the conscience of Northerners, black hands were, more and more, clasping white, and there was another verse: "Black and white together." The hymn was sung in triumph: on August 28, 1963, during the March on Washington which organizers had been afraid would be poorly attended, when the quarter of a million persons who had come to demand justice sent it thundering across the nation's capital—that was the moment when it became the anthem of the civil rights crusade of the 1960s. And it was sung in sorrow: when, eighteen days later, the four little black girls were killed in the bombing of their church in Birmingham, Alabama. As the pallbearers came slowly down the steps of the church, carrying the four small coffins, at first the only sounds from the throng—not only local residents but an astonishingly large number of people who had come from other cities—were sobs. There was no signal, but suddenly, all at once, several people began singing, and over the sobs of mothers rose up the words: "We shall overcome some day."

During the next summer—"Freedom Summer"—it was sung when the college students and the clergymen and the thousands of white men and women volunteers from the North were leaving to go down to Mississippi to try to win for black men and women the right to vote. ("The buses pulled up, and all belongings were piled aboard. But the kids refused to get aboard until we all stood in a large circle alongside one bus and sang 'We Shall Overcome' . . . with arms crossed, holding hands. . . . Then the departing kids got aboard.") After their arrival in Mississippi, the volunteers heard it in unexpected places. "We were sitting on the steps at dusk, watching the sun folding into the flat country. . . . Cotton harvesters went by—and then the sheriff—and then a six-year-old Negro girl with a stick and a dog, kicking up as much dust as she could with her bare feet. As she went by, we could hear her humming to herself, 'We Shall Overcome.' " It was sung that summer on the hot, sweaty nights in Mississippi's black churches, thirty-seven of which were bombed or burned that year. ("Tonight, at our mass meeting, as we were singing 'We Shall Overcome,' a girl was shot in the side and in the chest. We fell to the floor in deadly fear . . .") It was sung by the volunteers when they were being beaten, and Viola Liuzzo was singing it in the moment she was killed. And it sustained them. "I know the drudgery, the dangers and the disappointments," a college student wrote her worried parents. "I know what it's like to be so exhausted you feel as though you will drop. . . . Yet I also know what it's like to sing 'We Shall Overcome' with two hundred others till you think the roof will explode off the church." Wrote another volunteer: "Finally we stood, everyone, crossed arms, clasped hands and sang 'We Shall Overcome.' Ending every meeting of more than a half dozen with it, we sang out all fatigue and fear, each connected by this bond of hands to each other. . . . Together we were an army." Wrote another: "And then [we were] singing our freedom song, 'We shall over-come, we shall overcome . . .' We all joined hands and sang. . . . We sang with all our hearts—'Justice shall be done . . . we shall vote together . . . we shall live in freedom. . . .' "

And now, in March, 1965, the church song that had become the mighty battle hymn of the civil rights crusade had swelled to a new cre-scendo, for March, 1965, was the month of Selma, Alabama—of the Edmund Pettus Bridge and the long line of black men and women and children pledged to nonviolence marching toward the phalanx of troopers in gas masks and helmets, carrying guns and clubs, and, thanks to tele-vision, an entire nation had seen the swirling clouds of the tear gas, and, through the tear gas, the billy clubs swinging, and thudding as they struck, and then the mounted deputies spurring their horses forward and uncoil-ing their bullwhips. An entire nation had heard the screaming begin—and, as loud as the screaming, the cheers from white onlookers. That had been on Sunday, March 7. Two days later, when a club had smashed in his skull, the Reverend James J. Reeb of Boston became the second man killed—Jimmie Lee Jackson had been shot on February 18 in a nearby town—as a result of the Selma demonstrations. "Rarely in history," *Time* magazine reported, "has public opinion reacted so spontaneously and with such fury." That week, when a Jewish synagogue in Boston held a me-morial service for Reeb, the congregation softly hummed "We Shall Over-come" as the rabbi recited the Mourner's Kaddish for the dead. The hymn was sung in Detroit, where the Governor joined the Mayor and ten thou-

sand marchers, and in parades in scores of other Northern cities, and it
was sung in Selma, by hundreds of white clergymen ("Black and white
together / Black and white together / Black and white together some day
. . .") who had come from all across America in answer to Martin Luther
King's call for help. And, of course, it was sung—over and over, all during
that week—in Washington, in front of the White House, for if it was a
hymn of demand and defiance, the demands the civil rights movement was
making could, its leaders felt, ultimately be met only through the power
and the leadership of the President, Lyndon Baines Johnson, who, at the
same time, was a target of their defiance.

During the sixteen months since he had taken the oath of office as
thirty-sixth President of the United States, Lyndon Johnson had done
much for civil rights—including pushing through to passage a civil rights
bill in 1964—but, in the view of most of the movement, he hadn't done
nearly as much as he should have.

What were they asking for, after all, protesters felt, but the most
basic right of citizenship under a constitutional government—the right to
vote? It was ninety-five years since the Fifteenth Amendment to the Constitution had supposedly guaranteed that right, and they still didn't have
it. Of the five million blacks in the South old enough to vote, the overwhelming majority were still not registered. The figures in Selma were
typical for a small Southern town: out of 14,000 whites, 9,300 were registered; out of 15,000 blacks, 325. Despite the President's promises of
progress, little progress was being made. His Justice Department had filed
lawsuits, as had the Justice Department of his predecessor, John F. Kennedy, but the suits had been drifting along at a painfully slow pace. That
very week, as it happened, the protesters outside the White House, leafing
through the *Washington Post*, read that thus far in 1965 three out of every
four blacks who had applied for voter registration in Selma had been
turned down. For months after the passage of the 1964 law, even after its
inadequacies had been demonstrated, President Johnson had let civil
rights leaders know that he didn't think it wise to press for another bill
so soon. Now, with the violence raging in Alabama, Johnson had let them
know he would address a special joint session of Congress on Monday,
March 15, and had promised them that in the address he would submit a
voting-rights bill, a bill that would be stronger, but while some—a growing
number, in fact—of the leaders who had met with the President personally
were telling their colleagues that they believed in Lyndon Johnson's commitment to their cause, this belief was not widespread.

Worst of all, in the view of most civil rights protesters—most dam-
aging proof of the President's lack of sincerity—he wasn't even protecting
the marchers in Alabama. When Jimmie Lee Jackson had been murdered,
Martin Luther King had said, "He was murdered by the timidity of the

federal government that . . . cannot protect the rights of its own citizens seeking the right to vote." Now almost a month had passed since Jackson's death, a month of beatings and savagery—and the federal government, Lyndon Johnson's government, was still not protecting the marchers. Six days had passed now since Reverend Reeb had been killed, and there was still no one to protect the clergymen who had come to take Reeb's place. For almost four months, since the first marches in Selma had begun, black leaders had been pleading with the President to federalize the Alabama National Guard, or to send in regular Army troops—to do *something* to protect the demonstrators from the bullwhips and the clubs. Most of them had felt all along that Johnson wouldn't help; that was why King had called for the clergy. As his assistant Andrew Young had put it: "We didn't think they would send in the National Guard to protect black people. So we sent out a call to people of good will." And indeed Johnson hadn't helped. On Saturday, Alabama's Governor, George C. Wallace, had come to the White House to confer with him, and newspapers were reporting that the President had been very tough with Wallace—but the fact remained: the Alabama Guard was not federalized.

Not only did the protesters distrust his policies, many of them distrusted him. Although some civil rights leaders were now convinced of Lyndon Johnson's good faith, others were not, for they remembered his record—not the short record but the long one. He had been a Congressman, beginning in 1937, for eleven years, and for eleven years he had voted against every civil rights bill—against not only legislation aimed at ending the poll tax and segregation in the armed services but even against legislation aimed at ending lynching: a one hundred percent record. Running for the Senate in 1948, he had assailed President Truman's entire civil rights program ("an effort to set up a police state"). In the Senate, his maiden speech had been the lead-off address in a Southern filibuster against an attempt to impose cloture on debate and thus make passage of civil rights legislation possible. "We of the South," Lyndon Johnson had said, know that "cloture is the deadliest weapon" against the rights of a minority such as the South, and he, he had made clear, was part of that minority. At the conclusion of his eloquent, closely reasoned, ninety-minute-long defense of the filibuster, the Southern Senators, many aging now, had lined up at Lyndon Johnson's desk to congratulate this new recruit to their cause. The first person in line had been the Southerners' patriarch and leader, Richard Brevard Russell of Georgia, who later told reporters that Johnson's speech had been "one of the ablest I ever heard on the subject." Subsequently, the young Senator from Texas had been raised to the leadership of his party in that Senate by the Southern bloc, as the young hope of those aging men in their grim, last-ditch fight to preserve segregation. Until 1957, in the Senate, as in the House, his record—by that time a twenty-year record—against civil rights had been consistent. And although in that year he oversaw the passage of a civil rights bill, many liberals had felt the compromises Johnson had engineered to get the bill through had gutted it of its effectiveness—a feeling that proved correct. And constantly reminding them of Johnson's record, of course, was Johnson's accent, which was the slow drawl of the South; when Lyndon Johnson said "Negroes," for example, it came out, despite all that speech coaches could do, as "Nigroes," close to "niggers." And if, nonetheless, some of the leaders who had recently met with Lyndon Johnson were convinced he had changed, this feeling had not spread to the ranks: no matter how strong his words, most of the marchers outside the White House didn't believe he meant them; in the view of many, his actions— or lack of action—during this past terrible month had *proven* he didn't mean them. If, after years of opposition, he was in alliance with them now, they believed the alliance was reluctant, grudging. Very few of the tens of thousands—hundreds of thousands—of men and women, black and white, in the American civil rights movement believed Lyndon Johnson was wholeheartedly on their side. So now, on Monday, March 15, 1965, pickets had been marching in front of the White House for the eight days since the Edmund Pettus Bridge, walking in a long oval formation along the sidewalk outside the tall black wrought-iron fence that guarded the broad lawn that led to the Executive Mansion, carrying signs demanding that Lyndon Johnson take action, and singing. And the previous day, a Sunday on which churches across the country held services in memory of Reverend Reeb, fifteen thousand protesters had held a rally in Lafayette Park, across Pennsylvania Avenue from the White House, to protest "federal inaction"—Johnson's inaction, ultimately—"in the Alabama racial crisis." The rally ended with the singing of "We Shall Overcome." On the White House lawn, 350 Washington policemen formed a human wall reinforcing the wrought-iron wall, with White House guards and Secret Service men deployed behind them, but the mighty hymn could be heard clearly inside the White House, as could the words of a chant the protesters had adopted: "LBJ, just you wait / See what happens in '68." Speakers at the rally assailed his promises—"President Johnson's words are good, but they remain just that: words," one said—and his performance. His Administration, another speaker said, "has told the same old story in the Selma crisis. The minute there's violence, the Administration announces it's powerless to deal with it." There was little feeling in that crowd that Lyndon Johnson had any deeper commitment to its cause than he had shown in the past, so that the words "We shall overcome," sung outside the White House, were saying, in effect, that the cause would manage to win even without him. And now, on the evening the limousines were pulling away from the White House, the pickets were singing "We Shall Overcome."

Inside the fourth in the line of long, black vehicles that headed for the South gates, away from the pickets, a long double line of motorcycle outriders moving out ahead, Lyndon Johnson sat in the back seat, facing three of his assistants, his huge ears, outsized nose and jutting jaw accentuated by the light from the reading lamp behind him as he bent over a black looseleaf notebook containing the speech he was about to give to Congress. His massive bulk—he was more than six feet three inches tall, and weighed about 230 pounds—and the fierceness of the concentration with which he bent over the notebook and of the way his big hands snatched for the next page while he was still reading the one before it seemed to fill the car. He had entered the limousine without a word of greeting, and had immediately opened the notebook for a last-minute study of the speech. He said not a word during the ride to the Capitol. His eyes didn't look up from the notebook as the limousine passed the White House gates—with the pickets singing "We Shall Overcome" as if to tell him to his face, If you won't help us, we'll win without you. But one of the assistants riding with him had worked for him for almost twenty years, and saw his expression, and knew what it meant. "He heard," Horace Busby recalls.

WITH ALMOST the first words of his speech, the audience—the congressmen and Senators with whom he had served, the Cabinet members he had appointed, the black-robed Justices of the Supreme Court, the Ambassadors of other nations, a few in robes of far-off countries as if to dramatize that the world as well as America was listening, the packed galleries rimming him above—knew that Lyndon Johnson intended to take the cause of civil rights further than it had ever gone before. "At times history and fate meet at a single time in a single place to shape a turning point in man's unending search for freedom," the President said. "So it was at Lexington and Concord. So it was a century ago at Appomattox. So it was last week in Selma, Alabama."

He would submit a new civil rights bill, Johnson said—the Congress would have it before them that week—and it would be far stronger than the bills of the past. The strength of those bills had been diluted by compromise, he said, by compromise and delay; in the case of the last bill, just a year before, by a Southern filibuster which it took liberal forces eight months to overcome. In the minds of many in his audience as he spoke was the fact that he himself, on the previous bills, had often led the forces of compromise. "This time, on this issue," he said now, "there must be no delay, no hesitation and no compromise." But still no one among those Senators, congressmen, Justices, Ambassadors, not even the most perceptive, knew how far he was really going to go—for none of them could have predicted the words to come.

By submitting the bill, Johnson said, he was fulfilling the formal purpose of his appearance before them, but it was not merely a bill that he wanted to talk about. "Even if we pass this bill," the President said, "the battle will not be over. What happened in Selma is part of a far larger movement which reaches into every section and state of America. It is the effort of American Negroes to secure for themselves the full blessings of American life."

There was the briefest pause, as if he were gathering himself, and over his face came a look that the public, thus far in his presidency, had seldom seen, so careful had he been to wear a mask he considered statesmanlike and dignified. The eyes narrowed a little, and the jaw jutted, and the mouth, barely keeping itself from a snarl, hinted at it, and the tens of millions of people watching on television were looking into a face that many of those in the audience in the Capitol knew already—the face of a Lyndon Johnson determined to win.

"Their cause must be our cause, too," Lyndon Johnson said. "Because it is not just Negroes, but really it is all of us, who must overcome the crippling legacy of bigotry and injustice."

Briefly, he paused again. He always had so much trouble in his speeches with the emphasis on the words, but he got it right this time. The next four words fell like sledgehammers.

"And we shall overcome."

There was a moment of silence, as if, one observer was to say, it took a moment for the audience to realize that the President had adopted the rallying cry of black protest as his own, had joined his voice to the voices of the men and women who had sung that mighty hymn. And then the applause rolled across the Chamber.

And there were testimonies to the power of that speech even more eloquent than that applause. One took place in the living room of a local family in Selma, Alabama, where Martin Luther King and several of his aides were watching the speech on television. During all the years of struggle, none of his aides had ever seen Dr. King cry. When Johnson said "We shall overcome," they looked over to their leader to see his reaction. So they were looking when Martin Luther King began to cry.

Another testimony took place on the motorcade's return to the White House. As the limousines slowed to turn into the White House gates, the turn was made in silence.

The pickets were gone.

AFTER HE HAD STEPPED DOWN from the dais and was making his way out through the crowded center aisle of the House, accepting congratulations on his speech from Senators and congressmen who pressed forward to shake his hand, Lyndon Johnson had a few more words to say, to an audience of one: Emanuel Celler, the seventy-six-year-old chairman of the House Judiciary Committee.

While he was shaking Celler's hand, Johnson told him, with a friendly, boyish grin which he had found effective with the older man, that the formal draft of the voting-rights legislation would be ready in no more than two days, but that it would not be necessary for Celler's committee to wait even that long to begin its work on the measure. "Manny," he said, "I want you to start hearings tonight."

"Mr. President," Celler protested, "I can't push that committee or it might get out of hand. I'm scheduling hearings for next week."

In the midst of the crowd, Johnson's eyes narrowed, and his face turned harder. His right hand was still shaking Celler's, but the left hand was up, and a finger was out, pointing, jabbing. "Start them *this* week, Manny," he said. "And hold night sessions, too."

Celler did. In the Senate, the South staged an angry filibuster, but with Johnson using pressure and persuasion (civil rights leader James Farmer, seated in the Oval Office, heard the President "cajoling, threatening, everything else, whatever was necessary"), the bill was passed—its key provisions intact—with remarkable speed. And even before it was passed, the march from Selma to Montgomery had taken place. Segregationists lined the route again, but this time no one dared rush forward to strike a marcher. Standing between the hostile onlookers and the long line of black men and women and children were the FBI agents, and the federal marshals, and the National Guard troops and the regular-Army troops that Lyndon Johnson had sent, to make sure that no one would.

———

ABRAHAM LINCOLN struck off the chains of black Americans, but it was Lyndon Johnson who led them into voting booths, closed democracy's sacred curtain behind them, placed their hands upon the lever that gave them a hold on their own destiny, made them, at last and forever, a true part of American political life. He was to call the passage of the Voting Rights Act of 1965 his "greatest accomplishment," and the speech in which he presented that Act to Congress with the ringing words that touched a nation's conscience was indeed the high-water mark of the tides of social justice in his Administration. And there remain other legislative monuments to the accomplishments of the President who figuratively linked his arms with the arms of civil rights crusaders and clasped their hands in his; during the five years of the Johnson Presidency, great strides were made toward ending discrimination in public accommodations, and strides, if not great at least the first, toward ending discrimination in education, employment, even in private housing. Thurgood Marshall, a black face at last above the black robes of the High Court, through appointment by Lyndon Johnson, was speaking not of his own advancement but of that of his people when he said: "Thank you, Mr. President. You didn't wait for the times. You made them." In other areas of domestic social welfare as well, Johnson rammed to passage laws of which liberals had dreamed for decades: sixty separate education laws for the young and the poor; legislation that provided medical care for the aged and the poor. His "War on Poverty" was not crowned with triumph like his war on prejudice. Many of the laws he rushed through Congress in such unprecedented numbers—in a frenzy of legislation—as if, it sometimes seemed, he equated speed and quantity with accomplishment, were inadequately thought through, flawed, contradictory, not infrequently exacerbating, at immense cost, the evils they were intended to correct. But his very declaration of that war was a reminder—as was his overall concept of a "Great Society"—of government's responsibility to do more than stand idly by without at least attempting to strike blows against ignorance and disease and want. The presidency of Lyndon Johnson marked the legislative realization of many of the liberal aspirations of the twentieth century: in storming, on behalf of those laws, long-held bastions of congressional hostility to social-welfare programs, he used the power of the presidency for purposes as noble as any in American history.

But the fight for social justice was only one aspect of the presidency of Lyndon Johnson. In April, 1965, not a month after his Voting Rights speech, protesters were back outside the White House again. And this time, when they sang "We Shall Overcome," there was a new verse: "We shall live in peace."

Protesters outside the White House—every day, it seemed, month after month, year after year, for all the remaining forty-five months of his Administration. Flags outside the White House, and across Pennsylvania Avenue in Lafayette Park—not American flags but the flags of the enemy. Chants outside the White House: "Ho ho ho, Ho Chi Minh—the NLF is gonna win." Clenched fists against the Washington sky. Little flickers of flame as darkness fell—not the candles of earlier "vigils" for civil rights and peace, but burning draft cards. When civil rights protesters had sung "We Shall Overcome" outside the White House in 1965, they had sung it in defiance and demand, but when the hymn was sung now by protesters against the Vietnam War—sometimes the protesters were the same, so closely intertwined were the civil rights and anti-war movements—there was a new overtone to it, and the overtone was hatred. Before Lyndon Johnson's civil rights speech of March, 1965, the singers had in effect been saying to the President, we'll win even without your help; by 1966 and 1967 and 1968, they were saying, we'll win even though you oppose us. In 1965 Lyndon Johnson had been, in their eyes, a reluctant ally; by the end of his presidency he was the enemy to be overcome—a difference shown more clearly by other songs the protesters sang ("Waist deep in the Big Muddy / And the big fool says to push on. / Waist deep! Neck deep! / And the big fool says to push on") and by the signs they carried ("Hitler Is Alive—in the White House") and by the chants they chanted: "War criminal! War criminal! War criminal!"—and by one chant in particular, a chant that had become the battle cry of the anti-war movement: "Hey! Hey! LBJ! How many kids did you kill today?" New police regulations had recently limited the number of pickets allowed to parade on Pennsylvania Avenue, but there were still enough so that their chant could be heard inside the White House, and Lyndon Johnson heard it—and, of course, since it was being chanted constantly in anti-war rallies and parades across the country, he also heard it as he watched the television newscasts, night after night: "Hey! Hey! LBJ! How many kids did you kill today?" He would never forget it. In his retirement, at his ranch, during the silence of the nights in the lonely Hill Country of Texas, it still rang in his mind. He would sit and talk at the ranch of "young people by the thousands . . . chanting . . . about how many kids I had killed that day." He would talk of them chanting "that horrible song."

The protesters had returned in April, 1965, because that was the month in which the President sent American troops into offensive ground operations against an Asian foe.

When Lyndon Johnson became President, the number of American troops—advisers, not combatants—in Vietnam was 16,000; press coverage was relatively meager and muted; public interest small. And during his campaign, in 1964, for election to the presidency in his own right, Lyndon Johnson had pledged not to widen the war. "Some . . . are eager to enlarge the conflict," he had said during the campaign. There are even "those who say that you ought to go north and drop bombs," he said. But not him, he said. Or, he said, "they call upon us to supply American boys to do the job that Asian boys should do." But, he promised, over and over, "we are not about to send American boys nine or ten thousand miles away from home to do what Asian boys ought to be doing for themselves." Not a month after he took the oath of office following that campaign, the bombers were going north—in a program, "Operation Rolling Thunder," that would be enlarged and enlarged, and enlarged again, with

Johnson personally selecting many of the bombing targets. And in April, 1965, the President sent American boys—40,000 of them—ten thousand miles away, into a land war in the jungles of Asia.

"Lyndon Johnson told the nation / Have no fear of escalation. . . . Though it really isn't war / We're sending 50,000 more." By July, 1965, there were 175,000 men in Vietnam; by August, 219,000; by December, 1966, 385,000. By the time Lyndon Johnson left the presidency, 549,000 American troops were mired in a hopeless jungle war. By the end of 1966, more Americans had died in Vietnam than had been *in* Vietnam when Johnson became President. By the time the war ended, 58,000 Americans had died there; the polished black granite wall in Washington into which their names are chiseled is five hundred feet long. And that Vietnam Memorial wall commemorates the cost of the Vietnam War only in human lives—not in amputation and blindness and scars. The wall in Washington does not bear the names of young Americans wounded in the war. The wall would be far longer were it to bear those names. There are 288,000 of them.

How small a fraction of the cost to America of the episode that history has come to remember simply as "Vietnam" is represented even by these figures, moreover? How many American lives were wrecked in other ways, scarred inside with scars that would never heal? And what of the cost to which President Eisenhower referred when he wrote (in words he struck from his memoirs before publication), "The standing of the United States as the most powerful of the anti-colonial powers is an asset of incalculable value to the Free World. . . . Thus the moral position of the United States was more to be guarded than the Tonkin Delta, indeed than all of Indochina." By the time Lyndon Johnson left the presidency that asset had been squandered; were the American empire to live as long as Rome, would that asset ever be made whole?

And what of another asset, and its squandering?

March, 1965, had been a month of ringing words; April, 1965, was a month of whispers—whispers and lies. Making his decision to commit United States troops to the Asian conflict, Lyndon Johnson had warned participants in a crucial meeting in the White House that there was to be no mention of the new strategy to the press. When the truth crept out, almost two months later—in the words of one typically outraged editorial: "The American people were told by a minor State Department official yesterday that, in effect, they were in a land war on the continent of Asia"—Johnson ordered his aides to deny that such a decision had been made.

That had been one of the first duplicities, but it hadn't been the last. Nor did the duplicities concern only Vietnam. In an attempt to justify sending American troops into another small country, the Dominican Re-

public (in that same month, April, 1965), Lyndon Johnson told the press
and the American people that the American Ambassador had said that
otherwise "American blood will run in the streets." (He hadn't.) He said
that the Ambassador had said that he "was talking to us from under a
desk while bullets were going through his windows." He hadn't. Johnson
said that fifteen hundred innocent people had been murdered, some by
decapitation. They hadn't. He said that the revolution had been taken
over by "a band of Communist conspirators." It hadn't. Nor were the
duplicities confined to foreign affairs. They were present in the President's
discussions of the budget, of politics, of appointments—even of trip schedules. "Distrust of the President," as Theodore H. White put it, "was slow
in growing." But the duplicities continued and multiplied; "thus, men paid
attention to what he said and began to check his statements." And when
they did, they found that the President lied—lied about big matters and
small, lied not only about policy but about personal matters; his most
publicized such misstatement, that his great-grandfather "died at the Alamo," although his great-grandparents had not arrived in Texas until years
after the Alamo had fallen, was only one of many misleading remarks
about his personal history. A new phrase—"Credibility Gap"—entered
American political dialogue. It was printed in headlines, and on buttons,
even on buttons pinned to flak jackets; men who had been sent to Vietnam
on Lyndon Johnson's orders went into action wearing a button—"Ambushed at Credibility Gap"—that called their Commander-in-Chief a liar.

Television made the deceptions more evident, the truth more vivid.
To avoid debate in Congress, debate which might have revealed the scope
and intent of his conduct of the war, troops were raised by increasing the
draft quotas each month administratively, without calling up the reserves;
and the costs of the war were buried, as much as possible, in the Pentagon
budget. But Americans could watch, night after night on the newscasts,
American boys hacking their way through the jungles or reloading in the
tall grass. The viewers would hear the muffled explosions, and the voice-
over would tell them it was mortar fire, and the picture would bounce as
the cameraman ran for cover. Viewers could see what napalm looked like,
as the flames spread out—and they could see what the flames did to human
flesh, to civilians as well as to soldiers. A mood of disillusionment, disillusionment and rage, spread through America, a mood symbolized by
"that horrible song."

"It is difficult today to remember, much less . . . to understand, the
extent to which 'the President'—any President—was then revered, respected, feared," Tom Wicker, who covered the White House for the *New
York Times*, recalled in 1983. In times of foreign crisis, Wicker pointed
out, the last two Presidents before Johnson, right or wrong, had been able
to count on that reverence: Eisenhower after the U-2 incident, Kennedy

despite the Bay of Pigs; Kennedy until the very day he died could be certain of the nation's loyalty, almost fealty, in summit confrontation or missile crisis. And therefore when, in late 1965 or early 1966, while accompanying President Johnson to a speech in New York, Wicker for the first time saw protesters massed behind police barricades shouting, "Hey! Hey! LBJ! How many kids did you kill today?" the journalist says he "could hardly believe my ears."

But that was in 1965 or 1966. By 1968, reporters who followed the President had grown accustomed to the chant—for the chant followed the President, too: by the final year of his term, the only appearances that Lyndon Johnson, elected only four years earlier by the largest popular majority in history, could make without being hounded by pickets were at military bases.

With a note of sadness, Wicker wrote in 1983 that "the reverence, the childlike dependence, the willingness to follow where the President leads, the *trust*, are long gone—gone, surely, with Watergate, but gone before that. . . . After Lyndon Johnson, after the ugly war that consumed him, trust in 'the President' was tarnished forever."

That tarnishing revolutionized politics and government in the United States. The shredding of the delicate yet crucial fabric of credence and faith between the people of the United States and the man they had placed in the White House occurred during the presidency of Lyndon Johnson. Until the day of Kennedy's death—until, in other words, the day Johnson took office—the fabric was whole. By the time Johnson left office, the fabric was in shreds, destroyed by lies and duplicity that went beyond permissible political license, destroyed so thoroughly that Wicker could write that "The tragic irony of Lyndon Johnson is that the lowering of the presidency, not the Great Society of which he dreamed, is his most obvious legacy."

"We Shall Overcome." "Hey! Hey! LBJ!" The War on Poverty. Vietnam. The Great Society. Credibility Gap. The presidency, thirty-sixth in the history of the Republic, of Lyndon Baines Johnson was a watershed presidency, one of the great divides in American history, in the evolution not only of the country's policies both foreign and domestic, but also of its image both in the eyes of the world and in its own eyes. But it was not a triumphant presidency. Beside the bright thread, symbolized by the Voting Rights speech, that gleams through its tangled course runs a thread much darker.

THOSE THREADS, bright and dark, run side by side through most of Lyndon Johnson's life. In the first volume of this biography, a tall, gangling youth, humiliated and ridiculed during an impoverished boyhood in a tiny, isolated Texas Hill Country town that felt like "the end of the earth," earns at twenty-one a reputation as a "wonder kid of politics," and rises with spectacular speed both to a seat in Congress and to a toehold on national power, in his ascent displaying not only a genius for discerning a path to power but an utter ruthlessness in destroying obstacles in that path, and a seemingly bottomless capacity for deceit, deception and betrayal. Once he was in Congress, these traits were accentuated rather than softened—but along with them there was displayed a rare gift for mobilizing the powers of government to raise up the downtrodden. When he was elected—in 1937, at the age of twenty-eight—the two hundred thousand farmers and ranchers of Texas' Tenth Congressional District had no electricity, and, without it, were living a life of terrible drudgery, a life almost as bleak and hard as that of peasants in the Middle Ages. His victory in his long, difficult fight to "bring the lights" to the vast Texas Hill Country carried his constituents into the twentieth century. Johnson had displayed that capacity for compassion, and for the accomplishment that made compassion meaningful, before he was a Congressman, in fact; had displayed it as a twenty-year-old teacher in the "Mexican School" on the wrong—the Mexican—side of the railroad tracks in the desolate South Texas town of Cotulla. No teacher in that school had ever really cared if the Mexican children learned or not. He cared. Believing that speaking the language of their new country was crucial to their success, he insisted that his pupils speak English, spanked the boys and tongue-lashed the girls if they didn't, arrived at the school early and stayed late. And he didn't merely teach. He persuaded a reluctant school board to buy bats and balls and volleyball nets so that, although these children had no lunch, they could at least play games at lunch hour. He arranged activities with other schools—baseball games and track meets like the white kids had. To encourage his students to learn English, he formed a debating team, scheduled debates with other schools, and managed to arrange transportation, since for the Mexican School there was no bus. His coming to Cotulla, one of his students was to recall decades later—"It was like a blessing from a clear sky."

As the story unfolds in succeeding volumes, the threads will, again, run side by side. As Senate Majority Leader during the 1950s, Lyndon Johnson displayed a genius for manipulation and domination for the sake of his ambition, and for power for its own sake—he wrested from the Senate barons power no Leader had ever enjoyed before—but he also displayed a capacity for achievement on behalf of the dispossessed, beginning to pass social-welfare legislation for which liberals had long been yearning. And, of course, during his presidency, in the 1960s, the threads run side by side, darker and brighter than ever.

The two threads do not run side by side in this volume. The bright one is missing. For this volume is about a seven-year period in the life of Lyndon Johnson in which his headlong race for power was halted.

These seven years, the most extended such period in his adult life, begin in July, 1941, after his defeat in his first campaign for the United States Senate. During the next seven years, it appeared that he would never reach the Senate, much less realize the great ambition beyond the Senate of which he always dreamed but almost never spoke. During these years, he lost his toehold on national power. And with the death of his greatest patron, President Franklin D. Roosevelt, he lost even the aura of a White House favorite. For seven years, he appeared doomed to live out his political life as one of the 435 members of the House of Representatives; it seemed that the highest goal he could ever reach would be the chairmanship of a House committee. These were years of hopelessness and despair, seven years in what was for Lyndon Johnson the bleakest possible wilderness: a life without any political power that he considered meaningful. During these years, he came to the very verge of abandoning politics for a full-time business career, of leaving perhaps forever the world that was, in terms of his temperament and training and love, the world he was born to rule. Journalists would later write that Lyndon Johnson's years as Vice President were the worst years of his political life. They wrote that only because they hadn't known Lyndon Johnson during his later years in the House of Representatives.

During these seven years Johnson's lack of interest in the general legislative work of the Congress in which he sat, a lack of interest conspicuous since his earliest days in that body, became increasingly pronounced. And while he had previously done much for his district—had been not only a diligent and energetic but a creative representative—now, with his programs in place and being carried forward by an efficient staff, he implemented no significant new programs. In a state which returned its congressmen to office for decades, there was no realistic chance he would lose his seat, and there was, increasingly, a lack of enthusiasm in his representation of his district. He had been interested, involved in work for the district so long as that work held out the prospect—the imminent prospect—of leading to something more, but his interest waned the moment it appeared that the work might have to be the end in itself. Without the lure of new, greater power, the power he possessed was meaningless to him. Lyndon Johnson's interest in governmental accomplishment will return, dramatically, later. Here, in the years covered by this book, it scarcely exists at all. These seven years are years in which Johnson was all but totally consumed by his need for power, and by his efforts to obtain it. So in this volume can be seen—stark and unadorned—the traits which were later to divide a nation.

THESE YEARS include the genesis of Lyndon Johnson's fortune. He had always wanted money, but so long as the path to political power lay open before him, the other desire had been deferred. Now, with that path closed—perhaps forever—the deferring was over. He grabbed for money as greedily as he had grabbed for power, and his financial rise was as rapid and spectacular as his political rise had been. At the close of the first volume of this biography, Lyndon Johnson had less than a thousand dollars in the bank. By the end of this volume, he is telling intimates that he is worth a million, a substantial fortune at the time.

That growth, too, will continue, as the story continues. When, in 1963, Lyndon Johnson became President, his "family's" assets totaled perhaps $20 million. This son of an impoverished father from the impoverished Texas Hill Country, who for most of his life had no stated sources of income except his governmental salary, entered the Oval Office as possibly the richest man ever to occupy it. But in this volume, in which we see Johnson almost twenty years before he became President, we can focus on the most significant aspect of his accumulation of wealth. The dimensions are small in relation to the wealth to come, and only a single entity—a radio station—is involved, while later that one station will become a radio and television (and banking and land and cattle) empire. So here we can pursue, in detail and without complication, a subject that has been endlessly discussed but little understood, at least partly because of the dearth of detailed information: the role and significance of favoritism and influence in a democratic government. The birth and early years of the Johnson financial empire illuminate very clearly the subtle means by which favoritism and influence are exercised, and their effect on other individuals and on the body politic as a whole.

Throughout Johnson's entire political career, and during the twenty years since it ended, the Johnson fortune has been shrouded in secrecy and surrounded by carefully cultivated myths: that although its foundation—radio and television interests—lay in an industry every aspect of which is regulated by a governmental agency, the Federal Communications Commission, no favoritism or influence was involved; that the fortune was not his at all, but his wife's, seeded by an inheritance she received, and entirely controlled by her; that the fortune had, in fact, grown not because of any participation on his part (in response to inquiries made of him over and over again, over many years, he stated, over and over again, that he played absolutely no role in the business), but solely because of her business expertise and hard work; that although the burgeoning of the Johnson fortune may have been helped by twenty years of favorable FCC decisions, no one was hurt by those decisions. In this volume, the birth and early growth of the Johnson fortune are examined—and, under examination, the myths collapse.

THESE YEARS include the Second World War. Lyndon Johnson's six months in the United States Navy during the war have been treated with derision—as a story of opportunism or even cowardice—by detractors, and with praise—as a story of heroism—by supporters, but the actual story, as will be seen, is too complex for simplifications, and is strikingly revelatory of the violent contradictions in Johnson's character.

AND, FINALLY, these seven years are climaxed by the election which, in 1948, elevated Lyndon Johnson to the United States Senate, ended his seven years of despair, and thrust him back on the road to national power, an election in which almost a million votes were cast and which he won by eighty-seven.

His margin of victory in the 1948 election has been characterized as "the eighty-seven votes that changed history"—and they were. The Johnson Presidency was a watershed in American history, and without that election there would probably have been no Johnson Presidency. But there are additional reasons to examine that election in detail.

Among the many factors that contributed to the evolution of American history during his Administration, Lyndon Johnson's personality and character bore an unusually heavy weight. To understand that history, we have to understand that personality, and nowhere are certain facets of his nature more clearly visible than in the grim struggle of 1948, Lyndon Johnson's last chance for political survival.

During the forty years since it took place, moreover, the election in 1948 for junior United States Senator from Texas has become a small but enduring piece of American political history. When Johnson became President, and a wave of articles attempted to introduce him to the American people, that election was invariably prominent in every retelling of his career. *Life* magazine reminded Americans that an "87-VOTE 'LANDSLIDE' PUT HIM IN SENATE." "THE STORY OF 87 VOTES THAT MADE HISTORY" was a cover story blaring again from newsstands across the country. Years after his presidency, years after his death, that election remains ineradicably linked with his name. As Tom Wicker's 1983 article assessing his "legacy" explained: "Even had there been no war, it would not have been hard to distrust Lyndon Johnson. Hadn't he been elected to the Senate by only eighty-seven votes . . . ?" But the story of the 1948 election has been obscured by question marks; for forty years, Johnson aides and apologists have steadfastly denied that the election was stolen, or have said that even if it was, the theft was only a standard example of ruthless Texas politics. But the fact is that although Lyndon Johnson, largely through the legal genius of his ally Abe Fortas, managed, by a hairbreadth, to halt a federal court's investigation into the stealing of the 1948 election, nonetheless he stole it—and in the stealing violated even the notably loose boundaries of Texas politics. It wasn't eighty-seven votes that Lyndon Johnson stole to win in 1948, but thousands of votes—many thousands, in fact. Thanks in part to a manuscript, relating the details of the theft of the crucial votes, given to the author by the man responsible for the theft; in part to interviews with key figures in the election who had never previously spoken about it in detail; in part to the combining of hundreds of pages of transcripts of court hearings with scores of interviews, a previously bewildering picture comes blindingly clear.

AND THERE ARE yet other reasons for examining the 1948 campaign so closely.

This biography of Lyndon Johnson is intended to be a study not merely of his life but of American history during the years of that life. One of its focuses is the workings of the political power that shapes history, and in a democracy political power comes ultimately not from a gun's barrel or a monarch's manifesto but from a voting booth. Understanding political power in a democracy requires understanding elections. Explore a single individual deeply enough, Emerson noted, and truths about all individuals emerge. This is as true about campaigns as it is about men. Study a particular election in sufficient depth—study not merely the candidates' platforms and philosophies and promises but its payoffs, study it in all its brutality—focus deeply enough on all of these elements, and there will emerge universal truths about campaigns in a democracy, and about the nature of the power that shapes our lives.

Johnson's 1948 campaign is the perfect campaign to study, first of all because of Lyndon Johnson's genius in the art of politics. Election campaigns are the means to political power in a democracy, and in this campaign the means are used by a master—and can therefore be seen at their clearest and most effective. And it is perfect because of the man who was Lyndon Johnson's opponent in it.

Coke Robert Stevenson has been all but lost to history; yet for decades he was (and, indeed, among Texans old enough to remember him, he still is) a legend. He held the governorship of Texas longer than any man before him and was one of the most beloved public figures in the state's history: in one contested Democratic primary, the crucial election in a one-party state, he carried every one of the state's 254 counties, the only candidate for either of the state's two highest offices—Governor or United States Senator—who had ever done so in the history of Texas. But the legend of Coke Stevenson was based less on his political triumphs than on his political principles, which included a deep distaste for "politics" in its meaner sense. He campaigned almost entirely in the style of the Old West, in which a candidate simply drove from one county seat to another, delivering a speech in each to a small audience on the courthouse lawn. Decades after Stevenson's 1944 campaign, in which, against eight opponents, he won the Democratic primary with 84 percent of the vote (still the highest percentage compiled by a gubernatorial candidate in any contested Democratic primary in the history of Texas), a leading historian of the Texas Governorship wrote that that campaign was still unique: "Perhaps no other product of the primary system ever has won, or for that matter, ever will win again, the Democratic nomination with such a minimum of campaigning." The legend was based, moreover, on Stevenson's political philosophy—a fierce, self-taught Jeffersonian Democracy made fiercer by the influence of the harsh Texas frontier; for whether or not that philosophy was suited to a rapidly changing twentieth-century world (and, as his gubernatorial record demonstrated, it had all that philosophy's weaknesses as well as strengths), it possessed a deep emotional appeal to Texans in its uncompromising belief in individual enterprise and self-reliance, in freedom of the individual, in a view of government as a necessary evil at best, and in a near-reverence for the word "conservative." Most of all, Coke Stevenson was a legend because of his remarkable life. Known as the "Cowboy Governor," not only was he a true cowboy, his whole life, it seemed, was a Western epic, right down to the 1948 campaign, when, in an almost incredible confrontation on the main street of a dusty little South Texas town, Stevenson and his old ally, the renowned Texas Ranger Captain Frank Hamer, faced a band of Mexican *pistoleros* who had been ordered to prevent Stevenson from inspecting the disputed ballots that had taken victory from him and given it to his despised foe, Lyndon Johnson. Coke Stevenson was the living personification of frontier individualism, the very embodiment of the myth of the cowboy, a myth that still, today, reverberates through American culture with astonishing power.

BECAUSE OF the personality and philosophy of Lyndon Johnson's opponent, the 1948 campaign provides a unique view of the transformation of American politics in the middle of the twentieth century.

That campaign was the new politics against the old. Johnson was the new politics: electronic politics, technological politics, media politics. He didn't pioneer most of the tactics (except for one tactic, which had astonishing side effects: the use of a helicopter as a campaign device), but he brought some of these still-new devices to a higher level of sophistication, using them to maximum effectiveness. Scientific polling, techniques of organization and of media manipulation—of the use of advertising firms, public relations specialists, media experts from outside the political apparatus, of the use of electronic media (in 1948, radio) not only for speeches but for advertising to influence voters—the mature flowering of all these devices dates, in Texas and the Southwest, from Lyndon Johnson's 1948 campaign.

Stevenson was the old politics: the lone campaigner driving around a vast state speaking to handfuls of voters, no electronic devices to mediate between himself and them. Partly because Texas was changing from a rural to an urban state, mostly because the Johnson campaign demonstrated the effectiveness of the new techniques so convincingly that thereafter all politicians who could afford them adopted them, Coke Stevenson's campaign in 1948 was the last campaign of its type ever waged by a major candidate for a statewide office in Texas. It marked the end of an era in politics.

Furthermore, regardless of its date, the Stevenson campaign was not merely the last of the traditional, pre-media campaigns in Texas, but also as pure an example of that type as can be found. Coke Stevenson was not just the old politics; he was the perfect exemplar of that old politics. He was indeed what the historian called him: "unique." The absolutism of Coke Stevenson's campaigning—the rigidity of his refusal to employ modern political techniques—made the 1948 campaign as complete a contrast between the new and the old as can be imagined. The juxtaposition of opposites throws into bold relief the essential qualities of each. Today, television sound bites and commercials make and break candidates, and substance fades all but completely before the power of image. But the techniques of mass media manipulation are employed by both sides in campaigns, a fact which, despite extensive analysis, blurs understanding of the impact and significance of this manipulation. In the 1948 campaign in Texas these techniques were not employed by both sides. One candidate used them—to an extent unprecedented in the state. The other candidate refused to use them at all. And as a result, we can observe the impact of these techniques with a clarity that illustrates the full force of their destructive effect on the concept of free choice by an informed electorate. By studying this campaign we can, on the other hand, hark back to an era in which public opinion was molded, to an extent hardly imaginable today, not by a candidate's media advisers, but by the candidate.

. . .

THE 1948 CAMPAIGN was not only the new politics against the old, it was
political morality made vivid, as political techniques were made vivid, by
the sharpness in the contrast between the two principals.

The pattern of pragmatism, cynicism and ruthlessness that pervaded
Lyndon Johnson's entire early political career was marked by a lack of
any discernible limits. Pragmatism shaded into the morality of the ballot
box, a morality in which any maneuver is justified by the end of victory—
into a morality that is amorality. In the 1948 campaign, this pattern came
clearer than ever before, in part because of the lengths to which Lyndon
Johnson went in order to win—and in part because of the contrast between
his extreme pragmatism and Coke Stevenson's extreme idealism, which
makes Johnson's methods stand out in the clearest possible relief. The
Johnson-Stevenson campaign was merely an election in a single state for
a single Senate seat—one of hundreds of senatorial elections that have
been held in the United States. But if, upon close study, elections seem
to blur together and to have only meager larger significance, this election
is an exception to that tendency, because of the sharpness in contrast
between the philosophy, principles, strategy and tactics of the two candidates. The clash of such mighty—and violently contrasting—opposites
illuminates not only Lyndon Johnson's path to power but some of the
most fundamental ethical, moral and philosophical issues of American
politics and government in the twentieth century.

That campaign raises, in fact, one of the greatest issues invoked by
the life of Lyndon Baines Johnson: the relationship between means and
ends.

Many of the ends of Lyndon Johnson's life—civil rights in particular,
perhaps, but others, too—were noble: heroic advances in the cause of
social justice. Although those ends are not a part of this volume, those
ends are a part of that life: many liberal dreams might not be reality even
today were it not for Lyndon Johnson.

Those noble ends, however, would not have been possible were it
not for the means, far from noble, which brought Lyndon Johnson to
power. Their attainment would not have been possible without that 1948
campaign.

And what are the implications of that fact? To what extent are ends
inseparable from means?

Of all the questions raised by the life of Lyndon Baines Johnson, no
question is more important than that.

Part I

"TOO SLOW"

1

Going Back

ON JUNE 28, 1941, Lyndon Johnson seemed to have victory—yet another victory—in his grasp.

At the age of thirty-two, he had already won so many victories, and had won them so fast. A tall, lanky, big-eared young man from one of the most remote and impoverished regions of the United States, the Texas Hill Country, a young man with no money and only a third-rate education, by twenty-one he was already known as the "wonder kid" of Texas politics. At twenty-three, a congressman's assistant in Washington, he was the "Boss of the Little Congress," the organization of congressional assistants. At twenty-six, he was the youngest of the forty-eight state directors of the National Youth Administration, perhaps the youngest person ever entrusted with statewide authority for any New Deal program. At twenty-eight, plunging into a race no one believed he could win, he was elected to Congress. Now, at thirty-two, he was not only a Congressman but, having restored centralized financing to his party's congressional campaign and revitalized the moribund Democratic Congressional Campaign Committee with money from Texas oilmen and contractors to which he alone in Washington had access, he was a Congressman with power over other congressmen, national power. And when, in April, 1941, the sudden death of United States Senator Morris Sheppard opened a Senate seat, a paternally beaming Franklin Roosevelt allowed him to announce his candidacy in the ensuing special election from the White House steps, and Washington assumed Lyndon Johnson would be coming back a Senator—the youngest Senator, a Senator at thirty-two, well on the way to that vast ambition beyond the Senate of which he had spoken so frequently in his youth (and on not one recorded occasion since he had embarked on the road to it). All during the 1941 campaign, he assumed so himself. For the first time in his life, as week by week every poll showed him gaining on his leading opponent, Governor W. Lee ("Pappy")

O'Daniel, and then passing him and pulling further and further ahead, he was confident of success—euphoric, in fact. As late as midnight on June 28, Election Day, it appeared that the euphoria was justified.

But on that day, Lyndon Johnson made a mistake.

He hadn't made many, at least not in politics. If a single credo had guided his career, it was a belief that, as he was constantly telling his assistants, "If you do *everything*, you'll win." He was constantly drumming that adage into his aides, and the evidence of his life indicates that he had drummed it into himself. For more than ten years, at every stage of his career, he had done "everything," had worked unceasingly—as one assistant put it, "night and day, weekday and weekend." For more than ten years, in addition, he had planned and schemed and maneuvered, trying to leave no stone unturned, cautious and wary at every step. But that day, after ten years of ceaseless work and ceaseless vigilance—and after ten years of victories—he had relaxed. In the very moment of apparent triumph, he had, for perhaps the only time in his life in a crisis, let his guard down and given his opponents an opening.

Late in the afternoon of Election Day, the corrupt South Texas border bosses whose support he had purchased asked him when they should report the voting results from their counties, and he violated a fundamental rule of Texas politics: report your key precincts—the ones in which you control the result—only at the last minute so your opponent would not know the total he had to beat; otherwise, in a state in which not a few isolated rural precincts were "for sale," beating it would be all too easy. With a steadily widening lead feeding his overconfidence, Johnson had loftily told the South Texas bosses they could report their vote whenever they pleased. They reported immediately, and late that evening, even as headlines were proclaiming his victory and his supporters were parading him on their shoulders in triumph as he whooped and shouted in wild celebration, O'Daniel's strategists were making quiet arrangements. The next day, sitting at a telephone with his face turning ashen at the news, Lyndon Johnson found out that he had not won but lost. After ten years of victories, in this, his most important campaign, there was not victory but defeat.

Now Johnson had to go back to Washington, had to go back not as the youngest Senator, not as perhaps the brightest star in the new galaxy that in 1941 was rising over the political horizon, but as merely the Congressman he had been before. He had had the aura of the winner. Now he was going back a loser. So going back was hard.

And going back was made harder by the unusually powerful hereditary strain, famous in the Texas Hill Country, that ran through Lyndon Johnson's family, the Buntons. Generation after generation, the "Bunton strain" had produced dark-haired men well over six feet tall, all of whom had strikingly similar, and dramatic, features: a long nose that jutted far out of the face, a sharp jaw that jutted almost as far, huge ears with very long lobes. Their eyes, vividly set off by milky, "magnolia white" skin, were so dark a brown that they seemed black, so bright that they glittered, so piercing that they often appeared to be glaring. And the "Bunton eye" was no better known for its fierceness than were the Bunton pride and ambition: the phrases that Hill Country ranchers used about young Lyndon—that something "born in him," bred in him, "demanded" that he always be "in the forefront," "at the head of the ring"—were the same phrases that had been used about his forebears. Buntons possessed also a "commanding presence" and an "eloquent tongue" that led them to try, at an early age, to realize their ambition through politics. Lyndon Johnson, born on August 27, 1908, had been elected to Congress at the age of twenty-eight, the same age at which his grandfather had won *his* first elective office; Johnson's father had won his at twenty-seven. And going back was hard in part because of the poignant circumstances of Lyndon Johnson's youth. When he was thirteen, his father's sudden financial failure had hurled his family, in what seemed like an instant, from a respected position in the isolated little town of Johnson City to what Lyndon was to call "the bottom of the heap." The boy was condemned to live out the remainder of his youth in a continual insecurity that made him dread, month after month, that his family would lose the modest home that was all they possessed. Where once he had been able to charge more in stores than other children, now he could charge nothing at all, and had to stand watching while his friends bought candy because their parents had credit. The boy who, in the words of his favorite cousin, Ava Johnson, who grew up with him and loved him, "had to be the leader in everything he did, just *had* to, just could not *stand* not to be, had to win," was now the son of a man who "owed everybody in town," a member of a family held in contempt. He heard his father's acquaintances whisper as he passed on the street, "He'll never amount to anything. Too much like Sam." And going back was hard because the insecurity and humiliation aggravated the already powerful inherited strain that formed the base of his complex personality: he had to "be somebody," he had to be successful and appear successful; he had to win and be perceived as a winner. It was the interaction of his early humiliation with his heredity that gave his efforts their feverish, almost frantic, intensity, a quality that journalists would describe as "energy" when it was really desperation and fear, the fear of a man fleeing something terrible.

Making the return even harder—much harder—was the fact that he not only had lost, but had allowed victory to be stolen from him.

His brother, Sam Houston Johnson, said, "It was most important to Lyndon not to be like Daddy," and Sam Houston was correct. Their father, Sam Ealy Johnson, was idealistic, romantic, rigidly honest; in wide-open Austin, lobbyists who dispensed the "Three B's" ("beefsteak, bourbon and blondes") liberally to other legislators learned that they couldn't buy Sam Johnson so much as a drink. His colleagues called him "straight as a shingle," and despite this rigidity, he—an idealistic Populist with a remarkable aptitude for legislative maneuvering—compiled an impressive record in championing causes against the "Interests" and for what he called, almost with reverence, "The People." And the respect in which he was held by fellow legislators—decades later, one of them, Wright Patman, by that time a powerful United States Congressman familiar with the nation's most renowned public figures, was to call Sam Ealy Johnson "the best man I ever knew"—was mirrored in the adoring eyes of his son. As a small boy, Lyndon Johnson had tried so hard to imitate his father that people watching him laughed; he had tried to dress like him, right down to a scaled-down version of Sam Johnson's big Stetson hat. He tried to accompany him everywhere—"right by the side of his daddy wherever he went." As a teenager, Lyndon Johnson resembled his tall father not only in appearance—"the same huge ears, the same big nose, the same pale skin and the same dark eyes," recalls Patman, who was to serve with the father in the Legislature and with the son in Congress—but also in mannerisms, most notably in one very distinctive mannerism: when Sam Johnson wanted to persuade a listener of a point, he would drape one long arm around the shoulders of the man he was talking to, with his other hand grasp one of the man's lapels, and lean into him, talking with his face very close to the listener's. "Even as a teenager," Patman was to recall, "Lyndon clutched you like his daddy did when he talked to you." And when his father took Lyndon campaigning—Sam won six terms in the Texas Legislature—driving from farm to farm in a Model T Ford, stopping by the side of the road to share with his son an enormous crust of homemade bread covered with jam while they talked quietly together—that was a time of which Lyndon Johnson was to say, "Christ, sometimes I wished it could go on forever."

But it didn't go on forever. In the Hill Country, ideals and dreams brought disaster when they collided with the inexorable realities of that harsh land. Although, until Lyndon was thirteen, his father was financially successful, business was never what interested Sam Johnson. Texas legislators earned only five dollars a day, and then only on days when the Legislature was in session, but Sam was always available to drive endless miles over rutted roads locating elderly ranchers who didn't know they were entitled to a pension and helping them with their applications, or to lead long campaigns for better roads that would help farmers get their goods to market. His personal fortunes began to decline. And when, on a romantic impulse to make the whole Pedernales Valley "Johnson Country" again, Sam, ignoring the realities of the worn-out soil and the marketplace, paid far too much to buy back the old "Johnson Ranch," he plunged himself, seemingly overnight, into a morass of debt from which there was no hope of escape. Always a little resented by Johnson City because of his "air of confidence" ("the Johnsons could strut sitting down"), and because he preferred discussing ideas and principles of government rather than crops and the weather, Sam refused now to change his manner although he "owed everyone in town," persisted in wearing a jacket and tie instead of work clothes like every other man in Johnson City—and resentment turned to ridicule, ridicule climaxed by a roar of appreciative laughter at a barbecue when a potential political opponent said, "I tell you, ladies and gentlemen, Sam Johnson is a mighty smart man. But he's got no sense." Penniless, doomed to remain in debt until he died, unable to pay his bills in the stores he had to walk past every day, allowed to live in his house only because his brothers guaranteed the mortgage payments, he went to work on a road-grading crew that was building the highway for which he had fought in the Legislature, forced to wear work clothes at last. "He did a lot for that road, all right, Sam did," one man snickers in recollection. Lyndon's mother, also an idealist and romantic, who tried to teach her children that "principles" were the important thing, a delicate woman better educated than most Hill Country women (and less suited to the rough life), was unable to keep her five children neat, or even fed very well, and when she remarked, trying to explain the value of education, "Now is the time to put something in children's heads," the neighbors sneered, "Maybe she ought to try putting something in their stomachs."

The Johnsons became, in fact, the laughingstock of the town. Lyndon Johnson was to spend the rest of his youth in a poverty so severe that often he and his brother and three sisters would have gone hungry were it not for food given as charity by relatives and friends, food seasoned with small-town sneers and cruelty. He had to stand in Courthouse Square and watch his high school sweetheart drive by with another man because her parents would not allow her to date "a Johnson." "I saw how it made Lyndon feel," his cousin Ava says. "And I cried for him. I had to cry for Lyndon a lot." He was to work on the road gang himself, harnessed to a grader like a mule during a burning Hill Country summer and a freezing Hill Country winter. Lyndon's relationship with his father was transformed into one of resentment, tension, blazing clashes of wills, and competition as violent as admiration had once been. And this competition had one dominant theme. After his father's fall, it was terribly important to Lyndon Johnson that no one think that *he* had "no sense," sense as the rough, brutal world of the Hill Country defined the term: "horse sense," common sense, practicality, realism, pragmatism. Not only did he not want to be regarded as an idealist, or as a fighter for causes, he wanted to be regarded as a man who scorned ideals and causes as impractical dreams, as a man practical, pragmatic, tough, cynical. He wanted the world to see him not as merely smart but as shrewd, wily, sly. This was not, perhaps, a reputation that most men would have wanted. But, as Lyndon Johnson's demeanor proclaimed, it was the reputation he wanted, wanted and needed—because of the tears and terrors of his youth needed desperately.

Cultivating and manipulating older men possessed of power that could advance his ambitions, the young Lyndon Johnson employed obsequiousness and flattery so striking that contemporaries mocked him as a "professional son"—but that was no more striking than the openness with which he explained to them in detail his techniques of cultivation and manipulation, and boasted and gloated over his success in bending older men to his will. In both high school and college, he courted the daughter of the richest man in town. Not a few youths do that; few take the trouble that Lyndon Johnson took, in both cases, to make sure that his fellow students realized that the principal basis for the courtship was not love or sex but pragmatism. So widely did he make his motives known that his determination to marry for money became the subject of a joke in his college yearbook.

Each stage of his political climb was marked by perhaps the ultimate manifestation of pragmatism in politics in a democracy: the stealing of elections. At his rural college, where campus politics had always been so casual that the stealing of an election had not even been considered a possibility, he stole elections. On Capitol Hill, he arranged to have the ballot box in elections for the presidency of the Little Congress stuffed with illegal ballots, and then, if even that was not sufficient to give victory to him or his allies, he miscounted the ballots. He did this with an organization that had been only an informal social club of congressional assistants, a group so loosely organized and insignificant that a later president would say, in astonishment: "My God, who would cheat to win the presidency of something like the Little Congress?" He was always secretive about exactly what he had done—no one could ever prove anything against him—but on both College Hill and Capitol Hill, he made sure with winks, hints, his whole bearing, that everyone knew he had done *something;* as one of his college classmates, a friend, puts it, "Everyone knew that something wasn't straight. And everyone knew that if something wasn't straight, it was Lyndon Johnson who had done it." And at every stage—at college, in the Little Congress, in the big Congress—as soon as he was in the inner circle, he took pains to let everyone know he was on the inside, putting his arm around other insiders, whispering in their ear while ostentatiously looking around as if to make sure no one could overhear, strutting to display not only his power but the fact that he had obtained the power by trickery. His attitude proclaimed that if there were any tricks to be played, he would play them, that if any out-smarting was done, it would be he who would be doing it, that no one was going to outsmart *him*.

Until the 1941 Senate race, no one had. He had tried to steal this race, too—striking deals, buying county bosses. And he had, as usual, been unable to refrain from boasting about what he was doing. As always, he not only outsmarted opponents but displayed a deep need to make sure they—and the public—knew he had outsmarted them. But this time, at the last minute, *he* had been outsmarted. He who had stolen elections, who had been confident he had stolen *this* election, had had the election stolen from him instead. He had been cheated of victory—as if he, too, like his father, had been only a man who had "no sense."

So it was hard going back. His wife, who knew how hard it was, says, "I'll never forget the way he looked, walking away to catch the plane to Washington—striding off, looking very jaunty and putting extra verve into his step. It took a lot of effort on his part to act jaunty." That, she says, is "a memory of Lyndon that I will always cherish."

WHAT MADE IT EASIER was that he might not have to go back for long. The election for the full Senate term would be in July, 1942, only a year away, and Johnson intended to run in that election. And about a month after his return to Washington in July, 1941, he learned that if he ran, he would have a good chance of winning—for his great patron was his patron still.

Men who had observed Franklin D. Roosevelt's reaction to other politicians who had lost after he had allowed them to use his name were at first unsure what his reaction would be to a defeated Lyndon Johnson. Johnson himself had observed that after his predecessor as "Roosevelt's man" on the Texas delegation, his fellow Congressman W. D. McFarlane, had been defeated despite Roosevelt's endorsement, not only had he been unable to obtain even a low-level federal appointment, but he was never again allowed into the presence of the President who had once been so genial to him.

But, just as Roosevelt had during Johnson's senatorial campaign re-laxed his customary strictures against campaign assistance in his efforts to help this young man, for whom his aides said he had a "special feeling," so now his reaction to the young man's loss demonstrated that that feeling had not changed. After his defeat, Lyndon Johnson sent a note to Franklin Roosevelt.

Sir:

    In the heat of Texas last week, I said I was glad to be called a water-carrier—that I would be glad to carry a bucket of water to the Commander-in-Chief any time his thirsty throat or his thirsty soul need support, for you certainly gave me support nonpareil.

    One who cannot arise to the leadership shall find the fault in himself and not in you.

Sincerely,
Lyndon

    In the margin of the note, Roosevelt wrote to his appointments secretary, Edwin M. ("Pa") Watson: "General Watson—I want to see Lyndon." When they met, Roosevelt joked with the younger man: "Lyndon," he said, "apparently you Texans haven't learned one of the first things we learned up in New York State, and that is that when the election is over, you have to sit on the ballot boxes." The President had asked aides what he could do to cheer Lyndon up and had accepted a suggestion from Thomas G. ("Tommy the Cork") Corcoran, his political man-of-all-work, that the young Congressman be invited to give a speech immediately preceding the President's at the August national convention of Young Democrats in Lexington, Kentucky, an invitation that would give Johnson his first national exposure. And Corcoran, who was to recall that "in that 1941 race, we gave him everything we could—everything," was able, after checking with the Boss, to tell Johnson that in 1942 the giving would be at the same level.

THE INSTANT RAPPORT that had been struck between Roosevelt and Johnson at their very first meeting—in May, 1937, when the young Congressman-elect had traveled to Galveston to meet the President as he returned from a fishing vacation in the Gulf of Mexico—had gained Johnson admittance to a small circle in Washington, one that had revolved around Tommy the Cork, the stocky, ebullient, accordion-playing political manipulator; it had been Corcoran whom the President had telephoned, upon his return from Texas, to say, "I've just met the most remarkable young man," and to issue an order: "help him with anything you can."

    By 1941, however, with Corcoran's importance at the White House waning, the stars of the circle were Secretary of the Interior Harold L. Ickes and two Supreme Court Justices, Hugo L. Black and William O. Douglas, and it included a group of younger men who, like Johnson, were still in their thirties—men not yet influential in Washington, but who had, most of them, already begun to rise, and were rising faster now: a short, silent young Jewish lawyer from Memphis with olive skin, large, liquid eyes and "the most brilliant legal mind ever to come out of the Yale Law School," Abe Fortas, in 1941 thirty years old, who at Yale Law had caught the eye of Professor Douglas and had been the first man Douglas brought to Washington to assist him at the Securities and Exchange Commission; James H. Rowe, Jr., thirty-two, of Butte, Montana, and Harvard Law, who had caught Corcoran's eye, and then, after Corcoran placed him in a low-level White House job, Roosevelt's; Eliot Janeway, thirty, a Washington-based business writer for *Time, Life* and *Fortune* magazines; and Arthur E. Goldschmidt, thirty-one, known as "Tex," from San Antonio and Columbia University. There was a Southern tinge to the circle. Justice Black, of course, was an Alabamian, and so were two of the circle's most gregarious members, Virginia Durr, Black's sister-in-law, and her husband, Clifford, a lawyer and Rhodes Scholar, as well as their friend W. Ervin ("Red") James, a politically well-connected lawyer from Montgomery. Not only Johnson and Goldschmidt but a one-time Hill Country legislator for whom Johnson had once campaigned in Texas, Welly K. Hopkins, of Seguin, now chief counsel to John L. Lewis's United Mine Workers, and Assistant United States Attorney General Tom C. Clark, of the politically powerful Clark family of Dallas, were from Texas. In January, 1940, Johnson's most trusted adviser, former State Senator Alvin J. Wirtz, was appointed Undersecretary of the Interior. Wirtz was already acquainted with most of the group because of his work as counsel for the Tenth District's Lower Colorado River Authority and his shadowy role in the financing of other power projects, and political campaigns, throughout the West. A big, burly man with a broad, ever-present smile, he possessed a secretiveness concealed behind a carefully cultivated country-boy manner ("Slow in his movements, slow in his speech, but a mind as quick as chain lightning," Hopkins recalls) and a ruthlessness that astonished even hardened Austin political operatives ("He would gut you if he could. But you would never know he did it. . . . He would still be smiling when he slipped in the knife"). His charm ("terribly amusing, delightful," Virginia Durr says) and his avuncular manner ("Soft-voiced, very gentle—if you needed a wise old uncle and could have one appointed, he'd be the one," says Jim Rowe) quickly placed him near the center of the circle. Two of the most prominent members of the circle had, because of the vicissitudes of politics, left Washington, but whenever former National Youth Administrator Aubrey Williams of Alabama and former Congressman Maury Maverick of San Antonio visited the capital, cocktail parties were always arranged in their honor.

These men were bound together by adherence to Roosevelt and the New Deal—and specifically by a single issue, public power, the source of which, the giant hydroelectric power dams being built in the West, was

financed by Ickes' Department of the Interior; Fortas, Goldschmidt and
Benjamin V. Cohen, the other half, with Corcoran, of the New Deal's
fabled "Gold Dust Twins," had once occupied adjoining offices in the
sixth-floor suite of Interior's Division of Public Power. Most members of
the circle were veterans either of the fight for the crucial Public Utilities
Holding Company Act of 1935 and the subsequent skirmishes over ad-
ministering the Act or of the battles to build the huge dams which would
destroy the utilities' monopoly. There were differences among them—
most dramatically over civil rights; those, like the Durrs, who burned for
justice for blacks, were appalled by the attitude of friends like Wirtz, who,
once, when Virginia Durr asked him why he was opposed to giving blacks
the vote, told her flatly, "Look, I like mules, but you don't bring mules
into the parlor." But the public power issue was overriding. Wirtz, Mrs.
Durr was to recall, "wasn't a man of any radical sympathies at all, but he
did believe in government in the water thing."

They saw a lot of each other. The younger ones—the Rowes, Fortases
and Goldschmidts—lived within a block or two of each other in small,
rented houses in the Georgetown section of Washington that had until
recently been a slum but was rapidly being taken over and gentrified by
young New Dealers, and they would often get together in the evening for
informal dinners and back-yard cookouts. On weekends, the parties would
be in the riverfront garden of Hugo and Josephine Black in Alexandria,
or at the Durrs' gracious house on Seminary Hill with the big tree in the
back yard, or the Ickes' farm at Olney, Maryland. Before their return to
Texas to run for the Senate, Lyndon and Lady Bird had been regulars at
these gatherings, and Lyndon would invite the others for Sunday-after-
noon cocktails at the small, one-bedroom apartment he and Lady Bird
had rented in the Kennedy-Warren Apartment House on Connecticut
Avenue.

Johnson in fact had been at the center of this circle, in part for practical, political reasons.* He possessed something these young men needed:
access to Speaker of the House Sam Rayburn. During Johnson's early
years in the House, they had watched in amazement as he leaned over
and kissed the bald head of the Speaker, whose grim mien, fearsome
temper and immense power made most men wary of even approaching
him. And by the time, in 1939, that that entrée had been somewhat curtailed, Johnson had learned the levers of power in the House, and had

---

* Here, and in several other places, I have recapitulated material—including quotations from interviews—from Volume 1, *The Path to Power*, because it seemed to me
necessary to establish the context in which certain events of the present volume take
place. (Among the other places are the descriptions of Lyndon Johnson's early years
in Congress, his relationship with Sam Rayburn, Lady Bird's early years and the Rio
Grande Valley.)

cultivated the friendship of other House leaders. These young men from the executive branch were in constant need of information from the closed, confusing world of Capitol Hill, and Johnson obtained it for them. "I would call and say, 'How do I handle this?' " Rowe remembers. "He would say, 'I'll call you right back.' And he would call back and say, 'This is the fellow you ought to talk to.' " Then, during the 1940 campaign, they, and many Washington political insiders, had suddenly realized that the young Congressman possessed access to another valuable political commodity: cash and checks from those Texas oilmen and contractors for use in the campaigns of other congressmen; he was the conduit—the chief conduit—to sources of campaign financing of which the rest of Washington had barely even been aware.

Rowe, who had been the liaison between the White House and the revitalized Congressional Campaign Committee, had been impressed not merely with the money Johnson raised but with the astuteness with which he doled it out, and with which he handled a hundred other campaign chores from a single, centralized office. "Nobody had ever done this before," Rowe was to say. The members of this little circle were very good at politics; some were already, and some would eventually be, among the master politicians of the age. A master of a profession knows another when he sees him. "Counting" Congress—estimating the votes on bills important to them—was a frequent pastime at their parties. "He was a great counter," Rowe says. "Someone would say, we've got so many votes, and Johnson would say, 'Hell, you're three off. You're counting these three guys, and they're going to vote against you.' " "He was the very best at counting," Fortas says. "He would figure it out—how so-and-so would vote. Who were the swing votes. What, in each case—what, exactly—would swing them." And he was more than a counter. "He knew how things happened, and what made things happen," Fortas says. These men knew they had a much better formal education than he did, but they knew that in the world of politics it was he who was the teacher. Once they were discussing a problem, and what a book said about it, and one of the group said, "Lyndon hasn't read that." "That's all right," someone else replied. "We can tell him what the books say, and then he can tell us how to solve the problem." Money made him important to them in other ways, too; when, for example, Corcoran suddenly found himself out of the White House and looking for clients in his new law practice, Johnson saw to it that he was placed on retainer by Brown & Root, the Texas contracting firm, owned by George and Herman Brown, that had lavishly poured money into his campaigns.

Johnson was at the center of this circle for reasons not merely of politics but of personality. "There was never a dull moment around him," Fortas says. "If Lyndon Johnson was there, a party would be livelier. The moment he walked in the door, it would take fire." Quick wits flashed at these parties, and none flashed quicker than his. Grabbing little Welly Hopkins and pulling him up on a table in a Spanish restaurant to dance an uninhibited "flamenco," arranging elaborate practical jokes that included a surprise sixtieth birthday party that Franklin Roosevelt gave for Sam Rayburn after Johnson had lured him to the White House on the pretext that an angry President wanted to give him a dressing down, trading humorous notes with Fortas over the relative excellence of Texas and Tennessee pecans, organizing get-togethers ("He was a great one for spur-of-the-moment parties," Elizabeth Rowe remembers. "He'd call up and say, 'I'm about to leave the office. Get ol' Jim and come on out.' "), he was, in Mrs. Rowe's word, "fun." "He could take a group of people and just *lift* it up. That's what no one understands about Lyndon Johnson—that he was *fun!*" Women were very aware of him, of his big hands that were always touching shoulders and arms in a friendly manner, of the energy that made them describe him as "handsome" despite the outsized ears and nose, of the vivid contrast between the milky white skin and the piercing dark eyes and heavy, wavy coal-black hair and eyebrows. As for men, when they didn't hear from Johnson for a few days, they missed him. Once, Rowe telephoned Johnson's office "to see," as he wrote him, "if you had fallen in front of a train." "There has been a deadly silence around here for some time," he added. "Miss Gilligan [Rowe's secretary] says it makes this office very dull."

And he was more than fun. He was a dominant figure because of his physical presence—over six feet three inches tall, with long arms and huge hands, that aggressively jutting nose and jaw, and a flashing smile and eyes.

Adding to the dominance was an air of command. He had been giving orders for years now—to his assistants and, before that, to officials of the Texas N.Y.A. He was accustomed to being listened to: he carried himself with authority. And he had, as well, an air of belief. A superb raconteur, he was always ready with the latest inside stories about the great figures of Congress, mimicking them hilariously. And when he talked about two worlds of which his friends knew nothing—the world of Texas politics and vivid figures like Ma and Pa Ferguson, and the world of the Texas Hill Country—he spoke with a passion they never forgot, his voice now soft and confiding, now booming: the voice of a natural storyteller. Bill Douglas, an ardent outdoorsman and no mean conversationalist himself, loved to hold forth about the furies of nature he had witnessed on his Western trips; even Douglas's stories paled when Lyndon Johnson was talking about the rampages of the Pedernales or of Hill Country "gully-washers." And when Johnson spoke about the poverty in the Hill Country—and about what the New Deal's programs meant to his constituents—then, says Elizabeth Rowe, "his belief in what he was fighting for just poured out of him and it was very impressive." As the tall, skinny figure strode awkwardly back and forth in those narrow Georgetown living rooms, with clumsy, lunging strides, awkwardly flailing his arms to emphasize a point, he was, in the words of his friends, "eloquent," "spellbinding."

He was equally eloquent in explaining to these ardent liberals why, although he believed in liberal programs, he quite often didn't vote for them—and almost never fought for them. "I would reproach him very bitterly," Virginia Durr recalls. "Johnson would put his arm around me— Lyndon put his arm around all the girls—and say, 'Honey, I know you're right. I'm for you. . . . But we haven't got the votes.' " He didn't want to be associated with too many lost causes, he made clear. Says Jim Rowe, "Once I was pushing him for something liberal, and . . . he said, 'Just remember our old friend Maury Maverick isn't here any more. Maury got too far ahead of his people, and I'm not going to do that.' " But Johnson's attitude went beyond caution. He ridiculed—intensely and harshly—politicians who fought for ideals and principles. Says Helen Gahagan Douglas, the stunningly beautiful and intelligent actress who became part of the little circle after she was elected to Congress in 1944, but who had been invited to its parties whenever, in the years before that, she came to Washington, "He made fun of those who refused to bend. . . ."

When he was with the other, conservative, side—mostly in Texas, but with ultra-conservative Texas lobbyists in Washington and big businessmen visiting the capital—Johnson was just as eloquent on that side; "He [Johnson] gave the impression of being much, much more liberal than he actually was," conservative lobbyist Dale Miller was able to assure his friends. "He gave a lot more impression of being with the New Deal" than was actually the case. As for the Brown brothers, ultra-reactionaries both, their opinion is expressed by George: "Basically, Lyndon was more conservative, more practical than people understand. You get right down to the nut-cutting, he was practical. He was for the Niggers, he was for labor, he was for the little boys, but by God . . . he was as practical as anyone." Brown—who saw him with both sides since both Corcoran and Wirtz were on his payroll and Fortas was helping Brown & Root obtain a dam authorization (and whenever Brown visited Washington, Johnson made the suave contractor part of the circle)—marveled at Johnson's ability to make liberals think he was one of them and conservatives think he was one of *them*: "That was his leadership, that was his knack," he was to say. The more perceptive of the little circle saw this. "I was never sure whether some of Lyndon Johnson's votes were cast out of conviction or out of judging what Texas politics required," Mrs. Douglas was to write. "It was hard to tell; he never gave any indication. He was willing to make the compromises necessary, I believe, to stay in Con-

gress. . . ." Johnson, she saw, used his homey anecdotes to avoid having
to take stands on issues. "He protected himself by not being serious," she
said. "He was witty, he would tell stories, he was humorous. But . . . he
was loose, so he could go either way. . . . He was always aware that what
he said might be repeated or remembered—even years later. And he
didn't want someone to come back years later and say, 'I remember when
you said. . . .' " Watching him talk so much—and say so little—Mrs.
Douglas began to realize, she says, that Lyndon Johnson was "strong."
In Washington, she says, "everyone tried to find out where you stood.
But he had great inner control. He could talk so much—and no one ever
knew exactly where he stood." Although he talked so much, she says,
"he was one of the most close-mouthed men I ever knew." But these
practical men excused his refusal to be pinned down on issues. "It's a
defensible position in politics," Rowe says. And most of the little circle
were convinced that, at heart, Lyndon Johnson was liberal like them, and
those who believed differently excused him anyway; his refusal to take
stands made those of them who were tied to Lyndon Johnson by ambition
as well as affection feel more certain than ever that he was going far—
and they wanted to go along with him. Before his defeat in 1941, this
young Congressman had become not merely one of this little circle of
remarkable young men on the rise, but its center. Now, back in Washington, he was, despite his defeat, its center again.

THE SUPPORT he needed most in Texas was in place, too. During the
campaign, Johnson had used money on a scale that Texas had never seen,
trying, in the words of local observers, to "buy a state," and much of the
money—hundreds of thousands of dollars—had been generated by one
man, Herman Brown, the ruler of Brown & Root. Through federal contracts, Johnson had made Brown rich, and given him the chance to build
the huge projects of which he had long dreamed, and Brown had ordered
up contributions from dozens of subcontractors on Brown & Root dams
and highways and had, in giving from his own firm's coffers, gone to the
edge of the law and, some Internal Revenue Service agents were later to
contend, over that edge into the realm of fraud in order to finance Lyndon
Johnson's ambition. Brown wanted to make more millions, and to build
projects even huger. Representative Johnson had brought Brown & Root
millions of dollars in profits. What might Senator Johnson be able to do?
Now Herman's younger brother George delivered to Johnson his brother's
pledge: if Lyndon wanted to run in 1942, the money would be available
again—all that was needed.
    One problem was not solved. The mighty Sam Rayburn, Speaker of
the House of Representatives, had been very close to Lyndon and Lady

Bird Johnson. They had learned that his hard, expressionless face concealed tenderness and loneliness, the loneliness of a man who had no wife and children and who was too proud to ever admit he was lonely, who walked the streets of Washington alone on weekends with his face set as if daring someone to speak to him, as if he *wanted* to be alone, who went to few parties because he believed he had no gift for small talk. Rayburn's loneliness was accentuated by his lack of children. He saw in Lady Bird someone as shy as he had once been, and between the fierce Speaker and the timid young woman there grew a love similar to that between a father and daughter; she cooked his favorite foods the way he liked them, and made him, this man who never felt at home in Washington, feel at home. For some years, Rayburn had looked on Lyndon as a son; awakening in the hospital during a serious siege of pneumonia, the young congressional secretary found Rayburn sitting beside him, his vest littered with cigarette ashes from a night of smoking, ashes he had not brushed off because he was afraid that any movement would disturb the younger man. Seeing that Johnson was awake, Rayburn had growled: "Now, Lyndon, don't you worry. If you need anything, just call on me." It was Rayburn, the man who never asked a favor, who begged a favor for Lyndon Johnson, the appointment as Texas NYA director, and thereby gave the congressional secretary the upward boost he needed. And as soon as Johnson won his seat in the House, the Speaker had taken him into its inner circle, *his* circle, even into the sanctuary of sanctuaries, a little hideaway room on the ground floor of the Capitol in which, every afternoon, met Sam Rayburn's "Board of Education," a group of the great House barons—and twenty-eight-year-old Lyndon Johnson. In July, 1939, however, during the eruption of a long-smouldering feud between Roosevelt and Vice President John Nance Garner, Johnson saw his chance to replace Garner as Roosevelt's man in Texas, chief dispenser of patronage and power for the New Deal, and only Rayburn stood in his way. He betrayed the Speaker, fomenting, in concert with Wirtz, a feud between Rayburn and Roosevelt by leading the President to believe, inaccurately, that Rayburn, actually a staunch New Deal supporter, was its secret enemy. How much Rayburn learned about Johnson's role in poisoning the President's mind against him will probably never be known—around his personal feelings Rayburn had erected, decades before, an impenetrable wall—but he evidently learned enough, and for the next fifteen months, he was cold to Lyndon Johnson. Johnson's success in raising funds for the Democratic Congressional Campaign Committee in October, 1940—the fund-raising that had made him a force to be reckoned with by other congressmen—thawed the coldness somewhat, for Rayburn, aware of Johnson's importance in preserving the Democratic majority and thereby keeping him in the Speakership, was a man who always paid his debts. But the thaw did not extend to readmission to the Board of Education; all during 1941, Johnson received no invitation to the ground-floor hideaway. Encountering House parliamentarian Lewis Deschler late one afternoon on the landing of the staircase near the Board Room, he said, almost shouting, "I can get into the White House. Why can't I get into that room?" Nor did the thaw extend to more than perfunctory support for Johnson's Senate race that year; in Rayburn's own congressional district, in fact, Johnson ran very badly. And now, not long after Johnson's return to Washington in July, 1941, Rayburn's true preference became clearer. Another youthful public official of whom the Speaker was fond, Texas Attorney General Gerald Mann, a fiery New Dealer whose hometown was not far from Rayburn's own, had been a favorite in the 1941 race until Johnson entered, and there were those who felt that had Roosevelt not endorsed Johnson, thereby dividing the New Deal vote, Mann, rather than Pappy O'Daniel, would have been the victor in the Senate race. Now there were hints that Mann was Rayburn's preference for the 1942 race. The Rayburn problem was not an insuperable one, however, so long as Roosevelt held firm, and he did. When, in October, 1941, Mann came to Washington, the Speaker attempted to arrange for Roosevelt to meet him, telling Pa Watson that "a short visit with the President would help all [the] way down the line." Roosevelt refused to see Mann. Rayburn insisted, and an appointment was made for Mann's next trip to Washington, in December, but Johnson was quietly assured by Roosevelt's aides that the meeting would not change the President's choice. Other potential candidates— Representative Wright Patman, for example, and former Governor James V. Allred, a liberal and a Roosevelt ally—felt that, with Roosevelt so firm behind Johnson, there was no point in running.

Everything seemed on track for another run. A statewide Johnson campaign organization was being set up. The Brown & Root plane was flying the candidate back and forth between Washington and Texas, and from city to city across the state, as in late October, 1941, he began an unannounced campaign; during a tour of shipyards in Beaumont, the *Beaumont Enterprise* reported, "the central Texas representative whom the President has called 'My good friend' . . . shook hands with more people than the average politician could see in a week." And Johnson could scarcely restrain himself from making the announcement; asked at a private reception in Beaumont if he would run in 1942, he said, "When we have a prize fight" as close as the 1941 race had been, "it's usually considered close enough to call for a return engagement, don't you think?"

There was, however, an interruption in his plans: Pearl Harbor.

2

All Quiet on the Western Front

IN THE OPENING SPEECH of Lyndon Johnson's 1941 campaign, the line that had drawn the most enthusiastic applause was one he delivered after warning of the possibility of war, and of the need for America to be prepared: "If the day ever comes when my vote must be cast to send your boy to the trenches—that day Lyndon Johnson will leave his Senate seat to go with him." Finding as the campaign progressed that that pledge was a surefire crowd-pleaser in patriotic, militaristic Texas, with its glorious history of wars against Mexico and the Comanches, he repeated it day after day, in person and over the radio, on courthouse lawns in small towns and in big-city auditoriums. He played variations on the sentence. He promised that if war came, he would never ask for a desk job in Washington; that when the shooting started he "would be in the front line, in the trenches, in the mud and blood with your boys, helping to do that fighting." He promised that "If Hitler makes this an all-out war, I shall vote in the Senate for war. . . . And when I cast my vote I shall tear up my draft number and join the boys picked to defend our homes and our God and our liberties. I shall never vote for war and then hide behind a Senate seat where bullets cannot reach me." The promise to be "in the trenches" became almost the theme of his campaign. Printed on postcards, under the headline "WE NEED COURAGE LIKE THIS," it was mailed to hundreds of thousands of Texans. Gearing up for the next campaign, he constantly referred to it; when a reporter asked if he would run in the July, 1942, primary, he said, "I may be scrubbing the deck of a battleship by next July." And newspapers kept referring to it, too, friendly newspapers approvingly, hostile newspapers with considerably more skepticism, particularly in the Hill Country, where Lyndon Johnson's boyhood

and college acquaintances recalled instances—notable, in that rough society—of his physical cowardice. When, on October 7, 1941, Johnson
stated that Roosevelt's issuance of his "shoot-on-sight" order—authorizing American warships to fire on German submarines—meant that "the
United States is already in that war," Colonel Alfred Petsch, publisher of
the Hill Country's largest newspaper, the *Fredericksburg Standard*, which
circulated in Johnson's own Pedernales Valley, noted that when the Congressman had originally made his pledge, "a number of persons . . . sar-
castically characterized Mr. Johnson's fighting intentions," and added, in
thinly veiled sarcasm of his own, that it was now time for the pledge to
be redeemed:

> we still believe that Lyndon Johnson meant what he said during
> the campaign. We are confident that by his declaration of "being
> in the front lines, in the mud," he meant just that; and that his
> army service would not find him dressed in shining boots and
> spurs, reclining in an easy chair behind a desk "nowhere near"
> the front. . . .
>   The war being now at hand, according to Mr. Johnson's own
> declaration, his conduct will demonstrate to his critics and de-
> fenders what his campaign promise is worth. . . . So we feel
> certain that Congressman Johnson will soon be an enrollee in the
> United States draft forces. . . . We believe the Congressman will
> live up to his often repeated promises. But of course we may be
> wrong and the Congressman's disparagers may be right. It is up
> to Congressman Lyndon Johnson whether or not he will live up
> to his promise. . . .

Nor was the skepticism confined to the Hill Country. An editorial in the
San Antonio Light asked Johnson to enlist "some time ago."
      "Trenches," of course, had never been a serious possibility, unless
the United States Navy were to drastically alter its methods of operation,
for Johnson had enrolled as a Lieutenant Commander in the Naval Reserve about two years before. But after he had sat in the House on December 8, the day after Pearl Harbor, and heard Roosevelt's "Day of
Infamy" speech—in which the President told the nation, "Today all private plans, all private lives, have been in a sense repealed by the overriding public danger"—he and Warren Magnuson, a fellow member of the
House Naval Affairs Committee who was also a Lieutenant Commander
in the Naval Reserve, went to the office of Admiral Chester Nimitz, a Hill
Country native with whom both Congressmen were acquainted, and had
Nimitz sign forms placing them on active duty. That evening, Johnson

wrote Welly Hopkins, "When you get back to Washington, I may be 'somewhere on the Pacific.' Who can tell?"

One of the two young Lieutenant Commanders did indeed go to the Pacific. When the Navy balked at assigning a Congressman, and one with little training, to a ship heading into combat, Magnuson appealed to Naval Affairs Committee Chairman Carl Vinson, who "requested" that the Navy do so, saying that it would be invaluable to his committee to have a member with actual combat experience. Within a month, Magnuson was at sea, aboard an aircraft carrier that, during his five months on board, was the target of Japanese bombs, torpedoes and shellfire in battles off the Solomon Islands.

Johnson did not go to the Pacific. He went to the White House—to ask for a job in Washington. He took with him a letter requesting "active duty with the fleet," but it was *pro forma:* the subject he wanted to discuss was a proposal he had previously made to merge the National Youth Administration and the Civilian Conservation Corps into a single agency to be known as the Civilian Youth Administration. Now he wanted to make two new proposals to Roosevelt: that the new agency concentrate on wartime training programs, and that he be appointed its director. And when the President, in the midst of a somewhat hectic day, gave him no chance to do anything more than announce that he had gone on active service (the President simply "said he understood and told me goodbye"), Johnson didn't go back to Nimitz for assignment to a ship, or for any other assignment that might lead to combat, but to the office of his good friend and political ally—and substantial contributor to his 1941 Senate campaign—Undersecretary of the Navy James V. Forrestal, for a different type of assignment. In orders which he appears to have virtually drafted himself (a note from Forrestal asks, "Lyndon, how do you want these orders to read?"), the warrior was dispatched to Texas and the West Coast, for an inspection tour of shipyard training programs, and assigned to an office being established in San Francisco by the Navy for liaison with the government of New Zealand. Still lobbying for the Civilian Youth Administration directorship, Johnson didn't leave even for this assignment for another two weeks, during which time he sent Roosevelt a Christmas turkey "as big as a beef" and a note of reminder: "I am very hopeful that we can work out plans for consolidation of our youth agencies in a single agency for defense workers. Today, I'm leaving for the West Coast. When I return I will have a firsthand picture. I hope I may have a chance to put in my nickel's worth before an order is issued." When he did leave, he went with an entourage—his wife, who had brought along a portable typewriter so that she could type his letters; his administrative assistant, John Connally, who had enlisted in the Naval Reserve; and his old college friend and NYA subordinate, Willard Deason, who had been installed in a strategic post with the Bureau of Naval Personnel. And he arranged for billets for his troops in one of Los Angeles' best hotels. On January 2, 1942, he wrote Tom Clark, then an Assistant United States Attorney General in Los Angeles, "Will probably get out to Los Angeles the latter part of next week. . . . Will you put your Jew clothes on and contact Town House Hotel and tell them you have a couple of 'desperadoes' coming in that want a good rate on a double room." Arriving on the West Coast— to be greeted by a note from Roosevelt of thanks for the turkey and not a word about the reminder—the group traveled to shipyards in San Diego and San Francisco, with Lady Bird spending the days visiting "art galleries and all."

Johnson loathed his work with the liaison office; it was, he said later, "a paper-shifting job, placating the Navy and placating the New Zealanders; it was nothing; I had given up my seat in Congress for nothing."

Another reality of naval life was forcefully brought home to him on this trip in an encounter with an Admiral whom he failed to salute— and who called this oversight to his attention in a manner which he would, as President, recall jokingly as "rather memorable." Until that encounter, he was to say, "I did not fully appreciate that my uniform completely concealed my status as a congressman" or "the fact that I looked like any other junior officer and . . . was expected to salute my superiors."

After he was President, Johnson could joke about the encounter; it wasn't a joking matter at the time. Seated on the dais of the Naval Affairs Committee, he had watched Chairman Carl Vinson treat Admirals as if they were cabin boys; in his limited dealings with them, Johnson had himself become accustomed to their deference. In uniform, positions were reversed: Admirals, Captains and full Commanders would be giving him orders, and while in civilian life submission was customarily cloaked in civilities, in the military the reality of who gave orders and who took them was harsh and uncompromising. This was not a reversal he was prepared to tolerate. The woman who had worked alone with him in Richard Kleberg's congressional office, Estelle Harbin, had seen that: "He couldn't stand not being somebody—just could not *stand* it." Not only in Washington but in San Marcos, at college, it had been noticed that Lyndon Johnson could not endure being only one of a crowd; that he needed— with a compelling need—not merely to lead but to dominate, to bend others to his will, not to take orders but to give them. Of his boyhood, in Johnson City, a companion says, "if he couldn't lead, he didn't care much about playing"; this aspect of his personality had been expressed in a particularly striking fashion on the vacant lots where the boys played baseball. The young Lyndon Johnson, although a notably awkward athlete, certainly no pitcher, would give life to a saying usually used only figuratively: during the days of his father's affluence, he would, among those impoverished youths, often possess the only baseball; if he was not allowed to pitch, he would literally take his ball and go home. Now this pattern was repeated. After he had been in California for little more than a week, he asked the Navy–New Zealand Command for permission to "settle a personal problem" and hurriedly returned to Washington, to lobby Roosevelt for a high wartime office. Roosevelt gave him an appointment but no satisfaction. His dealings with Johnson had always been political, and in them the President had been the fox, but Franklin D. Roosevelt was the lion now, and he may have felt that a high administrative post for a young Congressman with administrative experience only as a state director of the National Youth Administration was not appropriate. Johnson did, however, make arrangements that would minimize saluting—and, indeed, any contact at all with Navy officers. He arranged to be relieved of his liaison duties. In the office directly across the hall from Forrestal's was Professor J. W. Barker of Columbia University, who had been named a special assistant in the Navy Department to study labor problems. Johnson met, and charmed, Barker, who asked that Johnson be dispatched, as his assistant, to make another inspection tour of training programs at West Coast shipyards. On January 29, Johnson, again accompanied by John Connally, left on this assignment.

THE HEADLINES that morning said "ENEMY 90 MILES FROM SINGAPORE" and "TWO MORE AMERICAN TANKERS TORPEDOED," and dispatches were reporting grim fighting on Bataan Peninsula in the Philippines and a great naval battle raging in the Macassar Strait. Johnson managed to leave the impression with his wife and staff that active service in a combat zone might be imminent, and Lady Bird believed this.

So did Sam Rayburn. When Johnson had risen in the House to face the unsmiling figure on the triple dais and say, "Mr. Speaker, I ask unanimous consent for an indefinite leave of absence," Rayburn's coldness toward Lyndon Johnson had melted in an instant. And before his first trip to the West Coast, Johnson wrote Rayburn. He was worried about the Speaker's health, he said; he hoped Rayburn would take care of himself. The letter was signed "Just one who respects you and loves you—LBJ." And now, when Lyndon and Lady Bird Johnson and John and Nellie Connally left for Union Station, where the two young men in uniform would board their train, Rayburn went along to see them off, standing silently amid the tumult of the giant concourse jammed with men in uniform going off to war, their women kissing them goodbye.

· · ·

THE NEXT TEN WEEKS were among the most tragic of the war. In the Pacific, the tiny garrisons on Guam and Wake Island were overwhelmed—the remnants of the decimated Pearl Harbor fleet had tried to relieve Wake's defenders but had been turned back—and Singapore fell. The battles of the Java Sea and Sunda Strait were lost, and the Navy reeled from blow after blow. America's eyes were on the Philippines—first on Bataan, where, through almost all those ten weeks, American troops held out in the face of terrible odds, and then on the underground tunnels of Corregidor, where 631 men of the last surviving regiment huddled around shortwave radios, hoping for word of a relief convoy, until they lost hope and stopped listening.

During those ten weeks, Lyndon Johnson and John Connally traveled up and down the West Coast, visiting shipyards in San Diego, Burbank, Los Angeles, San Francisco, Portland and Seattle. "We would go to the shipyards, and meet with Navy Training Officers and with contractors' representatives to discuss installing training programs and show them how to use the training manuals that Dr. Barker had developed," Connally recalls.

And, Connally says, "We had a lot of fun." They traveled by train, two tall, black-haired young Texans, dramatically handsome in their Navy blue and gold uniforms, having the good times of young sailors at war but not at sea. Jesse Kellam, Johnson's one-time subordinate at the Texas NYA and now its director, came out to the Coast to join them, ostensibly to facilitate the inculcation of NYA on-the-job training techniques in the shipyards. Although notably little inculcating was done, there was a lot of partying, and a lot of practical jokes: when Kellam got drunk at a party one evening, Johnson had a photographer fake pictures of Kellam and some girls, and in the morning showed them to Kellam, who pleaded with Johnson not to show them to his wife. On one train trip, with both Johnson and Kellam high, a post-midnight wrestling match got out of hand; Connally was able to break it up only by pouring cold water over them, and then pulling Kellam away from Johnson and locking him out of the compartment. "The next morning," Connally recalls, "we got into Sun Valley, Idaho. Johnson got off—he was in a good mood; his hat was turned up—he was saying good morning to people, and someone replied, It may be good for you, but you kept us up all night." The stops between trips were fun, too—particularly in Los Angeles, where the two officers were supposedly conferring with personnel of a shipyard there but spent considerable time in a more glamorous locale. Edwin Weisl, Sr., the politically powerful New York attorney and organizer of Johnson's northeastern financial support, was counsel for Paramount Pictures, and he flew out to Hollywood and, in Connally's words, "arranged things for us." Johnson and Connally went to screenings and to parties with movie stars, ate in the famous Paramount Cafeteria, where they met Veronica Lake and Alan Ladd and Bonita Granville; Cecil B. DeMille said, "I want to introduce you to the greatest young singer in America" and presented them to Deanna Durbin. Johnson had never been satisfied with the posed photographs of himself that he sent out to constituents by the thousands, and Weisl arranged for long sessions with a Hollywood photographer so Johnson could determine the poses in which he looked best. In an effort to reduce the ungainliness of Johnson's gestures during speeches, the photographer had the Congressman pretend to give a speech and photographed the gestures so Johnson could see them for himself. A voice coach was provided.

To at least one observer, Johnson seemed rather uninterested in the war. Alice Glass, a shade under six feet tall, with creamy skin and long, reddish-blond hair, a woman so spectacular that the noted New York society photographer Arnold Genthe called her "the most beautiful woman I have ever seen," was a small-town girl from Marlin, Texas, who had been installed as mistress of Longlea, an 800-acre estate in the northern Virginia hunt country, by the immensely wealthy publisher of the *Austin American-Statesman*, Charles E. Marsh, by whom she had borne two children. Witty, elegant, hostess of a brilliant table and a sparkling salon of politicians and intellectuals, she possessed a political acumen so keen that the toughest Texas politicians enjoyed talking politics with her; it was Alice Glass who devised the compromise ("Give Herman the dam and let Lyndon have the land") that pulled the Congressman and the ruler of Brown & Root off the collision course that, in 1937, had threatened Johnson's career. Alice Glass had been Lyndon Johnson's mistress for more than three years, in a passionate love affair of which Marsh, patronizing and paternalistic toward the young Congressman, was unaware. (In 1939, the publisher had helped Johnson financially by selling him land in Austin at a giveaway price. In 1940, he offered Johnson an oil deal that would have made him rich; Johnson refused it, because, he said, if the public knew he had oil interests, "it would kill me politically.") Observing Johnson's willingness to sit silently listening to Alice read poetry, knowing the risks he took in being the lover of the consort of a man so vital to his political career—this affair stands out in his life as perhaps the only episode in it that ran counter to his ambitions—the Longlea circle believed that his feelings for Alice were unique, a belief shared by Alice, who had told intimates that she and Johnson had discussed marriage. In that era, a divorced man would be effectively barred from public office, but she said that Lyndon had promised to get divorced anyway and accept one of the several job offers he had received to become a corporate lobbyist in Washington. As a result, she kept fending off marriage proposals from Marsh. "She wouldn't marry Charles after she met Lyndon," her sister, Mary Louise, says. The alacrity with which Johnson leapt into the 1941 Senate race when Morris Sheppard died, however, made her realize that her lover's political ambitions would always take priority, and that divorce was not a realistic hope, and, after the 1941 campaign, she finally agreed to marry the powerful publisher. But, an idealist herself who had first been attracted to Johnson because she felt *he* was an idealist ("a young man who was going to save the world"), she still believed in his idealism, and when, despite her marriage, he asked her to visit him in California, she went. He was, she felt, a young man on his way to fight a war or at least to participate in the war effort.

The contrast between Johnson's activities and the grim battles being reported daily in the newspapers was not lost on Alice, however, and she grew disillusioned. Years later, jokingly suggesting in a letter to a mutual friend, Brown & Root lobbyist Frank C. (Posh) Oltorf, that they collaborate on a book on Johnson, she said, "I can write a very illuminating hapter on his military career in Los Angeles, with photographs, letters rom voice teachers, and photographers who tried to teach him which was the best side of his face." Her sister says that "She was disgusted, just disgusted with him after that trip," although she was still powerfully attracted to him sexually. Alice's closest friend, Welly Hopkins' wife, says simply: "Lyndon was the love of Alice's life." As for Johnson, his feelings for Alice no longer precluded seeing other women.

After Alice returned east, "we had an interesting time up and down the West Coast," Connally says. In every city, the two young officers stayed at the best hotels—the Town House Hotel in Los Angeles, the Del Coronado in San Diego, the Empire in San Francisco. Sometimes the Navy paid; sometimes Alice's husband paid: Charles Marsh had arranged for Johnson to have the use of "due bills" (credits from hotels in payment for advertising) that hotel chains had given his various newspapers. The two young naval officers went on lighthearted shopping expeditions. In San Francisco, in a store owned by a Japanese named Matsomoto, who was about to be interned as an alien, "we bought robes and blouses at just giveaway prices—he followed us out into the street just begging us to buy more," Connally says. Connally purchased a gray silk robe with blue piping that forty years later was still one of his cherished possessions.

DURING THOSE TEN WEEKS, the movements of the Johnson Squadron were cloaked in secrecy. There were strategic reasons for this, of course. Back in December, when Johnson had entered the service, the *Houston Post*, a friendly paper, had noted that by going to the West Coast he had been "placed in line for possible early action against the Japs," but, friendly though the *Post* was, it had been compelled to add, "Of course, if Mr. Johnson should be merely getting himself a safe, warm naval berth for use as a pre-campaign headquarters and [to] cash in on his patriotism, the purpose of his entering the service would become obvious, and the voters would be certain to react accordingly." The *Post*, and voters in his own congressional district in Texas, might not, should they learn the nature and location of his activities as December passed into January, and January into February, March and April, view Sun Valley, Idaho, as the front line for "action against the Japs"; they might even view his job as "a safe, warm naval berth"—they might even "react accordingly." Another strategic reason involved Charles Marsh, who had business interests on the West Coast, and flew there while his wife was with Johnson. Wanting to visit Johnson, Marsh had his secretaries telephone Johnson's office in Washington to ascertain his whereabouts, but since Johnson's secretary, Mary Rather, was able to tell Marsh's secretaries that because of military secrecy, she did not know where Johnson was, the danger of the publisher dropping in unexpectedly on his wife and the young man of whom he was fond was averted.

The secrecy, however, extended also to the Navy. The movements of the two officers appear to have been almost as much of a mystery to their superiors as to the voters. Connally is careful to add to his description of the "fun" they had in California, "in spite of these little incidents, we were really working." Even so, their commanding officer appears to have encountered some difficulty in keeping track of their movements. On February 15, more than two weeks after Johnson had been dispatched to the Coast, Professor Barker was contacted, not by Johnson but by one of Johnson's secretaries in Washington, O. J. Weber, who said he would be forwarding some reports from his boss. "Where is that man?" Barker asked Weber. "Tell him to let me know where he's going to be so I can send him reports, orders, etc. from time to time or we'll get in a jam." When Weber provided Barker with an address at which Johnson could be reached, Barker wrote the Lieutenant Commander, "I'm very glad to know your whereabouts as we have had trouble getting any address to which to send mail. Please keep us advised." Johnson thereupon wrote Barker that "our messages and letters are evidently crossing each other." But the difficulties in communications—always, of course, a problem in a combat zone—continued. When, on March 5, Johnson sent progress reports on various shipyards to his superior, Barker wrote back that he was glad to have them, but added, "I've been wondering how things were progressing" in other assignments Johnson had been given before he left Washington.

One thing at which Johnson *was* working was politics. Every day, not one but several letters from his congressional office would arrive at the Empire Hotel in San Francisco with reports on various district problems—

ranging from appointments to the service academies and rural postmas-
terships to procuring for Austin businessmen priorities that would enable
them to obtain scarce raw materials; moreover, in Texarkana, where
Brown & Root was building a military depot, heavy pressure from the
Office of Price Administration was needed to reduce high rentals,
"which," Weber reported, "is forcing Brown & Root to lose many men
each week." Johnson would write instructions on the handling of each
problem in the margins of the reports, or would reply by letter if his
instructions were detailed. And he and Connally were also wrestling with
the larger political problem. In the first excitement of the outbreak of
war, and Johnson's going on active service, it had been assumed by everyone—including Johnson—that he would certainly not be running for the
Senate nomination in the summer of 1942, and he had promised to support
former Governor James V. Allred, a longtime ally, against Pappy O'Daniel. When Roosevelt had given Allred his blessing, Allred had formally
entered the race. But now, as the May 31 filing deadline drew closer,
although everyone else concerned still felt that Johnson could not possibly
run, Johnson was no longer so certain. The upcoming election would fill
one Texas senatorial seat for six years; the other was held by Tom Connally, re-elected just two years before and as immensely popular as ever.
Johnson felt, John Connally recalls, that "he might not ever have another
chance as good as this." Connally and Wirtz told him—Connally with the
diffidence of a subordinate, Wirtz with the quiet certitude that made him
the "only man Johnson listened to"—that running was not feasible; that,
as Connally recalls, "war fever was extremely high at this time, patriotism
was high, and it would have indicated he was more interested in his political future than the war." But Johnson appears to have been unwilling
to let even a war defer his ambition; he kept trying to find an excuse to
escape from his promise to Allred and to run. Although President Roosevelt made it clear that he wanted the Allred candidacy to go forward as
agreed, so that there would be no split in the liberal vote, Johnson refused
to drop the subject, and he and Connally analyzed the situation from every
angle, day after day—"this went on for weeks," Connally recalls—and
Johnson began quietly maneuvering to be "drafted" for the nomination.

He was also working diligently at obtaining promotion within the
Navy. While he was not reporting often to his superior, Professor Barker,
he was lobbying with Barker's boss, Undersecretary Forrestal, for a job
in which the roles of superior and subordinate would be reversed. And
he wrote to Forrestal's personal aide, Commander John Gingrich:

> All over the place there is in evidence great need of positiveness,
> leadership, and direction. There is much that I should be doing

that I am not. One does not function well without authority and responsibility.

When and if you or the Boss run into a problem that requires energy, determination, and a modicum of experience give me the word. I need more work.

Lady Bird says that the period from January to April of 1942 was "a very frustrating time of high hopes which didn't come to fruition. . . . That [was] a nonproductive few months, and he didn't like it a bit." A "constant stream of letters" was coming back to her, she says, "and after a while I could tell in his letters that there was an increasing frustration and feeling that he wasn't being useful, he wasn't getting the best out of his time. . . . Lyndon had been used to running his own show in Congress—and in the NYA, too."

In fact, her husband's hopes were higher than Lady Bird may have known. He apparently had in mind for himself a post in which he would no longer have to salute Admirals—because he would be an Admiral himself. At least an Admiral. He apparently had in mind a job in which he would be not only an Admiral but in a position to exercise authority over other Admirals. "He wanted something big in Washington, really big," Tommy Corcoran was to recall. "He had everyone working on it for him. Wirtz was working. . . ."

A letter from Wirtz at the time is more specific, and also casts light on Johnson's later contentions that during these months his sole aim was to get into combat. On February 23, 1942, Johnson's most trusted adviser, to whom he had been talking frequently on the telephone, wrote him: "I can appreciate how you feel and how much you would like to have more power to get things done." Wirtz said he had therefore attempted—unsuccessfully—to see Roosevelt and *had* seen presidential aide Pa Watson, and had "suggested that you be made Admiral and given the same comparative job in the Navy that Knudsen has in the Army."

William S. Knudsen had just been named a Lieutenant General and placed in charge of all production for the Army, giving him authority therefore over hundreds of factories producing billions of dollars' worth of war materiel (and over other Generals working on production). Johnson was lobbying to be placed in a similar position over all Navy production, and over the Admirals responsible for it. But Knudsen was a famous production genius, an immigrant's son who had risen from the assembly line to the presidency of General Motors and had thereby been in administrative charge of one of the nation's greatest industrial enterprises. The fact that Lyndon Johnson, who had never directed *any* industrial enterprise (unless one counts the Texas NYA, whose main function was to provide campus jobs for high school and college students), wanted a comparable job shows how lavish was his appraisal of his own abilities.

LOBBY THOUGH HE MIGHT at politics and promotion, however, his lobbying was yielding him nothing. Writing to the White House on March 7, he tendered assurances of his support for Allred, and then added a handwritten note, ostensibly to his friend, Roosevelt's secretary Grace Tully, that he knew she would show to the President:

> Things are very dull here with me. How I yearn for activity and
> an assignment where I can be reasonably productive. I hope
> sometime you run across something that you think I can do well
> 24 hours per day.

But the reply, from Roosevelt himself, contained a paragraph indicating that the President regarded the Allred nomination as all but settled; the only other line was, "I hope all goes well with you. My best wishes to you. As ever . . ."

And as March, the fourth month of war, drew to an end, time was running out for Lyndon Johnson. He had requested a transfer to Pearl Harbor—although what he planned to do there, without any service in or training for the Navy, is unclear. (As it was evidently unclear to his superior; in a letter that month, in which Barker expressed continued exasperation over the communications problem—"I have no address for you"—Barker wrote, "I don't see how we can find an excuse to send you to Hawaii.") Also unclear is the degree of enthusiasm with which Johnson was pursuing this request; if he was asking the White House for help in getting into active service, there exists no evidence of it in Roosevelt's papers, which contain requests from Johnson only for what Corcoran calls "something big" back in Washington. At least two of Johnson's older advisers—the two most aware of his true role in the war effort—now expressed, each in his own way, the feeling that Johnson was not trying hard enough to get into more active service. "Get your ass out of this country at once to where there is danger, and then get back as soon as you can to real work," the arrogant Charles Marsh wrote him. "If you can't sell the Navy on ordering you out, you are not as good as I think you are. . . . It [the work in Washington] may be in Man Power; it may be in running the congressional campaign; it may be in Congress. . . . But for God's sake, get going and quit talking." Alvin Wirtz's advice was, as always, tendered in his calm, courteous manner, but while considerably more understated than Marsh's, it was, in essence, the same advice. After assuring Johnson that he was still trying to get him a post in Washington comparable to Knudsen's, Wirtz added that "I am doubtful whether it would be altogether advisable for you to be called into the White House before summer and before you have some more active service."

The wisdom of Wirtz's advice was becoming clearer every day. Johnson may have felt that an important enough Washington post—one he was, moreover, ordered to take by his Commander-in-Chief in the White House so that he would have no choice but to accept the assignment instead of service in a combat zone—would redeem his campaign pledge to the people of Texas. But no such post had been offered—and what would the voters' reaction be if he left the Navy without ever having seen battle? The *Houston Post* ("if Mr. Johnson should be merely getting himself a safe, warm naval berth . . . the voters would be certain to react accordingly") was a friendly paper; what would the *San Antonio Light* say, or Colonel Petsch, or the none-too-friendly *Dallas News*, should he return to Congress without ever having been "in the trenches" or "on the deck of a battleship"—without, in fact, ever having been anywhere near a combat zone? Johnson's secretaries were continually giving inquiring constituents the impression that while the Congressman was, so far as they knew, at last report, on the Pacific Coast, he was there only en route to a destination thousands of miles farther west—the war zone in the Pacific—and indeed might be there already, for all they knew. But voters went on asking—out of solicitude—where the Congressman was. And on March 13, a minor state official and Pappy O'Daniel supporter, O. P. Lockhart, apparently having learned Johnson's true whereabouts, publicly suggested that if Johnson was going to spend the war on the West Coast, he might as well return to Washington, where at least he would be serving the district; Lockhart called on him either to resign from Congress or to return to it. Rushing out a reply, Wirtz said that "Lyndon Johnson is rendering patriotic and valuable service," but did not specify what it was. Marsh's managing editor, Charles E. Green, chimed in, writing that "government censorship does not permit me to say what Lyndon Johnson is doing. . . . But he's doing a job for his nation. . . ."

How long, however, could the reality of the situation be concealed? Even O. J. Weber was forced to give his boss a warning. In a letter on March 16, Weber wrote: "The matter of your being out of Washington is coming to a showdown and you're going to get caught no matter which way you jump. . . . Even if the President calls you back there will be that element which will say, I told you he wouldn't get in any trenches with the boys. Since the movement to recall members on duty with the armed forces is gathering momentum every day don't you think it is doubly important that you get on a boat and get to Pearl Harbor or some other place like that NOW and as quick as you can?" In another letter, Weber wrote: "We're going to have to have an answer [to voters' inquiries]. Any

way you take it the situation will be embarrassing." Other aides, back in
the district, were similarly warning Johnson that his constituents' curiosity
about his precise whereabouts and duties was rising, and Johnson's reply
to one of these aides, James Blundell, contained a note of defensiveness:
"I am under orders from the Secretary of the Navy, and the Commander-
in-Chief. I don't give the orders but I do take them. Today I am here,
tomorrow I don't know where I will be, but it will be where they think I
can do the most. . . ."

Even more ominously, inquiries were becoming increasingly insistent
from reporters on newspapers all over Texas, not out of suspicion but
simply out of eagerness to do articles about him. Newspapers had reprinted a cryptic message that Warren Magnuson had scribbled from
"somewhere in the Pacific": "Getting it, but am afloat." The Congressman's carrier, part of a task force that had raided Wake Island and the
Solomons, had just finished dodging torpedoes from a Japanese plane
while Japanese bombs rained down. Other congressmen were now in service. (Twenty-seven would eventually serve.) A third member of the
Naval Affairs Committee, Representative Melvin Maas of Minnesota, was
with the Marines in the South Pacific, where he would win, among other
medals, the Silver Star and the Purple Heart. Another Texan, Representative Eugene Worley, had become a Lieutenant Commander in the
Navy, and was in the South Pacific. Representative James Van Zandt of
Pennsylvania, also a Lieutenant Commander, was in the North Atlantic,
on a destroyer escorting convoys through U-boat-infested seas. Having
made during his last campaign a promise similar to Johnson's—to enlist
in the event of war and serve in the front lines—Representative Frank C.
Osmers of New Jersey had redeemed that pledge on the day after Congress had declared war: he had enlisted as a buck private and requested
assignment to a combat unit, with which he would later participate in the
Okinawa and Philippine invasions. Articles were appearing about *these*
congressmen. Still unwilling to abandon his political ambitions, Johnson,
as the months passed, had been unable to decide whether to file for the
Senate seat or for re-election to the House; the filing deadline for both
races was May 31, and no matter which election he selected, the announcement of his filing would focus attention on his war service, attention which, under the present circumstances, might prove disastrous for
either candidacy. If he wasn't going to get "something big" in Washington,
he needed to be in a combat zone when he announced. And there might
not be much time left, for Wirtz had let him know that the order recalling
all congressmen to the House, an order whose issuance would require him
either to resign from Congress or to return without ever having seen combat, was under active consideration at the White House. In desperation,
he headed back to Washington with Connally on April 13. In Washington,

he made no secret of the pragmatism with which he viewed the war, as is revealed by a diary entry made by a new White House aide, Jonathan Daniels, after meeting Johnson for the first time. Johnson, Daniels wrote, "wants for the sake of political future to get into danger zone though realizes talents best suited for handling speakers and public relations." After telling presidential secretary Marvin McIntyre he would wait around Washington as long as necessary to meet with Roosevelt, Johnson was finally given an appointment on Sunday, April 26. Judging from later communications, during this meeting he again sounded out Roosevelt about the Senate race—and the President again declined, this time firmly, to assist him. After a nudge from Forrestal, however, Roosevelt did assist him with his other problem. The President had decided to send a three-man survey team to report on the war effort in the Southwest Pacific. Two Lieutenant Colonels, one representing air forces, the other ground forces, from the War Department General Staff had already been selected. When Forrestal suggested Johnson as the Navy's representative on the survey team, Roosevelt agreed. On April 29 he was ordered to Australia.

On May 1, still unwilling to foreclose a senatorial race, Lyndon Johnson signed two applications, one filing him for that race, the other for re-election to his congressional seat, and told Connally, who would be remaining in Washington, to consult with Wirtz and make a final decision on which seat to file him for. Then, with Mary Rather and O. J. Weber acting as witnesses, he wrote out a will in longhand, leaving all his possessions to his wife, sealed the will in an envelope, and left for San Francisco. (Another envelope was sealed at this time; it was a large manila envelope, on which had been written, "To be opened only by JBC or LBJ." Inside is a leather carrying case containing four photographs, four of the pictures taken by Arnold Genthe of "the most beautiful woman" he had ever seen. Where Johnson placed the envelope at this time is unknown; it would later be kept in one of the locked filing cabinets in the office of his assistant Walter Jenkins, in which Johnson's most secret papers were stored.) On May 7, 1942, five months after Pearl Harbor, Lyndon Johnson boarded a huge PB2Y Coronado Flying Boat for the long flight to Honolulu—on his way across the Pacific to Palmyra, the Fiji Islands, New Caledonia, Australia and the war. He had brought with him at least one political accoutrement—scores of copies of his formal portrait—and waiting for him in Nouméa, capital of New Caledonia, was a brief reminder of politics: a telegram from the White House. Roosevelt apparently was concerned that Johnson might try to circumvent his strictures against a Senate race, and the telegram warned him off. It was signed by presidential secretary McIntyre, who officially spoke only in the names of Rayburn and himself—but Johnson knew whom McIntyre was actually speaking for. MUCH TALK DRAFTING YOU SENATE RACE. SAM AND I

THINK YOU SHOULD WIRE SOMEONE TEXAS YOU WOULD NOT CONSIDER. And when Johnson arrived in Melbourne, Australia, there was another reminder. Charles Marsh had been urging him to run for the Senate, but, Johnson knew, it was not Charles who had the brilliant political mind at Longlea. He had asked Alice for *her* advice, and for a report on the reaction to the suggestion that he be drafted for the race, and on May 31 he received it on the other side of the world: CHARLES BELIEVES YOU SHOULD FILE FOR SENATE. POLLS SHOW YOU LEADING. NO ONE ELSE SHARES HIS OPINION ENTHUSIASTICALLY. IF POSSIBLE, TELEPHONE. LOVE, ALICE MARSH. Whether Lyndon telephoned Alice is not known, but he got through on the telephone to John Connally. Calls from the South Pacific were limited in duration. "It had to be very short," Connally recalls. "He just asked, 'What did you file me for?' 'I filed you for re-election.' 'That's fine.' "

Those were the last reminders of politics. Then Lyndon Johnson headed into a war zone.

3

In the Pacific

IN MELBOURNE, Lieutenant Commander Johnson and his fellow "observers," Lieutenant Colonels Samuel Anderson and Francis R. Stevens, met General Douglas MacArthur, who paced back and forth in front of the maps on his wall as he gave the survey team from Washington an overview of the war in one of his famous *tours d'horizon*. The General's staff had arranged an itinerary for them: first they would inspect major industrial and training sites in the southeastern Australian countryside near Melbourne and then they would head more than a thousand miles north to the bases from which air raids were being flown against Japanese installations in the conquered portion of New Guinea. Recognizing the importance of a Congressman close to the President, the politically astute MacArthur had detailed a blue-ribbon escort team, headed by a Brigadier General, William F. Marquat, to accompany the observers.

The tour was conducted in the shadow of a war that was going badly. While the big Coronado had been crossing the Pacific, the Japanese had been capturing island after island. It was during Johnson's stopover in Hawaii that the first rumors of a great naval battle in the Coral Sea had begun trickling in; by the time he landed in Nouméa the rumors had become reports: of defeat, and of the loss of yet another aircraft carrier, the *Lexington*. With the Japanese now not only on New Guinea but on New Britain and Portuguese Timor, Australia itself was filled with fears of impending invasion—and of impending abandonment by its battered American ally. The lack of equipment was borne home to the three observers when they learned that the plane assigned by MacArthur as their transportation, an early-model B-17 Flying Fortress named *The Swoose*, had been grounded by lack of spare parts; after several days touring the Melbourne area, they were flown north on an ancient Australian airliner, first to Sydney, then to Brisbane, and finally to Townsville, in northern Queensland, for a visit to Garbutt Field, headquarters of the 22nd Bomb

Group. At a final briefing just before they left for Garbutt, they were told that a battle was shaping up at that moment, at a place called "Midway."

WHEN LYNDON JOHNSON arrived at Garbutt Field, on June 6, he found himself in a landscape almost as flat and barren as a desert; the trees were small and stunted, the undergrowth sparse. Amid the trees stood tents— old and frayed—and planes, twelve Martin B-26 Marauders of the 22nd Bomb Group, twin-engined medium bombers much smaller than the four-engine Flying Fortresses he had seen near Melbourne. Not one of the Marauders was unscarred. The three observers walked among them, looking at the blackened marks left by fires, at the small, neat bullet holes, at the gaping punctures caused by shell fire from Japanese guns, at the jagged, gleaming shards of metal that protruded from them. One Marauder, which had evidently been forced to come in with its landing gear retracted, lay tilted on its side, the tip of one wing on the ground, the propeller on that wing bent and blackened by fire. The other wing pointed to the sky; the engine on that wing, jolted loose by the crash, hung down. Around the planes scurried mechanics, frantically trying, with almost no spare parts available, to get them ready again for combat, hammering, welding, threading belts of fresh ammunition into machine guns. Other members of the ground crews were hoisting bombs, slim 100-pounders, big 500-pounders, into open bomb-bay doors. Watching them were crew members. Exhaustion and tension showed on their faces. Their uniforms were ripped and tattered. Some, because their uniforms had worn out and there were no new ones available, had donned Australian shorts, bush hats and cowboy boots. Some wore fresh bandages, stained with blood. Lyndon Johnson may have tried—and, for six months, had succeeded—to avoid being in a combat zone. He may have arrived in one finally only for what Jonathan Daniels had called "the sake of political future." But whatever the reason, Lyndon Johnson was in a combat zone now.

IF ONE CHARACTERISTIC of Lyndon Johnson was a boundless ambition, another was a willingness, on behalf of that ambition, to make efforts that were also without bounds.

As an NYA director to whom "hours made no difference, days made no difference, nights made no difference"; as an unknown twenty-eight-year-old running his first, seemingly hopeless campaign for Congress against seven older, better-known opponents, a race in which he drove himself so ruthlessly that a fellow politician, a man who worked terribly hard himself, said, "I never knew a man could work that hard"; at every stage in his adult life—as Congressman's secretary, Congressman, senatorial candidate—he had displayed a willingness to push to their very edge, and beyond the edge, the limits not only of politics but of himself. In every crisis in his life, he had worked until the weight dropped off his body and his eyes sunk into his head and his face grew gaunt and cavernous and he trembled with fatigue and the rashes on his hands grew raw and angry, and whenever, at the end of one more in a very long line of very long days, he realized that there was still one more task that should be done, he would turn without a word hinting at fatigue to do it, to do it perfectly. His career had been a story of manipulation, deceit, and ruthlessness, but it had also been a story of an intense physical and spiritual striving that was utterly unsparing; he would sacrifice himself to his ambition as ruthlessly as he sacrificed others. If you did *"everything*, you'll win." To Lyndon Johnson, "everything" meant literally that: absolutely anything that was necessary. If some particular effort might help, that effort would be made, no matter how difficult making it might be.

It would be made even if the effort required was the one that was, of all efforts, perhaps the most difficult for him to make.

One prominent aspect of Lyndon Johnson's makeup, particularly notable because of the rough-and-tumble world in which he had been raised, was his attitude toward physical danger, real or imagined. To Johnson City boys, wrestling and fistfights were normal parts of growing up. Lyndon Johnson had displayed a conspicuous hesitancy and timidity at participating in these activities, or at riding an unruly horse or diving from a not very high bank into the Pedernales River—at any of the routine roughhousing of youth. And at college, if a fellow student, antagonized by him, approached him to fight, Johnson would immediately, without a single gesture of resistance, fall back on a bed and kick his feet in the air with a frantic windmilling motion to keep his foe away, while yelling, "If you hit me, I'll kick you! If you hit me, I'll kick you!"—a scene which astonished other students, one of whom says: "Every kid in the State of Texas had fights then, but he wouldn't fight. He was an absolute physical coward."

Whether or not this view, widespread among his fellow students, is correct, certainly Lyndon Johnson had never been casual about his physical well-being; on the contrary, he had always been unusually anxious to avoid even the slightest exposure to violence, danger or risk. Never, in any physical encounter, had he conspicuously displayed courage.

But if courage was needed now, it would be there.

Lyndon Johnson was in a combat zone now, but he was in it only as an observer, not as a combatant. Yet recall by the President was imminent; he was never going to be "in the trenches" or "on a battleship"; this trip as an observer was to be his only direct participation in the war. And if he was never going to be a combatant, if the closest he could get to fulfilling his campaign promise, the only means now left to him of protecting his "political future," was to *see* combat—then he was going to see it.

On the night of his arrival at Garbutt Field, and on the next day, he, Anderson and Stevens talked to the airmen of the 22nd Bomb Group, hearing about the missions they had been flying.

The missions were mostly against the Japanese air base at Lae, on the northeast coast of New Guinea, and Lae was a tough mission. As Martin Caidin and Edward Hymoff report in their 1964 book, *The Mission*, the best available account of Johnson's experiences in the Pacific, just getting to the target was tough. Since, at nine hundred miles from Garbutt Field, Lae was outside the range of a B-26, the Marauders flew first to "Seven-Mile Strip," a primitive little American base hacked out of the New Guinea jungle on the south side of the Owen Stanley Range that towered up to ten thousand feet between it and Lae. The flight from Garbutt Field to "Seven-Mile," as it was called, was over the ocean. The men knew what was in that ocean: as one said, "so many sharks that we could fly low and actually see their fins and bodies cutting through the water." Occasionally, for sport, the machine gunners fired at the fins: then the water would turn red as other sharks tore apart those that had been killed or wounded. Just a week before, a badly hit B-26, returning from Lae, had fallen into the ocean; a Japanese pilot was later to write that he had seen "thirty or forty" sharks swarming around the crew members as they scrambled frantically to get into a life raft. "Suddenly one of them thrust his hand high above his head and disappeared. The others were beating frantically at the water. Then the second man disappeared. I circled lower, and nearly gagged as I saw the flash of teeth which closed on the arm of the third man. The lone survivor, a big bald-headed man, was clinging to the raft with one hand and swinging wildly with a knife in the other. Then he, too, was gone. . . ." After refueling at Seven-Mile, the Marauders took off for Lae—from a runway, surrounded by mountains and jungle, that was too short, that ran up and down a hill, and that was pocked with bomb craters so hastily filled with dirt and stones that sometimes the wheels of the heavily loaded planes would sink into one; just taking off from Seven-Mile, the pilots told the three observers, could be "pretty hairy." And almost as soon as they had taken off, they were over the Owen Stanley. Since a B-26 carried no oxygen equipment, the pilots sometimes attempted to fly through the passes in the rugged range, often during turbulent tropical storms (there were no facilities for forecasting weather), before swinging out over the ocean again—the Solomon Sea, it was called off New Guinea—for the best bombing approach to Lae. Antiaircraft fire over the target was heavy. The young men standing talking with Lyndon Johnson had flown through it so many times that they had given nicknames to various gunners; the most dangerous, they told him, was the one whose bursts followed so hard on one another that they had named him "Rapid Robert." And then there were the Zeroes, which would roar up to meet them, or swoop down on them, out of the sun. Johnson had heard reports that the Japanese fighter planes were less maneuverable than American planes; the American pilots corrected him: the Japanese planes were more maneuverable, they said. And, they told Johnson, the Japanese pilots were *good.* The three observers—the two Lieutenant Colonels and the Congressman in khakis—stood listening as they were told about the bombers that had been shot down, and about the planes that, battered, with one engine gone, had struggled home—over the ocean, and the sharks. The young airmen standing there at Garbutt Field that day, in their bush hats and shorts, had, Anderson was to recall, a "jaunty air," but as Lyndon Johnson talked to them, he was talking with men who were so familiar with death that they had evaluated its relative forms. One pilot described a recent crash in which a B-26, failing to clear the trees, had plowed into them and exploded in a great fireball. When the three observers expressed horror, the pilots told them that they didn't understand: after a crash, an explosion was a blessing, since the men in it died instantly; the alternative was burning to death in the wreckage. But the airmen's matter-of-factness could not conceal the odds against them: two weeks before, six B-25s from another squadron had raided Lae; five of the six had been shot down. Although the exact percentage of American bombers lost on raids against Lae in 1942 is unknown, one estimate is that on a typical raid, between fifteen and twenty-five percent of the planes did not return. The men with whom Lyndon Johnson stood talking among the battered planes of the 22nd Bomb Group were men who were face to face with death every time they took off on a mission. The following morning, their escort, Brigadier General Marquat, told the three observers that the 22nd Bomb Group's next mission against Lae would take place in two days, on June 9. Arrangements had of course been made for Anderson, as the Air Force observer, to fly on the mission, Marquat said, and now Stevens, Anderson's associate in Washington, said he was going also. There was no reason, Marquat made clear, for Commander Johnson to go: he was an observer for the Navy, and the Navy had no connection with this mission. Commander Johnson said he was going too.

AFTER AN EARLY DINNER at Garbutt Field on June 8, Johnson, Anderson and Stevens went to bed. The twelve Marauders had already taken off for Seven-Mile Strip, where they would refuel for the flight to Lae; the three observers were to be picked up at two a.m. by a B-17 that was bringing two Generals and other high-ranking observers to Seven-Mile to watch the Marauders take off.

A message had been sent ahead to the strip's commanding officer, Brigadier General Martin F. Scanlon—as Scanlon recalls it, "that an important Congressman would be arriving." The B-17 got to Seven-Mile late, so that the Marauders—loaded, fueled and ready to go—had to wait on the runways for the planeload of officers to land. But from the moment Lyndon Johnson stepped off the B-17 onto that rough little airstrip in the jungle, wearing khaki pants and shirt, a bulky, dark-blue Navy jacket without sleeves and his uniform cap, and, with a broad smile, shook hands with General Scanlon, he put everyone at their ease. "Affable, nice . . . doing a job and making very little fuss about it," was how Scanlon was to remember him. Introduced to Lieutenant Willis G. Bench, on whose B-26, the *Wabash Cannonball*, he had been assigned to fly, he shook hands and was led to his seat on the plane. Crouched over—there wasn't space enough in the Marauders for a man six-feet-three-inches tall to stand erect—he climbed into a narrow compartment behind the cockpit.

There was a further short delay before takeoff. During it, Johnson stepped off the *Wabash Cannonball* and walked away to urinate. Climbing back into the plane, he discovered that his seat had been taken by Colonel Stevens. Johnson was later to recall that he had told Stevens that he had been on the plane first, but Stevens, he said, "just grinned" and told him to "find another plane." Shrugging, Johnson got off the *Cannonball*—he left behind his movie camera and film—and walked over to another B-26, the *Heckling Hare*. Standing under the painted caricature on its fuselage— of a rabbit dropping bombs from a flying carpet—he asked the *Heckling Hare*'s pilot, Lieutenant Walter H. Greer, if he could ride on his plane. When Greer agreed, the tall man in the Lieutenant Commander's cap turned to the six other members of the bomber's crew and said he would like their permission, too, and when they gave it, he displayed during the several remaining minutes before takeoff "the amazing talent for meeting and greeting," for striking up instant friendships and intimacy, that had been astonishing people all his life. Sergeant Claude McCredie, the bombardier, was setting bomb fuses in the bomb bay, one of the last actions before takeoff, and Johnson started to ask him questions. "I was startled at the questions," McCredie was to say. "We've had the 'wheels' that came poking around before, but it was more effect than anything else. You can tell at once if a man really is interested. . . ." Then Johnson approached the tail-gunner, Corporal Harry Baren, and asked him his name. "We started to kibitz around," Baren said. "The moment you started talking to him, you liked the guy." Liked him so much, in fact, that "it suddenly dawned on me that this guy was really going along to Lae with us"—and Baren warned him of what was coming. "You're out of your goddam mind," he said. Baren and McCredie, who was listening, both recall the Corporal saying, "This ain't no milk run, believe me! You don't need to come along and get shot up to find out about conditions here, or the things we need: we'll *tell* you that. . . ." Johnson, Baren and McCredie were to recall, explained that "he had come to the Pacific to find out for himself what conditions were, and that the only way a man could ever know what things were like was to go out and see them with his own eyes, and to experience it for himself." And when Baren again "told him just how rough it was up there . . . all he did was grin." He kidded with the crew until the Marauders' engines, which had been idling, began to thunder, and Greer shouted down to his crew to board the plane. Donning a parachute—the harness had been adjusted for a shorter man, and there was no time to change it, so Johnson couldn't stand erect, but once inside the plane, he had to hunch over anyway—Johnson climbed into the cramped fuselage and sat down in a small cubicle on the right side of the plane just behind the cockpit. Across the narrow passageway, on the left side of the plane, was a small window. A clear plastic bubble, the "navigator's dome," was above him. If he stood on a stool, he would be able to look out the dome across the top of the plane.

Lyndon Johnson sat, seat belt on, parachute and harness bending him forward, as the *Heckling Hare* jounced down the bumpy runway and then laboriously groaned its way into the air with its heavy bomb load. The plane kept climbing—the squadron had to get over the Owen Stanley Range—and for a while, at fourteen thousand feet, the air was thin, but he had been warned that this would happen, and had been told that it wouldn't last long. The twelve B-26s divided into three formations, each formation a staggered V shape of four bombers; the *Heckling Hare* was in the third position in the last V. They flew for about an hour. Then they were nearing the target. In front of them, the first two formations were settling into their bombing runs, and then suddenly Captain Greer alerted his gunners: there were Zeroes ahead—ahead and above them. And then, without warning, the *Heckling Hare* staggered, and all at once Johnson could feel the plane slow down and begin to lose altitude; the generator that controlled the right engine had failed. Immediately, the plane began to drop behind the formation, and the *Heckling Hare* turned to head home. And then, in McCredie's words, "All hell broke loose."

A lone Zero was bearing in on them, charging across the sky. Bullets were smashing into the plane, and cannon shells were bursting against it, like shotguns being fired right beside your ear. The plane began skidding across the sky, diving wildly, trying to climb, diving again, then swerving, weaving, as Greer frantically jerked it through the air. Somewhere in those first few moments the pilot jettisoned the bombs to lighten the plane. "Here he comes!" someone screamed, and the Zero, which for a moment had overshot them because of Greer's maneuvering, was boring in again, and again the B-26 shuddered as it was hit. Its own guns were in action now, filling the plane with a steady rumble; it shuddered and shook from the recoil of the big machine guns in the tail and waist, the fuselage was filled with the roars and the explosions, and the smell of powder, and all the time the plane lurched and screamed back and forth through the air as Greer worked the rudders side to side—for long moments without result: "We were getting hit all over the place," McCredie says. "You could feel the bullets banging into the airplane. And those cannon shells . . ." The Zero was suddenly gone, and Greer was heading for a cloud bank that could spell safety, when suddenly a wave of seven more Zeroes was around them, and bullets and shells were smashing into the Marauder again, and again the plane was skidding and weaving wildly across the sky. And then McCredie, firing from the nose, had his machine gun jam, and Greer shouted at him to get back to one of the waist guns, and he started to crawl back along the narrow passageway, and as he did, he saw their passenger.

Lyndon Johnson was standing stooped over, so that he could see out that little window, and what he was seeing was three Zeroes. One would fake a pass, and when the guns of the B-26 followed him, the other two would come screaming straight in—straight at the plane, straight, it seemed, at that window, straight at him—with the leading edges of their wings spitting bullets, until, at the very last instant, the Japanese pilots dropped and zoomed under the B-26. "It was the kind of sight that scared you out of your wits," McCredie was to say. Johnson was looking steadily out the window. He turned as McCredie crawled by, and held up three fingers. He pointed out the window. "There're three out there to the left," he said calmly. And he smiled. McCredie took a look—one look—"I figured they were still laying off. But they were coming straight at us and firing! . . . The guns and cannons were all firing at us." McCredie pushed past. As he did, Johnson grinned at him "cool as a cucumber." Things seemed to get worse. The sky was filled with flashing wings with red balls painted on them as the Marauder struggled for the clouds. Radioman-gunner Lillis Walker had to leave his waist gun to crawl forward to the radio and find out if Seven-Mile Strip was clear for a landing. "It was rough. . . . The Zeroes stayed with us, working us over, like they were having . . . target practice." And then, as he crawled, "There was this passenger of ours. . . ." The passenger wasn't looking out the little window any longer. He had pulled out a stool, and was standing on it and looking out the navigator's bubble on top of the plane. There was a better view from up there. "From up there," Walker was to say, "that's a sight to scare the living daylights out of you. A couple of Zeroes were in front of us, and coming in, firing everything they had, and you're looking right into the face of death when *that* happens." Lyndon Johnson, the physical coward who was afraid of a fistfight, was looking into that face. He was, Walker was to say, "just as calm as if we were on a sightseeing tour. . . . Bullets were singing through the plane all around us and we were being hit by those cannon shells, and he was—well, just calm, and watching everything." He got down off the stool, so that Walker could push past to the radio. Walker recalls what Lyndon Johnson said as he passed. "Boy," Johnson said, "it's rough up here, isn't it?" And Walker recalls what he said in reply: "Yeah, I'm always scared up here." And he recalls what Lyndon Johnson did next. "He burst out laughing at me. I'm sure he felt exactly the way I did, but he just didn't show it. He didn't show it a bit."

Then, at last, they were in the clouds, and safe. After a while, they were home. Greer brought the plane in, nursing the bad engine, touching down without a jar. The crew climbed down to the ground. Several officers were rushing up to see if the Congressman was all right, but before he turned to them, Johnson had a last word for the crew. "It's been very interesting," he said. Then he grinned again.

NINE OF THE OTHER eleven Marauders returned to Seven-Mile Strip shortly after the *Heckling Hare*, having dropped their bombs on the Lae airfield and raced for home through the Zeroes, some of the Marauders skimming the ocean so low that the vacuum created by their propellers kicked up little whirlpools on the waves. Ambulances sped out, and wounded men were carried off the planes and taken to a makeshift hospital. Then came a wait as Johnson stood there with officers and men, until, finally, another plane appeared, riddled from nose to tail, the belly of the ship so shredded that the landing gear couldn't be lowered. A pilot ran to a radio, and talked the ship down to a belly landing; it slid to a halt in a cloud of dust. Then there was another wait, but there was no plane at the end of it. Many of the airmen had known there wouldn't be. They had seen one B-26, hit by shellfire from a Zero, fall through the sky, thick black smoke pouring from an engine, and crash into the water with shattering impact. Everyone aboard it was killed. That plane was the *Wabash Cannonball*, the plane in which Lyndon Johnson had been supposed to fly. In it when it crashed was his movie camera—and Lieutenant Colonel Francis Stevens, who had taken his seat.

LYNDON JOHNSON had seen combat, had been *in* combat, under fire, if only as an observer. The next day, he headed home, at five-thirty a.m., boarding the B-17 that would carry the two Generals and other high-

ranking officers as well as himself and his surviving fellow observer, Sam
Anderson, back to Australia—first to Darwin, and then on the long flight
south to Melbourne, where Johnson and Anderson would catch a Coronado PB2Y back to the United States.

On the trip home, there was one more adventure. During the first
leg, over what Johnson later was to recall as "El Paso desert country"
between Darwin and Clencurry, the plane's navigational equipment failed,
and the pilot became lost. After vainly flying for four hours in a box search
pattern (continually increasing the size of the boxes in hopes of finding a
recognizable landmark), with the Generals and other officers crowded into
the cockpit giving advice, the pilot, with fuel and daylight running out,
decided to land the plane in a pasture not far from a windmill and a ranch
house. With the officers and Lyndon Johnson huddled in the rear—Johnson was holding on to the tail guns for support—so their weight would
act as a brake to slow the plane after it landed, they hit the ground with
scarcely a jolt. Australian ranchers suddenly appeared, and, recalls one
of the crew, "Right away Lieutenant Commander Johnson gets busy. He
begins to get acquainted. They tell him where we are and some of them
go off to get a truck to take us into town where we can telephone, and
more keep coming, and Johnson is shaking hands all around, and he
comes back and tells us these are real folks—the best damn folks in the
world, except maybe the folks in his own Texas. Pretty soon he knows all
their first names, and they're telling him why there ought to be a high
tariff on wool, and there's no question he swung that county for Johnson
before we left. He was in his element. I know he sure swung the . . .
crew. He can carry that precinct any day."

And there was a medal. After an hour-long cross-country drive over
rutted roads to the nearest town—Winton—with the local sheriff, who
arrived with several ancient cars, an uneventful flight the next day to
Melbourne, and five days of rest and briefings, Johnson and Anderson
were suddenly summoned to General MacArthur's office on June 18, a
few hours before they were scheduled to leave for the United States.
Appearing irritated at Johnson, MacArthur said that of course Anderson
had had to take part in the air raid since he was an Air Force observer,
but that he couldn't understand why an observer for the Navy had risked
his life. Johnson replied, according to Anderson, that "many of the airmen
knew that he was a Congressman from Texas—that many were his constituents—and that he wanted to show them he would face the same dangers they had to face." MacArthur then listened for a while to what
Johnson and Anderson had to report. As they were about to leave, he
suddenly said that he had posthumously awarded the Distinguished Service Cross, an Army medal second only to the Congressional Medal of
Honor, to Colonel Stevens. Then he told the two men he was awarding

each of them the Silver Star, the Army's third-highest decoration. After a somewhat awkward pause, MacArthur said: "We don't have any Silver Stars out here. And the citations haven't been written yet." There was a supply of ribbons in his outer office, he said; "you can pick [them] up, and start wearing them."

And, as in so many crucial episodes in Lyndon Johnson's life, there was illness. Hardly had the big Coronado flying boat lifted off from Melbourne when he took to a bunk on the plane, feeling "terrible," and during the nine-hour flight he developed a fever. After their arrival in New Zealand that evening, Anderson brought him to a local hospital, where, Johnson wrote in his diary, he "got insulted." Navy doctors ordered him to the sick bay of a submarine tender in the harbor, but the next morning, anxious to get home, he refused their advice to stay, and flew on. That day, he began to shake badly with a chill and a high fever. Anderson and crewmen wrapped him in blankets; the pilot wanted to return to Nouméa, but Johnson insisted they continue homeward. By the time the Coronado set down that night in Suva, in the Fiji Islands, however, his fever was 103.6, and in bed in a hotel there he became delirious, and began vomiting. In a Navy hospital, sulphalhyzel brought his fever down, but when the Coronado left the next morning, it left without him. He had asked Anderson to get in touch with Admiral Nimitz in Pearl Harbor, and inform him of his condition. Nimitz immediately sent doctors to Suva, and after four days in the hospital Johnson left for Pearl Harbor, where he remained for treatment at the Navy Hospital until July 7, when he began the three-day flight to Washington, arriving there weighing 180 pounds, twenty-five less than when he had left. By July 10, White House aide Daniels would write, "Lyndon Johnson [was] back from his politically essential plunge into the Pacific."

On July 9, President Roosevelt released a directive ordering all congressmen in the armed forces to return to Congress. Of the eight Congressmen then on active service, four, including Vincent Harrington of Iowa, who was later killed in action, reacted to the order by resigning from Congress so that they could stay in uniform. Four, including Johnson, resigned from the armed forces. (In explaining his resignation, Johnson was to say, "I had been ordered out of uniform and back to Washington by my Commander-in-Chief.") He was back in the House, out of uniform, within a week after his return.

THE STORY of Lyndon Johnson's service in the armed forces during World War II, brief though it may be, nonetheless reveals violently clashing contradictions in his character.

During his 1941 senatorial campaign, except for an occasional reference to "scrubbing the deck of a battleship" as an ordinary sailor, he had repeatedly promised to "be fighting in the front line, in the trenches, in the mud and blood." But he had known when he had promised to "tear up my draft number" that he would not *have* a draft number—it was, indeed, at least partly so that he would not be eligible for the draft that he had had the foresight to obtain a commission in the Naval Reserve. (And, naturally, since the commission was as a Lieutenant Commander, scrubbing the deck of a battleship—or performing any other function of an ordinary sailor—was not a possibility, either.) He could, of course, have torn up the commission and obtained a draft number (or could have enlisted), but he did not do that.

What he did do, in obedience to orders that he himself had a hand in drafting, was to spend the first five months of the war trying to further his political future, while ensconcing himself in precisely the type of bureaucratic "safe, warm naval berth" he had promised to avoid. For five months, he delayed and stalled, making no serious attempt to get into combat while having what his sidekick John Connally was to call "a lot of fun." And when, after six months of the war had passed, he finally did enter a combat zone—when he no longer had any choice, when "for the sake of political future" he *had* to get into a combat zone, and get there fast—he went not to fight (in the trenches or anywhere else), but to observe. Despite flying more than 20,000 miles to reach that combat zone and return home, the only brush he had with the war there was to fly as an observer on a single mission, at the conclusion of which he left the combat zone on the next plane out.

Nevertheless, although Lyndon Johnson had avoided being at the scene of a battle as long as he could, once he was at it, his conduct was bold and courageous, nonchalant in the face of danger. If he had gone to the Southwest Pacific only so that he could later claim to have been in the war—and if he had been in that war for only one day—still, for that day he had been not a politician but a warrior. Ambition may have governed his war service as it governed his entire life, but, as had always been the case, in the service of that ambition he had done whatever he had to do.

NOTHING ABOUT JOHNSON'S WAR SERVICE, however, was more revealing than the way he came to portray it.

A great storyteller, he had a great story to tell, and he made the most of it. Hardly had he arrived back in Washington when he began telling it to journalists, inviting them to lunch, scheduling interviews, one after the other, with the AP, the UP, INS, *Time* magazine and Texas newspapers. Edwin Weisl, the counsel not only for Paramount but for Hearst Newspapers, was set to work contacting the chain's many columnists. If de-emphasizing certain facts—the precise length of his combat service, for example—was imperative, the guise of censorship and military secrecy made that de-emphasis easy; writing that Johnson had "distinguished himself 'Down Under,' " Walter Winchell told his readers that "the details of *how* he had distinguished himself would soon be released"; another journalist wrote that he had been on "an extremely secret assignment." The lead sentences in the articles that appeared—"Lyndon Johnson came home from the wars Monday"; "Fresh from the battlefields of the Southwest Pacific, with the boom of cannon from hostile aircraft still echoing in his ears"—were all that could be desired, and readers were told, in the Congressman's own words, about the "suicide mission" on which he had flown, and about "the harrowing flight home under fire" from Japanese Zeroes. His criticism of "incompetents" in high military positions and of shortages in equipment, of pilots forced to fly obsolete planes ("I would just as soon try to weather a storm riding on the tail of a box kite as I would to face the fighting Jap Zero with one of those Navy PB-Y crates some of those boys are now flying") made front pages not only in Texas but in Washington and across the country, as did copies of a picture taken of him at Seven-Mile Strip, which he had had the foresight to obtain from a news photographer.

Back in Texas a week after his return, he outdid himself. His demeanor was that of the battle-weary veteran who has seen war, and has been sobered by it. So sobered, in fact, that to one reporter "the congressman was noticeably a changed Lyndon Johnson." While in Washington the only reminder of his illness had been his loss of weight (weight which was rapidly being replaced), in Texas his weakness was so pronounced that only with difficulty could he summon up the strength to make speeches to his constituents. Sometimes, during a speech, he had to call for a chair in which to sit on the stage, so greatly was the effort taxing his energy. Sometimes he could barely make himself heard. At the Businessmen's Luncheon in Taylor on August 5, for example, he spoke, with evident strain, for some minutes in a voice so low that it was almost a whisper—"his talk went unheard by portions of the audience, as his recent illness prevented him from raising his voice"—until someone brought him a microphone. (At another speech, that very evening, in San Gabriel Park in Georgetown, Texas, his recuperative powers displayed themselves when he spoke for ninety minutes in his pre-war shouting style.) Whispering or shouting, however, his speeches, as one reporter wrote, "impressed and inspired" the farmers and ranchers of the Hill Country, many of whom had sons fighting overseas. "I have just returned from a tour of duty with some of the loneliest men in the world. . . . You may not know where your boy is tonight. Perhaps you have just had a letter telling you not to write to the old address again, not to send another bundle for a while." But of one thing they could be sure, he said: "your boy" is fighting bravely; he, Lyndon Johnson, had seen for himself the bravery, against long odds, of America's fighting men. And, he reminded them, he had been with those men. "I am happy to be here. How happy you don't know until you have been where I have been and have seen what I have seen," he said. He told his audiences that God had helped him return: "There are no non-believers at 12,000 feet with Jap Zero fighters around."

Good as the stories were, though, they grew better—and better. At first, they were improved only by exaggeration: in interviews and speeches, the pneumonia he had contracted became a more dramatic disease, and one evocative of the South Pacific jungles—dengue fever; the 25 pounds he had lost became 35 pounds, then 38 pounds, and then 40; the mission he had flown became missions; the 20,000 miles he had flown became 50,000 miles, and then 60,000; the time he had spent in combat was made to appear longer and longer.

Exaggeration is a normal aspect of war stories, only to be expected. With Johnson, however, exaggeration spilled over into something more— until the story of his wartime service bore little resemblance to the reality: which was that, exciting though his flight may have been, it was only one flight. He had been in action for a total of thirteen minutes. When, in December of 1942, five months after his return from this action, a reporter asked him, "Were you in actual combat?," he replied, "Yes, I was. I was out there in May, June and part of July. We exchanged greetings quite often. They paid us very busy visits every day for a time." After another interview, a reporter wrote that "the tall, dark and handsome Texan . . . speaks with deep emotion about the war," and no wonder: "He has had months of exciting active duty with the Navy. . . . He saw action in the South Pacific on sea and then on land in Australia. In the past year he has flown between 60,000 and 70,000 miles, part of the time in bombing raids. . . ." His actual role—as an observer, not an airman; an observer who had flown a single mission; an observer who had not had "months" of active duty and who had never been paid "busy visits every day for a time"—all but vanished from the telling; he portrayed himself as a war-scarred veteran of many battles on many fronts: by 1944, he was stating— in writing—"I lived with the men on fighting fronts. I flew with them on missions over enemy territory. I ate and slept with them; and was hospitalized with them in the Fiji Islands. . . ." And always the details became richer, more vivid. He began saying that because he had been too tall to fit into the parachute provided, he had flown without one; then he added another fillip: only one parachute had been available, and he had given it to a friend. The engine that had malfunctioned on his plane now, in his accounts, had been "knocked out" by Japanese Zeroes. Several of his crew had been wounded. In reality, his squadron had shot down a single Zero; in his retelling, the number steadily rose: "I saw fourteen of 'em go down in flames right in front of me." He even gave himself a nickname: he told a reporter that the men who had flown with him had come to admire him so much that they had named him "Raider" Johnson; that was how he had been known among the men of the 22nd Bomb Group, he said.

Especially significant was the fact that he persisted in these exaggerations, and added new ones, in circumstances that would have deterred other men. He began inviting journalists and friends to his house to see the "home movies" he had filmed on the trip before his movie camera was lost—to see them over and over again. At every dinner party at the Johnsons', it seemed, the movies would be shown, with a narration by the host, in a self-promotion so relentless that it made the guests smile even when they thought Johnson's narration was true. And because some repeat guests were hearing the narration more than once (not a few were hearing it more than twice), they could hardly help being aware that it was changing, that the story of Lyndon Johnson's war service was different every time they heard it. As they compared notes, the story became a joke among them. "Sometimes," says Harold H. Young, counsel to Vice President Henry Wallace, "you could hardly restrain yourself from shouting: 'Oh, bullshit, Lyndon.' " Sometimes their disbelief was expressed to his face, in derisive remarks only thinly veiled with laughter, during his presentation. His predilection for identifying each soldier or airman visible on the film who was from Texas similarly became a subject of ridicule; Ben Cohen, who had seen the film several times, said to him dryly: "Lyndon, now why don't you tell us the fellows who *aren't* from Texas? It would save you some time." Johnson could hardly have been unaware of the growing amusement and disbelief with which his stories were being received. But that did not stop him from telling the stories—and continuing to improve them.

ALSO REVEALING was the fact that he would persist in these exaggerations and keep adding new ones—until the story of his war service bore little relation indeed to fact—even under circumstances in which he must have been aware of the possibility that the facts might be checked: when he was President. In October, 1966, for example, when "Credibility Gap" had already become a phrase in common usage, President Johnson showed the home movies to a group of journalists gathered in the White House, and delivered a narration about his service during World War II.

Although some of the facts in the narrative were correct, the President also said: "During the months we [the three observers] were there, we must have talked to 10,000 men, flown to hundreds of bases. . . ." And, discussing the Lae mission—it is not at all clear from his narrative that this was the only mission he ever flew—the President said: "I lost some good friends on that mission. We came back with a lot fewer planes than we left with." On December 13, 1967, he was interviewed in the White House by a Texas journalist, Ronnie Dugger, generally hostile to him, who was writing his biography. In the book, Dugger wrote of the interview: "He not only let falsehood pass for truth, he faked his record himself. Telling me about the mission over Lae, he said that when twenty Zeroes attacked them, 'it was like shooting fish out of a barrel.' . . . Fourteen of the planes got the hell shot out of them. He saw Colonel Stevens' plane go down. He said that everybody who survived that mission got a Silver Star; everybody who died got the Distinguished Service Cross."

So deeply and widely mistrusted had Lyndon Johnson been at little Southwest Texas State Teachers College in the Hill Country that the nickname he bore during his years on campus was "Bull" (for "Bullshit") Johnson. And his fellow students (who used his nickname to his face— "Hiya, Bull," "Howya doin', Bull?") believed not only that he lied to them—lied to them constantly, lied about big matters and small, lied so incessantly that he was, in a widely used phrase, "the biggest liar on campus"—but also that some psychological element *impelled* him to lie, made him lie even when he knew the lie might be discovered, made him, in fact, repeat a lie even *after* it had been discovered, made him, in one classmate's words, "a man who just could not tell the truth." Now, in 1942, he was acquiring the same reputation in Washington.

More significant still was another reason for the skepticism about his war stories. Though he had flown only one mission, the story of that mission, told by him with the vividness of the master storyteller he was, was to some degree the story not only of a courageous man but of a patriot and idealist. Essential though such an image was to Lyndon Johnson politically, the image he needed in his inner life was very different. It was, as it had always been, very important to him that he be seen as shrewd, pragmatic, cynical—"different from Daddy." A shrewd, pragmatic man would have volunteered to place himself in danger only because of political necessity, so Johnson, almost as if he could not help himself, kept making clear, often to the very same men to whom he was telling the story of the courageous mission, that he had gone to the Pacific only for political advantage—only because he had, in terms of his ambition, no choice—and that, once there, he had done the absolute minimum necessary to safeguard that ambition. Before leaving for the Pacific, he had told Jonathan Daniels he wanted to go only "for the sake of political future"; after a conversation with Johnson now, after his return, Daniels noted in his diary that the trip had been "politically essential." The wink and the tear do not complement each other; even men fond of Johnson, hearing out of the same mouth a story of bravery and a story of pragmatism, found it difficult to give much credence to the first. They tended to doubt the story—including those parts of it (admittedly more and more rare) that were true.

But most significant of all was Lyndon Johnson's own attitude toward his war story: he was coming to believe that it was true.

The symbol of his belief was the Silver Star.

In one of his first interviews after his return to Washington, he told reporter Marshall McNeil that he thought he didn't deserve the medal. When McNeil apparently agreed with him (the reporter was later to comment, "He got it for a flight, not for a fight"), Johnson assured him: "Well, I'll never wear the thing." In at least one of his speeches in Texas, he went further, telling a responsive audience that he had refused the honor because "I believed that the small part I played in the trips [sic] did not entitle me to the same honor that went to men who risked their lives in daily combat." He drafted a letter of formal refusal ("My very brief service with these men and its experience of what they did and sacrifice makes me all the more sensitive that I should not and could not accept a citation of recognition for the little part I played for a short time in learning and facing with them the problems they encounter all the time. . . . I cannot in good conscience accept the decoration"), and then had the letter typed, ready for his signature.

It is indeed somewhat difficult to conclude that the medal was awarded for any considerations other than political. Lieutenant Greer, whose brilliant flying saved the *Heckling Hare*, did not receive a medal, nor did Corporal Baren, who shot down the Zero—no one on the plane received a decoration for the mission over Lae except the observer; in fact, some members of its crew were to fly twenty-five missions without receiving any medal, much less one as prized as the Silver Star.

But Johnson's attitude changed—and as with so many Johnson changes, the change was dramatic and total.

The letter refusing the medal was filed away, unsigned. All talk of refusal abruptly ended. Instead, not only did Johnson accept the Silver Star, he arranged to accept it in public. Several times. After purchasing the decoration (in an Army-Navy store in Washington), he took it to Texas, where in a number of public appearances it was affixed to his lapel as if for the first time; in Fort Worth, for example, the commander of the local American Legion post pinned it on him while a crowd of Legion-naires cheered and Johnson stood before them, head bowed, face somber, hardly able to blink back the tears.

And once he had it, he flaunted it; a medal for Lyndon Johnson was not a medal that was hidden away in a drawer. By the end of 1942, he had added a new item to his daily attire: a small silver bar with a star in its center. It was the "battle ribbon" emblematic of the Silver Star, and he wore it in his lapel for the rest of his life. And because the silver bar was unfortunately rather inconspicuous and audiences might therefore not notice it (and, even if they did, might not recognize it), Johnson intro-duced a gesture into his speeches: while referring to his combat service and the medal he had been awarded—and for some years his speeches were liberally studded with these references—he would place his left hand on his lapel and pull it forward and back, waving it, almost, to focus his audience's attention on the silver bar.

Had he once felt that he did not deserve the medal? Lyndon Johnson rapidly came to feel not only that he deserved it but that he deserved more: that the Silver Star was not a sufficiently high honor for such he-roism as his.

One of his protégés in Texas politics was a young attorney from McAllen, Joe M. Kilgore. "Fighting Joe Kilgore," he was called—with reason. Enlisting when the war began, Kilgore became an Air Force pilot, flew a twenty-five-mission tour over some of the most hazardous targets in Europe in Flying Fortresses, re-enlisted, and flew ten more. In a state that produced many heroes, Kilgore was one of the bravest. Once, seeing Nazi fighters swarming around another Fortress that had already been hit and crippled, the young pilot turned back into the face of the enemy, and flew cover for the other Fortress as it struggled home. He was awarded the Silver Star. After the war, Johnson brought Kilgore, now a promising young legislator, into his political camp. Constantly reminding Kilgore that he, too, had won the Silver Star, Johnson took great pains to make sure the younger man understood that in his (Johnson's) case that medal was not really sufficient acknowledgment for what he had done. "I had the Silver Star, and I kind of felt you got it for something special," Kilgore recalls. "I never heard [Johnson's mission] was anything more than a rou-tine raid in which he got shot at. And to hear the man complaining that he had gotten only the Silver Star for an experience that thousands of people had had was almost irrational," but "He bitched and bitched be-cause he only got the Silver Star." And, Kilgore came to realize, "he believed what he was saying. He believed it totally." During twenty years of political alliance with Lyndon Johnson, Kilgore came to understand, he says, that Johnson could believe whatever he wanted to believe—could believe it with all his heart. "He could," Kilgore says, in words that are echoed by the closest of Johnson's associates, men like George Brown and John Connally and Edward Clark, "convince himself of anything, even something that wasn't true."

It was that capacity of Lyndon Johnson's that, when one assesses his influence on history, proves to be the single most significant implication of his war service.

4

Lady Bird

AND WHAT OF THE WIFE he had left behind?

Claudia Alta ("Lady Bird") Taylor was not a person to whom other people paid much attention.

They never had. During her girlhood, in the East Texas town of Karnack, the reason was her manner. The lonely little girl whose mother died when she was five and whose older brothers were off at school for much of the year, lived alone with her father, a tall, burly, ham-handed owner of a general store and cotton gin, loud and coarse, who "never talked about anything but making money." While apparently fond of his daughter, he didn't know what to do with her and packed her off alone at the age of six, a tag around her neck for identification, to her mother's spinster sister in Alabama. Lady Bird (she was given her nickname by a nurse because "she's purty as a lady bird") was raised by her aunt, who moved to Karnack. Frail, sickly Aunt Effie "opened my spirit to beauty," Lady Bird says, "but she neglected to give me any insight into the practical matters a girl should know about, such as how to dress or choose one's friends or learning to dance." Lady Bird loved to read, particularly in a beautifully bound set of books that had belonged to her mother. She memorized poems that she could recite decades later, finished *Ben-Hur* at the age of eight. As for other companionship, the handful of students at Karnack's one-room school were almost all children of the itinerant black sharecroppers who worked her father's 18,000 acres of red clay cotton land; they seldom stayed for long, since her father was notoriously ruthless in his treatment of tenants behind in their rent. "I came from . . . a small town, except that I was never part of the town—lived outside," she says. During her high school years in nearby Marshall (she graduated at fifteen), the lonely little girl became a lonely young woman. Despite her expressive eyes and smooth complexion, she was considered plain, and her baggy, drab clothes seemed almost deliberately chosen to make her less attractive. To the other girls, preoccupied with dresses and dancing, and boys, she seems to have been almost an object of ridicule. Says one: "Bird wasn't accepted into our clique. . . . She didn't date at all. To get her to go to the graduation banquet, my fiancé took Bird as his date and I went with another boy. She didn't like to be called Lady Bird, so we'd call her Bird to get her little temper going. . . . When she'd get in a crowd, she'd clam up." In talking about her, they recall a shyness so profound that it seems to have been an active fear of meeting or talking to people. Lady Bird's own recollections are perhaps the most poignant. "I don't recommend that to anyone, getting through high school that young. I was still in socks when all the other girls were wearing stockings. And shy—I used to hope that no one would speak to me." She loved nature, boating on the winding bayous of Lake Caddo or walking along its shores ("drifts of magnolia all through the woods in the Spring—and the daffodils in the yard. When the first one bloomed, I'd have a little ceremony, all by myself, and name it the queen"), but the boating and walking were also usually "by myself." So deep was her shyness that, as a high school senior, she prayed that if she finished first or second in her class, she would get smallpox so that she wouldn't have to be valedictorian or salutatorian and have to make a speech at graduation. (She finished third.) The school newspaper joked that her ambition was to be an old maid.

Although she remained silent and retiring at the University of Texas, indications of determination and ambition began to appear. Instead of returning to Karnack when she graduated in 1933, as her father and aunt had anticipated, she insisted on spending an extra year at the university, so that she could obtain a second degree—in journalism, "because I thought that people in the press went more places, and met more interesting people, and had more exciting things happen to them." Attempting to overcome her shyness, she became a reporter for the *Daily Texan*, and forced herself to ask questions at press conferences. Nevertheless, the fight seemed to be a losing one. Except at press conferences, one friend recalls, "she was always pleasant, smiling, and so quiet she never seemed to speak at all." Her best friend, Eugenia Boehringer, despaired of making her more outgoing, or even of persuading her to change her style of dressing; despite the "unlimited" charge account her father had opened for her at Nieman-Marcus, she still wore flat-heeled, sensible shoes, and plain dresses that were much too large and of very drab colors. If her high school classmates remember a plain girl, her college classmates remember a plain young woman—in their words, drab, dumpy, a little plumpish, almost dowdy; painfully shy, and quite lonely. And despite her journalism degree, when college ended, she did return to Karnack. It was on a visit to Austin some months later, in September, 1934, that by chance, in the office in which Eugenia Boehringer was working as a secretary, she met Lyndon Johnson. Eugenia and Johnson were friends; through her, he already knew who Lady Bird was; he immediately asked her for a date and on that first date he asked her to marry him, which she did in November.

After her marriage, there was an additional reason that people did not pay much attention to Lady Bird Johnson: the way her husband treated her.

Upon their return to Washington from their honeymoon, he told her that he wanted her to serve him his morning coffee in bed; to bring him his newspaper in bed, so that he could read it as he sipped his coffee; to lay out his clothes, fill his fountain pen and put it in the proper pocket; to fill his cigarette lighter and put it in the proper pocket; to put his handkerchief and money in the proper pocket. And to shine his shoes. And she performed these chores. (When he first told her he wanted his coffee in bed every morning, she was to recall, "I thought, What!?!?!? Me?!?! But I soon realized that it's less trouble serving someone that way than by setting the table and all. . . .") And he made sure that everyone knew that she was performing these chores, loudly reminding her about her duties in front of other people. He was constantly inviting fellow congressmen, his own staffers, and friends like Jim Rowe, to their modest one-bedroom apartment on Kalorama Road at the last minute and telephoning Bird to inform her that another two guests—or ten—would be arriving shortly for dinner. And in these telephone calls, he did not ask her if she could handle the additional people, he simply told her—curtly— that they were coming. Often the invitees would be in the room with him when he telephoned. They heard his tone of voice.

The trip back and forth to his district, a trip that had to be made at least once, and usually more than once, each year, was a difficult one, since the 1,600 miles of roads between Washington and Austin were not the broad interstate highways of later decades; although Lady Bird was to recall that the distance could be covered in "three hard days," generally the trip took five days. After he was married, Lyndon Johnson no longer took that trip. One way in which Herman Brown repaid Johnson for the federal contracts he procured for Brown & Root was to place the company plane at the Johnsons' disposal. But only one Johnson used the plane. Lyndon Johnson flew back and forth. His wife drove—drove, after she had packed. Lady Bird disliked flying, but the principal reason she made the long drive instead of using the Brown & Root plane was that the Johnsons did not feel they could afford two sets of household furnishings or a second car. Every time Lady Bird drove from Washington to Texas and back, she took with her a carful of boxes. "For years," she would later recall, "my idea of being rich was having enough linens and pots and pans to have a set in each place, and not have to lug them back and forth."

And of course everyone in the Texas delegation was aware of this disparity in the Johnsons' travel arrangements. Says one Congressman: "He treated her like the hired help."

Lyndon Johnson possessed not only a lash for a tongue, but a talent— a rare gift, in fact—for aiming the lash, for finding a person's most sensitive point, and striking it, over and over again, without mercy. And he did not spare the lash even when the target was his wife—not that great talent was required to discern the rawest of Lady Bird's wounds: her terrible shyness, her dread of having attention called to herself.

Everyone was aware of the way he talked to her because he talked to her that way in public, shouting orders at her across a crowded room at a Texas State Society dinner ("Lady Bird, go get me another piece of pie." "I will, in just a minute, Lyndon." *"Get me another piece of pie!"*). "He'd embarrass her in public," recalls Wingate Lucas, a Congressman from Fort Worth. "Just yell at her across the room, tell her to do something. All the people from Texas felt very sorry for Lady Bird." If while entertaining friends at home, or while staying overnight at a friend's house, he saw some imperfection in her attire such as a run in her stocking, he would order her to change stockings, "just *ordered* her to—right in front of us," as her friend Mary Elliott recalls.

Also public were Lyndon's constant attempts to get Lady Bird to improve her appearance, about which she had always been so sensitive— to make her lose weight, to wear brighter (and tighter, more figure-emphasizing) dresses, to replace the comfortable, low-heeled shoes she preferred with spike-heeled pumps, to get her hair done more often, to wear more lipstick and more makeup. And after 1940, when John Connally married Ida Nell Brill, Johnson was able to flick the lash even harder. The dazzling Nellie Connally was everything Lady Bird was not— perfectly dressed, outgoing, poised, charming, beautiful; as a freshman at the University of Texas, she had been named a Bluebonnet Belle, one of the ten most beautiful girls on the campus; as a junior, she was named *the* most beautiful: Sweetheart of the University. After Nellie became a member of the Johnson entourage, Lyndon made sure that Lady Bird never forgot the contrast now so conveniently near at hand. "That's a pretty dress, Nellie. Why can't you ever wear a dress like that, Bird? You look so muley, Bird. Why can't you look more like Nellie?" Nellie, who had become close friends with Lady Bird, was distressed at such remarks. "He would say things like that right in front of whoever was present. 'Get out of those funny-looking shoes, Bird. Why can't you wear shoes like Nellie!' *Right in front of us all!* Now, can you think of anything more cruel?" Aware of Lady Bird's shyness, her almost visible terror at having attention called to herself, acquaintances said to each other: "I don't know how she stands it." And, of course, because of the complete lack of respect with which she was treated by her husband, they didn't have much respect for her. Seeing that in her relationship with Lyndon, her opinion didn't count, they gave it little consideration themselves. She talked hardly at all, and when she did try to talk, Nellie says, "nobody paid any attention to her."

Since 1938, moreover, Lyndon had been spending many weekends at Alice Glass's Longlea. Sometimes Lady Bird would accompany him, and sometimes he would leave her back in their little apartment in Washington. Whether or not she was aware of her husband's affair with Alice— and the Longlea circle was certain she was—weekends at Longlea must have been especially difficult for her: to Alice's adoring sister, Mary Louise, and to Alice's best friend, Alice Hopkins, both of whom knew of the affair, she was an obstacle to Alice's happiness, and, of course, she was not at home in the brilliant Longlea salon. No matter how many times he met her, Charles Marsh had trouble remembering her name; he was constantly referring to her as "Lyndon's wife." "Everybody was trying to be nice to her, but she was just out of place," Alice Hopkins says, and although the first part of that sentence may not have been true, the second was—and Lady Bird knew it; decades later, describing Longlea in an interview with the author of this book, she said: "My eyes were just out on stems. They would have interesting people from the world of art and literature and politics. It was the closest I ever came to a salon in my life. . . . There was a dinner table with ever so much crystal and silver. . . ." She appears to have felt keenly the contrast between herself and her hostess: "She was very tall, and elegant, really beautiful. . . . I remember Alice in a series of long and elegant dresses and me in—well, much less elegant."

THROUGHOUT LADY BIRD JOHNSON'S LIFE, however, there had been hints that behind that terrible shyness, there was something more—much more.

At the University, there had been her decision to get a journalism degree, and the courage with which she forced herself to ask questions at press conferences—and the glimpses her few beaux had beneath the quietness. One of them, Thomas C. Soloman, was to recall that for a time "I thought I was the leader." But, he says, he came to realize that "We had been doing what she wanted to do. Even when we went on a picnic, it was she who thought up the idea. . . . I also knew she would not marry a man who did not have the potentiality of becoming somebody." J. H. Benefield came to realize that the shy young woman "was one of the most determined persons I met in my life, one of the most ambitious and able."

Handed the task, customary for congressmen's wives, of escorting constituents visiting Washington, she carried out the assignment with unusual thoroughness, not only arranging the standard 8:30 a.m. tours of the Capitol but taking the visitors farther afield: to Mount Vernon and even Monticello. Realizing that her husband, despite his pre-nuptial avowals of fervent interest in culture and history, would never visit the Smithsonian or the Civil War battlefields, she made these tours with his constituents instead. And after a while, when a visitor had a question about a building they were visiting, the answer would be readily available. A friend came to see that "she must have read everything about the city of Washington and its history, and the Capitol, and Mount Vernon and Monticello; I don't mean just guidebooks but biographies of Jefferson and Washington. She knew everything—and I mean everything—about the gardens at Monticello and how Jefferson had planned them. She even knew about the Civil War battlefields. She had done a tremendous amount of work, without telling anyone." Asked a question, she would reply in a voice so soft as to be almost inaudible. "She would never say one word unless you asked," one Texan says, "but if you asked, she always knew the answer." Not only did she grant, eagerly, graciously, any favors that the visitors requested, she suggested other favors—hotel reservations, train schedules for a side trip to New York. "I early learned," she says today, "that CONSTITUENTS was spelled with capital letters," and she didn't forget their requests. Her husband had told her to get a stenographer's notebook and carry it in her purse everywhere, jotting down anything she had to do. She never forgot the notebook; it—and her diligence in crossing off the items written in it—would be remarked upon by her friends for the next forty years.

Even at Longlea, there were hints—although the Longlea "regulars" didn't notice them. She seemed always to be reading. One summer was to become enshrined in Longlea lore as "the summer that Lady Bird read *War and Peace*"; the scintillating Longlea regulars snickered because the quiet little woman carried the big book with her everywhere—even though, by the end of summer, she had finished it. When, during the loud arguments to which she sat silently listening, a book would be cited, Lady Bird would, on her return to Washington, check it out of the public library. One was *Mein Kampf*, which Charles Marsh had read, and to which he was continually referring. She read it, and while she never talked about the book at Longlea, when Hitler's theories were discussed thereafter, she was aware that, while Marsh knew what he was talking about, no one else in the room did—except her.

And there were other qualities—which were noticed even though their significance was not. To the regulars' condescension, Lady Bird Johnson responded with an unshakable graciousness. While Alice Hopkins says that Lady Bird "was just out of place," Mrs. Hopkins adds that

"If everyone was just trying to be nice to her," she would be nice right back, calm and gracious—"self-contained." Even Alice Glass's sister has to admit that there was something "quite remarkable in her self-discipline—the things she made herself do. She was forever working," not only on her reading, but on her figure—she had always been "dumpy," but in 1940 or 1941 the extra weight came off, and stayed off.

And as for her husband's affair with the salon's mistress, "Oh, of course," Lady Bird must have known, the regulars say. Wasn't her husband often going—without her—to Longlea when, as she could easily have determined, Charles Marsh was not at home? "I could never understand how she stood it," Mary Louise says. "Lyndon would leave her on weekends, weekend after weekend, just leave her home." But stand it she did. "We were all together a lot—Lyndon and Lady Bird and Charles and Alice," Mary Louise says. "And Lady Bird never said a word. She showed nothing, nothing at all."

When, at Texas State Society parties or other Washington social functions, her husband bellowed orders at her across the room, or insulted her, she never showed anything, either. She would sit silently, or say simply, "Yes, Lyndon," or "I'll be glad to, Lyndon," and she would do so as calmly as if the request had been polite and reasonable. People might say to one another, "I don't know how she stands it," but she stood it—and she stood it with a dignity that his shouts and sarcasms could not rattle, a dignity that was rather remarkable. But most acquaintances didn't really notice this. Their attitude toward Lady Bird Johnson was influenced by her husband's attitude toward her. She never tried to talk very much, of course, and when she did, she wasn't listened to very much. She was just a drab little woman whom nobody noticed.

AS FOR POLITICS, apart from entertaining her husband's guests and his constituents she had no connection at all with this major activity of his life.

During her husband's campaign for Congress in 1937—he had been unopposed in 1938 and 1940—she had, as always, had a welcoming smile and a warm meal for him and his aides at all hours of the night. But when, occasionally, someone—someone who didn't know her well—raised the possibility that she herself might campaign, the very suggestion that she might have to face an audience and speak brought such panic to her face that the suggestion was always quickly dropped. Sometimes she could not avoid standing in a receiving line at a reception for the Congressman— and although she would shake hands and chat with the strangers filing by, she would perform this chore with so obvious an effort that her friends felt sorry for her as they watched; the bright smile on her face would be as rigid as if it had been set in stone.

The 1941 Senate campaign was little different. She learned of her husband's decision to run only after the decision had been made; he didn't bother to tell her until after the press conference at which he told the public. Then he flew down to Texas to begin the campaign; Mrs. Johnson followed by car, so unessential was her participation considered. Having purchased a movie camera, she took pictures of Lyndon as he gave speeches, but they were for showing at home, not for use in the campaign. "I went around with my little camera, cranking," she was to say many years later. As she said this, she held up an imaginary camera in an amateurish way and pantomimed turning the crank, and as she did so, she hunched over a little, portraying—vividly—a timid little woman hanging back at the edge of a crowd, pointing a camera at her husband. Whatever she looked like to others, that was what Lady Bird Johnson looked like to herself. Did she have any other role in the campaign? "I packed suitcases and got clothes washed, and tried to see that Lyndon always had clothes; every day Lyndon went through three or four or five shirts. Traveling with him, trying to get him to eat a regular meal, or taking his messages. Just being on hand in his hotel to answer the phone so he can take a shower. And sitting on the platform at all the big rallies." And the few words she had to say on the rare—very rare—occasions when she represented her husband at a minor event ("Thank you very much for inviting me to this barbecue. Lyndon is very sorry he couldn't be here") were such an ordeal that they made her friends cringe. Her single attempt to contribute something more ended in embarrassment. She had been making big pitchers of lemonade, and baking batches of cookies, and lugging them to the campaign volunteers working in various offices around Austin, and she decided that on these visits, in order to thank the volunteers for their efforts and to spur them on to more, "I would give this little speech to them: 'Every single vote counts.' " She wrote and rewrote the few paragraphs of that brief talk, memorized it and nerved herself up to give it. But she evidently repeated it too many times. Meeting her on the street one day, a friend smilingly began to quote her speech back to her, and since the friend was not a campaign worker, Lady Bird felt that her speech had become a joke quoted around Austin. That was the end of her speechmaking in that campaign. Forty years later, she was to tell the author of this book that when the friend quoted her speech back to her, she realized, "Maybe it had made the rounds. I guess I gave the speech too often." Hearing a change in her voice as she spoke, I glanced up from my notepad. Mrs. Johnson was at that time sixty-eight years old. Her face was lowered, and she was blushing—a definite, dark red blush—at the memory of that humiliation so many years earlier.

As for the less public side of the campaign—the planning of strategy and tactics—the planners say that the candidate's wife was almost never present. "Well," she says, "I elected to be out a lot." Asked why, she replied: "I wasn't confident in that field." Was there also another reason? "I didn't want to be a party to absolutely everything," Lady Bird Johnson says.

BACK IN WASHINGTON after the campaign, she had a new apartment, in the Woodley Park Towers off Connecticut Avenue, much more spacious than the Kalorama Road apartment and with a living room that, she recalls, "just hung over Rock Creek Park, and was just filled with green." But an apartment wasn't what she wanted. "I had been yearning and talking about having a home," she recalls. The Johnsons had been spending about six months of the year in Austin, and every year they seemed to be living in a different apartment there—small and temporary. And in Washington, more and more of their friends were buying homes. "The central theme of my heart's desire was a house," she recalls, but there was no money to buy one. She and Lyndon had wanted children, but after seven years of marriage there were no children; she had had three miscarriages. In an attempt to solve what she describes as a "gynecological problem," she underwent an operation in Baltimore in September, 1941, but it did not appear to have been successful. "This was a sadness," she remembers, and changes the subject. But sometimes, despite herself, her sorrow slipped out; an old friend was to remember chatting with Lady Bird at this time, about other topics; every so often Lady Bird would pause, and a wistful look would cross her face, and she would say, "If I had a son . . ." or "If I had a daughter . . ." During the Fall of 1941, she was still taking constituents to Mount Vernon—she was to say she stopped counting after her two-hundredth trip—and she was very tired of those trips. Nellie Connally says, "She was like a sightseeing bus. That's what congressional wives did: they hauled the constituents around." During that Fall, she still entertained constituents at dinners—dinners at which her guests paid little attention to her. Anxious for something else to do, she enrolled, with Nellie, in a business school in Arlington, taking courses in shorthand and typing; years later, Mrs. Johnson, almost always careful not to say a derogatory word about anything, would say of the business school: "That was a dull, drab little place." And all during that Fall, the weekends at Longlea continued, as did the Texas parties at which her husband ridiculed her, or shouted orders at her. "The women liked her," Nellie Connally says. "Every woman sympathized with her. If they didn't like her for herself—and they did—they liked her because they saw what she had to put up with. It made what they had to put up with not so bad."

And then, after Pearl Harbor, when her husband, along with John Connally and Willard Deason, was preparing to leave on his first trip to the Coast, Lyndon said that she might as well get some use out of her typing classes and took her along to type his letters. Telephoning his congressional office every evening, he was told about problems in the district: about federal installations for which he had obtained preliminary approval before his departure—a big Air Force base for Austin, an Army camp in Bastrop County, a new rural electrification line—but that were now stalled in the federal bureaucracy; about scores of businessmen whose plans for construction or expansion of factories were stalled by lack of necessary approvals from federal agencies such as the new War Production Board and the Office of Strategic Materials; about letters and telephone calls—hundreds of letters and telephone calls—from constituents about routine pre-war matters, and about new war-related problems. There was no one to handle these problems. In Connally, Walter Jenkins and the brilliant speechwriter Herbert Henderson, Johnson had possessed an exceptional staff, but Jenkins had enlisted in September, Henderson had suddenly, unexpectedly died in October, and Connally's departure left no one in Suite 1320 of the House Office Building except apple-cheeked Mary Rather—charming, efficient, but only a secretary—and O. J. Weber, bright and aggressive but only twenty-one years old and with just a few months' experience. And the problems had to be handled quickly. If final authorization for the new military bases in the Tenth District was not pushed through, some other congressman would snap up the bases for his district. If constituents didn't get the necessary assistance in Washington, the feeling would spread that there was no one in the district's congressional office except secretaries, that the district was without adequate representation in Washington—at a time when a congressman was needed with particular urgency. Johnson had no idea how long he would be away from Washington, and if his absence was to be prolonged, voters might begin asking why he didn't resign his seat and let the district elect a new congressman. The political danger was real—and imminent. Let dissatisfaction mount and, with an election scheduled for July 25, 1942, he might, if he didn't resign, be replaced. Someone had to take over the office, to be in effect, in all but name, the Congressman from the Tenth District until the real Congressman returned. Someone had to handle a congressman's multi-faceted chores: to persuade Cabinet officers and high-level bureaucrats to cut through red tape and get the big projects moving again, to negotiate with the new wartime agencies on behalf of businessmen, to serve as the necessary link between constituents and federal agencies. Discussing the situation out on the Coast, Johnson, Connally and Deason agreed that choosing an ambitious young politician or lawyer from Austin, who might become a possible rival, was too risky. Moreover, the choice had to be someone who was not only totally loyal but who would provide a sense of continuity, someone who would make the district feel that the office was being run as if Lyndon Johnson were still there running it; someone, therefore, who was identified with Lyndon Johnson. It is unclear which of the men first suggested that the best choice—perhaps the only choice—was Mrs. Lyndon Johnson; she thinks it was Deason whom, to her astonishment, she first heard mention her name. Her husband at first dismissed the idea, but the more it was discussed, the clearer it became that it was the only solution. On their return to Washington, Johnson learned that he and Connally would soon be leaving again, on a trip whose duration was indefinite. He told Lady Bird she would have to do the job. And when, on January 29, 1942, he and Connally left for the Coast again, Lady Bird Johnson went to Suite 1320.

HER HUSBAND didn't make it easy for her. He did not, in fact, give her much of a vote of confidence before the staff; he appears, in fact, to have been unable to bring himself to tell Miss Rather and Weber that she was to be in charge of the office. He told her to write him daily letters listing the projects she was working on, and to leave wide margins, so that he could put instructions next to each item, but he told Weber and Miss Rather to write letters, too, and left the impression with them that he wanted them to report to him on how Lady Bird was doing.

At first, she didn't behave as though she was in charge. Confidence was a scarce commodity for Lady Bird Johnson. Asked years later about her early days in the office, she replies: "I was determined, and I wanted to learn. And I was scared." She went on attending business school in the mornings, and in the office she downplayed her role, to make it appear to the two secretaries that she was on a level with them: although she sat at her husband's desk as he had instructed her to do, she moved a typing table and a typewriter in beside his chair, and began to share the typing with the two secretaries—who at first treated her as a sort of apprentice secretary; there is a faintly patronizing note to Weber's report, in a letter he wrote to Johnson a week after she began working, that "Lady Bird is very industrious about her shorthand and typing at school." She let Mary Rather, who had experience doing it, make most of the calls to the departments and agencies.

But that changed.

Things weren't being done the way Lyndon would have wanted, she felt. She was signing all the letters from the office, and, reading them, she was finding misspellings. When she asked Mary and O.J. to correct them, they would correct them in handwriting, and the letters looked, she felt, rather sloppy. Lyndon had never let letters go out like that: one mistake, no matter how minor, and the whole letter had to be retyped, no matter how many times it had been retyped before. And she could not blind herself to the fact that insufficient progress was being made on the projects Lyndon would normally be pushing through the bureaucracy, and that complaints were already beginning to be heard from constituents; Weber himself was to report that "some people were already hollering that Lyndon Johnson had gone off of the job and his work wasn't being taken care of." She knew how important the efficient operation of his office was for the man she loved so deeply. And for her, too. Both of their lives were wholly bound up in his career. In her mind, he was at war—at any moment he might be facing the enemy; if he was actually having "an interesting time up and down the West Coast," some of it with Alice Glass, Lady Bird appears not to have been aware of that—and he should be spared worries about the office. That was the least she could do for him.

She knew, for she had heard their complaints over the years, how bitterly Lyndon's various secretaries resented being made to retype letters over and over again for minor mistakes. It was very hard for her to insist that Weber and Miss Rather retype letters over and over again. But she felt that it was necessary that she do so. And she did. Once, after she had handed a number of letters back to Weber for what she recalls as "small misspellings," she emerged unexpectedly from her office to find him smacking his fist on his desk in anger. But when he submitted another letter with a mistake, she handed it back to him.

She did things much more difficult—for there were people in Washington more formidable than Weber and Miss Rather.

"There was no doubt about it: O.J. and Mary knew more than I ever would," she recalls, "but I had one advantage. I had Lyndon's name, and he had a network of friends in the departments . . . and I could get my feet in the door when sometimes a secretary couldn't." "I had a complete picture of my complete lack of experience," she adds, "but I also had a feeling that nobody cares quite as much as you do about your business, and next to you, your wife. . . . They knew more, but perhaps I *cared* a bit more." She told O.J. and Mary that she would not be doing any more typing; from now on, she said, she would sign the letters they typed, and handle as many of the calls from the constituents as possible—and she would be dealing with the departments and agencies herself. And, she said, she would be getting in earlier in the mornings; she wouldn't be going to business school any longer.

Dealing with the departments and agencies. Corcoran and Rowe, and Lyndon's other friends in Washington, could make sure that agency heads and other high administrative officials accepted her telephone calls and, if a visit in person was necessary, could get her in to see them. But Corcoran and Rowe couldn't help her once she was in. For the previous twenty-nine years of her life, Lady Bird Johnson had never been able to make people listen to her, much less persuade them to do things for her.

She had to make them listen now.

Sometimes, when Lady Bird had an important call to make, Mary Rather, glancing into her office, would see her sitting at her husband's big desk, in her husband's big chair, "looking as if she would rather have done anything in the world rather than pick up that phone and dial."

But she always picked it up.

And if a phone call wasn't enough, if she had to go to see an official in person, she went to see him—even if the official was a Cabinet officer, even if the official was the most feared of Cabinet officers, Harold Ickes, the tart-tongued, terrible-tempered Old Curmudgeon himself. "There were some real scary moments," Lady Bird Johnson would recall forty years later. "One time I had to go and see that formidable man, Mr. Ickes." At parties, she had dreaded exchanging even a few words of social chatter with him; now she had to ask him to revoke an order relocating a CCC camp, and explain why, for political reasons, it should be revoked. But Ickes' secretary didn't keep her waiting too long under the giant moosehead that hung over visitors in his anteroom at the Department of the Interior, and when she was ushered in, "he really couldn't have been nicer." Peering at her over the top of his rimless spectacles, he listened to her story, and then said simply that he would look into the matter. But hardly had she returned to the office when there was a telephone call from one of Ickes' assistants. The matter had been worked out as Mrs. Johnson had requested, the assistant said.

DURING THE TEN WEEKS he and Connally were touring the West Coast, Johnson would sometimes telephone, and there was a constant stream of mail—her letters returned with Lyndon's orders in the wide margins, and letters he wrote with more detailed instructions—and the instructions at first were those that would be given to a political novice. At one point, he even complained to Weber about his wife: "Since she doesn't get pay she is irregular in writing, and I can't fire her—Can't you and Mary help me by persuasive reminders to write daily." Only a few paragraphs from his letters are known—Mrs. Johnson has not released the rest—but from this handful, the tone appears to have changed. When, as he had been leaving for the Coast, he had told her to write personal notes to key supporters in the district, he had done so with misgivings, but after copies of the first batch arrived, he wrote her, "Your letters are splendid. . . . I don't think I have ever sent any better letters out of my office." And when she began making occasional suggestions, he could hardly help starting to notice that they usually contained considerable insight, if not into politics, then into human beings; for example, they had decided jointly that she should include in her letters to constituents a reference to the fact that she was working without salary, but now she said she thought that was wrong—too self-serving. "I agree with you," he wrote. He wanted her to do more work, and more, and more—because, he wrote her, if she could do enough, "we would be invincible. Think of the effect it would have if 2,000 of our best friends in the District had personal notes from you written at the rate of 25 a day for sixty days. I don't know how you are going to find time to do all this and still take the people to lunch that I want you to take, and see the people in the evening that you must see, but I guess with your methodical planning you can work it out." There may have been some resistance in the office to taking orders from her, but on March 1 he sent a letter of "instruction about the staff's future responsibilities," and had her read it to the staff, and after that there was no question about who was in charge. Then, after ten weeks, he returned and learned almost immediately that he was going to the South Pacific; sitting at his desk, he wrote out his will leaving everything to her, had O.J. and Mary witness it, and left. "I remember how handsome he looked in his Navy overcoat," Lady Bird says.

The next weeks were a bad time for her. There were few telephone calls, and they were from Hawaii and then from New Zealand, and then there was one from Australia in which her husband said he was about to go into the combat zone; the weather in Washington was warm, and the windows in the Johnson apartment would be open, so that Gladys Montgomery, who lived in the apartment below, was awakened when the phone would ring "around three or four in the morning," and Mrs. Montgomery could not help overhearing the words with which Lady Bird ended each call: "Good night, my beloved." Then, for some time, there were no calls at all; the next word was a report that her husband was in a naval hospital in the Fiji Islands, dangerously ill. There were weeks of worry.

During these weeks, she ran his office. There were no longer any instructions in the margin of a letter to help her, although with a particularly thorny question she could call John Connally or Alvin Wirtz in Austin. She was on her own.

Every day brought some new problem to be solved. A relative of a constituent had died in Palestine, and a lawyer from Palestine was needed to handle the estate. When Lady Bird went to the State Department, she was told arrangements would have to be made through the British Embassy ("I didn't see the Ambassador—I wasn't that size of an applicant," Mrs. Johnson says—"but I did get to see" an official, "a very *nice* gentleman, with courtly manners. He said, 'Won't you join me for a bit of tea?,' and he reached into the drawer with an almost conspiratorial wink, and took out two lumps of sugar and dropped one in my cup and one in his").

"There were always mothers who said they hadn't heard from Johnny in months and months," she recalls. "Would I please find out where

Johnny was." There were "a whole lot of folks who wanted to get into
Officers Candidate School, knowing they were going to be drafted sooner
or later." There were the businessmen with half-completed plants "so you
had to plead their cause before the War Production Board or whatever.
. . . 'Strategic materials' and 'OCS' and lots of things became just a part
of your vocabulary. . . ."

And she learned she could solve the problems. "You know," she
would recall, "the squeaking wheel gets the grease. And if you keep after
the Army Department or the Navy Department or the Red Cross long
enough, and pester them enough, we could help them. For one thing, it
was down the street from us, and it was sixteen hundred miles from them,
so you could help them." The constituent got his lawyer from Palestine,
and Austin got its Air Force base, and a lot of Johnnys were located, and
Lady Bird Johnson heard mothers sobbing with relief on the telephone
when she told them that their son was alive, he just hadn't bothered to
write, you know how young men are.

She learned, moreover, that she could solve problems in her own
way. She could never use her husband's methods, but she could use her
own. If she was a squeaking wheel, it was a wheel that squeaked very
politely. Recalling forty years later the lessons she learned during the
summer of 1942 about helping constituents, she says: "If you'll just be
real nice about it, and real, real earnest, courteous and persistent, you
could help them." She never let her smile slip, or raised her voice, or said
a harsh word, but she never stopped trying to solve a problem—and a lot
of them were solved. Edward A. Clark, an Austin attorney who needed
a great deal of help, both for himself and for his clients, with the War
Production Board and other government agencies, and who had not
looked forward at all to having to rely on a woman, says: "When she took
over that office, she was wonderful. She gave wonderful service. And she
did it without ever raising her voice or fussing—she never shouted even
at a secretary. She thanked anyone who brought her a pencil. She was
just as sweet and kind to them. She was grateful to everyone." And as
she got the lawyer, and the Air Force base, and the other things the
constituents wanted, Lady Bird Johnson got something for herself, too—
something she had never had before: confidence.

"The real brains of the office were O.J. and Mary," she is careful to
say, in recalling 1942. "And yet I played a useful role."

When, years later, she would be asked how the summer of '42 had
changed her, she would always, as was invariable with her, put the changes
in the context of her husband. "The very best part of it," she would say,
"was that it gave me a lot more understanding of Lyndon. By the time
the end of the day came, when I had shifted the gears in my mind innumerable times, I could know what Lyndon had been through. . . . I was

more prepared after that to understand what sometimes had seemed to be Lyndon's unnecessary irritations. . . ." When, at the end of the day, Nellie or someone else wanted her to make still another decision—where to eat dinner, for example—she would "get almost mad at them."

But she also saw some changes that were not in the context of her husband.

"After a few months," she says, "I really felt that if it was ever necessary, I could make my own living—and that's a good feeling to have. That's very good for you, for your self-esteem and for your place in the world—because, well, I didn't have a home. I didn't have any children, and although I had a tremendously exciting, vital life, I didn't have any home base, so to speak, except for Lyndon, and it's good to know that you yourself, aside from a man, have some capabilities, and I found that out, er, er, er, to my amazement, rather."

Forty years later, Mrs. Johnson was renowned for her graciousness, her dignity, her poise under even the most difficult conditions, for the capability as a political speaker and as a President's wife that she had displayed as the First Lady of the United States. During interviews for this book, she was invariably helpful, cooperative, pleasant, but she seldom showed the depths of her emotions. When the interviews reached 1942, however, Lady Bird Johnson suddenly blurted out: "1942 was really quite a great year!"

SPEAKING OF THE QUALITIES that Lady Bird Johnson revealed for the first time while her husband was away at war, Nellie Connally says: "I think she changed. But I think it was always there. I just don't think it was allowed out."

After Johnson returned from the war ("I was shaken when I saw him," Lady Bird remembers. "He had been through a lot. He had lost [weight]. . . . My feeling was at once protective, and I wanted to get him a lot of milkshakes"), it was again not allowed out. Mrs. Johnson says that after her husband's return, "I did not go into the office regularly." Nothing could elicit from Mrs. Johnson's lips one word that could possibly be construed as a criticism of her husband. Oh no, she says with emphasis, she was not at all disappointed to stop working and return to her previous life. "I was glad to turn over the responsibility." The turnover was complete. Any illusions Mrs. Johnson may have held about now being included in her husband's political discussions were shattered at one of the first of those discussions, when she ventured to stay in the room after it began. "We'll see you later, Bird," her husband said, dismissing her. He treated her as he had before.

So impressed had Austin political and business leaders been with Mrs.

Johnson that one day, Ed Clark recalls, when a group of them were at lunch, someone said, "kidding, you know," "Maybe she's going to decide that she likes that office, and then he's going to wish he hadn't gone off to war." This joking became so widespread that it reached print in district newspapers; a letter to the *Goldthwaite Eagle*, for example, said that instead of re-electing Johnson to Congress in absentia, "I'd call a convention . . . and nominate Mrs. Lyndon Johnson for Congress to take her husband's place while he is fighting for his country. She would make a good congressman." The joking reached Johnson's ears—and after he returned, he took pains to put it to rest, to make clear that his wife's role as caretaker of his office while he was in the Pacific, and indeed her role in his overall political life, had never been significant. Once, in Austin, with a group of people present, he was asked if he discussed his political problems with Lady Bird. He replied that of course he did. "I talk everything over with her." Then Lyndon Johnson paused. "Of course," he said, "I talk my problems over with a lot of people. I have a nigger maid, and I talk my problems over with her, too."

In other areas, also, Lyndon Johnson treated his wife as he had before. On August 19, Alice Marsh wired Johnson: HOPE WE CAN HAVE THAT BIRTHDAY PARTY. Whether or not they did is not known, but Alice and Johnson resumed their affair. The weekends at Longlea started again.

Lady Bird's Aunt Effie knew how much her niece wanted a house, and now she told the young wife that she would pay most of the purchase price if Lady Bird found one that she wanted to buy. Moreover, there would be money from the estate of Uncle Claude Patillo of Alabama, who had recently died. By the Fall of 1942 his estate was being settled, and Mrs. Johnson was informed that she would eventually be receiving about $21,000. "Now we can go and get that house," she told her husband.

The two-story brick colonial at 4921 30th Place, a quiet street in the northwest section of Washington, was a modest eight-room house with a screened veranda at the rear, but she loved it. Her husband liked it too, but he insisted on bargaining and issuing ultimata to the owners. When they refused to accept his "take-it-or-leave-it" figure, the deal seemed dead. Coming home to their apartment one day, Lady Bird found her husband talking politics with Connally and asked if she could discuss the house with him. Her husband listened to her arguments, and then, without a word of reply, resumed his conversation with Connally as if she had never spoken. For once in her life—the only time in her married life that any of her friends can recall—Lady Bird Johnson lashed back at her husband.

"I want that house!" she screamed. "Every woman wants a home of her own. I've lived out of a suitcase ever since we've been married. I have no home to look forward to. I have no children to look forward to. I have nothing to look forward to but another election." In the retelling of this story, the denouement has a patina of cuteness. Johnson was reported to have asked Connally, "What should I do?," to which Connally is said to have replied: "I'd buy the house." This may not have been the actual dialogue, but by the end of 1942 the house was bought—for $18,000, about $10,000 of which Aunt Effie put up—and Lady Bird had her home. "You see," Mrs. Johnson carefully explains, "I didn't feel unhappy. I was happy about the house."

5

Marking Time

THE SIDEWALKS OF WASHINGTON were filled with uniforms by the time
Lyndon Johnson returned from the South Pacific—khaki and navy and
the off-grays of Australians and New Zealanders—and by the end of the
next year a surprising number of them sported service ribbons from different theaters of war, and then the ribbons bore the stars that signified
major battles: North Africa, the Solomons, the Aleutians, Sicily, the skies
over France and Germany. Seemingly endless caravans of Army trucks
and jeeps rumbled through the city on their way to the huge embarkation
areas north and south of the capital. Near the Mall, the drab wooden
"temps" hastily built during World War I and never torn down had
sprouted long wings and annexes. Soldiers with fixed bayonets walked
beats outside the tall iron fence in front of the White House, and the cars
that pulled up into the driveway disgorged Admirals and Generals. Washington was a city at war.

For a while after his return, Lyndon Johnson attempted to find a place
in the war—at, of course, a rank he considered appropriate. The job he
had his eye on now was Secretary of the Navy, and when, in October,
1942, the man in that job, Frank Knox, was away from Washington on
an inspection tour for the President, Johnson planted with Walter Winchell, Drew Pearson and other friendly columnists the rumor that Knox
was about to resign and that he himself was in line for the post. Noting
that if Johnson was appointed Secretary, he would be working with
MacArthur, Pearson wrote: "Lyndon Johnson as Secretary of the Navy,
Douglas MacArthur at the helm—that ought to be a good combination."
George W. Stimpson, the Washington correspondent for several Texas
newspapers, writing that the suggestion of Johnson's appointment "has
caught on like wildfire," said that if Johnson was appointed, he would, at
thirty-four, be the second youngest Cabinet officer in history; Alexander

Hamilton, Secretary of the Treasury at thirty-three, had been the young-est. ("Johnson," Stimpson wrote, "spent several months on active duty as a Lieutenant Commander, in the Southwest Pacific area. He ate, slept and fought alongside men in all branches of the service in half a dozen hot spots.") The wildfire, however, was limited to credulous journalists; Roosevelt, although still fond of Johnson, and willing to chat with him over breakfast, was apparently unwilling to consider giving him a high wartime post. Next came mysterious leaks (from Johnson, to reporters) of an imminent "secret government mission" to London—the kind of li-aison mission that Harry Hopkins was performing between Roosevelt and Winston Churchill, perhaps. ("Johnson," the Associated Press reported, "has been conferring almost daily at the War, Navy Department and the White House.") But there was no mission to London either.

Once Johnson realized that he was not to be given a high position in the war, the change in his attitude toward it was dramatic. In O. J. We-ber's recollection, "He regarded it as an interference with his agenda." He resented its demands on his staff, but, despite the strategic placement of Willard Deason in the Navy's Bureau of Personnel, and Johnson's in-fluence with Forrestal himself, the Congressman was defeated in a string of engagements with young aides, who, otherwise totally loyal to his ser-vice, persisted in regarding service to their country as a higher priority. Weber, for example, was so determined to serve that, after failing a Navy eye examination, he drank "gallons of carrot juice" in an attempt to im-prove his vision, and applied for enlistment as an Air Force communi-cations cadet. But every time he was notified to report for duty, Weber recalls, Johnson would say, "Well, I just can't spare you right now. I'll call someone and have him take care of it."

"This happened two or three times," Weber says, "and I really wanted to get in the war." The young secretary outmaneuvered Johnson by telephoning the colonel in charge of enlistments and telling him that the next time he received one of the Johnson-initiated telephone calls, the colonel should say that Weber was vitally needed in the Air Force. John Connally, who had been only temporarily deferring to Johnson's wishes in accompanying him to the West Coast, now refused to leave the Navy, and kept pushing for combat duty. After a staff job in North Africa, in 1945 he was finally assigned to the aircraft carrier *Essex*, operating off Japan, and rapidly won a reputation throughout the fleet for his coolness in directing the carrier's fighter planes as its group combat officer. A young Austin attorney, Charles Herring, turned out to be a competent replace-ment for Connally, and when Herring told Johnson that his number had been called in the draft, Johnson attempted to persuade him not to go, insisting that the opportunity of working in Washington was too good to pass up. Then when Herring said that his orders had already been cut, Johnson said, "Hell, I'll cancel that right now." And when Herring insisted on serving his country, Johnson exploded: "You're crazy!"

Not long after Johnson's return from the war, Roosevelt disappointed him in another matter. Johnson's possession of a measure of political influence that lifted him above the ranks of other junior congressmen was based on his fund-raising efforts during the 1940 elections. In a stroke of inspiration, he had seen in the moribund Democratic Congressional Campaign Committee an opportunity for personal political advantage. Obtaining an informal post with the committee, he had arranged for newly rich Texas contractors and independent oilmen to make contributions to it, with the stipulation that they be distributed at his discretion. This control over money urgently needed by congressmen running for re-election had given him their gratitude, and, in the House in general, a new respect, the first respect not based on his relationship with Roosevelt or Rayburn; his role with the campaign committee had given him his first taste of national power of his own. He had expected to perform the same role in 1942.

Between 1940 and 1942, however, Edwin W. Pauley, a burly, loquacious one-time oil-field roustabout who had become a successful California wildcatter, had emerged as a Democratic fund-raising force. His success in obtaining campaign contributions for the Democratic National Committee in 1940 had led Democratic National Chairman Edward J. Flynn, Boss of the Bronx and a longtime Roosevelt intimate, to name him the party's secretary, and in 1942, the President, impressed with him, appointed him treasurer. By October, journalists were referring to the oilman's fund-raising activities as "the great hot spell," for, as one wrote, "he turned on the heat to a degree that left many rich gentlemen permanently scorched," and succeeded in lifting the party out of debt. Antagonized by Johnson's aggressiveness—Johnson had been given only an informal post with the Congressional Campaign Committee in 1940 because of Flynn's objection to any formal connection—Flynn was not anxious to see him play even an informal role in the 1942 congressional campaigns. More to the point, because of Pauley's emergence, Johnson was no longer needed. His ace in the hole had been the fact that only he possessed access to the Texas oilmen; when, in 1940, Flynn had attempted to circumvent him and obtain their contributions himself, they had refused to contribute except through Johnson. Because of their common interests—and, in some cases, business ties—Pauley had access to the same money. When, in 1942, Flynn solicited Texas contributions, there was some reluctance—Brown & Root and liberal businessmen such as Stanley Marcus of the Neiman-Marcus department store refused to give except through Johnson—but when it was explained that handling all contributions through the National Committee would be more efficient, most of the big Texas contributors followed Flynn's suggestion.

Roosevelt appears to have wanted Johnson back in his 1940 role, but Roosevelt at war had little patience with politics. At a press conference, he responded to a political question by saying that too many reporters "haven't waked up to the fact that this is a war. Politics is out." To his aides, some of whom felt he did not understand that a poor showing by his party in the congressional elections would damage the President as well, he expressed similar sentiments. The battles on which the President's attention was focused that October were for Stalingrad and Guadalcanal, not Capitol Hill; only his direct intervention could have forced Johnson on Flynn, and that intervention was not forthcoming. Finally, on October 14, Marvin McIntyre told Johnson and the newest White House aide, Jonathan Daniels, whom Johnson had quickly cultivated, that the President would see them at 10:15 the next morning in the family quarters of the White House. But when the two men arrived, they were told, after being kept waiting in the Red Room, that the President would see them in his office instead. They went to Pa Watson's office right outside the President's, where they were joined by McIntyre. After a while, Watson said, "You gentlemen will not be in there for long, will you? Make it snappy." Johnson, "obviously getting his feelings hurt," according to Daniels, told Watson, "I have nothing to talk to the President about, he wanted to see us." Watson told the two men they should "go in and speak to him, even if just for a minute," but then Watson went into the President's office and when he emerged, he reported that the President had said that "maybe it would be better to see us later." Johnson strode out of the room. "It looked for a minute as if he had gone out in a pique," Daniels was to relate. By the time he and McIntyre caught up to Johnson, he had recovered himself; his face showed nothing; "he said he thought we were right behind him." But when Johnson attempted to get another appointment, Watson told him that the President had no time for political matters. At the last moment, Johnson wrote a concerned Rayburn that "these $200 droplets will not get the job done." What was needed, Johnson wrote, was to "select a 'minute man' group of thirty men, each of whom should raise $5,000, for a total of $150,000"; "there isn't any reason why, with the wealth and consideration that has been extended, we should fall down on this," he said. The money was indeed raised, but Johnson, having no direct role in the campaign committee, did not receive credit or influence. It had been money—campaign contributions to which he alone had access—that had given him his first lever to move the political world. Now that lever had been eased out of his grasp. In 1944, a single scene dramatized his loss. At a boisterous Democratic dinner in Dallas, at which Pauley announced to loud cheers and rebel yells that Texas had raised more for the party that year than any other state but New York, Johnson had to sit watching as State Treasurer Harry L. Seay presented the Californian with a $50,000 check—a check that represented the combined contributions of men who had once channeled their checks through *him*.

   In the House, as well as in the war effort, he wasn't being allowed to lead.

   A bare score of men—the Speaker, the Majority Leader and Whip, the most powerful committee chairmen—held genuine power in the 435-member body, and admission to this oligarchy was strictly by seniority. A handful of favored younger congressmen such as Johnson and Wright Patman who were granted entrance to Rayburn's Board of Education could drink with these men, but they couldn't rule with them. And the great Standing Committees of the House were run by chairmen answerable to no one—as was evident at every meeting of the Naval Affairs Committee, of which Johnson had been a member since he had been sworn in as the representative from the Tenth Congressional District of Texas in May, 1937.

   The committee's chairman, Carl Vinson, called the Navy "My Navy" and ordered its Admirals around like cabin boys. He treated his 26-member committee the same way. Slouched in the center of the two-tiered horseshoe of seats in the high-ceilinged committee room, glasses teetering on the tip of his long nose, mangled cigar dangling from his lips, his suits baggy and food-stained, his collar two sizes too big, the onetime country lawyer from a little town in Georgia ran the committee, one observer noted, "like a dictator," and scarcely allowed junior members like Johnson (who were addressed as "ensign") to question witnesses. When, occasionally, in questioning a witness, Johnson would essay a small witticism, Vinson would demand dryly, "Is the gentleman from Texas finished?" The gavel would crash down. "Let's proceed," the chairman would say. That committee, an observer said, is a "one-man committee. . . . On that committee, there are no disagreements"; the only voice that mattered was the chairman's soft Georgia drawl. For Lyndon Johnson's voice to matter on that committee, he would have to be chairman. Although deaths and early retirements among other members of the Naval Affairs Committee had elevated him from the lower to the upper tier of the committee horseshoe with unusual rapidity, Warren Magnuson, elected in a regular election and sworn in in January, 1937, three months before him, still sat between him and the chairman's gavel—and so did three other men, all of whom might be chairman before him—even if the Democrats retained control of the House. And none of the four could be chairman so long as Vinson was there (as indeed he would be there until 1965, when he retired at the age of eighty-one).

   There were other ways of leading within the House—but, as was seen in the first volume of this work, Johnson had never attempted them. His record on the introduction of national legislation—legislation which would have an effect outside his own district—had been striking. During his first six years in Congress, he introduced exactly one such bill: the bill to create a job for himself by merging the National Youth Administration and the Civilian Conservation Corps into a single agency, to whose chairmanship he hoped to be appointed. And if he didn't introduce legislation himself, he also didn't fight for legislation introduced by others. He didn't fight publicly. It was not merely laws that Congressman Lyndon Johnson didn't write, but speeches. His record in regard to "real" speeches—talks of more than a paragraph or two that were actually delivered in the House—had been as dramatic as his record on legislation. During his first months in Congress, in 1937, he delivered a brief memorial tribute to his predecessor. In 1941, he gave a speech advocating the extension of the Selective Service Act—the only other speech he had given in six years in Congress. In a marked departure from the usual practice among congressmen, he rarely even made use of the common device of inserting speeches delivered elsewhere in the *Congressional Record*; entire years had passed during which he had not employed this device even once.

He was as reluctant to fight on the floor of the House as he was to fight in the well. The liberal Southwestern congressmen known as "Mavericks" after their leader, Maury Maverick, were surprised when Johnson kept finding excuses to avoid attending their weekly dinners, but soon realized that while he professed to hold their views, he would not argue for them. Not that he would argue against them. As Representative Edouard V. M. Izac of California says, in an evaluation echoed by other congressmen: "He just simply was not especially interested in general legislation that came to the floor of the House. Some of us were on the floor all the time, fighting for liberal causes. But he stayed away from the floor, and while he was there, he was very, very silent." The record of Johnson's participation in House discussions and debates supports Izac's evaluation. As was seen in the first volume, that record is almost non-existent. Entire years passed without Johnson rising even once to make a point of order, or any other point; to ask or answer a question; to support or attack a bill under discussion; to participate, by so much as a single word, in an entire year's worth of floor proceedings in the body of which he was a member.*

His attitude toward taking public stands in the press was equally notable. Other congressmen might seek out reporters to comment on some national issue; Lyndon Johnson, starting to turn into a Capitol corridor

* The *Congressional Record* records not a single such instance of participation by Johnson in House discussions in 1937, 1938, 1939, 1942, 1943 or 1944.

and seeing a reporter standing there soliciting comments on a day when a hot issue was before the House, would whirl on his heel and hastily walk back around the corner.

He was as reluctant to fight for a cause in private as he was to fight in public. Some congressmen, even if rather silent in the well of the House or on the floor (although the *Congressional Record* indicates that few were as silent as Johnson), were effective in buttonholing fellow members in the House cloakrooms, or in the aisle at the rear of the House Chamber, where these "brass-railers" would stand with one foot up on the brass rail that separates the aisle from the members' desks. Johnson was not silent in the cloakroom or the aisle. Rather, he was friendly, gregarious—voluble, in fact. But, as Helen Gahagan Douglas observed, the volubility was a method of concealment. His colleagues on Capitol Hill observed what his classmates on College Hill had observed: that while Johnson was likely to dominate a conversation on a controversial issue, at the end of it none of his listeners would know his position on that issue. He would avoid saying anything substantive; if pinned down, he said what the other person wanted to hear. His avoidance of specifics was deft—as interviews with his colleagues reveal. While none of them can cite specific statements by Johnson to support their feelings, liberal congressmen believe that Lyndon Johnson was a liberal; conservative congressmen believe he was a conservative. Says the reactionary upstate New York Republican Sterling Cole, "Politically, if we disagreed, it wasn't apparent to me. Not at all." During his six years in Congress, years in which great issues had come before it, Lyndon Johnson had managed to steer clear of all of them.

Now, in the beginning of 1943, he broke new ground for himself, introducing a piece of national legislation—with the exception of the self-aggrandizing NYA-CCC merger proposal, the first such bill he had introduced in seven years—and rising on the floor to argue for it.

This fight ended in a fiasco. Johnson's bill, a draconian measure that would have curbed absenteeism in war plants by requiring the immediate drafting of any worker absent from the job too often, fell under the jurisdiction of the House Labor Committee, but Johnson introduced it instead in his own Naval Affairs Committee—without extending the courtesy of consultation to Labor Committee Chairwoman Mary T. Norton of New Jersey. When Mrs. Norton learned about the bill—after the Naval Affairs committee had reported it out favorably—she angrily confronted Vinson, who had to admit in embarrassment that he had incorrectly assumed that the Labor Committee had surrendered jurisdiction. She then demanded that the Rules Committee, which controls the flow of legislation to the floor, not allow this bill to reach the floor; and the bill died in the Rules Committee. Following this debacle, Lyndon Johnson did not make another speech in the House during the rest of the war. He did not introduce another bill. He had little to do with the workings of Congress. And whereas before the war, Johnson had been a dynamic and effective Congressman in improving the lives of his constituents through rural electrification and other public-works projects, wartime shortages of materials now brought such projects to a virtual halt. Work for the Tenth District was largely limited to servicing the requests of individual constituents, and for the duration of the war, increasingly this work was carried on not by Lyndon Johnson but by his staff. His political acumen and energy were, for the duration, no longer used for politics. They were used for making money.

6

Buying and Selling

*I have been unable to save much money in my life. I have been
in politics, and in politics an honest man does not get rich.*
     —SAM RAYBURN (whose savings at his death totaled $15,000)

DURING THE YEARS before the war, when the path to power lay open
before him, Lyndon Johnson had refused to risk a detour even for wealth.

He had wanted money during those years, wanted it passionately.
The lack of it—and the resulting insecurity—had underlain so many of
the terrors of his youth. Far from alleviating his fears, moreover, election
to Congress had seemed only to intensify them, particularly, say friends
with whom he discussed his financial situation, the fear of ending up like
his father, who had also been an elected official—six times elected to the
Texas Legislature—but who had died penniless, in the humiliating job of
a state bus inspector. So many times since Lyndon had come to Washington, he told these friends, he had seen former congressmen who had
lost their seats—as, he predicted, he himself would inevitably one day lose
his—working in poorly paid or demeaning jobs; again and again, he
harked back to an incident he could not get out of his mind: while riding
an elevator in the Capitol one day, he had struck up a conversation with
the elevator operator—who told him that *he* had once been a congressman.

When, during those pre-war years, he had been given small opportunities to improve his financial situation, he had accepted them eagerly.
In 1939, the paternal, immensely wealthy Charles Marsh, fond of gran-
diose gestures toward young men, offered Johnson a nineteen-acre tract
of Austin real estate at the giveaway price of $12,000. Lady Bird borrowed
the money from her father to buy it. Brown & Root graded and land-
scaped the tract and built a road out to it—and, for the first time, the

Johnsons owned property. Johnson had sought further opportunities; hearing that one of two businessmen he had casually introduced to each other at an Austin party in 1940 had later bought a piece of Austin real estate from the other, he asked the seller for a "finder's fee." The startled businessman refused to give Johnson anything, saying he had played no role in the transaction beyond the social introduction. Considering the matter closed—the transaction, the businessman recalls, was small, and the fee would not have amounted to "more than a thousand dollars, if that"—he was astonished, upon opening his front door to pick up his newspaper early the next morning, to see his Congressman sitting on the curb, waiting to ask him again for the money. And when he again refused, "Lyndon started—well, really, to beg me for it. . . ." George R. Brown, whom Johnson was constantly importuning, with increasing urgency, to find him a business of his own, had felt certain that if a substantial opportunity was offered, Johnson would leap at it.

But when the offer came, it was declined. During a vacation with Johnson and Brown at the Greenbrier Hotel in West Virginia in the autumn of 1940, Marsh, wanting to free Johnson from financial worries, offered to let the young Congressman purchase his share in a partnership with oilman Sid Richardson without a down payment, paying for it out of subsequent earnings. Johnson understood that the offer was worth at least three quarters of a million dollars, but after weighing it for a week, he declined with thanks, politely but firmly. I can't be an oilman, he said; if the public knew I had oil interests, "it would kill me politically."

Brown and Marsh had thought they had measured Johnson's political ambitions, had thought measuring them was easy, for Johnson was always talking about how he wanted to stay in Congress until a Senate seat opened up, and then run for the Senate, about how that Senate seat was his ultimate goal in politics. Never had he mentioned any other office, nor did he mention one during that week at the Greenbrier. But since being an oilman couldn't hurt him in his safe congressional district, or in a Senate race in oil-dominated Texas—since there was only one office for which he would be "killed" by being an "oilman"—after that week Brown and Marsh realized what Johnson really wanted, and how much he wanted it. Money and power—he wanted both. But the depth of his need for one was as nothing compared with the depth of his need for the other.

His rejection of money on that occasion, however, didn't mean that he stopped talking about it, or wanting it. A $10,000-a-year salary such as he drew as a Congressman was considered adequate by other young men in Washington, but it did not even make a dent in his needs. The suits that he had custom tailored, at Lentz & Linden in San Antonio, were the most expensive they sold—$195 apiece—and he purchased several at a time. Alice Marsh had taught him to turn the length and ungainliness of his arms to advantage by wearing custom-made shirts with French cuffs, and these shirts, monogrammed, arrived at his apartment in boxloads. His cuff links had to be solid gold, as did his watch; his shoes had to be of the softest leather—custom made—and his boots, custom made, were hand-tooled. He wanted not only maids, but a masseuse. He liked to give gifts, to pick up checks in expensive night clubs—possession of the resources to do so was very important to him. While he had been on the West Coast during the first months of the war, he had written O. J. Weber one day, "I waked up worrying about money," and he had told the secretary to send him "a list of all unpaid bills that have come in, and we will clear with you before they are paid," but after reiterating his concern about finances, he had gone on to ask for news about a new shipment of custom-tailored shirts he had ordered to wear with his Navy uniform (which had also been custom-tailored). Even before the war, after his defeat by Pappy O'Daniel, he had begun taking measures to improve his financial situation: employing George Brown as a conduit, he even made a few purchases of small oil leases that provided him with monthly royalty checks, purchases small enough, and made discreetly enough, so that they could be kept secret. But the amounts involved were insignificant compared with his needs. The Johnsons were constantly skimping—or at least one of them was; during a week in which boxes of custom-made shirts were delivered to the Johnson apartment, Mrs. Johnson set out, with her carload of boxes, on the long drive to Texas to save the cost of another set of dishes and household implements. As long as the path he had mapped out was open to him, he deferred his desire for money.

Now, however, with the path closed, it was deferred no longer. During the war, Lyndon Johnson grabbed for money as eagerly as he had grabbed for political power. Inexperienced in business, he displayed, for some years at least, little business expertise or instincts. But he didn't need any. For the basis of his business enterprise was not business but politics. His first step, in fact, was a case study in the use of political influence to amass wealth.

THE INSTRUMENTALITY was a radio station—KTBC, in Austin.

In few businesses was the role of government as crucial as in radio, for not only were the very licenses which allowed the use of the airwaves granted, and periodically renewed, only at the sufferance of the Federal Communications Commission, but the FCC possessed virtually unchallengeable authority over every aspect of a station's operations.

KTBC proved the point. Although radio was a booming business in 1942, the Austin station wasn't participating in the boom. The application filed with the FCC in December, 1935, by its three owners—a University of Texas law professor, A. W. Walker, and two attorneys, Robert A. Stuart and Robert B. Anderson (who became Secretary of the Treasury in the Eisenhower Administration)—for an FCC construction permit, the first step toward obtaining a license, wasn't even approved until nineteen months of bureaucratic red tape, which included six separate hearings, had elapsed. And although the owners had requested permission to operate virtually twenty-four hours a day, the permit they finally received, in July, 1937, allowed them only to share a frequency, 1120 kilocycles, with WTAW, the station of Texas A & M College, eighty miles from Austin; the FCC granted KTBC only the daytime hours, denying it the evening hours, the most valuable time on radio; KTBC was to be only a "sundowner," a station required to go off the air at sundown, as early as five o'clock during the winter months in which radio listenership was highest because inclement weather kept families inside. Given the lack of evening hours, it was almost irrelevant that 1120 (later changed to 1150) was too high on the dial for widespread reception because in the Austin area that end of the dial was already crowded with the city's other station, KNOW, and with two powerful San Antonio stations, WOAI and KTSA, whose signals, much more powerful than KTBC's, drowned out the Austin station except on a narrow frequency, and limited its range to the area immediately around the city. A "sundowner" had little chance of obtaining an affiliation with a national network. Businesses that wanted to advertise on the popular evening network shows would advertise on either KTSA, which was part of the popular CBS network, or on WOAI, which was an NBC network affiliate.

There had never been much money behind KTBC. The three owners had started it with an investment of only $27,000, and that had all been spent. Its "headquarters," located over the Austin School of Business in a small building on Colorado Avenue, consisted of a studio, a control room, three small offices and a classroom the station was allowed to use as a reception area when the school, as KTBC's lease put it, "does not have a class actually reciting there"; since the station could not afford the rental for even such modest facilities, it gave the school three hundred dollars' worth of air time a month in exchange. KTBC's only other physical plant consisted of an antenna and transmitter located on a plot of land north of Austin. The station's management was similarly makeshift. So amateurishly produced and written were its own shows that local merchants had little incentive to advertise on them. And they didn't. Each year, KTBC's financial picture worsened: in 1942, advertising revenues totaled $26,795, expenses $33,026; at the end of 1942, the station's debts were more than $19,000; the station had been kept afloat during 1941 and 1942 only by $5,000 in loans from Professor Walker, loans which consumed the last of his available capital. Employees were wondering from day to day when the station would go off the air for good. Better management would not have made much difference, however. So long as the conditions imposed by the initial license—the restrictions on its hours and its unfavorable location at the crowded end of the dial—remained, the station could never be very profitable.

But conditions could be changed, and changed quickly. For the restrictions on KTBC were, after all, restrictions that had been imposed by government. Lyndon Johnson had already learned, in obtaining lucrative "change orders" for Brown & Root on its Marshall Ford Dam contract, how easy it was to alter conditions imposed by government. Walker, Stuart and Anderson (and James G. Ulmer, a Yale graduate and radio entrepreneur who owned several Texas radio stations, and who had been given some form of interest in KTBC in return for his managerial expertise) wanted to change the severe restrictions on its operations; the reasons for KTBC's problems, Walker would say, were simply that "we did not have a network affiliation and we couldn't operate at night"; Ulmer was later to say that he had "completed all the engineering" data necessary for a contemplated application to the FCC for a change to a lower frequency and longer hours, but ran into more FCC delays unrelated to that change. And when, in frustration, the three owners tried to sell the station, they found that the FCC wouldn't even let them do that. In December, 1939, their "State Capital Broadcasting Association" had given an option to J. M. West, a wealthy oilman, rancher and publisher of the *Austin Tribune*, to purchase KTBC for $50,000, contingent on the required FCC approval of the transfer of the station's license to him. But in February, 1940, the FCC replied to the transfer application by revoking KTBC's license, stating that it had learned that Ulmer had a "hidden interest" in the station. The three owners responded that the FCC was mistaken, that Ulmer's interest did not extend to stock ownership. Wanting to make the point moot, however, since their only interest in the station now was to sell it, within a month, on March 25, 1940, they made arrangements that would "eliminate any monetary profit of any kind to which . . . Dr. Jas. G. Ulmer might ever become entitled to from the proceeds of the sale of said capital stock," although he would continue to manage the station. They then agreed to sell KTBC to West for $20,000— plus $12,000 to cover the station's debts at the time. Confident that they had certainly met any conceivable objection to the sale, the three owners again asked the FCC to permit the change of ownership.

The owners of KTBC may have moved quickly, but the FCC did not. It moved, in fact, not at all, for more than a year; although the Commission was finally to concede that Ulmer had indeed "completely . . . relinquished any . . . interest which he may have had" in the station's ownership, it did not issue this ruling for fifteen months, during which time KTBC was operating under a series of temporary licenses while hearings and bureaucratic complications dragged on. And when, on June 26, 1941, the FCC gave KTBC a regular license, it nevertheless did not approve the transfer to West—this time because he was a newspaper publisher, and the agency had recently decided to hold hearings on "Order 79," an overall policy that would bar newspaper publishers from owning radio stations; until these hearings were completed, the FCC said, all applications from publishers were being placed in a "pending" file. Nor did the delays stop there. In August, West died, and left his option to his two sons and a conservative Republican businessman from Austin, E. G. Kingsbery. When they petitioned the FCC for a ruling—*any* ruling, favorable or unfavorable—on the transfer request so that at least they would know where they stood, the Commission returned the petition, saying that it had been submitted in incorrect form. In 1942, KTBC was still snarled in bureaucratic red tape. By refusing to allow nighttime hours, the Commission was making operation of the station economically unfeasible for its owners. But since the Commission had refused, for almost three years, to rule on the Wests' option to purchase the station, and the option remained in force, the owners couldn't sell it to anyone else. The FCC was, in effect, forcing them either to operate at a loss, or to close down, thereby surrendering their license. But closing down would mean that Professor Walker would never get his $5,000 back; in addition, there was now also a $4,000 loan one of West's sons had made to keep the station going, a debt the owners felt obligated to repay.

They were frantic to sell. Walker wrote to FCC Chairman James Fly directly. He told Fly of the "hard struggle to keep this station on its feet." Only his loans had done so, the professor wrote, and "I have gone the limit of my personal ability" and could make no more. He was expecting to be drafted momentarily. There was, he said, no alternative to selling; he pleaded with Fly to allow the transfer of KTBC's license to the Wests. But the FCC still refused to approve the sale. Fly's only reply to Walker was that Order 79 continued to preclude FCC consent to the proposed sale of KTBC.

Ulmer was also frantic. Before his death, West, increasingly intrigued by radio's potential, had offered to buy all Ulmer's radio stations for $750,000, and to allow him to continue managing them. But, determined to have an outlet in the state capital, the oilman made his offer contingent on FCC approval not only of their sale, but of the KTBC sale as well: if Ulmer obtained FCC approval of the KTBC sale, the whole deal was on; if not, it was off. And Ulmer's money was running out.

And then, in 1942, Ulmer made a fatal misstep: he decided to retain an attorney who was known to have influence with government agencies, and the attorney he chose was Alvin Wirtz.

The two men had dinner one evening in Austin's Driskill Hotel, and Ulmer explained the situation. The big man with the broad smile could not have been more sympathetic. By the end of dinner, Ulmer thought he had retained Wirtz to represent the State Capital Broadcasting Association before the FCC; he was later to say that they had even agreed on a $10,000 retainer: $2,500 down, $1,000 a month for five months; the balance of $2,500 upon FCC approval. Wirtz told Ulmer to meet him at his office the next morning at nine o'clock.

But Ulmer did not know the man with whom he was dealing. At nine in the morning, Ulmer was in the waiting room of Powell, Wirtz, Rauhut and Gideon in the Brown Building. The secretary told him that Senator Wirtz hadn't come in yet, so Ulmer sat down to wait. He waited for some hours, from time to time looking at a picture prominently displayed on the wall, a picture of Lyndon Johnson, bearing a fond inscription. But Senator Wirtz never arrived. Finally, the secretary said that perhaps Ulmer should come back in the afternoon. And when he returned in the afternoon, the secretary apologized; Senator Wirtz, she said, had unexpectedly been called to Washington, and indeed had already left. She told Ulmer that Wirtz would be staying at the Mayflower Hotel, and Ulmer tried repeatedly to telephone him there, leaving messages. Wirtz never replied. In fact, Ulmer never heard from him again.

Ulmer never heard from the FCC about KTBC, either, and neither did the station's owners, or the holders of the option to purchase it, the Wests and Kingsbery. They did, however, hear from someone else: the man whose picture was on the wall of Wirtz's office.

Kingsbery was a conservative Republican and a tough businessman, but he was also a father. In 1941, Johnson had given his son, John, one of the coveted appointments to the United States Naval Academy at Annapolis. "He knew there were two ways through to me, my family and my money, and of those, the most important was my family," Kingsbery was to say. Now, when, just before Christmas in 1942, Kingsbery was asked to call on the Congressman, he brought him a present: a quart of pure cream. That was not, however, the type of present Johnson had in mind. Alluding to the appointment of Kingsbery's son, and then to Kingsbery's option on KTBC, the Congressman asked Kingsbery to give him the option. If he ever lost an election, he said, he would be out of politics, and "I have no means of making a living. I want to get into some business." Kingsbery was not particularly eager to exercise his option ("I understood the station was bankrupt") but felt an obligation to the deceased West not to do anything West's sons would not approve. He also felt, however, that he had an "obligation" to Johnson for his son's appointment, and he told the Congressman, "I'll recommend that they give it to you, and then we'll be even."

Johnson wanted someone more influential with the West brothers than Kingsbery to join in this recommendation; in fact, he wanted even more than a recommendation from George Brown.

Fearing that the ultra-conservative Wests would not want to sell this medium of public opinion to a "liberal," Johnson decided that the identity of the purchaser must be concealed; he proposed that Brown act as a front for him and pretend to the Wests that Brown & Root was the buyer. However, Brown recalls that he, unwilling to deceive friends, "told him he should do it himself"—that is, persuade them to sell. He knew Lyndon could persuade them, he was to say with a smile; convincing liberals that he was a liberal, conservatives that he was a conservative, "that was his leadership, that was his knack." Brown did not overestimate his man. He arranged for Johnson to meet the West brothers in Suite 8-F of Houston's Lamar Hotel—the Brown & Root suite that was the late-afternoon gathering place of the city's conservative rulers—led the three men to a room across the hall and shut the door behind them. "He went in there, and in an hour he had convinced them" that he wasn't a liberal, and he "had them liking him." Wesley West was to tell a friend, "I didn't like Lyndon Johnson, but by God I went over there, and he's a pretty good fellow." They agreed to give him their option to purchase KTBC.* Forty years later, George Brown, old now, almost blind, holding an interviewer's arm as he walked up to 8-F to take a nap after lunch, stopped and pointed to the door across the hall: "Right there, right in that room [824], is where he bought the radio station," he said. The Wests agreed to surrender their option on one condition: that the FCC approve the sale, which would be made not to Lyndon Johnson but to Mrs. Lyndon Johnson.

On January 2, Mrs. Johnson mailed Wirtz a check for $17,500 to be placed in escrow for the sale, and deposited $7,500 in her account in the American National Bank to be applied against the station's outstanding debts; when she had done that, Lyndon and Lady Bird's total remaining liquid assets may have been as little as $938 in the bank, plus $6,000 in savings bonds.

On January 18 the West brothers agreed to sell their option to her for $17,500 "subject to the approval of the FCC." On January 23, 1943, Mrs. Johnson filed an application (filled out by Wirtz), asking the FCC's consent to a transfer of control of KTBC from the old owners to her. On February 16, the Secretary of the FCC wrote, "The consent of the Federal Communications Commission is hereby granted." The Wests—first the

---

* In later years, Johnson propagated the myth that he had made a Christmas Day visit to the West Ranch to arrange the sale; he may have gone to the West Ranch, but the crucial meeting was in Suite 8-F at the Lamar—a place Johnson avoided mentioning whenever possible, since to anyone familiar with the Browns, it would be proof of his link with them.

father, then the sons—had been attempting for three years to obtain such a consent. Mrs. Lyndon Johnson had obtained it in twenty-four days.

BECAUSE KTBC WAS PURCHASED in his wife's name and she became president of the company and was active in its affairs, Lyndon Johnson was able to maintain for the rest of his life that the company, which was eventually to consist of a galaxy of radio and television stations, was not his but hers—all hers and only hers. Asked at a press conference during his presidency about a possible conflict of interest, he said there could not conceivably be any in his case "because I don't have any interest in government-regulated industries of any kind and never have had." He did not own the company, he said. "All that is owned by Mrs. Johnson." He derived no income from it, he said. He did not participate in its affairs, he said, and played absolutely no role in its decisions or operations. He repeated these assertions over and over—in terms that could not have been more unequivocal: "I have never received any funds or cast any votes in connection with it," he said on one occasion; on another, asked by reporters about the operations of KTBC, he replied: "I am unfamiliar with it." He had his lawyers repeat the assertions: "It was her station; don't let anyone tell you to the contrary," said Leonard H. Marks, an attorney who was an assistant to the general counsel for the FCC until 1946, when he entered private practice, in which he represented the Johnson interests. And his spokesman: "As you know," George Reedy, one of his press secretaries, said, "the President stated shortly after he took the oath of office that he had no television holdings. . . . As the American people know, the President had devoted all of his time and energy to the public business and he is not engaged in any private enterprise directly or indirectly." And his old friends: Elizabeth Wickenden Goldschmidt says, "I remember Lady Bird sitting there at their dining room table in Washington with all the books of the station laid out in front of her. She really worked very hard at running that station and she was a very astute businesswoman." During the Johnson Presidency, a number of reporters attempted to probe the Johnson empire. But their efforts were hamstrung by inadequate access to Johnson family financial records (which continues today), and by the reticence of KTBC employees, Johnson political aides, FCC commissioners and staff members and Austin businessmen; members of all these groups have become dramatically more candid in recent years. Moreover, during the 1960s journalists did not have access to memoranda and letters that can be found today scattered through a score of different files in the Lyndon Baines Johnson Library in Austin. Despite these obstacles, during the Johnson Presidency the enterprise of a handful of journalists—most notably ground-breaking efforts by Louis M. Kohlmeier, of the *Wall Street Journal*, John Barron, of the *Washington Star*, and William Lambert and Keith Wheeler, of *Life*—raised doubts about Johnson's assertions. But as Johnson responded to their articles with his own estimates of his assets, estimates far lower than theirs, and with forceful reemphasis of his assertions, his estimates and assertions were often repeated without much analysis by the bulk of the press, and the findings in the few pioneering articles became blurred in the public consciousness. In an "exclusive" article, one typical of the prevailing tone of press coverage, *U.S. News & World Report* stated in May, 1964: "This is a success which Mrs. Johnson scored on her own, while her husband was deeply involved in affairs of the House and Senate."

Johnson was especially emphatic about his role in dealing with the FCC: he said he had no role. And this, too, was repeated by the press, at least in part because it had no choice. *Life* magazine reported that "The FCC leans to a defensive attitude concerning its treatment of the Johnsons' radio-tv interests and insists that the President—either as representative or senator—has never tried to affect agency rulings. There is no evidence that he did intervene by word or deed." *The Wall Street Journal* stated that "FCC public records show not a single intervention by Representative, Senator, Vice President or President Johnson in quest of a favor for his wife's company."

But although in 1942 and 1943 Lyndon Johnson's political influence was not great, it was quite strategically situated in regard to the purchase of a radio station. In the "very close-knit group," in which, as Virginia Durr put it, "there was a great intertwining of both personal and intergovernmental relationships," three members were intimately connected with the governmental agency whose approval of the purchase would be necessary. Clifford Durr was an FCC commissioner, one of the seven-member board that ran the agency; W. Ervin "Red" James was Durr's chief assistant at the Commission. As for Lyndon Johnson's bluntest tool, barely a year into private practice, already becoming known as "the greatest wirepuller in history," Tommy Corcoran had many wires to pull in the FCC—including some that ran all the way to the top: both the Commission's chairman, James Fly, a former classmate of Corcoran's at Harvard Law, and its former chief counsel, William J. Dempsey, a thirty-two-year-old Corcoran protégé, owed their appointments largely to his influence. (Dempsey's predecessor, insufficiently responsive to a telephone call from "Tommy Corcoran at the White House," had found himself dismissed on twenty-four hours' notice.) And while Dempsey was now in private practice (sharing an office suite with Corcoran, with both men representing private clients before a notably accommodating FCC), many officials still at the top of the FCC were indebted to Corcoran for their jobs: the agency had, in the knowing Washington term, been thoroughly "Corcoranized."

Johnson also had at his command a weapon much more blunt than Tommy the Cork—and much more powerful. Sam Rayburn was as much a symbol of integrity in Washington as Corcoran was a symbol of the use of influence. Johnson was able to use Rayburn's name—feared throughout the capital—even though Rayburn might not be aware it was being used.

While radio stations were regulated by the FCC, the FCC was itself regulated—by Congress, which gave regulatory agencies their money and their powers. "The antennae of most commissioners," it would be written, "are sensitive to the faintest signals from Capitol Hill. . . ." At no agency was this sensitivity more acute than at the FCC. "Of all the watchdogs," Drew Pearson and Jack Anderson were to write, "the FCC seems the most eager to sit up and beg or roll over and play dead at the command of Congress." If the commissioners' antennae were sensitive to signals from congressmen, the antennae of Commission staffers were sensitive to the relay of such signals from the commissioners. Albert A. Evangelista, who during the 1940s, as an engineer in the FCC's Standard Broadcast Division, handled preliminary applications for radio station licenses, says that the process "was different when a congressman intervened." When a congressman contacted a commissioner about an application from a favored constituent, the commissioner would "route it to the right department." "If it was 'congressional,' it would get priority," Evangelista recalls. "When we got referrals from a congressman, that was something I had to work on right away." James E. Barr, who in 1943 was a senior engineer in the FCC's Standard Broadcast Division, says: "What you were afraid of was that" if you did not act favorably or fast enough on an application in which a congressman was interested, the congressman "would call a commissioner, and the commissioner would call and say, 'Put 'em on the air.' There was a lot more political influence in those early days."

And sensitivity had never been higher than it was at this moment. If there was a single year of maximum susceptibility to congressional pressures at the FCC, it was 1943, the year in which Lady Bird Johnson purchased her radio station. In 1943, the Commission was fighting with Congress not over increases in its budget or definitions of its power, but for its very existence.

Having learned that Representative Eugene Cox of Georgia, ranking majority member of the Rules Committee and a leader of the House's Southern bloc, had used a $2,500 "legal fee" from a Georgia radio station to purchase stock in the station, FCC Chairman Fly in January, 1943 (the month, as it happened, in which Mrs. Johnson was submitting her application to the Commission), had announced that the station's license would not be renewed without a public hearing. Cox's response was to call the FCC "the nastiest nest of rats to be found in this country." Charging that Fly "is guilty of a monstrous abuse of power and is rapidly becoming the most dangerous man in the government," Cox proposed the establishment of a House committee to investigate the FCC "Gestapo"—and around Cox's proposal crystallized Congress's long-building resentment of the New Deal and "bureaucratic dictatorship." The House named Cox himself chairman of the investigating committee—thereby, as T.R.B. wrote in *The New Republic*, "putting a judicial wig and robe on an accused man to try his own accusers." For the next six months, from January to July, 1943, the Cox Committee conducted an investigation characterized by the questioning in secret of witnesses who were summoned without warning and who were denied not only counsel but even access to transcripts of their own testimony. Against editorial criticism—"indecent," *The New Republic* said; the *Washington Post* editorialized that Cox "has perverted and distorted the important investigative functions of Congress to intimidate those who exposed his own corrupt practices"—Congress closed ranks; indeed, a second committee, the Communist-hunting Dies Committee, began to focus on the FCC. "All around Washington," one of the Commission's key staffers was to recall, "we heard it whispered that FCC would get it in the neck. We wondered where the ax would fall and how deeply it would cut." Then, in February, the FCC learned that the ax might cut very deeply indeed: an amendment, added to an appropriations bill, proposed eliminating all appropriations for the FCC, "thereby," as one representative put it, "cutting the Commission off without a cent, thus in effect abolishing it." As a liberal Congressman wrote, "all the confident forces of conservatism and reaction were arrayed behind that amendment," and "those forces constituted an unquestioned majority in the House." The FCC had, in fact, only one real hope on Capitol Hill, and it was Sam Rayburn, who was to recall, "I wrote the law that passed the Federal Communications Commission. . . . I was in on the borning," and who had proven before, more than once (most recently a year and a half before, in the extension of the Selective Service Act), that, because of the respect in which he was held and because of his unique force of personality, he could stand on the triple dais—alone against a majority of his colleagues—and bend the House to his will. Lyndon Johnson was "Sam Rayburn's boy"—that was common knowledge in Washington. The FCC could be expected to be sensitive to any requests from Sam Rayburn's boy. Furthermore, the Rayburn connection aside, the FCC, so short on allies in Congress, could be expected during this life and death struggle to be particularly sensitive to a congressman who was actively and energetically fighting in Congress on its behalf.

And that was precisely what this congressman was doing. During the very month in which Mrs. Lyndon Johnson was applying to the FCC, Lyndon Johnson, who had never before displayed any particular interest in that agency, was making himself its champion.

The assistance he gave was discreet, secret—and crucial. He didn't communicate with Durr directly. "Lyndon sort of kept away from me," the FCC commissioner was to recall; "we didn't talk about it." But Lyndon communicated with Durr's chief assistant, Red James, in late-night telephone calls during which, speaking in code—Rayburn was "the bald-headed fellow," House Majority Leader John McCormack "the Irishman," Cox "the chairman"—Johnson provided inside information, vital to the FCC, on the direction of the next congressional attack, and advice on what the Commission could do to counter it. "He was sort of acting as a spotter, telling us where to put the next shell, and giving us Sam Rayburn's reactions," Durr was to recall. Nor was Johnson's assistance to the Commission limited to information and advice. As the House massed more and more solidly against the FCC, its only hope seemed to be Rayburn's intervention, and Johnson was working to procure that intervention, playing on the Speaker's feeling that Cox's investigative methods (and his $2,500 "legal fee") were bringing his beloved House into disrepute; trying to overcome the Speaker's reluctance to set aside tradition and interfere with the internal workings of a committee. And on at least two occasions, when the FCC's cause looked particularly desperate, he succeeded in persuading Rayburn to come to its defense. At one particularly pivotal point, when the Commission learned that Cox was planning to make public an affair that the married Chairman Fly was reportedly having, James, in an attempt to head Cox off, took "this up with LBJ"—who took it up with Rayburn. Johnson reported Rayburn's reaction to James: the Speaker had "called the Chairman in, and told him, 'Now, Gene, there, Gene. There ain't gonna be no sex!' " Cox was a power in the House, but Rayburn was Rayburn, whom no man crossed; Cox's plans to publicize Fly's alleged affair were dropped—abruptly and completely. Then, in what was to be characterized as "an unusual and bold step" to procure Rayburn's help, Durr sent several petitions not to the Cox Committee but directly to the Speaker, setting out the facts about Cox's $2,500 "retainer" and asking the Speaker to remove Cox as the committee's chairman. And one midnight, James was awakened by a phone call: "This voice says, 'All right, no names. But today the bald-headed fellow met with the Irishman and the chairman. He said this, 'You've been my friend for thirty-five years, but I can't stand this any longer and you're going to have to step down!' " Cox was Rayburn's friend, but the House was Rayburn's love, and Cox was sullying its reputation. Cox abruptly announced his resignation from the investigating committee; as soon as he finished, Rayburn left the dais, stepped down into the well of the House and praised him, asserting that "my confidence in his honor and integrity is unshaken," words which were the price Sam Rayburn had to pay to preserve the honor and integrity of the House.

On February 17, 1943, moreover, Rayburn saved the FCC from more than an investigation. The amendment effectively "abolishing" the Commission was about to be overwhelmingly approved when the Speaker again stepped into the well for one of his rare speeches. His force seemed to fill the House Chamber. He had been the author of "the bill to set up the Communications Commission," he said. "Before that time there was chaos in communications. . . . I do not appeal to your prejudices or to your passions, but I do want to counsel with your reason. . . . There is only one agency in the United States of America, let me say to you, that has any control whatsoever over the air of the United States. Do you want by your vote to strike down that only agency?" The amendment was defeated; although the FCC's budget was slashed by twenty-five percent as a punitive measure, the Commission remained in existence.

Johnson was championing the FCC's cause not only in the Capitol but in the White House. When the Administration persisted in paying more attention to the war, he attempted to make it understand that, as presidential assistant Jonathan Daniels was to put it, "the Cox Committee investigation is a big job which is being ignored as a little thing," when, in fact, it was actually an anti-Roosevelt plot; "as I got it from Johnson," Daniels wrote in his diary, "anti–New Deal lawyers . . . hope to use this investigation of the FCC as a take-off for smearing the whole Administration or the important people in it."

ALL DURING THIS PERIOD, of course, Lyndon Johnson was seeing Clifford Durr socially in the evenings and on Sundays, sometimes at Durr's home, sometimes at his own. As was the case with the Cox investigation, he may have "kept away" from Durr so far as furnishing him with details of the KTBC application was concerned. Durr, a courageous Southern liberal (returning to Montgomery after his term on the FCC ended, in 1948, he and his wife would spend their lives fighting for civil rights there, often representing clients too impoverished to pay a legal fee), was the champion on the FCC of higher standards of programming—increased public service, for example, and fewer commercials. In the handling of more mundane matters, he often relied on Red James, a strikingly more pragmatic lawyer, whose later career would be intermittently intertwined with Johnson's, and Durr appears to have been unaware of many of the circumstances surrounding the KTBC application. And Johnson was, of course, seeing Red James, too—indeed, throughout this period, he was quite frequently bringing to see James the attorney who was handling the KTBC application: "During all this period of time, Alvin Wirtz used to come to Washington. I regarded Alvin Wirtz very highly, and he and Lyndon Johnson and I would get together and have a highball and go out to dinner, just shoot the bull about things, occasionally go over to Lyndon's house. . . . I would be working maybe at the FCC. Along about 4:30 in the afternoon I'd get a call from LBJ, and he'd say, 'Alvin has come to town. He wants to see you and wants you to come on over and we'll have a couple of drinks.' " (Did Wirtz represent them in the FCC matter? James was asked. "Yes. I'm sure he did.") And of course this was the period during which Johnson was making his late-night telephone calls to James. Whatever the reason, when Durr and James are discussing KTBC, even while Durr is saying, "I never got any pressures at all from [Johnson]," there emerges, not only in James' own words but in Durr's as well, an attitude that a disapproving observer was to describe as "government between friends."

Whenever, in later years, Durr was asked about the KTBC application, he was quick to point out that it was in Lady Bird's name, and to say that "Lyndon never had a thing to do with it."

> Bird came to me and said there was a chance to buy this radio station in Austin, and as I recall she said for about $22,000. She either had the money or could borrow the money on this inheritance she had of the Autauga County property. She could raise that much money, and she wanted to know whether I thought it would be a wise investment. So I gave her some figures on the earnings of well-run stations at the time. They were making an awful lot of money. . . . I heard generally around the FCC that this was a very poorly run station. I remember our engineers complaining about the engineering operations and getting all . . . frequencies and things of that sort. I told her that it seemed to me if she could get that station on its feet and get it well managed, it ought to be a very good investment.

There was nothing wrong with Bird's visit, Durr says.

> Now, there wasn't any skulduggery that I ever saw at the FCC. It was more or less the routine approval of the purchase of a station. This had to be approved by the FCC, but nobody else was in the picture. . . .

There was nothing wrong with that, Durr says. And, James, whom Bird also used to visit, makes the same point: "She used to come down and see me quite often and discuss matters, as she had a perfect right to do, unless they were adversary matters. . . ."

It is possible, of course, that during all their dinners and telephone conversations with Durr and James, Wirtz or Johnson did not mention the radio station to the two FCC officials. But Mrs. Johnson did, and after her visits Durr and James spoke to lower-level FCC staffers about KTBC—which, whether Durr and James intended this or not, would have signaled these staffers that their superiors were personally interested in the matter.

Not that all staffers needed to read such indirect signals. Lyndon Johnson may not, as Durr and James maintain, have been talking to them directly about KTBC, but his contention that he never intervened with the FCC would have fallen strangely on the ears of James Barr, who, as an official of the FCC's Standard Broadcast Division all during the 1940s, had to pass on some of Mrs. Johnson's applications. One day, while he was considering one of these applications, his telephone rang; when he picked it up, he found Mrs. Johnson's husband, Congressman Johnson, on the line. "He wanted to get a radio station, and what I remember is, he wouldn't take no for an answer," Barr recalls. "I can still hear him when I tried to explain: 'Now, Mr. Barr . . . Now, Mr. Barr . . . ' The thing that impressed me was that he was on a first-name basis with Red James." And although Johnson, Durr and James were reticent about telephone calls they may or may not have made, or influence they may or may not have used, Tommy Corcoran, never reticent about anything, was not. "I helped him out with that [the KTBC application]—all up and down the line," he said. With Fly? "I told you—all up and down the line," he said. And when he was asked whether the fact that Lyndon Johnson was a Congressman, a Congressman important to the FCC, had helped his wife obtain a radio license, Corcoran reacted at first only with silence, and a look of contempt that someone should have to ask so obvious a question. Finally he growled: "How do you think these things work? These guys [FCC staffers] have been around. You don't have to spell things out for them."

Moreover, about one significant point, Durr is incorrect. If "nobody else was in the picture," that wasn't because nobody else wanted to be.

While J. M. West had been anxious to enter the radio business, his sons and Kingsbery had not seemed to care one way or the other. Apparently feeling that Wirtz's silence was a signal that the sale to the Wests was never going to receive FCC approval, and fearing that behind-the-scenes maneuvering might be taking place in Washington, Ulmer, representing the station's owners, had, in 1942, let it be known in the Austin business community that if a new, firm offer for KTBC was received, the West option might be circumvented, surrendered or sold for a token amount. Several Austin businessmen thereupon expressed interest in KTBC at the same time that Mrs. Johnson was doing so. One prospective purchaser was William Drake, a lumber-company president who would later become Mayor of the city. Other businessmen recall that Drake was quite determined to acquire the station. Edward Joseph, one of the city's leading realtors and owner of a clothing store, says, "Bill Drake . . . made an offer on the station. . . . He made an offer on it, but Lyndon just reached out and got it from under him." (Joseph adds that "because of that . . . they sort of fell out and for a long time they were on the outs because of that.") Another businessman, more sophisticated in the ways of politics than Drake, took his experience with the FCC and Johnson more philosophically. He was William J. Lawson, a former Texas Secretary of State, who by 1942 had become a successful businessman in Austin. In partnership with two other businessmen, Lawson had recently acquired an FCC construction permit, the first step toward obtaining a license, for KBWD, a five-hundred-watt station in Brownwood, Texas, and it had proved to be a lucrative business deal. Obtaining a permit for a station in Brownwood, Lawson had found, was simple. He had simply sent in the application, and back—very quickly, as he recalls—had come FCC approval. The two businessmen (impressed by the financial possibilities of small radio stations—"This thing's a gold mine!" one said) bought out his share even before the license for KBWD was granted—for what Lawson considered a handsome profit. In 1942, Lawson recalls, "I wanted to do the same thing in Austin, with KTBC." But, he found, becoming the owner of a station in Austin was not as simple as becoming the owner of a station in Brownwood. After making a tentative agreement with Ulmer, Lawson sent the FCC a preliminary inquiry ("not even an application— it never got to the application stage") as to how to proceed, but, he says, "before I could get anything done, I got this odd letter—a form letter [not] even a dictated letter" that had the effect of discouraging him from proceeding further. Telephoning a veteran Capitol Hill staff member, D. Roland Potter, Lawson asked him to find out from his contacts at the FCC what had happened. Potter called back, telling Lawson that his contacts said that " 'Congressman Johnson was in to see us.' . . . They said that Congressman Johnson had indicated an interest in the license, and based on the information he had given them, I [Lawson] was financially unstable."

"Their excuse didn't make any sense," Lawson says. "They had already issued me one [permit], you know." Why would they find him suitable for one station and unsuitable for another? His financial situation, he says, had only improved since the Brownwood application. Lawson was very far from a political neophyte. He had been, in fact, a key strategist in Governor O'Daniel's victory over Johnson the previous year. And, being no neophyte, Lawson knew that this time Johnson had beaten *him*. He dropped any further effort to obtain KTBC. "I never made an issue out of it because I would have been fighting with the Congressman, and he had already made his point with the Commission," he explains.

Despite Durr's assertion, therefore, other prospective purchasers *were* in the picture—or, rather, might have been, if not for Lyndon Johnson's entrée, his access to the Commission's ear. Johnson, Lawson believed, had told the Commission that Lawson was "financially unstable." Untrue though this statement was, the Commission may have accepted it—because there was no one to refute it.

In courts of law, to the extent that only one side in a case has access to a judge, to that extent justice is diminished, since in such an *ex parte* proceeding the other side cannot be heard. The power of regulatory agencies such as the Federal Communications Commission is, in not a few respects, the power of a judge. But before the Commission, in the case of KTBC, the other side was not heard. The Johnson side—Lyndon Johnson, Lady Bird Johnson, Alvin Wirtz—could get appointments with an FCC commissioner and a top FCC staffer to discuss the Johnson application in person; the opposing applicant could get only "a form letter [not] even a dictated letter."

WHATEVER THE EXPLANATION, the shift in the FCC's attitude toward KTBC was dramatic after Lady Bird Johnson submitted her application to purchase the station. The five years during which the original owners had been dealing with the FCC had been five years of delays and red tape, or delays and unfavorable rulings—of slowness in every aspect of the bureaucratic process. From the moment the owners agreed to sell to Mrs. Johnson, red tape vanished, all rulings were favorable—and slowness was replaced by speed.

The speed was evident not only in the fact that her application to purchase KTBC, submitted to the FCC on January 23, 1943, was approved on February 16, 1943—in just over three weeks. It was evident also when, later that year, she applied to change the conditions under which the station operated. For the previous owners, changing the restrictions had seemed an insuperable obstacle. For Mrs. Johnson, changing the restrictions was no obstacle at all. In June, 1943, she applied to the FCC for permission to operate twenty-four hours a day—at a new frequency, 590 on the dial, a frequency so much more desirable than the old that the move alone would transform KTBC into a much more viable, and valuable, property. Not only would it make KTBC the first station that Austin listeners could get on their dials but 590 was at the opposite, uncluttered, end of the dial from 1150, an end so uncluttered in the Austin area, in fact, that KTBC would now be heard not only in Austin but in no fewer than thirty-eight surrounding counties throughout central Texas. Her application, abetted by a Wirtz-engineered application for daytime hours submitted by WTAW earlier that same month, was filed with the FCC on June 25. It was approved on July 20.

Was Lyndon Johnson's influence responsible for the change? Mrs. Johnson, Red James emphasizes, "had a perfect right" to "discuss matters" with him, "unless they were adversary matters." There was an adversary in this matter, because, as James was (perhaps inadvertently) to recall, the frequency "he [Johnson] wanted to change over to" was a frequency "where the dominant station was WOW in Omaha, Nebraska," and KWOW's broadcasts had previously reached south into Texas, a fact which KWOW used in selling advertisers airtime. "I think," James was to recall, "his lawyer talked to the lawyers for WOW and asked them if they would oppose it if he applied to go on that frequency. . . . They were a little upset about this. . . ." But, as James' own statement thus confirms, the fact that there was an adversary did not deter him from discussing the matter with Lyndon Johnson. And it didn't deter James from discussing the matter with other FCC officials.

And it didn't deter James from giving Lady Bird Johnson advice as to how to proceed, advice that may have carried with it the strong implication that the judges before whom her application would be argued if the adversary opposed her would not be wholly unsympathetic to her cause. James was to say that he discussed the case with a top FCC counsel and engineer.

They looked at the thing and said, "We don't see any particular problems about it." And I told Mrs. Johnson that, I told Lady Bird. I said, "Why don't you apply for it? You know, if they set you down for a hearing, so they set you down for a hearing, in a consolidated proceeding." So they applied for it and got it. The commission granted it.

They applied for it—not strange that the Johnsons decided to do so, after the chief aide to one of the judges told them in advance "why don't you apply for it?" The hearing would be a quasi-judicial proceeding, and a judge is not supposed to hear one side of a case without the other side having an opportunity to respond—as had been done. In addition to the lawyers for KWOW, at least two other persons were upset at the changes granted KTBC. After running into James Ulmer at a broadcasting convention, Leonard Marks, a Washington attorney who had left the FCC and was now representing KTBC, reported to Johnson that Ulmer was saying "that he had completed all the engineering on 590 and that you came in and stole it from him." (Ulmer added, according to a memo from Marks, that he would not write the story, "but whether he did so or not, somebody else probably would.") Also angry was Elliott Roosevelt, the President's son, who had gone into the radio business in Texas in partnership with oilman Sid Richardson. (Elliott's relationship with his father was strained at this time and he was receiving no help from the White House with his radio interests.) On August 31, 1943, after having lunch with Elliott, John Connally reported to Johnson that an angry Elliott had said during the lunch that "there was a controversy when KTBC got nighttime operations . . . but that Mr. Johnson had the skids greased with the commission."

Was Lyndon Johnson's influence—influence that translated into access and entrée into inside information and advance information—even more deeply at work? Had he known in advance something that no one else knew? Had he known, even before his wife bought KTBC, that if she bought it the FCC would change the conditions that had hamstrung the station in the past?

Lady Bird Johnson purchased KTBC in February, and in June made her application, the application that was so rapidly approved, for the change in hours and frequency. That was fast enough. But had Lyndon Johnson known even before June that such an application would be approved? In April, Lyndon and Lady Bird asked a Dallas radio announcer who had been the emcee of Johnson's traveling road show in the 1941 campaign, Harfield Weedin, to become manager of their new station, offering him a ten percent share of the profits. Weedin was reluctant to accept, because he felt that under the existing FCC restrictions on the station's operation, profits were unlikely. "You couldn't really make much money with just a daytime station," he says. But, he also recalls, Johnson assured him that "if I took the job, I would not be bothered with that"; the restrictions were going to be lifted "very shortly." Johnson said, "Look, the frequency is going to be changed. We're going to go full time. I have it in the works right now." He specifically told Weedin that the lifting of the restrictions was "all set," and Weedin believed him, because, Weedin says, Johnson understood that the restrictions were an insurmountable handicap. "Frankly," Weedin says, "I don't feel he would have bought it if he didn't know he was going to get those changes." The Johnsons' meeting with Weedin took place only two months after they had purchased the station, but Johnson was saying that the changes that would transform it were already "all set"—as indeed they very shortly proved to be.

Whether or not Lyndon Johnson had known of the changes in advance, they totally transformed the property his wife had purchased. She had, in effect, purchased 1150 on the radio dial. After FCC approval of her application for increased broadcasting hours and a new frequency, when a listener turned his dial to 1150, all he heard was static. There was no longer any station at that spot on the dial. The station was now at 590, which meant that it sounded different: louder, clearer. And it was on at night, when more people wanted to listen to it. Only its call letters were the same; otherwise, within months of the time Mrs. Johnson had bought a station so cheaply, that station no longer existed. (And at the earliest possible moment—as soon as the war ended and necessary materials became available—the transformation became even greater. In 1945, the FCC allowed KTBC to quintuple its power, from a thousand to five thousand watts, a change that meant the station could be heard in sixty-three counties.)

And if others had known that it could be so totally altered, would it have *been* so cheap? Might there not have been other bidders for so desirable a radio property? And would these other bidders have been so easily deterred as William Lawson had been? Indeed, would *Lawson* have been so easily deterred? Indeed, would the original owners have been willing to sell—to sell for so little—a twenty-four-hour-a-day station that was first on the dial, and that boomed out all over Austin and throughout central Texas? Would the owners have *had* to sell, if the property they owned had been the property into which it had now been so rapidly transformed by the FCC?

But no others knew—no others *could* know for sure, just as they couldn't be advised by a key figure in the FCC that they shouldn't worry unduly about a conflict with KWOW. And so there were no other bids for KTBC, and the owners of KTBC were willing to sell cheap.

LADY BIRD JOHNSON flew down to Austin, where, a station employee recalls, she "took one look at the layout and said, 'I don't know much about radio, but I do know about cleaning house.' She bought a pair of overalls, a bunch of brooms and mops, and some soap, and for a solid week she worked on that little walk-up, two-room [sic] station until it fairly sparkled." She studied KTBC's contracts with its advertisers to determine how much airtime the station owed them, and how much money the advertisers owed the station. She began trying to straighten out its books, which were a mess. In the legend which would be repeated to reporters year after year, these efforts were what turned the fortunes of KTBC around. "She worked eighteen hours a day for five months before we brought the station into the black," the employee says. Mrs. Johnson herself takes great pride in her industry during those early months. "The staff was infected with a sense of failure and uncertainty, and sloppiness had become a way of life in that little area, so we just gave it a good thorough cleaning up. I think it kind of improved everybody's spirits. It certainly did mine."

Mr. Johnson flew up to New York, where he called on William S. Paley, the president of the CBS radio network, and asked for a CBS affiliation, which would allow KTBC to carry the network's famous, nationally known shows, on which advertisers would be more eager to purchase time than on local shows, and for which higher rates could be charged. The affiliation was vital to KTBC, and Johnson knew it. "This is life and death to us," he wrote a former aide, Gene Latimer. At the time of his visit to Paley, the Federal Communications Commission was determinedly attempting to reduce the networks' control of independent stations, and Paley was leading an almost frantic fight to persuade Congress to reduce the FCC's authority over them by amending the law—Sam Rayburn's law—that had established the Commission. This was only the latest in a series of running battles between the networks and the FCC—battles in which the networks were continually appealing to Congress for help. Did the fact that this applicant for an affiliation was a congressman—"Sam Rayburn's boy"—have anything to do with CBS's decision in the matter? Paley and Frank Stanton were to cast the story in folksy terms. Paley would tell David Halberstam that Johnson had simply appeared in his office one day without an appointment; his secretary had come in to see him, Paley said, and "announced that there was a very tall Texan waiting out there in a big hat and boots who said he was a congressman." Paley went out to meet him, and the Texan, according to Paley, had said, " 'Mister Paley, I have this here ticket for a 250-watt [sic] station in Austin and I'd like to join as a CBS affiliate.' " Paley had sent the tall Texan to Frank Stanton, CBS director of research, who also handled some affiliate matters. Stanton says he looked at a map, found there was room for an affiliated station in Austin, and gave Johnson the affiliation.

Journalists may have regarded this story skeptically, but they felt they could not disprove it. In fact, however, it is possible to know what would have happened if a noncongressional station owner in Austin had applied for a CBS affiliation—for a noncongressional station owner *had* applied; had applied, in fact, several times. The other Austin radio station, KNOW, had been energetically attempting for years to secure a CBS affiliation. Every attempt had been rejected by CBS because the network already had an affiliate, KTSA in San Antonio, which could be heard in Austin.

CBS's DECISION in regard to Lyndon Johnson's request may have had nothing to do with his political influence. But his political influence had everything to do with many of the advertisers who bought time on KTBC.

The backers who had arranged for money to be contributed to his political campaigns now arranged for money to be contributed to his radio station. Herman Brown gave him some advertisers. Johnson told Harfield Weedin to go to the Houston offices of the American General Insurance Company, which had most of Brown & Root's insurance business, and American General's president, Gus Wortham, purchased fifteen minutes of airtime every night. Why did Wortham advertise on KTBC? "We twisted his arm," George Brown was to recall years later, with a smile. The New York attorney Ed Weisl, Sr., the chief financier of Johnson's campaign-funding efforts in the Northeast, who was powerful in both political and entertainment circles, gave him some advertisers. The Interstate Theater Chain, for example, bought fifteen minutes a night.

Many of these advertisers were—or during this period would become—connected with Everett Looney and Edward A. Clark, principals in the Austin law firm of Looney & Clark. Ed Clark was coming to be known, as Alvin Wirtz was already known, as a lawyer to go to in Austin if you wanted something from the federal government. Clark, a power in his own right, had never been intimidated by Johnson; he was too independent to take orders from any politician—and too astute: of all the men with whom Lyndon Johnson was associated in Texas, Clark was the one who, over the years, acquired and held the most power. He expressed the same philosophy as Herman Brown: if he invested in—"bought a ticket on," in his phrase—a politician, he wanted a return on that investment. And, through the radio station, he was to get it. What Johnson wanted was advertising revenues; what Clark wanted was recognition as a lawyer with influence in Washington—and both got what they wanted.

One of the powerful Texans with whom Clark would be associated for years was Howard E. Butt, of Corpus Christi, owner of the statewide H.E.B. chain of grocery stores. "I knew Mr. Butt's interest in politics," Clark says, and, he recalls, he knew Butt needed someone to help with problems he was having with federal agencies in Washington—particularly, during those wartime years, with the Office of Price Administration. So, Clark says, he advised Mr. Butt to advertise on KTBC. Because the station's records have not been released, it is difficult to learn any details about Butt's advertising, but it may have been done through companies whose products were sold in H.E.B. stores and who would advertise on KTBC and mention H.E.B. in their ads. In a letter written on October 27, 1943, Clark told Johnson, "I am today writing to Corpus so that Howard Butt will contact the advertisers whose products he sells at his stores in Austin so that he will have an opportunity to get coverage here." Butt soon found out how wise Clark's advice could be. In 1944, when the OPA was limiting each distributor's number of cases of grapefruit that could be harvested and packed in the Rio Grande Valley, Johnson intervened and persuaded the agency to allocate Butt 150,000 extra cases. "I was happy to be able to call Mr. Howard Butt after our conversation [about the grapefruit] today," Clark wrote Johnson on February 3, 1944, and, indeed, everyone involved got something out of this arrangement: Butt got 150,000 extra cases of grapefruit, and the profits from selling them; Clark got recognition as an attorney with influence in Washington; KTBC got advertising revenues.

Butt's was not the only company that Ed Clark advised to advertise on KTBC. Clark already had a connection with the General Electric Company, and on October 27, 1943, he was able to write Johnson that General Electric's popular "World News Today" program would be going on KTBC. "Thanks for the wonderful job on GE," Johnson replied. "That's the most important thing that has been accomplished lately." Among Clark's contacts were major oil companies, who worked together to exert political influence in Washington; one was Gulf Oil—Gulf wasn't a client of Looney & Clark, Clark says, "but I had friends there. I spoke to them about it [advertising on KTBC], and they understood. This wasn't a Sunday-school proposition. This was business."

Not all the advertisers came through Clark. Wirtz was on a retainer from Humble Oil, a subsidiary of Standard Oil. Humble sponsored football games on the CBS network, under an arrangement in which the giant oil company selected the stations which carried the games. KTBC was selected. Wirtz had other clients that wanted things from the federal government, and they, too, began to advertise on KTBC.

Local businessmen who wanted to obtain—or keep—contracts with the Army camps near Austin, or with the huge Bergstrom Air Force Base, got the idea, which was soon being openly discussed in the Austin business community. As one businessman puts it: "Everybody knew that a good way to get Lyndon to help you with government contracts was to advertise over his radio station." One example was the Jaques Power Saw Company. For one period, the only period for which records are available, the Jaques Company sponsored a six-day-a-week half-hour program. The purpose of the ads was not, says one Jaques associate, to attract business from listeners; Jaques did little business in Austin, the associate says. Rather, the purpose was to enable Jaques to sell power saws to the Army and Navy for use all over the country. In 1948, moreover, the company wanted to expand and needed a $1,250,000 loan from the Reconstruction Finance Corporation. When the application was filed, Johnson quietly spoke to at least one member of the RFC board, Vice Chairman Harley Hise, about it, and instructed Walter Jenkins to make subtle follow-up calls to remind the RFC that the Congressman wanted the loan approved. Jenkins did so, and as soon as the next meeting of the RFC board had ended, Hise hurried to a telephone and called Jenkins to tell him that the loan had gone through. (Jenkins communicated the good news to Jaques through its attorney, Everett Looney of Looney & Clark.) Other businessmen observed the pattern and followed it. Although they were ostensibly buying airtime, what they were really buying was political influence. They were buying—and Lyndon Johnson was selling.

Lyndon Johnson was always to maintain that his "wife's" radio interests were totally divorced from politics, and that, indeed, he, the politician in the family, had absolutely nothing to do either with acquiring KTBC's license, or, once it was licensed, with its operations. And Mrs. Johnson was indeed an integral part of the business. David Benjamin, who had been a salesman for KTBC under the previous ownership and stayed on, was impressed with the speed with which Mrs. Johnson brought order to the previously chaotic activities of the station's salesmen. "Mrs. Johnson knew who I had called on" and the results of the call, Benjamin says, "and she complimented me" or urged him on to greater efforts. Elizabeth Goldschmidt was not the only member of the Johnson circle who expressed admiration for Lady Bird's diligence, energy and business acumen. Leonard Marks says (after emphasizing that "It was her station—don't let anybody tell you to the contrary"), "Over the years, as the station prospered, I would go up to visit them at their home on Thirtieth Place on a Sunday. . . . She would have the reports of the week's sales, the list of expenses, and we'd go over them. She could read a balance sheet the way a truck driver reads a road map." In later years, moreover, Mrs. Johnson's role in the station's management greatly expanded, and her husband, in making major business decisions, began to rely more on her judgment, to a point at which Walter Jenkins, who was active in KTBC's affairs, said, in words echoed by members of the Austin business community, "I believe he came to trust her judgment almost as much as his own." Ed Clark himself says, "He trusted her judgment because she was never emotional, always calm. He would get angry. . . . He would get mad, cuss. She never got emotional. She—'This is too small to get mad over.' . . . She was always cool. Weighing things just on the basis of what made sense in business." Nevertheless, Mrs. Johnson's ability as a businesswoman was not the crucial factor in the acquisition of the station, or, once it was acquired, in its early growth. It was not Mrs. Johnson who negotiated with E. G. Kingsbery for his option to purchase the station. "I'm not sure I even knew there was a Mrs. Johnson," Kingsbery was to say. It wasn't Mrs. Johnson who negotiated with the West brothers. It wasn't Mrs. Johnson who telephoned James Barr at the FCC Standard Broadcast Division and "wouldn't take no for an answer." It wasn't Mrs. Johnson who saw William Paley and Frank Stanton in New York. It wasn't Mrs. Johnson who dealt with Ed Clark, and who procured an extra 150,000 cases of grapefruit for H. E. Butt, and who similarly worked within the government on behalf of other businesses which purchased advertising time on KTBC. It wasn't Mrs. but Mr. Johnson. Lyndon Johnson had worked at politics for years to achieve power; now he was working at politics to make money.

AND HE MADE IT.

Under its former owners, KTBC's income from the sale of advertising had been about $2,600 per month. During the first few months that Mrs. Johnson owned it, the income rose only to a little over $3,000 per month. But in December of 1943, the first substantial revenues from the CBS affiliation began coming in, the support of Herman Brown, Alvin Wirtz and Ed Clark was beginning to be felt, and advertising income rose to $5,645 for the month.

It rose more, rose faster and faster. In 1944, KTBC's average income from advertisers was $13,500 a month; in 1945, it was $15,300 a month; in 1946, it was $22,700 a month—more than the total amount Mrs. Johnson had paid for the station. In 1946 alone, the revenues from the property she had bought three years before for $17,500 totalled $272,500. Profits after expenses were also impressive. Mrs. Johnson soon began taking an annual salary (it was $21,500 by 1948), and the ownership also may have been withdrawing funds from the business by other methods; since sufficiently detailed KTBC records are not open, it has not been possible to determine the total amount of such disbursements, but one, in 1947, was apparently $80,000. Despite such withdrawals, however, KTBC's assets mounted rapidly. The end of the first era of the Johnson financial empire—the era in which his principal holding was Station KTBC, Austin— may be dated as 1952, because in that year it expanded into television, and its size and wealth soared to dramatically higher levels. But even before it entered that new era the station's assets—on December 31, 1951—were $439,000.

Until the end of his life, whenever the subject of the vast growth of the LBJ Company and associated business enterprises was raised, Lyndon Johnson would emphasize that he owned none of it ("All that is owned by Mrs. Johnson. . . . I don't have any interest in government-regulated industries of any kind and never have had").

These statements were, with rare exceptions, accepted by the press. Listing the holdings of the LBJ Company when he became President, the *Washington Star* agreed that "These holdings are not the President's." Presumably the journalists who looked into the Johnson finances did not examine the implication of Texas law, particularly the state's community property law, and most particularly the rights, under that law, of the spouse of a person who purchases a property with her own "separate" funds, such as an inheritance. Under that law, the spouse of that person—

such as Lyndon Johnson, spouse of Lady Bird Johnson, who purchased KTBC with her own inheritance—has indeed no interest in that property. He owns none of it. The spouse does, however, have an interest in the *income* from that property. He owns half of that.

James H. Rowe, Jr., recalls that "one day" after the radio station had been purchased, "he [Johnson] and I were walking the streets and talking, and he pulled a piece of paper out of his pocket, and said, 'I want to show you what this station made last year.'" Soon he was showing those papers—year-end figures for KTBC—to many friends. While the figures were small at first, these men recall that they got bigger—much bigger—each year, and were joined by figures for other investments. Soon, Johnson began pulling out columns of figures that, together, added up to his net financial worth. By 1948, the bottom line had seven figures on it. In that year, Lyndon Johnson began telling friends that he was a millionaire.

IN RUNNING KTBC, Lyndon Johnson was displaying the same intense involvement with every aspect of its affairs that was characteristic of his political career. Here is a letter to KTBC sales manager Willard Deason—one of many similar letters he wrote—from the man who said he was "unfamiliar" with the affairs of the radio station:

> Now, Bill, I am convinced that we can put some permanent business on the books this week and next week if we will plan and concentrate on a specific few. Last week none of our sales were really permanent, and the total sales for each person was very little more than his pay-check for the week. When this happens, we slip back and have trouble coming up.
>
> Show Jesse the attached letter I have written Jacob Schmidt and suggest to him that you or he, or both of you, go with Sam and see Mr. Schmidt personally. I had hoped you would present the deal you showed to Buttrey's to Yaring's after you had reduced it in half and would make some transcriptions of eight or ten word spots taken from Yaring's advertisements for them to listen to. I note instead you have pitched a Sunday program. I think Schmidt should be approached by asking him to give radio a fair test. In order to do this, he should give us a percentage of what he is now spending on the paper. We could do a better job for him, and we should contend to him that we can and will if he will give us a long-term opportunity. My idea would be that you and Jesse and Sam ought to get some Uncle Ezra transcriptions and some spot transcriptions taken from Yaring's newspaper ads and ask for a thirty-minute meeting with Joel Simon,

Leon, and Mr. Schmidt. You could do this because I requested you to if you think it would be easier.

I think we can and should sew up Ben Greig, Lawler, Prewitt, Schmidt, Yaring's, Red Arrow, Reynolds-Penland, and Swearingen-Armstrong in the next few days. Is there any chance of getting any Steck business?

Sincerely,
LYNDON B. JOHNSON

P.S. Bill, I don't know who Jim can help us with, but I should say Levine's, Louie, Lave's, and Ginsberg's if he is still on the other station.

IN RECRUITING A STAFF for KTBC, Johnson was using the same methods he had used in recruiting his political staff. There were, in Austin as in Washington, the charm and the promises deployed to persuade a man to leave his job and go to work for him.

When handsome, ambitious Harfield Weedin—already, at twenty-seven, program director of WFAA, a prestigious station in Dallas, and a well-known radio personality throughout Texas—arrived in Austin, the Johnsons showed him KTBC's offices and equipment. "I have seen run-down radio stations in my day, but never anything to compare with KTBC," Weedin was to recall. "The studio was a shambles, and the equipment . . . was third- and fourth-, maybe even fifth-hand. . . . My initial reaction was so awful I wanted to turn and go back to Dallas." But then, he was to recall, Johnson began to talk. "She was there, but he did most of the talking." And, he says, "he did quite a sales job on me."

The Congressman assured Weedin that the station would have unlimited hours ("very shortly they would go full time") and unlimited funds: "no money would be spared to make it Austin's leading station." He promised Weedin an employment contract which would give him not only security but ten percent of the station's profits, a promise which appealed to the young man since it would mean he was no longer merely a salaried employee. And Johnson promised Weedin something that meant even more to him than money: a title—general manager—and the authority that went with it; "They would turn it over to me to operate as I saw fit. . . . I could do anything I wanted in order to make it the station of their dreams."

"This was more like it," Weedin was to say. The more Johnson talked, the more he felt that "here was my great opportunity—a challenge that could pay off in the realization of my one remaining ambition: to be the manager of a successful radio station." Weedin asked for the Johnsons' assurance that he would be in charge, explaining, as he recalls, that since neither of them knew anything about the radio business, he had to be able to make decisions on his own. And the assurance was given: "They gave me *carte blanche* to do whatever I wanted to do, because I explained to them, That's part of the deal. . . . 'Otherwise I won't take the job.' "

And then, once the man had gone to work for Johnson, there came, in Austin as in Washington, the change. It wasn't as abrupt at the radio station as it had been in the congressional office because Lyndon Johnson, initially less knowledgeable about radio, was forced to rely on the knowledge of those he hired. At first, therefore, Weedin found himself dealing primarily with Lady Bird, and Lady Bird ("She is the most wonderful person in the world," he says) "was helpful mostly by giving me encouragement." Weedin did the hiring—he persuaded a friend, John Hicks, another young ambitious announcer in Dallas, to come to KTBC as chief announcer and program director. The vision that had been given to Weedin of unlimited funds for equipment turned out to be an exaggeration; he quickly found out, he recalls, that "Lady Bird did not have the unlimited funds I thought she had." There was not, in fact, enough to purchase even a new, urgently needed transmitter, but Weedin persuaded another friend, a crack engineer from Dallas, to come to Austin and repair the old one. Then they moved to new offices in the Brown Building. To save money, Hicks recalls, "we literally hand-carried that station from the business college; Lady Bird—she worked like a horse that day." (Her husband? "The Congressman was never around when you had work like that.") Weedin realized that "the most important thing was to get the station out of the red—but quick." To do so—to make the most of his "great opportunity"—he poured his talent and youthful energy into every phase of the station's operations. He hired two new salesmen but supplemented their efforts by going out as a salesman himself, although selling was not his field. The repaired transmitter, and the new 590 wavelength, gave KTBC a powerful, clear signal, and to make sure the station sounded professional Weedin himself delivered those newscasts that Hicks couldn't, so that KTBC had "professional voices." Establishing new rates for advertising, he persuaded KNOW not to undercut them, so that both stations would get more revenue. He selected and purchased the records for the music shows. He designed new stationery and promotional material for mailings. To make contacts with the Austin businessmen to whom he was trying to sell time, he put on quiz shows at luncheons of the Rotary, Kiwanis, Lions and other clubs, even delivering a five-minute "newscast" at Rotary meetings. His days began at six, because at 7:15 the "Wake Up with Weedin" show went on the air, and by that time he had to have written a newscast from the incoming teletype. As soon as he signed off at 8:30, he discussed the day's work with the salesmen, and dealt with the station's correspondence. By 10:30, he was out on the streets, calling on prospective clients, rushing back to the station to handle any problems. At 5:15 p.m. and again at six and eight o'clock, to give a rest to Hicks, who had been doing the announcing and newscasts all day, he did fifteen-minute newscasts, and then, fourteen hours after he had left for the station, drove home—to handle more business. "This," Weedin was to say, "was the toughest schedule I had ever had in my life." But for a while, he says, "all of us had that wonderful feeling of accomplishment. . . . And also as we looked at the profit side of the ledger . . ." By August, 1943, KTBC showed its first profit—eighteen dollars. By October, the monthly profit was hundreds of dollars. And after the CBS programs began coming through that autumn, it was thousands.

Gradually, however, the "wonderful feeling" faded. For the vision of "unlimited funds" to improve KTBC was not the only promise that was not being honored. The promised written contract, with its ten percent of KTBC's profits, did not materialize. During the first six months of the Johnson ownership, the Congressman himself did not come to Austin often, but when he did, Weedin would bring up the subject and the Congressman would stall. "Lyndon would never give me a contract because he could never decide if the ten percent was before or after taxes," Weedin says. In 1944, despite the station's substantial profits, Weedin was still receiving no money other than his salary—that inadequate salary, so much lower than his salary at his former station, that he had agreed to accept only because of the promise of a share of the profits.

But while the percentage had not been forthcoming, the other important promise that had motivated Weedin to come to KTBC—*carte blanche*, the assurance that he would really be in charge—had for a time been kept. As the station became stronger, however, that promise too began to be broken.

Weedin had been consulting almost daily with Mrs. Johnson, and the two of them had been getting along very well. As for the Congressman, during the first six months or so he left Weedin alone. "But once we got into the fact that we were making money and it looked like we were really on our way," that changed, Weedin was to say. He felt that the change was also due to the Johnsons' realization that "this thing was a hell of a lot—a great money-maker, and it was going to be bigger and bigger." Whatever the reason, "I did not have the *carte blanche* at the end of that time I had had in the early days." When Johnson was in Austin, he would come into the station and check the books. "Lyndon really took over. He was the one who made all the decisions. She wouldn't ever, I don't think, dare to tell me to do something without checking with Lyndon."

There was a more serious, if less tangible, source of tension between the two men. During the 1941 campaign, Weedin had become a fervent admirer of Lyndon Johnson. "He must have sold me, or somebody sold me, or I sold myself on doing whatever I could to get him elected. So I became a thorough Lyndon Johnson follower." For a time after Weedin went to work for Johnson at KTBC, this admiration grew even more intense—he believed that Johnson would be President of the United States someday; he proudly hung Johnson's picture on the wall of his office. Weedin's attitude toward Johnson was that of a younger man toward an older man who is his hero. Now, however, Johnson was not Weedin's candidate but Weedin's employer—and a new element entered the relationship. Attempting to define it, Weedin says, "The minute he walked in, he'd take over the room. . . . He had a tremendously commanding presence, and as everyone says, the one-on-one things, he was fantastic." He speaks of Johnson's "domination. . . . He never let up on that at all. He was a completely overwhelming man in person." And, he says, Johnson "intimidated" him: "He was the only person who could ever make me nervous." During their discussions about the station, "he would grill me."

> Whenever he would come in, I would be so up on things that I wanted to tell him that were going on, I'd done so much homework on everything to report to him, that I was a bundle of [nerves]. And I'm not a nervous man, but I was a bundle of nerves going in to talk to him. And he would start to ask a question and I would answer him before he would finish the question, because I knew what it was. And that used to infuriate him. He said, "Let me ask the question before you answer!" And the thing that made him mad, it was always the question he was going to ask, and I could answer it just from the first couple or three [words].

No matter how admiring, respectful and intimidated Weedin was by Lyndon Johnson, he couldn't be as admiring, respectful and intimidated as Johnson wanted him to be. Other employees of KTBC saw this. John Hicks recalls: "He wanted Harf to be a slave, and Harf just wasn't like that. He was young and eager, but he had a kind of dignity about him. He just *couldn't* be what Johnson wanted." He was very bright—and he *did* know the questions Johnson was about to ask. And that was too bright for Lyndon Johnson.

In February, 1944, Weedin received his induction notice from the Navy. Then he asked Lyndon Johnson for ten percent of the profits that KTBC had earned during the ten months he had been manager—the ten percent that Lyndon Johnson had promised him. These profits were approximately $50,000, so Weedin's share should, he calculated, be about

$5,000, and that was what he asked for. What was Johnson's reaction? "He was upset that I asked for it." At first he told Weedin that he wouldn't give him anything. At last he said he would give him a thousand dollars. When Weedin tried to negotiate that figure, Johnson made clear that the discussion was over: that was not only his offer, it was his final offer. "He told me that was what I was going to get," Weedin says. "So I took it."

WEEDIN'S EXPERTISE and contacts had been indispensable to Lyndon Johnson during the first months of the new ownership of KTBC, but with his other new employees the Congressman had more leeway, and as soon as they were hired he began inculcating in them the qualities he considered desirable in employees. At staff meetings—held frequently during his stays in Austin—he would combine appeals to naked self-interest and to higher ideals, including the ideal he held highest of all: "loyalty." Standing before them, hands thrust deep in his trouser pockets jingling change and keys, he would tell them that "We are building this station. It's going to be big. And you can grow along with it. Work hard, and be loyal, and you'll be rewarded." Sometimes he played the role of a father, one staff member recalls: "We're all one big family here, and we have to help each other and be loyal to each other." Sometimes he was more the high school football coach. "His staff meetings were like half-time talks," another employee says: " 'Every team has to have a quarterback, and I'm the quarterback. And I don't want anyone dropping the ball.' " And there were private meetings, in which he was more blunt. In public, he talked about "loyalty"; in private, he gave staff members his definition of that quality. "I want *real* loyalty," he told one young staffer. "I want someone who will kiss my ass in Macy's window, and say it smells like roses."

Despite all his efforts at instruction, however, he experienced difficulty in lining up the kind of team he wanted. In filling jobs in his political organization, his screening process had been deliberate and painstaking. For his radio organization, he was forced to hire people—to allow Weedin to hire people—whom he, Lyndon Johnson, hardly knew, and he was constantly being disappointed in them. In part, this was because they saw the way he treated Lady Bird. Ann Durrum Robinson, the station's continuity writer, says that "Mrs. Johnson didn't come down [to the station] too much. Mr. Johnson was the one who came down," but that several times she had lunch with her. And at these lunches—at any time he wasn't with her—"she came across as a very intelligent, capable person." But when the Johnsons were together, his treatment of her—"I'd really rather not go into the personal things. I'm a great admirer of hers, and I'd rather not. It detracts from her [to tell how she was treated by her husband]. I

feel disloyal to her if I tell what she took from him.'' Newswriter Jack
Gwyn says: "He talked to her as though she were a serving girl. So I saw
the way he used his family. He used his family without conscience.'' In
part, it was because they saw the way he had treated Weedin, using him—
and then refusing to keep his promise to him. And in part, it was because
of the way he treated *them*. They gradually came to realize that their
salaries were low—lower than those earned in comparable jobs on other
stations—and their hours were longer. "How long did you work?'' Mrs.
Robinson says. "You worked until the work was finished.'' She was working fourteen hours a day, for a salary of about thirty-five dollars a week,
and there was no pay for her hours of overtime. When several members
of the staff drove to Dallas one weekend to attend a meeting of a union
that was attempting to organize employees of radio stations, Johnson,
Jack Gwyn recalls, "was very upset. He called a meeting and said that he
was disappointed in us for doing that. He thought we were like a family,
and he would take care of everything. We had nothing to worry about.
He would take care of us. It was a firm way—like he was dealing with
recalcitrant children.'' Moreover, he at least attempted to treat them with
the abusiveness with which he treated the employees of his congressional
office. The KTBC offices had an intercom system, and if, when Johnson
was on the premises, he wanted to speak to someone, he would simply
flick on the switch that connected him with that person's office and begin
talking—without inquiring if there was a visitor present. "He'd just come
on and start talking,'' Mrs. Robinson says. And often he would say things
that KTBC staffers would not want anyone else to hear. "He might come
through the intercom angry, bawling someone out, when you were talking
to a sponsor,'' Mrs. Robinson recalls. "He could be very abusive.'' They
were afraid of being treated this way—and, after a while, of having no
choice but to be treated this way. As they got to know Lyndon Johnson,
some of the staff members grew afraid of falling under his power. "I think
he had a gift for getting from people whatever he wanted,'' Mrs. Robinson
felt. "I remember thinking that the Three E's of manipulation are 'en-
snare,' 'enthrall' and 'enslave.' And he was adept at any one of the three.''
Among themselves, some staff members talked of the dangers of becoming "enslaved" by Lyndon Johnson, who, they felt, tried to "get someone
so obligated that they couldn't [leave his employ]. . . . He would bestow
favors, to make it so worthwhile to be attached.'' Once you accepted a
favor, "there was a large amount of gratitude" that made it harder to
leave.

    So, for example, when Lyndon Johnson made his offer to John Hicks,
Hicks did not accept it on the spot. The offer was made, in March, 1944,
in Hirsh's Drugstore, on Congress Avenue. Johnson had told Hicks to
meet him there after he finished his last newscast of the day at ten p.m.

Normally, the drugstore closed at eight, but, as Hicks says, "when the Congressman wanted it open, it stayed open. They even kept a man there to make us sandwiches." And when Hicks arrived the Congressman was sitting there, slouched down in one of the booths along the right-hand wall of the restaurant, waiting for him. "Johnny," he said, "I want you on my team. Harfield's going into the service, and I'm going to need someone here at the station [as general manager]. And I'm going to need someone to represent me in Austin. I'm going to lend you ten thousand dollars. And I want you to take it and buy yourself a Cadillac car. And I want you to move to a [better] apartment. I want you to *be* somebody. Furnish the apartment. Get Regina a fur coat. I want you to join the Rotary and the Kiwanis, and *be* somebody here in Austin."

The young announcer was earning only seventy-five dollars a week. "Ten thousand dollars—that was more money than I had ever heard of," he recalls. But then, Hicks says, he asked Johnson, "Congressman, how can I ever pay you back?" And when Johnson replied, expansively, genially, with an easy, charming smile, "Johnny, don't you worry about that. You let *me* worry about that," Hicks suddenly felt himself drawing back.

"That was when I said, 'Uh, oh,' " he recalls. He wouldn't be able to pay the "loan" back—not in any foreseeable future—and Johnson must have known that. "I said, 'This man is buying something, and I don't know that I want to be bought. I'll be beholden to him.' " When the young man hesitated, Johnson elaborated on the further potentialities of his offer. "He said, 'I want you to know that I'm going to be President of this country someday. And you can come along with me. I want you on my team.' It was like he was saying, 'All right, boys. Here's the bandwagon. Hop on.' " But he also made clear what he expected in return. "He said to me that if I took the loan, 'I would expect your complete loyalty and cooperation in anything I want you to do. I will *give* total loyalty, and I expect total loyalty. If I call you up at two o'clock in the morning, and tell you to be somewhere, I want you on that horse.' " Hicks had seen what this man was like, and "I didn't want to be beholden to this man." So instead of hopping on the bandwagon, Hicks said, "Sir, I'm going to have to think this over," and he went home, in his car, which was not a Cadillac, to the "tiny" house he rented, and to his wife, for whom he would very much have liked to buy a fur coat, and talked it over with her. "We talked it over all night," Regina Hicks recalls. "Because not only was it a good way to get out of the service, but it was security." Says John Hicks: "I would never be able to save ten thousand dollars. It was very tempting. [I was] twenty-five years old, and with a brand-new baby boy . . ." Yet they decided to turn the offer down. "I knew that if I took that money from him, I would be *his* from then on. And I was a little too independent to be beholden to anybody. I knew that if I took his money, I would be on his team"—not just in broadcasting, but in politics, too.

THE NEXT DAY, when Johnson came into the station, Hicks told him he thought it would be better that he not take the loan, because he couldn't repay it. "You *are* crazy," Johnson said. And, Hicks recalls, that was all Johnson said: "It was like a curtain came down." The Congressman turned and left. So far as Hicks remembers, Johnson never spoke to him again. Since it was clear that he "had no future" at KTBC, shortly thereafter he resigned. But if Johnson didn't understand Hicks' refusal, Hicks' friends at the station did. Jack Gwyn, for example, says he understood perfectly. Had Hicks accepted the loan and purchased a house, Gwyn says, "I had this vision of a house with a huge picture of Lyndon Johnson over the fireplace."

   (Did someone else understand, even if she did not say so directly? Although Lyndon Johnson never repeated his offer, he did send an emissary. The evening after Hicks' refusal, Lady Bird, dropping by the Hickses' home, brought up the subject. She did so, however, in a noticeably "halfhearted" manner. And when John Hicks repeated his refusal, Mrs. Johnson said she understood, and she said so in a way that made Hicks feel that "she *did* understand." He and Regina were to speculate to each other that Mrs. Johnson "had seen other people take their ten thousand dollars and had seen what happened to them.")

GRADUALLY, Lyndon Johnson put together the kind of staff he wanted— composed of men who had demonstrated an unusual willingness to allow him to dictate their lives: Sherman Birdwell, who, as one of his boyhood playmates in the Hill Country, had followed Lyndon around obediently, attempting to imitate his mannerisms, an imitation he had continued while working for Johnson in the National Youth Administration; Willard Deason, who at college had served as Johnson's front man in his campaign to attain campus power, and who thereafter had demonstrated his unquestioning obedience by switching from a promising career in education to a career in law because Johnson told him to, and then, when Johnson decided another switch was in order, by leaving the law to work for Johnson at the NYA; Walter Jenkins, who had been in Johnson's service only since 1939, but who had made up for his late start by his willingness to work for his Chief "like a slave" and by a psychological dependence on him at least equal to that of his elders.

   The quality that was crucial to Johnson in the people he wanted working for him was revealed in his choice in 1945 of a new KTBC general manager, the job Harfield Weedin had once held. By this time, after Hicks' turndown, Johnson was culling candidates for positions in his radio office as thoroughly as he did for his political office. For each of the three or four final candidates, he took a separate page on a yellow legal pad, drew a line down the center of the page, and listed, on opposite sides of the line, the man's "assets" and "liabilities." For a long time he studied the pages. Then, on one of the pages, he underlined, on the "asset" side of the line, a single word—underlined it three or four times, decisively. The word was *loyalty*, and the name on the top of the page was *Kellam*.

As a youth, Jesse Kellam must have seemed an unlikely candidate for the Johnson team, for, as was seen in *The Path to Power*, he was regarded not as a man who took orders, but as a man who gave them. As a roustabout in the Texas oil fields, and later at San Marcos, as a 140-pound fullback who played without a helmet, Kellam had been noted for his viciousness as well as his toughness (once he deliberately fractured an opponent's ankle), and for his leadership abilities: although he was a full-back, he called signals; a teammate says: "In the huddle, Jesse spoke and we listened. He had command presence." But Johnson, the great reader of men, could read the most difficult text. Despite Kellam's toughness and command presence—and considerable ambition—when Johnson met him for the first time, in 1933, Kellam was a $100-a-month high school football coach in a backwater Texas town. After eight years in that job, he had, at the age of thirty-three, with Texas in the grip of the Depression, all but lost hope of finding a way out of the dead end in which his life was mired. Johnson, the twenty-five-year-old congressional secretary, had one, and only one, truly desirable patronage job—with the state Department of Education—at his disposal; he gave it to Kellam. When, two years later, Johnson became state director of the NYA, he asked Kellam to join his staff. Kellam did not want to leave the state job, but he did. And when Johnson resigned from the NYA to run for Congress, and needed someone he could trust to keep the NYA organization loyal to him, he selected Kellam as his successor.

Basic economic considerations may have played a role in tying Kellam closely to Johnson. The man who had gotten him his government executive position could have it taken away from him, and if that man turned against him, who would give him another one? "Lyndon had Jesse absolutely in his power," says someone familiar with both men. "And Jesse knew it." Now in 1945, that power was greater than ever. With the NYA disbanded, Kellam, returning from the Navy at the age of forty-three, had no job waiting. And although Johnson gave him a job, the KTBC general managership, he did not give him a contract, so Kellam had no security; responding to an FCC questionnaire a few years later, Kellam said he had a contract, "an oral one." This "contract," he said, included a provision for a percentage of the net profits. And who determined the percentage? The "station ownership." His economic dependence on Lyndon Johnson's pleasure was as total as ever.

But some of the considerations that tied Kellam to Johnson may have been more subtle than economic ones. Men who had observed the relationship between the two men had watched a powerful personality becoming steadily submerged in one much more powerful, until little trace of the first remained. Although Kellam was eight years older than Johnson, he called Johnson "Mr. Johnson." Johnson called him "Jesse." His gratitude for a word of praise from Johnson was almost painful to watch— although not as painful as his reaction to Johnson's anger. What Johnson said to Kellam behind closed doors at the NYA is not known, but on more than one occasion, when the door of Johnson's office opened, NYA staffers had been astonished to see Kellam, outwardly the toughest and most self-possessed of men, emerge crying. Now Kellam had his own office at KTBC. Johnson would enter it and shut the door when he wanted to confer privately with him. And more than once, when the door opened and Johnson strode out, staffers at KTBC passing the door saw Kellam sitting at his desk, tears running down his hard face.

Although Kellam enjoyed giving orders, in a coldly domineering fashion, from Johnson he took orders, with a slavish obedience. Some of the orders made other men marvel. One was to meet Johnson's plane when he flew into Austin. Since Johnson often traveled on private planes, his time of arrival was frequently uncertain. But that did not matter. If, for example, he would be flying from Houston after dinner with the Brown brothers, he would tell Kellam only that he would telephone him from Houston as he was leaving. So afraid was Jesse Kellam that he would miss that call that he would hardly stir from his office until it came. One evening, a member of the KTBC staff left something in the radio station's offices and came back late at night to pick it up. At first, he thought the executive offices were deserted because no lights were on in them. As he passed the office of the general manager, however, he saw, in the shadows inside, a figure behind the desk. It was Kellam, sitting alone in the dark, waiting for the phone to ring.

And it wouldn't be only at the Austin airport that Kellam would be in attendance. Once, a storm prevented a Pioneer Airlines flight on which Johnson was returning from a speech in Midland from landing in the capital. The pilot announced that they would land instead in Temple, sixty miles to the north. Johnson told the pilot to contact the Austin control tower. "My man" will be waiting for me at the Austin airport, he said. Tell him to drive to Temple and pick me up there. In Temple, the weather was again too stormy to land. The pilot announced he would try Waco, another thirty miles north. Johnson had the pilot notify the Temple control tower that when his man arrived, he was to be told to proceed to Waco. When the plane succeeded in landing there, Johnson had to wait an hour—but at the end of an hour, Kellam arrived. Says a man who was on the airplane, "He was following the plane around Texas. If he had had to go to Dallas, he would have gone to Dallas"—so that Lyndon Johnson's car would be available as soon as possible.

Kellam's loyalty to Johnson became famous in Austin. Says Ed Clark: "Johnson could tell him to do anything, and the only reply would be 'I'll be there.' He never had a conflict when Johnson wanted him. He never had plans. He would change any plans." Not only Jesse Kellam's career but his life was lived at Lyndon Johnson's pleasure.

As for Kellam's ability, that was held in lower esteem. In New York, in later years, as the Johnson media enterprises grew into multi-million-dollar properties, men who dealt with Kellam could not understand how such a man had come to be in charge of them. "I knew Kellam very well," says one CBS executive. "He was a nice guy, but he knew nothing about radio and television. He just didn't understand the business." They just didn't understand. Johnson was simply following with KTBC the pattern he had followed during his entire career. When he had been a young congressional secretary, two assistant secretaries, even younger, had worked under him. And it was not the brilliant, energetic but independent Luther E. Jones (later to be known as the "finest appellate lawyer" in Texas) whom Johnson selected to be a permanent member of his team but the other assistant, the more malleable, if considerably less talented, Eugene Latimer. He had followed this pattern in hiring men for the NYA, and for his congressional office, and in his recommendations for even low-level federal patronage jobs. As a general rule (the most notable exceptions in these early years were John Connally and Horace Busby), the men he picked were not the brightest available, nor the men with the most initiative or ability. They were, rather, the men who had demonstrated the most unquestioning obedience—not merely a willingness but an eagerness to take orders, to bow to his will. While he called it "loyalty," the capacity he prized most in his subordinates was actually the capacity for subservience.

JOHN HICKS was not the only man who fled from Johnson's embrace, fearing his domination. "I was one of his favorites," says Jack Gwyn. But when, one Sunday, during a confidential chat, Johnson said, "You know, I admire loyalty above everything else," Gwyn made the mistake of replying: "You're right. If you hire a man eight hours a day, he owes you eight hours a day." Johnson hastened to correct him. "I mean more than that," he said. "I don't mean just that kind of loyalty, I mean *real* loyalty.

Look at John Connally. I can call John Connally at midnight, and if I told him to come over and shine my shoes, he'd come running. *That's* loyalty."

Gwyn, to his surprise, suddenly heard himself replying: "Congressman, if anyone called me at midnight and told me to come over and shine his shoes, I'd tell him to go fuck himself." Johnson was immediately apologetic. "Well, I didn't mean it literally," he said. "I'm not gonna call someone at midnight." But, Gwyn says, the exchange had crystallized feelings that had been growing in him, and "I decided to leave. Johnson didn't demand a great ability. He demanded 'loyalty,' and what he meant by loyalty was a kind of total submission. If you worked for Lyndon Johnson, you sold your soul to him. You could see it happening to other people around you. You saw that Jesse Kellam had no soul of his own. You saw that other guys close to him no longer had souls of their own. You wrote [in *The Path to Power*] how he could reduce Jesse Kellam to tears. I saw that. And I've seen Kellam sit in that office of his waiting for Lyndon to arrive. If his plane didn't get in on time, or he [Johnson] had only said, 'I'll be there [sometime] Friday night,' he wouldn't leave. He would sit there until midnight if he had to. I was afraid it would happen to me." Gwyn took a job with an advertising agency in Fort Worth; "I just wanted to get out of there."

But although, after a while, almost all of the original staff members of KTBC—not only Weedin, Hicks, Gwyn and Mrs. Robinson but others who, forty years later, did not want their names to be used in a book about Lyndon Johnson—left the station, their loss was not an irreplaceable one. They were replaced—almost invariably with people willing to give Lyndon Johnson the kind of "loyalty" he liked.

7

One of a Crowd

DESPITE THE MONEY he was making in the years after he returned from his Navy service, these were not happy years for Lyndon Johnson. The men and women who had a chance to observe him most closely—as a youth, as a congressional secretary, as a Congressman—speak of Johnson's "low" times, when "he got real quiet," and "it was bad." These years were "very bad." Although he wanted money, had always wanted it, money was not what he wanted most—*needed* most—as George Brown had realized during that vacation at the Greenbrier. The hunger that gnawed at him most deeply was a hunger not for riches but for power in its most naked form; to bend others to his will. At every stage of his life, this hunger was evident: what he always sought was not merely power but the acknowledgment by others—the deferential, face-to-face, subservient acknowledgment—that he possessed it. *"You had to ask. He insisted on it."* It had been evident in the men with whom he surrounded himself, in the way he treated them, in his unceasing efforts, even as a junior Congressman, to dominate other congressmen, to dominate every room in which he was present, in fact, save only the bright, sunny oval room in the White House and Rayburn's dim basement hideaway in the Capitol. And the kind of power he craved he could never obtain from the radio business. Indeed, he came to realize—and intimates like George Brown and Edward Clark watched the realization growing in him—that in a sense, as the proprietor of a radio station whose income was derived from the sale of advertising time, he was often placed in a position antithetical to the one he wanted to be in. In asking a businessman to purchase time on his station, he was not conferring a favor—a transaction which would result in power for him—but receiving one. His use of political influence to grant the businessman a favor in return was still only a trading of favors, not a conferring. If he was a very well paid salesman, nonetheless selling, not buying, was what he was doing—with all that that implied in personal relationships. Says George Brown: "Ordering people around—well, you don't order around people you're trying to sell something to." Says Clark: "He wanted people to kiss his ass. He didn't want to have to kiss people's asses. And selling [radio] time—you have to kiss people's asses sometimes. In business you have to. He liked power, and so he was unhappy in business."

Politics, and only politics, could give him what he wanted. But in politics, he had no place to go. The summer of 1942—when Johnson had returned from the war—was the summer in which Pappy O'Daniel had won his full Senate term; that seat was therefore occupied until 1948. The term of the state's other Senate seat was up in 1946, but that seat had been held by Tom Connally since 1928. Connally was a power not only in Washington, where he was chairman of the Senate Foreign Relations Committee—it was the Connally Resolution that called for United States participation in the United Nations—but in Texas, where, as the author of the oil depletion allowance and other legislation favoring the oil industry, he was regarded as the champion of the state's dominant interest. A challenge to this picturesque figure—with his frock coat, string tie, and big black hat covering the head of senatorial gray hair curling at the back—would be merely quixotic. The Texas governorship was a possibility, and indeed in 1946 there would be speculation that Johnson would run for the governorship, but on Johnson's road map, the governorship—or any other state post—would be only a detour, a detour that might turn into a dead end. State office had no interest for him, he reiterated whenever the subject was brought up; years later, when John Connally was leaving Washington to run for Governor of Texas, Johnson would ask him, "What the hell do you want to be Governor for? Here's where the power is." As for appointive office, as he often explained to supporters, "You have to be your own man"—his own man, not someone else's; an elected official whose position had been conferred on him by voters, not by a single individual—who could, on a whim, take the position away. The ladder to his great dream had only three rungs, and appointive office was not one of them. Sometimes, as if he could not endure the frustration of his hopes, what he really wanted burst out of him, as it had with John Hicks in Hirsh's Drugstore—and as it sometimes did in Washington with old friends from Texas; one evening, alone with Welly Hopkins, he snarled: "By *God*, I'll be President someday!" He had mapped out his route so long ago, had mapped it out so carefully, had held to it so grimly, had plunged along it so fiercely. But now his progress was halted. He was stuck in the House of Representatives—that House of which he was only an insignificant member.

So these were very bad years for Lyndon Johnson.

.   .   .

AND THEY GOT WORSE.

With Roosevelt in the presidency, Johnson at least had the aura of a White House insider. Just after five o'clock in the afternoon of April 12, 1945, the telephone rang in the "Board of Education" room, and Sam Rayburn picked up the receiver. On the line was Roosevelt's press secretary, Stephen Early, asking to speak to Harry Truman. When the Vice President, who had been presiding over the Senate, arrived a few minutes later, Rayburn gave him the message, and Truman called Early, listened for a moment, and hurriedly left for the White House. Soon the news broke, and Sam Rayburn began to cry.

Lyndon Johnson was to say that when the telephone call came, "I was just looking up at a cartoon on the wall—a cartoon showing the President with that cigarette holder and his jaw stuck out like it always was. He had his head cocked back, you know. . . ." The cartoon may have provided him with inspiration. When a reporter, his friend William S. White of the *New York Times*, arrived to interview him for his reaction, he found Johnson standing with a cigarette holder in *his* mouth, and *his* jaw stuck out.

The interview, printed in the *Times* the next day, was dramatic: White wrote that the tall young Congressman stood in "a gloomy Capitol corridor," with "tears in his eyes" and his Rooseveltian cigarette holder clamped in "a shaking jaw," and cried out: "God! God! How he could take it for us all!" The article emphasized Johnson's closeness to Rayburn: Johnson told White that he had been in the Board of Education room when the telephone call came—an assertion which may not have been accurate.* It also emphasized his closeness to Roosevelt; recalling that the President had once sent him a photograph of his dog Fala inscribed "From the master to the pup," Johnson said, "He was just like a Daddy to me always; he always talked to me just that way. He was the only person I ever knew—anywhere—who was never afraid. Whatever you talked to him about, whatever you asked him for, like the projects in your district, there was just one way to figure it with him. . . . You could be damn sure that the only test he had was this: Was it good for the Folks. . . . The people who are going to be crushed by this are the little guys—the guy down in my district, say, who makes $21.50 driving a truck and has a decent house to live in now, cheap, because of Mr. Roosevelt." And it

---

* House parliamentarian Lewis Deschler was later to say that Johnson arrived at the Board of Education only after Rayburn had left, and asked Deschler, "Where's everybody?"

emphasized the closeness between their philosophies ("There are plenty
of us left here to try to block and run interference, as he had taught us,
but the man who carried the ball is gone—gone"), although the point was
also made that despite the closeness, independence had been maintained:
"They called the President a dictator and some of us they called 'yes men.'
Sure, I yessed him plenty of times—because I thought he was right—and
I'm not sorry for a single 'yes' I ever gave. I have seen the President in
all kinds of moods—at breakfast, at lunch, at dinner—and never once in
my five terms here did he ever ask me to vote a certain way, or even
suggest it. And when I voted against him—as I have plenty of times—he
never said a word."

The king, however, was dead. The day after Roosevelt's death, one
of Johnson's secretaries, Dorothy Nichols, asked him: "He's gone; what
do we have now?" "Honey," Johnson replied. "We've got Truman. . . .
There is going to be the damnedest scramble for power in this man's town
for the next two weeks that anyone ever saw in their lives."

Lyndon Johnson and Harry Truman were acquainted through a mutual friend: Sam Rayburn. Truman and Rayburn, two very tough, very
Democratic, politicians, got along well, and the Senator from Missouri
held a permanent invitation to the Board of Education. Sometimes Rayburn, invited to a social gathering of party elders, would bring Lyndon
along; at one such luncheon at the Mayflower Hotel to celebrate Truman's
nomination as Vice President in 1944, Truman received a telephone call
summoning him to a Senate vote, and Johnson volunteered to drive him
to the Capitol; once Truman, along with Rayburn and some other friends,
was a dinner guest in the Johnson home. And when the new President
delivered an address to a joint session of Congress on April 15, 1945,
Johnson wrote him a letter in the tone of an intimate friend: "Those of
us who know you so well were so proud of you today. . . . We in Texas
felt that you were a part of us long before you belonged to the nation."

Truman's reply, however, was little more than a form letter, and
during the months that followed Johnson had no other contact with him.
In May, Truman appointed Tom Clark United States Attorney General.
Johnson and Clark had been working together for years on a number of
matters involving the more confidential side of politics, including maneuvers to secure favorable rulings from the FCC for at least two mutual
allies, and Clark, who during the 1930s had been a lobbyist in Austin for
the Safeway grocery store chain (and for other major companies: a Texas
State Senate investigating committee found in 1937 that Clark had experienced "a tremendous and startling increase in earnings" after his law
partner became Texas State Attorney General), had helped persuade Safeway to advertise on KTBC. During Roosevelt's Administration, Johnson
had pushed vigorously for Clark's advancement up the Justice Department

ladder. On the day he was appointed Attorney General, Clark wrote Johnson a handwritten note: "I want you to be the first I write since the nomination . . . to you I will be ever grateful for a true friendship that opened to me opportunities for service." But Clark's appointment was almost the only bright spot for Johnson among the scores of appointments to the new Administration. He had assiduously cultivated—and won—the affections of many in the circle that surrounded Franklin Roosevelt; now Grace Tully and Marvin McIntyre were gone. There were new faces around the White House—dubbed by reporters the "Missouri gang"—and he knew few of them, none of them intimately. By July, he was writing to Rowe, still on naval duty in the Pacific, in the tone of a disgruntled outsider: "It is a different town today. . . . There is little to stimulate one to doing unbelievable things and such accomplishments as we are likely to make will be of the routine type. . . . Just what line [Truman's] subordinates follow has yet to be developed. I have contributed what I could in the way of counsel, but I don't know that much of it will be followed. Most of our old friends are bewildered. . . . My own course in political affairs is yet to be charted. We are giving serious thought to going back to the hill country in Texas and making our contribution to a better world from that spot." In succeeding months, he reached rather far in attempts to improve his acquaintance with the new President, sending him photographs to sign (including one, a rather far reach even for Johnson, of a picture taken five years before of then Senator Truman posing with Alvin Wirtz, and reminding Truman that Wirtz, "my closest personal friend . . . went into Missouri in 1940 to help in the campaign for the ticket"), and one of the huge Christmas turkeys that he had previously sent to Truman's predecessor, with a note explaining that he was sending it "Because of your friendship through the years; because of your many kindnesses to me; because I look forward to your company and your counsel in the years to come." He got the inscriptions ("To Lyndon B. Johnson, a grand guy and my friend") and thanks for the turkey, but little company or counsel: during all of 1945, in fact, Lyndon Johnson was in the Oval Office—to which he had once been welcomed with such warmth—exactly once.

Johnson's admirer Rowe was to explain the contrast between Johnson's treatment by Roosevelt and his treatment by Truman by saying simply, "You've got to have a reason to see a President." With Roosevelt, there had been reasons: Johnson's fund-raising capabilities; his role, through the Democratic Congressional Campaign Committee, as link between the White House and Capitol Hill; his role as "Roosevelt's man" (and spy) on the Texas delegation. Now his fund-raising and campaign-committee functions had been taken over by someone else, and Rayburn was Truman's man for Texas. But Rowe's explanation does not mention the paternal rapport that Roosevelt aides call a "special feeling," and that had led that President to break his own rules in lavishing campaign and other assistance on the young congressman. And Rowe's explanation also ignores Truman's feelings about Johnson—which were, in the early years of the Truman Presidency, quite different from Roosevelt's.

Lyndon Johnson's remarkable talent for cultivating and manipulating older men who possessed power that could help his ambitions—the obsequiousness so profound that scornful contemporaries referred to him as a "professional son"—had been exercised to the fullest on Sam Rayburn. He kissed the fearsome Speaker on his bald head, repeatedly told others, in Rayburn's presence, that the Speaker was "just like a Daddy to me"— and was in the Board of Education (and anywhere else he was in Rayburn's company) utterly deferential, respectful and admiring, "playing" this lonely older man like the "great flatterer" contemporaries called him. But Harry Truman had been a visitor to the "Board"; he had been present when Johnson was "playing" Rayburn. "He tried to play Truman the way he played Rayburn," says Board member Richard Bolling, a Congressman from Missouri. "But Truman had *watched* him doing it with Rayburn. So when Lyndon started doing it with him, he knew exactly what Lyndon was doing. And so it didn't work." During this period, Stuart Symington says, Johnson "tried to be friendly with the new President." But Truman, he says, "was a pretty sharp judge of character." Truman's daughter, Margaret, says that because her father had witnessed the professional son in action with Rayburn, "he never quite trusted him. . . ."

The situation grew still more discouraging. Johnson's chief remaining ally in the Administration's higher reaches was Secretary of the Interior Ickes; early in 1946, after testifying before a Senate committee that Edwin Pauley, nominated by Truman as Undersecretary of the Navy, had dangled before the Democrats a $300,000 gift from West Coast oilmen if the federal government were to drop a suit to obtain title to tidelands oil, Ickes resigned, a resignation Truman quickly and angrily accepted. Tommy Corcoran, once so influential with the White House, was so thoroughly disliked and distrusted by Truman that the President had ordered his telephone tapped. Johnson sought for chinks in the wall around the new President; when Truman's mother died in Grandview, Missouri, Johnson wrote him that he was donating a book in memory of the "first Mother of the Land" to the Grandview Public Library. Truman replied with a note that thanked Johnson but added, "I regret to advise you that Grandview has no Public Library. . . ." Johnson worked assiduously at cultivating two younger members of the Truman team, Clark Clifford and Secretary of the Air Force Stuart Symington, but, in Clifford's case, as Clifford later recalled, "It was a slowly developing relationship." With Symington, the results came faster, for the Secretary's fervent conviction of the need for an Air Force much larger than Truman was advocating dovetailed with Johnson's need to procure new federal contracts for the vast aircraft plants that had sprung up during the war on Texas plains. But the conflict between Symington's stance and Truman's meant that Johnson's closeness with the Secretary was attained only at the cost of more coolness from the White House.

Moreover, with the waning of the Roosevelt influence, conservatives had consolidated their political power in Texas. If Johnson was ever to run for the Senate, he needed their support, and needed to erase from their minds the impression that he was a New Dealer. In these post-war years, Harry Truman submitted to Congress an impressive new liberal agenda to end the wartime hiatus in social reform: increased Social Security benefits, a higher minimum wage, federal aid to education, pre-paid medical care, health insurance, and—in what would, if passed, be the first major civil rights legislation of the century—laws against lynching and against segregation in interstate transportation and laws ensuring the right to vote and establishing a permanent Fair Employment Practices Commission (FEPC). Speaking out as he had never before done in Congress, Lyndon Johnson in 1947 opposed most of Truman's "Fair Deal." The proposed civil rights program, he was to say, was a "farce and a sham—an effort to set up a police state in the guise of liberty." It is, he was to say, "the province of the state to run its own elections. I am opposed to the anti-lynching bill because the federal government has no more business enacting a law against one form of murder than another. I am against the FEPC because if a man can tell you whom you must hire, he can tell you whom you cannot employ."

One vote in particular helped consolidate the new image he was cultivating. Public resentment at the post-war wave of strikes and long-smoldering conservative anger at the power the New Deal had given to labor unions crystallized in the Labor-Management Relations Act of 1947—the "Taft-Hartley Act"—which curtailed union powers, outraging workers and labor leaders, who called it a "slave labor bill." Johnson voted with the congressional majority to pass the Act, and, after the President, in a stinging message, had vetoed it, voted with the bloc that successfully overrode the veto the same day it was delivered. His vote astonished, and enraged, the Texas unionists and liberals whom Johnson had been fervently assuring of his support throughout his previous ten years in Congress. "He was one of those who gutted us in 1947," H. S. (Hank) Brown of the Texas AFL would say years later. But it furnished the Dale Millers and George Browns with an additional talking point in their efforts to persuade fellow Texas conservatives that "he wasn't really as liberal as everyone thought he was." Lest his image, despite these votes, not be changing fast enough, Johnson in 1947 called in a favorite reporter, Lewis T. ("Tex") Easley, of the Associated Press, for an interview, after which Easley wrote that while "People all over Texas formed an impression over the years that Lyndon Johnson personified the New Deal . . . it would be an error to tag Johnson now as a strong New Dealer." In fact, Johnson seemed to be trying to say, that tag would always have been an error. "I think the term 'New Dealer' is a misnomer," he told Easley. "I believe in free enterprise, and I don't believe in the government doing anything that the people can do privately. Whenever it's possible, government should get out of business." George Brown's friends were starting to believe that maybe Brown had been right all along when he had assured them that despite Johnson's public posture during the Roosevelt Administration, in reality the Congressman had always been "practical." Helpful though his new stance may have been in Texas's ruling circles, however, it didn't do much for his popularity in the White House.

Newspapers and national magazines recounted cruises by the President and his intimates down the Potomac on the new presidential yacht *Williamsburg*, and described the President's frequent poker games. Johnson was on one cruise on the *Williamsburg*, but probably only one; he played in the poker games two or three times—when the games were held at the home of Rayburn's friend Secretary of the Treasury Fred M. Vinson, and Vinson invited him. As for the Oval Office, so far as can be determined, during all of 1946, Lyndon Johnson was in it exactly once— as a member of a delegation of congressmen. In 1947, he may not have been in it even once. As Symington puts it, "Johnson was just never part of Truman's inner circle at all." Horace Busby, who joined Johnson's staff late in 1947, noticed that during his first few months on the job, there was not a single message or telephone call from the White House. Not only was Johnson no longer a presidential protégé, he no longer possessed even a trace of the aura of an Administration insider. He was only a congressman. Even in his earliest days in Congress a decade earlier, he had been more than that.

And when, in 1948, an invitation to the Oval Office finally came, it was not the type for which Johnson had hoped. A Johnson suggestion to Truman, written by Busby, for a "re-examination" of the Administration's program of selling war defense plants to private industry, was released to the press, together with a follow-up letter. Shortly after a few brief paragraphs began clattering out on the wire service tickers, Johnson's office received a telephone call from the White House. The President would like to see Congressman Johnson the following morning at 11:15.

Johnson was very excited by the call. "The first thing he did was to go out and get his hair cut and his nails manicured," Busby recalls. He purchased a new pair of shoes. Hurrying to Lewis & Thomas Saltz, one of Washington's most prestigious men's clothing stores, he brought back a boxful of white shirts—"he wasn't buying them all; they were all different styles, and he just wanted to see which was the most suitable"—and a dozen "presidential" neckties. Calling in another young staff member, Warren Woodward, a dapper dresser, he consulted with him over shirts and ties, and then turned to the folding of his white pocket handkerchief. He wanted all four points showing ("none of this just a few points for him," Busby says) and precisely aligned, "so he spent part of that evening at his desk," folding and refolding the handkerchief, "and cursing it when it didn't come right." And the next morning, he kept darting out of his inner office to ask Busby and other members of his staff how much time he should leave for the taxi ride to the White House.

The President's interest, however, turned out to be not in Johnson's attire but in his political manners. Returning to his office about noon, Johnson did not enter through the outer office in which his staff members sat, but, using a key, through the door that led directly from the corridor to his inner office. The door between the two offices was open. Johnson silently pushed it closed.

"After a while, he buzzed for me," Busby says. And when Busby opened the door, his boss "was just an absolute picture of dejection." Truman, Johnson said, had been furious because he had released the letter to the press before it reached the White House. Johnson imitated the President speaking with his lips in a thin line and hardly moving, as the President did when he was angry. He told Busby that Truman had said, "Lyndon, I don't like to read my mail in the newspapers." (Johnson told Busby, "He's absolutely right. We didn't let him get the letter before the press had it. We've learned a lesson. We must never do it again.")

EVEN IN THE HOUSE OF REPRESENTATIVES, he was, during these years of 1945, 1946 and 1947, not gaining but losing ground.

The Speaker did what he could for him. Appointments to two prestigious new committees were in Rayburn's power, and he appointed Johnson to both the House and Senate Joint Committee on Atomic Energy and to the House Select Committee on Postwar Military Policy, most of whose other members were either chairmen or ranking members of their own committees. But while Johnson impressed David Lilienthal, the first chairman of the Atomic Energy Commission, who called him "an able young man, definitely liberal, shrewd, full of savvy," his attempts to carve out a prominent role for himself on these committees resulted merely in resentment from the other, more senior, members. On select and joint as well as regular committees—as in every phase of life in the House of

Representatives—seniority was the dominant factor. Ability couldn't circumvent it. Energy couldn't circumvent it. There was only one way to become one of the rulers of the House: to wait.

And then, in 1946, came two brutal reminders that even waiting was no guarantee.

In February, 1944, Representative Leonard W. Schuetz of Illinois had died, and in November of that year Warren Magnuson had won a Senate seat—and suddenly only two men (Patrick Henry Drewry of Virginia and Carl Vinson) sat between Johnson and the chairmanship of the House Naval Affairs Committee. Johnson had been inching his way toward the big black leather chairman's seat in the middle of the double horseshoe of the committee seats; now that chair had begun to seem within reach.* But Congress, stung by criticism of its inefficiency and inability to come to grips with the complexities of the Atomic Age and the post-war era, had established a bipartisan Joint Committee to study its own organization, and now, in July, 1946, the committee's recommendations were made, and some of them were adopted—including one for the merging of the House Naval Affairs Committee and the House Military Affairs Committee into a single new Armed Services Committee. On this new committee Vinson would be chairman, but since six Democratic members of Military Affairs possessed greater seniority than Johnson, he would no longer be third-ranking Democrat. Vinson's health and longevity (and Drewry's) suddenly became much less relevant to Lyndon Johnson's future. There were not two Democrats ahead of him now; there were eight.

Moreover, in November, 1946, for the first time since 1930, the GOP won control of the House. The victory was a potent reminder of the jaws of the seniority trap. Outwaiting or outliving the eight Democrats ahead of him might not help. If, when his turn in the Democratic line finally arrived, the Republicans were the majority, he still wouldn't be chairman.

As for the other possibilities for leadership in the body of which Lyndon Johnson had been a member since 1937, Johnson's post-war record was nearly identical with his pre-war record. He introduced one bill that would have an effect outside his own district in 1945: a minor measure, never effectively implemented, to give veterans priority in purchasing certain surplus goods after the needs of the federal government were provided for. He did not introduce a single piece of "national" legislation in 1946 or 1947. In 1948, he introduced a bill, whose details were never completely spelled out and for which he did not fight, to amend the Selective Service Act to "draft industries as well as men." By the close of his career in the House of Representatives at the end of 1948, the record

---

* During the 1940s, no one could have predicted the amazing longevity of Vinson's career in the House.

would be clear. During his more than eleven years as a member of the House, he introduced only four bills that would affect the country as a whole; in fact, since he introduced only three intra-district bills, he introduced only seven bills in all. Twenty other representatives entered Congress in January, 1937, and were still there at the end of 1948, so that their terms were roughly contemporaneous with his. One, Eugene J. Keogh of Brooklyn, an energetic legislator (who would later be responsible for the so-called "Keogh Bill," a pension measure), introduced 169 bills during those twelve years. Three other representatives among those twenty introduced more than one hundred bills. Many of the twenty introduced fewer than that, but not one introduced as few as seven. Johnson introduced fewer pieces of legislation than any congressman who served in Congress during the same years as he. As for passage of legislation, the record is little better. Of the seven bills he introduced, two—two that affected only his district—were signed into law. Twelve of the twenty congressmen had more bills signed into law than that. And since the two pieces of Johnson-introduced legislation that became law were bills affecting only his district, during Johnson's more than eleven years as Congressman no bill introduced by him that would have affected the people of the United States as a whole became a law of the United States.

His reluctance to fight for others' bills had, moreover, become even more pronounced. He refused to speak out for causes—refused, it sometimes seemed, to speak out on any issue with the exception of military preparedness; refused to take stands; refused to write not only laws but speeches. Was the *Congressional Record* crammed, month after month, year after year, with speeches delivered by congressmen in their home districts and then "revised and extended" so that they would be reprinted in the *Record* and thereby create the impression of involvement in national issues? Very few of those speeches were by Lyndon Johnson. Had entire years passed before the war in which he did not insert a single speech in the *Congressional Record?* Entire years passed now: 1944, 1945 and 1947. In regard to "real" speeches—talks longer than a paragraph or two actually delivered in the House—their paucity was likewise dramatic. During his first eleven years in Congress, he delivered a total of ten speeches— less than one a year. He refused also to fight in the press on national issues.

He refused to fight not only in public but in private. Helen Gahagan Douglas was a congresswoman herself now, and her earlier impression of Johnson's constant awareness "that what he said might be repeated or remembered—even years later" was confirmed. She noticed that at dinner parties Johnson still talked a lot—but he still seemed never to say anything substantive. She felt she understood those tactics. Lyndon Johnson, Mrs. Douglas says, was looking down a "very long road."

But he was making no progress along it. Instead, there were continual reminders that he was slipping back.

Once, his future on Capitol Hill had seemed so bright. He and Warren Magnuson had talked so often about how badly they both wanted to become Senators, and they had both assumed that it would be Johnson, with his access to the White House and to campaign funds, who would reach that goal first. But it was Magnuson who was sitting in the upper house. Indeed, during Johnson's years in the House, nine members had advanced to the Senate, while he remained behind. Johnson had once been the "baby" of the 21-man Texas delegation, and considered to have a bright future on it (when he had been sworn in at the age of twenty-eight, in fact, only two of the 435 members of the House were younger than he). Now, with his fortieth birthday—August 27, 1948—approaching, many members of the Texas delegation were progressing faster toward committee chairmanships or ranking memberships, passing him on the road to substantial power in the House. In a note of irony, there were no fewer than ten congressmen named "Johnson"; seven of them stood higher in the House hierarchy than he. Rayburn's friendship still gave him the aura of an insider, but it was only Rayburn's friendship that did so, and he was getting a little old to still be "Sam Rayburn's boy." He no longer possessed any power of his own, and since he could not resist trying to dominate other men, he was constantly being reminded of this. His attempts to act toward his fellow congressmen as he had acted when he had possessed at least a modicum of independent power—the power of giving them campaign contributions or, because of his White House access, administrative favors—aroused only resentment. Says Representative James Van Zandt of Pennsylvania: "When he wanted something, he really went after it. He would say: 'Now, goddamnit, Jimmy, I helped you on this, and I want you to help me on *this.*' " And, Van Zandt adds, "Johnson kept asking for favors, and he simply didn't have that many to give in return." He tried too hard—much too hard—to trade on what minor "help" he had given. "You can do those things once or twice," Van Zandt says. "He did them too frequently. People would get irritated."

The atmosphere which had surrounded Lyndon Johnson in the Little Congress (and, before that, at San Marcos) was now deepening around him in the big Congress. The powerful older men to whom he was so deferential were fond of Lyndon Johnson, as were a few—very few—of his contemporaries, most of them unassertive men such as Van Zandt or a fellow Texas Congressman, Robert Poage. With others, however, there was less fondness. Says another Texas Congressman, O. C. Fisher: "He had a way of getting along with the leaders, and he didn't bother much with the small fry. And let me tell you, the small fry didn't mind. They didn't want much to do with him, either." Even the admiring Van Zandt says that "People were critical of him because he was too ambitious, too forceful, too pushy. Some people didn't like him." In the House Dining Room, says Representative Wingate Lucas of Fort Worth, "guys would come [in] and sit down" at a table near where Johnson was sitting; they would greet all their fellow members nearby, except him. "And he would get up and say, 'Well, Joe, why in hell didn't you speak to me?' Well, they hadn't spoken to him because they didn't like him. They wouldn't put up with him." The situation was summed up in a symbolic gesture— a shrinking away. The old, hereditary Johnson habit of grasping a man's lapel with one hand and putting his other arm around the man's shoulders, holding him close while staring into his eyes and talking directly into his face didn't offend all fellow congressmen, some of whom liked the intimacy of the gesture, but more were offended. They would draw back from his hand, shrug away from his arm. And sometimes, if he didn't take the hint, they would react sharply. At least once, when he took a congressman's lapel in his hand, the congressman knocked his hand away. Without at least a modicum of power behind them, his techniques of manipulating men were ineffective, and earned him only unpopularity. With increasing frequency, moreover, his fellow members' eyes now betrayed something that to Lyndon Johnson was as unpleasant as dislike. Johnson was always reading men's eyes. He knew when his colleagues didn't even know who he was. And, with increasing frequency, that was the case. A new Representative, George Smathers of Florida, was sworn in in January, 1946. When, almost two years later, he saw, on the wall of Mrs. Douglas's office, "a big theatrical picture . . . of a shiny-haired fellow, I asked her who he was." Until that moment, Smathers recalls, "I wasn't even aware of his existence." Though Johnson had never spent much time in the House Chamber, had never listened to the speeches of others, he had, at least during his earlier years in the House, spent a lot of time in the cloakroom. Now he started going to the cloakroom less and less, and Van Zandt understood why. "He couldn't work up the enthusiasm any more."

Estelle Harbin, who had known Lyndon Johnson well when he was young, had said that he "couldn't stand being just one of a crowd—just could not *stand* it." Mrs. Douglas, who came to know Lyndon Johnson well now, when he was no longer so young, was to use similar words. "He never spoke in the House, you know, except on rare, rare occasions. He didn't spend much time listening to others in the House. He usually voted and then left the Chamber, loping off the floor with that great stride of his as though he was on some Texas plain." And "if he did remain, he looked the picture of boredom, slumped in his chair with his eyes half closed. Then suddenly he'd jump to his feet, nervous . . . restless, as if he couldn't bear it another minute." His days were punctuated with inconsequential, but painful, reminders of his lack of status and power. Posing for photographic portraits of the committees on which he sat hurt his pride. In the formal portraits of the committees at their daises, he was embarrassingly distant from the chairman. Informal portraits, such as one of the Naval Affairs Committee taken after a luncheon with James Forrestal at the Navy Department, were worse. Forrestal and several of his top deputies were seated in the single row of chairs, and officious committee aides made certain that the remaining chairs were occupied by the most senior congressmen; Johnson had to stand behind them, among the less senior congressmen, distinguished from the group only by his height. He "couldn't stand being just one of a crowd"—but, increasingly, one of a crowd was what he was.

Whenever, during these post-war years, Johnson attempted to assert his importance, he was only reminded of how little of it he possessed.

He was rebuffed even in an attempt to assert his power over one of his committee's young staff members. Thirty-year-old Bryce N. Harlow did not, in Johnson's opinion, show him sufficient subservience, so in 1947, the Congressman attempted, Harlow says, "to take me to the Johnson School." During a subcommittee discussion of a bill Harlow had drafted, Johnson suddenly asked him if some minor point had been checked with the Reconstruction Finance Corporation. The demand, says Harlow, who already, as congressional liaison during World War II for General George C. Marshall, had earned a reputation as an expert in legislation, was "ridiculous—it didn't have to be checked." He told Johnson so, and explained the reason. But Johnson turned to Subcommittee Chairman William E. Hess, of Ohio, and said contemptuously, "Well, Mr. Chairman, I move the bill be tabled until the staff member checks with the RFC and finishes the job he was supposed to do."

Harlow made the check as Johnson wanted, and said nothing further about it. A tiny, slender man (years later, taking the lectern at a Washington dinner, he would tell the audience, "Don't wait for the rest of me. I'm standing up"), soft-spoken, gentle and courtly, he may have seemed sufficiently malleable to be a prime candidate for the Johnson School, and the headmaster may have decided that a further lesson was in order. Shortly after the first incident, Harlow wrote "some report with a recommendation as to what the subcommittee should do"—just a standard report with the recommendation in the usual form—and, to his surprise, "Johnson requested an executive session." No sooner had the doors been shut than Johnson said, "I want to register a vehement protest against what the staff has done. It's an insult to the committee."

"I was astonished," Harlow recalls, "and so was Bill Hess. [Hess said,] 'What's eating you?' Johnson says, 'He's telling the committee what to do. He's telling us how to vote.' " And when Hess pointed out that

Harlow had only made a recommendation, as he had been instructed to do, Johnson, his voice heavy with sarcasm, said, "Let's just dissolve the Armed Services Committee, then. Let's just appoint Harlow to represent the Congress of the United States."

But Johnson had mistaken Harlow's character. Decades later, when a journalist could write that "Harlow is respected to the point of reverence in political Washington," one reason for the respect was that, devoted though he was to Presidents Eisenhower and Nixon, both of whom he served in high-level positions, he insisted on telling them what he believed, not what they wanted to hear. (When someone said, "It must take courage to tell a President he's wrong," Harlow replied, "It takes courage not to do it if you know you should. It may hurt you, but if you don't do it, you can't live with yourself. That's an expensive trip.") And Johnson also misunderstood Harlow's financial situation. "Lyndon would maneuver people into positions of dependency and vulnerability so he could do what he wanted [with them]," and "he thought he could do that to me," because, Harlow says, Johnson assumed that, like most staff members, Harlow needed the job. But Johnson didn't know that Harlow could return whenever he wished to the family textbook-publishing business, the Harlow Publishing Company, in Oklahoma City. After the executive session, when Hess told him, in Harlow's recollection, "Now, Bryce, don't you take this personally. I don't want you to get upset over this," Harlow replied by saying that "Johnson likes to pick on me. . . . This is the second time," that "I will not accept his further acerbity in the committee"—and that he was therefore resigning, immediately. Hess, knowing how perturbed Carl Vinson would be at the loss of the young staff aide for whose opinion the former chairman (and still ranking Democrat on the committee) had already developed great respect (he would promote him to chief clerk of the committee when the Democrats regained control of the House), telephoned "the Admiral"—who came to Harlow's office and attempted to persuade him to stay. And when Harlow refused, saying, "You listened to that, you saw what happened," Vinson took him by the arm, said, "All right, you come with me now, we're going over to see Lyndon," and, holding on to his arm, brought him over to the Speaker's Lobby, sat him down and summoned Johnson off the floor. He told Johnson to sit down, too, and then, sitting down himself between the two men, Vinson said: "Now, Lyndon, you put on quite a show this morning. And now Bryce is going to quit." The Admiral turned to Johnson and said: "We can't have that. So you're going to tell him you're not going to do that any more."

For an instant, Harlow recalls, he thought Johnson would refuse, but then "he looked at Carl, and he said, 'Oh, hell, forget it, forget it. We'll get along all right. Don't you worry about it.' " Johnson made the apology

so swiftly and smoothly that it scarcely seemed like an apology. But that
was what it was. Lyndon Johnson had been made to humble himself before a staff assistant.

REMINDERS OF his lack of power darkened even his social life. While he
had been stuck on the same rung of the Washington ladder, other members of the little circle of ambitious young men had been climbing, some
to impressive heights. He had helped Tom Clark get his first job; Tom
Clark was now Attorney General of the United States. Abe Fortas had
been only an SEC staffer when they met, and then Under Secretary of
the Interior. But in 1946 Fortas formed a law firm with Thurman Arnold
and Paul Porter, and that firm became a power unto itself in Washington.
Even Mrs. Douglas, so admiring of Lyndon Johnson, says that "after Abe
got his law firm, Lyndon Johnson was nowhere compared to Abe Fortas."
Because of the force of Johnson's personality, his charm, and the respect
in which he was held for his political acumen, Lyndon Johnson was still
very much a part of the circle, as popular as ever, still missed when he
was away in Texas. Yet it was noticeable that the center of gravity in the
group was shifting somewhat; Fortas, for example, "held forth at length"
more now than previously, Mrs. Douglas says. Johnson had always had
the habit of falling asleep at dinner parties if he was not the center of
attention, of putting his chin down on his chest when someone else began
to talk, closing his eyes and dozing off for as long as twenty minutes before
"he woke up talking." He was going to sleep—or pretending to go to
sleep—quite often now. When he gave parties in the Johnson home on
30th Place, the guest list was usually impressive, and the guests truly liked
him; he made them like him. But, as his friends could see, some of the
guests were there primarily because they knew that Sam Rayburn would
be there, and sometimes this unpleasant fact was rather obvious to the
host.

THERE WERE HUMILIATIONS even back in his own district, even in matters
so minor as office space.
    Instead of procuring space in a private building in Austin, Johnson
had begun demanding offices in the United States Courthouse. Judges and
District Attorney Jack Roberts had objected, saying that they were already cramped, but Johnson had gone over their heads to Attorney General Tom Clark, who had discreetly arranged for him to use a two-room
suite when District Court was not in session. But when, in 1946, Johnson
had his name and title painted on the door of the office he had been
loaned, he went too far. Needing the room for his own staff, the District

Attorney ordered the custodian to scrape off the lettering. "Subsequently," as Baxter Taylor, Jr., a real estate officer of the federal Public Buildings Administration, reported to a superior, "Mr. Johnson visited the office, discovered the removal, and objected most vehemently." The enraged Congressman telephoned John L. Nagle, the Building Administration's deputy commissioner for real estate management, but Nagle only referred the matter to Taylor, who, after a delay of some months, reported "there is no space in the building . . . for Mr. Johnson's use." Johnson was forced to ask Clark for help, and Clark secured an office for him in the Travis County Courthouse instead, but only after more bureaucratic delays, to each of which Johnson reacted with a rage that masked his sense of humiliation over the incident, which had become widely known—and a source of amusement—in Austin.

IN 1946, moreover, Johnson, who had not encountered serious opposition in his four previous re-election campaigns, was opposed by Austin resident Hardy Hollers. Hollers was a respected attorney, but a political neophyte without even a semblance of a campaign organization. He was running against an incumbent who had compiled a spectacular record of improving the lives of his district's impoverished farmers and ranchers with giant rural electrification projects and implementation of other New Deal programs, and whose flooding of the district with federal installations such as the giant Bergstrom Air Force Base and federally financed bodies such as the dam-building Lower Colorado River Authority meant that a staggeringly high percentage of its voters relied on a federal paycheck—and who had created a political machine that was also probably without equal in any other congressional district in Texas. Johnson's margin, while large—he received 42,980 votes, sixty-eight percent of the vote, to 17,782 for Hollers and 2,468 for a third candidate, Charles E. King—was less impressive when viewed against the tendency of Texas voters to routinely return incumbent Senators and congressmen to office—and against the fact that the only district-wide daily newspaper, Charles Marsh's *Austin American-Statesman*, had the tone of a Johnson campaign brochure. Political observers were, in fact, rather startled both by the size of the anti-Johnson vote and by the bitterness against the Congressman that surfaced during the campaign.

More significant was the reason for the bitterness. Hollers called his campaign "a crusade against corruption in public office," and its focus was Johnson's finances and ethics. Johnson, Hollers charged, had "enriched himself in office," and had enriched his friends as well, during a time in which other men in the Tenth Congressional District had been off at war. He noted that Johnson's three senior advisers, Wirtz, Clark and Looney, represented the oil companies and the big private utilities Johnson claimed he was opposing; the name of Brown & Root was raised, and, for the first time, publicly linked with Johnson's; the Congressman, Hollers said, was "an errand boy for war-rich contractors." "If the United States Attorney was on the job, Lyndon Johnson would be in the federal penitentiary instead of in the Congress," Hollers said. "Will Lyndon Johnson explain how the charter for KTBC, owned by Mrs. Johnson, was obtained? Will Lyndon Johnson explain . . . his mushrooming personal fortune?" Johnson's vigorous contention that he played no role in the affairs of his wife's station was not convincing in a small city in which the link between KTBC's advertising and the Congressman was an open secret among the city's businessmen. As an Austin journalist was to write: "Never again, after this campaign, was Johnson free from the belief . . . that he used his public power to get money for himself." Lady Bird was aware of the effect of the 1946 campaign. "That was a watershed," she was to say. "It was the first time we had ugly things said about us. We ceased to be the young shining knight." And her husband was aware also—even if the subject was a source of pain to him. (Once, he asked Ed Clark the reason that he was not more "loved" in the district for which he had done so much. "That's simple," Clark said, with his customary candor. "You got rich in office." Johnson leaped to his feet without a word and strode from Clark's office.) The fact that one out of every three voters had opposed him, in a district to which he had brought such great economic benefits, preyed upon his mind so incessantly that he could not stop talking about it. "He simply could not understand how any of them came to oppose him," a friend would recall. He wanted, *needed*, from his constituents not merely support but affection, and never again was he able to make himself believe that he had it.

ADDING TO JOHNSON'S ANXIETY, during these years, was another consideration—one which at times seemed to loom before him more ominously than any other.

According to family lore, Johnson men had weak hearts and died young. All during his youth, Lyndon had heard relatives saying that. Then, while he was still in college, and his father was only in his early fifties, his father's heart had begun to fail, and Sam Ealy Johnson had died, in 1937, twelve days after his sixtieth birthday. Sam Ealy had two brothers, George and Tom Johnson. George, the youngest of the three brothers, suffered a massive heart attack in 1939 and died a few months later, at the age of fifty-seven. In 1946, at the age of sixty-five, Tom suffered a heart attack, and in 1947 he had a second. Lyndon Johnson, who had always been deeply aware of his remarkable physical similarity to his tall, gawky, big-eared, big-nosed father, was convinced—convinced to what one of his secretaries calls "the point of obsession"—that he had inherited the family legacy. "I'm not gonna live to be but sixty," he would say. "My Daddy died at sixty. My uncle . . ." He had no patience with attempts to argue him out of this belief; once, when Lady Bird was trying to reassure him that he would not die young, he looked at her scornfully and said flatly: "It's a lead-pipe cinch." The long, slow path to power in the House might be the only one open to him, but it was not a path feasible for him to follow. Whenever it was suggested that he might make his career in the House of Representatives, he would reply, in a low voice: "Too slow. Too slow." Rayburn had begun trudging along that path early—he had been only thirty years old when first elected to Congress in 1912—and it had taken him twenty-five years, until 1937, to become Majority Leader; he had not become Speaker until 1940, at the age of fifty-eight. But Sam Johnson had died at the age of sixty. And what if the Democrats should not be in control of the House when Johnson's chance came? The path to power in the House—the silence, the obeisance—was not too narrow for Lyndon Johnson, who could follow surefootedly the narrowest political road. But it was too long. He had managed to break the trap of the Hill Country; he might not be able to escape the trap of the seniority system before he died.

There was, moreover, another point of comparison with his father, one about which he spoke with his brother (and perhaps only with his brother). Sam Ealy Johnson had never been able to recover from the single great mistake he had made: the payment of that ruinously high price for the Johnson Ranch. Lyndon Johnson had made one mistake—in that 1941 Senate race. Was he, too, never to be able to recover? Was he never to get a chance to come back? His early rise had been so fast; now his career had been stalled—he had been stuck in the House for nine years, and then ten and eleven. He talked endlessly about his fate—about the election that had been "stolen" from him, about the bad advice he had received not to contest that election because he would soon get another opportunity, about the war that had prevented him from using that opportunity, about the ingratitude of the young men who had not, upon their return from the war, rejoined his organization. And worse—in the words of one aide, "much worse"—were the times when he wasn't complaining, when, alone with only one or two aides, his voice getting very low, he would talk dispassionately, almost without emotion, about his chances of advancing in his political career, about his chances of advancing in the House of Representatives, in which he had now spent so many years—the House, to which he had come when he was young, and in which he was trapped, no longer young. "Too slow. Too slow." Horace Busby says: "He was thirty-nine years old. He believed, and he believed it really quite sincerely . . . that when a man reached forty, it was all over. And he was going to be forty in 1948. And there was no bill ever passed by Congress that bore his name; he had done very little in his life. . . ."

THE 1941 OPERATION for the "gynecological problem" that may have caused Mrs. Johnson's three miscarriages had apparently not been successful, and the "sadness" the couple felt over their lack of children continued. Then, in 1943, at the age of thirty, Mrs. Johnson conceived again. The child, born on March 19, 1944, in the tenth year of her marriage, was a daughter, named Lynda Bird in a combination of the father's first name and the second part of "Lady Bird." At the hospital, Johnson telephoned Sam Rayburn and Carl Vinson with the news, and then his mother. Lady Bird had had a difficult time in labor, and her doctor had suggested she have no more children, but the Johnsons continued trying. On the morning of June 13, 1945, Mrs. Johnson awoke in intense pain, and with a high fever. But, Johnson was to recall, "she insisted that it was all right for me to go to the office. The minute that I left the room, she called the doctor." A friend from Austin, Virginia Wilke English, was staying with them, and, Mrs. English recalls, before the ambulance arrived, "she started hemorrhaging just very, very badly." As Lady Bird Johnson was being carried out the door on a stretcher, however, she made the men stop so that she could give Mrs. English some instructions. "There was a manila envelope that was addressed to Jesse Kellam," Mrs. English recalls. "And it took thirty-four cents worth of postage and I was to put that on and to mail it that day. It had to go out that day." And, Lady Bird continued, she had invited guests to a dinner party the following evening ("Mr. Rayburn was coming," and two other guests), and the party was not to be canceled. There would be no problem, she said; their maid, Zephyr Wright, could take care of Lynda Bird, and could cook the dinner, and Mrs. English should act as hostess. "There's no use to cancel it because Lyndon has to eat anyway, and they're all invited," Lady Bird explained. (Says Mrs. English: "Man, I couldn't believe that.") At Doctor's Hospital, where her illness was diagnosed as a Fallopian, or tubular, pregnancy, Mrs. Johnson's temperature reached 105 degrees. Blood transfusions were needed. Her condition was listed as critical, but after an operation she recovered, although when she returned home, she was forbidden for some time to walk down the stairs. In 1946, Mrs. Johnson became pregnant again, and on July 2, 1947, Lucy Baines Johnson was born. Johnson was later to joke that the two daughters were given the same initials as he and his wife had because "it's cheaper this way, because we can all use the same luggage," but to an aide with whom he was as intimate as he was with Horace Busby, he would be more frank: "FDR— LBJ, FDR—LBJ," he told his young assistant. "Do you get it? What I want is for them to start thinking of me in terms of initials." "He was just so determined that someday he would be known as LBJ," Busby explains.

HIS MOODS SOARED and sank, but when they sank now, they seemed to sink lower—and to last longer. The years 1946 and 1947—1947, when Lyndon Johnson marked *ten years* in the House which he had been anxious to leave almost from the day he got there—were filled with periods of deepening depression. With his younger aides, for whom it was important that he be the confident leader in whom they could safely repose their own confidence, he wore a mask of self-assurance, but people who knew him better were worried about him. "He lost some of his drive, periodically pausing in the middle of his still-crowded work day to stare out the window with a troubled look in his eyes," his brother was to write. "He might spend a half-hour that way. Then he would suddenly busy himself with paper work and long phone calls, driving himself and his staff as never before." A severe eczema-like rash on his hands, always a sign of tension and unhappiness, had bothered him intermittently for years. Now it returned, and remained, making his fingers terribly dry, scaly and painful. Doctors prescribed various ointments, and he often had parts of his fingers wrapped in gauze, but to little effect. Lubriderm, a purple-colored salve, brought temporary relief, and Johnson often kept a bowl of it on his desk, and would continually dip his hands into it. The rash was particularly annoying when he was signing his mail, because the edges of papers made little slits in the dry, raw skin, and even a drop or two of blood could mess up a letter. Gene Latimer, who returned to work for Johnson in May, 1946, would see him "driving himself late at night . . . signing mountains of letters with his right hand frequently wrapped in a hand towel to keep blood from dripping"; Latimer said the rash "made him suffer with each signature." But when Latimer begged his adored "Chief" to stop signing, Johnson just shook his head. The signing routine seemed to soothe him, Latimer felt, as if, thinking about the mail, he was able for a while to stop thinking about his larger problems. Johnson was smoking more and more—three packs a day; he seemed now always to be holding a cigarette, and his fingers were stained yellow with nicotine. Sometimes, lighting a fresh cigarette, he bent over, head low as he took his first puff, inhaled deeply—"really sucking it in," an aide says—and sat like that, head bowed, cigarette still in his mouth, for a long minute, as if to allow the soothing smoke to penetrate as deeply as possible into his body. These years were punctuated, as were other periods of crisis throughout his life, by sickness; just after New Year's Day in 1946, for example, he was hospitalized in Austin's Seton Infirmary. His illness was variously referred to in the press and in letters to constituents as "flu" or "pneumonia," and some of his symptoms were consistent with these diagnoses. Other symptoms, however, were not. Asked about Johnson's hospitalization, two aides use the term "nervous exhaustion." Walter Jenkins said also, "It was bad." No one is willing to describe the illness in detail. Whatever its nature, recovery was not rapid. On January 19, Johnson's aides were responding to inquiries by saying that "he hopes to return to Washington almost any day now," and was still in Texas only because of an inability to obtain train or plane reservations. He was still in Seton Infirmary a week later, however, and when, after almost a month in the hospital, he returned to Washington, he was confined to his bed in his house there. On February 7, he wrote his cousin Oreole that "I am still having trouble with my throat," and was undergoing a new round of tests at a hospital. On February 12, he was still ill. In March, he was hospitalized for one of his recurrent, painful attacks of kidney stones, and in October, he spent another three weeks in the Seton Infirmary and then in the Mayo Clinic in Rochester, Minnesota, for a bronchial infection, the third time he was hospitalized that year.

Another Senate election would be held in Texas in 1948—an election in which, he, Lyndon Johnson, would be a longshot, not only against the incumbent, Pappy O'Daniel, but against any one of a number of candidates who had statewide reputations, for if his 1941 campaign had brought him recognition across the entire state, the intervening seven years had largely erased it: his name was little known to the electorate outside his own district. And he wouldn't have Roosevelt's name behind him this time. His chances of winning a 1948 election were not good.

Moreover, while the 1941 campaign had been a special election to fill the seat opened by Morris Sheppard's death, 1948 would be a regular election. Texas law prohibited a candidate from running for two offices in the same election. To run for the Senate, he would have to relinquish his House seat, and if he lost the Senate election, he might not be able to take the Tenth District seat back from his successor. And would he even want to return to the House? If he returned, it would be without even the seniority he had accumulated. And why would he want to return even with seniority? The House held nothing for him. *Too slow. Too slow.* If he lost in a race for the Senate in 1948, he might well be out of politics— the politics which were his life—forever. He could hardly bear to take the chance, to risk so much, on a single throw of the dice. "At first," he was to tell biographer Doris Kearns, "I just could not bear the thought of losing everything."

But what choice did he have? Other public officials in Washington would not take such a risk, if taking it meant they might, should they lose, have to leave Washington; other congressmen and Senators talked of how they were anxious not to return to the towns or cities from which they had come because they would miss the excitement and glamour of Washington, or the ability to be at the center of things. But it wasn't the excitement or glamour that Lyndon Johnson most wanted, that Lyndon Johnson needed, that Lyndon Johnson had to have. It was power. To stay on in Washington without it was intolerable to him. And since power, substantial power, was not possible for him in the House, he had no choice, really. He had to try for the Senate. However great the sacrifice he might have to make—the sacrifice of his House seat—to enter the Senate race, however long the odds against him in that race might be, he had to enter.

To his young aides, and to the young supporters like John Connally and J. J. ("Jake") Pickle who were not his aides but whom he would need, he maintained a pose of indecision, but to the men he depended on most and who would guide his campaign—Herman and George Brown, Alvin Wirtz, Ed Clark—he said that he would try once more, that he would make another run for the Senate in 1948. If he lost, he told them, he would not attempt to re-enter politics. After almost twenty years, after so much effort and striving, his career had boiled down to one last chance.

FOR A TIME late in 1947, after he had made his decision, that chance appeared to brighten. During that year, Pappy O'Daniel's popularity had been rapidly eroding because of his buffoonery on the Senate floor, and because of reports of his profiteering in Washington real estate, and it was becoming apparent that O'Daniel was deciding not to run again.

But then came rumors—confirmed in an announcement on New Year's Day, 1948—that Coke Stevenson, a former Governor of Texas who two years before had retired from office and presumably from public life, would enter the race. O'Daniel was one of the greatest vote-getters in the history of Texas. Coke Stevenson was a much greater vote-getter, by far the most popular Governor in the history of Texas, a public official, moreover, who had risen above politics to become a legend.

Part II

THE OLD AND THE NEW

8

The Story of Coke Stevenson

IN ALL THE VAST and empty Hill Country, there was no more deserted area than the seventy miles of rolling hills and towering limestone cliffs between Brady and Junction, about eighty miles west of Johnson City. Only a few widely scattered ranch houses dotted that area; for long stretches, after night fell, not a single light marked a human presence. Beginning in the year 1904, however, there was one light. It was the light of a campfire. Each night it was in a different location, for it marked the camp of a wagon traveling each week back and forth between Brady and Junction. Lying in the little circle of flickering light cast by the fire was a single person: a slender teenage boy. He would be lying beside the fire on his stomach, reading a book.

The boy was the son of impoverished parents. He was determined to be something more, and his determination had led him to haul freight between Junction and Brady. Older men, deterred by the loneliness of five nights alone each week in the trackless hills and by the seven dangerous, often impassable, streams that would have to be forded on each trip, had refused even to try to do that. But the boy had tried, and had succeeded. The little freight line was beginning to pay. Yet he was determined to be something more. He wanted a profession, and had written away to a correspondence school for textbooks on bookkeeping. And at night, he would be studying them, in the little circle of light from his campfire.

The boy was Coke Robert Stevenson. And if that scene—the single circle of light in the dark and empty hills; the boy within that circle, studying to get ahead; the courage and ambition which had brought the boy out into the emptiness—symbolizes the legend of the West, so, indeed, Coke Stevenson's whole life was the raw material out of which that legend is made.

His father was an itinerant schoolteacher who would travel with his family—Coke, born in 1888, was the oldest of eight children—to remote communities on the Texas frontier and offer to hold a "term of school," usually about three months, for thirty dollars a month. Coke, named after Governor Richard Coke, a Confederate veteran who in 1873 wrested the government of Texas from the Carpetbaggers and freed the state from the injustices of Reconstruction, got his only schooling in his father's classes; in his entire life, he had twenty-two months of formal education.

The Stevensons' poverty had forced Coke to go to work at the age of ten, building fences and digging irrigation ditches on nearby ranches for a dollar a week. By the time he was twelve, he was a cowhand on a ranch; at fourteen, while his father and mother homesteaded in Kimble County, deep in the Hill Country, the slender, dark-haired, serious-faced boy was herding steers in the fierce winds that whipped across the rugged mesas of the Continental Divide, in New Mexico. By that time, he wanted a ranch of his own, wanted one desperately. Asked in later years what his early ambitions had been, he replied: "I never had any doubt. I wanted to be a rancher." His mother noticed that out of every pay he received, no matter how small it was, her son was careful to save something.

When Coke was sixteen, his father opened a small general store in Junction, a little town in Kimble County wedged between high, green hills on the banks of the Llano River. Stocking the store was a problem; it was as hard to bring manufactured goods into the Hill Country, cut off from the rest of Texas not only by its hills and its vast distances but by the lack of roads and railroads, as it was for Hill Country farmers and ranchers to get their produce out of the Hill Country to market. A railroad had that very year pushed a line as far as Brady, some seventy miles away, but the Brady-Junction "road" was no more than a rough, rocky trail winding over the steep, jagged hills; in rainy spells it turned into a ribbon of mud. And rain made the seven swift Hill Country streams between Brady and Junction swell and race, and fording them could be dangerous even for a man on horseback; the thought of bringing a loaded wagon across all seven of them twice on each round trip was daunting. Men saw only danger in that trip; for Hill Country farmers and ranchers, one writer said. "the task of bringing in supplies and getting the fruits of their labor to market was an arduous one even when the roads were at their best. It was more than man and beast could stand when conditions were at their worst." But while Coke Stevenson saw the danger, he saw something else as well. Years later he would tell a friend: "I saw opportunity." With his savings he bought a wagon and six horses.

To induce merchants to use his "freight line," he knew, he would have to maintain a regular schedule. He announced he would make a round trip every week, even though that meant logging more than twenty miles a day.

Six-horse teams were generally driven from a seat on the wagon, but the old trail-drivers with whom Coke had bunked in his ranch jobs had told the boy how such teams had been driven in the early days on the frontier, and that was how he drove his: sitting among them. By riding the lead horse, the one on the left in the wheel team closest to the wagon, he could spur him on, and could reach the one beside him, too, with a kick; he used the whip on the other four. It was harder to sit a saddle all day than to sit on a wagon seat, but you could control the horses better, and get the most out of them.

The trip was as hard as men had foreseen. It would be many years before Coke Stevenson could bring himself to talk about the months during which, every day, "you had to make twenty miles a day" over those rocks and ruts with little chance that, should a wheel or an axle break or any of a thousand other possible mishaps occur on those "seldom traveled trails," someone would come along to help. When, decades later, he did talk about those months, men who knew the Hill Country and who could picture the difficulties he had surmounted would look at him with awe. He would unload his freight in Brady, fall asleep exhausted in the wagonyard, and be up before dawn the next morning to load up again and head out on the road back. When it rained out on the trail, he slept underneath the wagon; when it rained for several days, he would be wet through for several days. When the wagon mired in the mud, there was no one but him and the horses to get it out; "once I got stuck so bad in a mudhole that I was there eleven days," he would recall. The rain kept falling; at night he was so wet and cold that he burrowed into the load of freight for warmth. But, as a friend was to write, "rare was the occasion when he did not maintain his schedule, and the confidence of his customers grew with each successfully completed trip." And opportunity had, indeed, been there. Carrying "anything from a bolt of linen to a windmill," he earned enough to buy a second wagon, which he hitched behind the first, and he filled that with goods too. He began to make money: forty dollars a month, he would later recall.

But a freight line was not what he had always wanted, and by this time Coke Stevenson had decided there were better ways of getting what he wanted. He wrote away for the textbooks, and each night on the trail, after he had cooked dinner and rubbed down the horses (one of his brothers was to recall how Coke "treasured those six horses; they were all he had"), he would build up the campfire and lie on his stomach in the circle of its light and teach himself bookkeeping. During those evenings the teenage boy's only companions in the dark hills would be the horses and the books; a friend to whom, years later, Coke Stevenson talked about his experiences described them as "evenings of loneliness."

After two years of freighting, when he was eighteen, the opportunity for which he had been hoping appeared. Two brothers from England opened a bank in Junction. When he applied for a job, however, what he got instead was an insult. "The president," Stevenson would recall, "laughed at the idea of a freighter being a bookkeeper, but said that, since no Negroes were in the town, he could use a janitor" to sweep the floor and clean out the cuspidors. Men who knew Coke Stevenson in later years knew how quick a temper he had. But they also knew that he never showed it. As long as it was in a bank, the janitor's job might "work up to something" better than freighting, he felt. Although it paid only half the forty dollars a month he had been earning, he took it. Some months later, the bookkeeper became ill and the president asked Coke if he could keep the books for a while. After he showed that he could, he was made bookkeeper, and then, at the age of twenty, cashier.

But he was still not earning enough money to buy a ranch—and by this time he had found the ranch he wanted, the ranch of his dreams.

One day, following the canyon of the South Llano River through the hills southwest of Junction, Stevenson had come to its low, broad, shimmering falls. Beyond them, framed against the canyon's limestone walls, a herd of deer grazed in a riverbank meadow until his horse was almost among them, and then leaped gracefully away, white tails flashing. As he watched, Stevenson was to recall, a flock of wild turkeys strutted out of one of the groves of spreading, sparkling-leaved live oaks that dotted the bank. In the river's clear, rushing water, tall herons and cranes stood like statues.

Splashing across a ford, he spurred his horse up the far bluff, and came out onto broad, rolling upland pastures. Large swatches were covered with cedar, but cedar could be cleared away, if a man was willing to put in the necessary effort. And while in most of the Hill Country the beauty of the landscape was a trap, concealing from would-be ranchers the aridity of the climate, this was one of the few spots on the vast Edwards Plateau in which water would not be a problem. Two miles or so down river was a hundred-foot bluff, and from its face, from under a thick outcropping of rock, a sheet of water almost a hundred yards wide cascaded to the river below. This was called the "Seven Hundred Springs," because although subsequent exploration would reveal that the cascade came from a single spring, the rivulets pouring down the face of the rock gave the illusion of coming from many. Pushing through the cedar brakes in the pastures atop the bluff, Stevenson found hidden among them one stream after another, all clear and cold enough so that he knew them to be spring-fed, a source of abundant water. In later years, reporters traveling to that spot to interview Stevenson would marvel at its beauty. The river, one wrote, is "as pretty a stream as you could conjure up in your dreams." Twenty-year-old Coke Stevenson determined in the instant that it would be the site of his house, and the land around it his ranch. He wrote away for more books.

This time they were law books. He studied them at night, this young man with so little formal education, after the bank closed, in the office of a Junction attorney, using the attorney's books as well; during the almost five years that he was studying, townspeople grew accustomed to seeing the light burn late in the attorney's office; sometimes, they said, it burned all night. During the nights, too, he built a home in town, for himself and his bride, Fay Wright, the ebullient, charming daughter of the local doctor. He built it with his own hands, working by the light of a lantern, using the lumber from two old frame houses that he tore down so that he would not have to spend the money he was saving to buy his ranch. In September, 1913, Stevenson rode out of the Hill Country to San Antonio to take, and pass, the examination for his law degree. Early in 1914, he received his first substantial legal fee. With that and his savings, he bought his ranch—520 acres at the falls of the South Llano—for eight dollars an acre.

In that year, however, his life took a turning he *hadn't* planned.

It was due to a number of qualities that he possessed.

Some were physical. Coke Stevenson was tall—a little more than an inch over six feet—and strong; slender, but wiry, and with broad shoulders and big hands. He held himself very erect, and had a slow, careful, deliberate way of looking around him from the doorway before he stepped into a room—like, in the words of Texas historian T. R. Fehrenbach, an old gunfighter squinting "carefully down both sides of the street, evaluating the men, the weather, the lay of the land, before emerging into the sun—the famous, careful, Southwestern stare." He was very quiet. He had, a reporter says, "the original poker face." Although his friends say he had a "wonderful sense of humor," only his friends knew it. He seldom laughed out loud, "but you'd suddenly look at him, and see those big shoulders shaking, and know Coke was enjoying the joke more than anyone." On serious matters "Coke kept his own counsel, he was slow to speak," another friend says. When he did speak, it was in the low, slow, Texas cowboy drawl, and each word seemed carefully chosen. And when he spoke, other traits emerged, including one that even opponents define as "sincerity." He quickly earned a reputation as an outstanding courtroom advocate. "Coke would never say a word that he didn't believe, and that shone through," a fellow attorney says. "When he spoke to a jury, the jury believed him." So did people outside the courtroom. Coke Stevenson didn't talk much, but when he talked, men listened. The tall young attorney in cowboy boots and ill-fitting suits was, without meaning to be, a leader of men. Nineteen fourteen, the year in which Stevenson bought his ranch, was a year in which Kimble County ranchers, always on the verge of financial disaster because of the thin, poor soil, the difficulty of getting goods in and out to market, and the recurring Hill Country droughts, were pushed to the very brink by a new menace: livestock thieves. It was suspected that the rustlers' leader was the son of the county's most prominent, and popular, family. Capturing him red-handed might mean gunplay; prosecuting him would mean antagonizing his family. Solving the rustling problem would be a dangerous yet delicate job; the County Commissioners asked Stevenson to do it—as the new county attorney.

Stevenson had never considered holding public office, he was to recall: he accepted the appointment only on condition that he could resign it as soon as the crisis was over.

Enlisting the help of Frank Hamer, already famous as perhaps the toughest of the Texas Rangers, Stevenson "lay out" with Hamer in the hills night after night waiting for the rustlers, captured them, and found that their leader was indeed the young man who had been suspected.

The capture turned out to be the easy part of the job. At the time, Stevenson was to recall, he had little concept of public life. Receiving a crash course in the subject now, he didn't like it at all.

Claiming he wasn't guilty, the young man's family said that the new county attorney had arrested him only to make a name for himself with a sensational case; other Kimble residents felt that even if the young man *was* guilty, he should have been let off with a warning because of his family's contributions to the county. During the months the case dragged on, Stevenson's reaction to the criticism was dramatic: he refused to reply to it by a single word. And when the case ended—with the young man convicted and in jail—Stevenson without a word went back to the hills with Hamer, to "lay out" again to trap the rest of the rustlers. Soon the news was out: Kimble was a good county for rustlers to avoid. But as Stevenson was leaving his first public office, he was given a second, for Kimble had another problem now—one even more serious than rustling.

It was Stevenson's own fault that he was given this new position. During the previous year, 1917, the trail to Sonora, the only route from Junction to the west, had washed out, becoming, as one chronicler put it, a "quagmire" so "hopeless that even a single horse had difficulty getting through." Trying to repair the trail, Junction's citizens had organized a work party along the lines of a barn-raising, with every man bringing his own pick and shovel. But little progress was being made because the men were being given no direction—until, in his quiet, slow-speaking way, Coke Stevenson began giving it.

As he made suggestions, the crowd of boisterous men quieted, and listened to them, and followed them. Stevenson had the men return to their ranches to get wagons, and then had them fan out with the wagons, each carrying a team of men, across the hills to bring back the largest boulders they could find. The boulders were rolled into the mud, and when they sank from sight, more were brought until they rose above the surface. Then smaller rocks were added until the trail was restored. The ranchers thought the job was done, but Stevenson suggested that maybe it wasn't. As long as they had put in so much work already, he said, maybe the trail should be smoothed out, made more like a real road. He had the men take their wagons to nearby streams, bring back gravel from the stream beds, and spread and level it over the rocks.

Now, in January, 1918, the road situation throughout Kimble County had become more critical. Much of the rest of Texas was being linked together, by roads and rail, but the Hill Country was almost as isolated as ever. Laying tracks through hills was too expensive in a sparsely populated district, so railroads generally shunned the Hill Country. Most of America was entering the Automobile Age; a State Highway Department had been established in Texas, and construction of paved roads was under way in other sections of the state. But with a few exceptions (the most notable was the Fredericksburg-Austin highway being built in that very year because of the heroic efforts of the Representative from that area, Lyndon Johnson's father, Sam Ealy Johnson), Hill Country roads were as rudimentary as ever. Without rail connections to the rest of the state, trucks or wagons were the only means for the area's ranchers and farmers to get their produce to market, and because of the condition of the roads, their produce was often spoiled by the time it got there. With more and more roads being built elsewhere in the state, the competitive position of ranchers throughout the vast, isolated Texas Hill Country was steadily worsening, even before the terrible drought of 1916 and 1917. Nowhere was the situation more critical than in Kimble County. There were two hundred motor vehicles in Kimble in 1918, but in all that huge county, larger than the state of Rhode Island, there was not a foot of paved road; moreover, as a Hill Country chronicler wrote, "No semblance of a system of roads connected them with the outside world." One evening in January, Junction's elder citizens met in the bank; "This group of men had recognized that Junction and Kimble County had reached an important milestone; that it either must go forward or be lost in the shuffle of progress." Their only hope was "to give the county some modern roads and to provide access to the markets of the state." They decided to pass a $150,000 bond issue to finance road construction, but they knew the work wouldn't get done unless someone "took hold of the job and got it started on the right track." Coke Stevenson wasn't even at the meeting at the bank; he had had enough of public service. But if it wasn't for him, everyone knew, there would still be no road to Sonora. The young lawyer was sitting at home with his wife, reading in front of a fire, when, late in the evening, the phone rang, and he was summoned to the bank, where he was asked to accept the nomination for County Judge, the county's chief administrative officer. At first he flatly refused, but so serious was the situation that, finally, feeling he had no choice, he accepted, on two conditions: that under no circumstances would he be asked to accept a second two-year term, and that he would not have to campaign. His friends did the campaigning, and he won easily.

During his two years as County Judge, other qualities in Coke Stevenson became apparent. One was an unusual ability to persuade men to sacrifice for the common weal. Although $150,000 was more than the county's taxpayers could afford, it wasn't enough for the job. And Stevenson felt that none of it should be spent on right-of-way; the land, he said, should be donated, since its owners would benefit from the road. This proposal had been broached before, and rejected. Now, at a number of public meetings, Stevenson spoke of how individuals should cooperate for the public good. The right-of-way was donated. By the end of the two years, Junction was linked by road with every other major town in the county. And it was being linked with the outside world. Rivalry had for years existed between Junction and Kerrville, a town in neighboring Kerr County, which lay between Kimble and San Antonio. But Stevenson persuaded Kerr's Commissioners to co-sponsor a joint mass meeting of the two counties at which Stevenson argued that Kerr should build a road that would meet Kimble's at the border and link the two county seats. When he had finished speaking, in his slow, quiet way, Kerr agreed to do so. The agreement meant that Kimble would have a passable road most of the way to San Antonio.

To build the roads, the man who had taught himself law taught himself engineering. Kimble's hills were laced with small streams and steep slopes. Building elevated bridges was prohibitively expensive, so roads would have to dip down to the streams, crossing them on roadbeds laid just above water level, and up again. Stevenson knew nothing about engineering and little about mathematics. But he cut miniature car wheels out of cardboard, figured the ratio with the Model T wheel, traveling at twenty-five miles per hour, the standard of the day, and tested the miniature wheels on various concave surfaces to determine the proper "roll" of the dips. It was, one writer was to say, "testimony of the character of the road he built" that the Junction-Kerrville Road, the first piece of improved highway in all the immense distances between San Antonio and El Paso, was still in use more than twenty years later.

By the end of his two-year term, Coke Stevenson's fame had spread through the Hill Country, and a delegation called on him to ask him to run for Congress. Slow and thoughtful though he generally was, he answered this request quickly. "My public life," he was to recall in later years, "came about by accident. I did not deliberately set about entering public life. On the contrary, each time I held an office, it was for the purpose of getting a particular job completed." The jobs—rustler-hunting and road-building—were over, and, he said, so was his time in "public life." In 1920, he returned to his law practice. During the next eight years, the reputation of this self-taught lawyer continued to spread; from all across the vast Edwards Plateau men traveled to Junction in the hope that Coke Stevenson would represent them in cases ranging from intricate land-title suits to murder. He would never defend a man charged with livestock theft, cardinal crime of the Old West, and he would never accept a client, no matter how large the offered fee, in whose innocence he did not believe. Yet the docket for a single court term at Junction lists "C. R. Stevenson" as defense attorney in twenty-seven out of thirty-two cases. His reputation spread further; attorneys and judges from Houston and Dallas and San Antonio returned from Hill Country courts to tell their colleagues that in a little town in the middle of nowhere they had just watched what one of them called "one of the greatest trial lawyers in the history of Texas." Sometimes he would try a case in a big city, and courtroom observers realized that that assessment was correct. Judge A. B. Martin of the Texas Court of Criminal Appeals said that Stevenson was "the best all-round lawyer" he had ever seen. Although he refused proffered partnerships in big-city law firms as quickly as he had refused a congressional seat—he just didn't want to leave the Hill Country, Stevenson would say—he soon was reportedly being asked to try more lawsuits than any attorney in Texas. Before the end of his career, one writer reported, he had "written land marks" in law books and the legal reports of the state: monuments of a wholly self-educated attorney that attorneys from great law schools studied. Together with friends, he founded many small businesses in Junction—a hardware store, a title-abstract company, the first Ford automobile agency in the area; on Friday and Saturday nights, he ran the first motion-picture show in Junction, operating the projector himself—not that any of these businesses, in the cash-poor Hill Country, generated much cash profit. He was one of the organizers of a new bank—the First National Bank of Junction—and became its president. At the time he did so, the Junction State Bank, at which he had started as a janitor, asked him to continue as its attorney even though he was now president of a competing bank; as one biographer put it, this "stands as a sincere tribute to the respect in which Stevenson was held by his fellow townsmen"; Coke Stevenson, it was said, was so honest that he could represent the two competing institutions at once. But Stevenson didn't spend most of his time in town; he spent it at the ranch, and whatever money he made—from the law practice, from the hardware store, from the bank—he put into that ranch. He purchased a second five hundred acres, and then a thousand more, and then another thousand; by 1928, he owned more than six thousand acres of the beautiful, spring-watered property he had come upon so long before.

On the site, below the falls, that he had picked out for his home years earlier, he now built it, with his own hands. Several years later it burned down, and he built another house, also with his own hands. This one had a wing solely for his books. His self-education had progressed from the practicalities of law to its philosophy and theory, and then to government, to history and to biography. In the Hill Country, where books were so rare—Junction, like Johnson City, had no library; most families owned only one book: the Bible—he had created a substantial library. He would read at night, but also in the mornings, before daylight. He rose very early every morning, and put on a pot—a battered old graniteware pot—of very strong coffee. Then he would sit down with a book. Friends who stayed at the ranch remember sometimes getting up at four or five in the morning to go to the bathroom, and seeing a lamp burning in the living room, and in its circle of light, Coke Stevenson reading, his huge, gnarled, powerful hands tenderly holding the book. "He treats his books like friends," one man would recall. "None of his books has a turned-down edge" to mark the place; "none has notes on the margin—if notes are needed, he makes them on a piece of paper and inserts them at the place. . . ."

Fay designed this new house—a sprawling, spacious, two-story structure with three great archways in front, and above them a long terrace. Coke built it—a room at a time as funds were available. (It would take him ten years to complete it.) To implement his wife's drawings, he sent away for books on architecture and taught himself the rudiments of that profession. The house was somewhat Spanish and romantic in design, and it was built so that it couldn't be destroyed. Underneath the bright Indian rugs that covered them, the floors were of concrete; the ceiling and supporting beams were of concrete reinforced with steel; the walls—thick walls—were of concrete and native stone. A visitor said it was so solid that it was "seemingly indestructible"; another compared it to "a fortress." And it was, in a rough way, very impressive; towering up to the twenty-foot ceiling of the "baronial" living room was a huge, "unbelievable" stone fireplace. It was a stone Fay particularly liked that was found on a ridge some miles from the house; Coke lugged every stone home in a tow sack. Describing the house, the beautiful, clear river near it, the shimmering falls, the herons standing in the river, the beavers splashing nearby, the herds of deer so tame they ate out of Coke's hand, a writer who was Coke's friend would call the Stevenson Ranch "a Dream

Ranch—the dream of a 10-year-old boy who always knew that he wanted to be a rancher."

The ranch *was* a fortress, or at least a refuge from the world. Since Coke had refused to build even a rough low-water bridge across the South Llano, the only way of reaching it was by fording the river, which was not infrequently too high to be forded. He refused to have a telephone on the ranch. The closest town was Telegraph, a mile across the river, and that "town" consisted of one building: a store. (The town had no telegraph; it had been given its name because telegraph poles had been cut from trees near there during the 1850s.)

"He loved that ranch," says his nephew, Robert Murphey. From time to time he had a hired man or two helping him, but mostly he worked it himself. He cleared it with his own hands—whole tracts of it; Coke Stevenson's fame as a lawyer was no greater than his fame as an axman: he could swing a big double-bit ax with such accuracy that he could take a knot out of a log in a single stroke. He fenced the ranch himself. So hard was the Hill Country land—seldom more than a few inches of soil over limestone—that sometimes sinking a post, particularly a big corner post, required dynamite ("if," Murphey says, "you can imagine having to dynamite a posthole"), but most of the time Stevenson used a cutting bar, a heavy steel bar with a sharp edge on it, raising it above his head and slamming it down, over and over, with all his strength. "He loved the land, and he never let a day pass on the ranch that he didn't do something to improve the ranch—move a rock, sink a post, whatever," recalls Murphey, who would later live there for some years. "He kept a bunch of old tools in his car, so if he saw something that needed doing, he could do it on the spot. That doing something on the ranch every day—that was one of his prideful things." No matter how busy he might be with legal or bank affairs, he let nothing keep him away for the crucial days in a ranchman's year: goat- and sheep-shearing, and cattle-branding—his brand was "CS" on the left hip, nothing fancy. "I don't suppose there's been a calf on my ranch that I haven't branded myself," he was to say.

He relaxed there, too: he and his wife played with their son, Coke, Jr., and, a visitor says, "sometimes acted like they were still two kids themselves." Once, when the South Llano was high and fast, he bet Fay that he could drive his Model T two miles right down the middle of the river to the house, did it, and, when he had won, jumped out, yelling like a boy.

BUT HE WAS to be lured into spending time away from that refuge. After eight years, he was to find himself back on the road he had decided not to take: the political road.

In part, he came back to that road because of his wife.

"Mother believed that Papa was a great, great man who should serve the people," Coke Stevenson, Jr., says. She was a leader herself; Fay Wright Stevenson was later to be called "the most beloved [woman] that official Texas has ever known." During the 1920s, she became active in the local branch of the Eastern Star, and then president of the Texas chapter of that international organization; the more time she spent in the capital, the more convinced she was that her husband could lead men on a stage much larger than the Kimble County Commissioners Court—and she believed, quite deeply, that he should. Much as she loved the ranch, she did not believe Coke should spend his whole life there. She began urging him to run for office again.

In larger part, perhaps, he returned to that road because of his reading.

He had read the practicalities of the law, and then the principles behind them; "He buried himself in . . . the history of the law," a friend was to say. Then he read history and turned more specifically to government and its theories, and, the friend says, "he became lastingly inspired with the principles set forth" in two documents: the constitutions of his country and his state. He read the two constitutions—and took their words—as literally as he read his Bible, and his reverence was no less deep. "He . . . adopted them to the bosom of his heart."

The Constitution of Texas, drafted in 1876 by delegates (many of whom had worn the Confederate gray; several had been Confederate generals) representing a people who had seen, under a decade of Carpetbagger rule, the injustices of which government was capable, was, as the Texas historian Fehrenbach puts it, "an anti-government instrument." It not only bound the Legislature within very tight limits but said the Legislature would henceforth no longer meet every year but every other year because, as one Texan said, "The more the damn Legislature meets, the more Goddamned bills and taxes it passes!" It was no more lenient with the executive branch: the powers of the Governor were reduced to a point where he was one of the weakest in America. "If future State Governments prove burdensome or onerous, it ought not to be the fault of this Convention," one of the delegates said, and, indeed, the convention's handiwork made it, in Fehrenbach's words, "almost impossible for government in Texas to be burdensome or onerous in the future." The spirit behind the Constitution was the spirit of farmers and ranchers; however much they believed in education, pensions or government services, the taxes fell on them and their land. The Constitution was the embodiment of what Fehrenbach describes as "a lasting philosophy that no Legislature or Governor was to be trusted"—as a result, one analyst concludes, "everything possible was done to limit the power of all branches of government." It was a document more fitted to be the Constitution of the older, agrarian South than of an emerging industrial state, but, as Fehrenbach says, "None of these [limitations] was controversial; they were what the people wanted." Indeed, the people wanted them still; every attempt to modify them had been voted down.

The philosophy embodied in the Texas Constitution dovetailed with the philosophy of the man who studied it in the light of a predawn fire in his ranch house by the South Llano; its character was his. Thrift, frugality—parsimony, in fact—the Constitution enjoined these on government as he had enjoined them on himself: the saving that had begun at the age of ten; the diligently kept account book; "in him," a friend was to write, "there is an ingrained hatred of debt of all kinds." Limits on government; the devotion to individuality, to free enterprise, to individual freedom— he had lived his entire life by those principles. And the lessons of his life—almost the only lessons, in effect, that he had had—had convinced him that the Constitution was correct. He had saved, stayed out of debt, foreseen his own destiny, known what he wanted, fought, with the aid of no one but his wife, to get it—and had he not attained his dream? His whole world added to that conviction. If the phrases of the Texas Constitution were phrases out of the nineteenth century—well, the Hill Country in which Coke Stevenson lived was, really, a nineteenth-century world.

The Constitution of the United States could, of course, in some ways be read as a document that restricted government in the name of individual freedom—Jefferson had been among those who so read it—and that was the way Coke Stevenson read it. He liked few novels; history was his romance. This man who had taught himself history, who had read in it so widely, had a love of history—in particular, the history of his state, the proud heritage of Texas—almost religious in its depth. (On his ranch, he had found an old log cabin; when he learned that it had been built by Jim Bowie not long before he rode off to his death at the Alamo, Stevenson built a shelter around the cabin to protect it from the elements so that it would stand as long as possible. He erected a flagpole in front of his ranch house, and on March 2, Texas Independence Day, and other state holidays, he would, with no one around to watch but his wife and son, solemnly raise, in those lonely, empty hills, the Lone Star flag.) And he believed that the very essence of that heritage—independence, freedom— was embodied in those two constitutions. Now, in the 1920s, he was coming to believe that the government of Texas was doing violence to that heritage and those principles. The inefficiency of the state government— in particular, the antics of a Legislature whose lack of responsibility must, he felt, lead to higher taxes—troubled Hill Country ranchers. No one in Austin seemed interested in economy, they said—of course not, it wasn't their own money they were spending. The particular issue that angered him was a proposal to float a bond issue—huge, in terms of the time—to improve the state's highway system. Stevenson recognized the urgent need for highways, but a bond issue meant debt. And in the plans being floated for highways, the needs of the Hill Country were being neglected along with those of West Texas, and he thought he knew the reason why: these ranching areas were underpopulated and did not have enough weight in state politics. Stevenson began to tell friends, in his quiet, slow way, "The ranch people need representation."

Although he had no intention of providing that representation himself, in 1928, eight years after he had left public office, the legislative seat from his district fell vacant, and once again a delegation of fellow ranchers asked Coke Stevenson to represent them in government. Once again, he refused. But the only candidate who was nominated, a politician from Junction's rival town of Kerrville, was, in Stevenson's view, a free-spender "of whose political philosophy I did not approve." He tried to persuade a number of conservative ranchers to run. When they all refused, at the last minute Stevenson agreed to make the race, and won.

ALMOST FROM the day he arrived in Austin in 1929, he was, an observer wrote, "a marked man"—marked by the same qualities that had marked him in the Hill Country.

Austin was still the city of the "Three B's" ("beefsteak, bourbon and blondes") that it had been when Sam Ealy Johnson had been a legislator there ten years before; Congress Avenue was still lined with bars and whorehouses at which lobbyists maintained charge accounts for cooperative legislators; beneath the great dome of the Capitol the Legislature met in an atmosphere so raucous that it sometimes seemed almost indistinguishable from the nightly scene at the bar in the Driskill Hotel. Coke was an unusual figure against this backdrop. He was more silent than ever. He had taken to smoking a pipe, and he seemed never to be without it. When he was asked a question, he would light the pipe, staring down into its bowl as he did so, or puff deeply on it, thinking before he answered. Years of clearing timber and hauling stones and pounding postholes into that hard Hill Country rock had broadened his body so that it matched his great shoulders, and he was as erect as ever and still had the same slow, careful Southwestern stare and the same way, so graceful for a big man, of walking lightly on the balls of his feet. He liked drinking with the boys, who were legislators now rather than ranchers, and he was, in his quiet way, soon as popular at the Driskill Bar as he had been in Junction. When a party was being organized for a hunting trip, he was usually one of the first ones asked. And men who went hunting with him learned that behind that stolid exterior was a sense of humor. Some of

Coke's "gags" would, in fact, become staples of Austin lore. During a hunting trip with several fellow legislators and a lobbyist, for example, a rancher, an old friend, called Stevenson aside and told him that in one of the back pastures where the men were to hunt was an aged horse—an old family pet—so infirm that it should be destroyed. The rancher asked Stevenson to do it for him. Stevenson agreed. As the hunters' car was passing the horse, he asked the driver to stop, and got out.

"I think I'll just kill that ol' horse," he said, and, taking aim, shot it in the head.

His companions, unaware of the rancher's request, stared in amazement. "Why did you shoot that horse?" the lobbyist finally asked.

"I just always wondered what it would feel like to shoot a horse," Stevenson drawled. Pausing, he stared hard at the lobbyist. "Now I'm wondering what it would feel like to shoot a man."

But although, in Austin, Stevenson was with the crowd at the Driskill Bar, he was in a way not of it; there was a reserve, a dignity, about this tall, broad-shouldered silent man with that watchful stare that set him apart from the crowd. And of course he was set apart from many legislators by something else, too. "You just instinctively knew that Coke Stevenson was not someone you could approach with any kind of an offer at all," one lobbyist recalls today. "I mean, did you ever see him? If you ever had—if you ever saw that stone stare when he got angry—you would know what I mean. No one would have *dared* to offer Coke Stevenson a dime." And although he was a regular at the Driskill Bar, he regularly left it early to return to the house where he lived quietly with Fay (Coke could never bear to be separated for any length of time from his wife). "Coke's off readin' again," his friends would say. (Of course they did not know the extent of that reading: who else in Austin was awake at five a.m.?)

Much of his reading during these years was not of books but of legislation, proposed and actual; of state budgets; of memoranda submitted to legislators by state agencies, that went generally unread. His reading at the ranch had given him a rare command of governmental philosophies, principles and theories; now he was gaining as well an understanding of the minutiae and intricacies of state government so detailed that it would become legendary in Austin. "I think Coke really hated politics," an Austin politician says. "Truly *hated* it—the deals, the maneuverings. It just went completely against the grain of the man." But he loved government—loved it and knew it as few men did. "If you started talking about wheeling and dealing—trading votes, whatever—what you got from Coke was that stone stare. Sometimes it wasn't that he was angry; it was just that he was bored. But if you were talking about what government should do and why we should do it, then you had his interest." He was soon deeply respected in that political city—not as a politician but as a public official, a public official who felt that a legislator's responsibilities extended beyond the district that had elected him. Not only did he quickly secure the passage of legislation needed by "ranch people," he was instrumental in the passage of laws with broader—statewide—significance.

The man who so hated waste saw waste everywhere in the government of Texas, and set out to stop it. Learning that there was no auditing whatsoever of the expenditures of state agencies, he wrote, introduced and pushed to passage a bill establishing the office of State Auditor. To end the state's antiquated bookkeeping practices, which effectively prevented not only taxpayers but public officials from monitoring state expenditures, he pushed for, and won, enactment of laws making the state's bookkeeping more efficient. One of his biographers was to say that "As he saw it, the issue was glaringly simple. From the time he was a youth, he had written down in his ledgers . . . every personal expenditure he made. He knew where *his* money went. . . . The taxpayers were entitled to know where their money went." Asked the purpose of these laws, he said: "To get the people out of debt."

He didn't want their money wasted on roads, either, as much as he understood the need for a modern highway network. Governor Ross S. Sterling was proposing a constitutional amendment authorizing the huge highway bond issue—more than $300,000,000—to be financed by a gasoline tax. Waste and corruption in highway-building were already a joke; the solution, Stevenson said, was not to give the Highway Department more money, and spend still more on debt service for the bond issue. He proposed an alternative plan: use the gasoline tax revenue not for the service on new debt, but to retire the old debt—the bonds already issued by individual counties to build roads within their own borders. This would ease local tax burdens; it would "get the people out of debt." Use the balance of the gasoline tax revenues to build new highways—but on a pay-as-you-go basis. He had calculated how many miles of highways could thus be built annually, Stevenson said, and it was enough to meet the state's highway needs, particularly since none of the new revenues would be spent on new debt service. The highway lobby—oil and gas companies, road-building contractors—massed against him; at times it seemed that Coke Stevenson—and his philosophy—were all that was standing against legislative approval of the constitutional amendment. But he stood. Passage required the vote of two-thirds, or 100, of the 150 House members. "Gradually the number of affirmative votes climbed as the pressure was skillfully applied," a historian has written. "The number of affirmative votes finally reached 99, but Number 100 never was obtained."

There was, moreover, a new huge proposal—for improvements in the state's prisons. Stevenson had known bookkeeping and highway-building;

he didn't know prisons—so he set out to teach himself about them. He visited all the state prisons in Texas, visited them and slept in cells with the convicts. He visited prisons in the Northeast. And the reforms he then proposed not only improved Texas prisons, but did so at a fraction of the cost of the Governor's proposals.

Stevenson had pushed his auditing, bookkeeping, highway and prison legislation in quiet talks with his fellow legislators. He received little public attention. But his fellow legislators had learned about him: his rare speeches on the floor of the House commanded unusual attention; in the towering red-granite Capitol in Austin as in the little Kimble County Courthouse, when Coke Stevenson spoke, men listened. He spent not a minute more in Austin than he had to; as soon as the House adjourned each week, he and Fay would be on the road back to the place they loved. It was still, with no bridge, as cut off from the world as ever. And there was still no telephone; Stevenson had refused to have one installed. If someone urgently needed to get in touch with Stevenson, he would call the party line in the rickety, somewhat lopsided little general store in the "town" of Telegraph and the owner would ride over and notify Coke, who would ride back and talk. In 1933, there was an urgent call. His fellow legislators had caucused and had decided he would be their next Speaker. (Accepting, he made clear that he would still not put in a phone. "The darn thing would be ringing all the time," he said. "If it's important, they'll get in touch with me.") When he was Speaker, he still snatched every moment possible to be on the ranch. As adjournment neared each week, Fay would have their car waiting outside the Capitol. Banging down his gavel to end the session, Coke would stride out of the House Chamber, and within minutes would be on the road—speeding along the 166 miles back to the world he and Fay had created.

He was a rather unusual Speaker. No matter how loud the shouting became on the floor of the House, he never raised his voice. At first, he was criticized for what Austin political observers called "loose herding": refusing to assert tight control over the 150 representatives. He didn't mind the term; what was the alternative?—the tactics that would later be called "arm-twisting"? He wouldn't engage in that, he told intimates. There should, he believed, be time for debate, for reasoned consideration of issues; that, after all, was one of the purposes of a legislative body. And perhaps there were other philosophical reasons as well. Once, there was what a friend recalls as "a terrible ruckus on the floor," and Coke was doing nothing to quiet it down, and someone asked why not, and he said, "As long as they're not voting, they're not passing any laws. And as long as they're not passing any laws, they're not hurting anybody."

But the critics began to realize that the House was accomplishing more than ever before, and they began to realize that this was because of the new Speaker. His pipe had somehow become part of the legislative proceedings. He used it instead of a gavel, tapping gently for order with its stem. And sometimes, as an observer wrote, when debate was "hot and heavy," he would stop proceedings to ask one of the battlers "to lend him some pipe tobacco." Then, apparently concentrating deeply on the task, he would load the tobacco into his pipe, tamp it down and light up, not looking back at the members until it was drawing well. By this time, the observer noted, "the members had usually cooled off and settled in their seats." Sometimes he would lighten the tension with a joke, delivered deadpan; once, when the chaplain did not arrive to deliver the invocation, he told the members: "Well, I guess you fellows will have to be on your own today." But, while he never raised his voice or appeared to lose his temper, members learned not to try to push him. Observers said, as one put it, that "they have never seen a man as unruffled as Stevenson when the parliamentary battling gets sharp and tough. A bland smile on his face, Stevenson squints slightly through the blue haze of smoke from his pipe, rules—unchallenged—on this point of order and that . . . complaint. With dignity, and the right amount of cleverness, he tosses in a bit of kidding . . . humoring them slightly, but never giving in."

Then there were his quiet, private conversations with legislators. "Whenever anyone went to visit Mr. Stevenson, they did most of the talking," one observer said. "He was a good listener. He never did volunteer." But somehow, at the end of the conversation, freshmen legislators found they knew how to get their bills through the House and even veterans found they had been persuaded to compromises that would accomplish what they had wanted all along. "Hardly a man in the Legislature can say that Stevenson has not given him help when he needed it most," a reporter was to write. With an ability unusual among Texas legislators of that era, he managed also to be friends—in some cases, close friends—with the lobbyists who were an integral part of the Austin scene, while not surrendering the state's interests to theirs. After listening to a lobbyist ask a favor on behalf of the president of one of the state's major corporations, Stevenson said, "Well, you can tell him I ain't about to give him the dome of the Capitol." As the lobbyist left, discomfited, Stevenson added: "But you can tell him I ain't about to give it to anyone else, either." And, the lobbyist recalled, "that worked, when Coke was the man saying it. It wasn't only that he was so utterly honest. It was that he was so completely fair and just." Being *fair* was, in fact, important to him; he used the word frequently. "He was always concerned about this," a friend says. "He said, 'What has kept this country is that it's a country of laws. Otherwise, it's all influence. When your man is in, it's all right, but when the other man is in . . .' " A reporter wrote that "his legion of friends among present and former representatives swear that Stevenson was one of the greatest speakers and presiding officers in the history of all Texas houses. . . . Few days pass that some unforgettable act of his as Speaker is not told, perhaps an act cutting a Gordian knot in rules to get a job done, a joke he told. . . ." One observer wrote that even "most of those who have strongly opposed Stevenson's political viewpoints . . . admit that as a presiding officer, his manner of operation borders on the verge of genius." The House gave him its own tribute. More and more frequently, at the end of a trying day's session, it would rise and applaud its leader. He was a leader of men in Austin as in the Hill Country, and in 1935, at the end of his term as Speaker, the same thing happened in Austin as had happened in Junction: until that time the Speakership had always been "a one-term-and-out deal"; nonetheless, Coke Stevenson was asked, by a delegation of House members, to do what no Speaker in the history of Texas had done before and serve a second consecutive term.

The delegation's plea was echoed by Fay, who had become almost as widely known in the Statehouse as her husband. "She was so bubbly. She was as outgoing as Coke was quiet. She was so friendly. She made so many friends, and she never made friends for political reasons. She just loved people. And she and Coke—they made a terrific team. Coke and Fay were a beloved couple in Austin." Her husband's success in the capital had confirmed her belief that he "should serve the people," Coke, Jr., would say. "She didn't want him to be just a rancher again." Moreover, the same conservative beliefs that had impelled Stevenson to come to Austin in the first place were now impelling him to stay. Governor James V. Allred, a New Dealer, was proposing to push through a whole wave of New Deal reforms in Texas. Stevenson had supported the New Deal during its first years; he thoroughly approved of the measures by which it had alleviated the Depression. But now he felt the emergency was over. It was time for government to resume its former, smaller, role. Instead, it seemed to be steadily growing bigger. He wanted to fight the trend.

Nonetheless, after some weeks of weighing the delegation's request, Stevenson was deciding not to run again but to leave the Legislature and return to his ranch. Exposure in depth to politics and politicians had only deepened his distaste for them, he told friends. Then, however, Allred made a mistake. The Governor attempted to push Stevenson into retiring. New Dealers who had contributed heavily to both Allred's campaign and those of certain House members put pressure on these legislators to support Allred's choice for Speaker, and Stevenson learned what was happening. This was just what he had been opposing all his life, he said: the power of the federal bureaucracy and of federal money was being used to influence a state's internal affairs. He agreed to defy the Governor and run again. On the day of the vote, Fay stood in the doorway of the House Chamber, holding a huge bouquet of red roses. As each legislator approached, she asked him: "Are you for Coke?" To those who said yes, she handed a rose. Eighty members of the House were wearing them during the vote, sixty-eight were not: the man who hated politics had become the only politician in the history of Texas to succeed himself as Speaker. The legislation Stevenson pushed through during the next two years, including the establishment of a teachers' retirement fund, liberalized provision for workmen's compensation for state employees and the reorganization of state agencies, made his second term as Speaker "a landmark period in the history of the State Legislature."

As his term was drawing to a close in 1937, Stevenson looked up from his desk to find a delegation of legislators standing before him. Without a word, one of them handed him a petition—signed by more than a hundred members of the House—asking him to serve a third term. Stevenson refused on the spot. Every office he had run for, he was to say, he had taken not for personal ambition but for a principle or to accomplish "a particular job." Because some of his work for his "ranch people" was unfinished, he reluctantly agreed to serve one more term as an ordinary legislator, but said that after that he would never hold another public office.

He was wrong there. In 1938, popular State Senator Garrett H. Nelson, declaring his candidacy for lieutenant governor, proposed amending the state Constitution to establish a unicameral legislature. Stevenson felt that Nelson's proposal would remove one of the most vital bulwarks against the growth of government power. "Many measures that pass one house [but] ought never to pass into law are defeated in the other house," he was to explain. "It [a bicameral legislature] is a safeguard in behalf of the public." None of the various candidates whom Stevenson attempted to enlist to oppose Nelson were willing to run. Stevenson feared that Nelson might win, and that the victory would encourage supporters of the proposal. He entered the race for lieutenant governor.

IT WAS STEVENSON'S FIRST statewide race. He had been elected to office by his fellow Hill Country ranchers, by his fellow legislators—by people who knew him, and who knew the depths concealed by silence and a poker face. This was the first time that he had had to campaign among strangers—and such campaigning was very hard for him. "It was not easy for Coke Stevenson to ask anyone for anything," says his nephew, Bob Murphey, who was later to spend a lot of time watching him campaign. "For him to ask someone to vote for him—that was very hard. Underlying everything was that Coke Stevenson was not a politician as anyone would define a politician. He was not a social person. The dinner party, the cocktail hour, the niceties of a reception—he just didn't like that. Coke

Stevenson couldn't work a crowd. He wasn't a backslapper. He couldn't do the 'Hi, there! Sure good to see you! Lookin' for your vote Saturday!' He didn't have the perpetual grin showing his teeth all of the time. Campaigning did not come easy for him. For him to go into a town and walk the streets . . ."

It was more than shyness that made him a most unusual candidate.

In Texas politics, 1938 was the year of W. Lee O'Daniel, whose dulcet voice had mesmerized rural Texans through years of crooning his own songs ("Beautiful, Beautiful Texas," "The Lay of the Lonely Longhorn," "The Boy Who Never Grew Too Old to Comb His Mother's Hair") and delivering fundamentalist, evangelical homilies on a daily radio program advertising his Hillbilly Flour. Now, running for Governor although he had absolutely no previous political experience (he had never even cast a vote), touring the state in a red circus wagon with his famous Hillbilly Boys and his beautiful daughter, Molly, and his fiddler son Patty Boy, "Pass-the-Biscuits-Pappy" was drawing the largest crowds in the history of Texas—and was revolutionizing Texas politics. Other politicians, including several of Stevenson's opponents, rushed to sign up their own country-and-Western ensembles, and Stevenson's advisers suggested he get one, too. Stevenson put an end to the discussion by saying, coldly, "I've got a record, and if that ain't good enough—well, that's all I've got."

He was just as adamant about other—more traditional—political apparatus. He refused to issue a platform, or to make campaign promises. A platform, he said in his dry way, was like a Mother Hubbard dress: it covered everything and touched nothing. Platforms and campaign promises were meaningless; politicians issued them or made them, and then as soon as they were elected forgot them. They were phony, he said, and he wasn't going to have anything to do with them. Voters could know what he was going to do, he said; all they had to do was look at what he *had* done. He wasn't going to change.

Platforms and promises weren't the only accoutrements he dispensed with. "This of course was in an era when a politician who was running—the first thing he did was go out and get a loudspeaker and bolt it to the top of his car," Bob Murphey recalls. "Then, when he drove into a town, he could drive around and his driver could drum up a crowd with it. But Mr. Stevenson would not drum up crowds. And he said he wasn't going to have no loudspeaker." No loudspeaker? He wouldn't even have the customary signs—"Stevenson for Lieutenant Governor"—painted on his car. "I don't want to go into no town looking like a circus wagon," he said. He wouldn't even have a bumper sticker. So, with the exception of a few formal speeches, and a few—very few—radio talks, the Coke Stevenson campaign consisted of an unadorned dust-covered Plymouth pull-

ing into a little town with absolutely no fanfare or advance preparation—
or crowds.

Nonetheless, a Coke Stevenson campaign stop was not an unimpres-
sive event.

The reason was the candidate. The car that pulled into the little towns
all over Texas may have been ordinary, but the man who stepped out of
it wasn't.

"He had a real physical presence," recalls one reporter. "He was the
kind of a man—he stepped into a Courthouse Square, and people said,
'Who *is* that man?' Maybe they didn't know him, but they knew he was
somebody." There were his big shoulders, which seemed to have grown
even broader over the years, and his big jaw, and the way it was always
tilted up. There was the way he held himself—as tall and erect as ever—
as he looked around the square with that slow, quiet, careful "Southwestern stare," and there was his weathered face, with the sun wrinkles
spreading out from his eyes, and the glint in those eyes, tough and friendly
at the same time. And there was the way he carried himself as he walked
into the Courthouse or up to a little group of men who had been chatting
in the Square. In fact, men who saw Coke Stevenson campaigning in those
small towns pay him what is for Texans a very high compliment indeed.
They liken him to the movie hero who for decades was the embodiment
of what Texans admire. "That rugged appearance," says Murphey. "That
face that was so tough, but with a faint smile and that little sparkle always
in his eye. The way he carried himself: erect, that big chin up. The strong,
silent type—that was him. Coke Stevenson going into the Courthouse was
John Wayne walking into the saloon. Here's *The Man*. Here's our leader."

Even shaking hands, he had, as a reporter puts it, "a quiet dignity."
He would approach three or four men sitting on a bench in front of the
Courthouse. "Say, can I butt in there long enough to introduce myself?"
he would ask. "I'm Coke Stevenson." Then, as a reporter wrote, "he
grinned good-naturedly and stuck out a big hand." Or he would walk into
the Courthouse, or into a café. "Say, can I get acquainted? I'm Coke
Stevenson, and I'm running for Lieutenant Governor." Says Murphey: "I
don't think I ever heard him say, 'I'd like your vote,' or anything like
that. He just couldn't do that." In fact, he said very little. "When he was
with them, he would listen to them, as much if not more than he talked.
And when he talked, he showed them he knew their problems. The farmers, the ranchers, the people who worked with their hands—they felt an
affinity for him. Because he was *them*. And they felt it."

Yet he was also something more—as was apparent when he spoke on
the Courthouse Square or at a Rotary or Kiwanis luncheon. Coke Stevenson never talked long. His speeches were very simple. He made no
campaign promises; a reporter was to write that Coke Stevenson never

once in his entire career promised the people of Texas anything except to act as his conscience dictated. He had made a record in Austin, he said. The record was one of economy in government, of prudence and frugality, of spending the people's money as carefully as if it had been his own, of having government do only what the people couldn't do for themselves. That last point was very important, Stevenson said; it was always tempting to have government come in and solve problems, but every bit of government help came with strings of bureaucratic regulation attached, and every string was a limitation on the most important thing we possess, and have to leave our children—the thing that made Texas and America great. Freedom. Individual liberty. Every time that you accept a government program that you don't really need, you're giving up some of your freedom for a temporary gain; you're selling your birthright for a mess of pottage. And Coke Stevenson speaking in front of the Courthouse impressed voters with the quality with which he had, as a young lawyer, once impressed juries inside. Says one political observer: "You knew he meant every word of what he was saying. You knew he was sincere. You just looked at him, and you said, 'I can trust him.' " Journalists ridiculed this campaigner who refused to try to make news with his speeches or to make advance preparations, so that often he arrived in a town without anyone even knowing he was coming. But sometimes Stevenson would return to a town some weeks after his first appearance. And had the journalists not been so cynical, they might have observed that while on the first visit he had had to introduce himself around the Courthouse, on the second trip that would not be necessary. Nor, in fact, would it be necessary for him to walk into every office in the Courthouse. Recalls one politician: "The minute he got out of his car, the word would be passed: 'Coke Stevenson's here.' And the people would come out of the Courthouse and the stores to meet him." Not understanding the significance of this, however, journalists were startled when, in the first Democratic primary (the Democratic primaries were the crucial elections in a one-party state), this unlikely candidate defeated Senator Nelson, and three other candidates, to win a place in the runoff, although he finished 46,000 votes behind the leader, Pierce Brooks of Dallas. In the runoff against Brooks, Stevenson waged the same, seemingly foolish, type of campaign, and finished 46,000 votes ahead.

AT THE INAUGURATION in January, 1939, one of the great spectacles in Texas political history—it was staged in the University of Texas Stadium, the only arena large enough to hold the crowds of farmers who had thronged into Austin from all over Texas to see Pappy O'Daniel sworn in, with nearly a hundred college and high school bands (and the Hillbilly

Boys) playing and a chorus of ten thousand high school children singing—
Stevenson seemed very out of place. "Interspersed between much fiddling
and guitar playing, in the garish carnival atmosphere," the tall, serious
man delivered a speech, which he had laboriously written and rewritten,
on his two beloved constitutions. (Together, he said, they formed an "or-
ganic law," a "charter of human liberties." That charter "is now being
assaulted by the lovers of an extravagant and bureaucratic government
and by them it is termed to be outworn," he said. But "modern improvements do not change fundamental principles. . . . Let us cherish the old.")
Reporters asked him if, now that he was Lieutenant Governor, he would
have a phone installed on his ranch. No, he said.

With Governor O'Daniel almost totally ignorant of the mechanics of
government and unwilling to make even a pretense of learning (he passed
off most serious problems with a quip, appointed to key posts men with
no experience, submitted legislation that he knew could not possibly pass
so that he could blame the Legislature for not passing it, vetoed many of
the significant programs passed by the Legislature), the state deficit soared
to $34,000,000, state employees were frequently paid in warrants which
would be accepted by stores only at a discount, and the state government
was all but paralyzed—until the Lieutenant Governor stepped in to run
it. For three years, largely through his quiet, private conferences with
legislators, he kept the government afloat. But Austin's sophisticated political observers considered Stevenson too serious to have a future. His
speeches were not on politics but on government—on the *principles* of
government, of Jeffersonian democracy hardened by frontier individualism. More and more, one principle was emphasized. "Why do thinking
people cherish liberty?" he asked.

> Because the accumulated wisdom of past ages has demon-
> strated that people are happiest individually and make the great-
> est advancement collectively when the . . . essential elements of
> liberty and independence prevail. . . . The blessings of happiness
> and prosperity have flowed from the rock of individual effort.
> Now it is proposed to subsidize individual effort. Grants and
> loans of money to municipal and civic enterprises are sought and
> accepted by citizens who apparently do not realize that the price
> of such benefits is the surrender of a corresponding amount of
> liberty and freedom. . . . We must solve our problems by the
> rules of law prescribed when we set up this government. . . .

Newsmen deplored the closely reasoned tone of his speeches, and the
lack of emotion in his voice—because Stevenson has no "radio sex appeal," the *State Observer* said, "his political future is uncertain in these

days when the ether waves rule the political scene"—and politicians agreed. "The trouble with him," one state Senator said, "is that he insists on talking to a man's intellect, not his prejudices." He ran for re-election in 1940, campaigning the same way he had before, again violating every aspect of conventional political wisdom. He had no platform, made no promises and almost no formal speeches, simply driving from one little town to another and talking to small groups of people. He had two opponents. One received 113,000 votes, the other 160,000. Stevenson polled 797,000. (That figure was 100,000 more than was polled in that same election by the still immensely popular O'Daniel, who, with an enlarged band, toured the state in a new campaign vehicle—a white bus topped with a papier-mâché dome of the Capitol.)

The next year, 1941, O'Daniel tried to move up to the United States Senate—against Lyndon Johnson. Although Johnson at first appeared to have stolen the election, O'Daniel's growing instability, and the growing paralysis of state government, had alarmed the state's establishment, as had a campaign pledge by the rabidly prohibitionist Governor to ban the sale of beer and liquor within ten miles of any military base. This pledge could cost "Beer, Inc.," the state's powerful beer and liquor lobby, tens of millions of dollars should O'Daniel remain in the Governor's chair, so brewery lobbyists, "out-stealing" Johnson, saw to it that Pappy went to Washington instead—and on August 2, 1941, Coke was installed in the Governor's chair in which Fay had for so long dreamed her husband would sit.

Fay had to be carried to the Inauguration. A few months earlier, doctors had told Coke she had cancer, and was going to die. She was placed in a wheelchair draped in red satin and carried onto the speakers' stand, and, in the words of one observer, "remained smiling and radiant throughout the half hour's ceremony." She never appeared in public again. When she died, five months later, the Legislature commissioned her portrait, and it was hung in the Capitol.

AT THE INAUGURATION, Fay had heard Coke speak words she had often heard before. "To me the plan of government of our forefathers is a divine inspiration. . . . It is a government of laws and not of men." And, he said, now that he, as Governor, was the man who held power, the lesson he must remember was to be restrained in its use, for "Even if it means submerging his individual opinion as to what the law ought to be, the chief executive still must respect the majesty of the law. He must restrain his own opinions if those opinions should run contrary to the law." At the end he quoted Shakespeare: "This above all—to thine own self be true."

Coke Stevenson's Administration, which would last until January, 1947, revealed both the strengths and the weaknesses in so conservative a concept of government, particularly when the weakness was accentuated by a lack of the formal education that could have given him a broader perspective on the views he had obtained from his solitary reading. And his record as Governor made apparent also the narrowness of viewpoint of a man brought up, and successful through his own efforts, in a land as hard as the Hill Country. His response to problems with which he was familiar contrasted sharply with his response to problems to which his upbringing in that isolated country made it difficult for him to relate.

Because Mexicans had for years come to the Hill Country to pick crops—and because Stevenson had long suffered for the hardships he had seen them undergo—now, as Governor, not only did he press a reluctant Legislature to pass a resolution calling for Mexican immigrants to be "entitled to full and equal accommodations" in public places, he took an unprecedented step for the state by creating a Texas Good Neighbor Commission, which actively investigated incidents of discrimination and tried to promote local solutions. But there were almost no Negroes in the Hill Country, and Stevenson accepted all the Southern stereotypes about that race. He refused to intervene in wartime race riots in Beaumont, or to investigate a lynching in Texarkana. His life of hard physical labor made him sympathetic to the individual workingman, and he succeeded, against the wishes of the state's powerful manufacturers, in strengthening its unemployment compensation system. But, wary of organized labor, particularly the unfamiliar big-city unions, believing that labor's power had become excessive, he tacitly approved harsh anti-union bills conceived by Herman Brown and Alvin Wirtz by refusing to use his veto and allowing the bills to become law without his signature, although he was later to feel that some of them went too far. His lack of formal education hurt most after the O'Daniel-dominated Board of Regents of the University of Texas dismissed liberal university president Homer Rainey. The Rainey dismissal caused lasting damage to the concept of academic freedom at the state university, and Stevenson's refusal to intervene in this controversy revealed that he did not adequately grasp that concept. As he had refused to offer platforms when he was running for office, now he would not propose overall legislative programs, fearing he might unduly influence an independent branch of government. In Jefferson's time, such opposition to government *per se*—such fierce frontier individualism—might have made Stevenson a real democrat; in the more complicated mid-twentieth century, his reluctance to make use of the powers of his office allowed the continuation of the vacuum in Texas government in which special interest groups—the Texas oilmen, natural gas and sulphur companies, Brown & Root and their subordinate contractors—who had no such reluctance to interfere in government had long exerted undue influence in the legislature.

Yet Coke Stevenson's Administration also demonstrated the strengths in the frontier philosophy of government. When he came to office, Texas ranked near the very bottom of the forty-eight states in social welfare programs, largely because under the state's tax structure the men reaping fortunes from their exploitation of its natural resources paid back only a pittance to the state. As Lieutenant Governor, Stevenson had succeeded in obtaining from the Legislature a meaningful tax increase (even the liberal *State Observer* had to admit that despite his conservatism, he "did as much as any man to enact the biggest tax bill in state history"), and now he improved social welfare services more than they had been improved under past Governors, and more than they would be improved under any Governor for years to come. For example, Texas ranked 38th among the states in spending on education when Stevenson came to office; it ranked 24th when he left. For decades, Governors had come to office promising substantial increases in the woefully inadequate pensions the state paid to its older citizens; under Stevenson the pensions were tripled. He made these gains with a very subdued style of governing. He governed not by dramatic special messages or by the noisy, unproductive confrontations with the Legislature that had characterized state government for years, but by conferences with individual legislators and state officials. Arriving in his office, they would find that their proposed bills or budgets had been blue-penciled—Stevenson kept a supply of blue pencils on his desk for that purpose—and they found also that the man who had done the editing knew at least as much about their departments as they did, so that his arguments for reduced spending were hard to resist. The confrontations ceased, as abruptly as if a strong hand had turned off a spigot, and so did the incessant, argumentative and costly special sessions of the Legislature. Somehow, without confrontation or drama, the economies that Stevenson wanted so badly to bring to government took hold, without reductions (and in many areas, with increases) in the level of governmental services.

When liberals later criticized him for having had "no program," Stevenson would reply, "Well, that's not exactly right. I had a program. It was economy." Within that definition, he was very successful. The $34,000,000 state deficit he inherited at his inauguration had become a surplus of $35,000,000 by the time he left office. His program may not have been broad enough to remedy decades of backwardness in social welfare programs. It was, however, a program of which the people of Texas approved. "Mr. Stevenson has given Texas an economy administration," said one newspaper, and "that's what the people want." Even his liberal critics conceded that he was "as liberal as the people."

HE WAS WHAT the people wanted in other ways, too.

Because of his reluctance to talk about himself, Coke Stevenson's story had been little known outside Kimble County. But as his inauguration neared, reporters drove out to Kimble, and learned about his life—and presented their new Governor in epic terms.

"A man who brands his own cattle and cooks his coffee in a two-bit pot, Lt. Gov. Coke Stevenson, ranch-toughened and self-educated by campfire light, will become Texas's 33rd Governor," one of the earliest stories announced. "Coke Stevenson is a product . . . of the frontier before the rough edges were smoothed away," said another article. "Named after the lion-hearted Richard Coke, he smacks of the West. . . . That rare political asset of birth in a log house is his. He knew the feel of a saddle from babyhood. . . . 53 years old, 6 feet 1 inch in height, big-boned, spare of frame, possessor of a face furrowed with heavy lines and browned almost to mahogany hue, he [is] the Abraham Lincoln of Texas." The articles emphasized the struggles of his youth. "In the section where he grew up, the land was sparsely settled and schools were a luxury. . . . At the age of 10 years, he was taking his place in the saddle. . . . At 16, he entered into his first business venture. . . ." The articles talked of his freighting over "seldom traveled trails," of how he had educated himself during "evenings of loneliness." Headlines called him the "HORATIO ALGER OF THE LLANO." "He started out as a legislator and ended up as governor," said one article. "But that's nothing. He started out as a bank janitor and ended up as its president." The headlines called him the "LOG CABIN STATESMAN," the "COWBOY GOVERNOR." Stevenson's appearance and personality were also part of the epic: his taciturnity and his caution before speaking (even the bellwether liberal weekly, the *State Observer*, conceded that "Coke Stevenson makes fewer public statements than any other man in Texas political life today, yet is credited with greater wisdom"). So was the "statuesque Stevenson physique"—particularly after reporters happened to be present when, at a visit the new Governor made to a Lumbermen's Meeting in Lufkin, he was asked if he would like to take a turn in a log-sawing contest. As he walked over to join the burly lumbermen, the reporters saw that he was bigger than all but the biggest of them, that his shoulders were broader. Taking his place without removing his hat or his suit jacket (or his pipe from his mouth), he grabbed the big saw, nodded to signal that he was ready—and won. The fact that Stevenson was a great hunter and explorer was part of the epic; indeed, while he was Governor, he was once snowed in in the Rocky Mountains in Colorado for two weeks, and emerged leading two horses, each with a big buck slung over its shoulders; during the 1940s, few white men had explored Texas' Big Bend Country, the rugged, all but deserted mountain ranges in the southwest swing of the Rio Grande, but Coke Stevenson, a reporter wrote, has "walked or ridden over nearly every foot of it." Coke's ranch became part of the epic ("that famous ranch without a telephone," as one reporter called it, that rugged, isolated paradise at the falls of the South Llano), as did his love of his ranch, his eagerness to hurry back to it at every opportunity, his determination never to miss a shearing or branding ("Come hell or high water, legislature or no legislature, he'll be at Junction at the proper time to attend to those two chores"). So was the simplicity of his life style: as Governor, he still rose by five o'clock, brewed his own coffee in his old battered coffee pot, sipped it as he did his reading, and then ate his breakfast in the kitchen of the Governor's Mansion at a metal-covered worktable. As often as possible, he ate his dinner in the kitchen, too, instead of in the Mansion's ornate dining room. He still had no pictures of politicians in his office—just a photograph of two bucks fighting, and, after January, 1942, one of Fay. His coffee pot, and his coffee-drinking, became a part of Texas political folklore; once, when reporters were pressing him for an answer on a recent development, he said, "Listen, I'm too old to burn my lips on boiling coffee"; often thereafter, when pressed on an issue, he would say, "we'll just let that cup cool a while"—and reporters started calling him "Coffee-Coolin' Coke," to symbolize his caution. The reporters may have intended the nickname to be derisive, but Coke himself liked it—and so did the voters. His coffee pot and his pipe—which seemed never to be out of his mouth; if he wasn't actually smoking it when photographers arrived to take his picture, they would ask him to do so.

Strong and silent—Coke Stevenson's personality was the embodiment of what Texans liked to think of as "Texan." And so, indeed, was the whole story of his life, for in Texas, in 1941, the frontier was little more than a half century away. Some Texans had grown up on what still was the frontier; or their parents had, or their grandparents had, and had told them about it. The story of Coke Stevenson was a story they could relate to: when a Texan was told about making twenty miles a day—day after day, week after week, month after month—with a heavy-loaded wagon over rocky trails and across swollen streams, he could appreciate what that meant; Texans understood about the sleeping out in the rain, and about repairing the broken wheel spokes and rims and axles, about nursing the horses, and about loneliness. And it was Texans' deep love for the land—the soil that they had had to fight so hard to wrest from the Indians and the elements—that made their Governor's love of *his* land so meaningful to them. His hatred of bureaucracy, his distrust of the federal government, his belief in independence, hard work, free enterprise—all this struck a particularly clear chord in Texas. It was the "big country" that "fed big dreams" and that had drawn so many people fleeing the restrictions of a more orderly society, trading safety for danger, as long as with the danger came independence and the chance to create their own empires by their own efforts. It was a state, moreover, in which an unusually virulent mistrust of the federal government was a part of not-so-distant history; the settlers of the Texas frontier—and their descendants—firmly believed that the federal government had, inadvertently (some said, deliberately), protected the murderous Comanche raiders with its policy of not pursuing them and of preventing settlers from retaliating. And distrust of *all* government had been fostered by the Carpetbaggers—against whom, of course, the man for whom their Governor was named ("the lion-hearted Richard Coke") had fought. As the only state to enter the Union as an independent republic (it had been the Republic of Texas from 1836 to 1845), Texas was uniquely proud of its heritage. And Coke Stevenson's image *was* Texas. He was, in the words of one headline, "AS TEXAN AS A STEER BRAND." "Almost everybody calls him the 'typical Texan,' " the *Observer* noted. He made Texans remember why they were proud of being Texans. As a San Antonio reporter put it in April, 1942, after she visited "that beloved individualist," "Well, folks, Texas has a real Texan for Governor. The kind of man who has brought Texas fame in song and story. The kind that will give Texas back its faith in patriotism, in the ideals of 1776 and 1836. Coke Stevenson is like a fresh Texas Centennial celebration. He makes us live all over again many things that marked Texas pride and progress of a hundred years." The tone of this article was not unusual. Another began:

> In fancy: students of and true believers in the democratic way of government dream of witnessing the ascent to high office of a man who is imbued with faith, steeped in the fundamentals of constitutional government, and inherently honest.
> In fact: through a combination of patience, hard work and a quirk of fate, Texas has that sort of Governor.

"And," as Bob Murphey puts it, "the most important thing about the image was not just that it was wonderful, but that it was *true*—and that people saw it was true." In the summer of 1942, a year after he had stepped into the office Pappy O'Daniel had vacated, Coke Stevenson ran for Governor in his own right.

O'Daniel was campaigning in the same election (Lyndon Johnson was in the Navy at the time, of course) for a full term as United States Senator—and Pass-the-Biscuits-Pappy was running the same way he had run before, with shows and bands and hillbilly music. He was more popular than ever—and he endorsed one of Stevenson's five opponents, Hal Collins, a wealthy, spellbinding orator who, as one reporter wrote, "was out on the town squares with one of the hottest bands ever to make a political circuit." Stevenson's advisers pleaded with him all one long evening, to get a band himself, to do *something* to draw crowds. "Boys," Stevenson said at last, "there'll be no danged music." There was no platform, either. He said the same thing he had said when he had refused to issue one during his campaign for Lieutenant Governor: voters knew what he was going to do, because of what he *had* done; he had a record, and he wanted to be judged on that record. He refused to make a campaign promise. He refused to answer his opponents' attacks on him. "I have never made" any personal attacks "on anybody, and I am not doing it now," he said. "I would not want any public office if I had to win by such tactics." He campaigned the same way he had before, driving around the state, stopping in every town on his route to talk to small groups of voters. In that Democratic gubernatorial primary, the crucial election in a one-party state, Collins and the other four candidates received a total of 299,000 votes. Stevenson received 651,000. His 68.5 percent of the vote was the highest percentage that had ever been recorded in Texas in a contested Democratic primary. No candidate for Governor in the state's history, not famous campaigners such as "Pa" Ferguson or Pat M. Neff or Dan Moody, not even Pappy O'Daniel himself, had won by so overwhelming a margin. In the general election that Fall, he again ran far ahead of O'Daniel. O'Daniel had stormed out of Fort Worth waving a flour sack in one hand and the Decalogue in the other and had become one of Texas' greatest vote-getters. Coke Stevenson had ridden quietly out of the Hill Country and had campaigned without ever raising his voice—and had become an even greater vote-getter. In 1944, he ran again. This time the attacks were led by three-time State Attorney General Gerald C. Mann, who, in a trial balloon, spent the Spring of 1944 harshly attacking Stevenson. Stevenson refused to reply.

He didn't have to reply. "Ever a statesman and never a politician," a typical editorial said of him, and in fact even "statesman" did not adequately describe his image among Texans. To them, Coke Stevenson was not a politician but a hero. The nicknames pinned on him by journalists to mock his caution, and his deliberation in making decisions—Coffee-Coolin' Coke, Calculatin' Coke—did not stick, or became instead symbols of admiration for the qualities that the journalists were mocking. The nickname that did stick was more admiring. He had become known simply as "Mr. Texas."

Mann's attacks shattered against this silent granite image. That year, Stevenson's eight opponents received a total of 15 percent of the vote.

Stevenson received 85 percent, smashing the record he had set two years before. To this day, no gubernatorial candidate in the history of Texas has won nearly so high a percentage in a contested Democratic primary. He accomplished another feat perhaps even more impressive. He carried every one of the state's 254 counties, the only gubernatorial candidate in the state's history who had ever done so in such a primary. The leading historian of the Texas governorship was to write in 1974 that, thirty years after Coke Stevenson's campaign of 1944, which consisted of "several radio speeches and occasional appearances at public gatherings" (and, of course, some driving around Texas), his campaign was still unique, and perhaps would always be so; "perhaps no other product of the primary system ever has won, or for that matter, ever will win again, the Democratic nomination with such a minimum of campaigning." Stevenson's entire career had been unique. Because he had served more than a year of O'Daniel's gubernatorial term before winning two terms of his own, Coke Stevenson had been Governor longer than any other individual in the history of Texas. Before that, of course, he had been the only Speaker of the Texas House of Representatives ever to succeed himself. He was also the only man in the state's history who had held all three of the top political posts in state government: Speaker, Lieutenant Governor, Governor. Set against such a record, it seems almost incidental that he had run for public office twelve times—once for County Judge, five times for state legislator, twice for Speaker, twice for Lieutenant Governor and twice for Governor—and had never been defeated. The man who had not wanted to go into politics, who had violated most of the rules of Texas political campaigning—who had been considered a terrible campaigner— was, in fact, not only the most popular Governor in Texas history, but, in a state that had produced many remarkable political careers, his career had been perhaps the most remarkable of them all.

In 1946, he was asked—by newspaper editorials, by politicians, and by letters pouring in a flood into the gubernatorial mansion—to run for an unprecedented third term as Governor. Polls showed that his popularity was as immense as ever; even the liberal *Austin American-Statesman* was forced to report that he was so idolized in the capital that one state official "seems to believe that when he dies, he will go to Coke Stevenson." (The *American-Statesman* also admitted that although it had frequently criticized Stevenson's record, "He sincerely wanted to leave the State better off than it was when he came here, and he probably will.") Stevenson refused even to consider a third term. He felt that the prohibition against it was an unwritten article of his beloved Constitution, and as such inviolate. When his term was over, he stuck his old Stetson on his head, and went home to his ranch.

.   .   .

DESPITE SPECULATION that Stevenson would run for the Senate in 1948, at first, Coke's friends knew, he intended to stay home. "What people didn't understand was that he loved that ranch, truly loved it," says Ernest Boyett, who had been his executive assistant. "He had built it with his own hands, after all. And it symbolized everything he had wanted and dreamed of as a boy, and had fought for in life, and had gotten against very long odds. And it was beautiful."

But when Coke got back to the ranch, the ranch was different. Fay wasn't there.

"It had always been him and Fay," says Boyett. "Him and Fay against the world. Now he was alone." He had asked Coke, Jr., and his wife, Scottie, to come and live with him; his son, he had hoped, would practice law with him in Junction. But the young couple didn't want that kind of life, and stayed in Austin. "When he left the governorship, he had intended fully to go out to the ranch and stay there," his nephew Bob Murphey says. "But there was no one there."

He tried to stay. Because he had no telephone, it was difficult for his former supporters and political allies to get in touch with him, and he tried to keep it that way, still refusing to have a telephone installed. His mail was brought out once a week from Junction, and each week, it seemed, the mail sack grew heavier, with letters typed on the embossed stationery of Houston and Dallas firms, and written in pen or pencil on ruled pages torn from school notebooks, with letters bearing postmarks from every corner of Texas. He didn't open most of the letters—because he knew what they would be asking him to do.

Friends, visiting him, saw his loneliness. Murphey, now a young lawyer in Nacogdoches, loved him, and Stevenson's friends asked—Coke himself would never ask—Murphey to live with him for a while. Murphey agreed, arriving on Labor Day, 1947, and saw that the legend of Coke Stevenson was true.

"We lived like men out of another time," Murphey recalls. Their life was one of utter simplicity. It was a life of work. Rounding up cattle and goats, branding, shearing. Driving postholes, repairing fences, clearing cedar. Murphey considered himself a good worker, but he came to feel that his fifty-nine-year-old uncle could work him to death. "He never stopped, and he never got tired," Murphey recalls. At the end of the day, the two men, covered with sweat, would strip off all their clothes and bathe in the freezing river, using buoyant Ivory Soap so that if a bar was dropped, it would float instead of sinking. Then they would have dinner: beans and salt pork or beans and bacon—or just plain beans. After dinner,

Murphey would generally go to bed early—from exhaustion, and to stay as warm as possible. "The only heat in that house was from the fire" in the great fireplace, "and that house would get *cold!* I slept upstairs, and before I went to bed, I would stand close to the fire and toast myself back and front until I was sweating, and then run upstairs as fast as I could and jump into bed."

The stories about Stevenson's reading were true, too, Murphey saw. "He got up at four a.m.," he says. "I don't mean five, I mean four. I would get up to go to the bathroom, and I'd see him sitting there in front of the fire reading. That was when he did his reading, because when the sun came up, he wanted to be out on the ranch." With sun-up, Stevenson would be out milking the cows—in weather that was sometimes so cold that before Murphey could water the horses, he would have to break the ice that had formed overnight in the trough. "Sometimes, you suddenly remembered that this was the former Governor of Texas milking cows, standing buck-naked washing himself in the river, eating the same beans every day—you could hardly believe it. But there was no pretense about Coke Stevenson, none at all. He was what he was—and that was it." Once, driving into Junction, he and Murphey saw a car stopped on the road with a flat tire. While Stevenson was helping the driver change it, he tried to avoid telling him his name. When he was finished, the driver asked him point blank. "Coke Stevenson," the big man muttered, and got back into Murphey's car as quickly as he could.

But Murphey saw that his uncle was very lonely, and he had after all been the center of a very different world for many years. And Murphey had opened the mail, "and," as he recalls it, "the letters all said the same thing: 'Come back. We need you. Run for senator.'" Nor was Stevenson happy either with national political developments—the return to what he called constitutional values that he had hoped would follow Roosevelt's death was not nearly fast or thorough enough for him—or with the role, or lack thereof, of that buffoon O'Daniel, who was representing his beloved state in the Senate. Stevenson had agreed to a request from an old friend, R. M. Eagle, to address the Texas Lumber Manufacturers Association in Lufkin in October, 1947. At the end of the speech, Eagle, thanking him for coming, said, "We hope the Governor's public life is not closed." The audience began to applaud. Then one lumberman stood up, and then another, shaking their fists in the air. And then the whole audience was on its feet, roaring. Stevenson left without responding, said hardly a word on the long drive back to Junction, and the next morning was out at sun-up milking the cows as usual. But no one who knew him—including Murphey—was surprised when his uncle scheduled a radio broadcast for New Year's Day, 1948. Listening to it, Lyndon Johnson learned that among his opponents for the Texas senatorial seat would be "Mr. Texas" himself.

9

Head Start

TEN DAYS AFTER Stevenson entered the race, Johnson got a break. A 56-year-old Houston attorney, George E. B. Peddy, announced that he was entering also. In 1922, Peddy, then a youthful state legislator, had polled 130,000 votes as a candidate for United States Senator. During the intervening twenty-six years, he had not run for any public office, but he had been an officer in both world wars and was widely known, and respected, in veterans organizations. He was, moreover, regarded as a symbol of uncompromising conservatism, and his numerous family was well known in ultra-conservative Deep East Texas. He had no chance to win, but he certainly would draw a significant number of votes in East Texas—and the votes he would draw would be Coke Stevenson's.

Nonetheless, polls could not have heartened Johnson. A Belden Poll taken in February, by which time it was obvious that O'Daniel would not be running, showed that Stevenson was the choice of a higher percentage of voters than Johnson, Peddy and all minor candidates combined.

Nor could he have been heartened by the attitude of the press—which was that of course Coke would win. Who could possibly beat him? The only question was whether the former Governor would win a majority in the primary on July 24, or whether Peddy, and other minor right-wing candidates, would siphon off enough of the conservative vote to deny him a majority and force him into a second primary, which would be held, if necessary, on August 28. As one writer put it: "That strong, silent man on his isolated ranch in the Hill Country fastness holds no public office at this time, but he is considered . . . the most potent political force in the state."

LYNDON JOHNSON's career had been marked at every stage by a repetition of vivid patterns in both his political behavior and his personality.

Now, in this crucial, perhaps final, moment of that career—in this long-shot last chance—these patterns re-emerged, sharper than ever.

One pattern was the use of money as a lever to move the political world.

Stevenson's campaigns had always been adequately financed, not that his type of campaigning required much financing. Although his incorruptibility annoyed big business lobbyists, big business contributed to his campaigns nonetheless, because of their Darwinian survival-of-the-fittest philosophy into which his laissez-faire philosophy so easily shaded, and because his "economy" style of government was agreeable to men who felt that it was their taxes that paid for government services. Stevenson's campaigns, however, had been financed on the traditional Texas scale— a rough rule-of-thumb, occasionally violated, among Texas politicians was that a respectable statewide campaign could be waged for between $75,000 and $100,000. Johnson was thinking of money on a completely different scale. He always had. His first campaign for Congress, in 1937, had been one of the most expensive congressional campaigns—possibly *the* most expensive congressional campaign—in the history of Texas. During his first Senate campaign, in 1941, men handed him (or handed to his aides, for his use) checks or envelopes stuffed with cash—checks and cash in amounts unprecedented even in the free-spending world of Texas politics—and with these contributions of hundreds of thousands of dollars, he had waged the most expensive senatorial campaign in Texas political history. Now, in his last chance, he planned to use money on a scale unprecedented even for him.

He had it to use. After Johnson's 1941 Senate campaign, George Brown had delivered to Johnson Herman Brown's pledge to finance a second Senate campaign as lavishly as he had financed a first. Since that time, the federal contracts Johnson had helped Brown & Root obtain had gotten bigger; profits had mounted from millions of dollars to tens of millions—and at the same time fierce Herman Brown had glimpsed the wealth that could come to his company through the efforts of a Senator, rather than a mere Representative. In 1947, the pledge was renewed again; if Lyndon wanted to run, the money would be there—as much as was needed.

COKE STEVENSON may have been immensely popular in Texas. But in the state's third-largest city, San Antonio, and in the area south of San Antonio, the broad, gently undulating "brush country" covered with cactus and mesquite and dotted with small towns that slopes gently two hundred miles southward to the Rio Grande River and Mexico, popularity was not the coin of the political realm.

San Antonio's "West Side" was a sprawling Mexican-American slum, containing perhaps 60,000 residents, and, as journalist John Gunther was to write, "The way to play politics in San Antonio is to buy, or try to buy, the Mexican vote, which is decisive." Lyndon Johnson had, of course, been buying votes on the West Side for years: in 1934, buying them on behalf of then-Congressman Maury Maverick, he had sat in a room in the city's Plaza Hotel behind a table covered with five-dollar bills, peeling them off and handing them to Mexican-American men at the rate of five dollars a vote for each vote in their family; in 1941, he had bought votes on his own behalf, purchasing them wholesale instead of retail by arranging for the distribution of generous lump sums of cash to Mexican-American leaders who would make the direct purchases themselves, and whose organizations would make sure that voters got to the polls and voted for the approved candidate. Through a number of devices, moreover, the purchase of many West Side "votes" was accomplished without voters being involved at all. Opposition poll watchers and election judges at some West Side precincts might be persuaded—the going rate for such persuasion was only about ten or twenty dollars for a clerk, but it might be as high as fifty for a judge—to leave the polling place after the polls closed. Then the doors would be locked, the ballot boxes or voting machines would be opened, the names of persons who had paid their poll tax but had not actually voted would be added to the list of persons who *had* voted, and a corresponding number of votes would simply be added to the total of the purchasing candidate. There were more than 10,000 votes available on the West Side that were, political leaders in Texas estimated, in effect, for sale.

South of San Antonio, in "the Valley," geographically the area bordering the Rio Grande but in political parlance also including the counties which adjoined them to the north, there were cities—Laredo, Harlingen, Corpus Christi—with similar Mexican-American and black slums, and similar voting practices. Entering these slums was like entering a foreign city. As for the rest of the Valley, with its tiny communities scattered thinly across the brush country, only the arbitrary drawing of a border made these counties part of the United States. Their inhabitants were predominantly Mexican, their language and culture predominantly Spanish; they clung to the customs of their homeland across the Rio Grande. Their dozing towns, strung along the river, "bore," as one traveler wrote, "an appearance as foreign as their names"—San Ygnacio, Santa Maria, La Paloma, Los Indios. Their houses were thatched adobe huts, or *jacales*, one- or two-room structures of willow branches daubed with mud, around which swarmed dogs and goats and chickens. Inland, the names of the towns were more Anglo—Alice, Alfred, Orange Grove, Freer—and the Mexican sections often consisted of little wooden buildings with corrugated tin roofs, or of buildings up on cinder blocks or stilts because of huge termites which, in some towns, seemed to swarm everywhere; but whatever the materials used in their construction, the homes in these sections were still hovels—rickety shacks crowded together—and in their yards were the same goats and chickens. These Mexican-American inhabitants were largely illiterate; the Valley as a whole had one of the lowest literacy rates, if not *the* lowest, in the entire United States. And they had, as historian V. O. Key, Jr., noted, "only the most remote conception of Anglo-American governmental institutions." In the near-feudalistic regions of Mexico from which they came, serf-like dependence on a local leader, the *patrón* or *jefe*, had been the custom, as one observer noted, "from time immemorial," and they continued this custom in the United States. Since many of the Mexicans worked on the great South Texas ranches—the huge King Ranch alone employed more than seven hundred *vaqueros*—the *patrón* was often the ranch owner. The cattle barons, historian Douglas O. Weeks wrote, "established themselves as lords protector of those Mexicans who became their tenants and ranch hands," with the *vaquero* giving "unquestioning loyalty" to the ranch owner and regarding his wishes "as law, the only law he knows." But some of these *patrónes* were political bosses—ruthless, in some cases vicious, men who walked the streets of the dusty little towns in their domains surrounded by armed unshaven *pistoleros*; politics was violent in the Valley. A reporter from Philadelphia who journeyed there in 1939 found "as hard-bitten a political crowd . . . as Texas ever saw. . . . Each [county] has its own iron-fisted boss, who would make Philadelphia's Jay Cooke or New York's Jimmy Hines look like pikers."

On Election Day, *pistoleros*, sometimes appointed "deputy sheriffs" for the day, herded Mexican-Americans to the polls. Each voter was handed a receipt showing he had paid his poll tax (usually these taxes had been purchased by the *patrón* or *jefe* months before and kept in his safe to, as Key puts it, "insure discipline and orderly procedure"). In some Valley precincts, the voters were also handed ballots that had already been marked (in most of these towns, voting machines were not in use); according to one description,

> The Mexican voter . . . was marched to the polls, generally by a half-breed deputy sheriff with two six-shooters, a Winchester rifle, and a bandoleer of ammunition, to perform the sovereign act of voting. He entered the polls, one at a time, was handed a folded ballot which he dropped in the box, was given a drink of Tequila, and then was marched out, where he touched the hand of one of the local political bosses or some of his sainted representatives.

In other precincts, matters were managed less crudely: the voters were told whom to vote for, but were allowed to mark their own ballots. (Of course, the guards accompanied them into the voting cubbyholes to guarantee that the instructions were followed.) In still others, even more privacy was allowed. Large tents, guarded by deputies, would be erected near polling places; inside, voters were given pre-marked "sample" ballots to be substituted for real ones or, in another device, a piece of cord on which knots had been tied; when the voter placed this "string" next to the ballot, the knots would indicate the candidates for whom he was to vote. Privacy in casting a ballot did not guarantee its secrecy. Upon arriving to vote, each voter had his name, in accordance with Texas law, registered on a "poll list" with a number beside it—the number of the ballot he would cast. The ostensible reason for this law was to keep a person from voting more than once, but it also had the effect of allowing election judges to determine how a citizen had voted, if they wished to do so. Some *patrónes* dispensed with all these complications. An attorney for one of them—a *patrón* who let his voters keep their poll tax receipts—recalls his procedure: "Go around to the Mexicans' homes. Get the numbers of their [poll tax] receipts. Tell them not to go to the polls. Just write in a hundred numbers, and cast the hundred votes yourself."

The number of votes at the *patrónes'* command was not necessarily limited by the number of eligible voters. Since voters over the age of sixty were not required to pay poll taxes, and since poll tax lists were checked only irregularly to eliminate the names of those who died after sixty, "in the Valley," as one expert on the subject puts it, "the 'machine' votes the dead men." Nor was American citizenship necessarily a requirement; on Election Day, voters were recruited in saloons on the Mexican side of the Rio Grande and brought across in truckloads to vote on the American side. Starr County was "an excellent location for bringing voters from across the border," a commentator notes. In Webb County, the small town of Dolores had about 100 American citizens—and in some elections recorded as many as 400 votes. The votes of these *patrónes* were generally delivered as a unit. The Valley's controlled vote—generally estimated at between 20,000 and 25,000 votes, deliverable to the favored candidate by margins as large as ten to one—was euphemistically lumped together in Texas political parlance with those 10,000 votes from San Antonio's West Side, deliverable by a heavy majority, as the state's "Hispanic vote" or "ethnic vote" or "bloc vote." In total, this "bloc" might mean a plurality to the favored candidate of perhaps 25,000 votes. In perhaps no other region of the United States was so large a "bloc" of votes deliverable en masse.

In obtaining the support of this bloc, cash was often a decisive consideration. The power of these border dictators was matched by their greed. To some of these petty despots, votes were a commodity like any other—a commodity to be sold. The best history of politics in the Valley states flatly: "The State candidates who have the most money to spend usually carry these machine counties."

TO REACH the seat of power in the Valley in 1948, a visitor drove into San Diego, in Duval County, a town 130 miles due south of San Antonio (and unconnected to the larger city by any road—there was no direct road link between San Diego and the north; the town looked only south). The visitor drove past the dull red brick County Courthouse to a building just beyond it. At first glance, it was a long, low, graceful white stucco structure with a sloping roof of red Spanish tiles, and elaborate, intricately wrought iron grillwork, seemingly rather heavy in comparison with the rest of the building, over the windows and doors. Closer inspection, however, revealed that the windows were opaque, and the doors were of solid oak, several inches thick. And that heavy grillwork, which covered every opening, was anchored very solidly indeed in the walls. The spaces between the designs with which the grillwork was so prettily decorated were rather narrow, so that it would be difficult to push something, such as a gun barrel, through them with much freedom of movement. And, to increase the difficulty of shooting into the house, the grillwork jutted almost two feet out from the walls. As a reporter was to realize, "The building is constructed to withstand a siege."

Going inside, the visitor found himself in one of several offices staffed with secretaries and business executives. But behind them, on two benches that flanked another massive door, were, as the reporter was to write in 1951, "swarthy Latins wearing typical red, high-heeled boots, sombreros and six-shooters, whom the natives know as . . . bodyguards." Behind that door the visitor met a short, stocky man in his forties who was usually dressed in a conservative, double-breasted business suit, a carefully knotted necktie, gold-rimmed spectacles and a broad smile, and who, as a writer put it, "possesses the practiced charm of the successful sales manager he resembles"—until you noticed the hard, piercing fixity of his eyes even when he was relaxed, and the way that stare could change in an instant into a blazing glare at the slightest hint of opposition.

He was George Berham Parr, the Valley's Boss of Bosses, the son of Archie Parr, the legendary Duke of Duval, and now Duke in his own right. The Parrs had ruled Duval County since 1912, when Archie sided with the Mexicans after an "Election Day Massacre" in San Diego, the county seat, that left three Mexicans dead. (Later, Archie's chief political rival was shot in the back while eating in a San Diego café.)

No matter how frank they are about other matters, the great men of

Texas politics—the John Connallys, the Ed Clarks, the George Browns—
don't like to talk about George Parr. They downplay the role of money
in their relationships with him. "In counties like . . . Duval, by and large
those fellows took care of themselves," Connally says. "You might give
them a little money," but not much. And some journalists today, in writing stories about Texas in the 1940s, also portray the Parrs as mesquite
Robin Hoods, taking from the rich and giving to the poor; the support
the Parrs received on Election Day, according to this theory, came not
from intimidation but from friendship. George Parr himself, as one reporter puts it, "denies he had ever made a penny from politics."

The friendship was certainly there. In the Dukes of Duval, the Mexicans in the Valley had found a replacement for the *patrónes* on whom
they had depended in Mexico, and they were grateful. But there were
also somewhat darker shades to the story. As another journalist, writing
not in a later decade but at the time, put it, "The facts completely puncture Boss Parr's long-standing claims that he is in politics merely for fun."
In 1949, William H. Mason, a radio commentator in Alice who had criticized the corruption in Jim Wells County, would be shot to death by one
of Parr's deputy sheriffs; some contemporary observers of "The Land of
Parr" say political murders were not uncommon there, nor were beatings
handed out to Duval residents who attempted to oppose *El Patrón*, nor
were other forms of intimidation. The reporter who knew Valley politics
best in the post-war years, James M. Rowe, who covered the region for
the *Corpus Christi Caller-Times*, wrote:

> It is not easy for the average person to imagine what it was
> like . . . to oppose Boss Parr in his own county. A word from
> him was sufficient to get a man fired from his job or denied
> welfare payments or surplus commodities distributed to the
> needy. Merchants who opposed him faced the sudden loss of
> most of their trade. Little farmers and ranchers were intimidated
> by the *pistoleros*.

And the true color of the story was green, if not precisely the green
of Sherwood Forest. Under Texas law, beer retailing licenses had to be
approved by the County Judge. In Duval County, only one license was
approved, for a company owned by the County Judge: George Parr. But
this income from beer was not enough for Parr. In the rest of Texas, beer
cost twenty cents; in Duval, it cost a quarter; visitors to the Valley who
asked why were informed that the extra nickel was for "George." Parr
owned oil wells. But their income was not enough. To obtain more oil
rights, he erased clauses from land leases filed in the County Courthouse
he controlled. He took kickbacks on road construction contracts—accord-

ing to some sources, a kickback on every road construction contract awarded in Duval County. In 1932, for example, a contractor's representative had placed $25,000 in cash "in a little black bag" and had delivered it to him. But kickbacks on contracts were not enough. He formed a construction company, and awarded all the contracts to himself. For failing to report the $25,000 in income he pled guilty to tax evasion, and in 1934 received a suspended two-year sentence. But he went right back to altering oil and gas leases, and in 1936 was forced to serve nine months of that term.

Seemingly, no amount of money was enough. Some of Parr's income certainly was returned to the people of Duval and the other counties he controlled; when they needed money for medicine or funeral expenses or other emergencies, they had only to go to his office, or to the nearby Windmill Café, where he would eat lunch while dispensing favors—protected every moment by guards cradling Winchester rifles and watching over him through the café's large plate glass window; a burly *pistolero* stood at his shoulder while he gave his ear to petitioners. Parr himself always sat with his back against a wall. But the largesse thus distributed accounted for only a part of his expenditures. He made a lot of money— in 1944, he and his wife paid taxes on an income of $406,000—but no matter how much he made, it was insufficient to support a life-style that became increasingly ducal. He had a large, impressive home in Corpus Christi and a palatial home in San Diego—and to see that house, surrounded by low walls and lush landscaping, with balconies, swimming pool, large servants' quarters and high arches leading into an interior courtyard, and doorways entering lavishly furnished rooms, to see it standing, gleaming and white, amidst the pitiful shacks of his constituents, was to be reminded that in the Duchy of Duval workers on county construction projects, the projects from which the Duke was becoming rich, earned the minimum wage, forty cents an hour or sixteen dollars for a forty-hour week, and to understand the indignation of a contemporary reporter who wrote, "Despite his enormous wealth, much of it gained directly from the taxpayers, I found no record of his ever having attempted to improve the living conditions of tens of thousands of Latin Americans forced to exist in squalid slums, on near-starvation wages, throughout his domain." He had a racing stable of twenty-five blooded quarter horses, and so that he could enjoy the racing in the style he preferred, he had built a private racetrack, complete with automatic starting chutes and judges' stand; at it, he raced horses against those of other ranchers, with betting on the races, and when he bet, he bet big—as much as $15,000 on a single race.

The Duke of Duval, as he was named by journalists (in his domain Anglos called him "George B," his Mexican nickname was Tacuacha, "the sly possum"), owned a lot of land, but he wanted more. In 1945, the 57,000-acre Dobie Ranch came on the market, and he didn't have the money to buy it. On April 24 of that year, the Duval County Commissioners Court approved a payment to him for $250,000, and he exchanged that check for a cashier's check made out to the executors of the Dobie estate, and on June 13, another $250,000 payment followed the same route. He was later to say that he had merely "borrowed" the half million dollars (although when the Internal Revenue Service discovered the loan, in 1954, it had not yet been repaid). The next year, he again didn't have enough money to pay his taxes; "therefore," as Rowe was to write, he "returned to his 'bankers,' the Commissioners Court. A further payment of $172,000 was authorized." Parr was constantly in need of money to pay his *pistoleros*. The numbers of his "deputy sheriffs" were constantly increasing—"because," as one San Diego resident recalls, "George B knew [people] would kill him if they could." Always his life-style grew more and more lavish; the parties he threw for associates at the Dobie Ranch became subjects of wild rumors. In 1948, his wife was suing for divorce; and he was going to have to make a cash settlement of hundreds of thousands of dollars. If greed was a characteristic of many of the border-county dictators, their leader was the greediest of them all.

George Parr's control extended into Brooks and Jim Hogg counties, and into four other counties, through alliances with other, less well known, petty despots who ruled along the Rio Grande—Judge Manuel Bravo of Zapata County; Judge Manuel Raymond of Webb (a figure, one chronicler wrote, so secretive that "little is known of him except rumor," who ruled Laredo "with an iron hand"); Sheriff Chub Pool of La Salle; and the "Guerra boys," four brothers who, at Parr's sufferance, ran Starr County. Until recently, Parr's control had extended over Jim Wells County, which adjoined Duval, but the young Mexicans who had gone off to war came back more sophisticated, more independent, less willing to follow slavishly "George B's" orders; in 1948, a reform movement was contesting twelve of Jim Wells' thirteen precincts. The thirteenth precinct—"Box 13"—was the poorest Mexican district in Alice, the Jim Wells county seat, and in that precinct order was maintained by Parr's enforcer in Jim Wells County, Luis Salas, a burly six-foot-one, 210-pound native of Durango who had fled Mexico after fatally wounding a man in a barroom brawl. Salas, known as "Indio" because of his swarthy appearance, was feared for his savage temper and immense physical strength. Once, during a vicious fistfight he had with the owner of a restaurant in Alice, the owner's wife screamed at her husband, "Stop! Don't you know who you are fighting? He is the man they call the 'Indio.' " (The owner didn't take her advice: Salas beat him senseless and, while he was lying on the floor, picked up a barstool and systematically wrecked the restaurant; when the police chief arrived, and the owner's wife asked him, Aren't you going to arrest him?, the chief replied, "No, lady, you better thank the Lord that Luis did not kill your husband.")

Parr appealed to Salas' smoldering sense of racial injustice—Salas never forgot the shock with which, when he reached the United States, he saw his first "Mexicans Not Served Here" sign; "He [Parr] used to tell me, 'Look, Indio, all these *gringos* that come to me for help, I make them pay for their ambitions, they have to crawl. . . .'" If they were in a room with Anglos, Parr would speak to him in Spanish, calling them *"cabrones"* (cuckolds). Parr also appealed to Salas' sense of machismo—Parr applauded the "guts" with which he followed his orders—and to Salas' need for status: Parr gave him badges (as a city policeman in Alice, a deputy sheriff in Duval, Jim Wells and Nueces counties) to legitimize his brutality and allow him to use it enforcing his *patrón*'s law; a car—a new black Ford; even a chauffeur to drive him around. And he gave him money— more money than Salas had ever seen: hardly had they met when Parr handed him ten hundred-dollar bills, saying with a lordly indifference which Salas admired: "Spend this money among our voters, and if you need more, just come to San Diego." Says Salas: "Through my hands, every election year, passed thousands of dollars. . . . Every election year, we had to buy poll tax receipts—just for only that thing, took a great amount of money, also on Election Day, pay for the autos, pay for election judges, pay for clerks, etc., etc. . . ." Between elections, too, "I always had plenty of money to spend. People asking for money account they had sick people, or need to go to the hospital—we never said no, that was George's orders, that was what made him famous and powerful. George told me: 'Don't be afraid to spend money; it does not come from my pockets, comes from candidates.' . . . I spent money the way George told me: I go into a saloon, throw at them a ten-dollar bill. 'The drinks are on. . . .' Always had plenty of money to spend." In return, Parr's fearsome "Indian," who carried a big revolver on his hip, destroyed the businesses of men who tried to remain independent in politics (" 'Indio, I want his place closed. Close his place, burn the shack or eliminate him.' . . . [The owner] made a movement to reach something behind the bar, I gave him no chance, I threw two bullets in his direction, and he went out in a hurry [through] the back door. . . ."), taunted Parr's opponents into fistfights ("Of course I was always the winner due to my physical strength. . . . My political enemies, I know they were scared of me"), and made sure that Jim Wells County (and especially Precinct 13, in Alice) voted the way Parr wanted. "In all these years, George told me to give our candidates 80 percent of the total votes, regardless if the people voted against us." There was little trouble about doing this. "I had control of most of the Mexican-Americans in the county, they voted the way I tell them to vote." And if occasionally less than 80 percent of the voters voted for Parr's candidates, that did not matter; Parr's candidate would receive 80 percent of the vote anyway, for Salas, as the presiding election judge in Box 13, was the official who "counted" the ballots.

Salas says that he was "the right hand of George B. Parr in Jim Wells County" for "ten years of violence, crime and killings due to the ambition of crooked politicians." And he was very proud to be Parr's right hand. He worshipped Parr—"he did not give a damn for nothing"—and was proud of his *patrón*'s power ("George's office at San Diego always was crowded, especially in election year. . . . He stood there like a king") and of his friendship: "I had the confidence of such a great man. . . . As long as I live, I will never forget this man, and when I gave him my word to stay by his side regardless, I meant it, so up to date I still worship his memory."

Money had purchased Parr—had purchased the entire Valley, in fact—for Lyndon Johnson before, in 1941. The purchase had not been cheap, for Pappy O'Daniel had paid high for the Valley in each of his previous campaigns: just the year before, when O'Daniel had been running for Governor, he had received 95 percent of the Valley's vote. Negotiating the price for Johnson, however, was Alvin Wirtz, and Wirtz had a long-time business relationship with the Parrs. He had personally bargained with old Archie, with whom he had served in the State Senate, for the Parr-controlled votes in Corpus Christi during a 1928 attempt to unseat Congressman Harry Wurzbach. (After that election, Wurzbach charged widespread election fraud—and made the charges stick.) By 1941, with Brown & Root's money behind him, as well as the money of two other clients, Lone Star Gas and the Humble Oil Company, Wirtz was so important a supplier of the commodity prized by Valley politicians that they had to make pilgrimages to his hometown northeast of San Antonio. Recalls one of them: "He [Wirtz] would never mix and mingle with us down here. We'd have to go up to Seguin to see him. He was very powerful." At a crucial stage in the 1941 negotiations, moreover, Johnson himself had telephoned the Duke of Duval. In 1940, in the seven rural South Texas counties controlled by Parr, O'Daniel had received 95 percent of the vote; in 1941, O'Daniel received 5 percent of the vote, there was a scattering of votes for other candidates and Johnson received more than 90 percent of the vote.

The abruptness—and extent—of this decline in O'Daniel's popularity in the Valley startled even politicians who had become inured to its political mores. "It was nauseous to learn of the returns from such corrupt stinkholes as Duval and Starr Counties," one said. "Money bought every Mexican vote. . . ." An observer in Cameron County said: "We have a

situation in this State that is worse than Pendergast, Kelly-Nash and Boss
Hague crookedness ever was. How can one expect honest men and clean
government to survive such a system?"

In the Valley, as in Texas politics as a whole, Stevenson had been
the exception. The border bosses had always supported him by the traditional wide margins, but not for the traditional reasons—rather, during
the first primary of his initial race for Lieutenant Governor because Austin's conservative politicians and business interests who found his philosophy compatible persuaded the bosses to back him; in the second primary
for no other reason than that the inexplicable O'Daniel (who had purchased the Valley that year) included him on the list of candidates he had
never met but whom he was supporting (as one rebel Laredo politician
said, "The machine localities are straight behind the candidates O'Daniel
endorsed"); in Stevenson's races thereafter for reasons not financial but
strategic: because his immense popularity made victory a foregone conclusion, and the *jefes* wanted to be with the winner, and not antagonize
a Governor whose disfavor might interfere with their rule. Money was
never a factor in the Valley's support of Stevenson—he treated the *jefes*
with the same indifference and independence that he displayed toward
other powerful political figures. (And, of course, as Ernest Boyett, his
executive assistant, notes, "Why shouldn't the Old Man have been" independent of the Valley bosses? To a candidate who carried Texas by
hundreds of thousands of votes, the Valley was not a significant factor in
the electoral equation.)

In 1948, however, the *patrónes* were not going to be behind Stevenson. During the war, their politics had clashed with his patriotism—and,
as anyone who knew Stevenson could have predicted, that conflict could
have only one result. Late in 1944, George Parr and Judge Raymond of
Webb County had asked the Governor to appoint E. James ("Jimmy")
Kazen, a member of a politically powerful family and Raymond's relative
by marriage, to the recently vacated post of Laredo District Attorney.
Stevenson, however, had also received a visit from the commanding general of the huge Army Air Force base in Laredo—who pleaded with him
to appoint a District Attorney who was not tied in with the local political
machine. "He said the prostitutes were running wild; half of his men were
sick," recalls Boyett, who was present during this visit. "Mr. Stevenson
felt we were at war, and politics be damned." He appointed another man.
Raymond—and Parr—never forgave Stevenson for this slight, and Johnson took full advantage of the opening. During the war, he cemented a
friendship with *El Patrón*. One of Parr's intimates says that "for years"
Johnson would make visits to San Diego, driving past the Duval County
Courthouse and pulling up in front of the low building with the pretty red
tile roof and the massive grillwork. Inside, he and Parr would talk alone,

sometimes sending out for hamburgers to the nearby Windmill Café; Johnson always wanted them to "double the meat." Says another Parr intimate: "Everybody knew about it, but nobody was present to see or hear." Others say that such visits were actually rare, but that Johnson would make frequent telephone calls to Parr, sometimes chatting for an hour or more. Whatever the means of communication, the communication was there. The definitive word probably comes from Frank B. Lloyd, Parr's hand-picked District Attorney in Alice, and, with his brother, Edward, a member of Lloyd & Lloyd, the Alice law firm through which most Parr business in Jim Wells County was handled. "George and Lyndon were very close," Lloyd says. "He [Johnson] didn't make public spectacles [of trips to Alice] like some of the politicians did. But there was the telephone." About one thing all of Parr's associates are agreed: he was fond of the Congressman. As one of Parr's biographers puts it: "he liked Johnson's style and guts." Luther E. Jones, Johnson's one-time assistant in Richard Kleberg's office who was, for eight years during the 1940s, Parr's most trusted attorney, says, "He liked him. They were good friends, dear friends. It was a real working together there." Additional cement was troweled on after Tom Clark was appointed United States Attorney General by President Truman in 1945. A pardon for his 1932 income tax conviction was important to Parr, primarily because the other Valley *jefes* would regard it as proof of his power, and of his ability to protect them in Washington from investigations by federal agencies. Parr had applied for a pardon in July, 1943, and Johnson had attempted to help him obtain one. These attempts were unsuccessful as long as Francis Biddle was United States Attorney General. But on February 20, 1946, the pardon was granted—and Parr gave Johnson full credit for this. As for the still firmer cementing necessary for the 1948 campaign, that was again left to Wirtz. On the eve of the campaign, a deal was sealed. George Brown will say of it only that "We helped him [Johnson] down there [in the Valley] through Wirtz." No details are known. But Parr told Salas, Salas was to recall: "Listen, Indio, concentrate on the senatorial race. Be sure we elect Johnson."

Coke Stevenson was going into the campaign with his great popularity. But before the campaign began, Johnson had a 25,000-vote head start.

PURCHASING votes in the Valley was traditional in Texas politics. Johnson was thinking of other ways to use money in the campaign that were not traditional at all—ways that would, in fact, revolutionize Texas politics.

Politics was already changing, becoming more scientific, more technical, more media-oriented. Polling, for example, was growing more common. But no politician in Texas had ever used polls as Johnson wanted to use them. A statewide poll in the 1940s cost about $6,000, so politicians commissioned them sparingly, perhaps once a month, three or four during a campaign at most. Johnson wanted polling done not monthly but weekly, and each week he wanted nearly identical polls done not by one firm but two or three. "He wanted to be able to compare them on every point," Ed Clark recalls. Johnson was talking not about three or four polls but thirty or forty. And as Johnson explained to his advisers what type of polls he wanted, the more perceptive of them realized that their Chief was talking about something new to politics: he wanted polls that revealed not only voter preferences, but the depth of those preferences, how the preferences were changing—and how they might be changed: "He was interested in what today we would call the degree of strength support, in trends and in interest in [specific] issues," John Connally says. Issues, to Johnson, had never been anything more than campaign fodder; caring about none himself, he had, in every campaign he had run, simply tested, and discarded, one issue after another until he found one which, in his word, "touched"—influenced—voters. ("We didn't care if the argument was true or not," recalls one of his college allies. "We just kept trying to find one that touched.") Now he would no longer have to guess which issues were "touching": a scientific measurement would be available to him. Such in-depth polls would cost more than ordinary polls. At first, Clark blanched at the cost. "I didn't know where he was going to get the money for it," he says, But then he realized that, in this campaign, cost was not a consideration. "Whatever was needed would be there."

Radio had, of course, been an integral part of politics in Texas ever since Pappy O'Daniel had started selling himself instead of flour, but no politician, including O'Daniel, had ever used radio with the sophistication with which Johnson was planning to use it. In the past, radio politics had meant speeches, mostly by the candidate, occasionally by supporters. Johnson, knowledgeable about radio because of his KTBC activities, of course, wanted not only speeches but "produced," slicker, shows, with scripts and music, professionally written, directed and narrated. And he wanted to use radio on a scale it had never been used in a political campaign. He wanted to be on the air himself every day, several times a day—over a statewide network of stations. He wanted key supporters—Judge Roy Hofheinz of Houston, for example—on the air frequently, also over statewide networks. Since a single statewide broadcast cost between $5,000 and $8,000, Connally realized that Johnson was talking about an expenditure unprecedented in Texas campaigning, which traditionally had placed considerable emphasis on a candidate driving from county seat to county seat, speaking at each County Courthouse, giving occasional radio addresses. Connally realized that Johnson was talking about revolutionizing Texas politics. Thanks to polling, Johnson would be able to discover exactly what issues "touched" Texas voters. And when he found one that touched, he could hammer it into the voters' consciousness, in speeches on the radio, in ads on the radio, in ads in newspapers, in mailings—with a repetition whose scale alone would be a significant factor in the transformation of Texas politics that he was planning. And Connally also realized how money could specifically help against a candidate like Coke Stevenson. With the media politics Johnson was planning, the influence of money is magnified. "In politics you have to say something over and over to get voters to be aware of it," Connally explains. "One-day play—that's all you get out of any speech." But Stevenson, he felt, would go on making speeches, and not making much use of the media. And even if Coke wanted to, Connally felt, he couldn't. Media meant money, and, Connally says, Coke Stevenson "didn't know how to raise money." And Stevenson *wouldn't* want to; he had been campaigning the old way for so long, and so successfully, that he wouldn't realize the power of the new politics—until it was too late. "He didn't know how to advertise, he didn't know how to use the press. . . ." "Ol' Coke," Lyndon Johnson's bright young men felt, was not going to change. The 1948 campaign would, therefore, be a dramatic contrast—on the one hand, a lone campaigner traveling from town to town by auto, speaking on Courthouse lawns to small audiences; on the other hand, a candidate whose words would be brought several times each day into homes throughout Texas. Ol' Coke would campaign in the old way. Lyndon would campaign in the new. And, his men believed, no matter how popular Coke was, no matter how snugly his views dovetailed with the views of the electorate, because of the new way, Lyndon Johnson had a chance. Talking about it almost forty years later, John Connally grew excited: "This [the 1948 senatorial campaign] was the beginning of modern politics," he says. "You saw—you have this in your book [*The Path to Power*]—the small level of money" that had been employed before. "And this was the first big election in Texas since 1941. It was the dawn of a whole new era in politics." Other young men recall their excitement at the time. Joe Kilgore says Connally and Johnson came to the Valley in 1947, when he was still a young state legislator from McAllen. For several days, Kilgore recalls, the three men drove around the Valley, and "the entire conversation was political. The entire conversation was how he would run the campaign. . . ." The possibility that Stevenson might run was explored. At the beginning of these long days in the car, Kilgore had not believed that any candidate could possibly defeat the beloved Cowboy Governor. But after those days, Kilgore had changed his mind. "He [Johnson] had a better understanding of campaign organization than Coke Stevenson did—of the use of radio, of the use of the press, of the organizing of local political people. He was fascinating. Knowledgeable. I felt, 'He can win!' "

10

"Will!"

IN THIS CAMPAIGN—his last chance—personal as well as political patterns that had marked Lyndon Johnson's entire career emerged stark and unadorned.

Almost every great crisis of his career had been accompanied by a crisis in his health, for example, but he had done his best not to let it interfere, complaining endlessly, loudly, violently about the illness, but, even while complaining, refusing as long as possible to give in to it, fighting against pain and weakness with an endurance that was more than physical, spending his energy with a prodigality that would have exhausted the energy of a well man—and then finding more energy. In his first, desperate campaign as an unknown candidate for Congress eleven years before, he had kept going for days while complaining of stomach cramps, unable to eat, gagging and vomiting when he tried to choke food down, doubling over in pain yet refusing to cancel a single speech or a single long day's campaigning over bumpy Hill Country roads. He had kept going for so many days while making these complaints that his aides no longer took them seriously—until, two days before the election, during a speech in a County Courthouse, he could not, even by grasping the railing in front of him, hold himself erect any longer and consented at last to be taken to the hospital, where doctors found his appendix on the point of rupturing and operated immediately. Now, in this, the greatest crisis of his career, illness flared up again—and again Lyndon Johnson fought the weakness with his will.

For several days before he formally entered the campaign on May 12, he had been feeling the familiar dull abdominal ache, accompanied by nausea, that by now he knew signaled the formation of another kidney stone, and the pain grew steadily worse. Doctors advised a few days of bed rest in the hope that the stone would pass, but Johnson said there was no time for that. Then, a day or two before the Saturday night rally in Austin's Wooldridge Park that would open his campaign on May 22, the ache changed into the sharp, gripping, radiating cramps in the back and side of "kidney colic," a pain that comes and goes in waves so intense that medical textbooks describe it as "agonizing" and "unbearable"; "few bodily complaints . . . demand immediate relief so urgently," one says; doctors class kidney colic as one of the three or four most intense pains that a human being can suffer. The nausea grew worse; he began gagging on food when he tried to eat; sometimes he vomited. More significantly, he was running a fever, a sign that infection was beginning. The doctors increased the doses of painkiller—probably morphine and Demerol—which gave him temporary relief, told him that this stone did not appear to be passing, and reminded him that so long as the stone passed within a few days, probably no permanent damage to the kidneys would result, but that if it did not pass, the danger of irreparable loss of kidney function was real. It was time, they said, to consider an operation to remove the stone. The operation was a relatively simple one, but, Johnson was told, the recovery period would be a minimum of six weeks. Election Day was nine weeks away. If he had any possibility of catching Coke Stevenson, an operation would end it. The campaign would, in effect, be over. His political career would be over.

Johnson refused even to discuss the possibility of an operation. He had had stones before, and he had always passed them, he said. He would pass this one, too, and as soon as it passed everything would be okay. "I'll pass it, I'll pass it," he said. "I've had this before. Just leave me alone." Early on the morning of the Wooldridge Park campaign kickoff, however, both the pain and the fever became more acute, and every time he attempted to eat, he gagged. The pain, and the worry about its effect on his campaign—on his last chance—combined with the fever and the tension that always preceded crucial public appearances to produce a frenzy that came close to hysteria. One of his speechwriters, Paul Bolton, arriving that late afternoon at Johnson's Austin apartment to give him the final draft of the evening's speech, encountered Dr. William Morgan, Johnson's physician, on the stairs. When he asked Dr. Morgan how Johnson was feeling, Bolton recalls, the doctor "just shook his head. He wouldn't say a word. My heart sank." And when Bolton entered the apartment, the Congressman was standing in the middle of the living room, "mother naked—obviously sick, and obviously he had been shot full of painkillers." He began to rant, his arms flailing. Lady Bird was attempting to soothe him, and to get him dressed for the speech, but with little result. "I was aghast," Bolton recalls. "I was scared half silly." During the few minutes before Lady Bird shooed the speechwriter out, Johnson kept saying he was determined to give the speech, but Bolton remembers that he did not believe that was possible. The speechwriter drove to Wooldridge

Park "very much in a turmoil." But then, right on schedule, Lyndon John-son's car pulled up to the park and the Congressman got out. As he waved to supporters and told Lady Bird to go up on the stage ahead of him, he was poised, smiling, "all dressed up," Bolton recalls, "in his well-tailored clothes, looked like he was feeling beautiful." He didn't merely walk onto the stage, which had been cleared of everybody except his wife and his mother (both dressed completely in white); he ran out onto it, "head thrown back," Bolton recalls, "hands in the air," flung his Stetson into the crowd with a carefree, sweeping gesture; "he was a great figure of a triumphant warrior going to war."

The speech itself, broadcast over a twenty-station network, repeated themes ("Peace, Preparedness and Progress") familiar to Johnson's sup-porters. Its tone was militaristic. "Preparedness" is the only weapon with which to halt the "surging blood-red tide of Communism," he said. "Only the narrow straits of the Bering Sea separate Alaska from the menace of Eurasia, and in frozen winters a man can walk those straits. Moscow is only eighteen hours in the air from Detroit. . . ." America "must not surrender to the barbaric hordes of godless men in Eurasia. . . . We must stand up to the war-makers and say, this far and no farther." On civil rights, he attacked President Truman's attempts to create an FEPC ("be-cause if a man can tell you whom you must hire, he can tell you whom you cannot employ"), and to end the poll tax (because "it is the province of the state to run its own elections"). He was against proposed laws against lynching "because the federal government has no more business enacting a law against one form of murder than against another." As in 1941, he was trying to act statesmanlike and senatorial, which meant that he bellowed the speech. But after he finished, he shook hands with the audience—and didn't leave until he had shaken every hand offered.

Bolton's astonishment at Johnson's performance was no greater than that of Dr. Morgan, who was to say later that he had given Johnson "several shots of pain killer [probably morphine] that day and that he didn't know how in the world a man could keep functioning in the pain that he was in from a kidney stone." During the night following the speech, Johnson's condition did not improve. But he was scheduled to leave his house at seven a.m. for a four-day campaign swing through the Panhandle. It was a vital trip; the Panhandle was the first area targeted in the campaign because he was so little known there, and no time could be lost in trying to make a dent in Stevenson's support there. And tied into the tour was an event—still secret—which Johnson believed would dramatize what he could do for Texas as a Senator. Midway in his tour of the Panhandle, he was to break off for a trip to Dallas. There he would meet Air Force Secretary Symington, and following the meeting he would return to Wichita Falls to make a dramatic announcement: that city's Morris Sheppard Air Force Base, whose closing had been scheduled, would remain open. Symington was flying to Dallas just to meet personally with Johnson, so that the Congressman could say that he had, in the meeting, persuaded the Secretary to reverse the previous decision and keep the base open. If Johnson couldn't be there, the announcement would lose much of its drama. At seven a.m. Sunday, Johnson was at the front door of his house, waiting to go.

Sunday was a long day. From Austin the candidate, accompanied by speechwriter Bolton and twenty-five-year-old war veteran Warren Woodward, Johnson's adoring congressional aide, flew north to San Angelo and then on to Abilene and Lubbock, rushing to the telephone in each airport to call the local newspaper publisher and influential supporters; arriving that evening in Amarillo, he first gave a speech over the local radio station and then held a series of meetings with his press supporters and the key oilmen there.

Because Woodward was going to be Johnson's personal attendant, John Connally had been unable to avoid giving him some details of the candidate's physical condition, although, following Johnson's injunction to secrecy, he had told him as little as possible, and had certainly given the young ex-pilot no inkling of the possible seriousness of Johnson's illness.

Prepared or not, however, Woodward soon knew that something was very wrong—and rapidly getting worse. By the time they arrived in Amarillo that first evening, he recalls, "I noticed him beginning to perspire and look feverish. It was obvious that he was getting progressively more uncomfortable." He gave him the pills Dr. Morgan had sent along, and aspirin, and "he just kept going."

Monday and Tuesday were worse. The periodic waves of agonizing pain, which might last an hour or more, had begun radiating now from the back around into the groin, and then, finally, down into the testicles, a signal that a stone has passed from the kidney into the ureter, the narrow tube that connects the kidney to the bladder. Johnson's fever, moreover, was obviously climbing; by noon on Monday, Woodward was worried "about having enough shirts"; Johnson's face seemed constantly covered "with beads of perspiration." Although he always perspired profusely, this was especially dramatic; Woodward gave the candidate a new shirt at every opportunity—six or seven a day—but they seemed to be soaked through almost as soon as Johnson put them on. Choking down even a few mouthfuls of food grew harder and harder, and finally he gave up trying to eat.

But he didn't give up campaigning. He could get relief from the pain by lying down; the moment he stood up, it got worse. On Monday and Tuesday, however, not only did Lyndon Johnson drive hundreds of miles

between the small cities in the Panhandle—Borger and Pampa and Mo-
heetie and Floydada—in which campaign appearances had been scheduled, he walked the streets for hours shaking hands, and made speech
after speech to Chambers of Commerce and service clubs. On Tuesday,
the candidate's fever was clearly higher. The terrible cramps grew so bad
that sometimes in the privacy of a car or in a bathroom, he would double
over, clutching his groin and gasping for breath. But that was only in
private. In public, on speakers' platforms or on the streets of a town
shaking hands, voters might have noticed that the candidate was sweating
a lot, but the only expression they saw on his face was a smile, and his
handshake was as firm and friendly as ever. Tuesday was a very long day.
Johnson's first appearance was at six a.m., and at eleven o'clock that night
he was still shaking hands. And from the beginning of that day to the
end, Lyndon Johnson never left a room until the last hand in it had been
shaken. He cut not a single line out of a speech. The "unbearable" pain
was being borne. Somehow, Warren Woodward says, "he got through
those days."

All this time, of course, the young aide was first suggesting and then
begging his Chief to see a doctor. "It was perfectly obvious that he was
getting more sick as those days went on, and as I look back on it now, it
was because this stone was not passing and it was throwing more poison
into his system," he says. Each suggestion was rejected. "It never entered
his mind that he wasn't going to pass this stone," Woodward says. "Therefore he felt it was a personal trial of his; he just had to tough it out until
that stone passed. So all we could do for him was try to keep his fever
down by aspirin and maybe some medicine for pain. That was it, and the
rest was up to him. And that was his mood. . . ." Johnson ordered Woodward not to tell anyone at campaign headquarters back in Austin that he
was sick, just to say he was fine.

Tuesday night, however, was, in Woodward's phrase, "a wild night."
At about eleven o'clock, Johnson, together with his two aides, boarded
a Pullman for the three-hundred-mile trip to Dallas and his meeting the
next afternoon with Symington. Bolton disembarked midway on the trip,
in Wichita Falls, to prepare for Johnson's return there the next night,
when he was to give the speech announcing that the Sheppard Air Force
Base would remain open. Woodward's lower berth was directly across
from Johnson's, and Woody didn't get much sleep. By this time, his temperature soaring, Johnson was suffering alternately from what Bolton says
were "the most severe fever and chills I had ever seen," and throughout
the night Johnson would shout across the aisle: "Woody!" Jumping up,
in his pajamas, Woodward would cross the aisle, and open the drapes
curtaining off Johnson's berth. "Get this window open!" Johnson would
say, and Woodward would see that sweat was pouring off him from his

fever. "Finally," Woodward recalls, "the fever would pass and he'd maybe doze off for a little bit." Woodward would close the window. Then a chill would come. The chills were very bad. "He was just shaking uncontrollably." Woodward got the porter to collect all his spare blankets and pile them on Johnson, but they didn't help. "I'm freezing, Woody! I'm freezing!" Johnson would cry. He asked Woodward to get into bed with him, and Woodward did, and wrapped his arms around him "to try to give some heat from my body over to his and try to keep him warm." Then "when he would start the perspiring period," Johnson would order Woody, "Get this window open!" and then, after a while, shaking and shivering with cold again, he would order Woody to get back into his berth and hug him again. Sometimes Johnson would doze, and Woodward would return to his own berth, but he never got more than a few minutes' rest before Johnson's voice would be shouting "Woody!" across the aisle.

The next morning at nine, when the train arrived in Dallas' Union Terminal, Woodward, absolutely alone now with a desperately ill candidate (and alone also, since Bolton was back in Wichita Falls, with the knowledge of the severity of the illness), managed to get Johnson dressed and over to their suite at the Baker Hotel, where the Congressman went to bed. He asked Johnson if he could summon a doctor, or at least telephone headquarters back in Austin and tell them what was happening. "He said no, that he was still determined that the stone was going to pass." For some hours, Johnson lay in bed, "literally just racked with fever and chills." Although he had not eaten for almost three days, he had no appetite; Woodward tried to get him to eat, but Johnson couldn't; when he tried, he would have vomited, Woodward explains, "but there was no food in him, so he only gagged." Occasionally, he would groan. By this time, Woodward was convinced that Johnson could not possibly get back on a train, return to Wichita Falls and make the scheduled speech. He asked whether he could at least telephone Bolton in Wichita Falls and tell him to cancel the speech, but Johnson, he recalls, "continued to believe" he would be able to make the speech, and refused to listen to any suggestion that he wouldn't. "He was going to Wichita Falls with an important message. The Air Force base was going to be kept open. There just wasn't any way he was going to miss this opportunity." Johnson was, in Woodward's careful words, "getting a little more irritable about this time." Woodward did not telephone anyone. But by the afternoon, Woodward could not bear it any longer. He felt that if Symington knew the situation, he could persuade Johnson at least to get some medical assistance. "You have to remember I was a First Lieutenant, and this was the Secretary of the Air Force, but I screwed up my courage."

When the front desk telephoned to say that Symington was on his way up, Woodward gave Johnson a new shirt, and met Symington and

General Robert J. Smith at the door, and, in the few moments before Johnson dressed and appeared, "poured out my problems to them. I told them, 'I'm not able to convince him that we should get a doctor. He is a very sick man, and he'll probably fire me for telling you this, but I'm here by myself, and I've just got to turn to someone, because I know when I see a sick man, and this is a very sick man. Yet he's determined to go to Wichita Falls. He's determined to have this conference with you, Secretary Symington. And I don't know what to do.' "

Had Woodward not told the two visitors that Johnson was sick, they would never have known. When the young aide finished whispering to them, he called, "Congressman, they're here now." The door to the bedroom opened, and there was Lyndon Johnson, beaming at his visitors. "He pulled the door open and sprang out with all the energy and vitality just as if nothing was wrong," Woodward recalls. "Full of energy! Ready to go! My God! *Will!*" Sitting down with Symington and Smith, Johnson "conducted the conference and they worked out all the arrangements." And, Woodward is convinced, Johnson would not have said a word to the two men about his physical condition had not Symington, in a diplomatic way, "after the business was over, got the conversation around to his health obliquely: 'How are you feeling, Lyndon?' " Gradually, some of the truth emerged.

Even then the job of persuading Johnson to obtain medical assistance had to proceed by slow degrees. For some time the candidate flatly rejected his visitors' urgings that he see a doctor, insisting he didn't need one. But the longer he sat talking, the harder it became for him to conceal his pain, and he began to shiver uncontrollably. Even then, he would not agree to be examined by a doctor, but only to talk to one over the telephone; he allowed General Smith to telephone a Dallas urologist with whom he was acquainted to discuss the situation and ask if something could be prescribed to make Johnson feel better. The urologist, R. F. Van Duzen, refused to prescribe without examining the patient, and Johnson, by now trembling and barely able to hold himself upright in his chair, finally agreed to an examination. Arriving at the suite, Dr. Van Duzen, Woodward says, "took one look at him, and said, 'This is a sick man, a very sick man, and he needs to be in the hospital.' "

Recalls Woodward: "The Congressman just said no, he wasn't going to have anything to do with this at all and he wasn't going to go. Finally, [Symington] talked him into doing this. Finally, he consented to going. . . ."

But only for tests, and only for a few hours. "He envisioned it— 'Maybe I'll get a shot and a couple of pills.' He didn't view it in the light [that he would have to stay in the hospital longer than a few hours]. That was the only reason he agreed to go." And only under what Woodward describes as "great-secret conditions." Johnson authorized Woodward to telephone Bolton and order the speechwriter to deliver the speech he had written himself—but not to hint at the real reason for Johnson's absence; Bolton was to announce that the candidate had been flying to Wichita Falls but had been delayed by bad weather. No one but Bolton was to be told *anything*, Johnson told Woodward. *No one!* Not his wife, not his campaign headquarters, not Alvin Wirtz, not John Connally—no one was to know that he was in a hospital. As for the hospital staff, of course, they were not to be told the identity of their new patient.

By the time he arrived at the hospital, however, Johnson was doubled over in agony, gasping for breath, retching and gagging, unable to stand for more than a few moments at a time. His temperature was over 104 degrees. As attendants dressed him in a hospital gown and placed him in a wheelchair, he heard Dr. Van Duzen say he would have to remain in the hospital overnight, but he did not protest as he was wheeled down a corridor to a laboratory for tests. When the tests were completed, and he was being wheeled to his room, he vomited—over himself and an orderly and a nurse.

(A few minutes later, there was a poignant postscript. As Johnson had entered the hospital, he had said to Woodward, "Don't leave me, Woody." The faithful Woodward stayed at his side—except as Johnson was being wheeled to his room. A nurse had insisted that Woodward fill out the admittance forms, and Woodward had stopped—"maybe as long as five minutes"—to do so. But it was during those five minutes that Johnson vomited. When Woodward reached him, Johnson said, "Woody, don't *ever* do that to me again!" The astonished Woodward didn't know what he had done. "You left me," Johnson said. When Woodward tried to explain that the nurse had insisted he fill out the forms, Johnson said, "I don't care. You don't work for her, you work for me. You stay with me. I called you and you weren't there. I don't want you to leave me. Don't leave me when I need you." Thirty-six years later, when Woodward was being interviewed, he was still laboriously trying to excuse his lapse: "He didn't really need me. He had thrown up and soiled himself, and it was a sort of messy situation, but he had orderlies and nurses and all sorts of people to handle it, and he was well cared for. I was maybe gone as long as five minutes. It was indicative of the fact that he didn't like to be left alone. . . .")

Woodward saw that keeping Johnson's identity from the hospital staff was impossible. A small crowd of nurses, orderlies and doctors had been following his wheelchair down the hall "because they knew Congressman Johnson, knew who he was. . . ." Word was bound to leak to the outside world. Johnson was insisting he would be in the hospital only overnight. "I'll pass it, I'll pass it," he kept saying. "I'll be out of here in the morning." But even if he was there only overnight, didn't headquarters have to be told? Woodward asked Johnson if he could call Connally now, and Johnson said he could. But he told Woodward to tell Connally he was not to inform anyone else:

> Tell him not to release it to the press, that I'm just going to be here overnight and they just want to run some tests. Just tell him not to say anything to the press about it. I'll pass this stone during the night. I am reaching the point, sort of the crisis, and I'll pass this stone and I'll be out tomorrow. We'll pick up the schedule. You tell John that.

FEARING THAT the conversation might be overheard by the hospital's switchboard operator if Woodward were to make the call from his room, Johnson told him to make it from an outside phone. Woodward did—from a nearby drugstore. Connally said one thing that gave Woodward a sense of relief: Mrs. Johnson would be on the next plane to Dallas. The youthful aide realized that when she arrived the load of responsibility that he had been carrying alone would be shifted to Lady Bird's shoulders. But when Connally heard of Johnson's prohibition against telling the press his whereabouts, he said, "That's just ridiculous." Woodward returned to the hospital to tell Johnson that Connally said there was no choice but to tell the press, that "he thinks you can't have a candidate for the United States Senate and a Congressman in a hospital in downtown Dallas," canceling speeches and interrupting the campaign schedule, without reporters finding out about it.

By this time, Woodward was to recall, Johnson "really was not in complete control of his thinking. . . . There was an element of delirium from this high fever that he had. . . ." He told Woodward to tell Connally to do as he had been told: "You just tell him that I *order!*" But when Woodward made this call, Connally said, "Well, it's too late; I've already done it." Reporters had begun calling headquarters to ask why Johnson was canceling the Wichita Falls speech that evening, Connally said, and he felt he had no choice but to give the true reason, since they were sure to find it out anyway.

Woodward had expected Johnson to explode over this news, but when Johnson heard it, "a sort of calmness came over him and a sort of resignation." He said, "Well, I guess I might as well withdraw. Get your notebook." Dictating a statement irrevocably withdrawing from the campaign, he told Woodward to telephone Dallas newspapers immediately, and read it to them. "Do it right now," he said. "I'm out of this."

The young man didn't know what to do. He felt his Chief was in no condition to make a decision which might well end his entire political career, but he knew he could not make Johnson change his mind. "I'd learned not to argue with him," he says. And Johnson's tone had been very firm. "He was out. He had made a decision." When Woodward nonetheless screwed up his courage and tried to suggest that Johnson wait a bit, Johnson said angrily: "Do it right now." Recalls Woodward: "He was very, very firm in telling me to do it right that moment."

Years later, Woodward would say, "Can you imagine what would have happened if I had done that? The whole course of history—we might not even have had Vietnam or the Great Society." But, he would say,, "Every now and then the Lord takes care of you. God protects us kids." As he was walking out of the hospital room to carry out Johnson's orders, Woodward thought of something he could say to persuade Johnson to delay issuing the withdrawal statement—perhaps the only thing he could have said that would have persuaded Johnson to delay—and instead of leaving the room, he said it, and in so doing performed what was perhaps the greatest service that the devoted young man was ever to render to his leader, although he was to be associated with him for another twenty years. He said: "Why don't you wait until Mrs. Johnson gets here."

"THAT BOUGHT SOME TIME," Woodward recalls. "I told him that she was in the air right that minute, flying up to Dallas, and that it was in fact time for me to go out to meet her. I said, 'Let's go ahead and make the announcement, but let's do it after she gets here. She would want to be here when you do it.' . . . That, in his fevered condition, seemed to ring a bell with him." Johnson told Woodward to pick Lady Bird up; "then we'll call the press in and we'll announce this thing together."

On his way to the airport, Woodward did something else of which he was to be proud. "Halfway out to the airport," he recalls, "I suddenly said, 'Oh, my God! If some reporter calls him, he'll probably tell him he's withdrawing, and everything will be all over.' I stopped the car, and ran into some store and called back to the hospital and I got the [nurses'] supervisor and I told her, 'Absolutely no calls! Absolutely no visitors!' Under no circumstances was he to have any phone calls put through to his room or any visitors of any kind until Mrs. Johnson got there. I said he needed his rest. I said, 'He is to be isolated. No one is to see him or talk to him.' And, you know, I put the stopper in the basin just in time, because sure enough the phone calls began to come in while I was at the airport, but no one was put through to him."

And when Lady Bird arrived, all at once many of the problems seemed to vanish. "I had not had any sleep, I was about at the end of my line, and I was never so glad in my life to see anyone as I was [to see]

Mrs. Johnson," Woodward says. On the way to the hospital, he explained the situation. She didn't say much, but "she was calm and understanding and seemed to know exactly what to do." As soon as they walked into her husband's room, "she took over very completely." When Woodward slipped out, she was talking to Johnson "soothingly and quietly." Woodward could see that "he felt reassured having her there." And when, some time later, Woodward re-entered the room, "somehow or other the notion of withdrawing from the race seemed to kind of fade into the background. . . ."

In fact, what was on the Congressman's mind now was not withdrawal but food. The bed rest—and a massive shot of morphine—had made him feel better, and, with the hospital's kitchens already closed, he told Woodward, "Get me something to eat." When Woodward returned with a warm "Dutch oven" from the hotel, he found that the Congressman was in some respects very much back to normal. Woodward had brought a big helping of bacon and eggs, and, he recalls, "it looked like a feast to me; I couldn't remember when I had eaten last." But Johnson, sitting up with the tray on his lap, looked up at him and said, "Well, you've done it again." Woodward couldn't see anything wrong.

"Now, Woody," his Chief said, "*Why? WHY?????* Is this the way you want to do things all your life?"

"What's wrong?" Woodward said.

"There's no salt and pepper."

THE NEXT MORNING, the stone still had not passed. Johnson's fever was up again. And reports of his hospitalization were in the Dallas newspapers, and Johnson had seen them, and, in Woodward's careful phrase, "he was concerned about that." Finding that there had been little if any change in the position of the stone during the night, Dr. Van Duzen was saying that an immediate operation—the operation that would mean the end of the campaign, and perhaps of his career—was imperative.

During the morning, however, Woodward took a call in Johnson's hospital room from Jacqueline Cochran. The famous aviatrix had flown to Dallas in her twin-engined Lockheed Electra to hear Symington speak at a meeting of the Air Force Association, and she had learned from him of Johnson's illness. In her brusque manner, she said that a friend, Dr. Gershom J. Thompson, was the chief urologist at the Mayo Clinic in Rochester, Minnesota; that Dr. Thompson was a world-renowned expert at removing kidney stones through cystoscopic manipulation rather than through operations; and that she was ready to fly Johnson to Rochester that afternoon.

An important consideration to Johnson was that there would be a familiar face at the Mayo Clinic: his personal physician, Dr. James Cain, Alvin Wirtz's son-in-law, was on the clinic's staff. But even that consideration faded before the political: he was afraid that a trip to Minnesota for medical treatment would be taken as a slur on Texas doctors. "I don't want anyone to think that I can't get all the medical attention I need right here in Texas," he said, in Woodward's recollection, and ordered Lady Bird to "call Jackie and tell her no." But after a long conversation between Mrs. Johnson and Miss Cochran, "it was decided" that he would go; "Mrs. Johnson played a large part in that decision." Taken to Love Field in an ambulance, Johnson was placed on a bed that had been made up in Miss Cochran's Electra, and flown to Minnesota. (Although being moved had intensified his pain again, Johnson remained in command of his staff—even if it consisted of only a single aide. During the flight, Miss Cochran came back to check on the patient and told Woodward, who had been chatting with her about the thirty-five missions he had flown over Europe during the war, to sit in her pilot's seat while the co-pilot flew the plane. Johnson, who had been dozing, awoke and saw Woodward sitting in the pilot's seat. Rapping sharply on a table, he got Woodward's attention, and when the young man hurried back, snapped, "Woody, don't we have enough problems without you trying to fly this plane?" and told him to let Miss Cochran do all the flying.)

Hospitalization at Mayo's didn't solve the problem. Dr. Thompson was indeed expert at cystoscopic manipulation—inserting a cystoscope in the penis, running it up through the urethra and the bladder and then into the ureter, and then inserting a nylon loop in the cystoscope and using it to pull out the kidney stone—but only for a stone near the lower end of the ureter. It was general medical practice not to use a cystoscope on kidney stones high up in the ureter because of the danger that the cystoscope would puncture the ureter. And the physicians felt, moreover, there was little chance that the procedure would work in this case. When Johnson explained the necessity in political terms of avoiding surgery, the doctors were sympathetic, but said that in medical terms surgery would shortly be unavoidable. A stone as large as Johnson's appeared to be was probably almost completely obstructing the kidney, and eventually such an obstruction can cause the kidney to stop functioning. In addition, the patient had been running an infection-indicating fever for more than a week, and an infection in the kidney can lead to an abscess and gangrene. The prognosis was rapidly becoming one in which there could be no more waiting; the situation was nearing a stage at which it might be life-threatening. A few more days was the outside limit of the time the doctors felt they could afford to delay. So, for three days, Johnson waited, while doing everything he himself could think of to jar the stone loose: going out in a car, he had Woodward drive him over bumpy roads; in the clinic he walked up and down the stairs; holding on to Woodward for support, he bounced up and down—even jumped up and down—as hard as he could bear to. These exercises produced no result except increased pain and weakness. Says Woodward: "There was no change in his thinking. He was going to pass the stone. He wasn't going to *let* them take it [out] any other way. He was going to pass it, he was going back on the campaign trail."

During the three days, he acted, in fact, as if he was still campaigning. He persuaded the doctors to have three telephones installed in his room, and with the help of Lady Bird and Woodward he worked them constantly, waving nurses impatiently out if he was talking—and, indeed, refusing to stop talking even while a nurse was actually giving him treatment, telephoning not only Wirtz and Clark but supporters all over Texas, trying to convince them that he felt fine, that his physical problems were minor, that they were all but resolved, that he would soon be back on the trail, that in the campaign itself things looked good, that he was pulling up on Ol' Coke, that he was going to win; according to one report, in a single day he made sixty-four such calls.

But the reality was the stone—the stone that wouldn't move. The reality was the pain that morphine only partly dulled, the pain that wouldn't stop, the pain and the weakness. If the stone didn't move, all the telephoning in the world wasn't going to help him—and it wasn't moving.

Finally, on Sunday, May 30, the doctors reluctantly agreed to attempt the cystoscopic manipulation as a last chance—the very last chance—to avoid surgery. Johnson was wheeled away and given a general anesthetic, and for forty-five minutes Mrs. Johnson and Woodward silently paced outside the operating room, lost in thought, she about her husband, Woodward, as he was later to relate, not only about Johnson but about politics, because "the realization was dawning on me by this time that if they were unable to remove the stone this way . . . they would have to operate surgically. And in fact the campaign would be over." The doctors emerged and said that the procedure had been successful—just barely successful. (They said that "Had it been lodged any further up, they wouldn't have been able to do it.") According to one report, no kidney stone as high in the ureter as Johnson's had previously been removed at the Mayo Clinic. With the stone gone, Johnson's recovery should be rapid, they said, and Johnson could return to the campaign in a week.

HE WOULD RETURN to the campaign, of course, with almost two weeks lost. When he had begun the campaign, he had had nine weeks before the first primary, a terribly short time to make up ground on Coke Stevenson. Now he had only seven.

And he had made up little ground, if any. The news he was receiving in the hospital was not good. In the first place, there wasn't very much of it. His staff at his campaign headquarters in the Hancock House in Austin was sending him all the newspaper clippings on the race, but on June 1st, campaign assistant Roy Wade was forced to report, "I have no clippings. There were none in the Texas press today," and Wade's June 2nd letter began: "Again, very little news."

Even worse, there had been little shift during the week Johnson had campaigned before he entered the hospital. The last Belden Poll released—on May 16—before the campaign kick-off in Wooldridge Park had stated that Stevenson was the choice of 64 percent of the state's voters; Johnson had 28 percent. Private polls taken now showed no significant change in those figures. The Wooldridge Park speech had made little impact, nor had the series of talks he had given in the Panhandle; all the pain he had endured on the Panhandle trip had resulted in virtually no narrowing of the margin there, Johnson's polls showed. "Peace, Preparedness and Progress" wasn't working.

But Stevenson's campaign was. The former Governor was driving from one small town to another, accompanied only by Murphey and, occasionally, a public relations man, Booth Mooney. Arriving at each town, often unannounced, he would introduce himself to people on the main street or in the Courthouse Square, chat with them, ask them if they had any questions he could answer and, if they did, stop and answer them. He told the people he met that he would say a few words before he left, and in every brief talk ("I've never been very strong on making political orations. I'd much rather listen to you"), he repeated that if they sent him to Washington, he would do as he had done in the past: uphold constitutional government; make sure that America remained strong enough to be secure against Communism; oppose extending federal controls over individuals and businesses; encourage free enterprise and "economy" in government. "You know what I did in Austin to keep your state taxes down"; in Washington, too, he would try to eliminate "waste" and "extravagance." There was no news in such a campaign, of course; newspapers, as one Texas historian points out, "could give no account of the various conversations into which the candidate entered daily with the hundreds of people whose hands he shook as he introduced himself. . . . The Stevenson campaign dropped from sight. . . ." The meager newspaper coverage it attracted was couched in the mocking tone customary when "sophisticated" journalists discussed the Stevenson campaign style. "Candidate Stevenson was in Tyler Saturday, according to a message from his press agent," one reporter wrote, alluding to the fact that the press was not quite certain of his whereabouts. But Johnson, who knew small towns, was more aware than reporters of the effectiveness of Stevenson's quiet handshaking. And the former Governor had been out shaking hands all the time Johnson was lying there in Minnesota.

Then, on June 1, Stevenson made a radio speech, his first of the campaign, and Johnson was able to pick it up in his room at the Mayo Clinic. Without mentioning Johnson by name, Stevenson discussed the Congressman's references to "the barbaric hordes of godless men in Eurasia."

"There are men in this nation today who go about over the country as apostles of fear," Stevenson said. "They tell us another war is just around the corner. They are prophets of doom, howlers of calamity. We must—they tell us—be afraid." Such men, Stevenson said, were trying to manufacture an "emergency" based on fear. Such hysteria was not necessary. America must build up its defenses, he said; it must help Europe rebuild from the effects of the war because a rebuilt Europe would be a bastion against "economic and propaganda assaults" from Russia, and America must always be vigilant. But, he said, America should not get hysterical about a Red menace. "We can be vigilant without being frightened." And, Stevenson said, "I don't believe you are afraid. We are descendants of men and women who have fought and won both the battles of war and the battle of peace."

Part of Johnson's reaction to that calm, sincere voice which he knew was so effective with voters was rage; his harassment of nurses increased in intensity and he brought up the withdrawal statement with Woody. "I know you didn't send that," Johnson snarled at him. "And I won't forget." Part was something else, particularly after Woody had been sent back to Houston to make preparations for a speech that Johnson was planning to give there following his release from the hospital. With his departure, there was no longer a need for Johnson to keep up a front of optimism. All Mrs. Johnson will say of this week was: "He was depressed, and it was bad."

But there was no way out now. The deadline for filing for election to his congressional seat had passed, and he had not filed. He had burned his bridges. It was going to be the Senate, or nothing. "I just could not bear," he later recalled, "the thought of losing everything." But he *was* losing everything.

11

The Flying Windmill

OUT OF HIS DESPAIR, he emerged with a new strategy. It was unveiled in the first speech he made after returning to Texas, an address over a state-wide radio network that was delivered from a studio at a Houston radio station instead of in Hermann Park, customary site of political rallies, "because he had been out of circulation" and his advisers felt there was now so little interest in his candidacy that attracting a crowd would be impossible and a rally in the park only an embarrassment; in fact, Woodward had to "work like a dog" even to get fifty or so people to the studio. (One of them, invited to fill out the crowd, was Woodward's mother.)

It was very different from Johnson's earlier speeches. Previously, he and his advisers had agreed that attacking Stevenson personally would be a mistake. Because of the respect, indeed, almost reverence, in which the former Governor was held, such attacks had always boomeranged in the past. But now, in desperation, he attacked. Stevenson had said he opposed a Truman plan to provide federal aid to raise teachers' salaries because of provisions which Stevenson feared would increase federal control of schools. On this stance, popular in Texas, Stevenson could not be criticized, but Johnson used Stevenson's statement to bring in another issue, so that he could criticize the ex-Governor on *that* one. "While I was sick at Mayo's," Lyndon Johnson said, "a calculating, do-nothing, fence-straddling opponent of mine, who three months ago said he had no platform, got off the fence for the first time to oppose the teacher salary increase. I challenge my calculating opponent to tell Texans tomorrow if he favors withdrawing federal aid from five hundred thousand world-war veterans, men who did not sit at home when Old Glory had to be carried to every corner of the globe."

Two aspects of Johnson's attack were significant. First, its implication—that Stevenson might be opposed to federal aid for veterans—was totally false. As Johnson was well aware, Stevenson was in favor of such aid, and indeed had already proposed that it be increased. Equally significant were the words in which the attack was couched: "calculating, donothing, fence-straddling"—and, as the speech went on, with Johnson elaborating on his falsification of Stevenson's record, he referred to him directly: "Mr. Calculator," "Mr. Do-Nothinger," "Mr. Straddler."

Johnson's advisers were appalled. "Taking on Coke Stevenson was a very tricky thing to do," Jake Pickle recalls. "He was very popular." When, in dismay, local Johnson managers throughout the state contacted Claude C. Wild, a veteran Texas politician who had been given the largely honorary title of campaign manager, Wild assured them there would be no repetition. But Wild was wrong. By the end of the week, Johnson was attacking "Mr. Fence-Straddler's" courage. "A man ought to have the courage to stand up and say what he believes in," he said. Then he orchestrated attacks on Stevenson's honesty, having allies charge that the former Governor had pardoned a record number of criminals. Johnson had hoped this charge would be effective with voters who remembered that alleged sales of pardons by a previous Governor, Jim Ferguson, had become an accepted part of Texas political folklore. The Johnson camp said that the proof of the charge lay in the record number of pardons Stevenson had issued. Stevenson refused to reply to the charge, but state prison officials, queried by reporters, explained that the Johnson number had been arrived at by lumping together with true pardons two- or three-day passes given to convicts to attend the funerals of family members or to visit sick relatives—and pardons faded away as a campaign issue. Then Johnson circulated charges of corruption in an option that the Magnolia Petroleum Company had purchased to test for oil on land Stevenson owned. Stevenson refused to reply to this charge, either; surrounded in Austin by reporters asking for an answer, he said he would not attempt to defend his honesty, "as my private life is an open book and my record of public service is too well known to the people of Texas to require repetition. . . . If my record does not warrant my election to the Senate then I ought to stay at home. The people know enough to make their own choice." At the annual dinner of the Austin press corps, however, Stuart Long, one of Johnson's allies among the journalists, shouted a question at Stevenson about the Magnolia option while he was speaking, and Stevenson lost his temper. Turning to Long, his face set in the "stone stare," his voice so low it could hardly be heard, he explained the circumstances of the lease. Since everything said at the dinner was off the record, his reply was not preserved, and the details are not remembered. But reporters who were there—even Johnson supporters—remember how ashamed Long looked when he sat down. "Well," he whispered to Horace Busby, "I guess I was sure wrong about that." And that issue, too, thereupon dropped out of the campaign. But Johnson simply continued trying other "issues" that were nothing more than attacks on Stevenson's integrity. Coke Stevenson's strongest point was his reputation. Lyndon Johnson had decided his only hope was to destroy it.

TOGETHER WITH THE NEW STRATEGY came a new weapon.

It was a helicopter.

Despite their use in the war, helicopters were still almost unknown in civilian life; so far as Johnson could ascertain, no candidate had ever campaigned for political office in one. But some months earlier, Woodward, familiar with them from his Air Force service, had suggested that Johnson do so, because its use would ease one of the greatest difficulties in campaigning across a state eight hundred miles long and almost eight hundred miles wide, in which half the voters still lived in small towns to which roads were often inadequate and which were so far apart that much of any campaign was wasted in traveling between them. Attending a demonstration in Washington staged for congressmen by the Bell Helicopter Corporation, Johnson had perceived an additional advantage. Few Texans had ever seen one of these strange-looking aircraft; its arrival in a small town would be an event. Drawing crowds to campaign speeches was extremely difficult in Texas not only because of the people's distrust of politicians but because of the long distances they had to travel to reach a "speaking" and because the time these trips took was too precious to farmers and ranchers to be wasted. Politicians had tried everything from barbecues and watermelon feasts to a special train chartered by one candidate to haul voters to a speech from all across the state, but the only attraction that had ever worked had been Pappy O'Daniel's famous hillbilly band. Maybe, Johnson felt, a helicopter could be a drawing card for him the way the Hillbilly Boys had been for Pappy. Returning from the demonstration, he had told Warren Woodward: "Woody, that's the best idea I've ever heard!"

As Johnson had weighed the idea, however, he had come to feel that its advantages were outweighed by its drawbacks. The logistical difficulties of keeping an aircraft in operation over so vast an area were formidable. Most of this early generation of helicopters could carry fuel enough for only about 150 miles of flight, which would necessitate several refuelings every day. Helicopters could use only ninety-octane gas; some airports stocked it, some didn't—and most Texas towns didn't have an airport anyway. The helicopter would therefore have to be refueled from trucks, which would carry the gas in fifty-gallon drums. If the helicopter missed its connection with a truck, it would be forced down: the candidate could find himself stranded in a town or a field, an object of ridicule in the press—ridicule that could be fatal to a candidacy.

Fuel was only part of the problem. It was unusual for helicopters to be in the air more than an hour or two a day, and campaigning obviously demanded far more daily flying time. Not only fuel trucks but a mechanic would have to follow the craft back and forth across Texas in case it broke down. And what if it broke down and couldn't be repaired? What if, in some remote part of Texas, a needed replacement part wasn't available? That, too, could strand a candidate. Each night the helicopter would require servicing, and then would have to be guarded against curious people wanting to handle its valves or rotors. And the crowds attracted to hear the candidate speak would be attracted not to a courthouse or a schoolhouse but to an open area; explains Woodward: "If you are going to land in a field, there's no electrical sockets out there and you had to find some way to get your sound system wired in. . . ." So many things could go wrong in the daily hurly-burly of even a traditional campaign; why add to the normal difficulties the problems of traveling in a still largely unfamiliar form of transportation?

Safety factors had been the decisive consideration. Since the idea was to attract people, landings would have to be in or near populated areas; people unfamiliar with a helicopter might stray into its path or, once it had landed, might wander into the whirl of its rotor blades and be injured or killed. "CANDIDATE'S HELICOPTER KILLS FARMER"—that would be the end of the candidate's hopes. It was fine to say that the landing area would be roped off and guarded, but among the crowd would be children—how could you be sure that a child might not dart out between the guards and be injured? As more and more such problems presented themselves to his imagination, Lyndon Johnson had decided that using a helicopter was simply too risky a gamble. But things had changed. Now he was losing—losing everything. He took the gamble. On June 10, a big four-passenger blue-and-white Sikorsky S-51, sixty feet long and with three twenty-four-foot-long blades on its main rotor, piloted by James E. Chudars, an Air Force veteran who was one of the few pilots with substantial helicopter flying time, and carrying an ace mechanic, Harry Nachlin, left the Sikorsky Aircraft plant in Bridgeport, Connecticut, and headed southwest. Cruising at about ninety miles an hour, it arrived at Love Field in Dallas three days later. The next day, a public address system was installed in the baggage compartment behind the seats, a large speaker was lashed to one of the landing gear struts, "Lyndon Johnson for U.S. Senator" was painted on both sides, and the day after that, Chudars' passenger arrived for a test flight. Chudars noticed that Johnson seemed to have remarkably little interest in the machine to which he was going to be entrusting his life. When they were up in the air, what Johnson was watching was not the control panel but the faces of people on the ground. He was watching to see if their faces lifted to look at the helicopter.

And they did.

THE WEEK before the helicopter arrived had been a bad week, one of the worst, his aides say, in Lyndon Johnson's political life. His attacks on Stevenson had dismayed many of his advisers, and, even worse, had failed to arouse interest among voters. Stevenson was shrugging off the attacks, and so was the press. The press was, in fact, less and less interested in the senatorial race. On June 13, Margaret Mayer, of the *Austin American-Statesman*, reported that with only six weeks to go, voters were still reacting to the candidates' efforts with "a withering lack of enthusiasm." Johnson's announcement during that week that he would be "the first candidate to use a helicopter in political history" (to defuse the issue of its cost, he said that it, and its pilot, had been chartered and donated to his campaign by a group of "107 Dallas war veterans") had been greeted with misgivings from most of his staff, and with lack of interest in the press—except for occasional bursts of ridicule: a typical headline on a typically brief article about the announcement said: "JOHNSON TO GIVE 'EM PIE FROM THE SKY." Under the headline "LOOKEE, MAW—THAR'S THAT CONGRESSMAN," a *Houston Post* article said: "Asked what would happen if the sudden arrival of the helicopter stampeded some neighbor's cows through his kitchen, a spokesman for Johnson's headquarters said after a moment's thought, 'no comment.' " Peddy said only, "I hope he doesn't get hurt and have to go back in the hospital." This reaction, however, demonstrated only that in politics as in other fields, a revolutionary innovation may not be immediately recognized as the stroke of genius it is.

On June 15, the Tuesday following his brief test flight, Johnson took off at dawn, flying east out of Dallas. At his first stop, in Terrell, the landing site that had been selected by the advance man was a baseball diamond so far outside town that the crowd was small. Johnson, recalls Busby, "just *flogged* the man with his tongue." But at the next town to the east, Canton, the site was a vacant lot adjacent to the Courthouse Square, and the crowd was better—and at the next, Lindale, over in East Texas now, Johnson told Chudars to try circling over the little town several times before landing. As the pilot did so, and the roar of the helicopter's Pratt & Whitney 985 engine filled Lindale's streets, people poured out of their houses and stores, staring up at the sky. Then, when Chudars was over the Lindale High School football field, Johnson told him not to descend immediately, but to hover above the field, holding the helicopter as stationary as possible, so that people would realize where he was going to land. And as the helicopter finally settled gently down, Lyndon Johnson could see latecomers running through the streets to see it at close range.

Wednesday morning's newspapers carried stories about the senatorial candidate who, as one paper put it, was "flitting around in a strange sort of flying machine" that could go straight up and down and stand still in mid-air and that looked like a "flying windmill" (because of its tail rotor with its three four-and-one-half-foot-long blades), and there had been time now to place spot announcements on local radio stations. The word was also being spread by telephone, as East Texans who had seen the helicopter on the first day called relatives and friends in towns Johnson was to visit Wednesday to tell them not to miss it. All that day, Lyndon Johnson flew back and forth near the Louisiana border, over the thick pine forests that covered the rolling hills of the East Texas counties of Upshur, Cass, Lamar and Marion, before heading off to Texarkana, at the northeasternmost corner of the state. When he passed over a town too small to merit a landing, the helicopter would hover over its main street while he shouted down through the loudspeaker, relying on notes from his advance men, "This is Lyndon Johnson, your candidate for United States Senator. How's the gang at Morgan's Drugstore?" or "Give my regards to Will Overton." And as he neared a town where a landing was scheduled, he could see below him not only people running through the streets toward the landing site, but, in the countryside outside the town, plumes of dust moving along the dirt roads. Farmers had loaded their wives and children into their cars and were racing to see the helicopter land.

By Thursday, the Associated Press had given the helicopter a name, "The Johnson City Windmill," and the Windmill was flying west, leaving the pine forests behind as the land below changed into blackland prairie; for hours, Chudars and Johnson flew along the broad Red River Valley on the state's northern border, hovering over some towns while Johnson shouted down from the air, and at intervals cutting south to land for speeches in Omaha, Mount Pleasant, Mount Vernon, Bogota, New Boston, Clarksville and Detroit. The last stop of the day was Paris, in Texas terms not a town but a small city, with its twenty-four thousand residents. The streets of Paris, laid out following a fire that had all but leveled the city in 1916, were unusually wide. Wide as they were, however, as the Johnson City Windmill settled to its landing, they were jammed, not only the sidewalks but the streets themselves, with people waiting to see it. That evening, Johnson gave a radio speech from a Paris station. Afterward, back in his hotel room, he made his nightly telephone call to his headquarters at the Hancock House. Claude Wild had something to tell him. All that day, telephone calls had been pouring in from mayors and other public officials not only in East and Northeast Texas but all across the state, requesting that the itinerary for the "Flying Windmill" include their town. Communities that generally had little interest in a visit from a politician were asking—in some cases, almost pleading—for a visit from Lyndon Johnson.

WITH THE EXCEPTION of Coke Stevenson, candidates for the United States Senate did not generally travel with only one or two assistants—and certainly this candidate didn't. He needed at least one secretary, more than one speechwriter—he was, after all, giving both morning and evening radio addresses daily—as well as a man (Woody) to carry his suitcases, his boxes of monogrammed shirts and Countess Mara ties, his traveling case crammed with throat sprays and lozenges, skin ointment and pills. Now he needed, in addition, a helicopter mechanic, and someone familiar with the aircraft's landing requirements to be on hand at each stop to arrange vital crowd-control precautions. The microphone he used for speeches on the ground had proved unsuitable for mid-air speeches because it picked up too much noise from the helicopter motor, so a second, more sensitive, microphone was installed and hooked up to the loudspeaker lashed to the landing gear; a radio engineer—from KTBC—was needed to keep both microphones in working order. And he wanted, he now decided, a radio announcer—he selected KTBC's Joe Phipps—to announce his arrival from the air as the helicopter was coming in to land. He wanted *everything*—everything included, of course, sound trucks to tour towns to prepare their inhabitants for his coming ("You could do every street in these little towns twice in an hour," an aide recalls). And, to the astonishment of even his most hardened aides, he wanted a band, a hillbilly band. Was a helicopter a drawing card? Well, so was a band. A band playing at the landing site for an hour or so before the landing would help attract a crowd. He wanted a band. And whereas Phipps and perhaps one other person could fit into the helicopter, the band, the mechanic, the speechwriters and the rest of the entourage would have to travel by cars, cars which could not keep up with the helicopter. A score of unanticipated problems further complicated logistics, and although the red-and-blue tank trucks of the 'Umble (counsel: Alvin Wirtz) were supposed to be positioned along the helicopter's route, they were continually missing connections. Inability to prevent children from swarming around the helicopter and turning its valves necessitated a safety check after each stop.

But the helicopter was worth all the trouble. By the second week, the routine of "advancing" it had become more thorough. Residents of each town it was to visit could hardly have avoided reading about it, either in their local weekly newspaper, which would be filled with advertisements and articles (often written by the Johnson staff) or in their mail (for each delivery seemed to contain a reprint of another newspaper article on the

"Flying Windmill" or another letter or postcard reminder of the time of its arrival) or in the flyers that seemed to be pressed into their hands on every shopping trip to town. They could hardly have avoided hearing about it, either on the radio, in spot announcements that were repeated over and over on the local station, or on their telephone, for Johnson advance men, arriving in a small town, simply went through the skinny local telephone directories name by name until every resident had been contacted. Or from their children, who would come home to announce that school was being let out for the day so that they could see this modern aeronautical marvel, or from Johnson campaign workers who came to their door to tell them about it. People could hardly avoid seeing Johnson's picture, too, for Johnson was dispatching men to place posters in shop windows and on trees, urging his workers on with the same phrase he had used in previous campaigns: "I want it so you can't wipe your ass on a piece of paper in that town that hasn't got my picture on it." Recalls one of these campaign workers: "He said he wanted posters up on every light pole—and he meant *every* light pole; I was driving with him once, and there was one pole—just one pole—without a picture of him, and, my God, I have never heard one human being talk to another human being like he talked to that poor guy who had missed that pole." By the day on which the Flying Windmill was scheduled to arrive, these small towns, in which there was so little to disturb the ordinary round of life, and the surrounding countryside had been made to feel that its visit would be an extraordinary event. As a sound truck roamed the town that day, reminding its residents that "It's coming at three o'clock! The Johnson City Windmill! The Flying Windmill! The plane that can stand still in midair! The plane that can fly backwards! It's going to be landing on the high school field. Come meet your next Senator, Congressman Lyndon Johnson," small boys would ride their bikes over to the landing site and leave them sprawled on the ground while they played and waited, the old men who ordinarily lounged around the Courthouse Square would saunter slowly over, determined to be unimpressed, the town's businessmen, and farmers and ranchers from the countryside, would arrive in two and threes, standing talking with their hands on their hips and their big hats pushed back on their heads, and mothers would come carrying their babies. There would be quite a crowd.

And then people would hear the hum in the sky.

They would generally hear it some minutes before they could actually see the helicopter, but finally someone would shout, "There it is! Over yonder!" and someone else would shout, "Look, it's coming!"—and people would begin pointing to the dot in the sky that was growing rapidly larger. As it drew closer, the hum became the distinctive, rhythmic, beating, chopping sound of the rotor blades flailing through the air, and then the helicopter was overhead—the roar of its engine filling the sky, the long blades whirling—gleaming blue and white in the sun, seemingly as big as a house (and, indeed, sixty feet long and fourteen high, with those three long rotor blades, about as big as many of the stores in those little towns). And as it slowly descended, the roar of its engine, revving up to full power to hold the chopper steady, would become even louder, and the onlookers would be caught in the wind from those long whirling blades. Men would grab their hats to keep them from blowing off; women would put one hand to their heads to keep their hair in place, and would hold their skirts down with the other; mothers clutched their babies in their arms; fathers reached for their sons' hands and held them tight. The helicopter would settle to the ground in a last roar, a swirl of dust and pebbles swept into the air by its blades, a flurry of advance men would rush to guard the tail rotor, and then the motor would be cut off—and for a moment there was silence. Says the reporter Margaret Mayer: "Coming down on those rural people in those little towns who had never seen anything like it, with that tremendous roar and the dust swirling up, it was an awesome thing. As it was approaching, there was a lot of hurry-up: late-comers rushing to get there. But as it actually started to come down, there was silence—the silence of awe." And then the door of the helicopter would slam open. A long arm would swing out into the silence holding a broad-brimmed light gray Stetson hat, and then, in a sweeping gesture, would fling the hat into the crowd. And out into the silence stepped Lyndon Johnson.

The people, except for the small boys running to retrieve the hat, would be standing as if stunned, but Johnson didn't wait for them to come to him. In three or four long strides, while the rotor blades were still slowly revolving above him before coming to a halt, he would be out among them, reaching for hands, and after he had shaken a few, he would step back to the side of the chopper, where a wooden box would have been set up for him as a platform, don his microphone harness, and begin his speech, standing beside the machine that looked even bigger close up, and beside the huge white letters of his name.

After the speech, announcer Phipps would take over the microphone and talk—"Come meet Congressman Johnson. He's been a friend to the people of his district. He got them lights. He got them roads. He will be a friend to all the people of Texas"—while Johnson circulated through the crowd, shaking hands. Men and boys would walk over to the helicopter. Watching them, Harry Nachlin saw that "they all wanted to put their hands on it." To the mechanic's astonishment, many, not knowing what to do with the aircraft, did what they would have done with an unfamiliar automobile: kicked the helicopter's tires as if testing them for soundness.

The boys and girls crowded around Nachlin asking questions: "How fast does it fly?" "What makes it go forward?" "Can it really go backward?" "Can it really go sideways?" "What does the tail propeller do?"

There was drama in the takeoff, too. "The blades of the tail rotor came down pretty close to the ground," Nachlin recalls, so Phipps "would be shouting through the helicopter's public address system: 'Get back! Get those kids back! Watch out for those blades!' " When a space had been cleared, Chudars would start the engine and the roar would begin, and the blades would begin to creak and turn and beat the air again. The dust would lift and swirl, and the townspeople would back away. The Johnson City Windmill would lift off the ground in a roar that was one of the loudest noises they had ever heard, rise straight up about ten feet and then circle higher into the sky. As the crowd watched, Chudars would put on a little show over their heads: making 360-degree turns on a dime, wheeling the craft sharply to the left and the right, flying backwards or sideways. "They were the most modest of maneuvers, really," Woodward says. "He wasn't doing any trick stunts or anything. But to see an airplane fly backwards . . ." When Woodward had been a little boy, his grandfather had taken him to see Charles Lindbergh land in Abilene during his triumphal tour of the United States in the *Spirit of St. Louis*, the plane in which he had flown the Atlantic. "Today, with television and all, kids don't get thrilled any more. But then—that helicopter was new and revolutionary and different. These small towns—they had so few events in their lives. And this was an event. To see that helicopter come in thrilled those kids the way I had been thrilled to see the *Spirit of St. Louis*. It was a real *event* in their lives." And then the little show would be over; suddenly, the helicopter would whirl and clatter away across the sky, a tiny dot, disappearing, leaving behind comments that seemed to be the same in every town. Nachlin and Woodward and other men who followed the helicopter would remember them decades later: "Did you hear that chopchop? That's why they call it a 'chopper.' " "Did you feel that wind? Boy!" In those fundamentalist small towns, people were reminded of something in the Bible. Recalls a Blanco woman: "After it [the helicopter] left, a Bible student said that the Bible says that people will float through the air. He said, This is just the beginning. This is the beginning of a new era. We will see all sorts of changes from now on."

THE SOUND TRUCK had left as soon as the helicopter appeared, of course, racing off, not for the next town—two or three trucks were "leapfrogging" towns in order to keep up with the helicopter—but for the town after that or the one after that. Some of the cars carrying advance men would have left before Johnson finished shaking hands, to get a head start. But other drivers, including most of the reporters, would wait until the helicopter took off. Then they would pull out in a cloud of dust, trying frantically to keep up with the machine roaring overhead, not wanting to lose it. Because, between his stops in towns, Lyndon Johnson was putting on quite a show.

When, flying over the largely empty landscape between towns, he saw ahead of him a group of men—five or six members of a railroad track-repair crew working on a track, for example—he would jab a forefinger downward and Chudars would land beside them. Johnson would jump out, run over to them, shake their hands, hug them and give them his campaign leaflets, and then run back to the helicopter and roar up into the air again, leaving the men staring after him.

Sometimes the reaction of such targets of opportunity to the totally unexpected roar from the sky and the abrupt descent upon them of the weird-looking machine was not one of unbridled enthusiasm. In East Texas, for example, a dozen cotton-choppers, seeing the Flying Windmill suddenly wheel and head for them, dropped their hoes and ran in terror for the shelter of a nearby wood. Such reactions did not, however, deter the candidate. The helicopter was too fast for the cotton-choppers; before they could reach the wood, it was above them. As they froze in their tracks, he shouted down over the microphone: "Hello, down there! This is your friend, Lyndon Johnson, your candidate for the United States Senate. I hope you'll vote for me on Primary Day. And bring along your relatives to vote, too."

The targets did not have to be as large as these groups. As the helicopter charged across the vast plains of West Texas, in particular, anything moving on the flat, featureless brown landscape below could be seen for miles, and Lyndon Johnson sometimes seemed to be following the rule that if it was moving, he shook its hand. The pilot, asked once how often Johnson made him land for a handshake, replied: "Wherever we saw more than two people and a big dog."

Nothing in his path could escape. Was there an isolated farmhouse ahead? Into the midst of a peaceful farm setting—wife in her kitchen, baking, perhaps; farmer milking under a tree—the S-51 would suddenly swoop with the Pratt & Whitney roaring. "The chickens thought it was a bird coming down to get them," Busby recalls. "They would go berserk, flying up and hitting the fences." Cows would gallop awkwardly away in panic to the farthest end of the pasture, the milk bucket having been kicked over. Horses would squeal and rear in their stalls. And there in the front yard, broad smile on his face, campaign brochures in hand, would be a man saying: "Howdy, Ahm Lyndon Johnson, your candidate for United States Senator. Just droppin' in to say good mornin'."

Merely because a town was too small to merit a landing didn't mean that it would be ignored—not if it lay in the path of the Johnson City Windmill. Approaching some tiny hamlet in the middle of nowhere, Chudars would be ordered to hover above it. A great voice would come down out of the sky. "Hello, down there," it would say. And as people ran out of homes or stores to stare open-mouthed up at the helicopter, the voice would continue: "This is your friend, Lyndon Johnson of Johnson City. Your candidate for the United States Senate. Just saying good morning." Thanks to the efficiency of his office staff, some of the residents were greeted by name. "Hello, there, Mr. Sam Price. This is your friend, Lyndon Johnson. I'm sorry we can't land today, but I want you to know that I'm up here thinking of you, and I sure do appreciate your kind letter and comments. I just want you to be sure and tell your friends to vote for me at election time."

FOR THE PRESS, of course, or at least for those members of it willing to drive fast enough to keep up, this made good copy. "Hovering his helicopter close to the red farm land," a reporter wrote, "Johnson exchanged greetings with many workers in the fields. Flying low over a dusty road near Montgomery, the 'Johnson City Windmill' caused an old-fashioned buggy to burst into a spirited trot. Not since Pappy's hillbilly band had the folks in the piney woods had such a show." After a day racing along the Rio Grande, another wrote, "Johnson brought people rushing out of their homes and places of business as he circled cities in the thickly populated valley, waving his hat and urging the people to come and see him speak." Seeing the helicopter start to descend between scheduled stops, reporters jammed on the brakes, pulled over to the side of the road, ran across the fields to be on hand when Johnson talked to a farmer or to a group of field workers, and that night wired details of the conversation to their city desks. Coverage became more and more dramatic. Articles talked of his "fast-moving campaign," "his whirlwind campaign," of the "great excitement" and "crowds blocking the street" when he landed in a town, of the people "gaping" as the "whirlybird" went through its routines. The datelines—"With the Johnson City Windmill at Ballinger," "With the Flying Windmill at Dermott"—picked up the spirit; the headlines got bigger and blacker: "JOHNSON'S COPTER HEADS FOR GEORGETOWN"; "JOHNSON STUMPS COTTON PICKERS VIA HELICOPTER"; "JOHNSON AND HELICOPTER TO BE IN TARRANT TODAY"; "JOHNSON IN 24 PUBLIC APPEARANCES IN DAY." In a campaign which had made little news, there was big news now: not the import of the candidate's speech but the vehicle in which he arrived to deliver it. The helicopter was, in fact, national news: *Time* magazine, for example, reported (in an article headlined, "Hello, Down There") that "Long Lyndon Johnson, one of Texas' most ebullient congressmen, has introduced the first new gimmick in Texas politics since the hillbilly band and the free barbecue. . . . Out in the bottoms and the back country, the Johnson City Windmill wowed the citizenry." The pro-Stevenson *Dallas News* acknowledged that the Senate race had become "the campaign of the Flying Windmill."

And, of course, the bigger the headlines became, the bigger the crowds became, each fueling the other. On the final day of June, Johnson's first stop was in the Central Texas town of Bangs. The population of the town was 756. Reporters, making a person-by-person count of the attendance, found "more than 700" people waiting when Chudars set the S-51 down in Bangs' Main Street. And, the *Austin American-Statesman* reported, "that was the smallest crowd of the morning."

"At small towns and large towns, Johnson crowds far exceeded expectations," the *American-Statesman* said. In Coleman, where 2,500 of the town's 7,500 people jammed onto Main Street to see the helicopter, sheriff's deputies and Johnson's advance men had to push people back into stores to clear enough space for it to land. Day after day, rural Texans were coming to see the Johnson City Windmill in numbers such as had come to see no previous candidate in Texas history—no candidate, that is, except one: Pappy O'Daniel had drawn such crowds—and Pass-the-Biscuits-Pappy had won every race he entered. Thanks to the helicopter, statewide campaigning in Texas, which had always been a candidate's nightmare, had suddenly become a candidate's dream. All at once those terrible Texas distances had virtually evaporated; now all at once you were freed of those rutted, bumpy rural roads and were cutting effortlessly cross-country, over hills and rivers and lakes. And now when you approached a town, a town in which a campaigner would once have been apprehensive that no one except a handful of campaign workers and a score of voters would be waiting to hear him, now, as the helicopter neared the town, Johnson would suddenly see—on the single main street, or around the patch of green which from the air signified the Courthouse Square or the high school football field—not scores of people but hundreds. And these people wouldn't be standing around with the traditional studied, blank-faced small-town indifference that ordinarily made speaking to them difficult; circling the town, Johnson would see people running through the streets so as not to miss his arrival, and as he hovered and began to descend, he looked down on a sea of upturned faces—people waiting for him.

What politician—what human being—would not have been exhilarated by such a response? Lyndon Johnson, always elated by the slightest sign of respect or affection from the public, was exhilarated, particularly after a day of touring his own Tenth Congressional District, flying over the Hill Country in which he had spent the youth of anxiety and shame and humiliation that made respect and affection so necessary to him.

Heavy rain fell all that day in the Tenth District, but rain couldn't keep the people away. A hundred people were waiting for the Johnson City Windmill on the lawn of the high school in Bastrop on the plains below the Hill Country, a sizable crowd for Bastrop, and there were about two hundred in the Courthouse Square in Giddings. Before the next stop, at Brenham, the helicopter was delayed for half an hour because a fuel truck did not arrive on time, but when he reached Brenham the crowd was still there. Then the helicopter headed west toward the Pedernales Valley. Along the roads—the roads on which he had worked as a laborer, harnessed like a mule—a long caravan of cars raced after him, for the regular entourage had been supplemented by some dozen campaign aides who had driven out from headquarters in Austin. The aides sped through the hills blowing their horns, every car bearing, tied to its radiator, a big picture of him, and overhead the helicopter circled each town it passed— Stonewall, where his father had lost the Johnson Ranch forever; Johnson City, where young Lyndon and his brother and sisters had lived out the rest of their youth in dread of losing their home there, too; Fredericksburg, where Lyndon had been beaten up at the dance; San Marcos, where Carol Davis had refused to marry him. The big helicopter circled each town again and again, Chudars banking the aircraft so that as the townsfolk came out on their front lawns and into the streets, they could not miss the name "Lyndon Johnson" written in such big letters on its sides. The rain was heavier now, and visibility was limited, but when he got close enough to Taylor to see the high-school football field, he saw some three hundred automobiles parked there. The helicopter came down on the far side of the field, away from the cars. The people waded through the mud to reach him. Another crowd—huge by Hill Country standards— was waiting in Georgetown, and at the end of his speech there, he held a little press conference. Did flying in the helicopter make him uneasy, one reporter asked. "No," Johnson replied. "It gives me confidence." Was he tired from the long day's campaigning, another reporter asked. "Happy tired," Johnson said. "I know I am sweeping up votes like a whirlwind. I just feel it in the crowds." Heading back for Austin, where he was to spend the night, he passed over the little town of Round Rock. Ordering Chudars to circle lower and then lower still, and then to hover over Main Street, Johnson picked up the microphone and leaned out the window. The helicopter was low enough so that he could see the individual faces of people he knew staring up at him, mouths agape, and he called to them by name. He had invited *Houston Post* correspondent Jack Guinn to ride this leg of the trip with him, and, Guinn was to report, "We were close enough to witness smiles of astonishment on the faces of the citizens." Landing at Municipal Airport in Austin, Johnson was greeted by a roaring crowd of supporters. Among them was his fellow Congressman John Lyle, of Corpus Christi. "That thing sure makes a lot of noise," Lyle said. "That thing sure gets a lot of votes," Lyndon Johnson replied.

THE HELICOPTER was not the only cause of Johnson's elation as June drew to a close and the campaign entered the final month before the primary. The other was a mistake—a grave one—made by his normally cautious opponent. The Texas chapter of the American Federation of Labor, meeting in Fort Worth, endorsed Coke Stevenson for Senator—and Stevenson did not repudiate the endorsement.

The AFL endorsement was to prove one of the great ironies in Texas political history. It was given not out of enthusiasm for the ex-Governor, who had tacitly supported the Brown & Root-backed anti-labor Manford bills, but out of deep hostility toward Lyndon Johnson. For years Johnson had assured Texas labor leaders that he was a New Dealer, "100 Per Cent" for labor's great friend Roosevelt; then, believing that Johnson was what he said he was, the embattled, struggling unions of Texas had gone to him for help, and had found no help at all. Since FDR's death, moreover, in his stance against Truman's Fair Deal and his support of the Taft-Hartley Act, Johnson had openly opposed their aims. And his alliance with the hated Herman Brown had convinced them that while Stevenson had resisted them, Johnson had deceived and betrayed them. They saw their endorsement now as an opportunity for revenge.

But their action was to backfire. So weak were unions in Texas—utterly unable, even in the cities, to mobilize their members—that their support could not help, could only hurt, a candidate. Anti-union sentiment was fierce in rural Texas, which identified unions with labor racketeers, big-city corruption, big-city ethnic groups; a widespread theme in the state's monolithic press, expressed in 295 editorials during a four-month period in 1948, was that strikes should be abolished because they were part of a Communist conspiracy to overthrow America. When Stevenson learned by telephone of the unexpected endorsement, he was so shocked that, recalls reporter Charles Boatner, who happened to be traveling with Stevenson and Bob Murphey that day, after the former Governor returned to the car, "he just seemingly for ten minutes didn't say a word, and [then] he said, 'Well, I'm going to accept it; it will do me less harm to accept it than to fight it.' "

Attempting in later years to understand their enigmatic "Old Man's" failure to repudiate the endorsement, Murphey and advisers such as Ernest Boyett would speculate that his reasons were less political than personal. Every time he switched on the radio in the car, it seemed, he heard a Johnson speech or a Johnson advertisement calling him a "do-nothinger," or "an old man." "He never said a word," Murphey recalls; "just sometimes he'd roll down the window and spit." But those few men who had an opportunity to observe Stevenson during the campaign saw that his contempt for Johnson had been confirmed, and that dislike for his opponent had turned into something deeper. "He felt there was no way he could lose much of the conservative vote," Boyett says. "And he thought that maybe with it [the endorsement], he could pick up some of the liberals as well, and really rub it in. And by this time he really wanted to rub it in to Lyndon." Whatever the reason, however, Stevenson's failure to repudiate the endorsement gave his opponent's campaign something it needed: an issue. "Peace, Preparedness and Progress" hadn't caught on, and neither had anything else Johnson had tried. A helicopter could draw people to see a candidate, but he needed an argument to convince them they should vote for him. Now he had one; in the previously invulnerable armor of Coke Stevenson there had appeared a chink.

Lyndon Johnson's college debating partner, Elmer Graham, could have warned Stevenson what would happen next. The strong point of Lyndon's debating style, Graham says, was his devastating instinct for the jugular, his "knack of finding a weak point in the other team's argument" and, once he had found it, making the most of it.

Johnson issued a statement charging that the endorsement was the result of a "secret deal." "Labor leaders made a secret agreement with Calculating Coke that they couldn't get out of me," he said. "A few labor leaders, who do not soil their own clothes with the sweat of honest toil, have met in a smoke-filled hotel room in Fort Worth and have attempted to deliver the vote of free Texas workingmen. . . . I think the laboring men should ask their leaders . . . why they wanted the unions to . . . endorse a candidate who did not have the courage to sign or veto the state's vicious anti-labor law when he was Governor." The "labor leaders" made it worse—by rising to Johnson's bait. The AFL convention had not endorsed Coke Stevenson because of any "deal," one AFL leader, Wallace Reilley of Dallas, said the next day; it had endorsed him because his opponent was Lyndon Johnson—and Johnson, by his years of support of anti-labor bills in Congress, "has disqualified himself in the eyes of the working people of Texas." After Reilley offered a resolution terming Johnson's statement "a deliberate lie," the six hundred "boiling mad" delegates, the *Dallas News* reported, jumped to their feet, roaring in anger and shaking their fists as they approved it. But the headlines which reported their action—"INFURIATED AFL DELEGATES VOTE TO GET JOHNSON"—only helped the man they hated.

Then Johnson sharpened the charge. The "secret deal" to which Stevenson had agreed in return for AFL support, he said, was that if Stevenson was elected to the Senate, he would vote to repeal the Taft-Hartley Act—the act that was almost sacred in Texas as the symbol of the state's flaming anti-union sentiment. In speech after speech, over the radio and in the small towns to which the helicopter was carrying him, he demanded that Stevenson "tell the truth" about this "secret deal" he had made "with labor dictators." Stevenson, Johnson said, had sold his soul for the labor vote; "he's a yearling with the labor boss brand on his hip." Johnson's charge was untrue. Coke Stevenson was not opposed to the Taft-Hartley Act; he was in favor of it. From the time it had first been proposed in Washington, he had explained to supporters, in his slow, painstaking way, that although he was in general opposed to legislation increasing government regulation of any institution, he was in favor of such regulation when an institution became a monopoly and thereby gained power so great that only government could check its abuses in the interests of the public. Organized labor, he had told intimates, had become a monopoly, and was abusing its power. And Johnson *knew* his charge was untrue; says Paul Bolton, who, under Alvin Wirtz's guidance, was writing most of Johnson's speeches on the labor issue: "We knew it wasn't true, and I almost felt ashamed of what I was writing sometimes; Coke was so honest, you know. . . ."

Moreover, there had been no "secret deal"—or at least not one involving Coke Stevenson. The gulf between Johnson's charges and the truth was deepened by the fact that Lyndon Johnson *was* receiving "secret" support from labor leaders. The support came in the same form it had taken during Johnson's first campaign for the Senate seven years before, because he had maintained his ties to the labor movement in the Northeast. As in 1941, substantial amounts of labor cash were raised there and either sent to Texas by Tommy Corcoran and Jim Rowe, or brought in person by Welly Hopkins; on his return trips Hopkins carried recordings of Coke Stevenson speeches that had been carefully edited by Johnson's aides to make Stevenson sound more conservative than he was, and that therefore helped Corcoran and Rowe raise still more money from labor and other liberals in Washington and New York to defeat this "Neanderthal." (Johnson had, with more justification, used the same tactic in his race against O'Daniel in 1941.) Once Hopkins, chief counsel for John L. Lewis' United Mine Workers union, arrived in Texas to hear Johnson excoriating John L. Lewis. "He was saying things that kind of hurt my ears, and that I hated to hear," Hopkins was to recall. "I knew the political reasons for it, but it made me feel a little badly." But he had been sent to Texas to help Johnson, and he did so, contacting UMW supporters, and bringing papers—which he will describe only as "various documents that Corcoran and Jim Rowe had helped me get—a copy of some sort of document, a government document or some correspondence—not for public use but that were informative to Lyndon." But these labor connections were kept secret—Hopkins was to recall that he went to Texas "just informally and [as] quiet as I could [and] purposely stayed away from Lyndon's headquarters." So Johnson was free, in a violently anti-labor state, to make the most of labor's endorsement of his opponent.

Stevenson made one attempt to answer the charge, although he did so as he had always answered questions in the past, not making a short reply but explaining the political philosophy that had led him to his decision. In an interview with the *Abilene Reporter-News* on July 3, he said: "My policy is to let everyone alone unless he needs regulating. But when any segment of society becomes a monopoly, it needs to be regulated. I think the Taft-Hartley Act is all right as far as it is needed to keep down a monopoly." When Boyett and other advisers suggested that the last sentence might need clarification, Stevenson refused to issue any. One reason was that he felt he had been making statements with similar careful qualifications during his entire public career, and the people of Texas had always understood them, particularly in light of his consistent record. The people of Texas would understand this one, he said; of course people knew where he stood on Taft-Hartley, and on organized labor, he said. Who could possibly believe he would vote to repeal that Act? And he did not repeat his statement before the first primary. It appeared in the press—in just a few newspapers, really—only once.

But behind Stevenson's refusal to repudiate the AFL endorsement lay also Lyndon Johnson's genius at "reading" men. Johnson had read Coke Stevenson now, and he knew his weakness: his fierce pride, particularly a pride in his reputation for honesty and truthfulness. All his public life—from the time he had been a young county attorney and opponents had attacked his handling of the rustling case involving the son of the prominent Kimble County family—he had refused to utter a single word of reply to personal attacks. So Johnson, to keep him from replying, made the attacks personal. Not only did Johnson himself, and his supporters, in radio broadcast after broadcast, continue their attack on the "old man," ridiculing his lack of courage, impugning his honesty; not only did they "demand" that Stevenson "tell the truth" about his "secret deal" on the Taft-Hartley Bill; but the demands were deliberately couched in language that, Murphey says, "anyone who knew Governor Stevenson knew he would never reply to." For example, Johnson backer Ed Leach, editor of the *Longview Morning Journal*, wrote to Stevenson "demanding" that he speak out: "I would like to ask you to . . . break a precedent by stating your position on anything, but particularly on the Taft-Hartley Law." Johnson had read his man: Stevenson responded just as Johnson had known he would respond. Since the personal attacks concerned his "refusal" to say whether he was for Taft-Hartley, it became a matter of pride for him not to say whether he was for it. He said he would not "be drawn into a name-calling exchange." Voters knew his views on organized labor, he said; he hadn't changed, and they could be sure he never would. And because his support of Taft-Hartley had not been widely publicized, Stevenson's stance allowed Johnson to claim that Stevenson had never disclosed his views; indeed, newspapers would state repeatedly that the former Governor had made no statement about Taft-Hartley.

Stevenson's response was based not only on philosophy but on the buttressing of that philosophy by a lifetime's experience. Time and time again during his long career, candidates had attacked him personally and he had been advised to reply, and time and time again he had refused, always giving the same reason: his record would speak for him—the voters knew where he stood; he hadn't changed; the voters would therefore know the charges were false. And, naïve and unrealistic though this reasoning had seemed, time and again it had been proven correct—attack after attack had shattered against his image, in part because his image was so close to the truth that there were no cracks in which the charges could lodge; the charges had indeed been false, and the voters had indeed not believed them.

But Stevenson didn't understand that, as Boyett puts it, "Lyndon Johnson wasn't like other candidates." He didn't understand that Lyndon Johnson's campaign wasn't like other campaigns, that it was something new in Texas politics. Never before had attacks against Stevenson been repeated day after day, week after week, not only on the radio, that powerful medium, now, for the first time in Texas, being exploited to its fullest, but in weekly newspapers, daily newspapers, in campaign mailings, so that voters heard and saw the charges against him, it seemed, every time they turned on the radio, read a newspaper, opened their mail. Never before had there been a campaign in which the same phrases were drummed into voters' consciousness so constantly all through June and July. "Secret deal"? Perhaps Coke Stevenson felt he wouldn't dignify the charge by denying it. But dignity was a luxury in a fight with Lyndon Johnson, a luxury too expensive to afford. Perhaps Stevenson had too much pride to deny the charge. Pride was a luxury that an opponent of Lyndon Johnson could not afford. Once Johnson found an issue, true or untrue, that "touched," he hammered it—until people started to believe it. He had one that touched now; he had found the jugular and he wasn't letting go. The charges Johnson was making against Coke Stevenson were false—manufactured out of whole cloth, in fact. They were as false as any charges that had been made against Stevenson in the past.

But, this time, people were beginning to wonder whether they might not be true.

Even the former Governor's strongest supporters were beginning to wonder, as was shown in a column which expressed the views of the Dallas conservatives. "Mr. Leach's letter to Mr. Stevenson was a trifle discourteous, it is true," Lynn Landrum wrote in the *Dallas News*. "But it seems reasonable to expect that Mr. Stevenson in his own way will inform the public on this matter, which now seems to have become a critical issue in the race. The people of Texas . . . are substantially in favor of the Taft-Hartley Act. . . . They will want to know Mr. Stevenson's views."

Within a startlingly short time after Johnson had begun campaigning by helicopter, his private polls had shown him cutting into Stevenson's lead, and every day that gap had narrowed. On June 20, a new Belden Poll had been published. Stevenson was no longer leading him by 64 percent to 28, but only by 47 to 37, with Peddy having 12 percent (minor candidates had a total of 4 percent). The erosion in Stevenson's popularity, Johnson's more experienced advisers had realized, was not as great as it seemed at first glance, since Peddy had had only an insignificant 3 percent in the May poll, and his backers, conservatives, would return to Stevenson once Peddy was out of the race. But now Johnson's polls showed that since the AFL endorsement, the gap had closed still further. After weeks in which it had seemed that nothing could erode Stevenson's popularity, there was an erosion at last.

WITH HIS HELICOPTER and his issue, Johnson's mood veered from depression to elation. His euphoria was intense. Often, when his aides came at five a.m. to wake him, they found him already awake, and if he wasn't, he woke the moment Woody gently touched his shoulder. And, Woodward recalls, "he started at full speed. The minute we woke him up, he hit the ground running," giving orders and gulping coffee while he shaved. As he headed out the door of his room for his daily 6:45 a.m. broadcast, one staffer would call "He's moving out!" to alert the others downstairs, for they would have to scramble to keep up. As he passed them, his strides were long and his arms were swinging; "he was," in the words of the adoring Woody, "a general moving out in front of his troops."

After the broadcast—as stilted and stentorian as ever, the engineers in the studios of the little local stations frantically turning dials in an attempt to modulate his voice—he headed for the chopper. Charging from morning to night across the bare brown plains of West Texas, the Johnson City Windmill was landing in eight or nine towns each day now; Johnson was speaking in towns that few candidates for statewide office had ever visited; the helicopter was enabling him to do, on a statewide scale, what he had done in the Tenth Congressional District during his first campaign: to go to the people "at the forks of the creek." Many of them—perhaps most of them—had never seen a candidate for the United States Senate before. But they saw Lyndon Johnson, saw him and heard him talk.

He talked, for example, about his combat experiences—or what he said were his combat experiences. His service in the war was, of course, one of the major themes of his campaign. One of Woody's assignments was to transfer the Silver Star bar to the lapel of whatever suit jacket Johnson was wearing that day. When possible, he wanted to be introduced by a veteran—preferably one whose service, and sacrifice, had been dramatized by the loss of a limb; in Spur, for example, Johnson would ordinarily have been introduced by his most powerful and prominent supporter, a physician named Brannen, but it was arranged that Brannen would introduce Jake Vernell, a veteran who had lost a leg in the war, and that Vernell would be the man who introduced the Congressman. So successful was the Johnson campaign in locating pro-Johnson amputees for this task that the percentage of men introducing Lyndon Johnson who still possessed all their limbs was surprisingly small. And the introductions stressed the war service: "Congressman Johnson was fighting in the Pacific until he was recalled to his congressional duties." Particularly effective was a broadcast over a statewide radio hookup by veterans who told the story of their own war exploits and tied them in to Johnson's—or what they thought to be Johnson's. Typical of the newspaper coverage of the broadcast was the lead in the *Austin American-Statesman*: "Seven World War II heroes, young men new to politics, told why they are supporting Congressman Lyndon Johnson . . . [who] was awarded a Silver Star by General MacArthur for gallantry in combat action. . . ." But no one else could talk about Johnson's exploits the way Johnson could talk about them.

"I shared your boys' experiences," he would say in those small towns in which war heroes were revered and in which so many families had lost a son. "I said that if war was declared, I'd go to war beside them, and I did." He would point to the pin in his lapel or wave the lapel back and forth at the audience (or, when carried away by enthusiasm, would yank off his jacket and hold it over his head, with the lapel stretched out). "That's the Silver Star. General MacArthur gave it to me." He had made sacrifices just as their boys had, he said. He had intended to run in the Senate election in 1942, he said, "But when that election came around I was in the jungles of New Guinea."

And, he said, I know what it is to see boys die, because I had a friend die. "He was the boy I roomed with," Lyndon Johnson said. "He was a country boy, too. He was a pilot, and he flew a B-17, and he was a Colonel. His name was Francis Stevens, but we all called him Steve." They had been on a mission together, Johnson said, and Stevens' plane had been shot down, and he had perished in the crash. And to him, Lyndon Johnson, had fallen the task of collecting Steve's personal effects and mailing them to his mother. "I sat in that little room we had shared together, and I got all the letters his mama had written him, and I tied them up to send back to her. And I packed up his clothes. I remember I rolled up his socks. They smelled bad, but they were his, so I sent them to his mama, too."

And though his wartime experiences were somewhat exaggerated, the telling was tremendously effective—particularly when he tied the experiences in with his pleas for "preparedness." "Peace, Preparedness and Progress" might be the words he used during his stilted radio broadcasts, but here, face to face with the people whose votes he needed, he used different words. It cost us a lot of lives because we weren't prepared when the Japs attacked, he said. "I'd rather save lives than money," he said. "It's either your boys' lives or tax rebates for millionaires."

These words touched a deep chord in his listeners. One of the hands he shook after his talk at Graham was that of a farm wife. "My boy died on Iwo Jima," she said. "I know what you mean." At Sweetwater, an old man approached Johnson and tried to say something, but had to stop when he began to cry. And the press coverage of his war record was all that could be desired: talking about Lady Bird's concern for his safety in a helicopter, the *Port Arthur News* reported that Johnson said "that his wife didn't show particular concern when he was flying in B-29s, helping bomb one Japanese island after another into submission three years ago. His flights over jungle wastes and the limitless expanses of the ocean 'were all right by her, for she realized the job had to be done,' the Congressman says. 'But when she heard that some of my old wartime buddies were volunteering to fly me all over Texas to meet the voters in a helicopter, she threw up her hands. . . .' "

AND HE TALKED about his opponent.

He had emerged from the hospital determined to try to destroy Coke Stevenson's reputation, and he had been concentrating on doing so in his formal speeches, with attacks that had been growing steadily more personal. He kept calling his sixty-year-old opponent "an old man." Stevenson had retired to his ranch, Johnson said, and the only reason he was running for the Senate was that he had discovered that Senators were paid $15,000 a year. Stevenson wasn't planning to do any work for that money, just collect it as if it were a pension, Johnson said. "I am not for the fifteen thousand dollar pension you'll be giving this old man if you elect him." And then, somewhere near the end of June, Lyndon Johnson changed his mode of attack—in a stroke of pure political genius.

Washington had learned of Lyndon Johnson's gift for mimicry, of the accuracy with which he could capture a man's traits and imitate and exaggerate them in a devastating form of mockery. Now he began to use that gift in the small towns of Texas on the man who had for so many years been a hero in those towns.

The people's very familiarity with the former Governor, and with his well-known mannerisms and phrases, made him a good target. Johnson's mimicry took the form of an interview in which he played two parts: a reporter and Stevenson. First, playing the reporter, he asked a question— "What are your views on federal aid to education?" perhaps. Then, taking a step away, he turned, as if facing the reporter, and played Stevenson. Out and up came Lyndon Johnson's jaw in an imitation of Coke's. His hands went to his hips, in the former Governor's habitual stance when answering questions. And he rocked back and forth on his heels as Stevenson did while thinking, and paused for a while before answering. "Ah believe in constitutional government," he finally said. "Are you for or against the seventy-group Air Force?" the "reporter" would ask. Jaw; hands; rocking—in flawless imitation. The long pause which had given "Coffee-Coolin' Coke" his nickname. Finally: "Ah believe in constitutional government."

"It was perfect," a reporter said. "It was Coke to the life." The only element missing was Coke's pipe. And then, suddenly, Johnson had an inspiration. While performing his imitation one day, he noticed a farmer right in front of him smoking a large corncob pipe. Reaching out, Johnson grabbed it, stuck it in his own mouth, and added it to the act. Now, after his "reporter" asked Stevenson, "How do you stand on the 70-group Air Force," his "Governor" hurriedly stuck the pipe in his mouth as if panicked by the question and drew deeply on it, puckered up his eyes in mock concentration until he finally removed it, studied it for another long moment, and then said: "Ah believe in constitutional government." At every stop thereafter, Johnson would borrow a pipe from some man in the crowd. "With one eye on the labor bosses in Fort Worth and the other eye on the millionaires in Houston, he sits and smokes," Johnson would say. He would place the pipe in his mouth, stick out his jaw, put his hands on his hips, and rock back on his heels until he had the crowd giggling. Then he would mutter through the pipe stem: "Ahm for states' rights." "And what do you think about federal aid for veterans?" Long pause. "Well, I don't want to move the county courthouse to Washington."

Then, having made the crowd receptive, he could launch into a stronger attack. These savage personal onslaughts were directed against perhaps the most respected public official in the history of Texas. They were a great gamble, part of the great gamble that Johnson was taking in the whole campaign. From Jacksonville, Horace Busby reported: "The

Congressman has gone berserk. He is using a satire on Stevenson." But, Busby added, the satire "seems to be going over with the crowds fine."

PEOPLE WHO HAD KNOWN HIM for years said they had never seen Lyndon Johnson so "high." He had always deeply needed crowds and the feeling from them of acceptance and warmth and respect—now, thanks to the helicopter and to his own gifts, he was getting that feeling. "When he got in a crowd of people, that was when he was at his happiest," Woodward recalls, and "these were very special crowds for him." "He really *thrived* on the helicopter, and on the crowds that would come out," Margaret Mayer recalls. "He was energized, he was really charged up."

He was, in fact, carried away, at times all but out of control. A key to his handshaking method of "taking their hand first" was to reach for the people coming toward him to shake his hand, and in effect pull them past him. Shaking hands on the flatbed truck after the speech, he would sometimes be so excited that he would not only forget the pain in his cracked hands but would pull on voters' arms so enthusiastically that the voters needed all their alertness and physical strength to avoid being yanked off balance as Johnson pulled them past. "He was just *throwing* little old ladies past him," Busby recalls. "Woody and I stationed ourselves below the platform in case any of them needed to be caught." "When he was shaking hands, that was when he got most charged up," Margaret Mayer recalls; "It was just like he was plugged into electricity." During the handshaking, of course, KTBC announcer Joe Phipps was delivering over the helicopter microphone a nonstop spiel about the Congressman's accomplishments, and sometimes the Congressman became absolutely carried away by enthusiasm as Phipps' voice boomed out: "Come meet Congressman Johnson. He got roads for the Tenth District. He got lights for the Tenth District. If you elect him, he'll get lights for *you!* He'll get roads for *you!*" Sometimes, as Phipps' voice was filling the air, his subject, shaking hands on the truck, would shout to the announcer across the heads of the crowd: "Tell 'em about me, Joe! Tell 'em about me!"

Then the helicopter would take off, and Lyndon Johnson would be up in the air again, charging across the face of Texas, circling closer and closer to farmhouses to the accompaniment of pandemonium in the chicken coop and panic in the stable, landing beside railroad repair crews and little groups of farm workers so he could hug them and give them leaflets. (Occasionally, the pilot would simply circle the workers as Johnson bellowed down and showered them with great handfuls of campaign literature, but only occasionally. "He would rarely pass [a group] without going down," Busby recalls. "I would say, 'Hell, they're not going to vote.' He drew himself up in one of his more noble poses, and said: 'Son, they're *people!*' ") Seeing a train roaring along beneath him, he insisted on Chudars dipping low above the flat prairie and then racing the train for miles, the S-51 gradually passing the long line of freight cars as the engineer tooted his whistle in excitement. Circling a town where he was to land, he would lean far out of the helicopter window, waving his gray Stetson at the people below while he shouted, "Come to the speaking! Come to the speaking!" Above larger cities he went wild. Coming into Port Arthur (where the *Port Arthur News* was to proclaim the next day, under the headline "IT LANDS ON ROOFS AND IN PASTURES!," that "Candidate Lyndon B. Johnson's 'flying windmill' is probably the greatest political innovation since the invention of the ballot"), he circled the downtown shopping area again and again at a height of three hundred feet, leaning out of the helicopter window and yelling down through a megaphone (the helicopter's public address system was broken that day): "Hello, Port Arthur! Hello, Port Arthur! You look wonderful down there! Hello, Port Arthur!" while showering the city with his leaflets. Between cities, he urged Chudars to fly faster. And in his enthusiasm, Lyndon Johnson leaned out of the helicopter and, in the words of one reporter, "whipped his Stetson on the plane's flanks as though it were a bronco" that he was urging on to greater speed.

Following him was quite an experience, too.

Advance man Sam Plyler would leave each stop as soon as the helicopter touched down, because he had to be at the next stop before it arrived to make sure the landing area had been cleared, and he needed all the head start he could get. "Sam drove wide open, as fast as the car would go," Chudars recalls. Even so, if the town was some distance away, Plyler couldn't be sure he would make it in time, and as he sped along, he would keep darting backward glances into the sky to see if the black dot had come into view behind him. The other cars would wait until the helicopter lifted off, and then they would race out after it. There was quite a line of them. One car carried mechanic Nachlin and the radio engineer—and a two-way radio linked with Chudars, so that Nachlin could be summoned without delay in case engine trouble forced the helicopter down. Another carried a secretary and a speechwriter, generally Paul Bolton, and his typewriter. Another carried Busby—and *his* typewriter. Then there was a car for Woody, and his suitcases filled with the candidate's shirts, ties, pills, lozenges and hand creams. Sometimes there was a car for the band. Their absences for the campaign had cost the band's four members their radio station job, but Johnson had told them not to worry: "Some day you'll sing on the steps of the White House." And then there were the reporters' cars, more and more of them as the Flying Windmill became bigger and bigger news. Quite a caravan careened across Texas that summer—advance men, secretaries, speechwriters, aides, reporters, band members, sound truck operators—all of them, in Frank Oltorf's phrase, "driving like hell" along highways or narrow country roads, going just as fast as they could, while scanning the skies and hoping to make the next town before the Windmill landed.

State troopers stopped them. Once, waved over by a trooper, Plyler pleaded that he had to get to the schoolyard in the town up ahead because the helicopter was going to land there and he had to make sure no children got hurt. The trooper said, "Okay, I'll follow you. If that helicopter doesn't come in there, you're going to jail." And Plyler roared off again, the trooper flooring his gas pedal to keep up.

Tires blew out. Oltorf remembers a blowout while he was doing eighty on a narrow bumpy road, and how he was almost unable to get the car under control. Engines blew out. When a car was disabled, the driver simply abandoned it, like a dead horse by the side of the road, and flagged down another; the important thing was not to miss the Windmill's next landing. (Until the end of their lives, these men and women would tell stories about the summer they followed Lyndon Johnson and his Flying Windmill around Texas; as Oliver Knight of the *Fort Worth Star-Telegram* would write about one trip, "That mad dash from Navasota to Conroe in which I dodged stumps at 70 MPH just to keep up with that contraption will ever be green in my memory.") At the landing site, there would be the brief respite while Johnson gave his speech, and shook hands. And then he would clamber back into the helicopter, and the advance men would push back the crowd to clear enough room for the takeoff, and the mechanics, secretaries, speechwriters, advance men, aides and reporters would run back to their cars and screech off again in their long, frenzied dash back and forth across the state of Texas.

Dorothy Nichols was to be asked what she remembered about the 1948 campaign. "Three hours of sleep," she would reply. Three hours of sleep—or less.

And she remembered wet hair. Like the rest of the staff, Mrs. Nichols would recall, she had to be awake every morning at five, and after the early morning broadcast would spend the entire day racing frantically from town to town trying to keep up with the helicopter, at each town being given a long list of telephone calls to make or memos or speeches to type at the noon or evening stops.

> We tried to make every speech, but at any rate we had to get to
> the noon rest stop ahead of him, because we had his luggage.
> . . . We . . . had to get the hotel all in order for him to come
> in, unpack his suitcase, because he would get into his pajamas
> and get in bed and have a rest. So, that was my job. I was valet,

in other words. Then, at night, there would always be a meeting after dinner, a local meeting. So it was late hours. I . . . had to tuck him in bed and give him his pills and try to remember whether he had taken them or not, which sometimes was hard. I'd get to bed about three-thirty every morning and roll up my hair. Those were the days when we put pin curls in our hair, wet, and I would wake up at five o'clock every morning and comb it out, and it was still wet, but I did it again the next night. I took a book to read . . . a whodunit . . . and read the same sentence on page thirteen every night.

The original plan had been for Mrs. Nichols to stay with the candidate as secretary for the whole campaign, but that plan survived only until the campaign's first weekend, when she arrived back in Austin with the candidate, and reported in at the Hancock House. "They took one look at me at headquarters . . . and . . . realized that I couldn't take it all the time," she recalls. It was decided that for the rest of the campaign, she, Mary Rather and Dorothy Plyler would alternate on the road, one week on and two weeks back at headquarters, where the pace was less inhuman. Even with this schedule, however, by the end of the campaign the three women would be exhausted. "And," as Mrs. Nichols was to point out, "we were only doing it one out of every three weeks. He was doing it all the time."

Even when he was supposed to be resting, they came to realize, he wasn't. At the noon rest stop, Lyndon Johnson would indeed get into bed. But when someone came to waken him after an hour or so, he would almost invariably be awake—awake and ready with a long list of things to be done, things he had thought of during the hour. He had been "on the phone the whole time," Mrs. Nichols would say, or "he had somebody—local people or somebody on the staff—in there planning."

The afternoons would be long—hour after hour of flying across country, hovering over towns and speaking from the air, landing at farmhouses or in cotton fields, and, eight or nine or ten times a day, delivering a speech in a town, then shaking the hands of every member of the crowd. And evening brought no respite; often, Johnson would arrive at the town in which he was to spend the night just in time to race to his hotel, strip off his wringing-wet clothes, take a quick shower, dress and head out for the evening's event—a rally or a Rotary Club or Chamber of Commerce banquet—at which, after a reception, he would give a formal speech. And after the dinner (and the handshaking) would come an informal reception for prominent local supporters and financial contributors—identified as "FC's" (for "Fat Cats") in briefing memos for the day—either in Johnson's hotel suite or at the home of one of the fattest of the cats, receptions that were quite important because they gave Johnson an opportunity to meet new supporters, or to cement relations with those he knew only slightly—and to allay the fears of so many of them that he might secretly be a liberal after all.

In his initial instructions to his schedulers, Johnson had been very firm about the necessity for ending his evenings early. "You don't make any converts after ten o'clock," he had said. Before ten, therefore, Woody and other aides would begin trying to move visitors out of the room. But after the visitors had left, there would be a long list on yellow legal note-pads of people who had been trying to reach him that day, and the calls were returned—every one. "He did not spare himself," Woodward recalls. In Washington, the importance of callers was weighed, and many calls were not returned. Now, however, every name represented someone he needed. And before he went to bed, every name on the list would have a line through it and a brief notation for a follow-up letter to be sent in his name by headquarters. Sometimes a name on the list would represent a potential gain of only a single vote. The call was made. Shaking Johnson's hand after a speech in Kandalia, an elderly man mentioned a favorite nephew, James H. Knapp, who was an attorney in Arlington, a town near Dallas. In Arlington, Johnson telephoned Knapp to give him his uncle's regards, and ask for his support. (Knapp was not home when Johnson telephoned, but Johnson wrote him a letter, and in it said: "I am taking the liberty of dropping a note to your uncle.")

And as soon as he hung up the telephone, it seemed, it would ring— and it might be Alvin Wirtz or Ed Clark or Claude Wild or John Connally with some matter that had to be discussed and thought through, and the thinking had to be clear, no matter how tired he was, for calls from these men were important. And the candidate would be telephoning headquarters himself—making call after call, every time he thought of some item, no matter how minor, that might help his campaign. Wild urged him to stop. "Worry yourself about as few of the details of the campaign as you possibly can," the veteran campaign strategist said in a hand-delivered memo. "You can't run an organization with the perfection you might like to see it with volunteer and scattered help." Wild had heard how exhausted Johnson was, and he said the important thing was to "keep yourself physically in shape to continue your fine campaign." The others knew better than to try to stop their Chief from worrying. Eleven o'clock would pass, and then midnight and then, often, one o'clock, and two—and Lyndon Johnson, gaunt and haggard under his tan, would still be lying in his underwear on the bed in a sweltering small-town hotel room, cigarette in one hand, telephone in the other, trying to do "everything." Woody came to wake him at five, and often Lyndon Johnson was already awake, with more items on a list, more things his restless mind had thought up during the few hours in which he had been supposed to be sleeping. And when he left the hotel for that early morning broadcast, which was to be followed by the breakfast speech, and then by the grueling day in the helicopter, he left with those long strides and swinging arms. "He groused about no breaks," Woodward would recall years later, "but if there came a day when every minute wasn't filled," then he was furious.

Ed Clark, who had seen so many campaigners, said of Lyndon Johnson's 1937 campaign for Congress, "I never saw anyone campaign as hard as that. I never thought it was *possible* for anyone to work that hard." If that campaign had been Johnson's main chance, *this* campaign, the 1948 campaign, might be his last chance. Was 1937 the hardest Lyndon Johnson ever worked? Ed Clark would be asked. "Oh no," Clark said. "In 1948, he worked harder."

THERE WAS A SINGLE PAUSE in this headlong rush: one brief time-out for a visit unconnected with politics. On June 2, his helicopter grounded in Waco by high winds, Lyndon Johnson was touring nine North Central Texas towns by car, and one of the towns was Marlin. His official schedule in Marlin called only for a speech, a handshaking tour and quick courtesy calls on two or three local officials. Without the helicopter he was running very late by the time he reached Marlin, and as he fell further behind schedule there, his aides warned him that unless he hurried he might have to cancel the last two or three towns he was supposed to visit. But before he left—as his advance men were urging him into his car for the drive to the next town—he suddenly said: "No. There's someone I have to see here." Cutting off his aides' protests, he said curtly: "This is something that has to be done." He had his local campaign manager drive him to the home of Alice Glass's mother, and, while his staff fretted outside, looking at their wristwatches, he had a long, leisurely visit whose significance they could not understand.

THOSE WHO KNEW HIM realized the toll being exacted by his frantic pace. Walter Jenkins had seen his Chief drive himself to the verge of exhaustion before, but now, Jenkins saw, "he was more tired than he had ever been." Others saw frenzy, a frenzy that came close to hysteria.

One reporter, interviewing him, watched Johnson sit in a chair for a few minutes, jump up, sit in another chair, jump up again, pace around the room, lie on the bed, jump up and sit in a chair again, and wrote: "he's just too nervous to remain still." And as he moved restlessly from chair to chair, he puffed cigarettes, lighting one from the end of another; he rubbed big gobs of purple salve into his hands; he tilted back his head and sprayed his throat with a vaporizer and his nose with an inhaler; he gulped pills from a variety of bottles on the dresser; he stuck lozenges in his mouth and in his nervousness chewed instead of sucked them, so that he had to keep putting new ones in his mouth.

Intensifying this "nervousness" was the cocoon of optimism in which he was wrapped. In town after town, the report from his local campaign manager was glowing: he was pulling up on Ol' Coke; he was ahead of Ol' Coke; they had never thought anyone could give Ol' Coke a run for his money but by God, Lyndon, you're doing it! This, of course, is standard in any campaign, for local leaders are prone to be overimpressed by the aura of excitement which surrounds the candidate on his visit to their area, and are anxious moreover to let the candidate know how well they are doing on his behalf, but it was intensified in Johnson's case by the well-known violence of his reaction to any news that was not good; no one wanted to be the one to give him such news, and as a result he did not receive much of it. And while ordinarily his keen political instincts would have helped him to give such optimism its appropriate weight, he was even further charged up now by the peculiar nature of this campaign—both his and Coke's. Crowd size had always augured political success in Texas; thanks to his helicopter, he was in many areas drawing unprecedented crowds, and their response was good. And it was not merely the testimony of his own managers and of his own eyes that contributed to Johnson's euphoria, but what he read: the results of that last poll, which showed such substantial gains; the articles about his opponent's candidacy. Even Peddy was blanketing the state with radio speeches and developing a surprisingly strong campaign organization in Houston and some East Texas counties—and what was Coke Stevenson doing? Still interrupting his campaigning to attend to the shearing or the branding on his ranch, still driving from town to town, shaking hands, chatting with people, seldom giving a speech, and when he did speak, saying the same old things; as for radio talks, when Stevenson took to the air on July 16, it was only the third speech he had given in three months. In it he said he would "do as I have done in the past": uphold constitutional government and be a good steward of public funds. He said he favored aiding the Western nations of Europe, keeping America strong, opposing extensions of federal control. "The people of Texas know me," he concluded. "I don't have the money to hire an army of paid workers all over the state or to write a letter to every holder of a poll tax. But I have something more valuable. I have friends and supporters in every county in Texas who know the principles I stand for and who like those principles." Reporters said there was no news in the speech, that it was essentially the same talk he had been giving, several times each day, in the small towns to which he traveled. They said there was no news in his campaign. Indeed, during the previous few weeks, reporters had all but stopped covering Coke—for what, after all, was there to report? For days at a time, the ex-Governor all but vanished from view in the media. The scant coverage he received was not infrequently tinged with ridicule; a typical article described one of Coke's campaign days as "five towns and 95 handshakes." Johnson was seeing thousands of people each day, shaking hundreds of hands, was on the radio morning and night—and, often, noon. By all the standard indices of campaigning, he was doing well—and Coke was doing very badly.

Also playing a role in Johnson's feelings, it may be, was the depth of his need to believe what he was hearing and reading, to feel that he would succeed in his last chance. One of the typical violent alterations in Lyndon Johnson's moods had occurred. He was as euphoric in late June as he had been depressed early in the month. The prospect of victory always made his conduct as overbearing as the prospect of defeat made it humble to the point of obsequiousness. And now he was confident of victory. By the end of June, he was so euphoric as to be all but hysterical, a candidate at the point of irrationality.

He found it impossible to control himself, it seemed, even before the public he was trying to court. The slightest thing that went wrong triggered explosions of a kind with which his aides had long been familiar but which could only antagonize voters. Once, he arrived at a meeting where he was not supposed to give a speech and learned that the organization expected a short talk. Wheeling on his hapless advance men, he screamed, as the club members looked on: "I thought it was just gonna be coffee, doughnuts and bullshit!" On another occasion, advance man Cliff Carter had arranged to have the principal of Robstown High School and a delegation of teachers and students on the steps to greet him. Pleased, Johnson told Carter he wanted to shake the hands of every student in the school—in fact, every student in the whole city. That would take hours. "We don't have time, sir," Carter said, and produced the list of all the stops he was already scheduled to make. Johnson didn't even look at the paper; instead, he looked at Carter. As the principal observed the intensity of Johnson's glare, the hand he had extended to welcome the candidate slowly dropped to his side. The smiles faded from the faces of the delegation. There was a long silence. Then Johnson said, in the low, threatening tone that his aides feared more than any other: "Are we gonna join the Can't Do It Club right here on the steps of Robstown High School?"

Hotel lobbies became stages for violent scenes. There might be a brief delay in registration or a bellboy might be slow in arriving to take the candidate's bags. Johnson would shriek at the desk clerk or bellboy in public as he screamed at Woody or Mary Rather in private, while other patrons stared in astonishment. Hotel suites became stages, too. "He never got a meal that he didn't find fault with," Horace Busby recalls. "I just couldn't stand it: the way he'd beat up on the waiter or waitress. He would send back the food: 'Tell the cook I never saw so much fat on a piece of meat.' He would ring the bell and tell the desk clerk: 'This may be the worst hotel I've ever stayed in.' " The suites became stages even when the audience was the audience he most needed to impress favorably: local political leaders and their wives. "I'm talking about explosions, tirades," Horace Busby explains. "Especially explosions against the women who worked for him: 'Everyone in this outfit is against me!' That kind of thing." Local politicians "would come into his hotel suite with their eyes all aglow over the opportunity to meet him—all enthusiastic—and you could just see the light turn off." "His behavior was hurting him with local politicians," Busby says, and with their wives, whom they had often brought along to meet the great man, and who were even more shocked than their husbands at his abusiveness, particularly toward his female secretaries. If Johnson realized the effect his conduct was having, however, he seemed unable or unwilling to change it.

AND, BUSBY SAYS dryly, "his nudity was inappropriate."
    Nudity? Rooms in many small-town hotels had only hand basins, with communal toilets at the end of the hall. These bathrooms were small and hot, and it was cooler if the door was left open, so often Johnson left it open. Not a few voters therefore saw the candidate for the United States Senate sitting on the toilet, and described that sight to relatives and friends. Once, in Corsicana, Busby says, several key local supporters arrived at his suite with their wives for a private social hour following a speech. "He received them nicely, but then it was time for them to leave, and they didn't. He kept looking over at me to get them out of there," but the supporters were oblivious to Buzz's hints. "They were lost in rapture." So, Busby says, "right in front of them, he just starts undressing." When he had taken off his tie and shirt and they still hadn't left, "he started taking off his pants. The ladies started looking at the ceiling," and someone said maybe it was time to let Mr. Johnson get some rest.

HE COULDN'T CONTROL HIMSELF even with—or in front of—the press. He cultivated the reporters covering the campaign, at times with exaggerated flattery, at times with touches of unique political genius. One device he employed, and perhaps invented, was to introduce the members of the press to the audience at small towns. This impressed audiences and gave the townspeople a sense of identity with his campaign—in the case of an Allen Duckworth of the *Dallas News* or Jack Guinn of the *Houston*

Lyndon Johnson posed by a Hollywood
photographer (overleaf and right), and
(below) with John Connally, March, 1942

Lieutenant Commander Johnson (above) at Seven-Mile Strip and (below) with a pilot

One of a crowd: Johnson at a 1945 Navy Department luncheon for members of the House Naval Affairs Committee. In the front row are Representatives Margaret Chase Smith, Patrick Drewry and Carl Vinson, Secretary James Forrestal, Colonel Maas and Under Secretary Ralph Bard

Lady Bird with Lucy Baines,
August, 1947

Johnson with Lady Bird and his mother during his 1946 re-election campaign

Above: With John Connally and Fighting Joe Kilgore

Right: George and Herman Brown

Above: Johnson listening to Ed Clark's
speech at a 1945 homecoming
luncheon for Admiral Chester Nimitz
in Austin. At left: Governor Coke
R. Stevenson.

Right: With Alvin Wirtz

Lyndon Johnson and his staff at the House Office Building, Spring 1948: Glynn Stegall, Mary Rather, Warren G. Woodward, Walter Jenkins, Horace Busby, and Doris Seeliger

Coke Stevenson at 21

Stevenson, center right, as a
bookkeeper in the Junction
State Bank

Stevenson at the ranch

Fay Wright Stevenson

Stevenson, as Speaker of the Texas House (right), watches Governor Miriam ("Ma") Ferguson take the oath of office in 1933. On her right is her husband, former Governor Jim Ferguson.

Stevenson as Speaker of the Texas House of Representatives, 1933: above, at Speaker's podium; below, with delegation of schoolchildren

Governor Stevenson.
Below, with the dying Fay, at his inauguration in
August, 1941.

"Mr. Texas"

Coke and Marguerite
("Teeney") King Stevenson in
1954. Below, Teeney
Stevenson at the falls of the
South Llano.

Johnson and the Flying Windmill. Behind them, a Texas thunderstorm.

The Old and the New: Coke
Stevenson, above, at a
Lumbermen's Meeting; right,
Johnson comes to town

The meeting and the greeting

George Parr's machine and Ballot Box 13. Left to right: Deputy Sheriff Stokes Micenheimer, Hubert Sain, Givens Parr, Ed Lloyd and Barney Goldthorn. *At right:* Luis Salas, Parr's feared enforcer.

Texas Ranger Frank Hamer

Showdown Monday: Coke Stevenson surrounded by reporters after the
Democratic Executive Committee meeting in Fort Worth

Lady Bird and Lyndon enter the Federal District Court in Fort Worth. The man behind Johnson is Alvin Wirtz.

George B. Parr,
the Duke of Duval

Abe Fortas (below)

Lyndon Johnson and Tom Clark outside the Truman campaign train in San Antonio

President Harry Truman greets Johnson on the campaign train

The climax: the Alice courtroom—ballot boxes in foreground—minutes before the hearing was halted by U.S. Supreme Court Justice Hugo Black. Coke Stevenson is seated at center.

Senator Lyndon Baines Johnson, January 3, 1949. He and Senators J. Allen Frear, Paul H. Douglas and Robert S. Kerr pose with Senate President pro tempore Arthur Vandenberg (left).

Post, whose names were familiar; "when you're in a town of eight hundred or nine hundred people, why they like to . . . see the [face] of the byline they read," Charles Boatner of the *Fort Worth Star-Telegram* explains— while at the same time making the reporters feel like celebrities. But the flattery alternated with harsh tongue-lashings over the slightest hint of criticism in their stories. He even ridiculed them for no reason at all, displaying as he did so that keen insight into other men's feelings that enabled him to wound them so deeply. Dave Cheavens of the Associated Press was, recalls fellow reporter Margaret Mayer, "a fat, chubby little fellow . . . a sweet man, a great fellow, but really fat and sensitive about it." At one town Cheavens was scheduled to board the helicopter after Johnson's speech and ride to the next town with him. The helicopter was parked on the far side of a broad plowed field from the speakers' platform. After the speech, Johnson was hurrying across the field, his long legs enabling him to stride over the furrows. Cheavens, scrambling awkwardly after him, was falling farther and farther behind; Johnson shouted over his shoulder, "C'mon, Cheavens. Won't those little fat legs of yours carry you any faster than that?" "It was the type of thing that Johnson seemed to think he was entitled to say," Mayer says. "He could be quite mean to the reporters. . . . He thought he could get away with things like that. . . ." And, indeed, he could, because, in Mayer's words, "Johnson had courted favor with publishers all over the state." Reporters whose coverage of the campaign displeased him were transferred off the campaign—or fired.* Jack Guinn's articles in the *Houston Post* were impartial, but impartiality was not what Johnson had in mind from the newspaper whose publisher, former Governor William P. Hobby, had so admired Sam Ealy Johnson. Frank Oltorf was Johnson's campaign manager for one of the North Central Texas districts, but Johnson knew that Hobby was fond of Oltorf, a distant cousin. Telephoning Oltorf one evening, Johnson told him to ask "The Governor" if he could cover the Johnson campaign. Oltorf did so, and the Governor agreed, although Oltorf's only previous newspaper experience had been as the paper's student stringer at Rice University. (Asked how he would characterize his campaign stories for one of the state's largest newspapers, Oltorf says with a small smile: "They were adequate. And they certainly weren't unfriendly." "Did the editors rewrite you much?" Smile. "No.") Some reporters got their first view of Lyndon Johnson's relationship with subordinates during

* During one of his trips to North Texas, Johnson had spotted an article in the little *Palo Pinto Star* which did not meet his standards for reportorial accuracy. He ordered a former NYA assistant, Tony Ziegler, to "get in touch" with a local supporter, Judge Pat Corrigan of Mineral Wells, "and see if it could be stopped." Corrigan shortly informed Ziegler "that Mr. Brown, who is with the *Palo Pinto Star*, is no longer with them."

this campaign, and it upset them so deeply that occasionally one would attempt to intervene. One evening, the candidate had some of the top state political reporters in his suite, "talking to them, stroking them." But he "wanted something from Mary Rather and he spoke roughly and crudely to her . . . using obscenities that shocked even these hard-bitten reporters." After a minute or two, Felix McKnight of the *Dallas News*, burst out, "You can't talk to her like that! Apologize to her!" But "Johnson was totally oblivious to what he had done"—and, it appeared, "Mary was, too. She was used to it." The moment passed away without an apology. But almost none of this feeling showed up in so much as a hint in the reporters' articles.

He could not control himself even when on stage before the voters he was wooing. As his confidence grew, he seemed to feel that he had them in his grasp as he had his subordinates—and he began to treat them the same way. Circling a town in the S-51, as Phipps urged over the loudspeaker, "Come to the speaking, come to the speaking," he would grow irritated if the response was below expectations. Snatching the loudspeaker from Phipps, he would do the urging himself, and even through the loudspeaker's distortion, what Busby calls the "umbrage" in the voice was clear as it bellowed: "Come on out to the *speaking!*" During his speeches, anything less than total attention from his audience evoked the same reaction. Most politicians display affection for the children of potential voters. Johnson, however, was not particularly fond of children in any circumstances, according to Busby, and although their presence was necessary to attract their parents to his helicopter landings, he didn't intend to tolerate any nonsense from them. If there were childish antics in the crowd, the candidate would stop talking. And, Busby says, "I learned one thing: if he stopped—*hide!* You weren't going to like what happened next." Busby took his own advice—literally. Once, when Johnson stopped and stared down into the crowd at a little boy who was "talking or something," Busby says, "I went behind a tree. He kept staring at the boy, and finally said: 'Ahm not going to go on until the mother of this squirt comes up here and dusts his britches.' "

Receiving reports of Johnson's behavior, Alvin Wirtz attempted to calm him down, and his telephone calls worked for the first hour or two each day, but by mid-morning his quiet counsel had faded before the visions of victory dancing in Johnson's head. He had added to his speeches now a chant in which he asked audiences to join, and if the participation of the public wasn't always enthusiastic, there was usually enough of a claque on hand to make things sound as if it was. "Ain't gonna be no runoff." Johnson would say, "I'm gonna win without a runoff. Now let's hear it!" And the crowd—led by the claque—would chant "Ain't gonna be no runoff."

Whatever the young men in the Hancock House may have believed, the older, more experienced men in the Brown Building knew there was no realistic possibility of that prediction coming true. Johnson might do far better than had been expected, they felt, but as for polling more than half the vote?—the chant, they felt, was a campaign device; no one could seriously believe it might happen. But Ed Clark, talking one night in late June to the candidate, a candidate utterly in the grip of euphoria, came to a shocking realization: Lyndon Johnson believed it.

AND THEN, on the Fourth of July weekend, came the Texas Cowboy Reunion.

The Reunion had been begun in 1930 by Texans concerned by "the thinning ranks of true cowboys," the embodiment not just of a way of life but of the spirit and principles that made Texas so special. Its sponsors had picked a perfect site, a little town, Stamford, that sat on the vast rolling plains of West Texas like the set of a Western movie, right down to the headquarters of a working ranch, the Swenson Ranch, which was located on the town square, with its façade bearing the ranch's famous SMS brand with two backward S's. Stamford was located in the very heart of what had been the land of the "mustangers," the men who captured wild horses and drove them to Northern markets; children in this area grew up to the stories of the mustang stallions—Black Devil, Star Face, the Pacing Wild Stallion and, best remembered of all, Midnight, the great black herd leader who for years had outwitted men to keep his mares and foals free. By 1948, the mustangs had gone the way of the buffalo, but the great herds of cattle stretching to the horizon were still there, and so were the cowboys who herded them, sitting lonely guard against the horizon, and so was the cowboy's way of life; as one writer put it, "throughout this part of Texas the atmosphere of the West prevails" so strongly that automobiles almost look out of place. The Reunion's founders had designed it to preserve and revitalize the cowboys' traditions and skills by holding bunkhouse dances, chuck-wagon meals and a rodeo in which participation was limited to "nonprofessionals" to ensure that only "true cowboys," men who were still actually working the range, would compete; ranches sent their top hands to the three days of roping, cutting-out and riding contests that were held over each Fourth of July weekend. During the war, the young men of the ranches, the sons of the ranch owners and their cowboys, had gone off to fight, and the Reunion's founders had feared the event would die away, but after the war, it actually became bigger than ever. Families would come from all over the Panhandle and West Texas, some in pickup trucks but an astonishingly large percentage in chuck wagons, which would stand in a huge encampment on an area set aside outside of town near the fifty acres of horse and cattle corrals around the rodeo grandstand. In 1948, the attendance was more than twenty-five thousand.

Coke Stevenson arrived on a morning during which, as Bob Murphey drove him across the plains, he had listened to Lyndon Johnson assailing him; in his radio broadcast that morning, Johnson had said: "Old men killed Woodrow Wilson's plan for the League of Nations, old men in the Senate. I could say pipe-puffing old men, but that might look like a reference to one of my opponents." He himself had fought in the last war, Johnson said, unlike his opponent; "I didn't sit and puff my pipe when our country was at war." Arriving at Stamford, Stevenson was told that a big crowd of reporters was on hand—not to see him but to see Johnson's helicopter, which was scheduled to land at the rodeo site later that day. A Johnson sound truck was driving through the town taunting him: "Coke, if you've never seen a helicopter, here's your chance." The reporters crowded around him, asking him to hold a press conference. "I'm not here for politics," he replied. "I'm here to be with my friends." Since he would be riding in the parade, he had brought along his black boots, and he bent down and tugged them on.

TWO RIDERS carrying huge flags, one the Stars and Stripes, the other the Lone Star, were first in the parade, and behind them came six pretty girls in cowboy regalia on six white horses, leading the famous Cowboy Band of Abilene's Hardin-Simmons University also in cowboy regalia, playing Sousa marches. And then came the riders—hundreds of them, who had been milling around in giant corrals waiting for the parade to start—in a long column of threes. There were so many of them that even over the music you could hear the thudding of hooves.

Coke Stevenson led them out.

He had felt it was not right for a candidate for office to be leading the parade, and his old friend Bill Swenson of the SMS, president of the Reunion, had said he would ride beside him, but as the parade began, Swenson reined in his horse so that he was a few steps behind, and Stevenson was alone.

He was riding "Pal," a big, magnificently muscled Palomino, but Stevenson, with his great shoulders and the erectness with which he held himself in the saddle, seemed almost too big for him. He was still wearing a brown business suit and his gray Stetson hat without the wide brim, but the crowd watching him come saw a man riding like the cowboys behind him, sitting easily, deep and back in the saddle with a lot of leather showing in front, where it was most comfortable for the horse. Made nervous by the music and the excitement, Pal shied and pranced at first, but Stevenson calmed him down.

There were no cheers, but as he rode, people called out to him. "Hello, Coke." "Hey, Coke." "Howdy, Coke." He called back. "Hello, Jack." "Hello, Bill." A reporter realized that what he was seeing was "an exchange of greetings from old friends." At first the calls were scattered, but as he rode along, there were more and more of them until they were almost a continuous chorus; along the whole line of march, what you heard between the noise of the band fading ahead and the noise of the hooves mounting behind was, as one reporter wrote, "one constant [greeting] from the sidewalk crowds," a quiet but immense outpouring of affection.

And there was a gesture, too. It was a cowboy gesture, a peculiarly Texas gesture, in fact, for cowboys do not tip their hats except to ladies. As men said "Hello, Coke," they would touch one or two fingers to the brim of their Stetsons and then point the fingers toward the big man riding by. Even men who didn't call out made that gesture; every man in the crowd was making it, it seemed. To Murphey, standing on the porch of the hotel watching his uncle ride toward him, it looked as if hands were rising and touching hat brims in a long wave as Coke Stevenson passed by, "almost in a kind of salute."

And it wasn't only old men making that sign of respect. The young men in the crowd—the sons and grandsons of the old ranchmen who had settled this range—were making it, too. Their fathers and grandfathers had told them the story of Coke Stevenson, about the young boy starting up the freight line and studying at night in the lonely hills, about the young rider herding cattle up on the Divide, about the founding of the famous ranch, about the love story of Coke and Fay, the young wife who had believed her husband should be Governor, about the rancher who as Speaker and Lieutenant Governor and Governor had never become a politician, had never betrayed his standards, which were, of course, their standards, too, about their beloved "Cowboy Governor"—their own Governor. And as he came closer, the big man sitting so erect and calm on the prancing horse, the young men, too, touched the brims of their hats in salute. Behind the crowd—wherever there was space—were pickup trucks parked in a long row. Their owners, mostly young couples, would be standing in the backs of the trucks with their children so that they could see over the heads of the crowd. But often the children couldn't see. So, as Coke Stevenson approached, fathers and mothers would pick up their children and put them on their shoulders or hold them up in the air, so that they, too, could see "Mr. Texas" passing by.

After the parade, the 5,000-seat grandstand was filled to overflowing for the rodeo. Stevenson was sitting in the judges' box. Five other state officials and candidates for office were with him, and before the rodeo began the master of ceremonies introduced them one by one. The first five introductions were greeted by a polite but unenthusiastic sprinkling of applause. Then the announcer began, "Our beloved former Governor." And suddenly, before the announcer could finish, everyone was cheering. They were giving the rebel yell. They were throwing their hats in the air. Four or five riders who had been waiting on horseback against one wall to help in the events, caught up in the excitement, spurred their horses into a gallop across the arena, came to a rearing halt before the judges' box and waved their hats toward Stevenson. Everyone was shouting "Coke! Coke! Coke!"

BOB MURPHEY REMEMBERS how moved his uncle was by what had happened. Driving away from Stamford that night, Stevenson said: "Bob, the kind of people you saw today, remember them. The ranching business is changing; that kind of people—you won't see them again."

And Bob Murphey remembers what he thought when his uncle said that. "I didn't say anything," he recalls, "but I thought: Uncle Coke, we won't ever see your kind again, either."

THE REPORTERS who were waiting for Lyndon Johnson's helicopter at the Cowboy Reunion were disappointed. At his final stop before Stamford, the town of Aspermont, twenty-seven miles away, he had received a telephone call describing the reception Coke Stevenson was being given at the Reunion. He decided not to attend. Using the excuse that his helicopter was low on fuel because a truckload of gasoline had missed connections, he flew instead to Abilene.

BAD NEWS WAS WAITING for him there, too: the result of the latest private poll he had commissioned, and advance news of the latest Belden Poll, which was even then in progress and would be completed the next day. In the previous Belden Poll, Johnson had pulled closer to Stevenson: Stevenson had led Johnson by only 47 percent to 37 percent among voters whose preference had been decided; 23 percent of all voters had not decided. In Belden's new poll, the percentage of undecideds had dropped from 23 to 18, but Johnson's gains had all but come to a halt. Among voters with a preference, Stevenson still led him, 47 percent to 38 percent. (Peddy had 10 percent, the eight minor candidates a total of 4 percent.) The results, which Belden summarized as "almost the same as [the] results" of the poll a month before, were disquieting. During the month just past, the month of the great excitement over his helicopter, Johnson had picked up exactly one percentage point—and Coke had lost not even one. The percentages in Johnson's private poll cannot be found, but men connected with his campaign recall that its findings were even more unfavorable than Belden's.

For a candidate as sophisticated as Johnson in interpreting polling figures, the news was discouraging: since all the excitement about his campaign during the past month, the massive money poured into it, had not cut further into Coke Stevenson's strength, cutting further might well be impossible. During that month, Johnson's name had been brought before the voters in Texas not only by newspaper and radio coverage but in an unprecedentedly heavy wave of newspaper and radio advertising, direct mail, billboards, handbills. And Johnson, in his campaigning in so many small towns, had been brought before the voters in person. The result: no significant increase in his support. Had he reached the limit of his support—a limit above which he could not go? He had drawn hope in the early-June poll from the high percentage of undecided voters. Now a substantial number of those voters were no longer undecided, but, contrary to his firm expectation, they had not decided for him, at least not by any substantial majority; almost as many were going into Coke's camp as into his.

Most ominous of all, of course, was the fact that with 18 percent of the voters still undecided, Coke with 47 percent was very close to 50.1 percent, the majority which would make the first primary also the last. Lyndon Johnson's prediction—"Ain't gonna be no runoff"—might prove accurate, but not in the way he had intended. With only three weeks to go before the first primary, there was a strong possibility that despite Peddy's presence in the race, the first primary would be the last. Lyndon Johnson might well have to overtake Coke Stevenson in only three weeks. And study the poll results though he might that night in his hotel room in Abilene, they contained no indication that he could do it. They told him that he was on the verge of losing his last chance.

AFTER THAT NIGHT in Abilene, the euphoria was gone. It was replaced by desperation.

By coincidence, the next day, he got a new helicopter. The S-51, having reached the limit of mileage it could fly without a major checkup and overhaul, left on its return trip to Connecticut, and it was replaced by a 47-D model furnished, at Stuart Symington's request, by the Bell Helicopter Corporation. Dramatic as Johnson's campaigning had been before, now the drama was heightened. The 47-D was much smaller than the S-51, little more than a Plexiglas bubble, five feet wide, five feet long and five feet high, barely big enough to seat a pilot and a passenger at the front of a twenty-three-foot-long fuselage; it looked like a toy in comparison with the Sikorsky craft. Because it required so much less space in which to land, it could get in closer to the centers of population, where the landings were most effective, and its pilot, Joe Mashman, a thirty-two-year-old test pilot, could use its greater maneuverability to perform new crowd-pleasing stunts before and after landings. Its engine generated a meager 178 horsepower at best, and less in hot weather, so that with a load of any size, Mashman was to recall, "that little engine had to strain just to keep the aircraft airborne." Hardly had he landed in Austin when KTBC radio engineers arrived with an amplifier and a microphone which they told him the helicopter was going to have to carry—and which weighed a hundred pounds. Next, cars drove up with bundles of campaign literature for the candidate to distribute at unscheduled stops. And then the candidate himself arrived (he displayed no interest in the little craft, but "just got on and said, 'Let's go!' "). No one had told Mashman how big Lyndon Johnson was, and he was "dismayed" to find out; one look at him, the pilot was to recall, and "I knew I had a problem." Exacerbating the problem would be the necessity—caused by the candidate's insistence on landing as close to the center of town as possible—of taking off from constricted areas, which required rising steeply, often almost vertically, and thus using more power than if the helicopter could, as was normal, rise in a shallower climb. Although Mashman would keep the weight down by never filling the gas tank to capacity, for the remainder of the campaign, as the "Little Brother of the Johnson City Windmill" toured small towns all across Texas, almost every takeoff was an adventure. Mashman would lift off a few feet above ground, and then inch a little higher, hovering while studying his instruments to determine if he had sufficient "reserve," or unused power capacity, "to safely climb on out." Often, the instruments would show that he was using all the power the engine could generate just to hover, and he would have to return to the ground. The pamphlets would be unloaded and put in a car which would meet the helicopter outside town, at a location at which there would be more room, and less power, needed for takeoff. But sometimes that didn't help sufficiently. "Mr. Johnson, we've got to take the doors off," Mashman would say. If the fifteen pounds thus saved still wasn't enough, the only remaining jettisonable item would have to go. Mashman would set the helicopter down again, and the candidate would disembark, and a car would drive him to the site outside town. After a day or two, Mashman learned to evaluate the situation in advance. As he circled a town, with Johnson using the bullhorn to round up the populace, Mashman, if he "saw it was going to be tight," would tell his passenger he would be able to land with him, but not take off.

Johnson turned these difficulties to advantage. In the past, some of the people attracted to the landing site by the helicopter would drift away before his speech. Now Johnson devised a tactic to keep them from doing so. After the helicopter had landed, and he had told the audience to "come on around, and look at the whirlybird," he would, before beginning his speech, say: "My good pilot Joe tells me it'll be too dangerous if I take off with him because we wouldn't have enough power to clear those 30,000-volt high-tension wires over there. He's going to have to take off alone. And it's going to be mighty tight. I just hope and pray he'll be able to make it." Then, having, as Mashman puts it, "told the people of the impending daredevil feat," he would launch into his political speech. If people started leaving anyway, Johnson would ask them not to. "Now, folks, I want you to stay here and wait until Joe tries to get the Johnson City Windmill off the ground. He's going to need all the help he can get—he's going to need your prayers to get through this safely. We're all hoping that the good Lord sees that Joe gets over those high-tension wires over there. I know we'll all be here helping to pray for him." And indeed, as the pilot lifted off at the end of the speech, Lyndon Johnson would, in an effective climax to his little rally, lead the crowd in prayers for his safety: "Let's pray for Joe now. Good luck, Joe. We're with you, Joe. Help him, O Lord. Help this brave man make it out of here safely."

But Johnson was aware now of the limitations of helicopter drama. The polls had told him that. The helicopter could lure people out to meet him, it could even keep them around to listen to him. It couldn't persuade them to vote for him, not over Coke Stevenson.

Only he could do that.

Hard as he had worked before, now, during the three remaining weeks between the Fourth of July weekend and the first primary, he worked harder.

The summer of 1948 was a summer, day after day, week after week, of a laconic one-word weather forecast: *Hot*. That summer, the summer of Lyndon Johnson's last chance, was, in fact, one of the hottest summers of the century in Texas; it was a summer of terrible drought; and, in bone-dry East Texas, of widespread forest fires. Day after day, all across the vast state, the thermometer rose to near one hundred degrees by mid-morning and stayed there until sunset. Sunset brought only minor relief; the nights were little cooler. Few small-town hotels had air conditioning; after ten or eleven hours out in that blazing sun each day, Lyndon Johnson had to sleep at night in steaming hot rooms. During the day, moreover, the helicopter in which he was spending so many hours was no longer the big Sikorsky S-51, whose roof extended partly over the back seat, providing some shade there for Johnson; Chudars, who had to remain in the front seat to pilot the S-51, says that flying surrounded by unprotected glass on which the sun was beating down was as hot as "flying in a greenhouse." In the tiny Bell, there was no shade, nothing around Johnson and his new pilot but the curved Plexiglas bubble that intensified the sun's rays. Mashman, who had flown helicopters in Brazil for a year, had considered himself inured to heat, but that was only because he had never experienced "the Valley" during a drought. Even removing the helicopter's doors didn't help. "With the high humidity in the Valley, or Galveston or Houston, and the temperature in the nineties, the wind [from the open doors] didn't help because our perspiration wouldn't evaporate. We would be just dripping in there." Most landing sites were naked of shade, of course, since they had been selected because there were no trees or buildings on them. After landing the helicopter, Mashman could hunt up a tree, or a house, and take advantage of its shade. Johnson couldn't. Sometimes so brutal was the sun that Mashman, before leaving the helicopter, would slowly rotate the rotor blades until one of them was between the candidate and the sun, and Johnson would try to speak while remaining in that sliver of shade, but an eight-inch-wide rotor blade provided pathetically little protection. Campaigning in Texas during the summer of 1948 was, in the memory of those who were there, like campaigning in an oven.

Behind in the race—watching his last chance fade—Lyndon Johnson was campaigning longer and longer hours now, but no matter how long the hours were, they weren't long enough for him. There was no more talk about "breaks" in the schedule. Johnson wanted more speeches, more "hoverings" over towns too small for speeches, more handshakings—a break meant minutes lost, possible votes lost; he knew now that he needed every one. Woodward had thought eight or nine speeches a day—plus the morning and evening radio talks—the limit of the endurance even of Lyndon Johnson; now, in the first two days after the Fourth of July revelation, touring in the merciless heat of Texas' Gulf Coast, Lyndon Johnson delivered, in addition to his radio broadcasts, thirty-one stump speeches—and made fifty unscheduled stops to shake hands with cotton-pickers, farmers, or just a lone man driving a tractor. On the second day, he couldn't seem to tear himself away from Robstown, where, as a teen-ager who had run away from home, he had worked eleven hours a day in a roasting-hot cotton gin in which the air was so thick with dust and lint from the cotton being pounded into bales that men working in it often found themselves gasping for breath; his job had been tending a big steam boiler, and he had been constantly terrified that it would explode as other boilers had exploded in Robstown gins that year. By the time he arrived in Corpus Christi on that second day, it was just before dark; Mashman, who had been watching shadows close in around his craft, breathed a sigh of relief when he had it on the ground before total darkness. Jumping out of the helicopter and into a waiting car, exhorting the driver to greater speed, Johnson raced into the downtown area of the city and shook hands with passing pedestrians for hours. The next day's campaigning was summarized by a headline in the *Houston Post*: "JOHNSON IN 24 PUBLIC APPEARANCES IN DAY." The length of time he had been out on the road that day was summarized in a phrase in the story: "Sunup to sundown." On the following day, Thursday, July 8, thunderstorms hit the Gulf Coast as Johnson was flying along the coastline for a scheduled stop at Bay City. Ahead of the helicopter was swirling blackness; when Mashman said he couldn't land in the storm, Johnson ordered the pilot to circle the storm as close to it as possible so as to lose the least time on the way to the next stop, at West Columbia.

The speeches he was giving were different, too. He was scared now, as scared as he had been in his first campaign, in 1937. Now his chance wasn't his first but his last, and he was no longer the well-tailored "senatorial" candidate of the first few weeks of this campaign; he was the Lyndon Johnson of 1937 again, awkward, nervous, frightened—and one of the greatest stump speakers in Texas history.

He wasn't trying to act like a Senator now. He wasn't trying to act like a statesman. He was trying to win. The people in front of him held his fate in their hands. He told them he was one of them. "I'm a country boy, too," he told them—a statement which wasn't hard to believe as he stood there, tall and skinny, in his soaked-through shirt and bedraggled tie and wrinkled, baggy seersucker trousers, his face grimy and sweat-streaked. "I chopped cotton, I hoed my Daddy's fields." And because he was one of them, he told them, he understood how city people—like the people in Houston and Dallas who were backing Coke Stevenson—looked down on them. "They're saying I was a goatherder," he said. "That's right, I was. They say I was just a country schoolteacher. That's right, I was. But there's sure nothing wrong with that. I've had calluses on my hands. I worked on the first roads that ever got built in my county—with these hands. And I'm not ashamed of it. I'm proud of it." When he was young, he had gone through the trials their sons had gone through.

He had shared their sons' dangers, too, he told them. In the South Pacific, "This boy I roomed with—he was a country boy, too."

He had shared *all* their hopes and fears. As a boy, he said, he had lived on a farm that did not have electricity, and he had seen his sainted mother down on her knees every washday scrubbing clothes in a washtub, and "standing all day over that red-hot cookstove" ironing clothes with those heavy "sad irons" in a steaming-hot kitchen in midsummer "so that I and my brother and my sisters would be neat like the other kids." And as a Congressman, he said, he had helped the people of his district to realize their hopes and dreams. Getting electricity for his district hadn't been easy, he told them, and he told how the Rural Electrification Administration officials had told FDR that the population wasn't dense enough and how FDR had replied, "Oh, they breed pretty fast down there," and how the REA had then said, "Those people are too poor: they won't pay their bills." "The interests and the trusts—they were against us," Lyndon Johnson said. "The power companies and the utility barons, they said, 'You can't take lights out to those people. You can't sink poles in that granite.' Well, we got the holes in," he would say, "and we got the poles up, we put lights in twenty thousand farm homes. And do you know how many bills were delinquent? Not one. We can put REA lights in every rural home in Texas. We can build a blacktop road to every farm. We can pay our elder citizens a pension of fifty dollars a month. We can pay our teachers an extra four hundred dollars a year. We can guarantee the farmer minimum prices on farm products. We can build hospitals in every county."

When he talked about foreign affairs now, the phrases he used were phrases to which these listeners could relate. He played on their fears as he played on their hopes. America was in great danger, he told them. It was in danger from "the red tide of Communism," which was constantly planning a sneak attack. "Houston or Galveston could easily be the next Pearl Harbor." "This is off the record," he would confide, "but I can tell you that in 1951 another nation will have the atomic bomb. Twenty bombs in twenty places in twenty minutes could immobilize the United States." And, he said, it was not just the atomic bomb that Americans must fear. The next war, he said, would be a war not only of bombs but of germ warfare—whose horrors he vividly portrayed. Therefore, he advised his audience, they should pray. "From the time you say the blessing before breakfast in the morning until the last child is tucked in at night, pray that we will find the solution to the problem of peace." But prayer was not the only answer to the problem, he said. America must also be prepared. It must be strong. "Nobody would walk up and give Jack Dempsey a punch in the nose," he said. "And nobody is going to give us a punch in the nose if we're strong enough, too." That was the reason, he said, that he was for a seventy-group Air Force. Seventy groups? "I wish it were a hundred and seventy groups." We need "the best atomic bomb that money can buy," he said. And we must have a policy of not yielding an inch to the Communists. America must "draw the quarantine line and we would rather have it on the Mediterranean than on the shore of the Gulf of Mexico." The Communists, he said, are ready to move in on Berlin if

America yields one inch. "One inch," he would shout, shaking a long finger in warning. "One inch!"

He would say whatever they wanted to hear. To rural audiences, he shouted, "The day is over in Texas when people will work for sheepherders' wages while a few rich men skim all the cream," but to wealthy listeners—businessmen and oilmen in the Petroleum Club of Dallas or the Ramada Club in Houston—his vocabulary was not Populist but plutocratic and the cream—increasing the cream—was what he emphasized. He didn't merely say the oil depletion allowance should be continued; he said it should be increased, immediately, from twenty-seven and a half percent to thirty percent. Moreover, the government should set up a system of allocation of scarce materials to oil producers so that they would come first on the list.

In labor districts he was pro-labor, in anti-labor districts he was anti-labor, and in both districts he was very effective.

And when he talked about his opponent, he was just as effective. His listeners' respect for Coke Stevenson was the main obstacle between him and his dream. It had to be destroyed. And no one could destroy a reputation better than Lyndon Johnson.

Mimicking his opponent had become a staple of his appearances, of course, and it invariably got a laugh. But making his listeners laugh at Coke Stevenson was no longer enough; he had to make them angry at him. And as the sight of a corncob pipe in a farmer's mouth had given him inspiration, so, now, did faces in a window.

The window was in the second story of the County Courthouse in the North Texas town of Weatherford. On July 17, both candidates campaigned in the town. Stevenson had shaken hands and toured the Courthouse in the early morning and had then driven off to the next town. Some hours later, Johnson landed and was speaking in front of the Courthouse. The temperature that day was 106 degrees, and candidate and crowd were sweltering as he talked—when suddenly Johnson glanced up at the window, and saw Courthouse clerks and county officials peering out, and noticed that the window was closed and that there was an air-conditioning unit protruding from it. "Look up there," he shouted. "Look in the window. There's Coke up there. Folks, I'm out here talking to you man to man in the hot sun, and that's where Coke is, standing up there in that air-conditioned Courthouse looking down at us." Coke, of course, wasn't one of the faces in the window; he wasn't even in Weatherford any longer, but the people in the crowd didn't know that; recalls an observer, "He [Johnson] pointed up there, and sure enough there were people behind the window looking down. You couldn't see them clearly, and I'm sure everybody thought one of them was Coke, all nice and cool while they were sweating."

Thereafter, the heat and the air conditioning—the blazing sun and the fact that he, Lyndon Johnson, was out there in it with them—were staples of his speeches. "My opponent does his campaigning in the Ramada Club and the Petroleum Club—where it's air-conditioned," Johnson would say. "He does his campaigning at buffet lunches, with millionaires who think they're the bosses of this state. Well, I'm out here in the hot sun campaigning with you. Because I know who the bosses of this state really are! *You! YOU!!!* You who I meet in the squares and the fields, you who I meet out here in the hot sun—you're the real bosses of this state!"

The mimicking got laughs; this touched a deeper chord. "That's right, Lyndon," someone would shout. "You tell 'em, Lyndon!" And suddenly other voices would be shouting, too. "Tell 'em, Lyndon! Tell 'em, Lyndon."

"Yes, you're the bosses," he would shout to men and women who had to work every day—in fields or farmhouse kitchens—in fierce heat. "You're not sitting up in any air-conditioned rooms. And neither am I. I'm out here in the fields and the squares. And it's the people in the fields and the squares who are going to elect the next Senator of this state. He's going to be elected by *you*." "You tell 'em, Lyndon!" a voice would shout. Another voice would shout, "A-men." And all at once many voices would be shouting "A-men, Lyndon! A̲-men, Lyndon! You tell 'em, Lyndon!"

He told them more. In one speech, he said, "I'm not going to sling any mud in this campaign." Then he said that Coke was sixty-one years old (actually, he was sixty), and was campaigning for a job that paid $15,000. "Old" was a word he drummed into his listeners. "He's an old man," he said. "A big-bellied, pipe-smoking old man." And it was the "old men of the Senate" who had kept the United States from being prepared for the war. "We don't need any more big-bellied old men in the Senate." "Isolationist" was another word he drummed into his listeners—until he started using a stronger word: "appeaser." Stevenson, he said, "is an umbrella man." "He talks Chamberlain talk." "He wants another Munich." "You can put this in your pipe and smoke it: Texas is not going to send either an appeaser or an old man to the Senate, because the immediate job is not of appeasement but preparedness." Another word was "stooge." The proud Stevenson would pick up newspapers to see headlines like: "STEVENSON STOOGE OF AUSTIN LOBBYISTS, JOHNSON CHARGES." As Governor, he said, Stevenson had been the tool of the big oil companies and the "trusts and the interests," and now, he said, "these same men—who sit with Coke in air-conditioned hotel rooms—want to put their stooge in the United States Senate." The attacks grew harsher and harsher. Coke's refusal to make specific campaign promises, Johnson said, was designed to deceive the voters. "For too long, the voters have been deceived by candidates who spoke to you in glittering generalities, but who secretly engaged in double talk," by "this man with the slick tongue."

So powerful were Johnson's speeches now that even reporters and aides sometimes found themselves stirred by passages they had heard hundreds of times before.

Talking about the need for preparedness, from a flatbed truck in a little park in an East Texas county seat called Canton, he had gone through the routine about Colonel Stevens' "smelly socks" and was telling his audience that "never again must we send our boys through flak-filled skies unprotected." In the audience was Warren Woodward. He was ready to start the applause at the high points, but this wasn't necessary, so caught up was the crowd in what Lyndon Johnson was saying. Woodward himself was so moved that when Johnson said, "I've got this young man working in my campaign who flew thirty-five missions over Europe and his plane was hit thirty-five times, and I don't want him to ever have to go over there again unprepared; we have to give him the tools he needs," Woodward applauded and cheered along with the farmers and ranchers around him. And when Johnson unexpectedly added a new line to the routine, Woody cheered that, too, without at first grasping its relationship to him. "I want that young man to come up here," Johnson shouted, and Woodward shouted, "Yes, send him up!"—not understanding, he was to recall, that Johnson "was talking about *me*." "C'mon up here beside me," Johnson kept shouting, and Woodward kept shouting, "Yeah, go on up! Go on up!" until finally Johnson caught his eye, and "finally it dawned on me that I was that one that was supposed to go up," and that he had been shouting and leading the applause for himself. But when Woodward clambered up in the truck, "mortified" over the fact that he had been calling for his own appearance, he realized no one had noticed that he had been among the shouters, for the whole crowd had been as moved as he had been by the words of the tall, haggard, grimy, perspiration-soaked man on the truck. At speech after speech now, the crowds were caught up. "You could see the rapport building between himself and the crowd," Horace Busby says. Rural audiences, normally so reserved, would "start out at a distance, in a semicircle," he says. But as Johnson spoke, "almost every time, the semicircle would edge closer and closer to him."

Lyndon Johnson knew how to make the most of such enthusiasm, how to play on it and intensify it. He wanted his audiences to become involved. He wanted their hands up in the air. And, having been a schoolteacher, he knew how to get their hands up. He began, in his speeches, to ask questions. The first ones he asked of the kids who had been so enraptured by the helicopter. "How many of you are going to tell your folks to be sure to vote?" he would ask, and then, "How many of you are going to tell your folks to vote for Lyndon Johnson?" Wrote a reporter: "The hands would fly up as if Superman himself had asked it." Then he directed questions at the parents. "I'm traveling to places to see folks where no other candidate has bothered to go," he would say. "Am I the first candidate who's been here? Raise your hands if I'm the first candidate you've seen." The hands would go up. And he could build on his questions, too. When he was speaking in a town that he knew Stevenson and Peddy had not visited, he would say, "I keep reading about how many counties [the other candidates] have visited, how many miles they have traveled. Has anyone here seen another candidate?" If no hands went up, he would say, "C'mon, raise your hands if you've seen another candidate? Surely someone here has seen one of them? No one? No one has even seen another candidate. Well, you're seeing me. I'm here with *you*." Or if, when Johnson asked if anyone had seen another candidate, someone *did* raise his hand, Johnson would ask, "Where did you see him?" And no matter what the reply, Johnson had a line ready. If, for example, the responder said he had seen Stevenson in a hotel, Johnson would say: "What did I tell you? I'm out here in the hot sun with you people, and my opponent—my big-bellied, pipe-smoking opponent—spends his time campaigning in air-conditioned hotels."

As good as he was while he was speaking, he was better after the speeches. For after the speech came the meeting and greeting.

"He never just stayed on the [flatbed] truck or the platform, or, if the speech was indoors, on the podium," Woodward recalls. "He would finish a speech, and then he would *hurry* to the back door so he could shake hands. He didn't want anyone to leave before he had shaken their hand."

During the first weeks of the campaign—until, perhaps, that terrible Fourth of July weekend—he had rushed through the handshaking . . . in the description of Woodward and Busby, all but "throwing" people past. There was no throwing now.

The things he had been saying in the speech had made these rural Texans feel he was one of them. "They felt he was approachable," Woodward says. "They didn't hesitate to come over to him." And in a surprisingly large number of towns—not only in his own Tenth Congressional District and in the Fourteenth, for which he had worked for almost four years as a congressional secretary, but in other districts as well, through his NYA activities or his 1941 senatorial campaign—he knew personally one or more of the people crowding around him, and through the "favorable" list his staff had compiled for each town he was able to put names to faces. And when he saw someone he knew, Lyndon Johnson's face would, in the words of one observer, "just *light* up" with pleasure. He would reach out for him, and call the man's name. "Old Bob," he would say. "How you comin'?" He would put his arm around Bob's shoulders. "How *are* you?" he would ask. "Ahm awful glad to see you. Well, the last time ah saw you was when you came up to Washington to see Dick Kleberg. Ah hope you haven't been up again without comin' by to say howdy to me? You haven't. Well, ah hope you'll come up again, and we can chat for a while." "At almost every stop," Woodward says, "there was someone he had done something for." The "favorable" cards—and that remarkable memory—enabled him now to make the most of what he had done. "Someone would introduce himself, and say, 'Lyndon, do you remember my boy, John? You helped him get his disability.' 'Ah sure do. Ahm glad ah could help him. What's he doin' now? How's he comin?' " And when the man had told him, he would say: "That's *good!*" Or "Is there anything ah can do for him?" And "How's your missus?" Or they would ask him for new favors. "Lyndon, my boy—you know he was in the service, and he was hit in the leg. I need him to help out on the farm, but, Lyndon, he can't plow, and they say he can't get any disability, and I don't think they're doing right by him." And Johnson would turn to Woodward, who would be standing there with his notebook: "Woody, get that boy's name, and we'll look right into it."

The rapport was cemented—or, if there had been no previous connection, created—with physical affection, with hands and eyes, or, in the case of women, quite often with kisses. He would call older women "Mother" or "Grandma" even if he had never met them before, and hug and kiss them, and say a fond, respectful word to them. Often, when he would reach out to hug a woman, she would giggle and back away, and when he had kissed one, and the other women saw what was coming, they would retreat out of his path. But "he would come after them," recalls a man who watched this. "He'd go across the room after them," and when he caught them, Lyndon Johnson would take one of their hands in his and put his other around their shoulder and bend down and kiss their cheek, and these elderly farm women would receive the kiss scrunched down a little in embarrassment with their faces turned away, but with their faces aglow: "you could see they just loved this attention."

With men, the rapport was cemented with a handshake—and a handshake, as delivered by Lyndon Johnson, could be as effective as a hug. "Now, July 24 is Primary Day," he would say, "and I hope you will lend me your helping hand." And he would reach out and grasp the farmer's hand, looking down into his eyes. "What's your name?" he would ask. "Where're you from? What's your occupation?" And he would always have a relevant sentence or two ready to add. If the farmer said he had two sons, Lyndon would ask what they were doing, and if the farmer said they were studying agriculture at a college, Johnson would say, "Well, they're learning a lot of good things there, but people like you who know the land know stuff they can't learn from teaching, don't you?" Sometimes, in the midst of a crowd of strangers, he would stop and concentrate on a single person, as if he were back in a little Hill Country town again, running for Congress for the first time, and talking to a man he knew. He wouldn't take the man's hand at first. "Listen," he would say, standing before the man and looking into his eyes, his own face glistening with perspiration, his cheeks hollow with fatigue, and the shirt clinging to his body, "Listen, you know why I'm running for the Senate. I want your support. I want your vote. I hear tell that all the people down in your neck of the woods will listen to what you tell them. Will you tell them to vote for me? I need help. Will you help me? Will you give me your helping hand?" *Will you give me your helping hand?*—as he asked that final question, Lyndon Johnson would raise his own hand and hold it out in a mute appeal. When Johnson was only twenty-one, participating in his first political campaign, State Senator Welly Hopkins had concluded that the tall, gangling college boy had a "gift"—"a very unusual ability to meet and greet the public." Time after time now, Lyndon Johnson's hand would reach out to a voter—and the voter's hand would reach out in return.

THE HANDS with which he was doing this were terribly cracked now.

Dry and scaly as they had been before the campaign because of his eczema, the sun had baked them dryer. They looked almost like cracked leather marked with narrow lines of blood, for new cracks, deep, painful little knifelike slits, were constantly appearing in the skin. And many of the hands he was shaking were the hands of farmers, hard and strong, the hands of men who had worked with their hands all their lives. "Without meaning to, they hurt," says Horace Busby. And sometimes, in the crush after a speech, Johnson would momentarily forget to use the two-handed method or someone would grab his hand while he was still concentrating on someone else. Once, Busby was standing on the ground next to a flatbed truck, with steps on both ends, on which Johnson was shaking hands with members of the audience as they came up on the truck and filed past him. "All of a sudden I heard the damnedest yelp, like a dog had been hit." Busby looked up, and Lyndon Johnson "was down on one knee. He had been shaking hands with a big old guy in coveralls and a white shirt." But, as the young speechwriter watched, Johnson recovered himself and smiled at the farmer, and turned with a smile to the next person in line, and the next, and the next. At every stop, no matter how much it might hurt him to shake hands, he shook every one. He shook even those that were not offered to him. In small towns there was usually a little group of elderly men, the domino players from the Courthouse

Square, who would stand at the back of the crowd during the speech and after it would not approach the candidate, showing by the reserved look on their faces that *they* were not impressed by any politician (of course, elderly men like these were almost invariably Stevenson supporters). But when Johnson noticed such a group of men, he would, after he had shaken everyone else's hands, walk over to where they were standing to shake theirs; his cracked hand held out, and a broad, pleasant smile on his face.

HIS VOICE WAS CRACKED, too, and the throat sprays were not helping much more than the ointments were helping his hands. By the end of each day, it was a hoarse croak, but every time it seemed to be about to give out entirely, it would come back.

He was so tired. After spending July 15 accompanying Johnson on a tour of the Fourth Congressional District in Northeast Texas, District Chairman Fred Meredith asked Claude Wild to show the candidate mercy. "He had a mighty hard schedule that day," Meredith wrote.

> Upon arrival in Greenville that evening, we noticed the telling effects of this hard drive upon him. I don't know but what it would be well for John [Connally] and you to try to have him make fewer appearances for the balance of the campaign . . . because you are driving him to death.

In his reply, Wild didn't even respond to the suggestion about fewer appearances. What would have been the use? It wasn't his campaign manager who was driving Lyndon Johnson. Once, in these final weeks before the July 24 primary, the candidate was so tired that during his noon stop at a hotel, he decided to take a half-hour nap; changing into pajamas, he went to sleep. His aides, who had been watching with concern the toll being exacted from him, did not awaken him for two hours. When they did, his first look was at his wristwatch. His face tightened. He didn't take a nap like that again. Thereafter, as before, napping was something he did in the helicopter.

He would shout at Mashman over the roar of the engine. "Joe, I'm just too tired. I've got to rest." A moment later, he would be asleep. He slept sitting up, of course, since that tiny cockpit had no room in which to lie down: two twenty-four-inch-wide bucket seats occupied most of its sixty-inch width; between each seat and the door next to it (or the opening where the door would have been had there been a door) was a space of two and a half inches. As Johnson sat cramped in his seat, one set of the dual controls was between his knees, so that as he slept, held upright by his seat belt, his head slumping forward on his chest, his long legs were "sort of wrapped around the controls," his right arm all but out the open door. "There was so much noise and the cockpit would be shaking and vibrating, and the doors were off so the wind was whistling through it." The sun shining through the unshaded Plexiglas made the inside of the "bubble" glaringly bright. But Johnson would be sleeping, sometimes with his Stetson pulled down over his eyes for shade, sometimes with the hat still on the floor where an aide had placed it. Mashman found it incredible that anyone could sleep in such conditions, but he realized his passenger was just too tired to stay awake.

Sometimes Johnson, in the moment before he went to sleep, would tell Mashman, "We're going to fly over this town and, if you want to, slow down there and you can just say whatever you want, but I'm just too tired." He had found that Mashman could speak over the microphone, and the quality of the sound system ensured that no one on the ground would be able to tell who was really talking to them. So when the helicopter reached the town, Johnson would go on sleeping while Mashman, circling and hovering, would say through the microphone: "Hello, down there, this is your friend Lyndon Johnson, asking you to vote for me in this forthcoming election. This is Congressman Lyndon Johnson speaking, hopefully your next Senator. . . . We're sorry we can't land, but we're thinking about you." The blare of the public-address-system amplifier, lashed to the helicopter only a foot or two behind Johnson, had no more effect on him than the roar of the engine, or the vibration. As Mashman proclaimed, "This is Lyndon Johnson speaking," Lyndon Johnson slept on. Having completed his spiel, Mashman would climb and soar away. Glancing over at the exhausted man beside him, Mashman noticed how the sun pouring down on him made even sharper the grooves clawed into his cheeks by fatigue and deepened the dark, almost purple, shadows under his eyes. It glinted off the slits of blood on his hands. But as Lyndon Johnson slept in that cockpit filled with sun, he never blinked.

Johnson would never sleep for more than half an hour, Mashman recalls. Then, in an instant, he would be wide awake, and his first question, shouted over the engine noise, would be: "Are we on schedule, Joe?" or "How we doin' on time?" or "When are we going to get there?" And if the answer wasn't satisfactory—"Well, c'mon. We've got to get there, you know. *Come on!!*"

DURING THESE THREE WEEKS from the Fourth of July weekend to Primary Day, Mashman had a unique view of what the pilot calls Lyndon Johnson's "single-mindedness, his concentration, his determination"— words that are inadequate to describe either the intensity with which his passenger was focusing on his goal, an intensity that left no room for other considerations, or the ferocity with which he was fighting to reach it.

Mashman's view was unique because he alone flew with Lyndon Johnson during these weeks. He had been surprised—as had his predecessor, Chudars—by Johnson's total lack of interest in the helicopter; by the way, in an era in which helicopters were so new and "unproven that even many seasoned pilots shunned them," the Congressman had "just got on and said, 'Let's go' " the first time he had seen the aircraft, burying himself in his briefing papers and staying buried in them. Flying in the Bell was a substantially different experience from flying in the far larger Sikorsky: it vibrated much more, and was noisier; moreover, instead of sitting in a cockpit that resembled the cabin of a small airplane, a passenger was sitting, surrounded only by glass, as if he were simply perched five hundred or a thousand feet up in the air. But Johnson seemed not to notice.

During these weeks, Mashman feels, he came to understand the Congressman's lack of interest. The helicopter, he says, echoing the same words that Chudars uses, was to Johnson "only a means to an end"—the end being victory. This end, Mashman came to see, was so all-consuming that the means mattered not at all; no consideration that might interfere with victory could be allowed to intrude.

Not even personal safety. Because of Lyndon Johnson, during these three weeks Mashman flew constantly on a razor-thin margin of safety.

"He would urge you on," Mashman says. "He had a knack of getting everything there was to get out of you." And, the pilot says, "in the field of aviation, that's a very dangerous thing." Mashman says that "if he pushed you to the point whereby he was definitely wrong in doing so, and you definitely couldn't do it, if you just stopped and laid it on the line and said, 'I don't think this is a safe thing to do,' that we just can't do it, period—then he would back down and say, 'All right. You're the boss.' " Nonetheless, as day followed day, and Johnson pushed harder and harder, the "point" at which Mashman "stopped" edged closer and closer to the limits of safety.

The very act of "inching off" from inadequate landing sites with a too-heavy load, wavering in the air a few feet above the ground and then a few feet higher, and then struggling up into the sky, might have been disconcerting to the average passenger, but Johnson's only concern during such moments was in weighing the waste of time involved in this experimenting against the waste of time involved if he told Mashman to set down and let him out so that he could be driven to a rendezvous with the helicopter outside town: his only concern was which method would get him to the next town—the next audience of voters—faster.

The margin of daylight was another source of concern to Mashman—and, under Johnson's prodding, the pilot was constantly slicing that margin thinner and thinner. Since the helicopter was not equipped with night-flying instruments, Mashman had at first insisted that the campaign schedule allow him to be on the ground well before dark. Johnson was determined to cram the maximum number of campaign appearances into each day, and often he would run behind schedule; as the afternoon drew into evening, aides would warn him that daylight was running out, but the warnings were ignored, and Mashman found himself landing later and later, often in the dusk, just as darkness was becoming total. Years later, the pilot was to recall vividly the times he came in for a landing when he could barely see the ground.

Under Johnson's prodding, moreover, Warren Woodward was selecting tighter and tighter landing sites. One was located in Rosenberg, a small city of forty-eight hundred residents about thirty miles west of Houston. There, Woodward had been unable to find near the center of town "even a lawn" large enough for the 47-D to set down on. The only sizable flat area was the roof of a B. F. Goodrich Service Station. So Woodward ordered Mashman to land on the service station. No one was really sure if the roof would bear the helicopter's weight, and at the last minute Woodward had the roof shored up with beams hauled from a local lumberyard in wagons pulled by muleteams. The beams were in place—just—when the helicopter started to descend, but Mashman was more than a little worried about what would happen when its full weight settled on the roof. His passenger, however, was not; during Mashman's slow, anxious descent, Johnson lifted his head from his perusal of his notes for a single glance at the satisfactorily sizable crowd gathering to watch the daredevil landing. When they were down, his only reaction to the risk that had been taken was pleasure; the smile he turned on Woodward was, for once, wholly uncritical; "that's my can-do boy," he said.

Storms—even the violent late-afternoon Texas thunderstorms—were to Johnson nothing but an annoyance, an obstacle between him and his goal. Ahead of the helicopter, suddenly, one of those mighty columns of swirling blackness would loom up thirty or forty thousand feet high. Mashman might venture to mention it to his passenger. "Well, just keep on going," Lyndon Johnson would say. "We've got to get there." Willing though the pilot was to fly through a storm's turbulence, sometimes he would feel that the danger was simply too great because of the lack of visibility: he would be unable to see the ground, or even more than a few feet ahead, and of course the little craft was not equipped to fly on instruments. If he told Johnson he couldn't proceed, Johnson's initial response would be: "Well, are you sure, now?" If Mashman said he was, Johnson would defer to his judgment. Sometimes they would wait, hoping the storm would move away, hovering in midair close to its edge. At other times, the pilot would try to circle the storm and fly on to the next town, skipping one stop, with Johnson adjuring him to circle the storm as closely as possible so as not to lose a single unnecessary minute. But, more and more often, as the weight of Johnson's personality bore on Mashman's, the pilot found himself deciding to try to get through such storms—by flying under them, where he could see the ground. In order to see it, in the heavy rain, Mashman might have to descend as low as five feet off the ground, and would "just inch along," slower and slower, sometimes as slow as fifteen miles per hour, peering ahead through the sheets of rain to look for any obstacles: a building or an electric telephone wire; "many times we actually flew under high-tension wires," Mashman recalls. And all the time, of course, hanging above them was that mass of black clouds. The pilot himself was often "a little shaky" during such maneuvers, but his passenger wasn't; "All he wanted to know was, Are we going to get there on time?"

It wasn't, Mashman came to realize, that his passenger was weighing various considerations against the political necessities of the moment, such as getting to a rally on time, or cramming in one more stop before dark. Rather, it was that in his passenger's mind, there *were* no other considerations.

Mashman came to understand this fully after an incident in Marshall, Lady Bird Johnson's high-school hometown, on July 14.

The incident was the result of a form of stalling (its technical name was "settling with power") that occasionally occurred during those early days of helicopter flying. This stalling was caused by a combination of extremely hot weather, which reduced the engine's power, and a sudden shift in the wind when a helicopter was flying at a low altitude—so that the blades find no purchase in the air, and, as Mashman puts it, "the ship just begins to drop like a brick."

This phenomenon, which would be corrected in later generations of helicopters by a simple change in the angle of the rotor blades, was extremely rare; Mashman himself had never experienced it, and the first time he encountered it he did not realize what was happening. All he knew was that as he was flying at a height of between twenty-five and thirty feet along Marshall's main street on his way to a landing site in a park, with Johnson sitting beside him, studying his briefing papers, without warning "the ship just dropped out from under me"; he had lost power completely. His reaction was to jerk the controls toward him, a maneuver whose only effect was to cause the helicopter to pitch forward and drop even faster. As he sat there "with a feeling of complete helplessness," the helicopter fell like a stone, hitting the ground between two parked cars so hard that it bounced up into the air over one of the cars. Suddenly

Mashman found that he had power again. He regained control and continued flying to the park.

After they landed, just before Johnson stepped out to begin his speech, he said, "Joe, that wasn't where you wanted to land back there, was it?" His tone was one of mild curiosity. "No, no," Mashman replied. "We had a little problem. I'll tell you about it later." While Johnson was speaking, Mashman was preparing an explanation of what had happened, but in fact no explanation was required. Climbing back into the helicopter after the speech, Johnson immediately opened his next set of briefing papers and didn't ask about the sudden drop to the ground. He never asked. The helicopter in which Lyndon Johnson had been riding had fallen like a stone for twenty-five feet, had hit the ground so hard that it bounced higher than a car roof, and then, regaining power, had swooped up into the air again.

And, Mashman realized, Johnson hadn't really noticed.

AT SIX-THIRTY on the morning of July 24, Primary Day, George Parr came to the home of his feared Mexican-American enforcer, "Indio" Salas, and repeated his instructions: "Concentrate on the Senate race. Be sure we elect Johnson."

Salas, as election judge, presided over Precinct 13, the Mexican-American district of Alice, the county seat of Jim Wells County, where the polling place had as usual been set up in a large room in the Nayer Elementary School. In a vacant lot across the street from the school, Salas had arranged for the erection of the traditional Election Day tent—pyramid-shaped, about sixteen feet square at the base—and in front of it stood deputy sheriffs, wearing guns. It had been set up so that the Mexican-American voters who were herded into it by other deputies could be given their poll-tax receipts, their sample ballots or "strings"—and their instructions—in privacy. ("Inside we had a table," Salas recalls, "with plenty sample ballots to teach some of our voters how to vote; lots of them needed training.") There was a new development. Under Texas election law, each party was permitted "poll-watchers" to inspect the ballots, and the Jim Wells reformers, emboldened by recent successes, had actually dared to name two for Box 13, H. L. (Ike) Poole and young Jimmy Holmgreen, and when they arrived at the Nayer School just as the polls were opening at seven a.m., they handed Salas a paper: a judge's order designed to ensure an honest vote. But in George Parr's precincts, the law was not what was written on paper. Salas pointed to two chairs that he thought were far enough away from the table on which the ballots were counted so that the reformers could not get a good look at them. "I just ordered them to go sit in a corner and keep out of the way," Salas was to recall. "I tell you once more, I was so powerful I could do anything that pleased me." Then he whispered to the election clerks: "told them, Absolutely do not let them see the ballots." Poole, Salas was to say, "more or less obeyed" his orders, but Holmgreen objected when he saw Mexican-American voters pull out sample ballots and refer to them while marking their own, an obvious violation of the election law. Before noon, Salas began counting the ballots. Sitting at a table, he unfolded each ballot and called out the names on it; three clerks, sitting at the same table, marked down the votes on three separate tally sheets. Even from his chair in the corner, Holmgreen was to say, he could see the marks on the ballots, and he saw Salas calling out for Johnson votes that were actually for Stevenson. A brave young man, Holmgreen kept asking to inspect the ballots, as he was entitled by law to do. "He was up many times approaching the desk where the clerks were counting and reading the ballots," Salas says. "I told him, Better sit down." When Holmgreen persisted, Deputy Sheriff Stokes Micenheimer, a huge man, as fat as any cinema caricature of a Deep South deputy, with his belly bulging over his gunbelt, arrested him, marched him off to the city jail, and locked him in a cell. An attorney for the reformers obtained a writ of mandamus freeing Holmgreen and ordering Salas to allow the poll-watchers to see the ballots. "I just ignored same and again told Poole and Holmgreen, You just stay put, don't move from your chairs." Shortly after the polls closed at seven p.m., Salas announced the "vote" in Precinct 13—that single "box" furnished Johnson with the bulk of his 1,881-1,357 lead in Jim Wells County. And no "reform" opposition to Parr existed in the six counties— Duval, Starr, La Salle, Brooks, Jim Hogg and Zapata—controlled absolutely by the Duke of Duval. In Duval, Stevenson received 66 votes, Peddy 20, Johnson 3,707—98 percent of the total. In the six counties as a whole, Johnson received 90 percent of the total. His plurality over Stevenson in Parr's domain totaled almost 7,000 votes. In Judge Raymond's Webb County, he received 90 percent of the total, and a plurality over Stevenson of almost 6,000 votes. The districts of Corpus Christi that Anglo politicians called "Mextown" and "Niggertown" produced 4,000 more; those in McAllen and Edinburg, on the border, weighed in with more. Although San Antonio's West Side didn't produce as well for Johnson as had been expected, he nonetheless came out of that city and the Valley with the 25,000 votes he had expected.

Even including this bloc vote, however, Lyndon Johnson polled only 405,617 votes—34 percent of the total. Coke Stevenson had 477,077 votes, or 40 percent; Peddy had 237,195 votes, or 20 percent; and the eight minor candidates had 83,000 votes, 7 percent. Stevenson would have won without the necessity of a second primary had his fellow conservative George Peddy not polled an unexpectedly high total—largely, in the opinion of political observers, because of a mistake by the conservatives' daily Bible, the *Dallas News*, which the day before the election, confident that its favorite, Stevenson, would win even with a split vote, had loftily assured conservatives that they could vote for either Stevenson or Peddy without hurting the conservative cause.

Despite the conservative split, Stevenson had defeated Johnson by 71,000 votes. And when the second—runoff—primary was held on August 28, Peddy would be gone from the race. Political writers and observers agreed with virtual unanimity that Peddy's voters would now turn to the remaining conservative candidate: voters in the fourteen fiercely conservative East Texas counties that Peddy had carried were hardly likely to switch to the candidate identified as a liberal.

This assessment was echoed not only by newspapers—liberal and conservative alike—throughout the state but in Johnson's own camp, stunned by the extent of his defeat. (The shock was intensified for the younger Johnson aides—those who worked out of the Hancock House—because a last-minute Belden Poll, released on Primary Day, had, in contrast to earlier Belden Polls, shown that among "most likely" voters whose preference had been decided, Johnson had actually pulled ahead of Stevenson. The dramatic inaccuracy of this poll confirmed the feeling of the senior Johnson advisers—the Brown Building group—and of other Texas political observers that, in those relatively early days of polling in that state, identifying and predicting the preference of "most likely" voters was not reliable; the Brown Building group had not put much stock in the last-minute poll, which was, of course, at variance not only with their own private polls but, indeed, with virtually all informed Texas political opinion.) Stevenson's campaign manager, Morris Roberts, predicted that Stevenson would win "ninety percent" of Peddy's vote; "This is only natural. . . . The principles laid down by both Mr. Stevenson and Mr. Peddy are so closely identical it would be difficult to find a dividing line"—and in the somber discussions at the Hancock House and in the Brown Building, the consensus was that Roberts' estimate might not be too far off. The Johnson team had been confident that their chief would run close to Ol' Coke in the first primary, close enough so that Johnson would have a realistic chance of victory in the second. But the actual margin, Jake Pickle recalls, was "so imposing"—how could it possibly be overcome? "Making up seventy thousand votes in five weeks, particularly when we were sure that Coke would get most of Peddy's vote, too—it seemed impossible, absolutely impossible," Joe Kilgore says. Talk to a dozen Johnson aides about their feelings after the first primary, and one adjective recurs in almost every conversation: "Hopeless."

And this assessment was, in the privacy of the big back yard at Johnson's Dillman Street house, echoed by the candidate himself. Because local candidates would not be running, the pool of votes to draw from would be much smaller than in the first primary. "People do not come out to vote for a United States Senator," Johnson explained to Busby. "They come out to vote for the Sheriff or the County Commissioner." Most discouraging was that Johnson's percentage of the vote had been so low: thirty-four percent. The June Belden Poll had predicted Johnson's share of likely voters at thirty-seven percent. Despite the helicopter, despite the money, despite the frantic efforts of the past month, despite that month's intensified deluge of radio broadcasts and newspaper ads, Johnson had made no appreciable gain in the last month of the campaign. One explanation might be that, in conservative Texas, a percentage in the mid-thirties represented the upper limit of Johnson's potential vote. Asked for a comment on the first primary, Stevenson said laconically: "I think Johnson has pulled his weight."

THERE WAS ANOTHER possible explanation as well.

For more than a month before the first primary, unprecedented amounts of money had been devoted to persuading voters that Coke Stevenson had made a "secret deal" to help repeal the Taft-Hartley law.

Coke had hardly bothered to reply. The charge, he told intimates, wasn't true, but he didn't have to bother telling the voters that; they knew it without his telling them. The people of Texas, he said, wouldn't believe that charge no matter how often it was made. They wouldn't believe it because they knew him. They knew his record. They knew what he stood for. They knew what he would do in the future because they knew what he had done in the past. He had never betrayed them before—and he would never betray them now. And they knew that.

Coke Stevenson's belief flew, of course, in the face of all conventional political wisdom.

But, it now appeared, he had been right.

12

All or Nothing

ONE MONTH TO GO. One month to make up seventy thousand votes. One month to make Peddy's staunchly conservative followers turn against Coke Stevenson, symbol of conservatism. One month for Lyndon Johnson to save his political career. His entire life, it seemed, had boiled down to August, 1948.

And he couldn't even use his mighty weapon. "We were too far behind," Busby says. "Trying to draw crowds in little towns—that wasn't going to get you anywhere. We had to go into the cities." The cities, where a helicopter could not be used.

Every sacrifice had to be made, even one that may have been especially difficult: ending the abuse of helpless subordinates. Wirtz and Wild had been attempting for months to persuade Johnson to modify or at least conduct in private the explosions of violent, obscene rage at his staff (and, indeed, at non-staffers such as hotel waiters and desk clerks) which often took place in full view of local supporters. From town after town reports came in of tirades so shocking and unforgettable that they often negated all his efforts. But the suggestions from Austin that he abuse his assistants only in private had been ignored—as if the prerogative of venting his emotions at Mary Rather and Woody and Buzz whenever and wherever he felt like it was a necessity he could not deny himself.

Now, however, there was one month to go; he altered his behavior— with his customary thoroughness. The first witness to—and beneficiary of—the transformation was Horace Busby. Immediately after the first primary, the young press-release writer and idea man had been summoned from his desk on the first floor of the Hancock House "upstairs to where the big shots were meeting." There he received rather unwelcome news. He had been absolutely correct when he reported that the unprecedented size of Johnson's entourage was antagonizing voters, he was told. It had therefore been decided that on future campaign trips the candidate would be accompanied by only a single aide—"and guess who it's going to be."

Busby says he was designated for the assignment because "I had developed a reputation for handling his rages better than anyone else." But, he says, he had done the "handling" partly by becoming "very good at never being in his line of sight" when an explosion was imminent. As Johnson's sole companion, assigned to be constantly at the candidate's side, he would no longer be able to use that tactic. "I was," he recalls, "expecting the worst."

Therefore, he says, he was "shocked" when Johnson was "different than he had been during the first primary." Their next trip alone together was to El Paso, and on the plane "I was stunned. We were sitting side by side reading papers, and he was subdued. There was none of the volatility. We actually conversed." But even greater was his surprise at Johnson's behavior when they arrived at their hotel. Since their registration had been arranged in advance, Johnson could have gone straight up to his room, as had been his previous practice, but instead he went over to the desk clerk. "I'm Congressman Johnson," he said with a pleasant voice and smile. "You have a very fine hotel here. I've stayed in it before, and I'm looking forward to this visit." When the bellboy arrived in their suite with the luggage, Johnson told him, "I'd like to shake hands with you if your hands weren't so busy." When the bellboy put down the luggage, Johnson shook his hand. "Buzz," he said, "give the young man a tip." Then he changed his mind. "Son," he said, "he's a cheap tipper. I don't want him tipping you." And, Busby recalls, "he gave him five dollars."

And nothing prepared Busby for what was to happen the next morning. Johnson's first appearance would be an early-morning meeting, and he told Busby to get up at 4:15 a.m., so that he would have time to bring him coffee. The hotel operator failed to make the wake-up call, however. Busby was awakened at 4:45 a.m., not by the desk but by his boss. He was awakened gently. Johnson was sitting beside his bed. "He wasn't mad," Busby recalls. " 'Here, Buzz,' Lyndon Johnson said. " 'I went down and got a coffee and doughnut for you.' " For the entire month of August, Johnson rarely lapsed from his new code of behavior. Dressing for a dinner speech, Busby says, "he put in his own cuff links—I didn't have any of the valet services to perform that I was ill-disposed toward performing. Suddenly, Lyndon Johnson was taking care of himself." And there were few, if any, explosions. "He was a changed man."

ON MONDAY MORNING, July 26, both candidates left for Washington: Johnson for the special session of the "do-nothing" Eightieth Congress that President Truman had called to focus attention on its failures; Stevenson, in order to counter Johnson's charges that he couldn't be an effective Senator because he had no ties in the capital, for a brief visit to old friends like Tom Connally in the congressional delegation.

Lyndon Johnson's political genius had always enabled him to see opportunities for political gain where no one else saw them. He saw one now in Stevenson's trip to his turf, and he had a reporter Stevenson trusted casually ask the former Governor to hold a press conference while he was in Washington. Sure, Stevenson said. Stevenson, who had no faith in planes ("I never drove in anything with a motor that I didn't have to get out at least once to fix it"), traveled to the capital by train. Johnson flew, so he got there two days before Stevenson—and by the time Stevenson arrived, the trap had been set.

Johnson was well aware by now how Stevenson's pride could be turned against him: since he would always refuse to defend himself against a hostile question, particularly one asked in an insulting tone, simply ask him a hostile question, and, when he refused to reply, accuse him of "dodging" the issue. The question Johnson was most anxious for Stevenson to appear to "dodge," of course, was on Taft-Hartley. So, says John Connally, "We encouraged Marshall McNeil [Washington correspondent of the *Fort Worth Star-Telegram*], who had this very abrasive way of asking questions, to ask Coke where he stood on Taft-Hartley."

Johnson wanted the whole press conference "abrasive," and he made sure that other friends in the Washington press corps knew what questions to ask, and how to ask them. He told these friends that Coke Stevenson had been just another one of Texas' crooked Governors—that he had, in fact, sold pardons just like Jim Ferguson before him. He told them Stevenson was a "caveman," a "Neanderthal"—ignorant, isolationist, reactionary; a country bumpkin like Pappy O'Daniel. He told them that Stevenson had struck a "secret deal" with labor bosses to help repeal Taft-Hartley, and that he had been frantically dodging reporters' questions about that issue in Texas. He told them he hoped *they* wouldn't let Stevenson get away with such tactics in Washington. Johnson "not only primed, I would say he had briefed them thoroughly . . . on this man Coke Stevenson whom they had never heard of and never seen," Jake Pickle says. "It boiled down to the reporters actually asking and popping the questions and then riding him." By the time Stevenson arrived in Washington, "the reporters were waiting for him. Mr. Johnson and his friends, reporters like Drew Pearson, had the stage set." Hostile press conferences were rare in Washington in that era; this press conference, one reporter was to write, was "the most hostile in recent memory."

Hardly had it begun when Leslie Carpenter, a Washington correspondent for several Texas newspapers, including the pro-Johnson *Dallas Times-Herald* (Carpenter's wife, Liz, was a correspondent for other Texas papers), asked a question that attacked the former Governor's integrity.

Is the "large number of pardons granted in your Governorship an issue in this campaign?" Carpenter demanded. Bob Murphey, who had accompanied his uncle to Washington, saw Coke's jaw set, and knew what was coming. "I wouldn't know," Stevenson replied coldly. Johnson's charges about the pardons had been exposed as false in Texas, and the issue laid to rest there, but here in Washington it was raised again—in rapid-fire questions often couched in a sneering tone more suited to a prosecuting attorney interrogating an obviously guilty defendant. Reporters in Austin had become accustomed to Stevenson's deliberate way of answering questions—the slow drawl in which he always spoke—and had learned to wait for his replies. These reporters didn't wait, and while he was framing a reply to one question, they would be shouting others at him. Stevenson attempted once to explain that they were mistakenly lumping together "pardons" with three- or five-day "clemencies" during which prisoners were allowed to return home for a relative's funeral or a family emergency, but the reporters seemed not to understand.

The tone did not change when the questioning, led by Carpenter and young, aggressive Jack Anderson, a Drew Pearson legman, shifted to Taft-Hartley. Carpenter asked: "Do you think the Taft-Hartley law is a good or a bad law?"

Stevenson replied that the issue was too complicated to be answered by simply calling a law "good" or "bad," but every time he attempted to explain his more complex view of the issue, Carpenter interrupted him by simply repeating the same question. He did so five times, until Stevenson said: "That's a loaded question." Stevenson added, evidently referring to the statement he had made in Abilene on July 3, that he had made a statement on Taft-Hartley, and the reporters could look it up.

That evening, the pack of journalists again crammed into Stevenson's hotel room. Carpenter said that his paper could find no record in its files of his statement on Taft-Hartley, implying that Stevenson had lied. Then the reporter demanded: "Do you think the Taft-Hartley law is a good or a bad law?"

Stevenson lost his temper. "I'm not going to let the *Times-Herald* shape up my campaign," he said. Then, the *Dallas News* was to report, Stevenson "was also hammered at by Jack Anderson." Anderson's questions were couched in a tone that Stevenson was to liken to "cross-examination," and, Murphey was to say, "No one was going to cross-examine him." He was determined not to reply to questions asked in that tone. When Pearson's legman demanded, "What did you say about the Taft-Hartley law?" Stevenson angrily said only: "I couldn't repeat it from memory." "Could you give us the gist of it?" Anderson asked. "I might be able to," Stevenson said, "but I don't see any value in it." Stevenson's determination not to reply led him only into deeper and deeper trouble.

When Anderson kept demanding a reply—"All I want is a yes or no"—
Stevenson refused to give one, and when Anderson demanded to know
why, he said: "Because you all catch me here away from my notes and
put me under cross-examination." Well, Anderson said, "It seems like a
simple thing to remember how you stand." "The people of Texas know,"
Stevenson replied.

The questioning, by Anderson, Carpenter and McNeil, was finally
stopped by other, more neutral, reporters, who found their colleagues'
tactics repugnant. When Anderson said, "It appears to me you're trying
to carry water on both sides, Governor," another reporter, Bascom N.
Timmons, objected, even though he also represented a pro-Johnson paper. "That's an unethical question," Timmons said. Sarah McClendon,
who represented the *Beaumont Enterprise* and the *El Paso Times* as well
as other Texas papers, and who was already known as a fiery questioner
herself, was to say of that press conference: "It was lousy. It was one of
the lousiest things I ever saw."

Johnson would have been pleased by the tone of the questions at the
press conference; he must have been pleased, too, by the tone of the
stories that stemmed from it. The lead on Leslie Carpenter's article in
the *Fort Worth Star-Telegram*, for example, was that Stevenson "Tuesday
dodged a direct question, asked five times, as to whether he considered
the Taft-Hartley Labor law to be a 'good law' or 'a bad law.' " Liz Carpenter's article, in the *Austin American-Statesman*, said that "a dozen
newsmen . . . tried for 20 minutes to get an answer from him on the
question."

The cooperation of some of the reporters with the Johnson campaign
did not end with the filing of their stories. While Stevenson was on a train
back to Texas, Leslie Carpenter was dictating a message to Johnson suggesting follow-up questions ("Why don't you get some favorable reporter
to ask Stevenson something like this. . . . If Stevenson says 'No,' have
the reporter [say] . . . Then the reporter could say . . . I think we can
start the whole thing over with questions like this. Good luck and God
bless you"). Marshall McNeil was drafting a statement about Stevenson
for Johnson to deliver.

THE PRESS CONFERENCE became a pivotal point of the campaign because
of money—and what money could buy.

More money had been poured into Johnson's campaign than had ever
been donated to a politician in Texas, but that money was gone now,
spent. More money could be raised, however, for by this time, even if
Herman Brown had wanted to cut his losses, he couldn't. He was in too
deep.

None of the group whose fortunes were tied to Brown & Root—and, therefore, to Lyndon Johnson—could back out now. All of them were in too deep.

They knew it. More than a few of the younger members of Johnson's team felt that their Chief should seriously consider bowing out of the race without running in the second primary, so hopeless did they consider his position, but when one of them, Wilton Woods, ventured to raise that possibility to Alvin Wirtz, Wirtz replied, not with his customary smile, but with a snarl: "He's *got* to run it out now. There are too many people out on a limb now." Johnson's personal attacks on Coke Stevenson, so beloved a figure in Austin, had infuriated not only the former Governor but his longtime friends and allies in the State Legislature and bureaucracy, who, as Austin lobbyists like Wirtz and Ed Clark knew, would be less restrained in their use of governmental powers than Coke would be; there was, Clark recalls, real "hatred" for Lyndon Johnson in the corridors of the State Capitol. Clark, who had been aware when he had cast his lot with Lyndon Johnson five months before that "If I lost, I was going to be through; I was going to be out," now had additional fears. Now, he recalls, he was afraid that "We might be in trouble. They were going to punish us if they could." Asked whether some Brown & Root officials were afraid of being indicted, Clark replied, "That might happen. If you're in power, people will say what you want them to say." George Brown was to recall decades later that he and his brother feared that the bitterness engendered in Austin by the campaign might even endanger the continuation of the state road-building contracts that Brown & Root had been receiving for decades. After a normal campaign, Brown was to say, a "reconciliation" could be expected, but this campaign had been too bitter—and their opponent was too tough—for them to expect that. "In that second primary," he said, "it was all on the line." George and Herman had escaped—narrowly escaped—indictment on federal income tax charges for their financing of Lyndon Johnson's first senatorial campaign, largely (perhaps only) because they had a friend in power in Washington. In this second campaign, they had multiplied their illegalities—and if Lyndon Johnson lost, who would be their friend in power? Who was to be their friend with federal regulatory agencies, such as the Interstate Commerce Commission, whose jurisdiction included their Joe D. Hughes Trucking Company, or the Federal Power Commission, whose jurisdiction included their Big and Little Inch pipelines? "They [Brown & Root] were regulated in a thousand ways," says Clark, Brown & Root's attorney and lobbyist. "And [if Stevenson became Senator] Stevenson would have run them out of Washington. He would say, if anyone wanted to give them a contract, 'They're personally objectionable to me.' The Browns had to win this. They *had* to win this. Stevenson was a man of vengeance, and he would have run them out of Washington. Johnson—if he lost, he was going back to being nobody. *They* were going back to being nobody. That [second primary]—that was when the chips were down. That was the acid test. That was *it!* All or nothing."

Therefore, Ed Clark explains, "whatever he [Johnson] needed was available to him." Some of this financing was handled through the younger men, who would collect it—in cash—from Herman Brown or Wesley West in Houston or Sid Richardson on St. Joseph Island or Clint Murchison and Amon Carter in Fort Worth, or from big oil independents such as Harris Melasky in Taylor. Asked how much money was involved, John Connally smiles and says: "A hell of a lot. I'd go get it. Walter [Jenkins] would get it. Woody would go get it. We had a lot of people who would go get it, and deliver it. . . . I went to see Harris Melasky three or four times. . . . *I* handled inordinate amounts of cash." Connally says he can make no estimate of the amount of cash spent during the single month of August, 1948, but some idea of the scale emerges from an anecdote told by Charles Herring, the young Looney & Clark associate (and former Johnson congressional aide) who had been seconded to Connally for the campaign. No matter how fast the cash came in to Connally, Herring says, it went out at the same rate, and the telephone company, whose bill had not been paid, was threatening to cut off phone service. One evening, Connally told Herring: "I can get currency in Houston, but I've got to get it tonight." A private plane would take him to Houston, and he asked Herring to meet him at the Austin Municipal Airport on his return. When Connally arrived "at two, three o'clock in the morning," he was carrying a "brown paper sack like you buy groceries in." Inside, Herring says, was $50,000 in hundred-dollar bills. After counting it, the two young attorneys decided to stop for a snack at the Longhorn Café, an all-night diner. As they were driving home, Herring recalls, Connally "suddenly snapped his fingers and said: 'Where's that sack?' We had left it in the restaurant. Any bum off the street could have picked it up." But when they ran into the café, the brown bag was still there. When asked whether the $50,000 represented a substantial part of the cash spent in the primary, Herring looked astonished. "That didn't touch what you're talking about," he said. On another occasion during August, Herring says, Connally returned from a trip to Houston with $40,000 in cash, "took it home and hid it, and forgot where it was. For two or three days we couldn't find it." Connally thought the money must have been in a suit that had been sent to the cleaners, but no trace of it could be found. Herring said, "Maybe we'd better tell Johnson," but Connally, cool as ever in a crisis, never panicked, and told his assistant to tell nobody—"and," says Herring, "we didn't tell anybody about it. Except every cleaner in town." Finally the cash was found inside a shirt in Connally's shirt drawer. (Asked about these two incidents, Connally says only, with a grin: "I told you I handled inordinate amounts of cash.") Wilton Woods says that in 1941 he once carried $25,000 in cash from Herman Brown to Alvin Wirtz. During the 1948 campaign, he said, he made "several" trips carrying that amount—or more.

This immense supply of campaign financing meant that Liz Carpenter's story on Coke Stevenson's Washington press conference (including the erroneous implication that Stevenson had not made a "previous" statement) could be printed not just as an article in the newspapers that employed her but in many of the sixty daily and 488 weekly newspapers in Texas as an impressive advertisement with the headline: "EXACT WASHINGTON INTERVIEW OF STEVENSON DODGING ISSUES." Her article rolled off presses not just on newsprint but on the glossy paper of brochures sent out in direct mailings, and, in excerpted form, on penny postcards sent in repeated mailings so that the average Texas family would be able to see the name "Stevenson" connected with "dodging" over and over again. Some days after the press conference, Drew Pearson's column appeared with the key word used twice in the lead: "Ex-Governor Coke Stevenson of Texas . . . on a recent trip to Washington evaded more issues and dodged more questions than any recent performer in a city noted for question dodging." That column was reprinted, and tens of thousands—hundreds of thousands—of copies were sent to voters in repeated mailings.

Most important, the story of the press conference was repeated over and over on the radio. Johnson repeated it in his speeches, of course. These speeches were written by Paul Bolton. Describing what he wrote, Bolton says: "Repeat the same thing over and over and over—jumping on Coke Stevenson's having secret dealings with labor. You knew it was a damned lie [but] you just repeated it and repeated it and repeated it. Repetition—that was the thing." Johnson had respected and influential politicians repeat the lie in radio speeches broadcast in the areas where they were known. For example, Longview newspaper publisher Carl Estes, a power in East Texas, delivered a speech, written by Wirtz and his speechwriters, that was heard throughout his part of the state. Hailing Johnson's "outspoken championship of the Taft-Hartley law" during the fight for its passage in Washington two years before (a statement which would have surprised anyone who had been in Washington), Estes said:

> Mind you, the same labor bosses which Lyndon Johnson helped to force into the raiment of Americanism are now down here in free Texas, using Coke Stevenson as a willing whip with which to punish this courageous Congressman at the ballot box. If Lyndon Johnson is defeated, every CIO-PAC-AFL labor boss

in the country will hail the victory—"Operation Texas"—and the
march of decentralized industry to Texas, I warn you, will stop—
while Calculatin' Coke calmly lights his pipe.

Pleased with Estes' delivery of the speech, Wirtz ordered it rebroadcast
over a twenty-station statewide network, and reprinted in full-page advertisements in the state's leading newspapers.

As for his own stand on Taft-Hartley, Johnson said,

> My record on that bill has been made: I frankly stated it to
> the voters. I said my attitude toward amending it would be deter-
> mined by the recommendations of a joint committee of Congress
> set up to study the law in action. I said I would consider any
> recommendations of the committee except one. On one section
> of the law my opinion will not be changed. That's the section
> which requires the head of any labor union who seeks advantage
> under the act to file an affidavit that he's not a Communist, or a
> member of the Communist Party. I believe that every person and
> every organization doing business with the government . . . should
> be required to take a solemn oath that they are not Communists.

If this was something less than a firm endorsement of the Act—if,
indeed, it was no less equivocal than Stevenson's position—no reporter
pointed it out. (Indeed, a reporter wrote it. Marshall McNeil was quite
proud of his authorship of the Johnson speech.) Stevenson, still defiantly
refusing to reply to an opponent's charge, did not point it out either. Even
if he had, his reply might have been lost. Lyndon Johnson had one month
to make Texas believe that Coke Stevenson was a secret supporter of big-
city labor racketeers and had made a secret deal to repeal the sacred Taft-
Hartley Act. And during this month, Texans were told this by letter,
postcard, telephone calls from banks of phone workers, pamphlets, direct
mailings, radio advertisements and speeches, by ads in weekly newspapers
and by "articles" in the weeklies that were in reality also written in Johnson headquarters. The charge was drummed into voters by the shouts of
the scores of paid "stump speakers" Johnson had dispatched to crisscross
the state. Special attention was given to the conservative businessmen who
played so influential a role in Texas politics—and who had for years been
Stevenson supporters. "Transcripts" of the Washington interview were
mailed, with individually typed letters, to hundreds, if not thousands, of
"responsible businessmen." Such a campaign cost a vast amount of
money—but Lyndon Johnson had it.

And it wasn't only the shouts, but the whispers. One of the little-publicized factors of rural Texas politics was the men known variously as "missionaries" or "travelers" or "walking delegates" or "active campaigners." These were men influential with a particular ethnic group—for example, "You'd hire some popular Czech to go talk to the Czechs," one veteran of Texas politics says—or simply an individual well known in some remote rural district. Such men were for hire in every campaign. "You'd send a guy out to see the lay of the land," D. B. Hardeman explains. "He would walk around the streets, try to find out who was for who, go to the Courthouse. And they would talk around," spreading the rumors that their employer wanted spread. The missionaries were an effective political weapon, particularly in rural areas where voters were unsophisticated, uneducated and accustomed to relying on word of mouth for information. The missionaries knew what to say. "From previous campaigns they knew what people wanted to hear, and who to talk to."

Never in the history of Texas politics had these missionaries been deployed on the scale on which the Johnson campaign was deploying them. A lot of the cash that came in those brown paper bags went to the walking delegates. Asked, for example, how the $50,000 that Connally brought back from Houston was spent, Charles Herring says: "I saw him spend it. I saw him give it out. Our travelers would come by and pick up money." The Johnson campaign had between fifty and a hundred such delegates out on the road during the second primary and they each received between twenty-five and fifty dollars a day, plus expenses. Tens of thousands of dollars were thus spent to disseminate rumors about Coke Stevenson. Connally says the active campaigners were employed to "go around and spread propaganda. We'd contact a guy and give him walking money. To buy beers, that kind of thing. He'd just circulate, dropping these little tidbits. He'd go from beer joint to beer joint, and go into the Courthouses. He was a local guy, and no one would suspect he was employed in the campaign." And with their money, the rumormongers got their marching orders; says Connally: "We'd give them a party line. 'Did you hear Coke's not taking a stand [on Taft-Hartley]? Well, hell, he *can't* take a stand, you know. He made this deal. Well, no, he didn't say it publicly. But he said it to a lot of people in Austin when he didn't think anyone could hear, and one of them told me. . . .' " This whispering campaign was carried on not only by these travelers, of course; the rumors were spread by the thousands of federally paid employees of the state's twenty-nine Rural Electrification Administration cooperatives, and of the Department of Agriculture's Soil Conservation Service, and by employees of the Lower Colorado River Authority. And the whispers were very effective. "It was working," Boyett says. "These guys knew what to say. Lyndon had created the doubt: 'He'll vote to repeal that Act.' "

. . .

THE GREAT DANGER for Lyndon Johnson was that his opponent would reply to the questions about his stand on Taft-Hartley—for Johnson knew what the reply would be.

The Johnson strategists knew the truth about the charges they were making. They knew that Coke was really in favor of the bill they were claiming he was against. And if Coke simply said he was in favor of the bill, the issue would vanish—and with it any hope for a Johnson victory. So Johnson, confident now that if someone demanded that Stevenson do something, Stevenson would refuse, demanded again and again that Stevenson reply—in terms that he knew would make it even harder for Stevenson to reply. Calling the former Governor "pussy-footing" and "fence-straddling," he said in a typical speech: "Let's clear out the underbrush. The issue is plain. Has my opponent been gagged by the labor dictators? I challenge him to lift either his left leg or his right leg off the rail and get off one side or the other. Now is his chance to come clean with the people of Texas. It is his last chance." And as a further device to keep Stevenson from stating that he was for Taft-Hartley, Johnson now also predicted that the former Governor *would* state that—for the basest of motives. "It would be a peculiar circumstance if at this late date he should now decide . . . he is in favor of the Taft-Hartley Bill," Johnson said. Stevenson would be doing so, Johnson said, only because he had realized that his "true" feelings were costing him votes. The use of this tactic, too, was escalated from day to day. Under a headline that read "LIKE A BRANDED STEER—JOHNSON SAYS FOE TO BACK TAFT-HARTLEY," Hobby's *Houston Post* reported that Stevenson will "actually endorse the Taft-Hartley Bill" before the second primary in an attempt to deceive voters. Charging that Stevenson had tried "to be all things to all men," Johnson said that his own attacks on Stevenson's refusal to take a stand would force him to take one. Comparing the former Governor to "a freshly branded West Texas steer who tries to rub his brand off," the brand in this case being that of the state AFL, Johnson said, "If you folks will just stay with me, we will have him trying to get the AF of L brand off his left hip before this campaign is over."

Stevenson did not reply—for two weeks, during which Johnson's tactics had their effect. Speechwriter Paul Bolton, who says Johnson's speeches were false, says also that the speeches were working. "You watched [Johnson's] ratings go up those . . . weeks in the polls." Says Busby, a brilliant political analyst and strategist: "At the point at which Coke [in his Washington press conference] made the Taft-Hartley statement—at this point, he [Johnson] had no leverage to get back into the race, but the minute I saw [Liz Carpenter's] article, I said: 'This is our chance!' " "When Stevenson made his 'notes' reply, that was all we needed," John Connally says. "Johnson had an issue. Mr. Stevenson's strength came from his appearance of being a very solid, stable, thoughtful man. And a man who was above politics. Now . . . he looked indecisive. He looked vacillating. And he looked *political*. Which was destroying his image."

Stevenson's image was being destroyed even among the conservative businessmen who had known Coke Stevenson well—and who should therefore have been immune to the poison being circulated about his "secret dealings with labor." Many of these men lived in Dallas, which, in Busby's phrase, was "kind of the *de facto* headquarters of the right-to-work movement" in America. Their concern was both ideological—"Dallas," as Busby says, "had a singular number of businessmen who believed America had to be protected from labor unions"—and personal, for militant unionization in Texas would have adversely affected their pocketbooks. "The main concern" of the big Dallas businessmen, "the *employers*—was not to let unions take over the labor force in Texas. And they were just shocked to their toenails by this interview" (or, to be more precise, by Liz Carpenter's account of it). These businessmen read Stevenson's interview, and Johnson's advertisements and statements reminding them of the interview, "and concluded that Coke was making a secret deal with the unions."

Stevenson's little band of aides also knew almost immediately the effect that his refusal to answer Leslie Carpenter's questions would have among these conservatives, and their suspicions were confirmed by a telephone call. One evening just after Stevenson's return from Washington, the telephone rang in his hotel room while Ernest Boyett was present. On the line was Scott Schreiner of Kerrville, whom Boyett describes as "a lifelong friend" of Coke's. Schreiner had a question: "Well, Coke, how *do* you stand on Taft-Hartley?" To an old friend, Coke had no objection to replying. "Well, everyone knows where I stand. I'm not going to vote to repeal it." Boyett heard the reply, but he also recognized in the words "everyone knows where I stand" a disaster for the campaign, for he understood the true significance of the telephone call. "Even an old friend was starting to have doubts," he says. "Lyndon had planted doubts in the conservatives' minds about the Old Man: 'He'll vote to repeal the Taft-Hartley Act!' " But his boss still didn't understand, Boyett realized; he still felt that it was not necessary for him to reply. And, indeed, when Boyett and others attempted to persuade Stevenson to say in public what he had said on the telephone—the one magic sentence ("I'm not going to vote to repeal it") that could have neutralized Johnson's tactics—the answer was the same as it had been for three months now: " 'I'm not getting into a cuss fight with Lyndon.' " ("I would ask him to make a public statement every time I saw him," Boyett recalls with a sad smile. "He was just such a strong-willed person. . . .")

Exacerbating the reactionaries' doubts was a human consideration. Haters of Roosevelt and his New Deal—indeed, in Busby's words, of "everything Roosevelt stood for"—"they hated Johnson as a New Dealer. But when they saw Stevenson waver, they hated him worse than Johnson. To suspect that a former friend has betrayed you is worse than an enemy opposing you, and therefore they got very angry at Coke."

THE MISTRUST OF STEVENSON that Johnson had created among conservative businessmen increased Stevenson's difficulties, because these businessmen were, of course, the source of most of his campaign funds.

Immediately after the first primary, Stevenson's campaign manager had sent out letters soliciting contributions for the second race. But from some longtime supporters—including certain big contributors "that," Boyett says, "we had always counted on"—there was no reply. The checks that others sent in were often a zero short. "People who we thought would come in for a thousand or two thousand dollars would come in for only a hundred or two hundred," Boyett recalls. As a result, he says, "we had quite a bit less than we had expected." Boyett understood why. "Lyndon created the doubt: 'He'll vote to repeal that Act.' It cut the flow down to a dribble. Moreover," Boyett explains, "it wasn't just money we lost, but support." For the men who were no longer supporting Stevenson were the owners and managers of corporations. "In those days, if a popular executive with a company let it be known he was supporting a candidate, a lot of the employees would go along. And now some of the companies we had expected to support us, weren't." But the money aspect was crucial in itself. "We didn't have adequate funds to conduct a campaign."

IT TOOK Coke Stevenson two weeks to realize the damage that the Taft-Hartley "issue" had done to the reputation he cherished. "We didn't have any polls," Boyett recalls. "The Old Man didn't understand what it was doing to him." But calls from longtime supporters like Schreiner made him realize at last, and on August 11 Stevenson issued a statement on Taft-Hartley.

He made it in a letter to a friend, Sam Braswell, Jr., publisher of the *Kerrville Times*. "Sam," the letter said, "my stand on the Taft-Hartley law has never been a secret, although everything I have said regarding it has been deliberately misconstrued by my opponent in this race. I have said repeatedly in public statements and radio addresses that I think the effect of the Taft-Hartley law in curbing the labor monopoly has been a good thing for the country. I believe that you are sufficiently familiar with my public record to know that I have never kowtowed to any labor boss."

The *Dallas News* commented that Stevenson's letter proved that Johnson's campaign "has been largely waged against a straw man," for the letter "expresses the view that the Taft-Hartley Act has been of national benefit in curbing labor monopoly, the only real purpose at which it was aimed." The charge has always been "a little absurd," the *News* said, since "to anyone familiar with his [Stevenson's] long record in Texas administration obviously the accusation sought to portray him in a light utterly out of character." Coke himself pointed out that his statement was "nothing new—it is a restatement of what I said in Abilene," but his aides were pleased that he had finally made it; his letter would lay to rest once and for all Lyndon Johnson's accusations, they felt. And the *News* expressed the same opinion.

Which demonstrated only that they didn't know Lyndon Johnson.

He received the news in the midst of a day campaigning in San Antonio. He had to make three speeches in person that day and three over the radio, and to meet privately with the tough little postmaster, Dan Quill, and leaders of the "City Machine" and with the Mexican-American leaders who hadn't delivered for him in the first primary, and in between these speeches and meetings he shook hands in a park and at the city zoo, at the gates to industrial plants, with the workers crowding out at the end of their shifts, in downtown department stores, and in the teeming Mexican-American ghetto of the West Side. Towering above swarthy men in bright-colored shirts and old women in black rebozos, he abrazoed his way enthusiastically through the crowded, pushcart-jammed San Antonio slums. "Up one business block and down another, apparently unmindful of the more than 100-degree temperature," the Congressman moved, hugging, smiling, shouting, in a swirl of aides and voters. One by one, "reporters retired in defeat to the air-conditioned comfort of their hotel before the day was very old"; Johnson went on, hour after hour. But amid that turmoil and heat, the amazing political machine in Lyndon Johnson's mind never stopped clicking away. By mid-morning, he had devised a strategy to combat Stevenson's letter. First, he called in friendly reporters and planted doubts in their minds about the letter's authenticity. He understood there was some question about whether Coke had really written that letter, he told them; they'd better make sure he had before they got too excited about it. Didn't it seem strange to them that after all these weeks of refusing to make a statement, Stevenson had finally made one in a letter to the publisher of some obscure small-town newspaper instead of in a speech or press release? Had anyone seen the signature?

Two friendly reporters, Charles K. Boatner of Amon Carter's *Fort Worth Star-Telegram* and Robert V. Johnson of Hobby's *Houston Post*, drove the fifty miles to Kerrville, and the Houston reporter confirmed that the letter "was on stationery of the Stevenson headquarters at Austin and bore a signature which looked similar to the several signatures of the former Governor I have seen." But Johnson's tactic caused some newspapers to delay publication of the letter a day, and to give it smaller play than they would have on a first-day story, and it also clouded the letter just enough so that in some large papers it never received the major coverage it deserved; Robert Johnson's article, for example, said only that the letter "purported to give Stevenson's view."

But the main reason that Stevenson's letter had little impact was that Stevenson had little money. Now that the Old Man had made his statement, Murphey and Boyett and his other aides wanted it reprinted and broadcast. But printings and broadcasts cost money.

Lyndon Johnson, who *had* money, countered the letter with a barrage of broadcasts. On both August 13 and 14, he delivered three separate fifteen-minute radio talks, each over a thirty-station network that brought his voice into every town in Texas. The line he took was that Stevenson was still "dodging" the issue. Stevenson's letter, Johnson said, was "noncommittal. Texans think he has had plenty of time to give them a 'yes' or 'no' answer on whether he thinks Taft-Hartley is a good or bad law [and] whether he would vote to repeal it. . . ." Stevenson was still behaving like a frightened politician, Johnson said. "My opponent seems to be mighty interested in convincing the public he is not tied in with any labor bosses. Last June he accepted their endorsement with boasts. But under fire now from the other side he acts like he is ashamed of labor support . . . and is trying to rub off the brand."

To reinforce its candidate's statements, the Johnson campaign put on the air public figures respected in their various locales—and put them on in an effective way, often purchasing simultaneous time on every radio station, no matter how small, in an area so that listeners could not avoid the Johnson pitch. New reprints of the press conference articles were made, and new mailings went out. On August 15, Johnson, in another radio address, said, "By this time, nearly everybody in Texas has been forced to the conclusion that my opponent has established a world's record for refusing to declare his opinion on important issues." And indeed the impression in Texas still remained that Stevenson had entered into some kind of deal with "labor bosses." The ex-Governor's letter had been buried as completely as his earlier statement in Abilene. The *Dallas News* was to comment on Johnson's tactics: "With utterly unfounded allegation incapable of substantiation, he has striven to connect the AFL endorsement with a nonexistent deal to repeal the Taft-Hartley Act." But the tactics had worked: Johnson had not merely "striven" to connect the endorsement with a "deal"—he had succeeded in doing so. Turning the truth on its head, he had made a state believe not merely a lie, but a lie which defied logic. Texas had known Coke Stevenson's view about union bosses. But Lyndon Johnson was persuading a state that Stevenson's view was the precise opposite of what it really was.

The magnification of the power of money in the new media politics made such persuasion relatively easy. A substantial number of voters in Texas did not subscribe to a daily newspaper, and since many weekly newspapers never carried Stevenson's letter, these voters never read it; all they knew about it was what Lyndon Johnson told them. Few voters in Texas read the text of the letter more than once; they read, and heard, Johnson's interpretation of it over and over. Against an opponent who had so little money himself, this persuasion had, in fact, been easy. As John Connally is happy to explain: "You have to say something over and over to get voters to be aware of it. And he [Coke] didn't [do that]. He didn't advertise it, he didn't make an issue of it on the radio. So the press might be aware of the [letter], they might write a story about it—but nobody knew about it."

IN A FINAL TOUCH of irony, in Washington the presidents of four railroad unions endorsed Lyndon Johnson for Senator. Stevenson said, "This development is no surprise to Texans who are familiar with the real issues in this race . . . and with the past records of both candidates." But most Texans did not learn about the endorsement. There were few broadcasts and almost no mailings to drum home to voters that the supposedly anti-labor candidate had been endorsed by labor.* Nor, of course, were voters or businessmen aware that Robert Oliver, organizing director for the Congress of Industrial Organizations in Texas, was quietly lining up "a number of local (CIO) unions" in Texas cities to support Johnson, or that Welly Hopkins, general counsel of the United Mine Workers (whose president, John L. Lewis, was being assailed by Johnson on his noontime radio broadcasts), was drumming up labor support for Johnson and carrying campaign material back and forth between Corcoran and Rowe in Washington and Wirtz in Texas, or that a major source of funding for Johnson's "anti-union" campaign was David Dubinsky and other big-city union bosses, that in fact, unions in cities throughout the Northeast were shipping cash south to help the Johnson campaign. In almost every speech now, Johnson was reading the transcript of the press conference in which

---

* Asked about the difference in the candidates' positions on Taft-Hartley, Jeff Hickman, executive secretary of the state CIO, told a reporter that there was no difference. "The position of both candidates on the Taft-Hartley law is substantially the same. Both of them think it is a good law." But this statement was not even printed in many of the state's newspapers—and was buried in those that did use it.

Stevenson had refused to answer the questions about Taft-Hartley. The fact that Stevenson now had answered was all but drowned out in the flood of Johnson broadcasts, ads and pamphlets.

MONEY COULD BUY more than publicity. Money could buy men. George Peddy's votes were essential to any hope of victory, and Peddy's stronghold was in Deep East Texas, the little towns in the piney woods along the Louisiana border, the stronghold not only of Peddy strength but of Stevenson strength—of a conservatism as rock-solid as the Confederate state that Deep East Texas so closely resembled.

Johnson opened his second primary campaign there, in the very heart of Peddy country, in Center, county seat of Peddy's native Shelby County. In some ways it was a traditional East Texas rally, with farmers and their wives sitting on backless benches in the Courthouse Square, near the inevitable statue of the Confederate soldier, others remaining in their cars behind the benches and honking their horns to join in the applause. But the evidence of what money—unlimited money—could accomplish in even a hostile area was visible. As the *Houston Post* commented the next day:

> His [Johnson's] bid for votes in this section is obviously going to be a strong one. . . . Trees alongside the East Texas roads are decorated with his picture. His headquarters telephoned everyone in the Center phone book to get them out for the . . . speech.

Advertisements announcing the rally had not appeared merely in Shelby County newspapers, or on Shelby County radio stations, but all over East Texas, and the crowd—four hundred to five hundred persons, larger than anyone had expected—had come from as far away as Bowie County 105 miles to the north, to hear Johnson praise the native son in a bellow delivered over a full-size microphone strapped to his chest with a harness so that he could move around as he spoke. "I have not and will not speak an unkind word about Colonel Peddy. He was a man I liked and admired. . . . Colonel Peddy and I agreed on almost all the issues of the race."

But it wasn't Johnson's shouts that most strongly influenced Deep East Texas; it was the whispers of the missionaries. They had always had an unusually strong impact in these isolated little towns, so cut off from news of the outside world. Because of the affection for Peddy in these towns, the active campaigners were instructed to make the Colonel's friends believe that Stevenson was his enemy: "Well, you know, I was in Austin the other night, in the Driskill, and Coke came in, and you should have heard what he said about Colonel Peddy. He said . . ."

Did the Johnson campaign buy more than missionaries? At this crucial moment, according to men in both camps, Brown & Root swung into
action in East Texas with local subcontractors. The power of small-town
banks, on which local farmers are continuously dependent not only for
mortgages (and for refinancing of mortgages if they have had a bad year)
but for annual crop loans and loans to purchase seed, was mobilized.
Federal agencies with whom Johnson had influence—the Rural Electrification Administration, in particular—used their influence in East Texas.
And were more direct payments being made? Ed Clark, raised in San
Augustine and still owner of a home there, was asked in later years how
Johnson did so well in San Augustine, and throughout East Texas; Clark,
forthcoming on other points, will not discuss his home county. For reply,
he only raised a big hand and rubbed his thumb and forefinger together.
Forty years later, Ernest Boyett still vividly remembers his shock when
he began contacting East Texas political leaders whose support of Coke
Stevenson he had considered certain. "Almost the first two I contacted—
and they were key men—said to me that they couldn't support Coke this
time. I was so startled that words failed me. They had supported the Old
Man for years. But they said that they had been offered a thousand dollars
each to switch to Johnson. A thousand dollars was a great deal of money
for them. I remember one of them saying that he was getting older, and
he had to leave something for his wife. Well, what could I say to that?
They said they still believed in Coke, but that they would be throwing
their weight to Lyndon." Into Stevenson's headquarters poured similar
reports. Boyett recalls his thoughts: "My God! They're stealing East
Texas!"

SIMILAR TACTICS were being employed in rural counties all over Texas.
The impressions of a score of politicians who remember the 1948 campaign
are summarized in the reminiscences of a man who had the gift of grasping
the overall patterns in the Texas political scene, Ralph Yarborough,
United States Senator from 1957 to 1970.

> He [Johnson] had to turn it around *against* the Establish-
> ment. The old establishment had more of the infrastructure in
> these [rural] counties than Johnson did. The sheriffs, the county
> judges, the tax assessors. But they [Johnson and the Brown
> Building group] turned it around between the two primaries.
> They were able to do it so fast because of money. You can
> create a new structure fast if you have unlimited money. And
> they did. They were spending money like mad. They were spend-
> ing money like Texas had never seen. And they did it not only

so big but so openly. Nothing had ever been seen in Texas on such a scale, and they were utterly brash. They spent a lot of money. And they were brash about how they spent it, and they were utterly ruthless. Brown & Root would do *anything*.

They did it so big and so openly and so brash[ly] and so ruthlessly because they knew they didn't have a chance by conven tional political methods. Coke Stevenson had that race sewed up.

And they did it because they knew they had more at stake. They had an awful lot at stake.

For four months now, ever since May, Lyndon Johnson, and his money man, Herman Brown, and Alvin Wirtz had been trying to buy a state. They hadn't succeeded—so now they simply raised their offer.

To levels "like Texas had never seen."

COKE STEVENSON wasn't organizing the rural counties. During the first two weeks in August, he campaigned as he had always campaigned, driving around the state, shaking hands, talking to handfuls of voters about "principles" and the need for "economy" and "common sense" in government. The pro-Stevenson officials in these counties—legislators and former legislators, County Judges, men who were part of the traditional Texas political structure—were left to their own devices. There was almost no communication between them and Stevenson's Austin headquarters. Some of these men were actively working for Stevenson in the weeks before the second primary—and some were not.

Some, in fact, weren't even in the state. Well-to-do Texans try to escape the August heat by scheduling their vacations for that month. Many of Coke's "lead men" had been planning to go hunting in Canada. When they offered to stay home if they were needed, Coke's headquarters didn't make them feel they were needed. Nothing illustrates the lack of central coordination in the Stevenson campaign more clearly than the situation in two remote counties, Kinney and Hansford. These two Stevenson strongholds had given the former Governor a combined plurality of four hundred votes in the first primary. Because Stevenson was so far ahead, officials of these two counties felt the ex-Governor would not need their votes in the second primary—so they weren't holding one. And Stevenson headquarters was unaware of this fact. The overconfidence in Stevenson's headquarters was understandable: they were seventy thousand votes ahead, and how could they possibly lose the Peddy vote? By all the ordinary rules of Texas politics, their candidate had won.

. . . .

BUT JOHNSON wasn't playing by these rules.

From the earliest beginnings of Lyndon Johnson's political life—from his days at college when he had captured control of campus politics—his tactics had consistently revealed a pragmatism and a cynicism that had no discernible limits. His morality was the morality of the ballot box, a morality in which nothing matters but victory and any maneuver that leads to victory is justified, a morality that was amorality.

Johnson had already enjoyed considerable success in linking Coke Stevenson, adamant foe of organized labor though he was, with "big-city labor racketeers." Now he was to attempt to link the former Governor with another group: Communists. Coke Stevenson, Lyndon Johnson now charged, was a front man for a Communist conspiracy. Maybe Coke was an unwitting front man, Johnson said—and maybe he wasn't.

Johnson began this effort in a series of radio broadcasts (over state-wide hookups) that read into Stevenson's alleged failure to take a stand on Taft-Hartley a more sinister interpretation than any he had yet suggested. "Lyndon Johnson voted for the anti-Communist Taft-Hartley Law," Johnson said. "Lyndon Johnson will never vote to repeal this law. But my opponent has not yet made a public statement as to just where he stands on this measure that bans Communist control of labor unions." The next evening Johnson escalated the attack: "Birds of a feather" such as John L. Lewis, James C. Petrillo "and Communist Harry Bridges, whom I voted to deport to Australia years ago . . . have flocked together in a united effort to defeat Lyndon Johnson, who refused to wear their Red feathers in his hat, and they are using Coke Stevenson as their silent man Friday. . . . My opponent has refused to promise that . . . he will not . . . return control of labor unions to racketeering Communist leaders who take orders only from Moscow." By the following evening, he was implying that Stevenson's "refusal to promise" might mean that he had made a secret promise—"Does it mean that he would amend the law so that labor bosses could have secret Communist connections?"

Johnson seemed to think he could make Texans—at least rural Texans—swallow even so ridiculous a charge if it was repeated often enough. To reinforce his speeches—which were making Stevenson's Communist "link" more and more explicit—a new device was unveiled, aimed squarely at unsophisticated farmers. It was the inspiration of John Connally, who says that when he was a farm boy in Wilson County, "My first impression of politics in Texas was the *Ferguson Forum*," a simulated weekly newspaper printed during the campaigns of Governor Jim Ferguson. "People were all talking about it," Connally recalls. "It went into every rural mailbox. . . . Most of these rural people . . . read it and they believed it." Pappy O'Daniel had copied the *Forum* in his *O'Daniel News*. Now Connally ordered up the *Johnson Journal*—a four-page newspaper, written in Johnson headquarters but designed to look like a genuine weekly so that to the unsophisticated it would carry a newspaper's authority—and it was mailed early in August to 340,000 rural mailboxes. The *Journal's* theme was captured in its lead headline: "COMMUNISTS FAVOR COKE." Also reinforcing Johnson's speeches, of course, was the other campaign device that had proven so effective with unsophisticated voters. From the Hancock House, new marching orders were given to the missionaries: to fan out across Texas, calling on farm families, standing around in grocery stores, sitting in bars, dropping hints and innuendoes about Coke and "the Reds": "I'm not saying he is one, but listen. . . ."

ASSIDUOUSLY though he had, for years, privately cultivated Texas' wealthy reactionaries, Lyndon Johnson had always sought—for strategic reasons, it was true, but nonetheless he had sought—to preserve a measure of independence in his dealings with them. While he had run their errands and accepted their cash, he had kept a little distance between himself and them, partly because he never wanted to be allied completely with any position, partly so that he could claim to the Washington liberals that he was liberal at heart. But now this was to change.

The reactionaries' alliance with Coke Stevenson had always been tenuous; the former Governor, although in agreement on ideology, had always been too independent for their taste, too proud, not nearly subservient enough; not subservient at all, in fact. Richardson and Murchison and other members of their circle had assured them that Lyndon Johnson could "get things done" for them in Washington and that Johnson was not in reality the liberal he appeared to be, but before the first primary they had continued to give their support—their money, their influence over the votes of their employees—to Stevenson. Now, however, feeling betrayed by Coke ("He'll vote to repeal that Act!"), they were more disposed to give it to Johnson. But, prudent, practical men that they were, and determined to exact the complete subservience of the candidate who received that support, they put a price on it.

The price was that Lyndon Johnson should give a certain speech.

It was a speech not unfamiliar to Texas voters. They had, in fact, heard versions of it hundreds of times—delivered by W. Lee O'Daniel. For years, first as an announcer for Light Crust Flour and then for his own Hillbilly Flour, O'Daniel had exerted an immense influence over rural Texas through the radio talks he gave every day at a half-hour past noon over the dominant Texas State Quality Network, talks that were almost sermons about motherhood and religion and "Beautiful, Beautiful Texas," delivered, against a background of soft violins playing sentimental country-and-Western tunes, in the matchlessly warm, soft but firm voice

of a wise and wonderful "Pappy." "At 12:30 sharp every day," one reporter wrote, "silence reigned in the State of Texas, broken only by mountain music and the dulcet voice of W. Lee O'Daniel." Even after Pappy's
entrance into politics, he still spoke in the same time slot, but the speech
was different. It had in its many versions the same basic themes, which
played on the fears and prejudices of the unsophisticated and poorly educated listeners sitting over lunch on their farms and ranches. Its main
theme was the danger from Communists, who, Pappy said, had infiltrated
Texas industrial plants and—along with racketeers, "goons" and "mob-
sters" from the big cities of the Northeast—the state's labor unions. A
genius in demagoguery, he would reiterate certain phrases—"Communist
labor leader racketeers," "union thugs," and, after a labor incident in
Chicago in which a hand grenade was thrown, "pineapple-throwing Red
goons"—over and over; attempting to describe the speech—"Pappy's
Speech," as it came to be known in Texas political circles—one observer
recalls: "He would just drum, drum, drum with his little catch phrases—
'labor leader racketeers,' 'Communist labor leader racketeers,' 'pineapple-throwing labor leader racketeers': you just wouldn't think there
would be that many ways to get 'labor leader racketeers' into a sentence."

Pappy's speech embodied the ignorant and vicious side of Texas conservatism; it was the essence of everything that Lyndon Johnson had convinced his liberal friends in Washington he was fighting against in Texas;
indeed, during his 1941 campaign against O'Daniel, he had had Pappy's
speech recorded and sent to Washington to convince Corcoran and Rowe
(and Franklin Roosevelt, for whom they played the record) that Johnson's
opponent was a "Neanderthal" and that therefore their support of Johnson's candidacy should be increased. (This device had worked; says Rowe:
"That speech was the most unbelievable thing I ever heard.") When liberal or moderate Texans gave their reasons for despising Pass-the-Biscuits-
Pappy O'Daniel—and they despised him quite deeply—they often did so
by quoting "Pappy's Speech."

Because the twelve-thirty slot on the Texas Quality Network had become identified with O'Daniel, and because farm and ranch families had
grown accustomed not only to listening to it, but to believing what was
said on it, that time slot was, recalls Horace Busby, "the great prize in
Texas politics." It was controlled by a group of Dallas reactionaries, and
was not available to any liberal politician—or, indeed, to any politician
who refused to tug his forelock to them: when an unapproved candidate
tried to buy the time, the network simply said it was not for sale.

Early in August, 1948, Attorney General Tom Clark's brother Robert, a Dallas lawyer who represented the men who controlled that time
slot, approached Lyndon Johnson with a simple proposal. They would
support him—and give him the time slot—if he used it to deliver "Pappy's

Speech" as if it were his own. Of course, Clark explained, they didn't want him to give the speech just once; they wanted him to give it over and over, day after day, every day until Election Day, just the way Pappy would have done it. Lyndon would not even have to write it, they said. Pappy's old speechwriters would write it. All Johnson would have to do was read it, over and over, as evidence of his good faith, as public proof that he truly subscribed to Pappy's philosophy, which was, of course, their philosophy.

Horace Busby was in Amarillo with Johnson, staying in the same hotel, when the candidate received the first script. Having known nothing of Clark's proposal, the young aide had been surprised when he had noticed in the schedule that Johnson was to give a speech in that prized time slot.

No campaigning had been arranged for that morning, as Busby recalls: "He had a morning alone." Busby was in his own room, and Johnson summoned him. When he arrived, the candidate was looking through the script. "It was as though he had no life in him," Busby recalls. "He would sit down at a table, and . . . he would turn the pages. He would get up and pace and sit down again. Finally," Busby says, "he motioned me over [and said], 'Look at this stuff.' " Busby read the speech. He cannot recall the exact words but, Busby says, "it equated unionism with mobs. All about 'goons' and 'goon squads' and 'pineapples' [grenades] being thrown into the homes of honest union reformers, and extortion. The language was very rough."

"I don't know about that," Johnson said. "Sometimes politics asks too much." For what Busby describes as "an extended period of time," the candidate "was going through just an intense personal debate with himself." He paced back and forth, stopping every so often and staring at the ceiling, absent-mindedly jingling the change in his pocket—as if unable to decide whether or not to give the speech. He gave Busby some of the background.

> He named the men who were involved. He never said exactly
> what they had done. They had bought the time. They had put
> up the money. He said some of the largest *employers* in Texas
> had done this. Had defected from Coke and said if he would do
> these speeches that they would not only pay for it but that they
> would go to work with their people and get a turnout.

All the arrangements had been made, he said; in fact, one of Carr Collins' men was downstairs to handle the broadcast. But, repeating that "Sometimes politics asks too much" of a man, he also said, several times, "I'm going to call Bob Clark and tell him to forget it."

That call was not made. Instead, there followed what Busby calls "the rationalizing."

> Johnson said to me: "That man [Coke Stevenson] ought not to be Senator. He's the kind of isolationist who got us into this war, and he'll get us into another one. . . . The labor unions should not be supporting a man like Coke Stevenson who was against everything they were for; the unions were selling out the working people. . . ."

Suppose he refused to give the speech, he said; what would happen?

> Well, what it comes down to, Buzz, is this: I can [refuse to] make this speech and when I'm out of office I can go over to the union headquarters [in Washington] and tell them what a noble thing I did. And when I get over there, the receptionist is going to say, "Lyndon who?" And she's going to call upstairs, and then she's going to say, "Who are you with?" And then she's going to say, "I'm sorry, but there's no one who can see you."

And there followed what Ed Clark and others familiar with Johnson would call the "working himself up"—getting himself not only to believe what he was saying but to believe it enthusiastically. "He went off on a kind of 'rights of the people' soliloquy: 'Does Coke Stevenson care about the man who works for a living?' . . . The unions were selling out the working people—he really got pretty steamed up thinking his way through about the working people." When he had finished, Johnson picked up the script and walked out to give the broadcast. Busby, who believed he was so expert at reading Johnson's moods, knew that "when he pushed his hat back, he was in a good mood." To Busby's surprise—understandable surprise in view of the "intense personal debate" he had just witnessed— as Johnson picked up the script, "he pushed his hat back." Also "to my surprise," Busby, listening to the broadcast, realized that "he didn't try to cover up on any of the offending lines"; that, in fact, "he was expressive," reading the script very well, better than he read most speeches.

The reactionaries had demanded a stiff price for their support. Johnson paid it in full.

THE RESPONSE was all the candidate could have wished. Following the speech, he returned to the hotel, and, again while Busby was present,

There was a call from Bob Clark. Bob Clark had a gathering, and I could tell from Lyndon's end of the conversation that [everything had gone well]. And he was speaking with enormous respectfulness to them. And they were saying, We never expected you to do it, but you can count on us.

And there were more calls that night. The talk brought the ultra-conservatives in behind him. They just in effect joined the campaign.

. . . This gave a beneficial turn. . . . Before the end of the week, I felt enough electricity in the air that I thought we could win. And he did, too.

The polls showed that Johnson was indeed gaining. Now, when he called to ask John Connally, "What do you hear?," Connally had good news to report; "Particularly when Johnson got on the radio with the labor stuff, they [the polls] showed Johnson gaining," he recalls. The trend was especially strong in rural areas; Connally, an expert on rural voting, felt that the O'Daniel time slot—and the O'Daniel speech that Johnson was making in it—was, day by day, greatly increasing his share of the rural vote.

JOHNSON'S PRESENCE in the O'Daniel slot was a signal to Texas conservatives that he was approved by the conservative upper echelons. So the broadcasts, Busby says, "turned money that would have gone to Stevenson." Since the former Governor's campaign financing had always come from conservatives, the flow of Stevenson's funds, already drastically reduced, was cut off almost entirely. This, as Busby says, was important, because, by the middle of August, Coke Stevenson had had enough.

For three months, Stevenson's advisers had been pleading with him to defend himself against Johnson's attacks, trying to make him understand that Johnson was hurting his reputation, and, in the last few weeks, also telling him that Johnson was pulling dangerously close. For three months, they had been pleading with him with increasing urgency to attack Johnson, to make the public examine *his* record. For three months, Stevenson had refused to do so.

Two new developments appear to have made him change his mind. One was the insinuation that he was a Communist tool; according to one aide, the turning point came when, in a small town one day in early August, a farmer handed him a copy of the *Johnson Journal*. The other was the realization that although attacks on his reputation had never worked before, Johnson's attacks were working, that Texans were coming to *believe* that he was a Communist front, a "do-nothing" Governor who had accomplished nothing for the state, and an opportunistic politician without firm principles or beliefs who would trim his sails to the prevailing wind. After a grim meeting at Center, George Peddy's hometown, where twenty-five key Peddy supporters told him, "Coke, this thing is a lot closer than you think!," Stevenson agreed to say the things his supporters had for so long been wanting him to say.

He said them in two speeches in East Texas, each delivered in the traditional setting, on the lawn of a Courthouse in a county seat, one in Center, and one in Conroe. Despite the blazing heat, he spoke with his suit jacket on and buttoned.

The speeches combined a defense of his record with questions about Johnson's.

I don't like to make speeches like this, Coke Stevenson said. He had never made "a charge against any of my opponents." But, he said, "since things were said of me, I'd like to ask a few questions." And the questions he asked were the ones his advisers had been begging him to ask—the questions that had never been asked in public about Lyndon Johnson.

First, Stevenson listed seven major topics that Johnson himself had said urgently needed—and had needed, for some time—national action: an increase in old-age pensions; construction of more farm-to-market roads; control of inflation; reductions in income taxes; conservation of soil and water; control of Communist activities; investigation of Communist espionage. During his eleven and a half years in Congress, Coke Stevenson asked, had Lyndon Johnson ever taken any action on any of these problems? More specifically, had he ever introduced legislation that addressed any of these problems?

Stevenson went through them one by one.

When Lyndon Johnson had appeared before you, Coke Stevenson reminded his audience, when he "landed his helicopter on this very spot," the Congressman had talked—as he had been talking throughout the campaign—about the need for farm-to-market roads. Well, Stevenson said, during his own administration as Governor, hundreds—thousands—of miles of farm-to-market roads had been built all over Texas. But, he asked his audience, when Johnson spoke to you, did he mention anything *he* had ever done to get farm-to-market roads built? And, specifically, did Johnson tell you he had ever introduced a bill to help with the farm-to-market road program?

When Johnson spoke to you, Stevenson said, he talked about the need for increased old-age pensions. Well, during his own administration as Governor, old-age pensions had been tripled. Did Johnson mention anything *he* had ever done to get pensions increased? And, specifically, did Johnson tell you *he* had ever introduced a bill on the subject of old-age pensions?

Stevenson went through the other topics in similar detail. During his eleven and a half years in Congress, he asked, had Lyndon Johnson taken any action on such national problems? Had he introduced any bills to deal with them? And Stevenson asked a larger question. "When he was here," Coke Stevenson asked, "did my opponent tell you that he ever introduced any [such] bill in his entire life? Did he mention any law he offered in the eleven and one-half years he has been in Congress—any bill for the general welfare? When my opponent landed his helicopter on this very spot, did he tell you of any bill he ever introduced in Congress? Did he ever pass a bill which would aid the average citizen of the United States? Did he ever introduce a bill—a single bill? I can't find one. I can't find a single bill to help the average citizen that Lyndon Johnson introduced in eleven and one-half years. Ask him if he ever introduced a bill."

I don't like to make speeches like this, Stevenson repeated. I'm just giving you my record, and contrasting it with the absence of a record for the other candidate. "I'm just asking you if he had told you about introducing any legislation, and I think the answer is no."

WHEN, for the first time, public emphasis was placed on Lyndon Johnson's legislative record, the phrase summarizing that record—or the lack of it—was so dramatic that it leapt out of newspaper articles, even in pro-Johnson papers. "In the strongest speech of his entire campaign, [Coke Stevenson] lambasted his opponent, Lyndon Johnson, and demanded to know of 'one single bill' Congressman Johnson ever introduced in Congress," reported the *Houston Post*. The lead in the *Dallas News* said: "Lyndon Johnson, in eleven and a half years in Congress, never introduced a single bill which would contribute to the welfare of the people, Coke Stevenson charged." Some version of the phrase "not one single bill . . . in eleven and one-half years" appeared in virtually every daily newspaper in Texas.

During the next few days, moreover, Stevenson began to focus on aspects not only of Johnson's past record but of his present campaign. "It is no secret to any informed person that the other candidate is waging what is probably the most expensive political campaign in the history of Texas," he said on August 19. Where, he asked, was this money coming from—and why? "Could his money," he asked, "be coming from a few millionaires who owe [him] past political debts and hope for future political favors from him?" Stevenson even hinted—accurately—at another source of Johnson's money: "Could it be coming from the CIO?" Indeed, he said, part of "the huge expenditures" to elect Lyndon Johnson to federal office were being made with what were, in the last analysis, "federal taxes." As for himself, Stevenson said, he had kept his own campaign "on a very modest scale," as he had in the past. "I've never had a side-show or a brass band in my campaign. I was raised up in the ranch country, where a man is known for his character and the adornments he has," not the "adornments" he could buy. But, he said, he did not believe that Johnson's expenditures would make any difference. He believed that Texans would have enough intelligence to understand why the contractors and Hughes Aircraft were supporting Johnson. And he believed that Texans understood that he, Coke Stevenson, would never be "an errand boy" for contractors or oil companies. "I do not believe you are ready to sell the office of United States Senator to the highest bidder," he said. "I do not believe you want as your Senator a man who is able to call on secret sources for the multiplied millions of dollars that are being spent on behalf of the other candidate." These statements, too, received good play.

Good, but brief—too brief to be effective. "Repetition—that was the thing," Paul Bolton says, and the Johnson speechwriter is right. For Stevenson's charges to have significant impact on the campaign, Stevenson would have to repeat them in a series of radio speeches, and in advertisements on the radio and in newspapers, daily and weekly. They would have to be repeated in mailings of postcards and letters and brochures. They would have to be repeated in conversations, the conversations of "travelers" and other campaign workers.

Stevenson's advisers wanted repetition. Now that the Old Man had finally agreed to attack, they eagerly anticipated putting the attack on the air. But airtime cost money. Boyett and Roberts asked for money from the conservative businessmen who had previously backed Coke's campaigns. But their contributions, already slowed by the doubts Johnson had planted about Stevenson's stance on Taft-Hartley, had all but dried up because these were the men, many of them from Dallas, who had listened with Robert Clark to Lyndon Johnson reading "Pappy's Speech." During the last ten days of the campaign, Stevenson was indeed on the radio—but not often enough, and, except in a few instances, not to a sufficiently large audience. "We would have a statewide radio address scheduled," Boyett recalls, but often there would not be enough to pay all the stations to carry it. Frantically, he and other Stevenson loyalists would telephone county managers and ask them to raise the money to pay for their local station to carry it, but all too often this didn't work, either. "We would have to cut off stations." Stevenson's speech on Johnson's "huge expenditures," for example, was scheduled for statewide airing at 6:45 p.m., August 19, but at the last minute so many stations cut it off the air that substantial parts of the state never heard it. Stevenson's advisers had anticipated examining Johnson's record as a Congressman in a newspaper advertising campaign, and effective ads were written and designed; one asked Johnson, "If you have 'energy, initiative and independent judgment,' please refer us to one piece of legislation passed by the Congress during your eleven and one-half years that bears your name." But the number of such ads that appeared was pathetically small compared with the volume of Johnson ads that were appearing everywhere. Bolton was right: "Repetition—that was the thing." But Johnson had "turned" his opponent's money; his opponent couldn't afford repetition. The concept "not one single bill in eleven and one-half years" was a dramatic one, but it would not become generally known to the voters of Texas—because there was no money to make it known. Connally ("You have to say something over and over to get voters to be aware of it") explains scornfully: "So Coke makes a speech—so what? With one speech you couldn't sell anyone that Johnson wasn't an activist in the Congress. He had a reputation of being an activist. . . . One-day play is all you get out of any speech. He didn't make a big issue out of it. So the press might be aware of it, they might write a story about it—but nobody knew about it. With one speech, you can't sell anyone."

Under the old politics, Stevenson's charges, even without massive funds to publicize them, would have had a more substantial impact on the campaign. Under the old politics, radio, the prime consumer of campaign funds, was not nearly so great a factor, so stump speeches and newspaper articles had a greater relative importance, and good, if brief, newspaper play would have had more of an effect on a campaign. Limited though his airtime might be, the disparity between it and his opponent's would not have been so disproportionate. But this was the new politics—media politics, money politics, Lyndon Johnson politics. During the last two weeks of the campaign, despite the dropping of stations from his "network" broadcasts, most areas of Texas heard Coke Stevenson at least three or four times. Occasionally, one of Stevenson's supporters was on the air. Occasionally, there were in the big newspapers a few ads repeating his charges. During these last two weeks, Lyndon Johnson was on the air in every section of Texas at three regular times a day—every day; not only in Pappy's old twelve-thirty slot, but at seven-forty in the morning and seven-thirty in the evening; by mid-August, a Texas farm family had difficulty sitting down to a meal and switching on the radio without hearing his voice. Transcribed four-minute recordings were on the air at other times. His supporters were on the air, frequently on statewide networks, so often that, as one observer recalls, "it seemed like you could hardly turn on the radio without hearing about Lyndon Johnson." With the campaign roaring to a climax and newspapers focusing on it, news coverage of the candidates in newspapers was now fairly equal; but newspaper advertising was overwhelmingly Johnson's—and in many weekly newspapers, this space was as influential with readers as the articles, because the newspapers did not differentiate much between the two, and many unsophisticated readers couldn't tell the difference, anyway. As for direct mailings, Stevenson had few if any. Rural mailboxes were filled daily not only with the *Johnson Journal* but with mailing after mailing of letters and postcards. And always, of course, there was the conversational campaigning—the work of the "travelers." Only a massive barrage of Stevenson ads and mailings and walking delegates could have countered this, and there was no money to pay for them.

Stevenson's charges did not bother John Connally for a moment. *"So Coke makes a speech—so what?"* Connally's assessment of the situation was correct. Coke Stevenson had made charges about Lyndon Johnson— several charges. In effect, these charges went unheard. His charge that Johnson was, with his "huge expenditures," trying to buy the campaign, was drowned out, as were all his charges—by Johnson's huge expenditures.

THERE MAY HAVE BEEN another reason, too, that Coke Stevenson's attacks did not have greater impact on the campaign.

During the first primary, George Peddy had commented on what he called a "strange coincidence." In a radio address that he had hoped would provide a major boost to his candidacy, Peddy had advocated an increase in old-age pensions. On the very evening on which he made the address, however, Lyndon Johnson took much of the impact out of Peddy's proposal by making a similar proposal—in almost the same words.

Now others began to notice the same kind of coincidences. On August 18, for example, Stevenson said that he was "no new recruit in the fight against Communism." Almost simultaneously, Johnson was on the radio. "I am no recent convert to the fight against Communism," he said. On August 19, as Texas political historian Seth McKay puts it, "curiously . . . the two campaigners . . . on the same day accused one another of the same bad practices"—in almost the same words. In his speech in Austin that day, which claimed that Johnson's supporters were "waging what is probably the most expensive political campaign in the history of Texas," Stevenson added that money was being "spent like water" to defeat him. That same day, in Fort Worth, Johnson said in a radio speech that Stevenson's supporters were "spending money like water" to defeat him.

The coincidences went beyond phrasing. Meeting at the Driskill Hotel to plan strategy, Stevenson's inner circle of advisers had gradually come to realize that their plans were known outside the room almost as soon as they made them—although their only communication with the outside world had been over the telephone. Stevenson's schedule, for example, seemed to be known throughout Texas political circles even before it had been published—within minutes, in fact, after it had been decided on, although, Boyett says, during those minutes "the only time the schedule had been discussed" was on the phone. "We were absolutely certain that they were wiretapping our headquarters in the Driskill."

Asked about this, Connally has said, "We didn't do any wiretapping." He said that during the 1940s, "they didn't tap and tape like they do now." He also said, "Occasionally we would have a telephone operator—on her own"—listen in and tell us what was being said. "In those days, that was what happened: operators would listen in on the switchboard." Connally added, "We may have had somebody in his headquarters reporting to us." Was there in fact someone spying in Stevenson's headquarters? "I don't remember," Connally replied. Other members of the campaign, however, believe that the phone lines of Stevenson's headquarters were being constantly listened to, either by tapping or by operators listening in.

The repetition of speech themes and phrases by Johnson—whether based on overheard telephone calls or not, whether repeated the same or the next day—took the edge off Stevenson's belated efforts to attack, or at least to defend himself against his younger opponent. On August 19, for example, Stevenson made the point that Johnson's attempts to give himself a new, ultra-conservative, image squared poorly with his previous alliances with ultra-liberals in Washington; Stevenson pointed out that Henry Wallace had actively supported Johnson in his previous Senate race in 1941, and had even loaned one of his chief aides, Harold Young, to the Johnson campaign as a fund-raiser to obtain large sums of money from labor leaders in the North. "Are they [still] together to the extent that the money they are spending is coming from the same source?" Stevenson asked. This charge, which was accurate, might have been a telling point, but the next day Johnson stated that it was actually Stevenson and Wallace who were secret allies. In radio broadcasts that day he demanded, "What promises of support did he [Stevenson] extract from Henry Wallace when Wallace cooled coffee with him in the Governor's Mansion back in 1944?" (Wallace had visited the Governor that year during a tour of the Southwest.) And Johnson added, "I see . . . that the black bag of the labor bosses has finally arrived from the North to swell the slush fund being spent to defeat Lyndon Johnson." As the *Corpus Christi Caller-Times* commented: "The question by Johnson pushed the political merry-go-round full circle and left each candidate implying the other was—or had been—associated with the head of the Progressive Party." Who could blame voters, even those who were conscientiously attempting to follow the campaign, for being confused—and, in a sea of identical charges by both candidates, for being convinced by the candidate who could, thanks to the power of money, make the charge so much more frequently than his opponent?

. . .

DURING the crucial month of August, Lyndon Johnson even made use of his most reluctant weapon.

Months earlier, at the very beginning of the campaign, Johnson had personally ordered cards and placards with pictures of Lady Bird and his two daughters, and had commented with satisfaction upon seeing the finished product: "Coke can't do that." In competing for the "women's vote," he had told aides frankly, he possessed a significant advantage: he had a wife, and Stevenson didn't.

Attempts to maximize this asset had proven unsatisfactory during the first primary, because the confidence which Lady Bird Johnson had gained as a result of managing a congressional office and a business had not carried over into the area of her greatest timidity.

In the hectic swirl of Johnson campaign headquarters, the one constant was Mrs. Johnson's calm, warm smile. When, on her husband's rare days in Austin, staff members arrived at Dillman Street for an evening, or late-night, meeting, they had learned to accept as a matter of course the graciousness of her welcome, and, no matter how late the hour, a hot meal. Sometimes she quoted Kipling: "If you can keep your head while . . ." And, says Dorothy Nichols, during the frantic dark days of 1948 "I really believe she lived by [that poem]. She doesn't lose her head." Suitcases packed with her husband's medical supplies and carefully starched shirts were ready every time Woody screeched up to her door. But despite her husband's increasingly insistent demands that she make speeches, or at least personal appearances, on his behalf, during the first primary she had not done so. Her terrible shyness had always made public appearances of even the most undemanding variety such an ordeal that her friends had suffered for her on the rare occasions when she had been induced to stand beside her husband on a receiving line at some Tenth District event and, a bright smile set rigidly on her face, shake hands and try to chat with strangers filing by. As for making a speech, the very suggestion that she face an audience brought panic to the face of this woman who had once prayed for smallpox so that she wouldn't have to speak at her high-school graduation ceremony.

Although Mrs. Johnson was willing to do almost anything for her husband, making speeches was one thing she would not do—felt she *could* not do. There was, moreover, another impediment to her campaigning. Because of Texas' vast distances, personal campaigning—even appearing at receptions—involved airplane travel, and Mrs. Johnson was almost as afraid of flying as of speaking in public; she was often not only in terror but violently airsick as well. Finally, near the end of the first primary campaign, Alvin Wirtz, who always had more influence with her than any other of her husband's associates, suggested a way in which she might meet at least a few voters. Why not drive from gas station to gas station, purchasing only five gallons of gas at each stop, and meet the gas station owners and the hangers-on who were often around rural gas stations? This Mrs. Johnson finally agreed to do—as long as she didn't have to do it alone—and Mary Rather was deputed to accompany her. But this attempt lasted only a day or two. Then, one morning, as they were pulling into their third gas station, Lady Bird said to Miss Rather: "You ask them this time, Mary, I don't believe I can do it again."

After the first primary, however, there was only one month to go, and his wife's fears were no longer a luxury that Lyndon Johnson was prepared to indulge. "We need to get after the women's vote," Johnson told Busby. He told Lady Bird's friend Marietta Brooks of Austin, who was active in a number of statewide women's clubs, to telephone leading clubwomen throughout the state and organize "coffees" at which Lady Bird would meet the local clubwomen and give interviews to local reporters. And when aides ventured to mention that this would mean that Lady Bird would have to fly, Johnson said: "She'll fly."

She did—perhaps as much out of concern about what the humiliation of overwhelming defeat would do to her husband as for any other reason. In recalling her reasons years later, she would say: "We were overwhelmingly, vastly, horribly behind. . . ." Overcoming Stevenson's huge margin "looked hopeless, but at least I wanted to narrow that margin, just as much as I could, and make just as much of a showing as I could for myself and for him and all those folks who had already shoveled so much love and sweat and time and money into it."

Her first trip was to Corpus Christi on August 2. Mary Rather recalls that "We were all fanning out in various directions over the state that Monday morning, and if any had had time, they would have felt sorry for Lady Bird as she took off through gray rainy skies in a very small plane with one pilot and one traveling companion. . . ."

Lady Bird was so nervous that she had written out and memorized every phrase she was to say in the Corpus Christi interview—and it showed; asked if she thought helicopter campaigning was a good idea, she said she did because "I think a candidate ought to let the voters see one and to hear one's ideas." She said a Peddy supporter had telephoned her to say ninety percent of the Peddy vote would go to "Lyndon," and this was "a very happy generalization that we are going to strive to make a fact." But it *was* an interview—it was publicity, a pleasant article and photograph in the *Corpus Christi Caller*. And although she took plane trips back and forth across Texas all during August, a month in which the intense heat spawned almost daily thunderstorms, and the terror and the airsickness never got better, the fear of interviews eased at least a little;

after a while, Lady Bird was to say, she realized that "these people are just like me, so I had no reason to be scared." She never became less modest in her statements, but she became more effective. In Fort Worth, on August 24, she was still saying to a reporter, "My campaigning role is comparatively simple. I just pack and unpack and take care of Lyndon," but she was less reluctant to talk about herself, telling a reporter that she had studied to be a journalist herself but had gotten married instead, "so I became part of the news instead of reporting it." And, the reporter wrote, "Mrs. Lyndon Johnson, an attractive brunette whose roles as wife and mother have kept her in the background of her husband's public career, charmed two hundred Tarrant County women at a coffee Wednesday morning." Soon, in fact, her husband's top advisers, receiving reports back in Austin on her appearances, realized that she was becoming quite an effective force in the campaign. For one thing, Edward Clark says, unlike her husband, "She had never done anything unpopular. She had never done anything anyone could criticize." But, Clark says, it was more than that: "She was a great asset. She made votes everywhere she went."

One thing, however, she still resisted doing. When a reporter asked her that August if she planned to speak on her husband's behalf, she said: "I couldn't possibly make a speech!" Her husband was particularly insistent that she make one at the opening rally of the second primary, the rally in Center in Deep East Texas. Since she was from that area, and since her father was a political force there, even a few words from her would be a big help. But she said she simply couldn't. In a maneuver conceived by her husband to call attention to her despite her silence, she continually got up from her seat on the platform while her husband was speaking and adjusted the light on the podium, so that she was as visible as she could be without actually saying anything.

Now, finally, at the very end of the campaign, Lady Bird bowed to her husband's demands and agreed to take the step she dreaded most of all. She agreed to speak at the closing Johnson rally on August 27, the day before the election—in front of a crowd of some fourteen thousand people who would be jamming the San Antonio Municipal Auditorium, and in front of microphones that would carry her speech over a statewide radio hookup.

At least San Antonio was close enough to Austin so that she could drive there, but this proved a doubtful blessing. She and Mrs. Brooks were going to stop en route for a "coffee" in Seguin, but before they got there, their car skidded on wet pavement, veered off the road, overturned, and rolled over twice before coming to a stop in a ditch.

Lady Bird was bruised and shaken up but otherwise uninjured—and she didn't want anything to disturb Lyndon before his big rally. Depositing Mrs. Brooks, who was badly bruised, in a hospital, she drove alone to the Seguin reception, borrowed a dress from the hostess to replace her torn clothes, and shook hands with two hundred women with her usual smiling graciousness. Then she drove to San Antonio and made her speech.

During the next few days, mail poured into the Hancock House from political leaders (Abilene District Chairman Jay Taylor wrote, "Lady Bird was wonderful on the radio last night. Should have been on all the time!") and from voters (Mrs. W. S. Harris of Hays County wrote Johnson, "I heard your wife's sweet voice over the radio, and I thought what a comfort she was to you"); a Houston attorney and his wife, who had heard Mrs. Johnson's speech, were to write that they were waiting in line at the polling place on the "hot, muggy Election Day, being jostled by 'unwashed' members of our democracy," when his wife turned to him "with perspiration streaming down her face, and with makeup, hat and clothing somewhat bedraggled, and said, 'I want you to know that I am enduring this *only* on account of that lovely Mrs. Johnson.' "

After the speech, Lady Bird and Lyndon arrived at their San Antonio hotel room about midnight, and Johnson, as he would later recall, "told her we'd better get to bed." But Lady Bird said she was driving back to Austin that night for some last-minute campaigning on Election Day.

"As she changed for the trip," Johnson was to recall, "I saw these big bruises," and when he asked her about them, she had to tell him about the accident. But she drove back to Austin and was up early the next morning. She and Lyndon's mother and his sisters divided the Austin telephone book among them, and all Election Day they phoned people asking them to go to the polls and vote. She had a good line ready for reporters who inquired about the accident: "All I could think of as we were turning over was I sure wished I'd voted absentee." But she was prouder of the telephone calls, because all day she had managed to talk over the phone to absolute strangers without losing her nerve.

13

The Stealing

LYNDON JOHNSON had started the runoff campaign seventy thousand votes behind, and the Peddy votes had at first seemed likely to widen the margin. But almost day by day, it seemed, he was narrowing the gap.

And then, suddenly, during the last week or ten days of the campaign, it wasn't narrowing any further.

His young aides weren't aware of this. Amid the noisy bustle in the Hancock House, optimism mounted with each new report from Buzz or Woody of the record crowds Lyndon was drawing, and of their enthusiasm. The young men, like Connally and Herring, believed they were going to win. But in the quiet offices on the seventh floor of the Brown Building, where Alvin Wirtz, Edward Clark and Everett Looney, the senior partners in the law firms for which the young men worked, met with Herman and George Brown (and, whenever he was in Austin, with Lyndon Johnson), there was no longer jubilation. The reports coming into the Brown Building weren't from Buzz or Woody, but from more seasoned politicians, men who had watched a hundred campaigns, and who knew that crowds were only a part, often a misleading part, of a political story. Furthermore, they were receiving other information not available to the young men: the results of private polls. In these polls, which were being taken almost daily, Johnson had been steadily gaining ground on Coke Stevenson. And then, abruptly, as had been the case in the first primary, he stopped gaining. In a public poll, the Belden Poll, released on August 21, one week before the August 28 primary, the two candidates had leveled off, with Stevenson leading Johnson 48 percent to 41 percent with 11 percent undecided. Among voters considered most likely to vote (and who had a definite preference), Stevenson led Johnson 54 percent to 46 percent. These figures, Belden noted, were "practically the same" as in a poll taken the previous week. A Belden Poll released on August 27 showed that "there has been no great change in the potential strength of

Stevenson and Johnson since the first primary."* The men in the Brown
Building knew what the polls meant: Johnson had chipped and chipped
away at Stevenson's strength, but there was a solid core, a bedrock of
belief in Coke Stevenson, that had not been touched. Johnson had gained
on Coke—but he hadn't gained enough. He was going to come close. But
he was going to lose.

FOR THESE MEN it was all on the line now; it was "all or nothing." And
they knew what they had to do.

"Campaigning was no good any more," Ed Clark says. "We had to
pick up some votes." Votes in the numbers needed couldn't be picked up
by conventional methods, he says. "We needed blocs. Ethnic groups—
that was the place to go. . . . That meant going into the Mexican country:
the Rio Grande River, the border. . . ."

Johnson aides made trips down to the Valley again. They flew in
planes owned by Brown & Root, from an air terminal owned by Brown
& Root; the name of the company was not on the plane; the terminal was
simply called "Executive Air Services." Often the man who went was
Clark, the "Secret Boss of Texas," the man who "knew how to use money
without anyone ever seeing the money." "People went down half a dozen
times by plane—by private plane," Clark says. "They landed mostly on
private airstrips. I made several trips down there. I didn't stay overnight
any time I went down there"; there would be no names in a hotel register,
no servants in a private home who could remember and later, perhaps,
testify to the presence of these couriers. And they didn't see many people.
They didn't have to. In Webb County, Clark says, he saw only one man.
"Judge Raymond controlled the situation there just like I could take a
piece of paper and write my name. He not only appointed the county
judge, he appointed the county clerk, the election judges. He controlled
the election process. I did not discuss details with him. You didn't have
to know what he was going to do or how he was going to do it. You just
had to have a diplomatic talk with him, and tell him what was needed."

---

* This final Belden Poll also duplicated the single, aberrant category in the last-
minute poll before the first primary. This poll said that among all voters Stevenson led
Johnson 53 percent to 47 percent but, as had been the case in the last-minute poll
before the first primary, among the "most likely" voters, 6 percent were undecided;
among the rest, Stevenson led Johnson only 51.3 percent to 48.7 percent. But this
finding was discounted by Johnson's senior advisers, not only because it was reminiscent
of the single startling election eve finding that had predicted a Johnson victory in the
first primary—the finding that had proven so dramatically inaccurate (and had confirmed their feeling that the "most likely" category was not yet a reliable index)—but
because the results of their private polls were firm, and were even more favorable to
the former Governor than the public polls.

(Clark says he himself didn't give money to Raymond, or to anyone else.)

George Parr was left mainly to Alvin Wirtz. Neither of the two men is alive to discuss their dealings, but Luis Salas saw the result. Heavily though Johnson money had been spent before the first primary in the six counties Parr controlled, it was nothing to the way Johnson money was spent now. The Mexican-American political workers soon caught on. "Our people sure were spoiled. . . . They wanted money and more money," Salas says. But his *patrón* told him not to balk at any request. As Salas recalls it, Parr told him: "Luis, do not hesitate. Spend all the money necessary, but we have to have Johnson elected."

THE LARGEST single source of "ethnic" votes was, of course, San Antonio. Before the first primary, Johnson money had been poured lavishly into the Mexican-American slums of San Antonio's West Side, but leaders of the West Side machine had been lackadaisical, and Stevenson, a great favorite among Mexican-Americans because of his championing of their causes during his governorship (and, of course, the overwhelming favorite in the city's non-Mexican areas), had beaten Johnson in the citywide totals by more than eleven thousand votes. Johnson's key man in San Antonio had always been Dan Quill. After the first primary, the Postmaster had written Johnson that his organization could do better the second time around, although "We will need some money."

But no one was more skilled in the purchasing of votes in San Antonio than Lyndon Johnson himself, and he wanted another organization out working for him in San Antonio on the second Election Day as well, an organization that had never worked for him in the past: that of the city's feared Sheriff, Owen Kilday. "Dan Quill was a smart little operator," John Connally says, "but the man with the muscle in San Antonio was Owen Kilday."

The Kilday organization bore a very high price tag. "That was a sophisticated organization," Connally recalls. Election Day work was handled by Kilday's numerous deputy sheriffs. They would be responsible for hiring cars and drivers to round up Mexican-Americans and get them to the polls—and to make sure they voted correctly—and, Connally says, "They had a standard rate for a car and a driver, and they were paid handsomely": $250 for some deputies, $500 for others. "It takes a hell of a lot of money for an organization like that."

Did Johnson spend as much as $50,000 in San Antonio? "I wouldn't be surprised," John Connally said recently. But then he added that while that figure might be correct for the Kilday organization, "Then, of course, there was Valmo Bellinger"—the black boss in San Antonio; he had an organization, too. "Valmo had to have some help."

Huge sums of Johnson money were poured into the city. Whatever the price of the Kilday organization—and the Bellinger organization, and the Quill organization—Johnson paid it. Quill received a sum of money far greater than he had expected, and he came to realize not only that "the Kildays [were] not fighting us," but that Kilday and his many deputies were working in Johnson's behalf, and working hard.

Johnson made sure he got his money's worth. The final week of his campaign was a week of spectacle in the state's big cities. Flying into Dallas, Houston, Fort Worth and San Antonio in a private plane, he was met in each city by cheering, sign-waving campaign workers and a band playing "The Eyes of Texas," and then was driven—sitting atop the back seat of an open convertible and waving a Stetson—at the head of a caravan of banner-draped automobiles led by police motorcycles with sirens wailing, to greet crowds in the downtown shopping area and to speak at elaborate rallies that featured ten "star" Hollywood entertainers (and of course to make the customary three broadcasts a day over the statewide network). In San Antonio, the day before the election, the candidate, almost hysterical, shouted at a rally at the city's Municipal Auditorium that he was forty years old that very day—"You know, life begins at forty, and I hope to be the next junior Senator when I am forty years and one day old"—and massed bands played "Happy Birthday." It was the climax of a week of public pageantry spectacular even in the vivid history of Texas politics. In a motorcade led by police cars filled with dozens of Sheriff Kilday's deputies, and by jeeps, bearing immense photographs of himself, driven by uniformed war veterans, Johnson rode through San Antonio sitting atop the back seat of a convertible, with a Kilday (Congressman Paul) flanking him on one side, and Kilday's deadliest enemy, former Mayor Maury Maverick, flanking him on the other, symbolizing the fact that he had the support of both sides in the city's political wars. On his first two days in San Antonio, however, Johnson's most significant activities were not public but private: quiet meetings with leaders in that same Plaza Hotel in which, fourteen years before, he had sat in a room buying votes with five-dollar bills. In this election, Lyndon Johnson was going to run the West Side personally.

Johnson had been scheduled to vote in Johnson City on Election Day and then go to his Austin headquarters, but instead he spent the day—his third that week—in San Antonio. He was "riding the polls" on the West Side—on that West Side where "they'd just stuff the ballots in there," on that West Side where, after polls closed, some poll watchers were paid to leave, and doors were locked, and levers were pulled on voting machines. One of his middlemen, the city's Street Commissioner, Jimmy Knight, was to recall that Johnson gave him a thousand dollars in one-dollar bills for the expenses ("don't misunderstand me, it's not a pay-off or anything") of poll-watchers "because he, Lyndon Johnson, wanted to go around the polls," and "if the candidate gives the money, it has to be more. The price goes down immediately if somebody else but the candidate gives it to 'em, and the satisfaction is just as great." So as Johnson jumped out of his car at each polling place and walked among his workers, urging them on, the Street Commissioner followed him, handing out expense money: "You happen to inadvertently put your hands in your pocket and give 'em a couple of dollars and move on, you understand. You take this and put ten, fifteen, twenty dollars and put this in the crowd. . . ." If there was a touch of legitimacy to such "expense money," with other amounts of money handed out by the Johnson entourage in San Antonio that day the touch was less perceptible, and the amounts were much larger. And with the candidate's eye on them, Owen Kilday's deputies earned their money. All day they patrolled the West Side, looking not for crime but for votes. All that broiling-hot Election Day, Lyndon Johnson, with John Connally at his side, rode the polls in San Antonio—and only then did he drive to Johnson City to cast his own vote, Ballot Number 353, in the Blanco County Courthouse, two blocks from the house in which he had spent his youth after his father had lost the Johnson Ranch.

SOUTH of San Antonio, in Alice in Jim Wells County, "Indio" Salas, after a stop at the Election Day tent that had been erected across from the Precinct 13 polling place in the Nayer School, arrived at the school ready for trouble from the reformers' poll-watchers. But, he was to write, "this time had no trouble. They just sit in the place designated by me"—two chairs on the far side of the schoolroom, too far away to see the ballots. When the polls closed and Salas began to count the ballots, unfolding them and calling out a name to his three clerks, Jimmy Holmgreen felt that the election judge was counting for Johnson ballots that had actually been cast for Stevenson—and he was right: "If they were not for our party, I make them for our party," Salas was to reveal almost forty years later. But when Holmgreen jumped up and approached the table, Salas snarled at him, "You stay away from that desk. You sit over there. Sit down and don't interfere with my clerks." Holmgreen, not eager for another encounter with the huge Deputy Micenheimer, sat down. Salas and his clerks resumed calling out the votes: "Johnson." "Johnson." "Johnson."

No Election Day tents had been erected in neighboring Duval County. George Parr didn't need to make any preparations. He was just waiting for the telephone to ring to find out how many votes Lyndon Johnson needed.

THE EARLY RETURNS came mostly from three of the state's four big cities—Houston, Dallas and Fort Worth—because voting machines were in use in these cities, and they gave Stevenson a lead of more than 20,000 votes. Returns from the fourth big city that used machines—San Antonio—were unexpectedly slow, but the young men in the Hancock House, and indeed almost all observers, anticipated that when these returns came in they would substantially increase Stevenson's lead. The young men were sure that their Chief had been defeated; Lady Bird told a friend: "Well, it looks like we've lost. I guess we'll have to work real hard in the radio business now." Stevenson drove to his ranch with a group of old friends to sit by the South Llano, listen to the falls, reminisce over old victories—and celebrate this new one.

But neither Lady Bird nor the young men knew what the men in the Brown Building knew. Nor did Coke Stevenson. He had defeated Johnson by 11,000 votes—a 2–1 margin—in San Antonio in the first primary, but when, late that evening, the returns from San Antonio finally came in, he had not beaten him by a 2–1 margin this time. He hadn't beaten him at all. Johnson had beaten *him*. Kilday's deputies and Dan Quill had done their job: provide enough money, Quill had promised, and the West Side could be delivered. It was—and so was the adjoining black area. Some 10,000 Johnson votes had been produced in this vast slum—and despite Stevenson's previous popularity in San Antonio, the city's total vote this time was: Stevenson, 15,511, Johnson, 15,610. ("A remarkable turnaround," one observer was to comment.)

And by that time, the Valley was being heard from.

It was heard from all that evening, for the most part late that evening. Stevenson's lead was holding at 17,000 votes—and then Webb County reported 5,554 for Johnson, 1,179 for Stevenson—almost a 5–1 margin (and a plurality of more than 4,000 votes) for Johnson; Judge Raymond had delivered. New returns from Hidalgo County gave Johnson a plurality of almost 3,000 more; Cameron County's new returns pulled him 1,700 votes closer. Then Nueces County was heard from: a gain of 3,400 votes. And those were the counties with cities, and, in some precincts at least, voting machines. That evening returns were coming in also from the Valley's isolated, rural counties controlled by George Parr. In Precinct 13 in Jim Wells County, Salas had counted well. In previous elections he had given the favored candidate eighty percent of the vote; this time he had given Johnson more than ninety percent: 765 to 60. Thanks largely to that single precinct, Jim Wells County had given Johnson a total of 1,788 votes to Stevenson's 769. In the other rural counties, where there was no reform strength to speak of, Parr had been able to "count 'em" as he wanted. Brooks County reported 408 for Johnson, 110 for Stevenson. In Zapata it was 711 for Johnson, 158 for Stevenson; in Jim Hogg, 723 to 198. But even such overwhelming margins paled before the returns from the two counties in which George Parr's control was absolute. In Starr County, it was 2,908 for Johnson, 166 for Stevenson. And in Duval, Parr's home county, it was 4,195 for Johnson, 38 for Stevenson—a margin of more than 100–1. When the Texas Election Bureau closed for the night at 1:30 a.m., out of almost a million votes cast, Stevenson led by only 854.

BUT HE LED. And most of the votes were in. The next three days— Sunday, Monday and Tuesday—would be days of wild confusion; they always were in close Texas elections. Nearly a million votes had been cast, most of them on paper ballots. The judges counting them on Election Day in the precincts were often doing so with representatives of both sides looking over their shoulders and urging them to greater speed, interrupting them with arguments and with pleas for the latest totals. Then the totals were sent in by telephone, or by telephoning Western Union, whose operators also made mistakes, and were recorded at the Texas Election Bureau in a hectic Election Night scene. One common error was transposition of the two candidates' votes, because some lists had Stevenson's name first, others Johnson's. Transpositions, however, were merely one out of many possibilities for error. "In counting, copying and tabulating, the votes pass through the hands of eight different groups, between the voter and the final declared result," the *State Observer* noted. "With a million votes running the gauntlet of 'the Human Element' eight different times, there will always be mistakes regardless of the honesty and good intentions of the humans involved." Few persons familiar with Texas politics, though, were confident of the universality of "honesty and good intentions"; there was common knowledge in the upper levels of Texas politics of the precincts that were for sale, the "boxes" in which the County Judge wouldn't "bring in the box" (report the precinct totals to the Election Bureau) until the man who had paid him told him what he wanted that total to be. In close elections, precinct results were altered all through the state. Coke Stevenson's supporters included men who were veterans at these practices, and although they had been careless before Election Day, having neglected the preparations needed to assure that the "re-counting" would be in their favor, they were working frantically now—and they were on the alert against Johnson's attempt to do the same thing. An axiom of Texas politics held that "The lead in the runoff always wins"; in other words, the candidate ahead by the end of Election Day, at which time most of the vote had been counted, almost invariably won because he could "hold out"—delay reporting—enough boxes to keep a reserve to counter changes made by the other side; since both sides were changing votes, the side with the lead could keep the lead by changing enough votes to offset the other side's changes. Perhaps the only instance in modern Texas political history in which this rule had been broken was Lyndon Johnson's 1941 race, when he had, through overconfidence, allowed all his boxes to be reported early, thereby revealing how many votes his opponent needed to add—and foreclosing his chance to add any more of his own. Now, in the areas of Johnson's greatest strength, those whose votes had made the election close, observers felt he was again foreclosed. San Antonio voted by machine and those mechanically recorded tallies had been officially certified, and few changes were possible. And, as the dean of Texas political reporters, Allen Duckworth, was to write about Duval County but in words applicable to the Valley as a whole, "Duval always votes overwhelmingly, one way or the other," but "the county usually reports, practically complete, on Election Night." On Sunday, with Stevenson in the lead, his supporters were telephoning to election judges who had not yet reported their boxes to keep them out until they saw what Johnson would do—and they were confident that they could offset any move Johnson could make.

The "bloc vote" that Lyndon Johnson received with the help of the men in the Brown Building was substantial even for Texas. In the counties where George Parr "just counted 'em"—Duval, Starr, La Salle, Jim Hogg, Zapata and Brooks—the total reported on Election Day was 10,323 for Johnson, 1,329 for Stevenson, a plurality for Johnson of almost 9,000 votes. (To that plurality could be added the 700 votes from Box 13 in Jim Wells County.) Parr-controlled "Mextown" and "Niggertown" in Corpus Christi added another 3,000 votes to Johnson's advantage. And these were not the only "ethnic votes" that Johnson received from the area bordering the Rio Grande. He came out of the Valley—an area that included not only Webb County, where Judge Raymond "just wrote down what he wanted," and the six counties in Parr's domain but also Cameron, Hidalgo, Dimmit, Maverick and Nueces—with a margin of more than 27,000. The "remarkable turnaround" in San Antonio was achieved through the 10,000 votes he received in "ethnic" areas. Although key officials in both camps say that 10,000 was the number of votes controlled—on Johnson's behalf—in that city, the number of votes that were, in a term euphemistically used by these officials, "changed over" between the two primaries is only about 8,000. Even if the lower—8,000—figure is used, however, that figure, added to the Valley's 27,000 plurality, means that Johnson's plurality from the "bloc" totaled 35,000 votes.

If his total was impressive, his percentages were more so. In Duval

County, Lyndon Johnson received 99 percent of the vote; in the six counties of George Parr's domain combined, he received 93 percent. He was given 82 percent of the vote in Judge Raymond's Webb County. In the key Mexican-American and black sections of Corpus Christi, his percentage was 80 percent. In each of these areas, in other words, at least four out of every five voters voted for him. So he received a 35,000-vote plurality from areas in which the voting pattern was dramatically out of keeping with the normal patterns in a democracy. How much of that 35,000-vote edge can be said to have been "bought," either by payments to *jefes* and other political bosses who wrote down voting totals with little or no reference to the actual votes that had been cast, or by payments to bosses who rounded up men and women and made sure they voted as they were told to, or by payments to election judges who counted for Johnson votes that had actually been cast for Stevenson, or by payments to individual voters who voted in accordance with the payment they received, or by payments to deputy sheriffs who transported to the polls and directed the voting of men and women who did not even know whom they were voting for—how many of those votes were "bought" and how many would have been cast for Lyndon Johnson even had no money changed hands cannot, after forty years, be determined. But from the descriptions given by men familiar with the voting in the Valley and on the West Side that Election Day in 1948, it is apparent that the overwhelming majority of those votes—not merely thousands of votes but tens of thousands—fall into that category.

The dramatic disparity between the returns from the West Side and the Valley and the returns from the rest of Texas indicates the disproportionate significance that this area played in the election.

Coke Stevenson carried three counties in the state by a margin of at least 80 percent, two of them so tiny as to be of almost no significance in the election. In one, Kenedy County, the vote was 52–8, and in the other, Roberts County, it was 181–12. The third county was Gillespie, where the Johnson Ranch is located; Gillespie gave Stevenson 80 percent of its vote, 1,014–250. These three counties produced for Stevenson a plurality not of 35,000 votes but of 977; they were a minor factor in the election. Johnson's bloc voting was a major factor—the decisive factor. Without that plurality from the West Side and the Valley, he would have trailed Stevenson by a substantial margin.

Despite Johnson's harvest of these votes, however, he was still behind. His months of ceaseless campaigning, and his injection into the Texas political scene of unprecedented amounts of money, had narrowed the huge advantage which Coke Stevenson had enjoyed at the beginning of the long campaign, and had brought him within striking distance of "Mr. Texas." His purchased votes had brought him almost even. But he was still behind by 854 votes, and the men in the Brown Building feared that Stevenson was likely to increase his lead during the blizzard of corrections—honest mistakes and normal Texas "re-counting"—that were to come. And if their own candidate didn't make up that narrow margin, his loss would be as final as if he had lost by 100,000. Lyndon Johnson's political career was all but over—for want of fewer than a thousand votes.

THE ELECTION BUREAU closed at 1:30 a.m. Lady Bird begged Lyndon to get some sleep; he went into the bedroom and changed into pajamas, but a few minutes later he burst out, his hair as wild as his eyes. He spent the night in the little paneled den of the Dillman Street house, still in his pajamas, pacing back and forth or sprawled across the day-bed, and a telephone was always in his hand. In the Brown Building, Alvin Wirtz and Everett Looney were telephoning, too. Ed Clark was calling from his home. Lyndon Johnson had tried to buy a state, and, although he had paid the highest price in Texas history, he had failed.

So now he was trying to steal it.

The telephone calls were to local Johnson managers in thousands of precincts all across Texas. Some of the calls were to ask the managers to be vigilant against any Stevenson attempt to steal votes in their counties. But other calls had a different purpose: the local managers were being asked to "re-check," and, in the re-checking, to "find" a few more votes for Johnson. So far as can be learned—or at least proven—forty years later, Johnson personally made no telephone request that votes be added to his totals. Clark explains that the men in the Brown Building did not want the candidate to make such requests himself; when questioned as to whether that was because Johnson "might be *asked* if he had called," Clark nodded. Rather, the purpose of Johnson's calls was to reassure the local leaders that they would be with the winner when all the votes had been counted, and to give them a sense of personal contact with the candidate. "We weren't asking him to say anything illegal, but it was important that he give them recognition, that he tell them everything was going to be okay," Clark says. "Because we still needed them—to validate their votes, to stand behind them." Of course, it was not necessary for Johnson to make requests himself; others were making them on his behalf.

Some of the men who received these calls replied that technological considerations prevented them from helping. In San Antonio, Sheriff Kilday's chief deputy, George Huntress, received a telephone call from "the Johnson camp . . . inquiring into the possibility of additional votes." Huntress reminded "the person inquiring" that San Antonio now used voting machines, and that the results had been recorded. For other recipients of these calls, the considerations were ethical. The Johnson man who took the call in San Marcos replied that "of course he couldn't 'find' any more votes; the election was over." But other calls went to a more receptive man, a man who could "find" not just a few more votes, but a few hundred more. A politician in San Diego, county seat of Duval, who took one of those calls remembers: "It was Lyndon Johnson's office. It was very important that they get hold of George." Early Sunday morning a rumor began to circulate in Austin, and later that morning the rumor was confirmed. The Valley had already done a lot for Lyndon Johnson: a 27,000-vote plurality. But the Valley was going to do more. In particular, George Parr was going to do more. The Duke of Duval had given Lyndon Johnson a 100–1 plurality, more than 4,000 votes, in his county alone. Now, on Sunday, with Johnson behind despite the Duke's efforts, Duval County announced that there were more votes from the county to come. It had just been discovered, Parr's election officials told the Texas Election Bureau, that the returns from one of Duval County's precincts had not yet been counted; it was hoped to have them later in the day.

OUT ON THE BANKS of the South Llano, over a telephone that had been installed—on a tree—for Election Night, Stevenson had been hearing rumors of the Johnson camp's maneuvers. Confirmation came from one of his county managers in the Panhandle, who told the former Governor that he had just received a telephone call from someone in Johnson's headquarters who was under the impression that he was *Johnson's* county manager and who had asked him if he couldn't change at least three votes. "That was how we first learned what Lyndon was doing," Ernest Boyett recalls. "When he was behind, he got on the telephone to his managers around the state, and asked them if they couldn't change votes."

Stevenson remained calm; he might not be participating in, or even aware of, what his own allies might be doing in Austin, but he was certainly aware that such maneuvering was within the normal parameters of Texas politics. But then, early Sunday morning, he heard about the Duval announcement—which went beyond the parameters.

Stevenson and his advisers understood at once the significance not only of the fact that Parr was announcing that new votes would be coming in from the Valley, but of the fact that now, more than twelve hours after the polls had closed, these votes had not yet been counted, so that no one could tell how many each candidate had received. In later years, Johnson aides would argue that such a late finding of votes in the Valley was customary in Texas politics, but it wasn't. As Allen Duckworth wrote in the *Dallas News* that day, "The thing that brought protest from the Stevenson camp was the lateness of Duval's final report this time. The county usually reports, practically complete, on Election Night." George

Norris Green, whose book *The Establishment in Texas Politics* analyzes Texas elections in the 1940s, notes that Stevenson had won the Valley vote in his previous races but comments that "all of those votes had at least been turned in on time." Since few constraints limited Parr in the number of votes he reported ("he just counted 'em"), the effect of his turning in votes late would be that he could report almost any number of votes needed—which would mean that to a considerable extent the Duke of Duval could decide the result of any close statewide election all by himself; that the only limit would be the number of poll taxes he had paid. The 27,000-vote margin already given to Lyndon Johnson by the Duke of Duval and his allies in the Valley hadn't been enough to elect Johnson. So now, this Sunday, what, really, was George Parr doing but just waiting to see how many more votes would be needed? Jumping into his car, Stevenson accelerated so fast that he left a plume of dust behind him as he sped to Austin. But there was nothing he could do once he got there. All day Sunday, the Election Bureau was inundated in the usual blizzard of vote changes from all over the state, a few large, most small; but all day, looming over the counting of these ballots was that missing box down in the Valley.

For Coke Stevenson, Duckworth wrote, "The news came at dusk Sunday. It was bad, as expected." And it came at a strategic moment. All day, minor changes had in general balanced themselves out, and Stevenson had stayed ahead, by approximately the same 800-vote margin. Then, about seven o'clock, twenty-four hours after the polls had closed, upward revisions for Johnson came in from several Houston precincts— revisions in themselves so suspicious that there were immediate calls for an investigation. Suddenly, Stevenson was leading by a bare handful of votes. And then, at this crucial point, Duval announced that it now had its returns ready. The vote it had reported on Saturday night had been 4,195 for Johnson, 38 for Stevenson. Now Duval election officials said there had been 427 previously unreported votes in that "uncounted" precinct. Stevenson, they said, had received two of them; Johnson had received 425. Four hundred and twenty-five new votes (Duval's count was now Johnson 4,620, Stevenson 40) and for the first time Stevenson was no longer ahead in the statewide totals. "In the closest major race in the state's long political history," the *Fort Worth Star-Telegram* reported, "Lyndon Johnson rode into the lead of the U.S. Senate race Sunday night on a sudden tide of votes from Duval County." (No newspaper commented on a remarkable aspect of the Duval vote. Since another two votes would later be found there for Johnson, making Duval's final vote 4,622 to 40, 4,662 persons thus voted in a county in which only 4,679 poll tax receipts had been issued—the 99.6 percent turnout was an astonishing display of civic responsibility.)

On Monday, however, the Election Bureau received in the mail written returns from counties that had previously reported over the telephone, and there were the usual corrections made necessary by transpositions, discoveries of double-counting and simple mistakes in arithmetic—as well as, perhaps, other kinds of "mistakes." But Monday brought only one new return from the Valley—80 new votes for Lyndon Johnson in Starr County (final returns from Starr were Johnson 3,038, Stevenson 170; Parr's two key counties alone therefore gave Johnson an edge of more than seven thousand votes: 7,660 to 210)—and Stevenson received more benefits from the corrections than Johnson. Hour after hour all that day and into the evening, Johnson worked the telephone in his den, alternately sprawled, half reclining, on the day-bed and pacing back and forth across the little room, telephone in hand, lighting one cigarette from the end of another, the skin on his gaunt face drawing tighter and tighter, the circles under his eyes growing darker and darker—a candidate by El Greco. But by the end of the day, Stevenson had 494,396 votes, Johnson had 494,277—Stevenson led by 119 votes in what Duckworth, in a view echoed in newspapers throughout the state, wrote was "the most exciting Senate race Texas has ever known."

Tuesday brought more transpositions—including a sizable one from Eastland County in West Texas. When someone at the Bureau re-checked Eastland's 2,645–2,317 figures, which had had the higher figure in Johnson's column and the lower in Stevenson's, it was found that they should, in fact, have been reversed, and that change pushed Stevenson further ahead. And under Texas election law, seven p.m. Tuesday (seventy-two hours after the polls closed) was the deadline for precinct election judges to turn over to their county chairmen all ballot boxes, containing not only the actual ballots that voters had cast but the tally and poll sheets kept by election judges and clerks. At that hour, the Election Bureau announced it had "complete" (complete in the sense that all boxes had reported) returns in all of the state's 254 counties except for one box in sparsely populated Borden County, where about forty votes were supposed to be still unreported (and, of course, except for the two "Stevenson" counties Hansford and Kinney, which hadn't held primaries because Stevenson's men had not considered them necessary). At seven, the Election Bureau announced its final returns for the day: Stevenson, with 494,555 votes, was 349 votes ahead of Johnson, who had 494,206. Election Bureau Manager Bob Johnson told a reporter that "there was little doubt the bureau's unofficial count would give Stevenson a majority." And, as the *Houston Chronicle* pointed out, "The [Election] Bureau, although it cannot actually elect an officeholder on the basis of its unofficial returns, has been consistently accurate during the thirty-two years of its existence. It has never missed naming the eventual winner." Indeed, the returns from each county had been checked and re-checked so many times by both sides that no further major changes were expected. Lyndon Johnson's second Senate race apparently had ended like the first; "Should Johnson lose by a few hundred votes," as Duckworth wrote, "it would be the second time he has been nosed out on his quest for a seat in the upper house." The blaring headlines—"STEVENSON LEADS BY 349 WITH ABOUT 40 VOTES OUT"—seemed to trumpet the death of his dreams.

LITTLE CHANGE in the situation occurred on Wednesday, September 1, the fourth day after the election. A day of checking and re-checking returns produced only seventeen revisions—most of them downward because of discoveries of double-counting—and these were so evenly divided between the two candidates that they virtually canceled themselves out, producing a net change of only thirteen votes. These were in Stevenson's favor, and his lead increased to 362 votes. "STEVENSON'S MARGIN FIRM," a typical headline said; the vote in the race for United States Senator from Texas seemed to have all but hardened into its final form.

Little change occurred on Thursday, the fifth day after the election. Eleven revisions reduced Stevenson's lead by a total of 11 votes to 351. Many newspapers were treating the race as over; "STEVENSON HOLDS FINAL VOTE LEAD," said the *Brownsville Herald*. His supporters exulted; in an editorial entitled "Good Senator by Bad Margin," the *Dallas News* said that "Texas has made a good senatorial choice. . . . It is a remarkable victory when it is clearly in the face of what in mere politeness may be termed 'bloc voting' in four [sic] Southwest Texas counties. Duval County had come quite close to being represented in Congress by a Senator of its own." Reporters found Stevenson at the Travis County Courthouse, performing legal work for a rancher who was his neighbor in Kimble County. Pressed for a statement, he said that "All the counties have been rechecked carefully," and he was sure he had won. And Stevenson's feelings were echoed by even the most cautious Texas politicians; the election seemed to be over.

But their feelings were incorrect. The Valley wasn't done yet. On Friday, September 3, the sixth day after the election, the Valley was heard from again.

Hardly had the Election Bureau opened at nine when corrections were reported from the Rio Grande: 43 new votes for Johnson from Dimmit County, 38 new votes for Johnson from Cameron County.

In particular, George Parr wasn't done. With Duval County poll taxes exhausted, no more votes could be produced in that county, of course, but there were other counties in his domain. One was Zapata, and Friday morning, Zapata produced 45 votes more for Johnson. Corrections came in from counties in other areas of the state that Friday morning, but all were small—none as big as those from the three Valley counties. At noon the Valley's 126 new votes had played the major role in reducing Coke Stevenson's lead to 157 votes, 494,096 to 493,939.

Another county in Parr's domain was Jim Wells, where the reformers' strength had forced Parr to exercise discretion on Election Day. The only precinct in that county that had been run as the Duke liked precincts run was Luis Salas' Precinct 13. The vote reported by Salas on Election Night, 765 to 60 in Johnson's favor, had provided the bulk of Johnson's 1,788–769 margin in Jim Wells. Now, on Friday morning, the Democratic Executive Committee of Jim Wells County was meeting to make its final certification of the returns and report them to the state committee. In the County Courthouse, one of the committee members, B. M. Brownlee, was unfolding the tally sheets and reading off the totals. The totals for the first twelve precincts were the same as those that had been reported on Election Night. Then Brownlee unfolded the tally sheet for Salas' Precinct 13. This total was not the same. The figure for Johnson, which had been reported as 765 on Election Night, was now 965—because, according to testimony that would later be given, someone had, since Election Night, added a loop to the "7" to change it into a "9". Johnson had 200 more votes.

At about 12:30 p.m. on Friday, with Stevenson's lead holding at 157 votes, Jim Wells County telephoned its amended return, including those 200 additional Johnson votes, to the Election Bureau—and suddenly, with virtually all the counting in the election over, Coke Stevenson was no longer ahead. Lyndon Johnson was ahead. With so few counties still to be reported—and only minor remaining changes to be made—those 200 votes from Precinct 13 were decisive. In the Bureau's final tabulations, Johnson had 494,191 votes, Stevenson 494,104. Out of 988,295 votes, he had won by 87—less than one hundredth of one percent.

14

Lists of Names

LYNDON JOHNSON HAD WON the election. Now he had to keep it won—and that was to be very difficult. For Coke Stevenson believed Johnson had stolen the election. And Stevenson decided to prove he had stolen it.

When the 200 new Johnson votes from Luis Salas' Precinct 13 in Jim Wells County were reported on Friday afternoon, Stevenson exploded. "A concentrated effort is being made to count me out of this Senate race," he said in a press release. "On Thursday at noon"—when the Election Bureau was reporting that he, Stevenson, was 381 votes ahead, and after the Bureau's manager had said that there was little doubt that he had won—Johnson had "issued a 'victory' statement and urged his friends to 'do their duty.' Almost immediately, last-minute 'gains' for my opponent began to roll in from those counties of South Texas which are said to be dominated by a single man. I would like to know how my opponent knew so much in advance of the 'revisions' being made today."

Johnson's response came fast—too fast. No "revisions" had been made, he said in a written statement. The explanation for the changes from the South Texas counties was simply that incorrect figures had originally been reported to the Election Bureau and that the correct figures had not been reported for some time. He had known the correct figures all along, he said. "The corrected votes in several of the counties which the Election Bureau has just used were reported to our headquarters Saturday night [August 28, the night of the election]." He had, he said, known ever since Election Night that he had won.

This statement did not help his case; as the *Dallas News* commented, the Duval County election chairman had announced on Sunday morning, August 29, that the ballots in Duval's last box, the box that was to turn out to contain 425 votes for Johnson and two for Stevenson, had not yet even been counted. How, then, could Johnson have known on Saturday night what the count would be? Two days later, Johnson made a statewide radio broadcast; in the final moments before he went on the air, he sat hunched over the microphone, editing and re-editing the text. During the eight minutes he spoke (the last two minutes were reserved for his wife), he changed his earlier statement: Now he said he had known the correct figures not since Saturday night but since Tuesday night (August 31). Then, shifting from defense to offense, he said, "The hue and cry about Duval County has taken so many, many years to develop." Many of Texas's most renowned Senators and Governors had received Duval's overwhelming vote over the years; Coke Stevenson had—each of the previous four times Stevenson had run for office. And neither Stevenson nor anyone else had ever complained before. "My opponent has accepted that vote," he said. "The newspapers have complacently reported the vote from the county, year after year." If Stevenson had evidence that votes had been bought in Duval, "it was his duty to present it to the grand jury. Lyndon Johnson did not buy anybody's vote." Furthermore, he said, "similar charges could be made about many counties which Stevenson had carried throughout the state."

This argument—that the Valley's vote for Lyndon Johnson was nothing more than the normal run of Texas politics—was always to be Johnson's contention, and it was to be stated and re-stated over the years by Johnson supporters, most notably Mary Rather, Walter Jenkins and Charles Herring. Evaluating this contention is made difficult by the conditions of Texas election records for earlier decades—in the case of lopsided elections, the votes in some counties are not even on record, either because the counties didn't report them or because the state, with the conclusion already sealed, didn't record them. Sufficient records are available, however, for analysis of the previous fourteen senatorial and gubernatorial elections—every such election since 1932—and for those elections, Johnson's contention is not correct.

In part, the differences between the 1948 election and earlier elections were only differences of timing and degree. Late amendments of returns were indeed, as Johnson said, common in Texas elections—but not this late. Johnson's 1941 race for the Senate, in which both candidates tried "to outsteal each other," had been marked by "corrected" returns, but the bulk of these returns for the Saturday election had been reported to the Election Bureau on Monday, mostly by county officials who excused even this much delay by claiming that no counting of returns had been done on the Sunday Sabbath; by late Monday, the election was in fact over, and the decisive votes were announced as soon as the Election Bureau opened Tuesday morning. Even that degree of lateness had been considered shocking—and now, seven years later, the decisive votes had come in not on Monday or Tuesday but on Friday, six days after the election.

One-sidedness (noticeably heavy votes for one candidate or another) was also common in late, "corrected" returns in Texas—but not this one-sided. The 1941 Senate race is typical. The corrections which gave Pappy O'Daniel the victory came from East Texas, and while the corrections shifted the trend in those counties, the shifts had at least a tinge of plausibility to them. The Election Night returns from a typical county, Shelby, for example, had been 46 percent for Congressman Martin Dies, 34 percent for O'Daniel, 11 percent for Johnson and 9 percent for Gerald Mann. After the 256 new votes reported from Shelby on Monday, the county's total percentages were: Dies, 44 percent; O'Daniel, 38 percent; Johnson, 10 percent; Mann, 8 percent. This shift of percentages had enabled O'Daniel to pick up 162 votes on Johnson, but in an inconspicuous manner. The shifts in other counties followed the same pattern. There were no countywide totals for O'Daniel anywhere comparable to 4,622 to 40.

And while these differences were only of timing and degree, there was a crucial third element that, when combined with the first two, made Lyndon Johnson's 1948 senatorial campaign something new in Texas politics. This was the fact that the unusually, perhaps unprecedentedly, one-sided votes which were decisive in Johnson's victory were cast at the direction of a single man, a man who, moreover, did not have to "vote 'em" but simply to "count 'em"—which meant that he could provide a candidate with additional votes simply by filling in new numbers on the printed "tally sheets" provided for a county's returns. This factor combined with the timing with which these votes were reported— at the last minute, after virtually all other votes had been recorded—to narrow the 1948 election, in its final, decisive stage, down to a single border boss waiting for a telephone call, and, when he received it, determining the outcome of an election by simply writing down whatever new numbers were required.

Johnson's contention that his vote from the Valley was nothing more than normal Texas politics ignores this crucial point. The reason that there had been no "hue and cry" over the Duval County or South Texas vote for "many, many years" was that for many years that vote had not played a decisive—or even a significant—role in any senatorial or gubernatorial election. Coke Stevenson now declared that Johnson's statement was not true. "This is the first instance in recorded history that those bloc voting counties have determined the result of a statewide election," he said. And beyond that, "This is the first time that the manipulators of the voting in these counties were not content with all-out bloc voting, but re-opened the boxes in secret long after the election had closed and stuffed them with a directed number of ballots." More than a score of Texas politicians who were active in the 1930s and 1940s, interviewed in recent years, unanimously disagreed with Johnson's contention—as do the only two surviving intimates of Coke Stevenson from the campaign, Ernest Boyett and Bob Murphey. More tellingly, the only three surviving members of the Johnson campaign's high command—John B. Connally, who would later be Governor of Texas; Edward A. Clark, who was for decades an immensely powerful figure in state politics; and George R. Brown, bankroller of scores of Texas elections—do not agree with it, either. Valley votes had never before been decisive in a statewide election, John Connally says. "Never. Never before 1948." Says Ed Clark: "I never did know of a situation like that. I just never did know of anything that was similar to what was happening down there in that area [in 1948]." And they explained why: the unprecedented size of the Parr-delivered vote in 1948, and the timing of the delivery. Over the years, Clark says, "a lot of different people" had been given top-heavy majorities down there, but these majorities "had never been" given after the votes had been reported. "See, down there one of the questions that was often asked, when five or six good friends got together, you understand, was 'Does that fellow vote 'em or does he just count 'em?' " And if he just "counted 'em," Clark explains, and could go on counting them after the election had been over for some days, he could decide the result of any close statewide election— just by counting more, as needed.

Edgar Shelton, after talking to his father, who was George Parr's lawyer, and to the George Parr intimates with whom his father put him in touch, had seen in 1946 "the possible dangers of those [Valley] machines." What, Shelton asked, "if we had two men running for an important office such as Senator or Governor, one of them being . . . dishonest? Assume that the dishonest man had secured a pledge of support from the bosses of the Valley, as he probably would. If the race were close and the honest man was ahead by only a few thousand votes with all of the returns in except from the Valley' . . . the election could easily be 'stolen' by having the Valley counties send in just enough votes to put the dishonest man in office. Thus the will of the people of the State would be denied by less than a dozen men, all political feudal lords of the Valley."

"This," Shelton wrote in 1946, "has probably not yet happened." Every longtime Texas politician interviewed agrees that, before 1948, it probably never had. Not even the most arrogant border dictator had ever dared to do that, they say. Indeed, when, two days after Election Day in 1941, Lyndon Johnson had asked George Parr to do precisely that, Parr had refused because his county's overwhelming majority for Johnson had already been recorded; he was later to tell friends that he had replied, "Lyndon, I've been to the federal penitentiary, and I'm not going back for you." Clark says, "I just never saw—now, there have been other close contests but," he says, never one in which there had been "a feeling that a result might be changed by an investigation of those controlled counties." (In addition, Clark ridicules the theory that Stevenson aides were also stealing votes on a widespread scale throughout the state. Asked about it, the "Secret Boss of Texas" laughs. "They didn't know how, and Governor Stevenson didn't know how," he says. And, Clark adds, in a view echoed by politicians familiar with Texas politics of the time, stealing votes on a widespread scale would have been impossible for Stevenson after Election Day even had he wanted to try it: "Preparations had to be made in advance for that sort of thing; contacts have to be made; it takes organization." The Stevenson camp, Clark points out, were so unprepared for the second primary "that they didn't even know that two of their counties weren't even holding a primary.") But George Parr had done now for Lyndon Johnson what Shelton had feared could one day happen. The unwritten laws, the ethics, the morals of Texas politics were so loose and elastic that it was difficult to break them. But Lyndon Johnson had broken them.

Stevenson was used to Valley politics. He had received the Valley's support in the past, not that its support had ever had any significance to his political career. But he knew the limits within which these politics operated—and he felt that it was by going beyond those limits that Lyndon Johnson had beaten him. The ex-Governor felt particularly strongly about the timing of those decisive changes in the Valley's vote. Johnson had claimed that the votes in Duval, Jim Wells, Zapata, Starr and other Parr-dominated counties had all been counted on Election Night, and that the counts had not been changed thereafter. Stevenson believed they had. He was certain that Johnson had, by those changes, stolen the election from him. Two things now motivated Coke Stevenson. One was personal: his injured vanity and pride, and the simple code by which he lived, the Code of the West. When someone stole something from you, you got it back—or at least brought the thief to justice. The other went beyond the personal. It was his belief, the belief so deep it was "almost like religion to him," in democracy and the law. If this could happen, if an election could so blatantly be stolen, neither democracy nor law could prevail.

He decided to do something about it.

First, he sent men to the Valley. The head of the team investigating Duval County, San Antonio attorney Pete Tijerina, says that when they began interviewing residents who were certified as having voted, "many said they hadn't. They told us their county commissioner had picked up their poll tax receipts and voted for them." But when the investigators tried to get these statements notarized, they found that no notary public in Duval County would do so. "We were stopped by sheriff's deputies, one of whom had a submachine gun. They said they [had] heard we had guns. We told them we had no guns, but they made us spread-eagle while they searched us. They then told us we had thirty minutes to get out of Duval County. We got out in that time."

To investigate in Jim Wells County, Stevenson asked the help of three young attorneys. One, Callan Graham, had been an impoverished youth in Junction during the Depression. Stevenson had encouraged him to take up the law, had loaned him his books and his office to study in, and, after Graham had been admitted to the bar "in the old-fashioned way" (without attending the University), had helped him through the early years of practice by quietly referring cases to him. Graham idolized Stevenson; he was proudest of his election in 1948 to the Legislature because his seat was the one Coke had once held. The other two lawyers, Kellis Dibrell and James Gardner, partners in San Antonio, had been agents of the Federal Bureau of Investigation, in whose awesome reputation Stevenson believed; Stevenson telephoned them and, in Dibrell's words, asked them to go and "see what we could find out."

The three young attorneys were ill equipped for the mission. "I had no badge or gun; I was a young lawyer," Dibrell recalls. "It was an awful big assignment and I didn't know where to start." And they were, frankly, as Graham puts it, "a little uptight going into this area we'd heard so much about." They had, he says, been warned at Stevenson's Austin headquarters "that they were known to kill people down there. . . . They said, 'Be sure not to wear a suit coat so they can see you don't have a gun.' " When the three young attorneys arrived in Alice, at the end of that jouncing 150-mile trip through the empty South Texas brush country, the atmosphere in the little town did not relax them. Unshaven Mexican *pistoleros*, wearing Colts or carrying Winchester rifles, stood in groups along Main Street, staring silently at the visitors.

The three young men had brought along a book on election law, but hardly had they arrived when they learned what so many visitors had learned before them: that Jim Wells County, like so much of the Texas brush country, was a land outside the law, in which printed legalities did not apply. The law stated clearly, Graham was to recall, that every citizen has a right to look at the election tally sheet, and at the "poll list," the list on which was recorded the names of individuals as they signed in to vote. "It is very clearly stated in the law, so we thought there'd be no problem." These lists were in the possession of B. F. (Tom) Donald, secretary of Jim Wells County's Democratic Executive Committee, and cashier at the Texas State Bank of Alice. That was George Parr's bank, but the three attorneys went to Donald's office at the bank, and asked to see the lists. "No," Donald replied. Recalls Graham:

We cited the law to him. That, in retrospect, was rather comical.
We said, "Well, here's the law right here. It says any citizen has

the right to see it." He said, "I know that. But you can't see them because they're locked up in that vault, and I'm not going to unlock the vault. That's why you can't see them." As I say, that's kind of comical now. He didn't say he wasn't going to show them to us, he said, "I won't open the vault. They're locked up in the bank vault, and I will not open it."

Donald's refusal to show the lists made the three lawyers suspect that they might contain the proof they were looking for: the proof that the Precinct 13 vote had been altered—that the crucial two hundred votes had been added to Lyndon Johnson's total after the polls had closed, and after the time on Election Night when the smaller total had been reported to the Texas Election Bureau. The lawyers went to see the "reform" members of the county's Democratic Executive Committee, who confirmed these suspicions. One reform member, B. M. Brownlee, said that he had seen the precinct's "tally list," from which the Executive Committee had been taking the vote prior to making its official report. And, as Brownlee was later to testify, "about, possibly, 200 tallies from . . . the end," the ink in which the votes were being marked "had changed." The tallies up to that point had been written almost entirely in black ink; after that point, they were all in blue ink. Harry Lee Adams, who had "snuck in" as new chairman of the Executive Committee while Parr "wasn't looking," had first been denied a look at the lists by Donald—although by law he, not Donald, was the official entitled to their possession—but, on a later visit to the bank, he had, although still denied possession of the lists, been allowed a brief look at the poll list. And his brief look, Adams said, had been enough. While he was jotting down the names of the individuals who had allegedly voted, he said, he had noticed that approximately two hundred names from the end—at Number 842, to be precise—the ink in which they were written had changed. Prior to Number 842, the names had all been written in black ink; beginning with 842, they had all been written in blue ink.

Brownlee and Adams' stories convinced the three lawyers that the poll and tally lists contained the proof of the dishonesty of the voting in Precinct 13; with the lists, they felt, they could get the names of all the final two hundred* voters and simply ask them if they had indeed voted

* In the different tallies of the election—in court testimony and at the Convention and in newspaper accounts—the number of additional votes for Johnson is sometimes given as 200 and sometimes 201. Stevenson is usually given two extra votes, but sometimes only one. This appears to be the result simply of careless or hurried arithmetic in the various tabulations. All accounts agree that the color of the ink changed approximately 200 names from the end, but all accounts also agree that the change occurred at Number 842, instead of about 825. Although it is impossible to determine the

in the election, and whom they had voted for. And the voters' testimony could be presented in a court of law. But Donald had refused to show them the lists. And they were not anxious to make another trip to the bank; they were, they admit, "intimidated" by the thought of walking again down that dusty street with men glaring at them and fingering rifles and revolvers as they passed.

So Coke Stevenson went to the Valley himself—and he took along with him a representative of another law enforcement body, one in which he, as a Texan, had even more faith than he had in the FBI, and one which was, in Texas, even more revered: the Texas Rangers. And he didn't take along just any Ranger, but one of the toughest Rangers of them all, a Ranger who was, in fact, a figure even more legendary in Texas than Stevenson himself. For just before he left Austin, he met Frank Hamer on the street.

Thirty years earlier, when Frank Hamer was a young Ranger and Coke Stevenson a young county attorney newly appointed to his first public office, the two men had "lain out" together night after night in the hills of Kimble County to catch cattle rustlers. During the intervening years, they had become hunting companions and close friends. And now, when Hamer heard that Stevenson was going to the Valley, and heard why he was going, he stared at him for a long minute. And then he said, "Well, I'll just go down there with you."

It was Frank Hamer who led the posse of lawmen who trailed Bonnie and Clyde for 102 days and set the ambush in which the famous bank robbers were finally killed, but that was only one of the episodes that had garlanded his career with glory. He first pinned on a Ranger's star in 1906, when he was twenty-two years old, six-foot-three, two hundred pounds, with broad shoulders and a lightning draw. His initial assignment was as one of the seventeen Rangers dispatched to curb the riots, punctuated by murders, which had been raging through the Rio Grande Valley for months despite the efforts of hundreds of federal troops. (The success of the seventeen led to the remark, possibly apocryphal, that came to symbolize the Texas Rangers: the sheriff of a mob-ravaged city telegraphed Ranger headquarters for assistance, and received word it would arrive on the next train. When the train pulled in, the sheriff was dismayed to see only one man disembark. "Only one Ranger?" he asked; "Only one mob," the Ranger explained.)

---

reason for this discrepancy, apparently about 17 names listed on the poll list did not show up as votes, either because the voters mismarked their ballots, which were then invalidated, or because the election judges misnumbered some of the first 825 ballots.

Hamer then became a "town tamer"—in a town, Navasota, that was very tough to tame. When he pinned on the city marshal's badge there, Navasota was a boomtown in which shootouts on the main street were so frequent that in two years at least a hundred men had died. After two years of what a writer called "Hamer's stern and unremitting justice," shootouts were a thing of the past; nobody wanted to incur Frank Hamer's wrath. Asked if he knew the marshal, a man replied: "Yes, *sir!* An' when I sees him comin', I jes' steps aside."

Not long thereafter, he was the state's key witness in a trial being held in a West Texas town. In an attempt to prevent him from testifying, a gunman jumped out from a hiding place and shot him at point blank range as he was passing on the street. Wounded in his gun arm and hand but still on his feet, Hamer, as one writer put it, "calmly observed that the man's gun had jammed." He snatched it out of his assailant's hand. A second gunman jumped out and fired. Barely missing Hamer's head, the bullet tore a hole in his Stetson. Seeing him still on his feet, the two assailants turned and ran. One kept running; he was to escape until he was later arrested. The other made the mistake of pausing for a last shot. By this time, Hamer, despite his wound, had his gun out in his uninjured hand, and shot him dead.

By the 1930s, Frank Hamer had been wounded seventeen times; at least twice he had been left for dead. He had killed fifty-three men. Despite his refusal to give interviews and his dislike of publicity, the tall, powerful Texas Ranger, with his black suit, his invariable courtesy, and his laconic speech, had become a mythical figure in Texas. Historian Walter Prescott Webb called him one of the "most fearless men in Western History." A Hollywood writer said: "It's embarrassing to describe Frank Hamer in these days of Westerns. One can hear about him . . . and then one realizes that Hamer is the real character all casting directors are striving for." His toughness had become mythical, too: looking down at Bonnie's bullet-riddled body in 1934, he had affected regret at having been forced to shoot a woman. But, asked in private about the climactic gun battle, he would say, "I sure did hate to bust a cap on a lady"—and smile. And his reputation—and his grim bearing—were weapons in themselves. During the Thirties, when he was more than fifty years old, he was called in to end the violence in a particularly bloody dock strike in Houston; walking out onto a dock on which swirled an angry crowd of striking longshoremen, Hamer approached the largest man he could find. "I'm Frank Hamer," the big Ranger said. "This strike is over"—and it was. In 1948, he was sixty-four years old and long retired from regular duty, although as a "Special Ranger," employed by the Texas Oil Company to protect its property, he was still allowed to carry a gun. He didn't wear it anymore, but when Coke Stevenson told him he was going to the Valley, he went home and strapped it on before they set out.

ARRIVING IN ALICE, they met Dibrell and Gardner in a room in the Alice Hotel, and were told that the election records were still being kept in the bank. Stevenson said he wanted to go there, and the two lawyers said that of course they would go, too. While they were up in the room, the whisper was running through the town: "Coke Stevenson's here! And Frank Hamer's with him!" A reporter walking into the Courthouse heard the name on all sides: "Hamer!" "Hamer!"

Hamer told the men in the hotel room to take off their suit jackets so that people could see they weren't armed. He took his off, too—so that people could see he was. They clattered down the stairs of the rickety little hotel and out onto the dusty main street and, in a scene that would be incredible were it not attested to by witnesses for both sides, walked the two hundred yards to the bank. The lawyers trailed a few paces behind. Coke Stevenson and Frank Hamer walked side by side, two tall, broad-shouldered, erect, silent men—two living legends of Texas, in fact—two men out of another, vanishing age, another, vanishing code, marching down a street in a dusty Texas town to find out for themselves, and prove to the world, how Lyndon Johnson had gotten the two hundred crucial votes.

Back in the hotel room, the two young lawyers had been a little disappointed at their first look at the legendary Frank Hamer. "He appeared to be an old man," Dibrell recalls. And then, coming out of the hotel, Hamer saw George Parr's *pistoleros*.

There were more of them this time. "Everywhere you turned there were people with guns on," Dibrell says. One group of perhaps five was directly in Hamer's path. Another, somewhat larger, was standing in the very door of the bank.

As he approached them, Hamer didn't even slow down. His biographers were to write that when he approached the first group, he said, "Git!," and at the second, he ordered, "Fall back!" The two young attorneys don't remember any words at all; they only remember how, walking behind the old Texas Ranger, they suddenly realized how big he was, and how he carried himself—and how his right hand was poised just above the butt of his gun, his fingers curled for the draw. And they remember how, as Dibrell puts it, "when Frank Hamer walked down the street, those clusters of people parted." The *pistoleros* in front of the bank, having stepped aside for Stevenson, evidently intended to follow the ex-Governor inside, but Hamer turned and stood in the doorway, his hand still poised above his gun. None of the men facing him moved. After a few minutes, they walked away.

INSIDE, Stevenson was confronting Tom Donald in his office. He said he wanted to see the tally sheet and the poll list and copy all the names on the poll list, and when Donald refused to allow him to do so, Stevenson, as he was to state in an affidavit, "advised him that I was being deprived of my rights under federal law"—and advised him also, in the dry words of the affidavit, "of the consequence thereof." Recalls the one reporter who was present, James M. Rowe of the *Corpus Christi Caller-Times*: "Coke was like a glacier—he could look really mean." Donald took the list and tally sheet from his desk, and showed them to Stevenson and his men, and for a few moments—a vital few moments—Dibrell and Gardner studied them intently. When they began copying names from the list, Donald said, "No, you can't do that!" and snatched it away, but the two lawyers had had time to memorize some of the names, and the numbers beside them, and they rushed out into the bank's outer room and wrote them down. They had been alerted by Adams and Brownlee as to the crucial points, and had looked at those first—and they had had time to confirm what the two local men had told them: that the last 201 names on the list (two hundred of whom were listed as voting for Johnson, one for Stevenson) had been written in the same ink, different from that previously used, and in the same handwriting, different from that which had previously appeared. They noticed, moreover, something that the two Alice men had not: that the 201 names were in alphabetical order—the first few names starting with 842 began with A, the next few with B, until about 915, when the end of the alphabet was reached; then the A's began again—as if whoever had been writing the names had miscalculated and gotten to the end of the alphabet too fast, and had thereupon simply gone back to the A's and started over. The two lawyers also did something that Adams and Brownlee had not done: they had memorized—and now wrote down—the last name in black ink, the name of voter 841. If the moment of change came at 842, who was 841, and what could he tell them? James Gardner had also looked at the tally sheet—and had made a discovery that dwarfed all the others: Johnson's partisans were arguing that the count of Precinct 13 had not been changed, that no one had ever said Johnson's vote total was 765, that it had always been 965. The certification on the tally sheet gave the lie to that argument, Gardner felt. "The certification showed that the vote for Lyndon Johnson was 965," he was to testify, "but it was evident from looking at the 965 that the 9 had been changed. It previously had been a 7. . . . The 7 had been worked over in pen and ink from a 7 around to a 9. . . . An additional loop [had been] added to the 7 to make a 9 out of it."

Armed with the names they had jotted down and those that Adams had obtained earlier, Dibrell and Gardner, together with Graham, set out to ascertain if these "voters" could furnish additional information about the balloting in Precinct 13. It turned out that they could furnish quite a bit.

Persuading them to give evidence was difficult, because of the atmosphere of fear—fear of Parr, of Luis Salas and his deputies, of Parr's lawyer Ed Lloyd, and, for the unsophisticated, all-but-uneducated members of Alice's Mexican-American community, of Anglos in general. One of Stevenson's attorneys was to remember vividly years later how one Mexican man told him, "People live longer down here if they keep their mouths shut." Nevertheless, evidence was given. The 841st voter on the poll list—the voter who, Stevenson's allies were convinced, was the last person who had in fact voted—was Eugenio Soliz, a twenty-eight-year-old worker on a county highway crew. And Soliz told them that he felt he probably had indeed been the last voter; he had arrived at the Nayer School voting place at about 6:40 p.m. on Election Day, twenty minutes before the polls closed. When he left some minutes later, after voting, "there was no else there voting besides me . . . and there was no one else coming up to vote." Would Soliz give an affidavit affirming his statement? Gardner asked him. Soliz said he would—and he did so, sitting in Gardner's automobile, while Gardner, resting a portable typewriter on his lap, took his statement down and a notary listened and attested to it. Although Soliz said he understood it in English, his statement was read to him in Spanish by Conrado Martinez, a local businessman, and Soliz signed it.

Then Stevenson's lawyers turned to the 201 names listed after Soliz on the poll list of voters—200 of whom, the tally sheet said, had voted for Lyndon Johnson. Brownlee had taken nine of these names down during his brief look at the poll list, and the young lawyers had jotted down additional names. They asked each of these people if they had voted for Lyndon Johnson. No, they replied, they had not; they had not, they said, voted for anyone. Without exception, the voters questioned said they had not been to the polls at all on Election Day. For one of these persons, twenty-one-year-old Hector Cerda, a college student, voting in Jim Wells County would have been difficult. He hadn't *been* in Jim Wells County that day, he explained; he had spent the day in the town of Pharr, 109 miles away, and had not returned until late that night, long after the polls had closed. For three other persons whose names were listed as voting, voting would have been even more difficult. They had been dead for some years.

．　．　．

Now, Coke Stevenson believed, he had proof that the decisive two hundred votes had been stolen—that they had not been cast by voters at all, that that number had simply been added to Lyndon Johnson's total several days after the election—and he believed that this proof would enable him to have these votes thrown out and give him victory.

They could be thrown out at either of two levels—local or state—and he moved on both levels at once. While what one newspaper described as "a small army of attorneys" went from house to house in Alice collecting affidavits, Stevenson swore to his own, summarizing the evidence of "fraud . . . errors and irregularities" in Precinct 13 already collected, filed it with the county clerk, and petitioned the Jim Wells County Democratic Executive Committee to meet and recertify a new, correct, tabulation of the county's votes to the State Democratic Executive Committee. Ten of the seventeen members of the newly elected county committee met. They heard their new chairman, Harry Adams, their secretary, Ike Poole, and B. M. Brownlee add to Stevenson's affidavit what they themselves knew about the counting of the vote at the Nayer School and about their own investigation; as a result, Poole was to say, "I am confident there are more than two hundred people shown as voting who did not vote." (Poole was also to tell reporters, "I helped gather the evidence and obtain affidavits from more than 200 such people.") The committee then passed a resolution which its members felt would eliminate the 200 votes once and for all; it was certainly unequivocal enough: "The Democratic Committee of Jim Wells County . . . has evidence of fraud and irregularities in" the county's Precinct 13, it said, and "it is the opinion of the [committee] that the certified report to the state committee was not a true and correct picture of the results of the election as held in [that] Precinct." Since the committee "had been denied" all records of the voting in Precinct 13, it could not determine the true vote, the resolution said, and it therefore could not draw up a new certification to replace the one already sent to the state committee; the state committee should therefore itself "determine the correct vote" and substitute it for the incorrect one. Later that day, the reformers on the committee, meeting among themselves, decided that the denial of the records need not handcuff them as totally as that resolution implied and that they could draw up a new certification themselves without waiting for the state committee; the certification could either return the Precinct 13 vote to the one originally reported Election Night, thereby removing 200 votes from Johnson's total or, since the fraud and irregularities in that precinct were, they felt, so widespread, they could throw out the precinct entirely, thereby removing 965 votes from Johnson's total (and 61 from Stevenson's). It is "expectcd," the *Austin American-Statesman* reported, that "an entirely new resolution of certification [will] be drawn up by the new [county] committee and presented to the Democratic State Executive Committee as a substitute for that filed by the outgoing committee." And, the committee members said, since they were legally entitled to those voting lists, why not move legally to force Donald to turn them over? There were lawyers in Alice who were not under Parr's domination; they would hire one to force the bank cashier to do so.

Stevenson's other recourse was his party. Its nominees would be determined—at the party's convention in Fort Worth that was to begin the following Monday, September 13—after reports from a "canvassing subcommittee," and from the full 62-member State Executive Committee. Customarily, the committee certifications were *pro forma*; as a result of court decisions, it was generally accepted that neither committee would seriously consider disallowing an individual county's certification. But there was nothing *pro forma* about this election, and the Executive Committee members were sufficiently sophisticated about politics to understand what had happened down there in Precinct 13 and in the Valley as a whole, and the implications for future close statewide elections. What had happened, others felt, was simply too raw, too blatant. Moreover, many of the committee's members were old friends of Coke's. In Fort Worth, Stevenson issued a statement saying he was prepared to appear before the Executive Committee "with proof that the returns in Jim Wells are not correct." They knew Coke: if he said he had proof, he had proof. When the committee members arrived in Fort Worth that weekend, reporters quickly realized that the Jim Wells certification was not considered a typical example of Texas election chicanery but an exceptional case— and was going to be seriously considered. "SENATE RACE MORE DOUBTFUL," the headlines suddenly said; "SPOTLIGHT TURNS ON SOUTH TEXAS"—on, to be more specific, a tiny town in South Texas. As the *Corpus Christi Caller-Times* explained, in a lead paragraph beginning with a rather unfamiliar dateline: "ALICE—Voting Precinct 13 at Alice—not Duval or Harris or Dallas counties—and its 1,027 disputed votes Friday became the issue that may decide whether Lyndon B. Johnson or Coke R. Stevenson will be the next senator from Texas." Reporters raced to the Valley. On Primary Day, James M. Rowe of the *Caller-Times* had been unable to interest any major newspaper or wire service in the reports from Jim Wells County. Now, he recalls, "all of a sudden people seemed to realize that a little town in Texas had elected a United States Senator." Under the headline "The Duke Delivers," *Time* magazine said: "Last week many Democrats from north and west Texas who never considered the dapper 'Duke of Duval' anything more than a local political princeling found he had become a powerful king-maker. In the stretch of one of the closest political races in U.S. history, he was the man most responsible for Congressman Lyndon Johnson's nomination over Coke Stevenson for the U.S. Senate." Texas newspapers were agog over "the biggest political story in the state's history." And Texas reporters began to zero in on the specific charge Stevenson was making. A reporter from the *Houston Chronicle* interviewed Ike Poole, and the headline over the interview said flatly: "200 VOTES GIVEN JOHNSON AFTER PRIMARY." For months the political headlines had drummed the words "Taft-Hartley" into public consciousness; now, suddenly and repeatedly, there was in the headlines a new word—"FRAUD."

Politics—the new politics—helped Johnson counter Stevenson's efforts. The influence of national politics and power on a state, already so evident during the campaign itself, was to intensify during the party's convention. The 1948 Texas convention had national political implications. In four Southern states, Democrats had broken away from the national ticket and formed the States Rights Party, which would, in November, carry these states for its presidential candidate, J. Strom Thurmond. For Harry Truman, far behind Thomas Dewey in the polls, it was considered imperative to keep Texas from deserting his party; the delegates chosen in May who didn't support him had to be ousted at this convention. The fight to do so would hinge on the ability of the "Loyalist" (in general, liberal) Truman Democrats to unseat the legally elected (by, in some cases, overwhelming margins) delegations from the "big" counties—Harris, Dallas and Tarrant—on the convention floor, a fight which was going to be very close.

Johnson made use of this fact. The liberals, more sophisticated than the run of Texas politicians, were aware of Johnson's true, less-than-liberal, record in Washington; although he was more liberal than Stevenson, their support of him had never been enthusiastic. More idealistic on the whole than other Texas politicians, many of them were as outraged as the conservatives over the manner in which Johnson had attained his 87-vote majority. But now feelings about the senatorial campaign were submerged in feelings about the presidential race. And Johnson told his men to take advantage of those feelings. They made an offer to the "Loyalist" leaders: the delegates with whom he would have influence at the convention—most notably the delegations from Austin, San Antonio and the Valley—would vote to unseat the States Rights delegations and vote to seat Loyalist delegations in their place. They would also vote for the Loyalist candidates for the new State Executive Committee which would be elected at the end of the convention and for Loyalist candidates to all other convention posts. In return, Johnson asked for only one thing. It was couched in legal terms: his men, headed by Wirtz (Connally was doing much of the legwork), were ostensibly asking for certification of the senatorial vote as it had been sent in by the individual counties, with no changes, and they claimed that this was the course prescribed by law. But what they were really asking for was plain to the Loyalist leaders. Says one of them, Robert Eckhardt, later a Houston Congressman and in 1948 a key figure in the Loyalist group: "Johnson was interested in preventing Box 13 from being opened. . . . His major purpose was not to permit the opening of Box 13." The request made them all the more aware of what the crucial Box was likely to contain, and ordinarily they might have balked, but now, as Eckhardt puts it, "It seemed much more important to a lot of us . . . that there not be a bunch of [presidential] electors that could throw away Texas votes" instead of giving them to Truman. So, in his words, "Connally and I connived on that," and the deal was struck.

PUBLICITY HELPED, TOO. Johnson countered Stevenson's charges of vote-stealing by saying—over statewide radio networks—that actually it had been Stevenson who had stolen votes, not he.

Stevenson's supporters "were strangely silent about the bloc vote which gave my opponent a 30,000-vote lead coming out of three big cities," Johnson said. Moreover, Johnson said, in Dallas "they have counted me out of 2,000 votes." And "nobody has asked for an investigation of . . . the River Oaks Box of Houston where Stevenson got eight out of every ten votes cast." In Brown County, he said, there was vote-switching. He had been cheated in rural counties as well. "You didn't hear of the Kenedy County bloc vote, where only eight votes were in the Johnson column," he said, and listed three other suspicious counties or boxes.

These charges would not have been very convincing to anyone who examined them closely. In Dallas, for example, there had been five changes in the returns, and not all of them favored Stevenson. Besides, they were the result not of late returns but of clerical errors; made by a clerk who typed a "9" instead of a "7" in a Johnson column, the most significant of them gave *Johnson*, not Stevenson, 2,000 more votes than he deserved. (Dallas' official certificate, as one writer pointed out, "corrected that error, and the final returns were certified, without protest from Johnson leaders, on September 4.") Johnson's reference to Stevenson's 30,000 total plurality in Houston, Dallas and Fort Worth as a "bloc" vote is totally misleading: in none of the three cities, which together cast a total of 173,627 votes—100,479 for Stevenson and 73,148 for Johnson—was there any pattern of "bloc" voting other than the normal heavy majorities for Stevenson in upper-income, conservative precincts and for Johnson in low-income, black and Mexican precincts (and in precincts with heavy concentrations of workers in defense-related industries). Houston's River Oaks Box "where Stevenson got eight out of every ten votes" was the city's wealthiest enclave; it always voted heavily for a conservative candidate. Nobody but Johnson ever suggested that there was any illegality in the voting there; in saying that "Nobody has asked for an investigation" of it, Johnson was correct—and nobody ever would. In Brown County, there certainly was a heated contest going on—however, it was not over the Senate election, but over the election of a County Judge. Ballots would indeed be ruled invalid there, but not because of anything to do with the Senate race.

As for rural counties, in Kenedy County, which Johnson charged was a "bloc vote," he was correct, but the "bloc" was only 52 votes. (Kenedy County consisted almost entirely of a division of the King Ranch, whose owners, the Klebergs, distrusted Johnson.) In the two other rural counties he mentioned, the totals were also minuscule. Not *one* of the state's 254 counties voted for Stevenson by ratios comparable to those Johnson received in the Valley. Votes were certainly stolen for Stevenson—Stevenson's totals were "corrected" in dozens of counties, just as Johnson's were "corrected" in dozens of counties other than the Valley counties—but in numbers so small as to bear no comparison to the majorities Johnson received in the Valley. Furthermore, the "corrections" in the totals of the two candidates after Election Day, corrections which followed the traditional Texas pattern, were so balanced as to virtually offset each other, and these corrections had no significance in the final result.

HAVING SEEN THE EVIDENCE, and filed his affidavit, Stevenson left Alice with Frank Hamer on Friday evening, September 10. Before him was the weekend, during which the reform majority of the Jim Wells County Democratic Committee was determined to meet and correct the county's voting tally before the State Democratic Convention began. At the far side of the weekend, at ten a.m. Monday, the convention would open in Fort Worth, to certify the result of the primary. All through that weekend, Coke Stevenson and Lyndon Johnson engaged in a grim, bitter struggle—and during it a pattern emerged that was to characterize the remainder of the fight between the two men. Stevenson was trying to get the ballot box and record of Precinct 13 open, to let Texans see the evidence that he and his men had seen—the loop added to change a "7" into a "9," and the two hundred ballots that supposedly supported that change. Johnson was trying to keep the records closed.

The pattern was set in the weekend's opening skirmish. The meeting of the Jim Wells Democratic Committee, at which reformers were planning formally to demand the records, and, whether or not they were produced, to throw out the tainted two hundred votes, might be convened at any moment. It had to be stopped—and it had to be stopped fast.

Behind the broad, amiable smile of Alvin Wirtz was the mind "as quick as chain lightning," the mind that was always thinking "three steps ahead" of his opponents. On Saturday morning, while the Jim Wells reformers were planning their strategy for the county committee meeting, telegrams were delivered to each of their homes—telegrams, signed by a judge, forbidding them to hold one.

Jim Wells County was in the state's Seventy-ninth Judicial District. The District Court was, Dudley Lynch writes, "George Parr's home turf," the judge, Lorenz Broeter of Alice, his "loyal supporter." But on this crucial Friday, Judge Broeter happened to be holding court in Starr County. It would take perhaps two hours to get there and locate him, and in two hours a meeting might be convened, a new certification made. There were, however, judges conveniently to hand in Austin. An affidavit was hastily typed up, and Lyndon Johnson signed it. In it Johnson charged that Stevenson, Hamer and Dibrell, as well as Adams, Poole and the other fifteen members of the Jim Wells committee, had "entered into a conspiracy for the purpose of causing the votes in Precinct No. 13 in Jim Wells County to be thrown out on the grounds of fraud and irregularity." Johnson claimed that Stevenson had threatened and intimidated Adams and Poole into calling a meeting of the committee to "make a new tabulation" and that Adams would call that meeting "at any instant, unless restrained." And Johnson therefore asked that a temporary restraining order be issued on the spot, without a hearing, to stop the committee "from making any new tabulation, or attempting to recanvass the votes in Precinct No. 13, or hearing any contest, or eliminating any votes on grounds of illegality, fraud . . . and from making, sending or filing with the State Democratic Executive Committee any returns" other than those already sent in—the ones containing the disputed two hundred votes— until Broeter could rule. Everett Looney hurried over to an Austin district judge, Roy Archer, of the 126th District, with the affidavit and a proposed injunction signed by him and Wirtz (Looney's name came first; Wirtz never put his name first on anything if he could help it), and the argument that unless the order was issued at once, Johnson would suffer irreparable harm from the committee's "conspiracy." Archer signed the order, and telegrams embodying it were instantly dispatched to every committee member.

Archer's order shocked attorneys knowledgeable in the state's election law; one historian was to state that the order "amazed and angered others not directly related to the proceedings or to the Senate race. . . . Lawyers across the state searched in vain for a legal precedent for an Austin judge restraining an official Democratic Party meeting hundreds of miles away in another county." Stevenson understood the reason for Wirtz's maneuver; it was, he said angrily, an "obvious attempt to prevent the truth from coming out of Jim Wells County until after the State Executive Committee has canvassed the returns on Monday." But a judicial order was a judicial order: when Adams, who of course did not feel he had been intimidated or threatened by anyone (at least not by anyone on Coke Stevenson's side), took Archer's telegram to an anti-Parr attorney in Alice, he was told bluntly what it meant: "Even if it [the election] was stolen, you're not to do anything." Wirtz's maneuver worked. "Of course we'll obey the law," Poole told a reporter; there would be no meeting until Judge Broeter ruled. And Broeter, George Parr's loyal supporter, notified of Archer's order, said he would hold the hearing—but not until Monday morning. Monday, of course, was the day of the state committee canvassing. And once the state committee had opened the Jim Wells returns—the returns which the present Jim Wells committee felt were false—and certified them, the feelings of the Jim Wells committee wouldn't matter.

WHILE HIS LAWYERS were fighting the rearguard delaying action in Alice over the weekend, Lyndon Johnson himself was engaged on the main front, in Fort Worth, five hundred miles to the north. He had rushed there on Sunday afternoon after dispatches from his lieutenants told him that, on this front, he was losing.

Two battles—two votes—would be waged on this front on Monday. The first vote would be taken by a seven-member subcommittee of the State Executive Committee, the party's ruling body, to canvass and certify (in theory, to examine and make official) the returns from the 252 counties that had held elections and then to make a report (in effect, a recommendation as to who the party's nominee should be) to the full, 62-member Executive Committee. The second vote would be taken by the Executive Committee on whether or not to accept the "canvassing subcommittee's" report: on whether, in other words, to recommend that the full convention name as the party's official nominee the candidate named by the subcommittee, or some other candidate.

In this election, the canvassing subcommittee's certifications of the votes from the individual counties would be more than usually crucial. Once it had made official the vote from Jim Wells County to the Executive Committee, the attempts of the reformers down in Alice to submit a revised return would be largely moot: the certified return (the original return) would now be in the hands of the Executive Committee, with the weight of the subcommittee's certification behind it. If, however, the subcommittee refused to certify the Jim Wells vote, the nature of the entire Johnson-Stevenson fight could change dramatically—and unpredictably; the range of possibilities seemed endless. But one clear possibility loomed as disastrous to Johnson's supporters: that the reformers in Alice would, before the subcommittee finished its work, submit a revised return—one with the two hundred disputed Johnson votes subtracted from the county total—and that the subcommittee would certify *that* return instead of the original, thereby giving Stevenson a higher total statewide vote than Johnson.

It was to forestall this possibility that Alvin Wirtz had obtained that temporary injunction forbidding the Jim Wells County Committee to revise the county's return. Without a revised return before it, the canvassing subcommittee could not of course certify it to the full Executive Committee; there would be nothing for it to certify except the original. On Monday, Johnson would be safe from a revised return as long as Judge Archer's injunction remained in force. That holding action in that District Court down in Alice was therefore the key to the subcommittee battle in Fort Worth. His attorneys felt Judge Broeter might well keep the injunction in force until some later date. But even if Broeter dissolved the injunction, Johnson would still be safe, so long as the dissolution did not come too early in the day. As far as the subcommittee battle was concerned, delay was the key; all that was required for victory was a delay of a few hours. Since the court hearing and the subcommittee's county-by-county certifications would be going forward simultaneously on Monday morning, there would be tense hours until Johnson could be sure that his attorneys back in Alice had delayed long enough. His attorneys assured him they would be able to do so.

The projections for Monday's second battle, the vote that evening in the party's 62-member Executive Committee, were, however, far less optimistic. The Executive Committee vote would be the decisive vote at the convention. "By custom," as Allen Duckworth wrote, the full 2,000-member convention "accepts without question the report of an executive committee on winners of primary nominations." Johnson's advisers felt that it was the Executive Committee vote that would decide the outcome of his long fight. And, polling the committee's sixty-two members, his advisers found to their consternation that a majority favored rejecting any report from the canvassing subcommittee that did not throw out the tainted Jim Wells votes and name as the Democratic nominee not Lyndon Johnson but Coke Stevenson. Clark and Connally, bitter enemies who agree on little, agree on the situation in Fort Worth that weekend—in the same three words: "We were behind."

No parade greeted Lyndon Johnson when he got off the plane in Fort Worth this time; he was met by worried faces and big, black headlines: "SHOWDOWN MONDAY." At the Blackstone Hotel, he was ushered into a suite that had been hastily redecorated "in modernistic decor" for his visit, and he put on a confident front for reporters. He had a "comfortable majority" on the Executive Committee, he said, and he was sure he would receive the certification. But after the press filed out, he was handed a sheet of paper on which the names of the fifty-five members of the Executive Committee who were attending the convention had been divided into two columns according to the preferences they had expressed—one column for him, one for Stevenson. The list of names in Stevenson's column was longer—several names longer. The committee's ruling would probably be decisive, he was told. If it voted against him, his fight was over. His career was over. And it seemed that that was what the committee was likely to do. "Just one vote difference there [in the Executive Committee] and it was all over," Ed Clark recalls. "One vote: if they had ordered [Stevenson's name onto the ballot] there wasn't going to be much we could do. It was over." Recalling that night, Ed Clark stops talking and sits for long minutes behind his desk staring off into space, remembering. "The state convention," he says at last. "That was when I thought we might lose."

Johnson's reaction to this news may never be known. Of those men who witnessed it only two were alive when research on this book began, and no matter how frank these two—Ed Clark and George Brown—have been in describing other episodes in Johnson's life, neither wanted to talk about this one. Clark, who was intimately associated with Johnson for thirty years and at his right hand in a score of crises in Texas, will say only: "I never saw him so worried about anything." Brown will say only: "He was wild." After some hours, he grew calmer. By the time Connally saw him, he was, in Connally's words, "frantic, but orderly—'Get me this one'; 'Get me that one' "—telephoning the Executive Committee members, and the men back in the members' home counties who could influence them. He was "calling all over the state to get pressure on the delegates any way he could." He interrupted his telephoning only to attend a barbecue for convention leaders, at which he arrived wearing a big smile and an air of confidence.

Johnson's telephone calls were not the ones that mattered most, however. He needed all his big guns on the line now, and, thanks to the planes at his disposal, he could get them there; despite all the pressure Clark had exerted in East Texas, some Executive Committee members from the East Texas districts were still on Stevenson's side. Clark was in his room when "Johnson called me and told me where to get a plane, and pick up Ben Ramsey [the Texas Secretary of State] in San Augustine so he could be in on the trouble we had up there." Soon Ed Clark and Ramsey were prowling hotel corridors together—the two most powerful men in East Texas, trying to bring the East Texas members into line for Lyndon Johnson.

And he had not just Clark and Ramsey but the man behind Clark and Ramsey. He had wheeled up his biggest gun of all. Telephoning Herman Brown in Houston, he asked him to come in person. No one who knew Herman, and who was aware of his contempt for politicians and his distaste for politicians in groups, thought he would come. "Herman Brown [had] never worked a convention in his life," his lobbyist Oltorf says. But he worked this one. Herman knew them all, it seemed. He knew the district judges and the county commissioners from the counties in which he had done road contracting work long before there was a Mansfield Dam, and if he didn't know the judge or the commissioner to whom a stubborn Executive Committee member might listen, he knew a subcontractor, a subcontractor who did work for Brown & Root or who wanted to do work for Brown & Root in the future, who knew the judge or commissioner. He knew the legislators with whom he had dealt on the Manford bills, and on a hundred other items, the men to whom he had sent envelopes filled with cash. And that night in Fort Worth, Herman Brown called in all his chits. It was necessary that he call them in, he told the recipients of his calls, because if Lyndon Johnson didn't win in the Executive Committee tomorrow, there might not be any more contracts—or subcontracts. The full, immense, weight of the economic power of Brown & Root was thrown behind Lyndon Johnson that night. Three of the seven absent committee members were contacted by Herman Brown, and leaders in their counties were telephoned by Herman Brown, and then Herman Brown's plane went and collected the members—and there were three new votes for Lyndon Johnson.

But Coke Stevenson's side was working the committee members, too—and working hard—and his side had legislative leaders and state officials and county officials who had had alliances with Coke through the long years, and all that night the fight went on. "Johnson knew damn well that Stevenson had some real pros on his side," Oltorf says. "They might not have been working during the campaign, but they were working that night." Lyndon Johnson didn't sleep at all that night—and neither did his men. Midnight turned into one o'clock, and one o'clock into two, and Lyndon Johnson's men worked the corridors and the bars in the big hotels. At two o'clock and three, Ed Clark's big hand was on the shoulders of committee members. "That was the longest night," Clark says. "I was up all night, and Ben Ramsey was with me, and he was up all night." But no one knew which candidate was ahead. In this fight the committee members were particularly anxious not to be joining the losing side. Recalls Clark: "People were asking me for a commitment that if they gave me their vote, they'd be on the winning side." But Clark had his code of honor. "I said, 'I cannot give that commitment.'" Some committee members were telling each side what it wanted to hear, so it was difficult to be certain even of some votes that had been promised. And as pressures and counter-pressures were brought to bear by both sides, votes kept shifting. "I knew we had turned around votes they still thought they had, and so I felt sure they had done the same to votes we still thought *we* had," Clark says. He was carrying around a list of the fifty-eight potential voters, he recalls, and he had to keep switching names from one column to the other. "I just didn't know how it was going to go," he says. The only certainty in the Johnson camp, and in the hotel room in which Lyndon Johnson sat all night amidst the bright modernistic decor in a shirt soaked with sweat, his face gray with fatigue and stubble, his eyes sunk in his head, hunched over a telephone and a list, was that, with those three new votes Herman Brown had flown in, it was going to be terribly close. Lyndon Johnson's fate was on the piece of paper lying on the desk in front of him—in that list in which votes were counted not in tens of thousands but one by one. And the list kept changing.

THEN it was Monday. "SHOWDOWN MONDAY."

As convention delegates and Executive Committee members were crowding into the Blackstone's high-ceilinged, dimly lit Venetian Ballroom at ten a.m., the lobby outside was filled with more delegates, and with tension. An elevator door opened and Lyndon Johnson stepped out, behind a phalanx of aides. His hair was slicked down so flat that it might have been pasted to his skull, the circles beneath his eyes were as dark as bruises, his skin, covered with nicks from the closeness of his shave, was sallow. As his entourage was pushing through the crowd, one of its members, Jerome Sneed of Austin, who was also a member of the Executive Committee, suddenly collapsed, gasping for breath and writhing in pain on the lobby floor from what appeared to be a heart attack (it was later diagnosed as ptomaine poisoning). Sneed was quickly surrounded by shouting, excited delegates—and by one man who was always calm, the man whose mind worked so fast. While other men knelt by Sneed's side and loosened his necktie and shouted for a doctor as he gasped in pain, Alvin Wirtz knelt by his side, scribbled something on a piece of paper and, handing it to Sneed along with a pen, told him to sign it: it was his proxy; Wirtz had saved a Johnson vote.

Johnson entered the ballroom in the midst of his aides, smiling, waving and reaching out to shake hands. Stevenson had arrived early, and was sitting quietly, puffing his pipe. As Johnson was passing Stevenson's seat, an enterprising newspaper photographer tried to persuade them to pose together. The two men were not far apart; "just for a moment, they looked like two dogs wanting to get at each other and held back by a leash," says a man who was between them. The moment passed; Stevenson's mask and Johnson's smile were back on, they turned away from each other, and Johnson and his entourage moved to another part of the big room. Pulling out a pack of cigarettes, Johnson lit one, drawing on it deeply; oblivious for once to photographers, he put on his eyeglasses.

After the seven members of the "canvassing subcommittee"—three neutral; two representing Stevenson; two (Wirtz and Alma Lee Holman of Taylor) representing Johnson—had been appointed, the ballroom was cleared, and at about 10:45 a.m. the subcommittee began its meeting there.

At almost the same moment, the District Court hearing began in Alice, so that for the next few hours, the two interlocking actions were proceeding simultaneously.

During those hours, therefore, the pattern—of Stevenson trying to open the Box 13 records and of Johnson trying to keep the records closed—became clear. And so did the tactics—haste in Fort Worth, delay in Alice—by which Johnson's men were trying to accomplish his aims.

In Fort Worth, Wirtz was attempting to hurry the subcommittee through its work. Stacks of big manila envelopes were piled on the stage of the Venetian Ballroom: the returns for 252 counties. Wirtz wanted to dispense with opening them. No sooner had the subcommittee meeting begun, with Democratic State Secretary Vann M. Kennedy reporting that on purely arithmetical grounds Johnson had indeed won by the eighty-seven votes previously reported, than Wirtz moved that the subcommittee, without any further deliberations, certify those figures as official and report to the full Executive Committee that Johnson was the nominee. And when this motion failed—the subcommittee's three neutral members agreeing with Stevenson's representatives that it was their function to canvass the election county by county—Wirtz kept urging the canvassing along. One of those manila envelopes contained the Jim Wells return, the return based on the tally sheet on which the "7" had allegedly been changed into a "9," the return which had given Johnson the 87-vote majority. At the moment, it was the only Jim Wells return. If the Jim Wells committee met and authorized one of its members to telephone the subcommittee and say that the return was being corrected, anything could happen. Once the subcommittee reached Jim Wells in its canvassing, and made the old return official, the danger of a new certification would be over. But the subcommittee was going through the envelopes alphabetically, and there were 122 counties between Johnson and safety. So Wirtz hurried the subcommittee along—and when the Jim Wells return was finally reached, and Stevenson's representatives showed some disposition to discuss it, Wirtz said, in a statement with which the neutral members agreed, that they could not do so: so long as the court restraining order was in effect, he said, the subcommittee was prohibited not only from changing the Box 13 vote but from investigating it—even, in fact, from discussing it.

In Alice, meanwhile, Johnson's representative, attorney Dudley Tarleton, was working to keep that restraining order in effect—at least until the subcommittee had finished its work. So, as speed was the order of the day in Fort Worth, delay was the order in Alice.

Stevenson attorney Wilbur Matthews considered the case so clear-cut that he thought the hearing in Alice wouldn't take long. No court should stop the Jim Wells committee from opening the records, investigating the returns, and, should the findings justify such an action, revising the returns—and, he said, nothing could be clearer: to support his view, Matthews read passages from the authoritative *Texas Jurisprudence*, which said flatly that because intra-party primary elections were not open to all voters but only to members of a political party, disputes in it were to be considered intra-party matters "of which courts are not to take cognizance." What could be clearer than that? he asked. Judge Archer's restraining order, he said, "has no parallel in the judicial history of the United States" and no justification under Texas law; it should be dissolved at once.

Tarleton's presentation was somewhat longer. He read, in what Matthews considered "a deliberate manner," Judge Archer's order and Johnson's petition asking for the order. He read "at length" from the primary election statutes. Then he started in on various court decisions. It was evident, Matthews was to write, "that he was stalling for time." He was still reading when Judge Broeter called a two-hour recess for lunch. And he was still reading when court resumed after the recess.* Tarleton's recitation may have been unnecessary. Early in the court proceedings that morning, an extra-legal occurrence had convinced Stevenson's attorneys, had any further convincing been needed, of the slimness of their chances of having the order vacated. The occurrence was the arrival in court of George Parr. Striding past the benches where other spectators sat, he pushed through the low swinging door into the section of the courtroom customarily reserved for attorneys and sat down at the table with Johnson's attorneys, relaxed and at ease, as if he owned the courtroom (which, of course, many of the persons watching him felt he did). His nonchalance

---

* The more substantive side of Tarleton's argument was studded with legalisms and technicalities. The laws forbidding state courts to intervene in primaries referred only to a first primary; second primaries were not mentioned, he said. County committees might be empowered to "convene" to certify precinct votes, but the laws did not mention "re-convening." To change the certification, he said, the Jim Wells committee would have to hold another meeting, and the law's omission made such "re-convening" illegal.

slipped only once; during a recess, the Duke of Duval was expansive and smiling as he explained to newsmen that the reports about his political influence were untrue: "You don't control votes," he said. Then a question, an innocuous one, annoyed him, and for just a moment the reporters saw the true face of George Parr. He "stopped short," one wrote; "His eyes seemed to pierce his glasses and his smile and hearty laughter" were replaced by what the reporter described as "a resolute expression." After the recess, he returned to the attorneys' table, where he bent his gaze on Judge Broeter. But despite Parr's presence, there was always a possibility of a miscarriage of the ducal brand of justice—always a possibility that the judge might rule for Stevenson and vacate the restraining order. Members of the County Democratic Committee, including Adams and Poole, were in the courtroom, hoping to be allowed to look at last into Box 13. So Tarleton took no chances. He delayed as long as was necessary. And his tactics served their purpose. At 2:30 p.m., a newspaperman brought a wire service bulletin into court. Reports conflict on its contents, but it appears to have stated that the canvassing subcommittee had reached Jim Wells County in its tabulations. It's "too late," Matthews told Judge Broeter. Dissolving the restraining order would no longer serve any purpose. "The case is moot and should be dismissed," he said in disgust.

Broeter did not dismiss the case. "I am not saying that there was fraud or that there was not fraud," the judge said. "If it so happens that our laws do not set out adequate means and speedy procedures to correct illegal acts I regret it," but "I do not make the laws. . . ." At three p.m., a rumor swept the courtroom that the subcommittee was refusing to certify the Jim Wells returns, and was waiting to hear what the court ruling was. Broeter thereupon gave the ruling. It was in favor of Johnson. The judge said he did not see how granting Johnson's request for an injunction would "interfere in any way with an election contest." Therefore, he said, he was continuing the injunction until such a contest was filed, or until the present case was heard on its merits. Until that time, no change could be made in the Box 13 tabulations. The case "failed in the face of the power of George Parr," Matthews was to write. Delay had been Johnson's purpose, and that purpose had been served. When the subcommittee had reached Jim Wells, there had been no new certification for them to look at.

UP IN FORT WORTH, however, Lyndon Johnson was now to receive a most unpleasant shock. His attorneys had assured him that in the absence of a new certification from Jim Wells County, the canvassing subcommittee would have no choice but to accept the old one and send his name to the Executive Committee as the party's senatorial nominee. But suddenly, without warning, the subcommittee was refusing to do so. When, with the county-by-county tabulation completed, Alvin Wirtz moved that the subcommittee certify Johnson's 87-vote majority, one of Stevenson's two representatives on the seven-member subcommittee, retired Major General Albert Sidney Johnson, objected. Declaring that the 87-vote majority included at least 202 clearly illegal votes from Jim Wells County, he moved to amend Wirtz's motion. His amendment would certify the returns from 251 counties—but not the Jim Wells returns. The "question of the correct and legal vote" of Jim Wells should be submitted to the full Executive Committee, he said—and until that correct and legal vote was ascertained, that county's votes should not be included in any tabulation.

Without those votes, Coke Stevenson was the party's nominee. Johnson jumped to his feet. Grabbing his sleeve, Wirtz pulled him down, and he and another of Johnson's attorneys, Charles I. Francis, made Johnson's argument, Francis almost screaming at Subcommittee Chairman W. B. Simmons that with a court injunction in force, "For this or any other committee to refuse to accept the vote as now certified would be violating that injunction." Simmons, however, ruled that the subcommittee could vote on General Johnson's amendment. Wirtz and Mrs. Holman voted against it, as did one of the subcommittee's neutral members, but the other neutral member voted with Stevenson's two representatives. With the vote tied, three to three, Simmons cast the deciding vote. It was for General Johnson's amendment, which thus carried, four votes to three, and became the subcommittee's majority report. Wirtz announced that he would make his motion a minority report, but that was what it was: a *minority* report. Johnson had been confident that, if only his attorneys could stall long enough down in Alice, he would emerge from the subcommittee meeting bearing its imprimatur as the party's nominee and with the two hundred indispensable votes from Jim Wells firmly certified as his. The stalling had worked, but not the rest of his strategy. He would be going into the crucial Executive Committee meeting with neither of those two advantages.

The vote had been taken at five o'clock. The meeting of the Executive Committee would begin at seven.

Now EVERYTHING HINGED on the Executive Committee. Several alternatives were available to it. It could adopt its subcommittee's majority report, and conduct its own investigation of the Jim Wells returns. It could adopt the subcommittee's minority report, and name Lyndon Johnson the nominee. Or it could disregard both reports, and simply name a nominee: Johnson or Stevenson. Whatever the exact wording of the resolution on which it finally voted, the fifty-eight members of the committee present in Fort Worth would in reality simply be choosing between the two men who had fought so long for the nomination. And still, as seven o'clock neared, no one knew whom the committee was going to choose. Committee members were still switching back and forth. Others, afraid of being caught on the losing side, were saying they would abstain, or were telling each side what it wanted to hear. George Brown asked his brother how it was going to go that night. His brother said he didn't know; all he knew, he said, was that it was going to be very close. Even as Ed Clark, weary from more than thirty-six consecutive hours of counting votes, was walking down to the ballroom for the meeting, he wasn't sure what the actual count was going to be. As he walked, he pulled out the rumpled sheet of paper on which he had been doing his figuring, and counted up votes for the last time. "I had it figured as a tie," he says.

Spacious though it was, the Venetian Ballroom wasn't nearly spacious enough to hold all the politicians who wanted to be present. Every seat, of course, was taken—and, it seemed, every foot of floor space, too. It was very hot; perspiration rolled down the faces of burly men with big cigars—by the time the meeting began, the ballroom seemed already filled with smoke—who were jammed so tightly together that they tried in vain to keep their expensive Stetsons from being crushed. Women members of the Executive Committee kept dabbing their faces with handkerchiefs that were already sodden.

"The whole atmosphere was tension," recalls the man who presided at the meeting, State Democratic Chairman Robert Calvert. Some of the spectators were there simply out of a desire to be present at one of the most dramatic moments in Texas political history, but others —those who were adherents of Lyndon Johnson and Coke Stevenson out of ideology or personal affection or who had personal stakes in the outcome of the vote—had deeper interests. Standing in the ballroom that evening were Jake Pickle and Raymond Buck and Fred Korth and John Connally, men who had, some of them many years before, tied their fortunes to Lyndon Johnson's star. Those men would remember their feelings until they died. "I was leaning up against a pillar in the back listening and trying to make tabulations but my heart was pounding so much that I could hardly write," Pickle recalls. "Because I knew what was involved."

Johnson had a lot of his men present; wavering committee members anxious to be with the winner might be swayed at the last moment by an impression as to who the winner was going to be. He was loudly cheered as he and Lady Bird walked to the seats that had been saved for him by two of his men in the front row and sat down, facing the committee. He smiled until he felt the ovation had gone on long enough. Then he lifted his hand, palm out, and the cheers stopped as abruptly as if he had turned off a faucet. "Is Coke here?" spectators asked each other. Then the former Governor was noticed, sitting inconspicuously in the middle of the audience.

Stevenson's lead attorney, Clint Small, a former district judge, focused on what the Stevenson forces considered the main question: whether or not a single precinct—a boss-dominated precinct notorious for the "bloc" pattern of its voting—was to be the decisive factor in a statewide election. "The issue," Small said, "is whether or not Precinct 13 in Jim Wells County is to elect a United States Senator." And, the attorney said, the issue was whether or not that single precinct was to elect a Senator with votes that were patently illegal. Lyndon Johnson, he said, was "trying to get the [Senate] office with votes of people who never appeared at the polls. . . . Every name that appears after 841 has been placed there after the closing of the polls."

Small said he was prepared to prove this charge. Although access to the voting lists had been illegally denied, the names of some persons alleged to have voted had been taken down. Affidavits had been obtained from those persons. Johnson's claque was heckling and booing Small now, in an attempt to drown him out, but Small read aloud the affidavits, in which each of the "voters" swore he had not voted. As he finished reading one, he asked the Executive Committee: "Are you going to put a man in the United States Senate on that vote? . . . They cold-bloodedly added the 202 votes that are deciding this Senate race. Don't count votes put in four or five days after the ballots were counted." Yelling above the shouts of Johnson's claque, Small told the committee, "This [the Jim Wells] certificate reeks with corruption and fraud. . . . They will say you have to take it whether it is good or bad. You don't have to take a certificate when you know it is false."

Opening the arguments for Johnson, John Cofer of Houston, one of the most renowned of the stem-winding, arm-waving school of courthouse lawyers, roared, "I believe in justice and right." During his arguments—together with those of Charles Francis of Brown & Root and Ed Lloyd of the Duchy of Duval—it became apparent, however, that their substance was rather that justice and right had no relevance to the work of the Executive Committee. Determining the legality of ballots, Johnson's lawyers said, in an argument which weighed heavily with many committee members, was the function of the state's District Courts; it was, in fact, Francis said, "contrary to law" for the committee to determine legality: under state law, the committee's sole function was to add up the voting totals sent in by the individual counties. "You are here [only] to count the votes," Cofer shouted, pounding the air with both fists. "You may or may not be able to understand law, but by the Holy Writ, you can count!" Turning to Coke Stevenson as he sat puffing his pipe, Francis jabbed a finger at him and said, "Coke Stevenson, if you don't think those votes were fair and accurate, you can take Frank Hamer with his pistols and have your day in court. We'll meet you there. That is where the law says election contests should be held." To rebel yells, shouts of "Pour it on!" and applause from supporters, Johnson smiled, then waved his hand for quiet.

As for affidavits, he had affidavits, too, Cofer said. "Are you going to let Mr. Small wave an affidavit, and then let me wave one?" he asked. "Well, I can wave two for every one he can wave." (He would not, however, do so at this time, Cofer said, because the place for affidavits was in court.)

Furthermore, Small's affidavits were worthless, Johnson's attorneys said, because they had been obtained by intimidation and threats during what Lloyd termed an "invasion" of his beloved Jim Wells County by "goon squads" which had terrorized innocent people. The "goon squads," Lloyd said, were Stevenson's lawyers, and Frank Hamer; ignoring the fact that Hamer had not been present when any of the affidavits were obtained (he and Stevenson had been on their way back to Austin at the time), Cofer bellowed, "He [Stevenson] went down there [to Alice] with a man who had a gun on his hip and said to these people, 'Swear to this.' None of you would try a Negro on the basis of affidavits obtained by a policeman, with a gun on his hip." The remainder of the arguments by the three attorneys on the affidavits also had racial overtones. "You are not going to deprive him [Johnson] of this election on affidavits obtained from Mexicans," Cofer said. "You just take a number, pick you a Mexican and let him make an affidavit."

For three hours the lawyers held forth in the sweltering, smoke-filled ballroom. Stevenson sat impassively. Johnson was hunched forward, one elbow resting on a knee, his face supported by his hand; his nervous fingers pinched and pulled the skin on his cheek, tore at the flesh around his fingernails. He was lighting one cigarette from the butt of another, and sometimes he bent over, sucking in the soothing smoke for a long minute. But only for a minute; then he would be hunched forward again, his eyes flickering around the room, watching everything, but mostly staring at the faces of the committeemen and women, trying to guess his fate. The voting began at 9:48 p.m.

The vote was on a motion to adopt the minority report Wirtz had drafted in the subcommittee instead of adopting the subcommittee's majority report, so an "aye" vote would be a vote that the Executive Committee certify Johnson as the nominee; a "no" vote would in effect be for Stevenson's certification.

At the beginning, the votes were mostly for Stevenson, including several from Executive Committee members Johnson had believed favored him. Men who were watching Lyndon Johnson would never forget how he sat there rigid and unmoving, appearing almost stunned, as the voting continued: "No." "No." "No." After 31 votes had been cast, Stevenson had 21 to his 10.

Then the tide changed, and vote after vote—including several that Johnson had believed would be for Stevenson—were for him. The vote was tied, and then tied again, this time at 28 to 28, and then the last vote was called, and it was for Johnson. He had won, 29 to 28. Pandemonium enveloped the ballroom; men pounded Lyndon Johnson on the back, women pushed through the crowd to hug and kiss him; cheers and rebel yells drowned out Chairman Calvert's attempts to gavel enough order out of the chaos to announce the vote; in the din no one noticed for some minutes that a committee member, Mrs. Seth Dorbrandt, who had voted for Johnson, was waving her arms and asking for the floor. Finally, as the noise was dying down in anticipation of Calvert's announcement, the chairman noticed Mrs. Dorbrandt and gave her the floor. She withdrew her previous "aye" vote for Johnson, saying she wanted to be recorded as "present, but not voting." (She later told reporters that "I believed by changing my vote it would make a tie and force the decision into the courts where I believe it rightfully belongs.") The vote was tied again. Spectators shouted to Calvert to call again the names of the five committee members who had been absent during the balloting. One after another, he called the names, and the first four, who had not come to Fort Worth, didn't answer. The fifth and last name was that of Charlie C. Gibson of Amarillo. Knowing that Gibson was in Fort Worth, John Connally had been searching for him and moments earlier had finally found him. In later years, when the story of the Executive Committee vote would be encrusted with myth, some of those myths surrounded Gibson's disappearance during the voting: it was said he had been missing when his name was called either because he had a headache or had dozed off in another room, or because he had gone to the bathroom. It was indeed in a bathroom that Connally found him, but, he says, Gibson was not there in order to use its facilities but because he had promised his vote to Johnson, and now didn't want to be caught on the wrong side. What he was doing in the bathroom, Connally says, was hiding; "He knew it was going to be close and he didn't want to vote." "Goddamnit, Charlie, get out there and vote!" Connally shouted. Just as Calvert was calling his name, Gibson burst into the room. "Aye!" he shouted. Johnson again led 29 to 28. At that moment Lyndon Johnson thought fastest; in the instant of silence that followed Gibson's "aye"—before pandemonium could break loose again—he called to Calvert: "Announce the results now, Bob, before someone else changes his mind." Calvert did. Lyndon Johnson had won. The margin had been a single vote, but he had won.

. . .

THE FULL CONVENTION the next day, tumultuous though it was on the surface, and crucial though it was for Truman's chances of holding Texas, was an anticlimax in terms of *Realpolitik*. The deal struck earlier between Wirtz and the Loyalists was consummated. Johnson's forces voted to seat not the Houston delegation that had won in May but a Loyalist delegation from Houston—whereupon States Rights delegations from Dallas, Tarrant and several smaller counties stalked out (in their bitterness, taking with them microphones, speakers, podium and even the organ, which had been rented by the host delegation; "AS TARRANT GOES, SO GOES THE FURNITURE," one headline read). Pro-Truman (and pro-Johnson) delegates swarmed into the Will Roberts Auditorium to take their places, thus giving the Loyalists overwhelming control of the convention. Johnson's aides "helped us on the seating," Eckhardt recalls. "In return we took care of the Johnson crowd on the ballot boxes. We didn't open the boxes." The Loyalists voted to place on various party committees—including the new Executive Committee and the canvassing committee of the convention as a whole—men and women who would oppose any investigation of the Jim Wells vote. That canvassing committee, on which Stevenson supporters had pinned their last hopes, was now, in the words of one observer, "a merry Johnson party." "It's stacked 99 percent against us; what good would a fight do now?" a depressed Clint Small asked. And, indeed, when the Executive Committee's minority report, the report charging Johnson with "palpable fraud and irregularities," was presented to the convention's canvassing committee, it was ignored; one committee member moved to table it, another quipped, "Let's put it under the table," and there was general laughter. When, that evening, at the convention's closing session, Governor Beauford Jester tried to speak, he was interrupted by shouts of "We want Johnson." A party official read the Executive Committee's majority report, the one carried by the 29–28 vote, amid swelling applause. Then permanent Chairman Tom Tyson called for an "aye" and "no" vote on the report, and there was a thunder of ayes. Then a roaring chant: "Johnson! Johnson!" The candidate and Lady Bird had been waiting in the wings, and they were escorted to the speaker's platform to a tremendous roar. He had had a hard fight, but he had won, he said. "This is the moment for which we have been waiting for one hundred weary days. . . . I am filled with so much gratitude towards my friends that there is no room for bitterness. The election is behind us. This is a great night for us. . . . To all of you, we say, we love our friends; we forgive our enemies." The next morning, the Johnsons rose early, left the Blackstone, were driven to the airport and boarded a plane for the

Gulf Coast, "to look on sand and water where there are no telephones." His aides, some of whom had been celebrating all night, were still celebrating. The morning's pro-Johnson newspapers exulted with them. The convention had been "a field day for Lyndon Johnson," the *Houston Post* said. "Hairbreadth Harry himself never experienced a more exciting run of adventures than those which brought to a hairbreadth, photo-finish climax the closest major political race in all Texas history."

"And," said the *Post*, "the most exciting thing about it all, from Mr. Johnson's viewpoint, was its happy ending."

ENDING? The fight that had gone on so long had not ended at all.

15

Qualities of Leadership

IN BELIEVING that the struggle with Coke Stevenson was now over, Lyndon Johnson and his aides (and Stevenson's aides as well) were not reckoning with the deepening sense of injustice the former Governor had come to feel—or with the implications of this feeling for a man with so fervent a belief in the law. Stevenson believed that an election had been stolen from him; that in itself was infuriating. But then, after he had set out to retrieve what had been stolen—after he had gone to Alice and obtained the evidence which, he believed, proved the theft—he had been told that, evidence notwithstanding, the law provided no recourse against that theft.

Lyndon Johnson, Stevenson felt, had used the law against him, not the law in its majesty but the law in its littleness; Johnson had relied on its letter to defy its spirit. Stevenson had first sought justice from the people who knew the truth best, the Jim Wells Democratic Committee itself—and that committee had been willing to give him what he sought, to meet together and throw out the tainted ballots. But the law—in the form of the injunction Johnson had obtained from a George Parr court—had prevented the committee from doing so. Then he had sought justice from his party at a higher level—from its Executive Committee—and the law had stopped him there, too, as Johnson's attorneys had convinced the committee that investigating the votes was "contrary to the law." In that Executive Committee, Charles Francis had told him, shouting, to his face, You can "have your day in court. We'll meet you there"—knowing even as he shouted that in the court to which he was referring, the State District Court, no effective action was possible before the case was made moot, and that no other state court would accept jurisdiction until after the District Court had ruled.

After the 29–28 vote against him in the Executive Committee, Stevenson had still hoped that the full convention would deal with the "palpable fraud and irregularities"—and then had come the quip, "Let's put it under the table," and the roar of laughter from the men with whom Johnson had stacked the convention. To Stevenson's young attorney friend from Junction, that laughter was symbolic. "That whole week, it was like Lyndon was laughing at Coke," Callan Graham says. "It was as if he was laughing in his face, and telling him that he was so smart that the law couldn't touch him. During neither of these proceedings, neither at the Executive Committee nor in the court, did Lyndon Johnson or his lawyers deny what we were saying. Their argument in both cases was that it didn't make any difference legally. They were just saying that, true or not, we couldn't do anything about it." And, indeed, when, after the convention, Stevenson met with his own attorneys in his hotel suite, most of them told him the same thing.

And that was an argument that Coke Stevenson could not accept. He loved the law that he had taught himself on the ranch, loved it as he loved his land, loved it with an intensity so deep it was almost religious, believed in its majesty, in its power to right a wrong. Now he had been told that the law was powerless to right the wrong that he felt had been done in this election. "For Coke, this just *couldn't* be true," says his nephew, Robert Murphey, "because if that was true, it would destroy something he had believed in all his life, something that was very important to him." He went out for a walk on the streets of Fort Worth, alone, and a reporter, encountering him, asked him if the long battle was now over. Coke Stevenson's big jaw came up. "Of course not," he said. "We're going to fight right on." And that night, while the convention was cheering Lyndon Johnson, and Johnson was celebrating and sleeping and then flying off for a vacation, Coke Stevenson was fighting. He and Dan Moody, another former Governor, who had volunteered to serve as one of his attorneys, met for a while and decided that since there was no help available in the state courts, they would go to the federal courts. Moody said that because the primary involved a federal office, Stevenson could sue under the federal civil rights statute because he had been denied a civil right: the right to have the votes in the primary counted honestly. He could ask for an injunction or restraining order that would forbid the inclusion of Johnson's name on the November ballot pending a full hearing in Federal District Court, and, should that hearing show that Johnson had been elected by fraudulent votes, he could ask for an order placing his own name on it instead.

Moody was too tired that night to draw up the necessary petition for a restraining order himself, but there was that young attorney who had written the report that the canvassing committee had so blithely ignored. Josh Groce was wakened in his hotel room by a telephone call. On the line was Coke Stevenson, whom he had never met, and Stevenson asked him to turn his report into a petition for an injunction. While Groce was doing this, Stevenson, with all his legal advisers gathered in his hotel room, discussed which of the three federal judges who sat on the United States District Court for the Northern District of Texas to present it to. There seemed no good choice. One of the three was irascible, erratic, a judge lawyers shied away from; the second was too much a "brass collar Democrat," one who would be eager to uphold the party's Executive Committee; the third, former Lieutenant Governor T. Whitfield Davidson, was noted not only for his formality in a courtroom but as a "strict constitutionalist," who might be predisposed against permitting federal intervention in a state election. But Davidson, while a fervent Democrat (he had been one of Roosevelt's first prominent supporters in Texas), was also noted for his independence, and it was decided to present the petition to him.

It had to be presented to him fast—before Johnson's name went on the ballot. Attorney Connie Renfro of Dallas telephoned Davidson's home and was told that the judge was vacationing on his sister's ranch, but no one seemed to know exactly where in Harrison—or perhaps Upshur—County the ranch was located; Renfro, leaving Fort Worth at midnight, spent all night driving around East Texas; dawn was breaking before he found it. Braving a rather fierce-looking watchdog, he found the tiny, white-haired judge already awake, brewing coffee—and learned that Davidson's insistence on the rules of court held firm even when the court was a ranch-house kitchen. The judge pulled a table into the middle of the room and sat at it as if behind a bench, had Renfro place a copy of the petition and proposed restraining order on it, studied them as Renfro read them aloud—and then, at 6:25 a.m. Wednesday morning, he signed the restraining order, setting the following Tuesday, September 21, for the hearing on whether to harden the order into an injunction. Speeding back to Fort Worth, Renfro filed the order with the clerk of the Federal District Court. Even as Lyndon Johnson was in a plane en route to his vacation, believing he was on the ballot at last, state election officials were being ordered to keep the Democratic line blank, at least until the hearing. Coke Stevenson went for another walk. He looked happier than he had for days.

ON SEPTEMBER 21, assured by his legal team that his argument against federal intervention in a state election was strong and that Davidson would be predisposed toward it, Johnson strode into Federal District Court in Fort Worth, at the head of a long line of lawyers, deeply tanned and wearing a broad, confident smile. His hair was sleek and shiny with pomade. The dark blue of his suit's heavy, rich fabric was broken only by the Silver Star pin and the precise points of the white handkerchief in his breast pocket. His white shirt was gleaming and starched. His necktie had a bright floral print. The pearl-gray Stetson in his hand was a 20X beaver. His wife was dressed as he liked her dressed, complete to the long feather curling up from her fashionable pillbox hat. The crowd in the oak-paneled, high-ceilinged courtroom was a political crowd: in the audience were Speaker of the House W. O. Read and other prominent state officials; Tom Clark's brother Robert and other political influentials; political reporters; even one of the candidates defeated in the first primary, Cyclone Davis. At the attorneys' tables sat political stars, not only Alvin Wirtz and Clint Small, but James Allred and Dan Moody; Allred, Moody and Stevenson—three former Governors of the state. As Johnson worked the crowded, noisy room, shaking hands, chatting in a relaxed manner, every inch the successful candidate, the scene seemed like a continuation of the convention that had so recently been held a few blocks away.

But this wasn't a convention but a courtroom, a courtroom very different from George Parr's courtroom in Alice. Just before Judge Davidson entered, a marshal told the men who had taken off their suit jackets to put them on, and then he called out, "No smoking, gentlemen." Coke Stevenson put out his pipe, Lyndon Johnson put out his cigarette. After the silver-haired jurist had taken the bench, in the words of one reporter, "just radiating dignity in a quiet way," some of the attorneys—former Governors and glittering political names—went on talking. "Now, gentlemen," the judge said, "I will ask you not to carry on any consultation in the courtroom. If it is necessary to direct attention to the next man, do it very quietly." The attorneys looked up at the judge, and sat down. The talking stopped. Whatever the outcome of Coke Stevenson's petition would be, that petition was going to be heard in a setting very different from any in which his battle with Lyndon Johnson had previously been waged, in the setting Stevenson loved—not in a noisy, smoke-filled convention hall, but in a quiet, high-ceilinged courtroom, in a court not of politics but of law.

And as soon as Moody began his opening argument, every trace of a smile was gone from Lyndon Johnson's face.

Moody's first sentences contained some news for Johnson. He said that Coke Stevenson was no longer charging election fraud merely in Jim Wells County; he was broadening his complaint. He was charging that fraud had also been committed in Zapata County. And he was broadening it still further—into the county whose vote totals had been perhaps the most indefensible of all. Fraud had been committed, Moody said, in Duval County. He was therefore no longer talking about two hundred votes, he said, but many more—thousands, in fact; he was to tell Davidson: "We expect to lay before this court testimony that will affect thousands of votes in this election."

And, Moody said, he was prepared to prove what he was saying. "The ballot box in one of the precincts in Jim Wells County was in what is known as common parlance, 'stuffed,' " he said. "That is to say, after the election had been held, and the votes counted, that additional votes were added." He had witnesses to prove it, he said. They had been brought to Fort Worth and were ready to testify; at that moment, Moody said, they were waiting in an office just down the hall.

Johnson's attorneys argued as they had earlier that whether Moody's statements were true or not, they didn't matter. Johnson had been defrauded of votes, too, they said—in Dallas County, in Brown County, and elsewhere. Any investigation of voting fraud in Texas would be "fatally defective" unless *all* voting fraud in Texas were to be investigated, "all of the irregularities, throughout the length and breadth of this great commonwealth," attorney John Crooker said. And if all the illegal votes were thrown out, Johnson would win by more than eighty-seven votes. They were prepared to argue the case on its merits, Crooker said, but not in this court: state court and state court alone was where this contest must be decided. And, he said, in terms designed to appeal to Davidson's "strict constitutional" views: "They now seek to have Your Honor extend the federal powers. . . . We ask no further encroachment of the federal powers in Texas than has already occurred. If there is anything any more important than the purity of the ballot . . . it is the power of the sovereign states that . . . ought to be maintained in all its strength."

Crooker said that his side had not even made preparations for arguing the case on its merits in Davidson's court, so confident was he that Judge Davidson would admit that his court was without jurisdiction. "Respondent Lyndon Johnson appears at this time solely for the purpose" of asking that Stevenson's request for an injunction be dismissed because federal court has no jurisdiction. That, Crooker said, is "the sole pleading now on file, and the sole purpose . . . of appearing here, because of our confidence that under the law this court has no jurisdiction."

Moody, however, replied that those arguments did not apply to a civil rights case. Stevenson's suit, he said, was being brought under a civil rights statute that allowed a federal suit in cases in which an individual has been deprived, "under cover of state law or customs or usage," of rights "secured by the Constitution of the United States." Stevenson had been deprived of such rights, he insisted: "The Constitution provides that a citizen has a right to become a candidate" and entitles him to an "honest count" of the vote. The plaintiff, moreover, was not just a candidate. He was a voter. "He has a right . . . as does every other voter in the state to have his vote honestly counted, honestly and legally, votes not thrown out and no stuffing of the ballot box."

And Moody argued also on broader grounds. "Under the law of Texas," he said, "there is no remedy to correct such a wrong" as Stevenson had suffered. But did that mean that there should be no remedy *anywhere?* That someone could commit fraud and be immune from punishment for it? He did not believe that, he said. "I decline to believe that the courts of the United States are impotent to detect fraud and punish [it]." And that was why the jurisdiction of this court had been invoked, he said. "The jurisdiction of the Court is invoked to prevent wrong."

It was not merely Coke Stevenson who had been deprived of a federal right—a right guaranteed by the Constitution—by what had happened in the Valley during this election, Moody said; it was every voter who had voted honestly and had had his vote in effect canceled by one put in the ballot box dishonestly. "Your honor," he said, "I can sum up in a word the nature of [this] suit. While it is an action in equity in the Federal Court, essentially it is a crusade for honesty in the ballot box and for the protection of the people of this state from fraud in election and from depriving the people of their honest choice in the election of a person to high office."

And then, before he recessed court for lunch, Davidson said a few words—and to the shock of Johnson's attorneys they did not seem to be the words of a judge who felt that he had no jurisdiction in the case, or that the legal questions were as cut and dried as they maintained. "The court wants to say one or two words off the record," he said. Wheeling around in his chair, he faced the two candidates, and spoke directly to them, in a low voice that the audience strained forward to hear. Under the present circumstances, the judge said, whoever won the nomination would win it under a cloud—and that cloud would not go away. "Public sentiment will crystallize into anti-Stevenson and anti-Johnson sentiment. . . . You will have the feeling among some in Texas that the winner has won on a technicality." No matter who won, there would always be a shadow on his public career. Therefore, the judge said, he had a suggestion—"and it is only a suggestion, off the record and will not be included in my decision": arrange to have the Democratic State Executive Committee place both names on the general election ballot, and "let the people of Texas decide the winner."

Stevenson needed no time to decide if he was willing to do as the judge suggested. "All smiles as the noon recess began," in the words of one reporter, he said, "Sure I'm for it. I'm willing to run it over." Pushing his way out of the courtroom, Johnson said, "No comment."

In a conference that noontime, Lyndon Johnson's ten attorneys advised him to accept Davidson's suggestion. It was hardly the suggestion, they pointed out, of a judge who doubted his jurisdiction, and, although Davidson had made no direct statement, the tone of certain other remarks by the judge indicated that he was likely to rule against them on the jurisdiction issue. If he took jurisdiction, there would be a wide range of possibilities, and most of them—an investigation of the South Texas boxes, for example—would be quite ominous for their client. Indeed, even the present hearing was ominous: those witnesses were waiting just down the hall; what if Davidson allowed them to take the stand? What might they say? Accept the judge's suggestion—settle the injunctive suit with the compromise he suggested—and the hearing would be over. In explaining their recommendation that Johnson compromise, the only one of the attorneys still alive, Luther E. Jones, says simply: "The uncertainty of the legal processes: who knew what was going to happen, particularly in a case as complicated as this. And, you know, lawyers like to compromise: any settlement is better than a lawsuit, that kind of thing." It was not inconceivable, his lawyers warned Johnson, that if Davidson held a full-scale trial on the issue, Johnson's name would not be on the ballot at all. "The compromise that the judge had suggested here was that both go on the ballot, and the feeling was that in that case [Johnson] would win": in a general election, the state's conservative vote would be split between Stevenson and the Republican candidate.

The team of ten lawyers offering Lyndon Johnson this counsel—offering it unanimously—included not only former Governor (and federal judge) Allred, not only Alvin Wirtz, Johnson's most trusted adviser, but, in Crooker and Cofer and Tarleton and Looney, a quartet of the most renowned and respected lawyers in Texas. When they gave clients advice, the clients usually followed it.

Lyndon Johnson did not follow it. During the next few days in that September of 1948—those days of crisis—he was to display vividly many of the most striking qualities of his nature. One was the fierceness and determination with which he grabbed for political advantage, grabbed it and, once he had it in his grasp, held on to it. He had the advantage now—he had the certification from his party—and agreeing to Davidson's compromise would mean relinquishing that certification, sharing it with the man from whom he had taken it. Another was the utter inability to comprehend the questions of morality or ethics raised by his actions, an utter inability to feel that there was even a possibility that he had violated accepted standards of conduct and might be punished for that violation. But, during this conference and during the following days, Lyndon Johnson was also to display many of the qualities that made him a leader of men.

Among those qualities of leadership was a willingness to take responsibility for his own fate. This quality had been a constant in his career. No matter how strong the lure, he had never tied himself inextricably to Roosevelt or to Rayburn or to Herman Brown. If he had not placed his faith in princes, he was certainly not going to place it in lawyers. He would make up his own mind. Another quality was decisiveness; he might delay for a long time studying a decision, but when the time came to make it, he made it. And if he had to make it without study, if he had to make it fast, he made it fast. Lastly, there was the sheer force of his personality, the dominance of Lyndon Johnson, face to face, over other men, even over ten other men, even over ten famous and respected men operating in the field (the law) of their expertise, not his. Lyndon Johnson might, as on this occasion, be leading men in a battle whose aims and methods would not bear scrutiny. But he would *lead*.

Having given him their expert and unanimous advice, the lawyers sat back, expecting him to accept it. Instead, in the words of Luther Jones, "Lyndon just hit the goddamned ceiling!" He was, Jones says, "truly angry." Part of his anger was directed at the judge, whom he cursed violently and viciously. "Maybe his temper was short because this thing was a nerve-racking ordeal, and it looked like that judge was going to take it away from him," Jones says. "He was outraged at this attempt to take his victory away from him. . . . It was just incredible that someone was doing this to him." And part of his anger was directed at *them*, at his lawyers. "He was very indignant" at their suggestion that he compromise, Jones recalls. "He said he had won the election, and he was not going to temporize; he was a citizen, and he had rights and he insisted on their being followed, and he didn't want to temporize *one bit*."

For almost two years, when they worked together in Washington, Jones had not only shared the same small office with Lyndon Johnson but had slept in the same small bedroom with him. But that had been fourteen years before. Powerful though Johnson's personality had been then, Jones, who had seen him seldom in the intervening years, had never before witnessed what that personality had developed into with increased age, and with power, and with experience in command. Witnessing it now, he was awestruck. "Lawyers like to compromise. And the compromise that the judge had suggested here was that both go on the ballot, and the feeling was in that case he would win. The lawyers were suggesting that Lyndon accept that. And many men would have accepted that. But Lyndon was just angry. Red-faced anger. The wildest kind of anger. He was outraged at their suggestion and he told them so. 'This is a free country! I won it fair and square, and you want me to trade it away!' "

There was not a trace of hesitation or diffidence in the way he spoke to "the best legal brains in the state," Jones says. "Lyndon Johnson is a man of force and power, and, boy, he exhibited it all that day."

Under the force of that personality, all other considerations melted away. If other arguments were raised, Johnson dismissed them. He didn't want any discussion, he said; the discussion was over. "He just said, 'I instruct all of you to proceed accordingly.' " And, indeed, there was no further discussion. Lyndon Johnson got up from the conference table, towering over his attorneys, and strode out of the room. After court had reconvened that afternoon, and Moody had formally accepted, on Stevenson's behalf, Davidson's proposed compromise, Crooker read the statement the attorneys had drafted after Johnson had left the conference room ("I received a majority of the votes. . . . I have a legal right to the nomination. . . . To voluntarily barter away that right would be to stultify myself and result in a betrayal of the Democratic Party"). What one writer called "the fight to the political death in Judge Davidson's courtroom" resumed.

THE NEXT DAY was worse for Johnson—for the next day was the day of the witnesses.

Johnson's lawyers made a last, frantic attempt to keep them from being heard. John Cofer's voice was shaking as he pleaded with Davidson, on personal and political grounds, to dissolve his restraining order without taking evidence; Stevenson's suit was nothing but a delaying tactic, Cofer said, and the delay might keep the Democratic line on the senatorial ballot blank in November. "They would rather have a Republican elected than have Lyndon Johnson as United States Senator," he shouted. Pointing at Lyndon and Lady Bird, he said such a result "would be doing a great wrong, a terrible wrong, to that young man there who has served so ably his people of the Tenth District. It would be doing a great wrong to that little woman there who has helped him bear the burden of his statesmanship." But Moody pointed out that it was not Stevenson who had first taken the election results to a court, and thus begun the chain of events that were keeping the ballot blank. "It was the defendant Johnson himself who went to a District Judge in Travis County to restrain the new officers of the Jim Wells committee from trying to see if the returns from that county were correct," he said, shouting as if he were on the stump again. "They didn't want an investigation of the facts. The man who is right has nothing to fear and welcomes an investigation." Stevenson was not planning to present all his witnesses at this hearing, Moody said, only enough to demonstrate conclusively to the court that evidence was available that would show fraud widespread enough to change the outcome of the election. Allred jumped to his feet to reply, and for a moment the two former Governors stood shouting at each other, but Davidson cut them both short with a sharp rap of his gavel. And then the judge told Moody: "You may proceed with the evidence." At last, after three weeks of maneuvering, witnesses were going to begin to testify in public, under oath, about what had happened down there in the Valley.

Only thirteen of them testified that day, but that was enough. The thirteen included Jim Wells Democratic officials H. L. Adams and B. M. Brownlee and, with Josh Groce questioning them, they both testified that George Parr's men had concealed the crucial poll list, and that there had indeed been changes on that list at the decisive point. ("Q: Mr. Adams, did you notice any change in the ink at any particular point on that poll list? A: Yes, I did. Q: Where did that change appear? A: With the number 842.") Groce introduced as evidence the list of names Adams had scribbled—and suddenly another aspect of the list was a matter of court record: "I call to Your Honor's attention on this list copied from the poll list . . . that from 842 down [the names] run in alphabetical order."

And while Johnson's attorneys had at least known that this particular evidence was coming, there was something new of which they had had no warning—and that came as a surprise to them. Groce had just asked James Gardner, one of the lawyers who had accompanied Stevenson and Frank Hamer to the bank, "Did you examine the poll list to see whether or not there was any changes?" Gardner said that he had, and that at the bank he had also gotten a look at a document no one else had seen, the certificate of the total vote—and that he had observed a change that no one else had mentioned: "The certificate showed that the vote for Lyndon Johnson was 965 but it was evident from looking at that 965 that the 9 had been changed. It previously had been a 7."

Three of Johnson's attorneys leaped to their feet as one, objecting. "That calls for an opinion and conclusion of the witness, highly objectionable," Allred shouted. Davidson upheld him, but when Groce reworded the question ("Just describe . . . what you did see"), Gardner said, "where it had been a 7 there had been an additional loop added to the 7 to make a 9 out of it," and this time when the attorneys objected, Davidson said, "I will hear it [the testimony]." When they went on arguing, the judge said firmly, "The court has ruled," and that crucial loop was a matter of record, too.

But, most important, there were the voters—or, to be more precise, the alleged voters. On that day, Wednesday, September 22, 1948, for the first time in a court of law testimony was given under oath about whether those two hundred votes, the votes beginning with the number 842, that had given Lyndon Johnson his victory had actually been cast for Lyndon Johnson—or, indeed, for any candidate. And if the oratory of Johnson's lawyers and supporters had beclouded this issue for three weeks, the terse answers of these witnesses cleared the air.

There was Hector Cerda, the student at Texas A & I who was listed on the poll list as Voter Number 920.

"Where were you on August 28th, 1948?" Groce asked. "At Pharr," Cerda replied.

Q: How far is that from Alice?
A: Approximately 109 miles, I believe.
Q: State whether or not you voted on that day?
A: I did not vote.
Q: You did not?
A: I did not vote, no sir.

There was Louis Salinas, listed as Voter Number 911. "Did you vote in the August 28th primary this year?" "No." There was Juan R. Martinez, listed as Voter 891. "State whether or not you voted in the August primary, on August 28th?" "No." There was Olivera Herrerra, listed as Voter Number 881. "I did not vote."

There was an affidavit from Eugenio Soliz, Voter Number 841, stating that he had arrived at Precinct 13 at about six-forty, that "there was no one else coming up to vote," and that he believed he was the last person to have actually voted. And now one of the witnesses was Enriqueta Acero, listed as Voter 842, which would have made her the voter after Soliz, and she testified that *she* had not voted.*

There was further testimony. During the previous three weeks of controversy, ever since the 965 Johnson votes in Precinct 13 had been reported, Johnson and his partisans had continuously argued that the Johnson vote in Precinct 13 had always been 965, that it had never been changed, that no one had ever said it was 765—that the election judge, Luis Salas, had reported it as 965 on Election Night, and that the report had simply been garbled in transmission to the Election Bureau. Now there was a surprise witness. "Call Charles Wesley Price," the court attendant said, and Johnson's attorneys looked around to see who he was. Price, a twenty-five-year-old resident of Alice, testified that he had been present at the offices of the *Alice News* at about eight o'clock on the night of August 28. At that time, Price said, "Luis Salas . . . brought the returns in from Precinct 13" so that a *News* reporter, Cliff DuBose, could tele-

---

* Allred produced his own affidavit from Soliz, saying that he could not read the first affidavit and that he had signed it because "I was very much afraid" of the "three very well dressed Americans" who had questioned him. But Groce recalled Gardner, one of the three men, to the stand. Gardner said he had typed Soliz's statement himself, sitting in a car with him "in the pouring rain" while Wroe Owens, another attorney, and Conrado Martinez and a notary public stood outside, that the statement had been read to Soliz in both English and Spanish before he had sworn to it and had had it notarized, and that no duress of any type had been used. And, of course, Martinez, the notary and Owens were all prepared to testify. Allred did not pursue the matter.

phone them in to the Election Bureau. Did you hear Salas say what the Precinct 13 vote was? Groce asked. Yes, Price replied. And what was the vote Salas reported? Allred jumped to his feet ("Clearly hearsay"), and Davidson upheld the objection, but it was obvious what Price was going to say—and would say, if the investigation continued, and testimony was allowed on this point. The truth or falseness of Johnson's claim that Salas had originally reported 965 votes for him could be determined, because Price—and DuBose as well—had heard the original report.

And there were witnesses not only from Jim Wells County but from Zapata County, whose revised final vote had been 669 for Johnson to 71 for Stevenson, and these witnesses testified that in Zapata, too, votes had been added for Johnson. As for Duval County, if Davidson agreed to hear the case on its merits, evidence would be available from that county, too, Moody promised (although Moody was also to point out that returns of 4,622 to 40—more than 100-1—might be considered fraud "upon their face"). "Sufficient illegal votes have already been proved in this hearing to have changed the result" of the primary, Moody said, and there were many other counties, too, whose returns "are loaded with fraudulent votes." Lyndon Johnson had not really won the primary, Moody said; his alleged victory was composed of thousands of "votes" that had never been cast.

When Davidson had ruled that the witnesses would be heard, Lyndon Johnson's self-assurance had visibly begun to drain away. His wife, despite her jaunty hat, was, an observer wrote, "even glummer than he was." During the testimony, Johnson kept darting hasty glances at Stevenson; Stevenson never looked his way. During recess, Stevenson, returning from the bathroom, encountered Johnson in the corridor outside the courtroom. "Howdy," Johnson said, assaying friendliness. Stevenson returned the greeting by briefly raising his hand; he did not reply.

And while the witnesses' words cut through Lyndon Johnson's arguments, there were also words that day from the judge—which cut deeper.

Davidson's ruling on the case contained at least a touch of indignation about Johnson's conduct in it.

If Stevenson's "allegations be true, then the complainant has been wronged," Davidson said. "He has had a seat in the Senate of the United States taken away from him. . . . [If] enough ballots were stuffed to have changed the result . . . manifestly, that is a wrong." And Johnson had presented not "one word of evidence" to refute Stevenson's charges. Indeed, not only had he refused to present evidence himself, he had effectively prevented anyone else from presenting it—or even from obtaining it—by securing that earlier injunction in a state court. Coke Stevenson had been entitled to see the poll and tally lists, the judge said, to determine the truth about the change in Jim Wells' vote. "It was the right and privilege of anyone interested in the vote to try to inform himself about that change which came quite late." Lyndon Johnson had prevented Stevenson from doing so, with that earlier injunction. "The effect of that was to . . . prevent the new county chairman and . . . Coke Stevenson . . . from making an examination [of the lists]." They had finally managed to obtain a glimpse of the lists but they had been stopped from making a copy—"They haven't been allowed to do so . . . yet." The very fact that the lists had been concealed made it more likely that a wrong had been committed, he said. The concealing of the lists "throws such a cloud on the fairness of the election that we think it should be gone into, and that the parties concealing this information must have been conscious of the fact that it would probably change the result of the election."

Then Davidson moved beyond the narrow specifics of the case to discuss what he felt were more basic issues. And when he did, the words he spoke were words Coke Stevenson had been waiting to hear for a long time. Because the terms in which Judge Davidson discussed the case were terms that lifted law above legalisms. As he spoke in his soft, calm voice, the shouting and the vocabulary of politics that had clouded the case seemed at last to fade away—to be replaced by what Davidson considered the issues of justice, of equity, of *right*, that the law was supposed to signify.

Lyndon Johnson's contention, the judge said, was that, whether or not Coke Stevenson had been wronged, the law was powerless to right that wrong. And with that contention, the judge said, he did not agree. "A sound principle of justice," he said, is "that there must never arise a wrong for which there is not a tribunal wherein there is a remedy. That is in fact the spirit of equity that has come down to us through the ages." The defendant, Lyndon Johnson, "admits there is no remedy. His counsel says, 'What can you do about it. We have no remedy [in law].' " That is why the plaintiff is here—in this court. And "here we are admitting that he has been wronged and laughing at him in his face, as it were, because he has no right. . . . Even if there was no statute on the books, this man would still have an equitable hearing in the court. He comes to a United States court, complaining that he has been deprived of a right. . . . And it is admitted by both parties that a right to determine that nomination exists nowhere if not in this court."

Of course the case fell under the federal civil rights statute, Davidson said. "Whenever I steal, whenever I misappropriate, whenever I stuff a ballot box, we are taking from a man that which is his. We are not only taking from him that which is his, but we are depriving other voters of their right to choose, by offsetting the vote they cast." And he was going to find out the facts in the case. "In cases of fraud," the judge said, "the rule is—throw open the doors and let the light in." Therefore, he said, he was continuing the injunction that kept Johnson's name off the ballot. And, he said, he was going to institute an investigation to determine if Johnson's name belonged there at all. The court "would like to see further the facts concerning Box 13 in Jim Wells County, also Duval County and Zapata County." He was therefore appointing Masters in Chancery, special officers of the court with full power to subpoena witnesses and evidence, to hold hearings in the three counties and submit written reports to him by October 2, the day before the deadline for placing names on the ballot. After seeing these reports, he would rule on whether the injunction should be made permanent. And the judge added a final note which Lyndon Johnson may, if possible, have found even less cheering than those which had preceded it. A trial might be necessary to determine if the injunction should be made permanent, the judge said. The Masters' "investigation is a preparation for trial." The trial would be on "the issue of fraud. If this fails of proof, then Lyndon Johnson is the United States Senatorial nominee, and he will move into the position with a clean bill of health. If he does not . . ." At this point, as one reporter wrote: "The judge paused, as if searching for words, then he spread his hands and shrugged."

   Johnson's attorneys repeated their now familiar argument that there had been fraud in many counties besides the three Stevenson was naming. "We are unwilling to try an election on the Jim Wells County vote," Cofer said. "There are other counties we would like investigated if there were time"—Brown County, for example, and Galveston and possibly Dallas. But Davidson called their bluff. "I will be glad to appoint Masters to investigate any counties" you name, the judge said. Allred declined the offer. "We're not in a position to give time to this thing in the next few days," he said. He said that the time of Johnson's attorneys would be taken up perfecting an appeal to a higher court. Davidson agreed to facilitate matters by granting a severance, a legal device allowing Johnson's attorneys to proceed with the appeal while the investigation was going forward. But, the judge emphasized, it *was* going forward: "The case on the facts will proceed."

LYNDON JOHNSON had worn another wide, brightly colored necktie to court that day, but by the time the judge had finished speaking, the face above the gay floral pattern was the face of a man confronted by the imminent death of his hopes and dreams. Beside him, Lady Bird seemed stunned. For weeks now, in court and convention, he had been fighting to have his name placed on the ballot as the Democratic nominee for Senator. But now, on September 22, the Democratic line was still blank;

Texas election officials had already sent to the state printers the sample ballot from which individual counties would print up their ballots, and this was a sample ballot, as the Associated Press put it, "unique in Texas political history because it includes no Democratic nominee for U.S. Senator." The Republican nominee, Jack Porter, was listed; the space for the Democratic nominee was empty. October 3 was the legal deadline for placing a name on the final ballots that would be used by voters on Election Day. If Johnson's name wasn't on the ballot by October 3, it would never be on it. Since Davidson had ordered his Masters in Chancery to report to him by October 2, theoretically the judge would be able to dissolve the injunction in time for a candidate's name to be included. But realistically this was little comfort to the Johnson camp now that they had heard the witnesses, for should the Masters' investigation confirm their testimony, it seemed all too likely that if Davidson did order a name to be placed on the Democratic line, the name would not be Johnson's. Ever since the additional votes from Precinct 13 had been reported on September 3, banner headlines in Texas newspapers had linked Johnson's name with victory, as he won in the Election Bureau tabulation, won in state court, won in the Democratic Convention. Now, in the headlines announcing Davidson's decision, it was no longer "JOHNSON WINS." It was "JOHNSON LOSES COURT FIGHT" and "JOHNSON LOSES COURT DISMISSAL PLEA"—"JOHNSON LOSES." And it was "COKE WINS PLEA TO BAR JOHNSON" and "STEVENSON WINS RULING BY U.S. COURT"—"STEVENSON WINS." In the opinion of many men in both camps, the headlines were an accurate summary of the situation. Recalls Ernest Boyett: "When Davidson handed down his ruling, we thought we had won."

MEETING THAT EVENING with his ten attorneys (now, in this emergency, supplemented by others) in a large conference room at the Texas Hotel, Lyndon Johnson was confronting, in what the *Austin American-Statesman* called "the greatest political controversy of all time in Texas," a legal situation so unprecedented and so tangled—and with so wide a range of possible outcomes—that, as the Associated Press reported, "In the midst of the confusion and present uncertainty . . . the best legal sources were unwilling to comment on what might happen." As one historian was to write: "Since there was no parallel or precedent even in the politically bizarre state of Texas, no one knew what would happen in the Senate race" if, by October 3, Davidson had not permitted Johnson's name to be added to the ballot. And the longer Johnson's attorneys discussed the crisis, the more daunting it appeared. For what, after all, were his options? A write-in campaign? That was an unattractive alternative. He might lose such a campaign to Stevenson. Moreover, far fewer voters would take the trouble to turn out on Election Day and write in a candidate's name than would vote for a name on the ballot. If Stevenson was also not on the ballot, the overall Democratic vote would be much smaller than usual, and Johnson would be dividing that write-in vote with Stevenson; even if he should defeat Stevenson, there was no certainty that in these circumstances he could defeat the Republican candidate.

Appealing Davidson's injunction to a higher court was a possibility, of course, and on appeal the injunction might well be overturned. But it was hard to conceive that this one could be overturned in time to get him on the ballot. Any appeal, his lawyers explained, would have to be heard first by the United States Court of Appeals for the Fifth Judicial Circuit, of which Davidson's court was a unit, and the Court of Appeals was not scheduled to convene until October 4, the day after the deadline. Even if they managed to persuade a single circuit judge, sitting alone, to stay the injunction—an unlikely event—Stevenson could then appeal that stay to the United States Supreme Court, whose fall term also began on October 4.

Johnson could do what he had been threatening to do for weeks: demand an investigation of other counties besides Jim Wells, Zapata and Duval. He could even demand a statewide re-count. Davidson had indicated his willingness to grant such demands. Those demands might, however, be unwise for many reasons—including the possibility that investigation might reveal as fraudulent more of his votes than Stevenson's. Moreover—the most brutal fact—the wisdom or folly of such a course was beside the point now. It might have been feasible in the last week of August, when the primary had been held. It was not feasible in the last week of September. A widespread investigation or a re-count could certainly not be completed by October 3. There was no time.

Another aspect of the situation had also to be considered.

Under Davidson's order, ballot boxes—including Box 13 from Jim Wells County—were going to be opened. Lyndon Johnson had been trying for weeks to keep those boxes from being opened. He had, through George Parr's court, stopped the county committee from opening them. He had, through his deal with the Loyalists at the convention, stopped the state committee from opening them. But they were going to be opened now.

Who could predict the ultimate result of that? The brief glimpse of the Box 13 poll list that the Alice reformers had snatched, supplemented by the testimony of a few witnesses, made it difficult to doubt that fraud had occurred in that precinct. What might be the result of a full inspection of the list, combined with the unlocking of the precinct ballot box (which allegedly contained, after all, not merely 200 but 965 votes marked for Lyndon Johnson)? And Box 13 was only one precinct. What would be the result of the Federal Masters' unlocking all the ballot boxes in Zapata County—and in Duval County, where, out of 4,679 persons eligible to vote, 4,662 had allegedly gone to the polls, and 4,622 of them had allegedly cast ballots for Lyndon Johnson? What would be the result of the Masters' examining all these poll lists? What would be the result of their taking testimony from not just thirteen but scores of witnesses? Dan Moody had already promised "testimony that will affect thousands of votes." What if he could keep that promise? What if the definitive, no-longer-deniable word *fraud* was successfully applied to Precinct 13 and to other precincts—and the truth about the Valley's vote for Lyndon Johnson was no longer a rumor but a fact? What would be the effect on his reputation? There had been no public hint as yet that Lyndon Johnson had participated personally in the obtaining of fraudulent votes that may have given him his victory, and perhaps no such hint would ever surface. But the votes would be linked with his name in the press: how could they not be?—they had been cast for *him*. If scores of ballot boxes were opened, scores of poll lists examined—and if, as Moody promised, thousands of fraudulent votes were found—would the public believe that such wholesale stealing of votes had been carried on without his knowledge? The implications reached beyond the state, as even pro-Johnson newspapers could not avoid pointing out; the *Fort Worth Star-Telegram* said the very "filing of the suit that alleges irregularities . . . may also be the grounds for 'black marking' Johnson in such a way that the U.S. Senate would not seat him even if all court action fails." And the investigation's implications reached also into the future—his future. Whatever its results, a full investigation could hardly fail to tarnish his name permanently—to link it indelibly with the greatest election scandal in Texas history. His seat in Congress was already gone: Homer Thornberry, having won the Democratic primary in the Tenth District, was assured of election in November. And he was in imminent danger of having his reputation tarnished so badly that even if he were to desire another political post—appointive or elective—he might not be able to get it. He was in danger of going through the rest of his life identified in the mind of the people of his state with Box 13. And as he met with his lawyers that evening, Lyndon Johnson realized that not one of them knew what to do.

THE SOLUTION to both his problems—getting on the ballot and stopping the investigation—was the same: Judge Davidson's injunction must be overturned—fast.

October 3 might be fast enough on the legal front, for a dissolution of the injunction by that date might allow his name to be placed on the ballot, but in the court of public opinion the verdict might already be in by that date: witnesses would have been heard, poll lists checked, ballot boxes opened—and conclusions drawn by the Federal Masters in official, public reports. Short as was the time before October 3, it was too long if he wanted to avoid the ineradicable "black marking" that the *Star-Telegram* had mentioned.

But none of the roomful of attorneys could think of any way to get the injunction overturned and the investigation stopped any sooner. "The rules were perhaps less clear than you might think," Luther E. Jones recalls. The lawyers went off separately and wrote drafts of an appeal. The greatest lawyers in Texas—"Allred wrote one, Johnny Crooker wrote one . . . Everett Looney wrote one . . ." Then they came back, and discussed them. There was no agreement, either on the broad ground for the appeal or on the specific arguments to be used. They couldn't even agree on the court to which the appeal should be made: some wanted to argue again before Judge Davidson, some to go directly to the United States Supreme Court. "Day moved on, and night came, and . . . it was late at night, and they still had not agreed on the opposition paper."

Exacerbating the problem was the fame and reputation of the attorneys involved. "These were talented lawyers but each of them was famous in his own right, and each of them had to tell stories—about his great courtroom triumphs, etc.," Jones says. "Antecedent to making effort, they had to reminisce, and the reminiscing was just awful, really, because it stopped the work."

The attorneys laughed and chatted—and as they did, time was running out on Lyndon Johnson's last chance. After hours of discussion, still "Nobody could agree on how to do it." Jones saw that "Mr. Johnson was getting impatient to a degree that's hard to describe, because they were not producing the thing that was needed." The crisis facing Lyndon Johnson could not be solved by Johnson's own genius, for that genius was political. It could be solved only by legal expertise. He had assembled a roomful of legal experts, some of the greatest legal experts in Texas. And none of them were helping him.

In this crisis, Lyndon Johnson responded with a vivid and dramatic demonstration of other qualities of leadership that he possessed.

One was an ability to think—fast and clearly—under intense pressure; to see, in a tense and tangled crisis, what was needed to solve it. Another was his genius not only in choosing men, but in using them for his purposes. To him, every man was a tool, and in difficulty he reached unerringly for the right tool. Now, facing a Gordian knot of seemingly insoluble legal complications, Lyndon Johnson reached for his sharpest tool of all. As the roomful of renowned lawyers went on arguing, he asked Alvin Wirtz: "Where's Abe?"

Wirtz telephoned Fortas' Washington office and learned that by coincidence, a very lucky coincidence, Fortas was at that moment in nearby Dallas, taking depositions in an anti-trust case. He was not at his hotel, though, and no one knew where to find him. Johnson telephoned Stanley Marcus. "Do you know where in hell I can put my hands on Abe Fortas?" he asked. "He's right here," Marcus replied. Fortas immediately flew to Fort Worth.

When he walked into the big conference room, Fortas was to recall, "It seemed to me that there were acres of lawyers," who were, it seemed, "having a great deal of controversy as to the next step to be taken."

Another of the qualities that made Lyndon Johnson a leader—the quality of his perhaps most admired by his Texas associates—was a toughness of mind: under intense pressure the self-pity and hysteria fell away, to be replaced by what was needed.

Explaining the problem to Fortas, the lawyers started talking all at once, interrupting each other. Johnson made them speak one at a time. All the time they were talking, with Fortas occasionally interjecting a question, Lyndon Johnson said not a word. When the lawyers had finished, Fortas recalls, "I said what I thought should be done."

His suggestion entailed an immense gamble. Lyndon Johnson's only chance of overturning Judge Davidson's injunction lay in Circuit Court or Supreme Court. The discussions in which the other lawyers had been participating that evening had been based on the assumption that in attempting to overturn the injunction, Lyndon Johnson would naturally use every chance he had. Abe Fortas was suggesting that Johnson not do that. He was, in fact, suggesting that Johnson deliberately throw away every chance but one—and risk everything on a single hearing before a single judge.

In the view of most of the attorneys in the conference room, the best legal chance of overturning the injunction was in hearings before the full Circuit Court, and then, if Johnson lost there, in a further appeal to the Supreme Court. Even though neither court convened for its Fall term until October 4, their hope was that if the injunction was overturned, some legal means would then be found of putting Johnson back on the ballot. During those long hours of shouted conferences, one attorney recalls, "dozens" of such means had been suggested.

Fortas' calm voice, pragmatic and precise, cut through those arguments. They were unrealistic, he said; there was no time for hoping now: if they won before a full court, additional court actions—additional hearings, additional delays—would be required to obtain the legal orders to get Johnson on the ballot, with Election Day itself always coming closer. And at every stage, Coke Stevenson could himself appeal. Fortas was to say later that he had been "confident" that in a hearing before a full court, Johnson would win. "This was alleged fraud, which in these circumstances was a state matter," he was to recall. "The federal judge enjoining the state election" had no authority to do so. But, he was to say, what good would that victory do? Victory before a full court meant defeat in the election.

Then Fortas turned to another legal avenue—bringing the appeal before a single judge—and now his reasoning was more complex.

Since a single Circuit Court judge could stay a lower court's injunction if that injunction would make ineffective a later judgment of the full court, most of Johnson's lawyers had been recommending making the strongest possible argument to a Circuit Court judge whose "strict constructionist" views and previous record made likely a favorable ruling. Fortas said that this course, too, would be unwise. Since the sole issue would be jurisdiction—whether Davidson had been correct in taking authority over the case—making such a plea to a single judge would smack too strongly of lawyers' simply asking one judge to overrule another. No matter how persuasive their plea, he said, a judge sitting alone would be far more likely to deny it than the full Circuit Court. In any case, the judge would almost certainly want to consider the issue for several days, to "take it under advisement"; should his ruling then prove unfavorable, no time for taking another course of action might remain before the October 3 deadline. Even if he granted the stay, too many days of consideration would, while giving Johnson a legal victory, doom his chances of being on the ballot. Fortas felt confident that the jurisdictional grounds would persuade a single Supreme Court Justice—particularly the Justice with administrative responsibility for the Fifth Circuit, Hugo Black—to do what a single Circuit Court judge would not: grant their plea for a stay of the injunction and thereby allow Johnson's name to go on the ballot. Getting the case before Black, however, represented a considerable problem. The Circuit Court route could not be bypassed entirely, since a Supreme Court Justice would be unlikely to hear a case alone until lower court avenues of appeal had been exhausted. "The problem was to get it up there in time in a way that would not result in a dismissal of it because it had not been passed on by the lower court," Fortas explained. "It would have been a mistake to go directly to the Supreme Court, to Justice Black, and bypass the [Circuit] Court of Appeals." But if they took the case to the Circuit Court—to a single judge of that court—the case might be delayed there until it was too late for a ruling by Justice Black to help. "A way had to be devised in getting a very quick hearing from the Court of Appeals," Fortas says.

Fortas told the assembled attorneys that he had thought of a way—a very risky way. In the first place, he said, no affirmative action at all should be asked from the single Circuit Court judge: that would complicate the matter and make a delay in the judge's decision more likely. The only relief asked should be for a simple stay of the injunction on jurisdictional grounds—the issue on which a single judge would be most un-likely to overrule a fellow judge; the issue, in other words, on which an unfavorable ruling to their side was most likely. Then, Fortas said, they should try to make an unfavorable ruling even more likely by presenting to the judge not a strong argument, detailed, full and persuasive, but a weak one, a plea offered in what Fortas called "a summary way," a way that was not particularly convincing. And to further ensure an unfavorable ruling they should try to select as the single judge not, as the other lawyers had been suggesting, a judge who seemed predisposed to rule for their client, but rather a judge seemingly predisposed to rule against him. The combination of these steps, Fortas said, was the best way of obtaining a quick decision from a Circuit Court judge—a decision that would be un-favorable, but that would be fast, fast enough to allow Johnson's lawyers then to present his case to Justice Black, and to be able to tell Black that the case had already been appealed (and lost) in Circuit Court. Before Fortas arrived, Johnson's roomful of attorneys had been trying to decide what was the strongest case they could present to a Circuit Court judge. Fortas was suggesting they present to that judge not the strongest case, but the weakest. Under his plan, the object was not to try to win in Circuit Court, but to lose—fast. Lyndon Johnson had two forums in which he might win an appeal from Davidson's decision—the full Circuit Court and then, if unsuccessful there, the Supreme Court. Abe Fortas was suggesting that he rely on only one, that, in fact, the first forum be surrendered—by deliberately losing in Circuit Court. He was suggesting that everything be staked on the gamble that Black would agree to hear the case as a single Justice—and that Black would, after hearing it, rule for them.

Deciding whether to adopt his plan was not, Fortas was to say, "par-ticularly difficult" on the "legal aspects" of the case. "What that [decision] mostly required was courage," he says. "A man's political life was at stake." His suggestion, he was to recall, "was not a conventional course of action. Lawyers like to do things by the book—*B* comes after *A*—and here we are skipping right through to *Z*." Moreover, the dangers involved in his plan were, he concedes, "tremendous." By forgoing the chance to have the Circuit Court rule, Johnson would be gambling everything on Black. "You're doing a one-shot instead," Fortas was to say, and if you lose on that shot, "You lose everything." But the "most brilliant legal mind ever to come out of the Yale Law School" had sliced its way through the other lawyers' verbiage to the heart of the matter. "Skipping right through to *Z*" was the only possible way that Johnson's name could appear on the ballot. So when Fortas had finished talking, there was dead silence. Not one of the previously voluble lawyers ventured so much as a com-ment. "Everyone was delighted to have me take the responsibility," For-tas was to recall with a tight, sardonic smile. But Lyndon Johnson was a leader of men. The silence was broken by the voice—hard, flat and decisive—of the man whose "political life was at stake," the man who would "lose everything" if Fortas' gamble failed.

"Let's do what Abe says," Lyndon Johnson said.

Fortas asked for a secretary, and went into an adjoining room. In what seemed an astonishingly short time he had returned with a one- or two-page outline of a brief. "That's all you need," he said.

THE NEXT DAY, they did what Abe had told them to do. Luther Jones translated Fortas' draft into a formal brief. The man known as "the finest appellate lawyer" in Texas considered himself honored to be allowed to work on a brief outlined by Abe Fortas. Jones was, as one magazine put it, "the man with probably the finest technical knowledge in the state," but he knew enough to know how his expertise compared with Fortas'. "It was a thing of beauty to watch the way he handled it," Jones would say. "He listened to all of us for perhaps an hour, took all our work and got a secretary, and in ten minutes came back with a very brief proposition. . . . You see, a super-expert doesn't need to beat around the bush. He knows exactly what needs to be done, and he does it." Jones himself flew—in a Brown & Root plane—to New Orleans to file the brief with the clerk of the Fifth Circuit Court of Appeals. Analyzing previous rulings by the court's six judges, a group of attorneys assembled by Tommy Corcoran in Washington found, in Judge Joseph C. Hutcheson of Houston, a jurist whose record strongly suggested an almost out-of-hand rejection of Johnson's plea; Hutcheson had once held, in fact, that a stay of a lower court injunction required the concurrence of at least three Circuit Court judges. In line with Fortas' strategy, therefore, it was to Hutcheson that Johnson's attorneys applied for a stay of Judge Davidson's injunction, and Hutcheson agreed to hear the application.

And in the event, the court fight unfolded precisely as Abe Fortas had predicted it would. At the conclusion of a four-hour hearing in his chambers in the federal Courthouse in Houston on Friday, September 24, Judge Hutcheson caused consternation in the Johnson camp by announcing that he would take the case under advisement. But the advisement lasted only five hours—for Lyndon Johnson, of course, five terrible hours of waiting: what if the judge delayed his decision too long? Summoning the attorneys back to his chambers that same evening, however, Hutcheson handed down his decision—the decision Fortas had forecast. Had Johnson's attorneys asked "that something affirmative be done," the matter would be more complicated, Hutcheson said, but "if you merely ask that" the injunction be stayed, "I can't do it. I am only one individual. I can't act independently" of the entire court in overruling another judge.

"It is quite clear that I, as a single circuit judge, have no power and ought not set aside or stay the injunction." The leaders of Johnson's Washington legal corps—Corcoran and the three senior partners of Arnold, Fortas and Porter—thereupon telephoned Justice Black at his home in Alexandria, Virginia, on Saturday to ask if he would hear their application for a stay of the injunction. Black agreed to do so, setting the date for Tuesday, September 28, to allow time for Stevenson to arrange for legal representation at the hearing.

HARRY TRUMAN'S campaign train pulled into San Antonio early Sunday morning, September 26. Waiting at the station to greet the President was a crowd of politicians—including one so altered in appearance since he had left Washington in May to begin his campaign for the Senate that Jonathan Daniels, who had not seen him in the intervening months, was startled when Johnson boarded the train. "I think the most dramatic time I ever saw Lyndon Johnson was on that trip," Daniels was to recall. ". . . He came aboard, looking like the damnedest tramp I ever saw in my life. He couldn't have shaved in at least two days, and he looked sick as hell. . . . If he lost at that point, he was pretty well licked for the rest of his life. He was going to be a great man or just another Texan, and at that point he didn't know and nobody else knew which it was going to be." Someone handed him a large drink of Scotch. His hands shook as he drank it. Johnson had been standing with other dignitaries, but went over to the crowd and began shaking hands—as if he couldn't stop.

For Lyndon Johnson, Monday was a day of applause. Whatever Truman's feelings toward him had been before, Texas was indispensable to the President's own re-election chances in 1948, and two of the men most important if he was to carry Texas were on the train with him: Sam Rayburn and Tom Clark. And, as Evans and Novak were to put it, "for all of his conservative transgressions during the 80th Congress, Lyndon Johnson would be infinitely preferable to the adamantly conservative Coke Stevenson in the Senate." And there were more immediate considerations: the President was anxious to keep Texas from joining Strom Thurmond's States Rights rebellion, and the people identified as States Righters in Texas were Stevenson's supporters. At stop after stop, the President, with Johnson standing beside him on the back platform, told the crowds, "My advice to you is to go to the polls on Election Day and send Lyndon Johnson to the Senate."

But there was another sound that day, too: the rap of gavels in South Texas courthouses. For a race began on this Monday, September 27, 1948—a race which would determine Lyndon Johnson's future. It was run in two little courthouses in the Rio Grande Valley and, two thousand miles

to the north, in the gleaming marble temple of the United States Supreme
Court in Washington, D.C. The two Masters in Chancery appointed by
Judge Davidson—William Robert Smith, for thirteen years United States
Attorney for the Western District of Texas, and J. M. (Mac) Burnett, one
of Smith's longtime deputies—issued subpoenas on Monday morning requiring election officials of Jim Wells, Duval and Zapata counties to appear before them and produce their counties' ballot boxes, poll lists and
tally sheets. The subpoenas were returnable that very afternoon: at three
p.m. that day, Smith would begin the Jim Wells hearing in Alice, while
Burnett simultaneously opened one in San Diego, the Duval County seat.
The testimony of witnesses would be taken expeditiously, the two Masters
announced; their hearings would be completed by Friday so that their
official written reports could be submitted to Davidson by the Saturday,
October 2, deadline the judge had set. In Washington, Justice Black's
hearing would not begin until Tuesday. Abe Fortas had assured Lyndon
Johnson that Black's ruling would be favorable because of the jurisdictional grounds, but favorable or not, the ruling might come too late. If
the poll lists and tally sheets were examined and the ballot boxes opened,
and if the evidence in them, combined with witnesses' testimony,
proved—proved definitively in public, in court, in a sworn, official record
summarized in the Masters' official reports—that in Jim Wells and Zapata
counties hundreds of votes, and in Duval County thousands, that had been
counted in Lyndon's column were not votes at all but simply figures added
to tally sheets on the whim of election judges, not even a Supreme Court
ruling could save his reputation. A ruling might not, in fact, be able even
to save his seat: *pro forma* though most Senate investigations of elections
might be, how could the Senate ignore proof—official, sworn, court records—of such patent illegality?

All that Monday and Tuesday, therefore, Johnson's attorneys in both
Valley courthouses employed delaying tactics—abetted by further demonstrations of the difficulty of obtaining evidence in a land outside the
law. The Masters' subpoenas had behind them the full authority of a federal court, but when United States marshals attempted to serve them on
election officials they were, in most cases, unable to do so. The witnesses
had disappeared. In Duval County, for example, more than fifty witnesses
had been subpoenaed. Only eight could be located; many of the others,
including election judges and clerks and County Democratic Committee
Chairman Campbell King, were reported to be "on vacation"—in Mexico,
where, of course, United States subpoenas had no force.

In Jim Wells County, subpoenas had been issued for three key election officials. When Smith gaveled his hearing to order in the Jim Wells
County Courthouse, Marshal W. W. Ainsworth reported that not one of
the three could be found. The most important official, Tom Donald, who

had had custody of the election records and had refused to open the bank vault to allow Coke Stevenson's attorneys to inspect them, had apparently left town that very morning—just about the time the subpoenas had been issued, in fact. And when Smith, over Everett Looney's objections, began to probe into Donald's whereabouts ("The Court" wants to "lay [its] hands on those records"), the Federal Master was informed that Donald had left town without telling even his wife where he was going or when he might return. That night, Donald telephoned her to say he was across the border in Mexico; he gave her no hint where in Mexico, however, or "what he was going to do" there, or how long he was planning to stay.

Those witnesses who were located, moreover, were in general somewhat less than helpful when they took the stand. Duval's County Judge, Dan Tobin, testified that he did not know the names of ten of the county's eleven precinct election judges—or any information to speak of about poll taxes, election returns or any other aspect of the election. Another Duval official said that "yes, many several thousands" of poll tax receipts had been financed by outside parties. He could not, however, recall who these outsiders were.

The evidence had disappeared, too. If any piece of evidence was crucial, it was the poll list and tally sheet from Jim Wells' Precinct 13. Coke Stevenson's lawyers, who had seen these documents, were convinced that if they were produced in court, their contents would prove beyond doubt that the election had been stolen for Lyndon Johnson.

The law required three copies of those documents: one copy sealed in the Precinct 13 ballot box along with the ballots, one copy in the custody of the secretary of the County Democratic Committee, and one in the custody of the presiding judge at that precinct, Luis Salas. Committee Secretary Donald, of course, was missing, but now Salas, previously missing, allowed himself to be found and served with a subpoena. As Stevenson and his attorneys, sitting in court, watched the burly former *pistolero* swaggering to the stand, they believed they were close at last to obtaining the proof they had been seeking.

They were wrong. Salas was quite relaxed as one of Stevenson's attorneys, C. C. Renfro, questioned him; he seemed to regard the proceedings almost as a joke. Renfro took him through the election procedure, and elicited from him the fact that he had indeed made the three required copies of the poll and tally documents, placing them in large manila envelopes, about two feet square, and had indeed put one copy in the ballot box, given one to the Democratic officials, and kept one himself.

And, Renfro asked, where is the one that you kept yourself?

"It is lost," Salas replied.

Salas had a further revelation to make. It emerged as he was explaining the circumstances under which he had lost his copy of the records. Following the election, he said, "there has been so much talk about this Box 13" that on September 15 he had decided to compare his copy with Donald's. "You see, I had been hearing a lot of talking that there was something wrong with the election. The election was level, nothing wrong with the election. I went to get the copies from Tom Donald to compare with mine." After Donald gave him the committee's copy, Salas said, he put both copies in his car and drove to a bar in Alice, the Baile Española. "I stayed there from five, I guess, until nine-thirty, something like that, and when I come back they [had] stole[n] everything from the car."

This revelation did not sink in for a long moment. Then Renfro asked, you mean "your copy and Donald's copy, too?—*both* lists were stolen? *Both* are lost?"

"Yes, sir," Salas said. The poll list and tally sheet that Coke Stevenson and his aides had seen at the bank had disappeared.

Salas had a few more points to make under questioning. He had indeed gone to the *Alice News* on the night of the primary, he said, and he had indeed seen the reporter Cliff DuBose there. But, he said, he had never told DuBose how many votes Johnson or Stevenson had received that day. "I never say *anything* about how many votes anybody got." According to Salas' testimony, DuBose was a rather uninquisitive reporter. "Did he ask you?" Renfro demanded in a voice that was by now indignant. "No, sir," Salas replied. Renfro, outraged, next asked Salas about the report that two hundred votes had been added. "It is not true," Salas said. Absolutely unruffled, he left the stand with a broad grin, to shouts from the crowd of "Viva, Luis Salas! Viva, Indio!"

THE SAME PATTERN of disappearing evidence was unfolding in Duval County as well—in Duval, where thousands of votes were at issue. Only eight of the fifty Duval election judges and clerks subpoenaed had been found, but as George Parr sat listening to their testimony, he may have felt that even eight was too many. For their testimony reinforced the widespread belief that in his county "they didn't vote 'em, they just counted 'em."

One of the eight was the presiding election judge at Precinct 6, Ernesto Benavides. He testified that after the polls closed on Primary Day, he made the required three copies of the poll and tally lists, placed two of them in the locked ballot box and left one, his own, at the schoolhouse at which the voting had been held. And where is your own copy now, he was asked. "I do not know," he said. When he had returned to the school four or five days later to look for it, "it was lost."

Burnett, the Federal Master, interrupted—quite sharply—to take over the questioning himself. Were the ballots from your precinct actually counted and included in the official total from the county? the Master asked. At first, Benavides replied, "I don't know." Then he hesitated. In front of him, in the crowded little courtroom, George Parr sat waiting to hear his answer. "Oh, yes, the votes from Precinct 6 were counted," Benavides said.

How was that possible? the Master demanded. You testified that the results had been given to Campbell King at the Courthouse that evening. "How did the county chairman obtain the returns from your box if you left a list at the school and the other two were in the locked box?"

"I do not know," Benavides replied.

Stevenson's lawyers believed a similar situation had existed at most of the other ten Duval precincts. During the three weeks since Coke's trip to Alice, they had found a surprisingly large number of men and women in the Valley willing to brave George Parr's wrath, and they had affidavits which they felt proved that few if any of the ten precincts had so much as bothered to file returns with county officials. Parr and his boys had simply written down any numbers they pleased, giving Johnson whatever totals the candidate or his aides said were needed: that was the explanation for the hundred-to-one majority; only the lack of sufficient poll tax receipts had stopped Parr from giving Johnson even more votes.

In Zapata County, there was a change in the wording of the script. Instead of the word "lost," synonyms were employed: "gone," for example, and "missing." There was, however, no change in the basic plot.

The key precinct in Zapata was Number 3, where the late correction six days after the primary had given Johnson forty-five crucial additional votes. The records from all four of the county's precincts, contained in four large manila envelopes, had been given to the County Judge, Manuel Bravo, by the county Democratic chairman, Josefa Gutirez, in Bravo's office. Mrs. Gutirez testified that when she—and the records—were subpoenaed by the Federal Master, she had gone to Judge Bravo's office to get the records back and bring them to the hearing. Judge Bravo had thereupon given her envelopes—three envelopes. They were from Precincts 1, 2 and 4. "I put four in and there were only three," Mrs. Gutirez said. "I don't know what happened to the other. . . . I didn't even know it was missing." Called to the stand, Judge Bravo said he didn't know, either. He had put four in his filing cabinet, he said, but when he went to get them, there were only three. "Number 3 was gone." Its "returns were missing."

Nonetheless, the two Masters did not let the missing witnesses and evidence stop their investigation. In the Jim Wells County Courthouse, for example, Stevenson attorney Josh Groce, after hearing Salas testify that the first two copies of the crucial poll list had been lost, told Smith, "Sir, I would like to suggest that there is one other copy of this poll list that is available. That is the one in the ballot box; and I would think that Your Honor, under the order of this court, would have the right to bring that ballot box into this court here, open the ballot box and take out only the poll list . . . and we request the commissioner [Master] so to do."

Johnson's lawyers leaped to their feet, Looney protesting that only "an express order of the District Court" could authorize the opening of a ballot box, Tarleton, his shock of shaggy white hair awry as he stamped around the courtroom, his arms extended upward as if to call the heavens to witness this contemplated injustice, invoking broader grounds: for a federal official to open a state ballot box, he shouted, would be a return to "the evil days of Reconstruction. . . . There is still the doctrine of states' rights. . . . Those ballot boxes . . . are secure in their sanctity under the law of this state and are not the subject of invasion by outside authority." But Smith was firm. "I have the power to order the United States Marshal to impound those ballot boxes, and the Marshal is so ordered," he said. Writing out the order, Smith handed it to Marshal Ainsworth, who served it on the County Clerk in his office down the corridor, and before the close of court Monday, twenty ballot boxes that had been used in the county's seventeen precincts had been carried in by janitors and piled up in front of Smith's bench. Some of the cylindrical, rather battered tin drums with removable tops (voters had placed their ballots in the drums through slits in the covers) were labeled with precinct numbers, some were not. Some of the drums were padlocked, some were padlocked but with keys dangling from the padlocks, some were unlocked. Presumably the twenty included the box or boxes from Precinct 13. Coke Stevenson, sitting motionless at a counsel table, may have felt that there in front of him, not five feet away, was the evidence he had sought for so long. One of Lyndon Johnson's allies had said it was Johnson's "major purpose . . . not to permit the opening of Box 13." Now a Federal Master had ordered Box 13 to be brought into court, and it was in the custody of a United States Marshal—ready to be opened. Whatever the condition of those tin drums—locked or unlocked, labeled or unlabeled—one of them either would or would not contain that last copy of Precinct 13's poll list. If the list was found, proving the legality or illegality of the two hundred decisive votes would be swift and relatively easy. If the list was not found, such proof would be difficult, but, in the opinion of the Master on whose report Judge Davidson would base his decision on making the injunction permanent, the mere fact that all copies of the list had disappeared would be highly significant. Monday had been a day of applause for Lyndon Johnson. There would be no applause on Tuesday. No crowd noise would obscure the rap of the gavels. The campaign would have narrowed to that race in court. On that Tuesday, in Alice, Texas, a Federal Master would begin opening the ballot boxes that were the heart of the investigation into Lyndon Johnson's senatorial campaign. On that same day, in Washington, D.C., Justice Black would be deciding whether to halt that investigation or to allow it to continue.

THE STARTING TIME in both Washington and Alice on Tuesday was nine-thirty in the morning, but, because of the different time zones, the hearing in Washington began an hour earlier. So close was the race that that sixty minutes' lead might make the difference. Filing into Hugo Black's walnut-paneled, book-lined chambers in the Supreme Court Building Tuesday morning was Lyndon Johnson's first team: Wirtz, Allred and four prominent New Dealers—Fortas, Thurman Arnold, Paul A. Porter and Hugh Cox. Appearing alone for Stevenson was Dan Moody, who had disdained the help of younger attorneys; the civil rights issue—the key issue that authorized federal jurisdiction, in the opinion of the young lawyers assisting Stevenson—was never raised. Sitting in a semicircle around the Justice's desk, as Black rocked in his swivel chair, the attorneys presented essentially the same arguments they had been repeating for a month in lower courts. Moody said the issue was fraud, whether it had been committed on Lyndon Johnson's behalf and whether Johnson should be allowed to benefit from it; in ordering the Masters' hearing, Moody said, Judge Davidson had been attempting "to prevent the reaping of a harvest from the perpetration of a fraud." Fortas said the issue was jurisdiction: election contests were "irrevocably and incontestably vested" in Texas state law and should not be supervised by a federal court. Weighing in with an argument that had significant political connotations during a year in which the balance of power in the United States Senate might hinge on Texas, Wirtz warned that if Stevenson succeeded in keeping Johnson's name off the ballot, "There will be no name of a Democratic nominee. The Republican nominee . . . will be the only candidate on the ticket."

Down in the Alice Courthouse, Parr had stationed a deputy sheriff next to the telephone in the County Judge's office. Allred had been given the number of that phone, and told to call the instant Black announced a verdict, so that in case the verdict was favorable not a moment would be lost in stopping the Alice hearing. Parr had ordered the lines kept clear for a call from Washington.

All Tuesday morning, with the lawyers still arguing before Justice Black, the phone did not ring. But although Federal Master Smith had planned to open Ballot Box 13 as soon as he convened his hearing Tuesday morning, he was unable to do so, because the box first had to be identified—and the person called to the witness stand to identify it was Luis

Salas. Laughing and joking, to the appreciation of friends in the courtroom, Salas managed to do a thorough job of sowing confusion about
which of the twenty tin containers was Precinct 13's. As Stevenson and
his attorneys sat grimly watching, unable to speed the process, Salas said
that the ballot box into which he had placed the poll and tally lists was
not among the twenty that had been brought to court. (How he knew that
was unclear, since he also said that he had placed no identifying mark of
any kind on it.) Then he said that Precinct 13 had had not one but two
ballot boxes. Smith directed that Salas inspect the boxes. One by one—
slowly—he looked them over and found for each one some reason why it
was probably not from his Precinct 13. Finally he tentatively—very tentatively—identified two. Thanks to the delay he caused, although the arguments in Washington lasted for almost four hours, when they
concluded—at a little after one p.m. Washington time—and Black announced he would retire to consider his verdict, down in Alice none of
the twenty boxes had been opened. At about the time that Black retired,
Smith announced a recess for lunch. The outcome of the race—between
Black's decision and the opening of Ballot Box 13—was still in doubt.

During that lunch recess, Salas was informed that the two men who
had actually marked the ballots would be put on the stand. If they were,
Salas was to recall, he was sure "they would be indicted." He told Ed
Lloyd: "This investigation going bad for us, Ed." If the two men were in
legal danger, he said, "I am going to tell the truth."

"Don't say anything yet," Lloyd replied in panic. "Hold your
horses."

After lunch, Salas returned to the stand, but none of the boxes had
yet been opened when, on Tuesday afternoon, a clerk summoned Dan
Moody and Johnson's sextet of lawyers to Black's chambers. The Justice,
he said, was ready to announce his verdict.

Black agreed with Fortas. "It would be a drastic break with the past,
which I can't believe Congress ever intended to permit, for a federal judge
to go into the business of conducting what is to every intent and purpose
a contest of an election in the state," he said. The issue, he said, in an
obvious reference to the balance of power in the Senate, is of "supreme
public importance. Not only are the parties interested, but the whole State
of Texas and beyond the state." Black disagreed with Moody's contention
that Stevenson had no other recourse but the federal courts. "What about
the Senate?" he asked. "The Senate is the judge of the qualification of
its own members, finally." While, he said, "fraud, very reprehensible
fraud" had been charged, fraud was a criminal charge "punishable as
crime if the charges are sustained." Therefore, he said, "I am going to
grant a stay until the full Supreme Court has an opportunity to consider
it." Under the procedure in such hearings, Johnson's attorneys had to

draft the order granting the stay. Instructing them to do so, Black said he would sign the order on Wednesday.

Trotting, almost running out of Black's chambers, Allred telephoned Alice and San Diego to notify Parr's men of the verdict, and within minutes Smith recessed his hearing while he went into the County Judge's office and telephoned Judge Davidson in Fort Worth to ask for instructions.

Reporters had told Davidson of the verdict, but they did not know precisely what Black had ruled, and the District Court Judge had received no official notification. He did "not yet know the scope of Justice Black's action," Davidson told Smith, but if it merely stayed the injunction, the Masters' hearings, "being more in the nature of a trial on the merits, would have nothing to do with the injunctive matter." Informed that Black's order was not yet drafted, and that Black would not sign it until the following day, Davidson instructed Smith to proceed with his hearing. Returning to the courtroom, Smith did so—over the furious protests of Johnson's attorneys. And when, a few minutes later, Salas finally completed his identification of the ballot boxes, the Master said: "The court is going to open the ballot boxes."

Jumping to their feet again and rushing to the bench, shouting at Smith, Johnson's lawyers stalled almost frantically to keep the boxes closed, Tarleton repeating his arguments that opening them would violate state laws and statutes, Looney saying, "if the practice permits, and I think it does . . . we should like time" to appeal directly to Judge Davidson for a ruling about the opening of the ballot boxes. But Smith said: "I have made my ruling." He had been appointed to find out the truth about Precinct 13, he said. That required the poll and tally lists, and two of the three copies of those lists had been lost. "There is nothing left for me to do but to look to the third place where they are supposed to be, and, if they are there, to examine them." Tarleton shouted that because of Salas' testimony, no one could even be sure which of the twenty boxes were Precinct 13's. Smith admitted that the attorney was correct, but added that "if they [the two boxes Salas had identified] are not [Precinct 13's] then I am going to open the rest of them." He slammed down his gavel. In a voice that reporters called "stern," he said: "We will open all the boxes if necessary." The covers of the two tin drums identified by Salas were secured not by locks but by baling wire twisted through the padlock hasps. Smith had Marshal Ainsworth bring him a heavy pliers. With them, he untwisted the wire of the two drums, and then he took off their covers.

One of the two drums was indeed a ballot box from Precinct 13, Jim Wells County. Despite his efforts to confuse the court, Salas had testified that on Election Day he had signed the back of each ballot, and when Smith reached into this drum he found that the ballots inside were signed

"Luis Salas." Pulling seven out at random (they bore numbers from 229 to 1010), Smith asked Salas formally, "I ask you if that is your signature," and Salas acknowledged that it was. Then the Master looked through the ballot box. It contained hundreds of ballots. It did not contain a poll list, or a tally list.

The second of the two boxes was not from Precinct 13. It contained ballots from Precinct 4. There were still eighteen boxes piled up in front of Smith, and the Master was determined to find out for certain whether the crucial lists were in one of them. If the lists were not in one of those boxes—either because when the second Precinct 13 box was identified and opened, the lists were not inside, or because there turned out to be no other box from Precinct 13 in the pile—that would mean that the third copy of the lists had disappeared like the first two, and in Smith's opinion, this destruction of every copy of Box 13's records would be "the most potent piece of evidence" of the illegality of the returns that had elected Lyndon Johnson. When Salas, recalled to the stand, continued to maintain that none of the other eighteen boxes was the other box from his precinct, the Master recessed the hearing until nine-thirty the following morning, Wednesday, and announced that he would open the rest of the boxes then.

THROUGHOUT THAT EVENING, lawyers worked in Washington to draft the text of an order for Justice Black's approval, and on Wednesday morning they presented it to him. Black retired to study it.

Meanwhile, in Alice on Wednesday morning, the climax of the Master's hearing was at hand. Jamming the benches of the little courtroom and lining the walls in the rear and the sides were witnesses—the witnesses who had testified in Fort Worth that they had not voted in Precinct 13 despite the fact that their names were on the poll list, and dozens of others, including the two men Salas feared would be indicted if they were put on the stand. The witnesses had been told that they would be called to testify that day—as soon as the Master had finished opening the ballot boxes. And Luis Salas was in court again, and during the night his resolution had hardened: he would not allow his election clerks to take the blame; if they were called to testify, he would take the stand again and, this time, tell the truth.

In front of Lyndon Johnson's attorneys were the ballot boxes, behind them and all around them were the witnesses: they were surrounded by the evidence they had been fighting to keep out of the record. Desperately hoping for the arrival of Justice Black's order, they made a new time-consuming motion that required a ruling from Smith. Parr's deputy sheriff was again stationed in the County Judge's office down the hall from the courtroom, waiting for the phone call from Washington that would keep the rest of the ballot boxes from being opened. But the call still had not come. "Let's proceed," Smith said. Because—perhaps unsurprisingly—the keys to the padlocks on nine of the eighteen boxes were missing, Smith sent for a locksmith, who began working on the nine locks as Smith began opening the other nine boxes. At one point that morning the Master let his feelings show through. As he was about to open a box, one that Salas said was not from Precinct 13, Tarleton said, "We object to the opening of that box because a witness has positively testified it was not Box 13." "That witness testified to a lot of other things, too," Smith said dryly, opening the box. The stream of frenzied interruptions by Johnson's attorneys continued. When Smith looked at ballots to see which precinct number they bore, Looney objected to his "examining . . . ballots from other boxes." I'm just trying to see if they are Box 13, Smith replied. "A violation of the sanctity of the ballot box," Tarleton shouted. "You have impeached the verity of the ballot when you have opened the box." Smith kept proceeding through the boxes. At the start of that Wednesday morning, eighteen had stood between him and the proof he considered "most potent." One by one, that morning, the eighteen were being opened. First came the nine unlocked boxes. None contained the ballots from Precinct 13. There were nine to go, and by this time the locksmith had opened them. The phone call from Washington had not come. The race was very close now.

Shortly after noon, Smith recessed the hearing for lunch. When he reconvened, at one-thirty, that phone in the County Judge's office had still not rung. Pointing at the nine remaining ballot boxes, the Master said: "Let's pass [them] up, please." He had opened two—neither from Box 13—and was lifting the top from a third when, at one-fifty, the phone rang. Allred was on the phone. Justice Black had just signed an order directing that all proceedings in the case be stayed "until further order of the Supreme Court." Shoving his way through the spectators jamming the courtroom door, the deputy sheriff ran up to Dudley Tarleton and whispered to him. The white-haired attorney, oratorical tricks forgotten for once, leaped up and without a word to Smith ran behind the sheriff to the County Judge's office, where Allred told him that Davidson had received Black's order, and had sent a telegram to Smith (and to Federal Master Burnett, in San Diego) ordering them to halt their hearings. When Tarleton returned to the courtroom and informed Smith of this, the Master telephoned Davidson, who confirmed Tarleton's report. Resuming his seat on the bench, Smith said, "Judge Davidson has just instructed me to close this hearing and proceed no further." He did so. The race was over. The third copy of the poll list had not been found (and never would be), but because seven of the ballot boxes had not been opened, no one would ever be able to prove definitively that all three copies had vanished. The hearings ended in anticlimax. Smith told the courtroom that he would be unable even to file a report. "I hardly see how I could make any findings . . . on a record wholly incomplete," he said. "The testimony was not all in, and one of the parties had not been heard and the other party had been heard only in part. . . . As a matter of fact the plaintiff had just begun to develop the case when we adjourned." To this, Groce added a statement poignant to Stevenson's adherents. "I am so full of what went on in Fort Worth which Your Honor does not know about."

Well, Smith repeated, the whole record is not in.

"It will be," Groce said.

GROCE WAS WRONG. On October 5, the Supreme Court refused to hear Coke Stevenson's petition that it consider Black's stay of the injunction. On January 31, 1949, the Court rejected Stevenson's petition for a trial on the merits of the case. The hearing Judge Davidson had ordered would never be resumed. The remaining ballot boxes were never to be opened. The testimony of the witnesses who filed out of the Alice Courthouse—and out of the Courthouses in Duval and Zapata counties—without being heard was never to be heard. The federal courts' investigation of Lyndon Johnson's 1948 senatorial victory was over. Definitive proof that the decisive two hundred Box 13 "votes" had not been cast was never to be obtained. Proof that thousands of other votes from the Rio Grande Valley—votes indispensable to Johnson's election—were not votes at all but merely numbers written on a tally sheet by border-county *jefes* would never be obtained. Evidence that some of these votes were "cast" by dead men would never be presented in a court of law. Abe Fortas' strategy had worked with only a few minutes to spare. But it had worked.

All other investigations were, in effect, over, too. Stevenson asked the Justice Department and the FBI to investigate the election. Attorney General Tom Clark agreed to do so, but the investigation showed, as one analysis put it, "a notable lack of investigative and prosecutorial vigor." An historian has written: "The FBI investigation . . . disappeared without a trace." Attempts by Stevenson partisans to interest the FBI and Justice Department more deeply in the case resulted only in "a fancy dance without a serious investigation"—as was also the case with a *pro forma* Senate investigation of the Texas senatorial election. After Lyndon Johnson easily defeated Republican Jack Porter in the November election, he was seated in the Senate.

16

The Making of
a Legend

ALTHOUGH LYNDON JOHNSON was now a Senator, interest in the 1948 election did not die down, and in 1952, it was fueled by an incident which created a sensation in the media in Texas. It involved one of George Parr's Mexican-American *pistoleros*, Duval County Deputy Sheriff Sam Smithwick, who in 1949 had shot to death a news commentator on an Alice radio station who had attacked the corruption of the Parr regime. Sentenced to life imprisonment, Smithwick, in 1952, wrote Coke Stevenson from the Texas State Penitentiary at Huntsville. He said that in 1949 he had "recovered" the missing "Box 13" from the Parr aides who had originally been ordered to dispose of it. He had hidden it, he wrote, and could produce the ballot box "if you are interested." He asked Stevenson to visit him at Huntsville to discuss "this matter in detail."

Receiving the letter at his ranch, Stevenson set out for the prison, but stopped in Junction to call and notify prison officials he was coming. They told him not to bother. Sam Smithwick, they said, was dead. He had committed suicide in his cell by tying a towel around his neck, attaching it to the window bars, and then slipping off his bed. Smithwick's letter, reproduced on the front page of the *Dallas News*, made headlines— banner headlines—throughout Texas, particularly after, as the *Fort Worth Star-Telegram* reported, "some guards and prisoners at the penitentiary had talked of the possibility that Smithwick" had been murdered. "Somewhere," that article said, "the thief who stole election records from Precinct 13 in Jim Wells County after the 1948 senatorial election squirmed uncomfortably."* A dramatic cartoon in the *News* depicted a terrified Lyndon Johnson cowering under the sheets in his bed, while above him a huge ghost held a locked box labeled "Precinct 13." No evidence whatsoever was ever adduced to link Lyndon Johnson with Smithwick's death, and there is no reason to believe such a link existed. Nevertheless, so widespread throughout Texas was the speculation that the death might be connected with the 1948 election that, after attempting at first to ignore the issue, Johnson was forced to issue a statement saying that disclosure of Smithwick's letter appeared to be "a continuation of a fight by a group of disgruntled, disappointed people." Johnson's statement did not, however, end the speculation, and it helped to keep the story of Box 13 alive in Texas. Year after year, references to it continued to appear in the state's newspapers and magazines (a 1976 *Texas Monthly* article on "Historical Markers You Will Never See" referred to the "group of dead men, who had risen from the grave to cast their ballots in alphabetical order" for Lyndon Johnson). It had become an enduring part of the state's political history. And when Johnson moved onto the national stage, the story followed him.

The national spotlight began to turn in Senator Johnson's direction in 1951, when he was named Democratic "whip"—assistant floor leader— and as it turned, its glare fell on these vivid episodes down in the Valley. National news magazines reported, as did the *New York Times Magazine*: "Exactly 87 votes in Texas put Johnson in the position to do his present job." The country was told how, in what *Collier's* called "a fabulous political and legal melee," these votes had been cast. It was told how, in the words of *The Saturday Evening Post*, "Johnson's attorneys rushed into court and obtained an injunction to prevent eliminating any votes on the ground of . . . fraud," how he had won at the convention only through a 29–28 vote, how Justice Black's ruling made "it . . . too late to do anything else to keep Johnson's name off the ballot." The national spotlight, in fact, focused on that previously all-but-unknown kingdom from which those 87 votes had come, and on its ruler. A second *Collier's* article that same year, an article on George Parr titled "SOMETHING IS ROTTEN IN THE STATE OF TEXAS," said, "His power reaches into Washington," and began with a description of the 1948 election:

> The outcome astounded the state and stunned Stevenson's supporters—because for six days after the election . . . the ex-Governor had been adjudged the winner. Then a single precinct

* Publication of this letter intensified suspicions among Stevenson supporters that the twenty boxes brought into the Master's hearing had not included the box that contained the poll and tally lists, that only one of the two Precinct 13 boxes had been in court.

had tardily "corrected" its count by adding 203 [sic] votes in its official return—*all but one for Johnson!*"

Not a few of these articles, moreover, mentioned a nickname by which Johnson was sometimes known in Washington: "Landslide Lyndon." His introduction to the nation came complete with the nickname, and with its provenance. As he made his entrance onto the great stage of history, still in a relatively minor role, he entered with that story attached to him.

All during the 1950s, as Lyndon Johnson rose to power in the Senate and came to dominate it, his nickname, and the reasons behind it, punctuated major articles about him. When, in 1959, he began running for President, the spotlight intensified and details emerged. *Look* magazine, in a long two-part biographical article that listed the hurdles "likely to arise before Johnson in a campaign for the Presidency," included "an allegation of fraud in his first election to the Senate." Its author, Bill Davidson, interviewed Stevenson attorneys who had investigated in the Valley, and read some of the court transcripts. The article concluded: "There is no evidence that Johnson had anything to do with the admittedly peculiar goings-on in Jim Wells County. . . . Johnson did, however, sign a petition for a court injunction that stopped . . . eliminating any of Johnson's votes. Since that time his enemies have labelled him 'The Senator from the Thirteenth Precinct.' " Even favorable articles, such as a generally laudatory cover story in *Time* magazine, mentioned the "suspicious 87 votes" and the "notorious Box 13."

The presidency brought a spotlight more intense yet, and with that new intensity the 1948 election was elevated from being part of a cover story on Lyndon Johnson to a cover story itself. At the height of his popularity, in 1964, when he won his great election victory, on newsstands all over the country was "THE STORY OF 87 VOTES THAT MADE HISTORY," the cover story of *U.S. News & World Report*: "The 87 votes . . . set him on the road to the White House. . . . If they had gone the other way, Lyndon Johnson probably would not now be occupying the White House. . . ." There again were the pictures of the pile of ballot boxes, of Parr, of Hugo Black, of Lyndon and Coke, of Lady Bird with a sad smile; there again was the map of Texas, with Jim Wells County outlined in red.

Distrust of Johnson grew during his presidency until, as Richard Rovere was to write in *The New Yorker*,

It seems . . . to be a fact beyond dispute that no other President has ever had to live in an atmosphere so heavy with distrust and disbelief as Lyndon Johnson. . . . What may well be a majority of the American people are persuaded that the President is a dishonest and dishonorable man.

And as more and more articles appeared attempting to analyze his character and his reputation, many of them turned to the 1948 election for clues. In a way, the most perceptive of these analysts said, the oft-repeated stories about that election formed in themselves a foundation for the misgivings. Tom Wicker, concluding in 1983 that "After Lyndon Johnson . . . trust in 'the President' was tarnished forever," added: "Even had there been no war, it would not have been hard to distrust Lyndon Johnson. Hadn't he been elected to the Senate by only eighty-seven votes, widely believed to have been stolen in Texas's notorious Duval County?" As a President passes into history, the perception of his character can sometimes be summarized by a single anecdote. George Washington, with his reputation for honesty and integrity, is often simplistically linked with the probably apocryphal incident of the cherry tree and "I cannot tell a lie." Lyndon Johnson, passing into history, was also linked in the public consciousness with a single incident, not apocryphal—an incident summed up in a precinct number: "Box 13."

EVEN AFTER Lyndon Johnson's presidency—even after his death—bursts of news about "Box 13" would still from time to time make headlines across the United States. The most dramatic were occasioned by "Indio" Salas. For twenty-nine years after the election, Box 13's election judge—the man, in the opinion of Coke Stevenson's partisans, most directly responsible for the "87 votes that made history"—steadfastly refused to discuss those votes publicly or privately. But in a 1977 interview with reporter James W. Mangan of the Associated Press, Salas said that Stevenson's supporters had been correct all along. During his testimony in the Alice Courtroom twenty-nine years before, Salas admitted, he had lied. Now, he said, he wanted to tell the truth. "Johnson did not win that election," he said. "It was stolen for him." And, he said, he, Luis Salas, had participated in the stealing.

Three days after the election, he said, he was summoned to George Parr's office in San Diego, where he found the Duke, Ed Lloyd, Alice City Commissioner Bruce Ainsworth—and Lyndon Johnson. Johnson, according to Salas, told Parr: "If I can get two hundred more votes, I've got it won." Speaking to Salas in Spanish, Parr asked him to add the two hundred votes. Salas refused, he says, but agreed to certify the votes as accurate if someone else added them. "I told him I would certify them because I didn't want anybody to think I'm not backing up my party; I said I would be with the party to the end," he says. That night, at about nine o'clock, in an office on the second floor of the Adams Building in Alice, two other men whom he refused to identify because "they were just following orders" added the votes as he sat watching. "I was right there when they added the names," he told the Associated Press reporter. "They all came from the . . . poll tax sheet . . . I certified. . . . I kept my word to be loyal to my party." He did so, he said, despite misgivings about the identical handwriting. (Asked by the reporter why the handwriting had not been varied, he replied, "How? Only two guys? How they going to change it? The lawyers spotted it right away, they sure did.") Noticing, moreover, that the two men were adding the names from the poll tax sheet in alphabetical order, he warned Parr that it was "a mistake" not to "mix up" the names. But Parr was too arrogant to accept advice. "I told George Parr, and he wouldn't listen to me. I said, 'Look at the "*A*". You add 10 or 12 names on that letter. Why don't you change it to the other—*C* or *D* or *X*—mix 'em up.' [But] George said, 'That's all right.' George was stubborn. He would not listen to anybody. But it was stupid."

Salas confirmed all the suspicions of Coke Stevenson and his supporters. The two hundred votes were only some of the votes he had stolen for Lyndon Johnson, he said. On the witness stand, he had sworn that "The election was level, nothing wrong with the election." Now he told the Associated Press reporter that the election had not, in fact, been "level" even before the two hundred votes were added. On Election Day itself, he said, he had, in the Nayer School, "called out" as votes for Johnson votes that had, in fact, been cast for Stevenson.

The Associated Press story was picked up by the nation's leading news magazines and by newspapers all across the United States. Once again, after almost three decades, the dateline "ALICE, TEX." was on the front page of the *New York Times*; once again, in a thousand headlines, the familiar words were linked anew with Lyndon Johnson's name: "LBJ ELECTION 'STOLEN,' EX-OFFICIAL SAYS." There were again the same references to "the notorious Precinct 13," to "the notorious eighty-seven votes," the same reminders that, as *Newsweek* put it under the headline "HISTORY: LBJ ACCUSED," "suspicions have persisted that Lyndon Baines Johnson stole his way into the U.S. Senate."

By 1977, of course, the Lyndon Baines Johnson Library was in full stride as the guardian of Lyndon Johnson's reputation. It swung into action. Director Harry Middleton assured a Johnson biographer, Merle Miller, that Salas' assertions were untrue. "I know Johnson didn't do what Salas said because that would have been *dumb*," Middleton said. That was enough to convince Miller. In his biography, *Lyndon*, Miller was to write that Middleton's remark was "perhaps the best comment on the Salas story." Using the public relations expertise of two one-time Johnson aides, Liz Carpenter and George Christian, the Library announced that it would open five thousand pages of documents relating to the 1948 campaign. That was a lot of documents to be absorbed quickly, particularly by reporters unfamiliar with a rather complicated historical situation, so they could be excused for focusing on a "memo" from Johnson (actually a draft of a 1948 press release) denying the charges ("I am without knowledge concerning the ballots in either Duval, Jim Wells or Zapata Counties. . . ."), as if this press release had greater significance than any of a hundred others issued by both sides during the investigation.

Johnson's supporters focused on Salas' statement that Johnson had been present personally at the meeting in Parr's office. Walter Jenkins, Mary Rather and Charles Herring held a joint press conference to assure the reporters who had descended on Austin that his presence in San Diego would have been impossible. They insisted that Johnson had remained at his Dillman Street home in Austin for the four days after the election, keeping tabulations on the vote-counting. "I was there all the time," Miss Rather said. "Congressman Johnson hardly left the house, except once to go downtown." Jenkins said, "It would have been absolutely impossible for Mr. Johnson to have been outside Austin for the length of time it would have taken for him to go to Alice [sic]." Their statements were hardly conclusive—all three acknowledged that their recollections of the hectic days twenty-nine years earlier were based solely on their memories, unsupported by any diaries or other documentation, and it would have taken no more than a few hours for Johnson to make the short drive to the Austin airport and fly the two hundred miles to San Diego in a Brown & Root plane and then return—but no confirmation of Salas' statement on this point existed. Many of the follow-up newspaper articles treated his statement with skepticism. The story faded inconclusively away.

The focus on that single point, however, enabled Johnson's defenders to obscure the fact that it was the only unconfirmed point in Salas' statement. Reporters' skepticism about his other statements would, perhaps, have been reduced had they been more familiar with the overall record of the case, particularly the transcripts of the testimony given by other witnesses during the Federal District Court hearing in Fort Worth and the federal Master-in-Chancery hearings in Alice and San Diego. The reporters believed that in his 1977 statement Salas was making new revelations. Actually, Precinct 13's election judge was only confirming testimony that had been given by others during those hearings. The principal doubt surrounding that testimony had been the doubt he had cast by denying what these witnesses had said. Now Salas was admitting that his denials had been false.

ANOTHER DECADE LATER, in March, 1986, I located Luis Salas in Houston. He was living with his wife, Tana, in a comfortably furnished mobile home in the large, pleasant back yard of the house of his daughter, Grace, and her family. The man who opened the door of the trailer bore, at eighty-four, little resemblance to Parr's fearsome "Indio." He was no longer tall and broad but stooped and slender, with gray hair, eyeglasses and a gentle manner. Throughout the interview, he kept glancing anxiously toward his wife, who was sitting in the next room, obviously in poor health. But his eyes were keen, and he was mentally alert.

I was asking questions about the 1948 election when Salas suddenly said, "I have written it all down." Walking over to a trunk, he bent down stiffly and pulled out a manuscript—eighty-five pages of it typed, obviously by someone unsure of the rules of punctuation, with nine additional handwritten pages attached—and handed it to me. A paragraph near the beginning says: "Reader, I don't know if my story is to your liking, writing nonfiction is hard, I had no schooling, please excuse my spelling and grammar, but I had to write this book, to leave it to my family, when I go beyond, my time is running short, and I want to finish without adding or subtracting parts that are false, or invented by my imagination, no, everything has to be exactly the way it happened." The title of the manuscript is "Box 13."

The manuscript is actually an autobiography, written in 1979. It tells in detail the story of Salas' youth in the little Mexican town of Bermejillo, while Pancho Villa's Mexican Revolution was raging; how he learned Morse code at fourteen and became a railroad telegraph operator; how "my Indian blood" made him a fighter and his size and temper made him feared until "my character was hardboil, cinic and arrogant, and never looked for trouble but if trouble came to me, I was right there." When he was twenty-three, he wrote, he shot a man who later died of gangrene from the wounds. The man's relatives swore revenge, and he fled Durango. "I was to become the wandering Jew," he wrote. For years, working as a telegraph operator, he lived in lonely little shacks along the lines of the Mexican National Railways until, in 1936, he crossed the border into the United States and settled in Alice; "I missed the mountains, here was endless flatland." In 1940, he related, he met George Parr, whom he revered and who gave him money, and a car and badges—and made him his enforcer. "My life changed with the power invested on me. . . . Wearing a gun gave me sense of security, but very few times, I used the gun, most of the disagreements I had were resolved with my fists, I weighed 210 pounds. . . . As long as I live, I never forget this man, and when I gave him my word to stay by his side regardless, I meant it, so up to date I still worship his memory."

In his manuscript, Salas attempts to explain his motives for writing it. One, he says, was to "show people the corruption of politics." This explanation becomes less convincing as Salas talks, because of the pleasure in his voice and on his face when he says, "Any vote for Stevenson [smile] I counted for Johnson." But in the manuscript he also gives other motives which ring more true. In part, he stated, he wrote his "book" because he wanted his children to know the story of Box 13, and indeed of his whole life. "Now is the year 1979," he wrote. "I am running short of time, feel sick and tired, but . . . before I go beyond this world, I had to tell the truth. . . . My wife Tana know why [he certified the two hundred votes] for Lyndon Johnson but my three children, they don't know why, when they read my book, I hope they will understand, and find me free from blame, I am certain they are not going to be against me." Before he died, he wrote, he wanted to put down the truth for them. And in part, he stated, he wrote his "book" because he wanted history to know the story of Box 13—and his role in it. The elderly, frail Mexican-American man sitting in the trailer in Houston felt very strongly that he was a part of history—a small but, in his view, a vital part ("I had to certify" the crucial two hundred votes; "we put L B Johnson as senator for Texas, and this position opened the road to reach the Presidency")—and he had written it "exactly the way it happened" so that history would acknowledge his role. His story, he wrote, is the story of "How an Indian boy raised in the rugged mountains of Durango came to this country and was involved in one of the most notorious scandals of politics that opened the road for L B Johnson to reach the presidency of this country, this is history like it or not, nobody can erase these facts."

Salas' pride, moreover, was clearly hurt that when finally, in 1977, he told the Associated Press the story he had waited so long to tell, "many people did not believe." "The people have a good reason not believe what I wrote in the book," he admits in "Box 13." "The reason is that I lied under oath." But, he said, the story he told the Associated Press was "the true story." As for the Johnson Library, quoting at one point from the transcript (which he refers to as the "questionnaire") of the Masters' hearing, he stops and says: "Reader it is a long questionnaire if you willing to read it all go to the Lyndon Johnson Library in Austin, of course you don't find there that we stole the election for L B Johnson." Perhaps, he wrote, if he put all the facts down in detail, in a book, people would believe.

During the years since he had written the manuscript, he had several times made additions to it. In some of them, he expresses confidence that eventually he will be believed. "May be I pass away before I see my book published," he wrote, "but some day it will come out, because it is part of history of the United States and people have the right to know the exact truth." At other times, as he grew older, he was more pessimistic. At one point, he wrote in hand, "I have been having trouble to publish, some publishers don't believe what I wrote is the truth." Later still, he wrote, "One thing worries me, and it is that I won't be here to see my book published. My time is getting shorter and shorter every day that goes by. . . ."

In "Box 13," Salas mentions two other reasons for coming forward at last to tell the story he had concealed for so many years. One is that George Parr died. "I gave George my word to stay at his side to the end," he wrote. "That end came when George died, that released me from my promise. . . ." The other reason he gives is yet one more reminder of the force of the personality of the former Governor of Texas, and of its effect on people who hardly knew him.

Salas wrote about the moment in the hearing in Alice when the Federal Master announced that Justice Black had ruled and that the hearing was over. As the announcement was made, he wrote, "I looked at Coke Stevenson and that gave the shivers. . . . Still remember the look in his eyes, frustration, despair and desperation, when we all heard. At that moment I had pity and compassion for the man, we stole his well-deserved candidacy, and I thought for myself [that I] brought disaster to another man not involved in no way with my projects. . . . When I was going out, all my friends shouted viva Luis Salas, in other circumstances may be that could be welcomed, this time I did not feel anything but remorse, knew very deep on me that I had wronged another human being." During the intervening years, Indio Salas wrote, he had been unable to forget the look in the eyes of that strong, silent man, and ever since, "The only remorse I feel is . . . for what we did to Coke Stevenson."

Indeed, Luis Salas relates in "Box 13," Sam Smithwick was not the only deputy sheriff from Alice who wrote Coke Stevenson a letter. He, Luis Salas, had written him also, Salas says. "I wrote him a letter asking forgivings, but he never answered."

"I don't blame him," Luis Salas said.

WHATEVER SALAS' MOTIVES for writing "Box 13," that manuscript—and his interview with me—adds details to the story of the 1948 election. The manuscript names the men who he says actually added the two hundred votes—Deputy Sheriffs Willie Mancha and Ignacio ("Nachito") Escobar— and explains why Salas refused George Parr's request that he add the votes himself. "I did not want them in my handwriting"; certifying the votes involved merely "giving another total," so he agreed to do that. "That night in the dark corridors of the Adams Building a President of the United States was made." Parr called off names from the poll list, Salas wrote, asking him if the person had voted, and if Salas said the person had not voted, Mancha would add that name to the poll list while Escobar added a Johnson vote to the tally sheet. The manuscript explains the two added votes for Stevenson: after they reached the requested 200 figure, "Nachito was a jolly man full of jokes, he said, let us give this poor man [Stevenson] a *pilón* [gift], and he added two votes making a total of 202." As to whether he, Luis Salas, had on Election Night reported the Johnson total as 765, Salas wrote that of course he had: "I told Cliff Dubose . . . Dinky Price was there, and he heard me. . . . Price was right, so there you are if the investigation had continued, they could easily had me indicted. . . ."

I asked Salas if I could copy the manuscript, and when Salas agreed, we went to a nearby stationery store and copied it on a Xerox machine. "Everyone is dead except me, Robert," he said. "And I'm not going to live long. But Box 13 is history. No one can erase that."

ON THE POINT in his 1977 statement to the Associated Press on which attention had focused—whether or not Lyndon Johnson himself had come to George Parr's office to ask for two hundred more votes—Salas said that he had recognized Johnson because during Johnson's campaign trip to Alice, Salas had been ill in bed and Johnson's campaign workers had brought him to Salas' house to meet this man who was so important to his hopes in the Valley.

On this point, Salas could be lying. Or he could be mistaken—given his very imperfect English, that is a strong possibility; he may simply have misunderstood the introduction of the man who came to his home. Or, on that campaign trip to the Valley, a Johnson aide who physically resembled the candidate could have done in Salas' home what Joe Mashman did from the helicopter: pretend he was Johnson to someone who could not tell the difference. Or Salas could be telling the truth; Johnson might have come to San Diego himself to ask for votes.

But the point is not nearly so significant as Johnson's partisans made it appear.

Although there is still a dispute over whether Johnson asked in person for the final, decisive 200 votes to be added to his total, there can no longer, thanks to the confirmation, in Salas' manuscript and interviews, of the sworn testimony of others, be any reasonable doubt that 200 votes *were* added to that total—six days after the election. DuBose had testified that Salas had originally given the total as 765; Price had testified that it had been 765. The only doubt about that fact had been cast by Salas' denial when he had testified. And now Salas was admitting that he had lied: "I told Cliff [DuBose] 765."

The two hundred votes that "changed history" are, in fact, once one retreats from the headlines, significant only because of their decisive timing. There is, thanks to Salas, no longer any doubt that in his Box 13 alone far more than two hundred votes were stolen for Lyndon Johnson. Jimmy Holmgreen had previously said so: "I saw dozens of votes that were for Stevenson counted for Johnson." Ike Poole had previously said so. And now Salas was saying so: "If they were not for Johnson, I make them for Johnson."

Even Box 13 as a whole, notorious as it became in American political legend, is hardly unique. In that precinct, votes were counted for Johnson although they had actually been cast for Stevenson, and further votes were counted for Johnson although nobody had cast them at all. But "there were hundreds of Box 13s in the Valley." Duval County gave Johnson 4,622 votes, and even the rudimentary investigation cut short by Justice Black's order showed that a high percentage of those votes had never actually been cast at all. The testimony in Zapata County had been presenting the same picture. In the three counties investigated by federal Masters in Chancery, therefore, the evidence was overwhelming that a high percentage of the 7,279 votes counted in Lyndon Johnson's totals were not cast at all or were cast for Stevenson. Similar conditions had prevailed in Starr County, which had given Johnson 3,038 votes. And what of the rest of George Parr's domain: his key "boxes" in Corpus Christi that produced 3,000 Johnson votes, for example? What of Judge Raymond's Laredo? No investigation was conducted there, but no Johnson adviser in a position to know suggests seriously that the 5,544 votes Johnson received in Webb County were "level." As for San Antonio—San Antonio where Lyndon Johnson "rode the polls" on Primary Day himself to oversee the vast West Side—Johnson's deputies on the West Side themselves boast of the votes that were "switched" for him there, and the estimate most frequently given is 10,000. Not 87 votes "changed history" and not 200, but thousands—many thousands, in fact.

Did Johnson ask in person—or just over the telephone, or just through men like Wirtz and Looney and Clark—for these votes? Johnson's followers deny Luis Salas' contention that in the case of Box 13 Johnson asked in person. But that denial would be significant only if it proved not merely that those particular votes were not stolen at Johnson's personal request but that he had no personal knowledge of what was going on in the Valley as a whole, and in San Antonio. And nobody is seriously suggesting that.

IN 1983, the Lyndon Baines Johnson Library obtained another item that might have been of interest in analyzing the 1948 senatorial election. It was an oral history interview given in that year by William R. Smith, the Federal Master in Chancery who had presided over the Precinct 13 hearing.

Smith's oral history leaves little doubt as to what his report to Judge Davidson would have said, had not Justice Black's ruling forced him to terminate his hearing. More important, it makes a point that articles on the election almost invariably overlook, possibly because it was so completely blurred by Johnson's oratory. Salas' confession in 1977 that he had lied on the witness stand had come as no surprise to him, Smith told the oral history interviewer. "I thought at the time he was lying." When the precinct election judge had testified that he had gone to the *Alice News* office on the night of the primary and not given the precinct's election returns to the reporter, "I didn't believe a word of that, because that's what he went there for. . . . I figured what the hell was Salas doing there if he wasn't there to give them the election returns."

But the lie that he, the Master, had found most significant was Salas' statement that he had lost the poll list and other records of the election. "I didn't believe a word of it," Smith told the interviewer. "[He] kept telling how these poll lists had been stolen and misplaced" and "I didn't believe that." That lie, to Smith, was pivotal, because the failure to produce the records was, to his mind, the crucial point in the case.

There's one thing that kept going through my mind during that whole hearing, which I thought was probably the most potent fact in the case. . . . At the hearing before Judge Davidson, the hearing before that old Judge [Archer] in Austin, and the hearing before the State Democratic Committee, if Stevenson were wrong about the illegally added votes, all the Johnson forces had to do was to bring the election poll list and the election return [tally sheet] of Precinct 13 and show it to them, that there hadn't been anything added, but they never did it. They never did do it. And if they had wanted to defeat Stevenson in the hearing before me, all they'd have to do is bring the official poll records of Precinct 13 of that day's voting and put them before me as proof. Of course, they may have done it later, but I didn't think they were going to. They hadn't ever produced it anywhere else. And to me, that was the most potent fact in the whole case, the fact that they had not brought these things in. That would have been a perfect way to refute the allegation of Stevenson. But they never did do it.

He had opened the ballot boxes in the hope of finding the Precinct 13 poll list, Smith said, "but I didn't expect to find it. If I had found it, I probably would have fainted. I didn't think it was going to be in there"— and, of course, it wasn't.

And what would his report to Judge Davidson have said? Smith was asked. "What are your conclusions?"

"I was very much of the opinion that the Stevenson people were right. . . . I firmly believe and have for years that the election was stolen in Precinct 13. I'm now convinced that [the votes] were added, 202 of them, after the polls closed. . . . I think Lyndon was put in the United States Senate with a stolen election, and I think he and everybody else knew it."

This statement by the Federal Master in Chancery is the most definitive word available on Precinct 13, since his report would have been the basis for Judge Davidson's ruling on whether or not to keep Lyndon Johnson's name off the ballot. But it is a statement that, so far as can be determined, has never appeared in print.

IN THE LANDSCAPE of Lyndon Johnson's life, already littered with stolen elections, the 1948 election was simply one more detail. Its larger significance lay in the increased clarity it gave to certain aspects of his character.

Prior to his entrance into campus politics at San Marcos, "no one," as another student recalled, "cared about campus politics." Elections— for class offices or the Student Council—were casual affairs. But Johnson saw in those elections an opportunity to obtain a measure of control, small but pivotal, over the fate of some of his fellow students. At this "poor boys' school," a diploma was for many students the only hope of escape from a life of poverty and brutal physical toil on their families' impoverished ranches and farms, and in the Depression, campus jobs, with their tiny cash stipends, represented the only means by which these young men could stay in school and obtain their diplomas. Johnson saw a method by which the victors in campus politics could obtain authority to dispense those jobs. And to obtain this power that no one else had focused on, he did what no one else on the sleepy campus had done: created, out of a small social club, a disciplined and secret political organization. And when, because of his personal unpopularity, the club could not, despite his organizing, win elections, he taught unsophisticated farm boys how to steal elections (and how to win them by other methods: "blackmailing" a popular rival woman candidate out of a race over a meaningless indiscretion, for example; "things we would never have dreamt of if it hadn't been for Lyndon"). College Hill's pattern was repeated on Capitol Hill in 1933 and 1934. The "Little Congress" of congressional aides was a social organization. But Johnson saw in its presidency a means of entrée to men of power. Again there were repeated complaints, this time from fellow Little Congress members, that he had "stolen" elections ("Everyone said it: 'In that last election that damn Lyndon Johnson stole some

votes again' "). When, in 1933 and 1934, Johnson was accused of "stuffing" a ballot box, he was not yet represented by Abe Fortas, and his
accusers succeeded in accomplishing what Fortas prevented Johnson's
1948 accusers from accomplishing: opening the suspected ballot box.
When the Little Congress box was opened, it was found that the accusations against Johnson were true. Again, as at college, what he had done
was unprecedented: no one had ever stuffed a Little Congress ballot box
before. (And, perhaps no one would ever stuff one again, for after his
departure the organization quickly reverted to its easygoing social role;
*"My God, who would cheat to win the presidency of something like the
Little Congress?"*) In his first campaign for the Senate, he stole thousands
of votes, and when they proved insufficient ("He [O'Daniel] stole more
votes than we did, that's all"), his reaction was to try to steal still more,
and his failure in this attempt was due only to his irredeemable tactical
error, not to any change in the pattern: in making the attempt he tried,
unsuccessfully, to persuade George Parr to go further than even the Duke
of Duval had ever gone before; ("Lyndon, I've been to the federal penitentiary, and I'm not going back for you.") At each previous stage of his
career, then, Lyndon Johnson's election tactics had made clear not only
a hunger for power but a willingness to take (within the context of American politics, of course; the coups or assassinations that characterize other
countries' politics were not and never would be included in his calcula-
tions) whatever political steps were necessary to satisfy that hunger. Over
and over again, he had stretched the rules of the game to their breaking
point, and then had broken them, pushing deeper into the ethical and
legal no-man's-land beyond them than others were willing to go. Now, in
1948, in his dealings with the Valley, he was operating beyond the loosest
boundaries of prevailing custom and political morality. What had been
demonstrated before was now underlined in the strongest terms: in the
context of the politics that was his life, Lyndon Johnson would do whatever was necessary to win. Even in terms of a most elastic political morality—the political morality of 1940s Texas—his methods were amoral.

AT FIRST—as long as an investigation of the result of the 1948 election
was still a possibility—Johnson's reaction to what had happened was defensiveness. No sooner had he been safely seated in the Senate, however,
than the defensiveness faded and was replaced by boasting.

    As was customary with Johnson, the reaction was embodied in homey
anecdotes and jokes—particularly in one joke, source unknown, which
had begun circulating in Texas almost as soon as the election was over.
Lyndon Johnson brought it to Washington and popularized it, telling it at
Georgetown parties, in the Senate cloakroom, on the Senate floor; re-

peating it even to reporters, who printed it. The story was related with evident enjoyment, and with the flair of a master storyteller, complete with accent. The accent was that of a small Mexican-American boy, named, variously, Manuel or Jesus. As Lyndon Johnson told the story, Manuel was sitting on a curb in a little town near the Mexican border one day and crying, when a friend came up and asked him what the trouble was.

"My father was in town last Saturday, and he did not come to see me," Manuel replied.

"But, Manuel, your father has been dead for ten years."

Manuel just sobbed louder. "*Sí*, he has been dead for ten years. But he came to town last Saturday to vote for Lyndon Johnson, and he did not come to see me."

The reaction was also embodied in an imitation, carried off with the flair of a great mimic. The imitation, performed at Georgetown dinner tables and in Senate Office Building hideaways, before audiences that included fellow Senators and reporters, was of George Parr. Cranking up an invisible old-fashioned two-piece telephone, Johnson would pretend to be Parr calling on Election Night, and shouting over the staticky connection between South Texas and Austin: "Lyndon, this is George. George Parr! Can you hear me, Lyndon? Can you hear me?" Johnson would then act out his own role. "Yes, yes, go ahead, George." Then Johnson would imitate Parr reporting the election results, always ridiculously lopsided in favor of Johnson. "Well, thank you, George," Lyndon Johnson would say with a grin. "That's mighty nice."

The imitation was "one of Lyndon Johnson's sidesplitting acts," Hugh Sidey would write. "Johnson was funny imitating Parr. The thought of Parr was funny."

And, of course, Johnson's reaction was embodied in his nickname. The identity of the coiner of that nickname cannot be definitively established, although it may have been Lyndon Johnson himself. But Johnson was among those who popularized it and made it a familiar part of the slang of insider Washington. "From the start, he disarmed suspicious senators he did not know by sticking out a hand and saying, 'Howdy, I'm Landslide Lyndon,' " Alfred Steinberg, a Capitol Hill reporter and Johnson biographer, was to write. During the first weeks after Johnson returned to Washington following the election, fellow Senators and friends would pick up the telephone to hear him drawl, "This is Landslide Lyndon calling."

Within a very short time, he stopped using the nickname, came to dislike it, and more than once flew into a rage at someone who used it. But it was too late to erase it from Washington's consciousness: the nickname was too vivid, and it had been circulated too widely, for it to be forgotten. And, of course, he never completely stopped telling the 1948-related anecdotes and jokes, and doing the sidesplitting George Parr imitation. Most contested intra-state elections are not items of intense interest in Washington: who, for example, would remember even a year or two later that another new Senator elected in 1948, Robert Kerr of Oklahoma, had also been charged with election irregularities? Loud though Kerr may have been on most subjects, he was discreet on that one. Texas's 1948 campaign had never been followed particularly closely in Washington except by Johnson intimates; awareness of that campaign would normally have faded fairly quickly. Instead, awareness grew—and became vivid. The campaign became a staple of Washington conversation. The joke, the anecdotes and the nickname had made it well known, had kept it in Washington's mind. Johnson's repetition of the anecdotes had, moreover, let Washington know that there was at least some truth in Stevenson's charges: Johnson's portrayal of Parr's telephone calls, for example, would hardly have led a listener to believe the charges were untrue. And the man who was repeating the joke and the anecdotes over and over, year after year, was the man accused of stealing the election. If there was anyone in Washington political circles who didn't know that the 1948 campaign was a good story, it was not Lyndon Johnson's fault. And everyone *did* seem to know. It was at least in part because of him that those first magazine articles in 1951 and 1952 which brought him to the nation's attention focused so strongly on that campaign. As years passed, the campaign became a minor American political legend, a legend with a decided tint of crookedness. And for some years the memory was kept vivid by the very man who had allegedly done the stealing. People hearing him reminisce about the campaign, or watching the grins and winks with which he joked and talked, could hardly escape getting the impression that the election *had* been stolen, and that he was not ashamed of that fact. Far from it. The impression he conveyed was of a politician who had outsmarted an opponent, done something illegal, and hadn't been caught. The impression he conveyed was of a man who not only was unashamed of what he had done, but who was proud of it—who boasted about it.

Among Washington insiders, of course, Lyndon Johnson had long been known as a political manipulator, a "wheeler-dealer." But this image had been unknown to the public at large—because Lyndon Johnson had been unknown to the public at large. So, by relating the 1948 campaign in detail, magazines first conveyed to a nationwide public the impression of Johnson as a manipulator, a schemer, a somewhat unprincipled and unscrupulous wheeler-dealer, of a deceiver proud of his deceits. First impressions are strong, and hard to dispel.

The image would, of course, become very important to Johnson's later career. But even more important was the fact that he had deliberately created and cultivated the image—because it was the image he wanted to project. The poignant reason he had wanted this image—the reason it had been terribly important to Lyndon Johnson that he be known as calculating, shrewd, tough, hard, ruthless, "practical" in even the most uncomplimentary connotations of that word—was all too easy to understand to anyone familiar with his heredity and with the carefully concealed circumstances of his terrible youth. He had been a "Johnson": a member of a family despised because it did not possess, in the term that mattered most in the Hill Country, "common sense." In particular, he had been the son of a man whose honesty and idealism had led him into ruin and disgrace and the road-building gang—and had led his son into the road gang, too. Lyndon's little brother, who understood Lyndon so well, said, "It was most important to Lyndon not to be like Daddy." Lyndon Johnson had to prove that he possessed the "common sense" his father had lacked. He needed respect for his pragmatism—needed it passionately—even if obtaining it meant portraying himself as a wheeler-dealer, a politician in the worst sense of the word. Had the public been aware of the humiliations of the early life of Lyndon Johnson, there might have been at least a measure of understanding of the pain-filled motivations behind the image. But there was no such understanding. There was only the image.

Alvin Wirtz had been worried that Coke Stevenson's lawsuit would "black mark" Lyndon Johnson. In a sense, Lyndon Johnson had black-marked himself.

WHEN, IN THE mid-1950s, Johnson began maneuvering for the presidency, he attempted to dispel the impression he himself had done so much to create of the circumstances surrounding the 1948 election. By 1964, running against Barry Goldwater, he was stating that the 1948 election had been honest, and that his margin of victory had been the result of Lady Bird's last-minute telephoning. But he was never to be able fully to restrain himself from gloating about his cleverness in defeating Coke Stevenson. In 1967, a Texas journalist and longtime critic who was writing a biography of Johnson, Ronnie Dugger, interviewed the President in his bedroom in the White House.

The topic was not the 1948 campaign, but Johnson, "rambling about other subjects," suddenly interrupted himself and told Dugger he wanted to show him something. Going into Lady Bird's adjoining bedroom, he rummaged through a closet and after five or ten minutes returned "beaming," holding a photograph. The photograph is of five smiling men gathered around the front hood of an automobile with a "Texas-1948" license plate. Balanced on the hood of the car is a ballot box, marked "Precinct 13." The men are Ed Lloyd, the attorney who ran Jim Wells County for

George Parr, and who was Johnson's leader there; Parr's cousin, Givens Parr; County Sheriff Hubert Sain; Sain's immense, pistol-carrying deputy, Stokes Micenheimer; and another Johnson ally in Jim Wells, Barney Goldthorn. As Johnson returned with the photograph, Dugger was to write, "he held it forward to me with a kind of pride. . . . The President watched my face as I searched the photograph for its meaning," and "as I got it . . . he grinned at me with a vast inner enjoyment."

Dugger asked the President for details about the picture, including "when it had been taken," but Johnson said not a word and "carried the picture back to its place in his wife's room." Some years later, however, Dugger mentioned the photograph to Luis Salas. "Yes, I know the one you mean," Salas said, and found his own copy of it. He showed it to Dugger, and said it had been taken on the day of the second primary in 1948—before the polls had closed.

For a President to preserve as a personal memento a photograph showing the notorious Box 13 in the possession of his political allies—a photograph which by implication proves that someone was indeed in a position to stuff it—is startling in itself. For him to display the photograph to a hostile journalist is evidence of a psychological need so deep that its demands could not be resisted. It is continuing evidence of the fact that not even his possession of the presidency had eased the insecurities of his youth.*

* Since there had been no box marked "Precinct 13" among the twenty brought into the Master's hearing, this was presumably the second box from that precinct, the one to which Salas had referred on the witness stand, and that was not brought to court.

17

A Love Story

THE 1948 Texas senatorial campaign marked the end of the old ways in Texas politics and the beginning of the new.

The Johnson campaign taught Texas politicians the power of the media. "After that," as Horace Busby puts it, "they saw that the way to reach the state was through radio." And, of course, the state was becoming more urban, less rural. "The exodus from the small towns had started." So, in subsequent statewide campaigns, candidates no longer campaigned as Coke Stevenson had campaigned in 1948. They no longer drove from one small town to the next. "You no longer made the circuit. The campaigning in the Courthouse Square died out. Coke's campaign was the last campaign of that kind ever waged in Texas."

Busby was speaking as he sat in a restaurant in Washington, D.C., looking back on the campaign of almost forty years before. He had been talking about it for several hours, and now he stopped. Then, after a long pause, he said he had one more point to make. "You should understand," he said. "Coke was good quality. He was a good quality legislator, Lieutenant Governor, Governor." There was another pause. "You should understand," Busby said. "He wasn't as bad as we cut him up to be."

BUT THE STORY of Coke Stevenson was not over when the fight for the Senate seat ended.

It was to continue for twenty-seven more years, more than a quarter of a century, for he lived until 1975, when he was eighty-seven; that number therefore had a double significance in his life.

After Justice Black handed down his ruling, Stevenson went back to his ranch—and his old life. A longtime friend, hunting companion and fellow widower, Emil Loeffler, a former mayor of Junction, moved in with him. Until she died in 1952, Stevenson's mother, who was in her eighties, would visit him for several weeks at a time; every morning, he would rise at four to read, cook the cornbread his mother liked, eat breakfast with her, and then, after washing the dishes, drive her around the ranch. Later, while she napped, he would do his chores, but only those that could be done near the house; during his mother's visits Coke was never out of earshot of the house.

He had lost none of his desire to improve the ranch, which he now expanded to more than fifteen thousand acres; he sunk the poles for new fences and corrals, sledgehammering 120 posts into the hard Kimble County rock himself because the work was so hard that he could hire nobody to do it. He practiced law from an office in Junction (he still refused to install a telephone on the ranch; prospective clients who couldn't find him in town had to drive out to the ranch), becoming a familiar figure again in the old Kimble County Courthouse. (To avoid any hint that he was using his influence with state officials he took cases mainly for Kimble County families he had known over the years "for fees . . . that I could write on a blackboard in my office for all to see and not be ashamed of a single one of them.") Many of the state's conservative business leaders had, once the excitement of the campaign had faded, reached the same conclusion as Busby, and realized they had been unjust to Stevenson, and they asked him to run—ample financing assured—for Tom Connally's Senate seat in 1952; he would, after all, be only sixty-four years old, they pointed out. He declined. "I would not want to be the junior Senator to Lyndon Johnson," he said. "It just wouldn't work. My belief in principles is too strong." He might run again, he said, but against Johnson—in 1954, when Johnson came up for re-election. To his friends, however, it was obvious that Stevenson had no enthusiasm for re-entering politics. "He hadn't lost interest in politics; he still read the news magazines and all, but he had lost interest in his participation in politics," his nephew, Bob Murphey, says. The stacks of mail—heavier than ever, containing now not only pleas for him to run but information on alleged 1948 vote frauds in scores of counties—piled up on the kitchen table, unanswered. His friends felt he was considering the race mainly because life on the ranch was, again, too lonely.

And then, in 1951, there was a new county clerk in the Courthouse. As a girl growing up on a Kimble County ranch, Marguerite King had been noted for her intelligence ("She was one of the brilliant ones," a friend recalls), and for her ability as a rider and a rifle shot ("I learned to shoot before I could hold the stock steady against my shoulder; I'd lean it on a rock or something," she says), but she had been nicknamed "Teeney" because she was barely five feet tall. Since then, she had left the Hill Country as one of the few young women from that isolated area to attend Baylor University, had married, been widowed when her husband, a pilot, had been shot down over Europe; and now, thirty-three years old, she had returned to Junction with her young son. But she was still petite and her nickname had stuck. "Teeney" was very quiet and serious, usually staying home reading ("biography, history—anything; I tried to read a hundred books a year"), but beneath the quietness was determination; in 1951, when the office of Kimble County Clerk became vacant, she ran for the job and was elected, becoming the first woman in the county's history to hold elective office.

The new county clerk was strikingly attractive: slender and shapely, with keen blue eyes, what friends called a "whipped cream complexion" and glowing, tightly curled, golden hair. Her friends kept suggesting the names of eligible young men to her, but they weren't interesting, she said; they didn't have anything to talk about. They didn't read.

She was still new to the job when, one day, Coke Stevenson came into her office to file a case, and she was unfamiliar with the procedures involved. She would never forget the quiet, calm, "*kind*" way he explained them to her. Then they began to chat. Recalling that day many years later, she says simply: "We found we had many things in common to talk about." Stevenson was in the Courthouse frequently, of course, and they had more talks. "He loved his ranch and his land," she recalls, "and he asked me if I'd like to come riding and see it. I would do that, and we would picnic on the river. That was how it all started, I guess."

He invited her to go deer-hunting, and that proved a little embarrassing: famous hunter though Coke was, Teeney turned out to be the better shot. He was very good with her son, Dennis, then nine years old; years later, Marguerite would recall that Coke was a "gifted speaker, whether to an audience of hundreds concerning the serious affairs of the State or Nation, or to one little boy begging for the fiftieth time: 'Tell me about the time you shot the bear.' " She saw that Coke "doted on all children" and thought it was sad that Coke, Jr., now chairman of the State Liquor Control Board and a big man in Austin, didn't visit the ranch more frequently so that Coke could see his two granddaughters. One day, when Bob Murphey came for a visit, instead of his uncle being alone, there was a beautiful woman with him. She seemed tiny beside Coke's height and big shoulders, and was much younger. But Murphey realized that that didn't matter. "I'll never forget the way she looked at him, and the way he looked at her. Uncle Coke was in love, and Teeney was in love with him." On January 16, 1954, without telling anyone—for Teeney hated "fuss" as much as Coke did—they slipped into a little church and asked the minister to marry them. (When the *Junction Eagle* learned of the wedding, the lead on its article told something of the near-reverence in which the groom was held: "Saturday, for the second time, Coke R. Stevenson, lawyer-ranchman and former Governor, took a bride from among his own people.")

After they were married, when Coke rode out over his ranch, Teeney rode beside him; she was a good enough rider so that when he was working with cattle, she could work with him, although she couldn't handle his big brown "cutting horse," Nellie, and Coke found her a black named Elgin with a very smooth gait. When he was doing work with which she couldn't help, such as clearing cedar or driving fenceposts, she would pack a lunch and bring it to him, and sit by him as he worked (worked, in his sixties now, hour after hour, swinging the huge sledgehammer as he had when he was young). Teeney seemed to want to spend every minute with Coke. Late in the afternoons they would swim in that beautiful river, with the herons and the cranes standing nearby, and the deer coming down to drink.

And as for Coke, he was a different man—or, rather, he was the man he had been when he was young, and had driven his car down the middle of the river on a bet. "I'm going to say a word about Mr. Stevenson now that you wouldn't believe," Bob Murphey says. "Bubbly. Uncle Coke was just *bubbling*. He just worshipped her." Murphey had a wife himself now, and she says, "He never walked in the kitchen that he didn't grab her and squeeze her and give her a big kiss. They were just so *happy* with each other!" Other friends, visiting the ranch, would watch Teeney and Coke reading together and talking. "They had the same kind of humor, the same way of looking at things," Ernest Boyett says. "That dry way of observing people. They could sit and talk for hours. If that wasn't happiness, I don't know what was."

And when, on January 16, 1956, the second anniversary of their marriage, they had a daughter, Jane, Coke Stevenson's love for the little girl became, for the people of the Hill Country, a part of the story that had become, during his own lifetime, a legend to the people of Texas.

He gave her a precious possession that he had obtained for himself during countless mornings with his books. He gave her history.

As soon as the little girl was old enough to understand (and she was old enough very young; at three and a half she was not only reading adult books but could speak fluent Spanish), Stevenson began telling her stories—wonderful stories—about the history of the United States, and of Texas—and of Greece and Rome. After she started school, on days when snow or ice made the roads impassable and she couldn't get to school, he and Teeney would take over her education themselves, reading to her. And when Jane was nine, Coke and Teeney started showing Jane history for herself. They had read her the accounts of the Alamo, of course, and of the battles of San Jacinto and Goliad and Sabine Pass, and they took her to all those sites, but they also ranged farther afield. They took her to see the Oregon Trail, reading Parkman's *The Oregon Trail* as they drove; the three of them followed the trails of Lewis and Clark. "And many of the other Western trails, too, trails we never hear of," Teeney recalls. "Coke knew all the trails." There was the Revolution and the Founding Fathers, and there were trips to Mount Vernon and Monticello, and there was the Civil War, and all the battlefields that made up part of the history that Coke Stevenson loved. By the time Jane was a teenager, she had been taken by her mother and father to every one of the forty-eight states, and to several provinces of Canada, also. And there was a trip to a place nearer home. Coming home from school one evening when she was eleven, Jane told her father and mother that her class had begun studying how the state government worked. Coke took her to Austin so she could see it work for herself; once again, there was the whisper in the halls of the Capitol, "Coke Stevenson's here," and people came out of their offices into the halls to see a tall, erect old man holding by the hand a skinny little girl in pigtails.

And she appreciated the gift. "Jane was a good student, and a good historian," Teeney says. "Those trips were *good*." She loved history, and she and her father were very close. A reporter who spent several days with Coke when Jane was twelve was struck by the slim, pretty girl, and by her relationship with her father. "Stevenson is gentle-voiced with her, calls her 'baby,' " the reporter wrote. "And you sense her love for the man who is big in her history books." And when she became a teenager, Coke Stevenson made for Jane what was, for him, the ultimate sacrifice. Newspapers across Texas chronicled it in amazement: "A telephone has been installed on the Coke Stevenson Ranch." "Well," Stevenson drawled, "you know how teenagers are."

"HE IDOLIZED THAT GIRL. He told me many times that he hoped he would live to see her grown," Bob Murphey says. He lived to see her nineteen years old and married to a young rancher, and not only did Coke live to a great age, respected throughout the Hill Country, a prophet with honor in his own country, but only in the last three or four years of his life did his health begin to fail; a reporter who went to see him wrote in 1959 that "at 71, the [former] Governor of Texas does hard manual labor six days a week." All through the 1960s, as he neared eighty, he seemed never to be ill, and he still ranged from Wyoming to Montana to hunt the big elk. And he still worked on his ranch. He had decided to build at least rough roads connecting its fifteen thousand acres, and he did—ninety miles of them—and he took pride in every mile. He never lost his desire to learn new methods; deciding in about 1963, when he was seventy-five, that he wanted to build a large garage for his tractors and other ranch machinery, he decided also that he wanted to build it without supporting columns, so that maneuvering the vehicles would be simpler. Sending away for architectural textbooks, he taught himself the science of canti-levered construction, studying these books as eagerly as, fifty years before, he had studied books to teach himself accounting, and law, and highway construction. He never lost his self-reliance, and his happiness and pride when he did something on his own. And as for the law, "Well," Teeney says, "Coke just *loved* the practice of law. And he had just the pick of cases now, from all over the state, and when he got a new case which was difficult," where the legalities were complicated, he was as enthusiastic and as eager about studying up on the law involved as he had been when he had first started reading law books. His love of his land, the land he had saved so long to buy, and his pride in the improvements he had made on it were so deep that visitors constantly commented on it. Taken on a tour, a guest remarked on the clarity of the water in a large "tank" or pond. "I built that," the host said. He had built it twenty years before, he said. The water was so clear because he had lined the pond with cal-iche, which he had lugged from another section of the ranch; sure, he said in response to the guest's question, "It was a *lot* of work." But, Coke Stevenson asked, surveying the results of his labor, "wasn't it *worth* it?" If there was a single aspect of the ranch that was dearest to him—with the exception of the falls of the South Llano ("How he loved that river!" Teeney would recall)—it was the springs which kept the ranch green and his cattle watered even during droughts that turned the rest of the Hill Country brown. Every time he discovered a new spring his enthusiasm over the discovery would be as full and pure as the excitement of a young boy.

The love between Coke and Teeney was striking, too, as was the contentment they brought to each other. They were to have twenty-one years together, and they seemed to fall only more and more in love. When he rode his ranch, by horse or car, inspecting it or cutting out cattle, Teeney still rode with him; when he was doing work in which she couldn't participate, she would still come, carrying lunch, and sit near him for hours as he worked. She began doing some of the research for his legal cases, so she was part of his life in the law, too. Says a friend: "It seemed like they couldn't bear to be apart for a minute." Says Murphey: "Uncle Coke told me many times how much joy she had brought him, and how he had never thought he would ever be this happy again."

Teeney made sure that the Stevenson ranch was no longer isolated. Her husband had friends—from his days as a young legislator, in fact from his days as a young cowman—all over Texas, and now Teeney invited them for visits. "It was sort of an Open House," one of these friends says.

"There were a lot of bedrooms in that house, and sometimes it seemed like they were all filled." In the evenings, Stevenson and his guests would sit around a mesquite campfire by the river drinking Ten High whiskey and swapping stories, while Coke got a good scorch on the steaks as big as saddle blankets.

COKE STEVENSON and Lyndon Johnson never saw each other again. Stevenson's hatred and contempt for Johnson never faded, and occasionally it would surface. Asked once, during Johnson's 1964 campaign for the presidency, to evaluate him, he said, after a long pause: "Well, of course, he is a very, how should I say, skillful politician," and dropped the subject except to say that he himself would vote for Goldwater. "I've been waiting a long time to see a turn toward conservatism." Those who knew him well knew there were still scars from the 1948 campaign.

But the scars were smoothed over by happiness. From the day Teeney agreed to marry him, Stevenson never again thought seriously about running in the 1954 campaign against Johnson—or in any other campaign. He simply had no interest in public office. His dream, after all, the dream he had conceived during those nights so long ago on the Brady-Junction trail when six horses had been all he owned, had not been to be Governor, or Senator. His dream had been to be a rancher. And now he could enjoy the realization of that dream. "He would have made a great Senator," Teeney says. "But he loved his ranch, and the life out here, and he *loved* practicing law. His life out here was more meaningful for him than it would have been any other way. And he knew that. He understood himself."

A columnist for the *Dallas News*, Frank X. Tolbert, came to visit the former Governor. Observing Stevenson's joy in the ranch, in the boyhood dream that he had turned into reality, witnessing the enthusiasm with which he still planned and built each new improvement, seeing the serenity of the quiet evenings by the river he loved, the affection between him and his wife, the love and respect in which he was held by wife, daughter, friends—by everyone around him—Tolbert wrote: "After spending some time with Coke Robert Stevenson . . . here by the green, rushing river, I'm wondering if he wasn't lucky to lose that Senate race by 87 votes."

Those who knew Coke Stevenson didn't wonder. Bob Murphey, who had witnessed, better than anyone else, how hard his Uncle Coke had tried to win the Senate race, says, "Thinking back on it now, I truly believe that getting beat for the Senate and marrying Teeney was the best thing that could have happened to him."

And a reporter who came to do a profile on the former Governor in 1969, when Stevenson was eighty-one years old, didn't wonder. Watching

Teeney come to meet him, the reporter wrote, "You sense . . . a protective motherly manner as she approaches her gray bear of a husband"—not that her husband seemed to need protection; he worked, the reporter wrote, "like a ditchdigger." Teeney insisted that Coke show the reporter the historic marker that had been erected by the Texas State Historical Commission on the lawn of the Kimble County Courthouse. The marker had been placed in honor of a Texas institution. "Coke R. Stevenson," it began. "Strong, Resourceful, Conservative Governor . . ." The reporter realized he was talking to "the only man in Texas who can look out his office window and see his own monument." He realized how proud Coke was of the marker—at least partly because it bore the key word. "A conservative—he's one who holds things together," he told the reporter. "He shouldn't fight all progressive movements, but he should be the balance wheel to hold the movement to where it won't get out of hand." He *had* been a conservative Governor, he said. "When I left office I left a thirty-five million dollar surplus." He mentioned the old-age pensions he had tripled and the public welfare payments he had increased and the prison reforms and the more humane treatment in state institutions for the insane, and the reporter realized how very proud Coke Stevenson was of his whole life. Then Teeney and Coke drove the reporter out to the ranch, and he saw the house, and the love with which it was filled.

Finally, they went down to the river. A rowboat was there, and Coke explained that "Jane rows upstream, me downstream," and Teeney broke in to say with a smile: "Then they both get tired, and I have to row." A recent flash flood had changed the contours of the banks, and as the boat moved along, Coke Stevenson, eighty-one years old, suddenly jumped up in the boat and shouted, pointing excitedly at an Indian burial mound that the flood had uncovered. And there were springs, new springs. "There's another one," he said. "And look! There's another!"

"He takes in the whole scene, waterfalls and deer and turkey and gentle flow of river," the whole panorama of the beautiful canyon, the reporter wrote. And then, still standing up in the boat, Coke Stevenson threw his arms wide, in a gesture of triumph and joy.

18

Three Rings

SENATORS OF THE UNITED STATES are sworn in in groups of four, and at ten minutes past noon on January 3, 1949, Lyndon Baines Johnson, with his wife and John Connally and Buzz and Woody watching from the crowded galleries above, walked down the Senate's red-carpeted center aisle beside Burnet R. Maybank of South Carolina, who was being sworn in for a new term, and two Senators-elect like himself, Robert S. Kerr of Oklahoma and Estes Kefauver of Tennessee. Standing stiffly above them on the dais, his right palm upraised, Arthur Vandenberg of Michigan, the Senate's president *pro tem*, read the oath—"Do you solemnly swear that you will support and defend the Constitution of the United States . . ."— and the four replied together: "I do." Then, after stepping to the parliamentarian's desk below Vandenberg, and signing his name in the Senate Register, Johnson walked to his seat in the last row on the Democratic side of the Chamber. Later that day, sitting in his new offices in front of a high arched window that framed the Mall and the Washington Monument, he was interviewed by Margaret Mayer of the *Austin American-Statesman*, who had followed him through most of his long campaign. Miss Mayer asked him "if it had all been worth it." He nodded, and winked. Then he strode out of his office and down the corridor to the elevator. He rang the elevator bell three times—the signal that a Senator was waiting.

The Senate into which Lyndon Johnson was sworn was as dominated by seniority as the House of Representatives. Power resided in the Senate "Club" or "Inner Circle," which consisted largely of the chairmen and ranking members of the Senate's great Standing Committees, and of four party leaders—two floor leaders and two assistant floor leaders or "whips"—who, unlike the Speaker of the House, were not formal officials of the Senate but in effect held the limited powers the committee barons deigned to allow them. The sole basis for accession to a chairmanship was

length of service in the Senate: a vacant chairmanship went to the man
of the majority party who had been longest on that committee—and once
a man became chairman, the post was his for the duration of his political
life; nothing, not even senility, could change that. As a result, six of the
fourteen committee chairmen were in their fourth or fifth Senate terms,
having served a quarter of a century or more. Neither energy nor ability
could circumvent the seniority rule. To become a leader in the Senate, it
seemed, required waiting—years of waiting.

Within just two years, in January, 1951, Lyndon Johnson would be
a leader, his party's whip—an assistant floor leader who, moreover, very
quickly began to invest that hitherto largely titular role with new significance. Just two years later, in January, 1953, he would be *the* Leader of
his party, only Minority Leader since the Democrats had lost control of
the Senate, but nonetheless the youngest floor leader in the history of the
Senate. From that seat in the back row he had moved in only four years
to the Democratic Leader's front-row, center-aisle seat, sitting at the head
of men who had served as many terms in that body as he had years there.
And within weeks of his election as Leader, he would begin to revolutionize some of the Senate's most sacrosanct traditions in order to concentrate the barons' prerogatives in his own hands. By 1955, with the
barons' power broken and the Democrats back in the majority, Lyndon
Johnson was the most powerful Majority Leader in history.

DEBTS,
BIBLIOGRAPHY,
NOTES
AND INDEX

Debts

DURING THE FOURTEEN YEARS in which this life of Lyndon Johnson has been going forward, librarians across the United States have come to know and respect Ina Caro, an indefatigable researcher of unshakable integrity who happens to be my wife.

For the first volume, in transforming herself into an expert on rural electrification and soil conservation, she spent long days driving back and forth over lonely Hill Country roads searching out elderly farm and ranch women who could explain to her—and through her, to me—the difference that these innovations made in their lives. For this volume, her work has been more with written materials. In pursuing them, she has crisscrossed the United States, spending weeks, for example, going through the papers of former Senator Richard B. Russell in a library in Athens, Georgia, those of Willis Robertson in a library in Williamsburg, Virginia, and those of former Presidents Franklin Roosevelt and Harry Truman in Hyde Park, New York, and Independence, Missouri. My beloved idealist has tracked the maneuverings of supreme pragmatists such as Tommy-the-Cork Corcoran and former United States Attorney General Tom Clark in the National Archives in Washington and in the Truman Library in Independence. These are major institutions. The librarians of tiny libraries in small towns all across Texas know Ina Caro as well. Over and over, she has searched through those libraries until she unearthed copies of weekly newspapers that the librarians believed no longer existed.

She does pioneering work. To cite one example: To find the truth about the fabled "West Side" vote in San Antonio, long a subject of rumor in Texas political circles, Ina wanted to analyze the precinct-by-precinct West Side voting records in a Lyndon Johnson senatorial primary during the 1940s. First she was told that the records no longer existed— an understandable misstatement since during the intervening forty years or so no one had looked at them. Finally she learned that the records did in fact still exist but were about to be destroyed—and had been stored meanwhile in an abandoned jail. Ina went to the jail, and analyzed the records—and what she found has enriched the book.

I could cite a hundred examples of how Ina's research has enriched these volumes. She is a true historian, in the highest sense of that term: what she is interested in is the truth, and nothing will deflect her from her search to find it. If there is a farm woman on a ranch a hundred miles, or more, away, over bad roads, a woman who might—just might—tell her something she hadn't been told before, Ina simply gets into the car and starts driving. If there is a possibility that some obscure folder, previously unopened, in the papers of some United States Senator in some out-of-the-way library will shed light on some maneuver of Lyndon Johnson, Ina will be up at dawn to catch the next plane out.

In a world that is hectic and frenzied, moreover, Ina Caro is quiet, and calm, and wise—and so are her judgments. When, after reading one of my chapters, she makes a comment about it, I have learned I'd better listen. There is a line in Shakespeare: "More is thy due than more than all can pay." I used that line in dedicating the first volume of this work to Ina, because it was so apt, and, as I finish writing this second volume, there is still no better line to sum up my feelings. Ina, of course, is a medieval historian in her own right, and now her own book—a wonderful book—is going forward.

I don't know what I am going to do without her help.

WHEN ROBERT GOTTLIEB, who edited my first two books line by line, left Knopf two years ago, he promised me that he would edit this book the same way.

Not a few of my friends who are writers or editors told me—some of them quite forcefully—that that would be impossible, that Bob's new position as editor of *The New Yorker* would simply be too time-consuming. I, however, never had a moment's doubt that he would do what he said, no matter how great the difficulties. He had given me his word, and I had learned about Bob Gottlieb's word.

And he did in fact edit the book just as he said he would edit it. After his long days at *The New Yorker*, he was sometimes too tired to edit the book in the evenings, so he did it on weekends, and we reviewed it on weekends, all through a very hot summer. I remember more than one weekend on which the rest of the literary world seemed to be in East Hampton, where I have a summer home, and Bob's family was in Williamstown, where he wanted to be—and we spent it together in New York City, battling over semicolons.

The editing process was not only as thorough as those on my earlier books, but the same in most other respects as well. He lavished on this book, as he had lavished on my other books, his talent, his energy and his unique editorial intelligence.

In only one respect was the editing process different this time. Whereas he had managed to edit my first and second books without once, in months of work, ever saying a single complimentary word about them in my hearing, this time, at the very end of the editorial process—as, in fact, we laid down the last page of the manuscript—he did say something. He said, "Not bad."

KATHERINE HOURIGAN, Knopf's managing editor, has given the same invaluable assistance to every stage of this book that she gave to both *The Power Broker* and *The Path to Power*. Her editorial judgments are characterized, in my opinion, not only by perceptivity but by an unflinching integrity that has only grown stronger over the years. For a number of reasons, this book presented daunting production problems. I have seen the ingenuity and the tireless effort she put into solving them—and I have appreciated it.

Those problems have also taxed the patience, ingenuity and strength of Andrew W. Hughes, the book's production manager at Knopf. I thank him for his help. Andy's father, Andrew L. Hughes, has served as my attorney on this work, as he did on my first two books. For the legal (and literary) advice which he began giving me while I was a reporter on *Newsday* and he was its general counsel, and which he has continued giving me ever since, I express to him, too, my deepest appreciation.

Among the many other people at Knopf to whom I am indebted, I must thank especially my old friends Bill Loverd, Nina Bourne, Jane Friedman, Janice Goldklang, Ellis Levine, Mel Rosenthal, Virginia Tan, and Sara Stemen.

I must thank as well a new friend, Sonny Mehta. It is wonderful to find in the publishing world an individual with both a discerning literary sensibility and an understanding of and sympathy for the aims and problems of writers.

Over the years, my agent, Lynn Nesbit, has always been there when I needed her. I value that relationship, and I am glad that it has continued.

THE STAFF of the Lyndon Baines Johnson Library have been, over many years now, of more help to me than I can easily express.

As always, Claudia Anderson has been of particular help because of her historian's instinct and the depth of her knowledge of the contents of the Johnson archives. Tina Houston, the Library's supervisory archivist, and Mike Gillette, Linda Hanson, Ted Gittinger, David Humphrey, Joan Kennedy, E. Philip Scott, Nancy Smith, Robert Tissing, Shellynne Wucher, Regina Greenwell, Irene Parra and Kathy Frankum deserve—and have—my deep gratitude for years of help.

For some years now I have also had not only the cooperation but the guidance of Dr. Richard A. Baker and Dr. Donald A. Ritchie, Historian and Associate Historian, respectively, of the United States Senate. While the assistance they have given me deals mainly with events that I describe in the next volume, I want to thank them now as well. Baker and Ritchie are both historians of great diligence and insight and I appreciate all they have done.

My thanks also to Dennis Bilger, Archivist, and Benedict K. Zobrist, Director, of the Harry S Truman Library; Betsey Hudon, Special Collections, The University of Texas at Arlington; Margaret Rose, Librarian at the Corpus Christi Public Library; Diane Bruce of the Institute of Texan Culture; Sharon Jenkins, Supervisor at the FCC; Audray Bateman of Austin; Louis Marchiafava of the Houston Metropolitan Research Center; Paul McGlaughlin at the Franklin D. Roosevelt Library; Claire Maxwell of the Austin Public Library; Paul K. Goode of the James C. Jernigan Library at Texas A&I, in Kingsville; Don Jacobsen at the Fort Worth Public Library.

A Note on Sources

THE RESEARCH for these first two volumes of my life of Lyndon Johnson, two volumes which together cover what I consider the "Texas part" of the work since in the volumes to come the focus will shift to Washington, has taken place over the past fourteen years. A portion of it has taken place at a single location: a desk—two and a half feet by four feet—in the Reading Room on the eighth floor of the Lyndon Baines Johnson Library and Museum in Austin, Texas, where, on periodic visits to the Library, I sat while the Library's archivists wheeled in to me on large wooden carts the document cases, some plain red or gray cardboard, most covered in red buckram (and stamped with a gold replica of the presidential seal), which contain the written materials—letters, memoranda, scribbled notes, transcripts of telephone conversations, speech texts—relating to my subject's boyhood, his early years as a schoolteacher, congressional aide, and Texas State Director of the National Youth Administration, his eleven and a half years as a Congressman from Texas' Tenth Congressional District and his 1948 campaign to become one of the state's two United States Senators. Other boxes contain his Senate Papers, which I have studied primarily for my third volume, but which of course contained more than a little information that helped illuminate that earlier period. In all, during those fourteen years, a total of 787 boxes were delivered to my desk. They contained, by the Library's estimate, 629,000 pages of documents. How many of those pages I read I don't know, but I read a lot of them.

The time I have spent at that desk has been a wonderful time—thrilling, in fact. From the first time I thought of becoming a biographer, I never conceived of my biographies as merely telling the lives of famous men but rather as a means of illuminating their times and the great forces that shaped their times—particularly political power, since in a democracy political power has so great a role in shaping the lives of the citizens of that democracy. What I set out to try to do was to examine the way power works in America in the middle of the twentieth century. I have been fascinated by political power ever since I was a reporter and realized how little I knew about it—and you can learn quite a bit about that subject if you just sit there and read enough documents in the Lyndon Johnson Library.

A single example—one of a hundred that could be given—will perhaps illustrate what I mean. When I was beginning the research, one of my first interviews was with Thomas G. ("Tommy the Cork") Corcoran, Franklin Roosevelt's political man-of-all-work and a Johnson intimate during his early rise to power. By this time I had found that the crucial time in which young Johnson was elevated from the mass of congressmen to a congressman with influence over other congressmen—a congressman with at least his first toehold on national power—occurred during a single month: October, 1940. When I asked Corcoran how Johnson had attained this power, Corcoran replied, in his gruff, cryptical way: "Money, kid. Money. But you're never going to be able to write about that." When I asked him why I would never be able to write about that, he replied, "Because you're never going to find anything in writing." For some years thereafter—perhaps three or four years—I felt that Corcoran was correct, but then, among those hundreds of boxes in the Johnson Library, there before me—suddenly—in Boxes 6, 7, 8 and 9 of the Johnson House Papers, to be exact, was the written documentation of what Corcoran had meant, and I was able to understand, and, I hope, to explain (in Chapter 32 of Volume I) Lyndon Johnson's leap to national power through the campaign contributions he obtained from Texas oilmen and contractors to whom he alone had access and that he distributed, at his sole discretion, to other congressmen.

HERE is a description of the papers in the Johnson Library that form part of the foundation of these first two volumes—and an explanation of how they are identified in the Notes that follow.

House of Representatives Papers (JHP): The memoranda (both intra-office and with others), casework, speech drafts and texts, and other papers kept in the files of Johnson's congressional office from 1937 through 1948. These papers also include records pertaining to his other activities during this period, records which were originally compiled by his staff in other offices, such as the records compiled in an office he temporarily rented in Washington's Munsey Office Building when he was raising money for Democratic congressmen in 1940, and records kept in his Austin campaign headquarters during his first campaign for Congress in 1937 and his campaign for the Senate in 1941.

More than 70 boxes of documents contain about 56,000 pages of material on his 1948 senatorial campaign. These include letters and memoranda from campaign headquarters in Austin to district leaders and campaign aides in the field; confidential intraoffice memoranda; communications between the Austin headquarters and Johnson's congressional office in Washington, and reports from local campaign managers on Johnson's activities and behavior in their districts. These boxes also contain memoranda sent back to Austin from Horace Busby, who traveled with Johnson during part of the campaign. Also in these boxes are Busby's "suggested releases" and speech drafts, including releases to be issued and speeches to be given by others. These boxes also contain poll tax lists, lists of the candidate's supporters, "contacts" and potential financial contributors (with notes about them), briefing papers for the candidate, newspaper clippings, schedules, and expense accounts. They include scribbled notes from one headquarters worker to another.

Lyndon Baines Johnson Archives (LBJA): These files were created about 1958, and consist of material taken both from the House of Representatives Papers and from Johnson's Senate Papers. It consists of material considered historically valuable or of correspondence with persons with whom he was closely associated, such as Sam Rayburn, Abe Fortas, James Rowe, George and Herman Brown, Edward Clark and Alvin Wirtz; or of correspondence with national figures of that era. These files are divided into four main categories:

1. Selected Names (LBJA SN): Correspondence with close associates.

2. Famous Names (LBJA FN): Correspondence with national figures.

3. Congressional File (LBJA CF): Correspondence with fellow Congressmen and Senators.

4. Subject File (LBJA SF): This contains a Biographic Information File, with material relating to Johnson's year as a schoolteacher in Cotulla and Houston; to his work as a secretary to Congressman Richard M. Kleberg; to his activities with the Little Congress; and to his naval service during World War II.

Pre-Presidential Confidential File (PPCF): This contains material taken from other files because it dealt with potentially sensitive areas.

Pre-Presidential Memo File (PPMF): This file consists of memos taken from the House of Representatives Papers, the Johnson Senate Papers, and the Vice Presidential Papers. While these memos begin in 1939 and continue through 1963, there are relatively few prior to 1946. While most are from the staff, some are from Johnson to the staff. The subject matter of the memos falls in numerous categories, ranging from specific issues, the 1948 Senate campaign, liberal versus conservative factions in Texas, phone messages and constituent relations.

Family Correspondence (LBJ FC): Correspondence between the President and his mother and brother, Sam Houston Johnson.

Personal Papers of Rebekah Baines Johnson (RBJ PP): This is material found in her garage after she died. It includes correspondence with
her children (including Lyndon) and other members of her family, and
material collected by her during her research into the genealogy of the
Johnson family. It also includes scrapbooks.

Personal Papers of Alvin Wirtz (AW PP): 25 boxes.

Senate Papers (JSP): The scope is similar to that of the House Papers. However, these files are far more extensive than the House Papers.
These papers include "Committee files" dealing with specific committees
on which Johnson served and the papers collected when he was Democratic Leader during the years 1951–60.

Senate Political Files (SPF): These files cover a time period from
1949 to 1960. They concern the consolidation of Johnson's position in
Texas following the 1948 campaign, the 1954 Senate campaign, and Johnson's 1956 bid for the presidency, as well as numerous county files. They
were made into a separate file by the Library staff.

White House Central File (WHCF): The only files in this category
used to a substantial extent in this volume were the Subject Files labeled
"President (Personal)" (WHCF PP). They contain material about the
President or his family, mainly articles written after he became President
about episodes in his early life.

White House Famous Names File (WHFN): This includes correspondence with former Presidents and their families, including Johnson correspondence when he was a Congressman with Franklin D. Roosevelt.

*Record Group 48, Secretary of the Interior, Central Classified Files
(RG 48):* Microfilm from the National Archives containing documents
relating to Lyndon Johnson found in the files of the Department of the
Interior.

*Documents Concerning Lyndon B. Johnson from the Papers of
Franklin D. Roosevelt, Eleanor Roosevelt, John M. Carmody, Harry L.
Hopkins and Aubrey Williams (FDR-LBJ MF):* This microfilm reel was
compiled at the Franklin D. Roosevelt Library at Hyde Park and consists
of correspondence to and from Johnson found in various PPF and OF
files at the Roosevelt Library. Whenever possible, the author has included the file number, by which the original documents can be located
at the Roosevelt Library.

Johnson House Scrapbooks (JHS): 21 scrapbooks of newspaper clippings compiled by members of his staff between 1935 and 1941.

Each document from the LBJ Library is cited in the Notes by the
title of the folder in which it can be found, the box number and the
collection in the Library. If no folder title is included in the citation,
the folder is either the name of the correspondent in the letter or, in the

case of files kept alphabetically, the appropriate letter (a letter from Corcoran, for example, in the folder labeled C).

WRITTEN DOCUMENTS can never tell the whole story, of course, and, as in the first volume, I have also relied heavily on interviews with the men and women closest to Lyndon Johnson during the seven years covered by this volume. Thirteen of the men and women who were, during these years, particularly close to Lyndon Johnson were alive when I began work on this book, and I have interviewed all of them, most of them in repeated, lengthy interviews. They are George R. Brown, Horace Busby, Edward A. Clark, John B. Connally, Thomas G. Corcoran, Helen Gahagan Douglas, Abe Fortas, Welly K. Hopkins, Walter Jenkins, Gene Latimer, Mary Rather, James H. Rowe, Jr., and Warren G. Woodward. (Busby and Woodward came to Johnson's staff later than the rest of this group—only during the last year of this period—but were quickly put on an intimate footing with him.)

During this time, Johnson's two principal assistants in his congressional office were Connally and Jenkins, both of whom joined his staff in 1939. Jenkins, who succeeded Connally as Johnson's administrative aide during this period, had helped me greatly with his recollections on the first volume; for this volume, he continued his detailed assistance until his final illness. He died in November, 1985. Connally refused during the entire period of research on my first volume even to respond to requests for an interview. Some two years after it was published, however, Governor Connally said he had read the book, and now wanted to talk to me at length. He told me that the only way in which he could free the requisite bloc of uninterrupted time would be at his ranch in South Texas. For three days there, we talked, from early in the morning until quite late at night, about his thirty-year association with Lyndon Johnson. Governor Connally had told me that he would answer any question I put to him, without exception. He was true to his word, and discussed with me—as indeed he also did at a subsequent lengthy interview—with considerable, and sometimes startling, frankness, perhaps a score of pivotal events in Lyndon Johnson's life in which he was a key participant. His interviews were especially valuable because, in more than one case, he is the only participant in those events still alive. I am all the more grateful to him because his silence about some of these events that he broke in talking to me was a silence that had lasted for decades.

During his years as a Congressman in Washington, Johnson was part of a quite remarkable group of young men and women: Benjamin V. Cohen, Thomas G. Corcoran, Helen Gahagan Douglas, Abe Fortas, Arthur Goldschmidt, Eliot Janeway, James H. Rowe, Jr., and Elizabeth

Wickenden Goldschmidt. These men and women—once the bright young New Dealers—gave me their time with varying degrees of generosity, but some of them were very generous indeed, and when the meaning of documents in the Library was not clear, they often made it clear. These men and women had ringside seats at Lyndon Johnson's rise to power. Perceptive as they are, they understood what they were watching, and they can explain it. The greatest single loss to my research, in my opinion, came with the death of Abe Fortas after I had had only a single interview with him. But even in that one interview, he explained things for which I would otherwise have had no explanation.

If many of the names above are known to readers familiar with American political history, the name of Edward A. Clark is not. The only high public position he ever held was as United States Ambassador to Australia during Lyndon Johnson's presidency. Because I rely on his recollections quite as much as on those of the more famous figures, however, I feel I should identify him. In 1936, this canny politician was already not only Texas Secretary of State but chief political adviser to Governor James V. Allred. Twenty years later, in 1953, as the most powerful lawyer and lobbyist in Austin, he was named "the Secret Boss of Texas" by the *Reader's Digest*. Thirty years after *that*—in 1982—he was still identified as "one of the twenty most powerful Texans." Of all the men with whom Lyndon Johnson would be allied in Texas, Clark was the one who would, over the long years to come, acquire and hold the most power in that state. More to the point, so far as my work is concerned, he was Brown & Root's lawyer—and, for twenty years, Lyndon Johnson's. When I finished the first volume of this work, I wrote that "over a period of more than three years, Mr. Clark . . . devoted evening after evening to furthering my political education." During these past seven years, the education has continued, to my benefit.

It is necessary, I think, to repeat in this note the note I made in Volume I about Lady Bird Johnson and my work. Lady Bird Johnson prepared carefully for our ten interviews, reading her diaries for the years involved, so that she could provide a month-by-month, detailed description of the Johnsons' life. Some of these were lengthy interviews, particularly one in the living room of the Johnson Ranch that as I recall it lasted most of a day. These interviews were immensely valuable in providing a picture of Lyndon Johnson's personal and social life, and of his associates, for Mrs. Johnson is an extremely acute observer, and has the gift of making her observations, no matter how quietly understated, quite clear. The interviews were less valuable in regard to her husband's political life. In later years, Mrs. Johnson would become familiar with her husband's work, indeed perhaps his most trusted confidante. During this earlier period, Mrs. Johnson was not familiar with much of the political maneuvering in which her husband was engaged, as she herself points out. Once, when I asked if she had been present at various political strategy sessions, she replied, "Well, I didn't always want to be a part of everything, because I was never . . . I elected to be out a lot. I wasn't confident in that field. I didn't want to be a party to absolutely everything."

Although from the first I made it clear to Mrs. Johnson that I would conduct my own independent research into anything I was told by anyone, for some time she very helpfully advised members of the semi-official "Johnson Circle" in Texas that she would have no objection if they talked with me. At a certain point, however—sometime after the interviews with Mrs. Johnson had been completed—that cooperation abruptly and totally ceased.

Selected Bibliography

ADAMS, FRANK C.: *Texas Democracy.* Springfield, Ill.: Democratic Historic Association; 1937.

ALEXANDER, HERBERT E.: *Money in Politics.* Washington, D.C.: Public Affairs Press; 1972.

ALLEN, FREDERICK LEWIS: *Only Yesterday.* New York: Harper; 1931.

ALLEN, ROBERT S.: *Our Sovereign State.* New York: Vanguard; 1949.

ALSOP, JOSEPH, AND TURNER CATLEDGE: *The 168 Days.* Garden City, N.Y.: Doubleday; 1937.

ANDERS, EVAN: *Boss Rule in South Texas.* Austin: University of Texas Press; 1982.

ANDERSON, JACK, AND JAMES BOYD: *Confessions of a Muckraker.* New York: Random House; 1979.

ANGEVINE, ERMA, ED.: *People—Their Power: The Rural Electric Fact Book.* Washington, D.C.: National Rural Electric Cooperative Association; 1980.

ASHMAN, CHARLES: *Connally.* New York: Morrow; 1974.

BAKER, BOBBY, WITH LARRY L. KING: *Wheeling and Dealing.* New York: Norton; 1978.

BAKER, GLADYS L., WAYNE D. RASMUSSEN, VIVIAN WISER, JANE M. PORTER: *Century of Service.* Washington: U.S. Department of Agriculture, GPO; 1967.

BAKER, RUSSELL: *The Good Times.* New York; Morrow; 1989.

BANKS, JIMMY: *Money, Marbles, and Chalk.* Austin: Texas Pub.; 1972.

BARNOUW, ERIK: *A History of Broadcasting in the United States. Vol II: The*

Golden Web: 1933 to 1953. New York: Oxford University Press; 1970.

BEARSS, EDWIN C.: *Historic Resource Study . . . Lyndon B. Johnson National Historic Site, Blanco and Gillespie Counties, Texas.* Denver: U.S. Dept. of Interior, National Park Service; 1971.

BEASLEY, NORMAN: *Knudsen.* New York: McGraw-Hill; 1947.

BELFRAGE, SALLY: *Freedom Summer.* New York: Viking; 1965.

BELL, JACK: *The Johnson Treatment.* New York: Harper; 1965.

BENDINER, ROBERT: *White House Fever.* New York: Harcourt, Brace; 1960.

BERMAN, LARRY: *Lyndon Johnson's War.* New York: Norton; 1989.

——— *Planning a Tragedy: The Americanization of Vietnam.* New York: Norton; 1982.

BILLINGTON, RAY ALLEN: *Westward Expansion: A History of the American Frontier.* New York: Macmillan; 1949.

The Biographical Directory of the American Congress, 1774–1971. Washington: G.P.O.; 1971.

BLACK, HUGO L., AND ELIZABETH BLACK: *Mr. Justice and Mrs. Black: The Memoirs.* New York: Random House; 1986.

BLAIR, JOHN M.: *The Control of Oil.* New York: Pantheon; 1976.

BORNET, VAUGHN DAVIS: *The Presidency of Lyndon B. Johnson.* Lawrence, Kansas: University Press of Kansas; 1983.

BRADLEE, BENJAMIN C.: *Conversations with Kennedy.* New York: Norton; 1975.

BRANCH, TAYLOR: *Parting the Waters.* New York: Simon & Schuster; 1988.

BRAY, HOWARD: *The Pillars of the Past.* New York: Norton; 1980.

BROWN, D. CLAYTON: *Electricity for Rural America*. Westport, Conn.: Greenwood; 1980.

BURNS, JAMES MACGREGOR: *The American Experiment*. 3 vols. New York: Knopf; 1982–89.

——— *Roosevelt: The Lion and the Fox*. New York: Harcourt Brace, and World; 1962.

——— *Roosevelt: The Soldier of Freedom*. San Diego: Harcourt Brace Jovanovich; 1970.

CAGIN, SETH, AND PHILIP DRAY, *We Are Not Afraid*. New York: Macmillan; 1988.

CAIDIN, MARTIN, AND EDWARD HYMOFF, *The Mission*. Philadelphia: Lippincott; 1964.

CALVERT, ROBERT W.: *Here Comes the Judge*. Waco, Texas: Texian Press; 1977.

CAROLI, BETTY BOYD: *First Ladies*. New York: Oxford University Press; 1987.

CHAMPAGNE, ANTHONY: *Congressman Sam Rayburn*. New Brunswick, New Jersey: Rutgers University Press; 1984.

CHESTER, LEWIS, GODFREY HODGSON, AND BRUCE PAGE: *An American Melodrama: The Presidential Campaign of 1968*. New York: Viking; 1969.

CHILDS, MARQUIS: *The Farmer Takes a Hand*. Garden City, New York: Doubleday; 1952.

——— *Witness to Power*. New York: McGraw-Hill; 1975.

COCHRAN, JACQUELINE, AND MARYANN BRUCKNUM BRINLEY: *Jackie Cochran: An Autobiography*. New York: Bantam; 1987.

COCKE, WILLIAM A.: *The Bailey Controversy in Texas*. San Antonio: The Cocke Co.; 1908.

CONNALLY, TOM, AND ALFRED STEINBERG: *My Name Is Tom Connally*. New York: Crowell; 1954.

CORMIER, FRANK: *LBJ, The Way He Was*. Garden City, New York: Doubleday, 1977.

CRAWFORD, ANN FEARS, AND JACK KEEVER: *John B. Connally: Portrait in Power*. Austin: Jenkins; 1973.

CROLY, HERBERT D.: *Marcus Alonzo Hanna*. New York: Macmillan; 1912.

DANIELS, JONATHAN: *The End of Innocence*. Philadelphia: Lippincott; 1954.

——— *Frontier on the Potomac*. New York: Macmillan; 1946.

——— *White House Witness, 1942–1945*. Garden City, New York: Doubleday; 1975.

DAVIE, MICHAEL: *LBJ: A Foreign Observer's Viewpoint*. New York: Duell, Sloan, and Pearce; 1966.

DEACON, JAMES. *Straight Stuff*. New York: Morrow; 1984.

DONOVAN, ROBERT J.: *Conflict and Crisis: The Presidency of Harry S Truman, 1945–1948*. New York: Norton; 1977.

——— *Tumultuous Years. The Presidency of Harry S Truman, 1949–1953*. New York: Norton; 1982.

DOROUGH, C. DWIGHT: *Mr. Sam*. New York: Random House; 1962.

DOUGLAS, HELEN GAHAGAN: *A Full Life*. Garden City, New York: Doubleday; 1982.

DOUGLAS, WILLIAM O.: *The Court Years*. New York: Random House; 1980.

——— *Go East, Young Man*. New York: Random House; 1971.

DOYLE, JACK: *Lines Across the Land*. Washington: Environmental Policy Institute; 1979.

DUGGER, RONNIE: *The Politician: The Life and Times of Lyndon Johnson*. New York: Norton; 1982.

DULANEY, H. B., AND EDWARD HAKE PHILLIPS, MACPHELAN REESE: *Speak, Mr. Speaker*. Bonham, Tex.: Sam Rayburn Foundation; 1978.

DUNAWAY, DAVID KING: *How Can I Keep From Singing: Pete Seeger*. New York: McGraw-Hill; 1981.

DUNNE, GERALD T.: *Hugo Black and the Judicial Revolution*. New York: Simon & Schuster; 1977.

ELLIS, CLYDE T.: *A Giant Step*. New York: Random House; 1966.

ENGLER, ROBERT: *The Brotherhood of Oil*. Chicago: University of Chicago Press; 1977.

——— *Politics of Oil*. New York: Macmillan; 1961.

EVANS, ROWLAND, AND ROBERT NOVAK: *Lyndon B. Johnson: The Exercise of Power*. New York: New American Library; 1966.

FAGER, CHARLES E.: *Selma 1965*. Boston: Beacon Press; 1985.

FARLEY, JAMES A.: *Behind the Ballots*. New York: Harcourt, Brace; 1938.

——— *Jim Farley's Story: The Roosevelt Years*. New York: Whittlesey House; 1948.

FEHRENBACH, T. R.: *Lone Star: A History of Texas and the Texans*. New York: Macmillan; 1968.

FISHER, O. C.: *Cactus Jack.* Waco: The Texian Press; 1978.

FLEMMONS, JERRY: *Amon: The Life of Amon Carter, Sr., of Texas.* Austin: Jenkins; 1978.

FLYNN, EDWARD J.: *You're the Boss.* New York: Viking; 1947.

FRANTZ, JOE B.: *37 Years of Public Service: The Honorable Lyndon B. Johnson.* Austin: Shoal Creek Publishers; 1974.

FRANTZ, JOE B., AND J. ROY WHITE: *The Driskill Hotel.* Austin: Encino Press; 1973.

―――― *Limestone and Log.* Austin: Encino Press; 1968.

―――― *Texas: A Bicentennial History.* New York: Norton; 1976.

FREIDEL, FRANK: *Franklin D. Roosevelt: Launching the New Deal.* Boston: Little, Brown; 1973.

――――, ED.: *The New Deal and the American People.* Englewood Cliffs, New Jersey: Prentice-Hall; 1964.

FRASER, RONALD: *1968.* New York: Pantheon; 1988.

GANTT, FRED, JR.: *The Chief Executive in Texas.* Austin: University of Texas Press; 1964.

GARROW, DAVID J.: *Bearing the Cross.* New York: Morrow; 1986.

GARWOOD, JOHN, AND W. C. TUTHILL: *The Rural Electrification Administration: An Evaluation.* Washington, D.C.: American Enterprise Institute for Public Policy Research; 1963.

GEYELIN, PHILIP L.: *Lyndon B. Johnson and the World.* New York: Praeger; 1966.

GILLESPIE COUNTY HISTORICAL SOCIETY: *Pioneers in God's Hills.* Austin: Von Boeckmann-Jones; 1960.

GITLIN, TODD: *The Sixties.* New York: Bantam Books; 1987.

GLAZER, TOM, ED.: *Songs of Peace, Freedom, and Protest.* New York: McKay; 1970.

GOLDMAN, ERIC: *The Crucial Decade—and After: America 1945-1960.* New York: Knopf; 1961.

―――― *The Tragedy of Lyndon Johnson.* New York: Knopf; 1969.

GOODWIN, RICHARD: *Remembering America.* Boston: Little, Brown; 1988.

GOODWYN, FRANK: *Lone-Star Land.* New York: Knopf; 1955.

GOODWYN, LAWRENCE: *Democratic Promise.* New York: Oxford University Press; 1976.

GOULD, LEWIS L.: *Lady Bird Johnson and the Environment.* Lawrence: University of Kansas Press; 1988.

GOULDEN, JOSEPH C.: *The Best Years: 1945-50.* New York: Atheneum; 1976.

GRAVES, JOHN: *Texas Heartland: A Hill Country Year.* College Station: Texas A & M University Press; 1975.

GREEN, GEORGE N.: *The Establishment in Texas Politics.* Westport, Conn.: Greenwood Press; 1979.

―――― *The Far Right Wing in Texas Politics.* Ann Arbor: University Microfilm; 1967.

GUNTHER, JOHN: *Inside U.S.A.* New York: Harper; 1947.

―――― *Roosevelt in Retrospect.* New York: Harper; 1950.

HALBERSTAM, DAVID: *The Best and the Brightest.* New York: Random House; 1972.

―――― *The Powers That Be.* New York: Knopf; 1979.

HALDEMAN, D. B., AND DONALD C. BACON: *Rayburn.* Austin: Texas Monthly Press; 1987.

HARWOOD, RICHARD, AND HAYNES JOHNSON: *Lyndon.* New York: Praeger; 1973.

HASSETT, WILLIAM D.: *Off the Record with FDR: 1942-1945.* New Brunswick, New Jersey: Rutgers University Press; 1958.

HEARD, ALEXANDER: *The Costs of Democracy.* Chapel Hill: University of North Carolina Press; 1960.

HEARD, ALEXANDER, AND DONALD S. STRONG: *Southern Primaries and Elections, 1920-1949.* Tuscaloosa, Alabama: University of Alabama Press; 1950.

HENDERSON, RICHARD B.: *Maury Maverick.* Austin: University of Texas Press; 1970.

HUMPHREY, WILLIAM: *Farther Off From Heaven.* New York: Knopf; 1977.

HUNTER, JOHN MARVIN, AND GEORGE W. SAUNDERS: *The Trail Drivers of Texas.* Dallas; The Southwest Press; 1929.

ICKES, HAROLD L.: *The Secret Diary of Harold L. Ickes.* 3 vols. New York: Simon and Schuster; 1953-54.

JENKINS, JOHN H., AND H. GORDON FROST: *"I'm Frank Hamer".* Austin: Pemberton; 1980.

JOHNSON, CLAUDIA ALTA (TAYLOR): *A White House Diary.* New York: Holt Rinehart & Winston; 1970.

JOHNSON, LYNDON BAINES: *A Time for Action: A Selection from the Speeches and*

Writings of Lyndon B. Johnson, 1953–64. New York: Atheneum; 1964.
—— *My Hope for America.* New York: Random House; 1964.
—— *Pattern for Peace in Southeast Asia.* Washington, D.C.: Department of State, GPO; 1965.
—— *The Presidential Press Conferences.* New York: Coleman Enterprises; 1978.
—— *This America.* Photographed by Den Heman. New York: Random House; 1966.
—— *To Heal and to Build: The Programs of Lyndon B. Johnson.* New York: McGraw-Hill; 1968.
—— *The Vantage Point: Perspectives of the President, 1963–1969.* New York: Holt, Rinehart and Winston; 1971.
JOHNSON, REBEKAH (BAINES): *A Family Album.* New York: McGraw-Hill; 1965.
JOHNSON, SAM HOUSTON: *My Brother Lyndon.* New York: Cowles; 1970.
JONES, JESSE H.: *Fifty Billion Dollars.* New York: Macmillan; 1951.
JORDAN, TERRY G.: *German Seed in Texas Soil.* Austin: University of Texas Press; 1966.
JOSEPHSON, MATTHEW: *The Politicos, 1865–1896.* New York: Harcourt, Brace; 1938.
—— *The Robber Barons.* New York: Harcourt, Brace; 1934.

KAHL, MARY: *Ballot Box 13: How Lyndon Johnson Won His 1948 Senate Race by 87 Contested Votes.* Jefferson, N.C.: McFarland; 1983.
KAISER, CHARLES: *1968 in America.* New York: Weidenfeld & Nicholson; 1988.
KEARNS, DORIS: *Lyndon Johnson and the American Dream.* New York: Harper; 1976.
KEY, V. O.: *Southern Politics in State and Nation.* New York: Knopf; 1949.
KINCH, SAM, AND STUART LONG: *Allan Shivers: The Pied Piper of Texas Politics.* Austin: Shoal Creek; 1973.
KOENIG, LOUIS W.: *The Invisible Presidency.* New York: Rinehart; 1960.
KOHLMEIER, LOUIS M.: *The Regulators: Watchdog Agencies and the Public Interest.* New York: Harper & Row; 1969.
KRASNOW, ERWIN G., AND LAWRENCE D. LONGLEY: *The Politics of Broadcast Regulation.* New York: St. Martin; 1982.
KROCK, ARTHUR: *Memoirs.* New York: Funk & Wagnalls; 1968.

LAHR, RAYMOND M., AND J. WILLIAM THEIS: *Congress: Power and Purpose on*

Capitol Hill. Boston: Allyn & Bacon; 1969.
LASH, JOSEPH P.: *Eleanor and Franklin.* New York: Norton; 1971.
LEUCHTENBURG, WILLIAM: *Franklin D. Roosevelt and the New Deal, 1932–1940.* New York: Harper; 1963.
—— *From Harry Truman to Ronald Reagan.* Ithaca: Cornell University Press; 1983.
LONG, WALTER E.: *Flood to Faucet.* Austin; 1956.
LOPES, SAL: *The Wall.* New York: Collins; 1987.
LORD, RUSSELL: *The Wallaces of Iowa.* Boston: Houghton Mifflin; 1947.
LOUCHHEIM, KATIE, ED.: *The Making of the New Deal: The Insiders Speak.* Cambridge: Harvard University Press; 1983.
LUDEMAN, ANNETTE: *A History of LaSalle County, South Texas Brush Country, 1856–1975.* Quanah, Tex.: North Texas Press.
LUNDBERG, FERDINAND: *America's Sixty Families.* New York: Citadel; 1937.
LYNCH, DUDLEY: *The Duke of Duval.* Waco: The Texian Press; 1976.

MacDONALD, BETTY: *The Egg and I.* Philadelphia, New York: Lippincott; 1945.
MAGUIRE, JACK R.: *A President's Country.* Austin: Alcade Press; 1964.
MANCHESTER, WILLIAM: *American Caesar: Douglas MacArthur 1880–1964.* Boston: Little, Brown and Co.; 1978.
—— *The Death of a President.* New York: Harper; 1967.
—— *The Glory and the Dream.* Boston: Little, Brown and Co.; 1974.
MANN, ARTHUR: *La Guardia.* Philadelphia: Lippincott; 1959.
—— *La Guardia Comes to Power.* Westport, Conn.: Greenwood Press; 1981.
MARSHALL, JASPER NEWTON: *Prophet of the Pedernales.* Privately published.
MARTIN, ROSCOE C.: *The People's Party in Texas.* Austin: University of Texas Press; 1933.
MATTHEWS, WILBUR: *San Antonio Lawyer.* San Antonio: Corona; 1983.
McADAM, DOUG: *Freedom Summer.* New York: Oxford University Press; 1988.
McCLENDON, SARAH: *My Eight Presidents.* New York: Simon & Schuster; 1978.
McKAY, SETH: *Texas and the Fair Deal, 1945–1952.* San Antonio: Naylor; 1954.
—— *Texas Politics, 1906–1944.* Lubbock: Texas Tech. Press; 1952.
—— *W. Lee O'Daniel and Texas Politics,*

1938–1942. Lubbock: Texas Technological College Research; 1944.
MCKAY, SETH, AND ODIE B. FAULK: *Texas After Spindletop: The Saga of Texas, 1901–1965.* Austin: Steck-Vaughn Company; 1965.
MILLER, MERLE: *Lyndon: An Oral Biography.* New York: Putnam's; 1980.
MILLER, WILLIAM: *Fishbait.* Englewood Cliffs, New Jersey: Prentice-Hall; 1977.
MOLEY, RAYMOND: *After Seven Years.* New York: Harper; 1939.
———— *27 Masters of Politics.* New York: Funk and Wagnalls; 1949.
MONTGOMERY, RUTH: *Hail to the Chiefs: My Life and Times with Six Presidents.* New York: Coward-McCann; 1970.
———— *Mrs. L.B.J.* New York: Holt, Rinehart and Winston; 1964.
MOONEY, BOOTH: *LBJ: An Irreverent Chronicle.* New York: Crowell; 1976.
———— *The Lyndon Johnson Story.* New York: Farrar, Straus; 1964.
———— *Mr. Texas: The Story of Coke Stevenson.* Dallas: Texas Printing House; 1947.
———— *The Politicians: 1945–1966.* Philadelphia: Lippincott; 1970.
———— *Roosevelt and Rayburn.* Philadelphia, New York: Lippincott; 1971.
MORGAN, TED: *FDR.* New York: Simon & Schuster; 1985.
MORISON, SAMUEL ELIOT, HENRY STEELE COMMAGER, AND WILLIAM E. LEUCHTENBURG: *The Growth of the American Republic.* New York, London: Oxford University Press; 1969.
MOURSUND, JOHN S.: *Blanco County Families for One Hundred Years.* Austin: Nortex Press; 1979.
MURPHEY, BRUCE ALLEN: *Fortas: The Rise and Ruin of a Supreme Court Justice.* New York: Morrow; 1988.

NEWLON, CLARKE: *L.B.J.: The Man From Johnson City.* New York: Dodd, Mead; 1966.
NICHOLSON, PATRICK J.: *Mr. Jim: The Biography of James Smither Abercrombie.* Houston: Gulf; 1983.
NOONAN, JOHN T., JR.: *Bribes.* New York: Macmillan; 1984.
NORRIS, GEORGE W.: *Fighting Liberal.* New York: Collier Books; 1961.
NOUSE, EDWIN: *Three Years of the AAA.* Washington, D.C.: Brookings Institute; 1938.

OLMSTED, FREDERICK LAW: *A Journey Through Texas.* New York: Edwards & Co.; 1857.

O'NEILL, WILLIAM L.: *American High: The Years of Confidence, 1945–1960.* New York: Free Press; 1986.
OVERACKER, LOUISE: *Money in Elections.* New York: Macmillan; 1932.

PEARSON, DREW, AND JACK ANDERSON: *The Case Against Congress.* New York: Simon & Schuster; 1968.
PELZER, LOUIS: *The Cattleman's Frontier.* Glendale, Calif.: Clark; 1936.
PERRY, GEORGE SESSIONS: *Texas: A World in Itself.* New York: McGraw-Hill; 1942.
PHILLIPS, CABELL B.: *From the Crash to the Blitz, 1929–1939.* New York: Macmillan; 1969.
———— *The 1940s: Decade of Triumph and Trouble.* New York: Macmillan; 1975.
———— *The Truman Presidency.* New York: Macmillan; 1966.
PHILLIPS, WILLIAM G.: *Yarborough of Texas.* Washington, D.C.: Acropolis; 1969.
PICKRELL, ANNIE: *Pioneer Women of Texas.* Austin: Jenkins/Pemberton Press; 1970.
PIERCE, NEAL R.: *The Great Plains States of America.* New York: Norton; 1973.
———— *The Megastates of America.* New York: Norton; 1973.
POOL, WILLIAM C., EMMIE CRADDOCK, AND DAVID E. CONRAD: *Lyndon Baines Johnson: The Formative Years.* San Marcos: Southwest Texas State College Press; 1965.
PORTERFIELD, BILL: *LBJ Country.* Garden City, New York: Doubleday; 1965.
PRESLEY, JAMES: *A Saga of Wealth: The Rise of the Texas Oilmen.* New York: Putnam's; 1978.
PROVENCE, HARRY: *Lyndon B. Johnson.* New York, Fleet; 1964.
Public Papers of the President. Lyndon B. Johnson, 1963–64. Vol. I.

RAMSAY, MARION L.: *Pyramids of Power.* New York: Bobbs-Merrill; 1937.
RASMUSSEN, WAYNE: *The Department of Agriculture.* New York: Praeger; 1972.
REDDING, JOHN M.: *Inside the Democratic Party.* New York: Bobbs-Merrill; 1958.
REEDY, GEORGE: *Lyndon B. Johnson.* New York: Andrews & McMeel; 1982.
RESTON, JAMES, JR.: *The Lone Star: The Life of John Connally.* New York: Harper & Row; 1989.
ROSENMAN, SAMUEL I., COMP.: *The Public Papers and Addresses of Franklin D. Roosevelt.* 13 vols. New York: Russell & Russell; 1969.

ROVERE, RICHARD: *Final Reports*. Garden City, New York: Doubleday; 1984.
RUST, WILLIAM J.: *Kennedy in Vietnam*. New York: Scribners; 1985.

SALE, KIRKPATRICK: *Power Shift*. New York: Random House; 1975.
SAMPSON, ANTHONY: *The Seven Sisters: The Great Oil Companies and the World They Made*. New York: Viking; 1975.
SCHANDLER, HERBERT Y.: *The Unmaking of a President; Lyndon Johnson and Vietnam*. Princeton: Princeton University Press; 1977.
SCHAWE, WILLIEDELL, ED.: *Wimberley's Legacy*. San Antonio: Naylor; 1963.
SCHLESINGER, ARTHUR M., JR.: *The Age of Roosevelt*. 3 vols. Boston: Houghton Mifflin; 1957–1960.
—— *The Imperial Presidency*. Boston: Houghton Mifflin; 1973.
—— *Robert Kennedy and His Times*. Boston: Houghton Mifflin; 1978.
SHERRILL, ROBERT: *The Accidental President*. New York: Grossman; 1967.
SHERWOOD, ROBERT E.: *Roosevelt and Hopkins: An Intimate History*. New York: Harper; 1948.
SHOGAN, ROBERT: *A Question of Judgment: The Fortas Case*. Indianapolis, New York; Bobbs-Merrill; 1972.
SIDEY, HUGH: *A Very Personal Presidency: Lyndon Johnson in the White House*. New York: Atheneum; 1968.
SIMON, JAMES F.: *Independent Journey: The Life of William O. Douglas*. New York: Harper; 1980.
SINGER, KURT D., AND JANE SHERROD: *Lyndon Baines Johnson, Man of Reason*. Minneapolis: Denison; 1964.
SMITH, GENE: *The Shattered Dream*. New York: Morrow; 1970.
SMITH, MARIE D.: *The President's Lady: An Intimate Biography of Mrs. Lyndon B. Johnson*. New York: Random House; 1964.
SOLBERG, CARL: *Oil Power*. New York: Mason/Charter; 1976.
SPEER, JOHN W.: *A History of Blanco County*. Austin: Pemberton; 1965.
STEHLING, ARTHUR: *LBJ's Climb to the White House*. Chicago: Adams Press; 1987.
STEINBERG, ALFRED: *Sam Johnson's Boy*. New York: Macmillan; 1968.
—— *Sam Rayburn*. New York: Hawthorn; 1975.
SUTHERLAND, ELIZABETH: *Letters From Mississippi*. New York: McGraw-Hill; 1965.

TAYLOR, C.: *Rural Life in the United States*. New York: Knopf; 1952.
Texas Almanacs: 1939–50. Dallas: *Dallas Morning News*.
THOMAS, WILLIAM L., ED.: *Man's Role in Changing the Face of the Earth*. Chicago: University of Chicago Press; 1956.
TOLBERT, FRANK X.: *Tolbert's Texas*. Garden City, New York: Doubleday; 1983.
TRUMAN, MARGARET: *Bess W. Truman*. New York: Macmillan; 1986.
—— *Harry S Truman*. New York: Morrow; 1973.
TUGWELL, REXFORD G.: *The Democratic Roosevelt*. Garden City, N.Y.: Doubleday; 1957.
TULLY, GRACE: *F.D.R., My Boss*. New York: Scribner's; 1949.
TURNER, KATHLEEN: *Lyndon Johnson's Dual War: Vietnam and the Press*. Chicago: University of Chicago Press; 1985.

U.S. DEPARTMENT OF AGRICULTURE: *Rural Lines, USA*. Washington, D.C.: Rural Electrification Administration.
—— *Yearbook of Agriculture, 1921, 1925, 1940*. Washington, D.C.: G.P.O.

WEBB, WALTER PRESCOTT: *The Great Frontier*. Boston: Houghton Mifflin; 1952.
—— *The Great Plains*. Boston: Ginn; 1931.
—— *The Texas Rangers: A Century of Frontier Defense*. Austin: University of Texas Press; 1965.
WEBB, WALTER PRESCOTT, AND H. BAILEY CARROLL, EDS.: *The Handbook of Texas*. 3 vols. Austin: Texas State Historical Association; 1952–76.
WHITE, OWEN P.: *Texas: An Informal Association*. New York: Putnam's; 1945.
WHITE, THEODORE: *America in Search of Itself*. New York: Harper; 1982.
—— *In Search of History*. New York: Harper; 1978.
—— *The Making of the President, 1960*. New York: Atheneum; 1961.
—— *The Making of the President, 1964*. New York: Atheneum; 1965.
—— *The Making of the President, 1968*. New York: Atheneum; 1969.
WHITE, WILLIAM LINDSAY: *Queens Die Proudly*. New York: Harcourt Brace and Co.; 1943.
WHITE, WILLIAM S.: *The Making of a Journalist*. Lexington: University Press of Kentucky; 1986.

432   Selected Bibliography

WHITE, WILLIAM SMITH: *The Professional: Lyndon B. Johnson.* Boston: Houghton Mifflin; 1964.

WICKER, TOM: *JFK and LBJ.* New York: Morrow; 1968.

WILLIAMS, JUAN, ET AL.: *Eyes on the Prize.* New York: Viking; 1987.

WILSON, H. HUBERT: *Congress: Corruption and Compromise.* New York: Rinehart; 1951.

WILSON, RICHARD W,, AND BEULAH F. DUHOLM: *A Genealogy.* Lake Hills, Iowa: Graphic; 1967.

WOLFE, JANE: *The Murchisons.* New York: St. Martin's; 1989.

WOODWARD, BOB, AND SCOTT ARMSTRONG: *The Brethren.* New York: Simon and Schuster; 1980.

WPA: *Texas: A Guide to the Lone Star State.* New York: Hastings House; 1940.

——— *Washington: City and Capital.* Washington, D.C.: G.P.O.; 1937.

WYATT, FREDERICA BURT, AND HOOPER SHELTON: *Coke R. Stevenson: A Texas Legend.* Junction, Tex.: Shelton Press; 1976.

Notes

ABBREVIATIONS

AA-S	Austin American-Statesman
AS	Austin Statesman
CCC-T	Corpus Christi Caller-Times
CR	Congressional Record
DMN	Dallas Morning News
DT-H	Dallas Times-Herald
FWS-T	Fort Worth Star-Telegram
HC	Houston Chronicle
HP	Houston Post
NA	National Archives
NYT	New York Times
OH	Oral History
SAE	San Antonio Express
USN&WR	U.S. News & World Report
WP	Washington Post
WSJ	Wall Street Journal

LBJL	Lyndon Baines Johnson Library
JHP	Johnson House Papers
LBJA CF	Congressional File
LBJA FN	Famous Names
LBJA SF	Subject File
LBJA SN	Selected Names
PP	President (Personal)
PPCF	Pre-Presidential Confidential File
PPMF	Pre-Presidential Memo File
WHCF	White House Central File
WHFN	White House Famous Names File

Introduction: Ends and Means

History of "We Shall Overcome": Glazer, *Songs of Peace, Freedom, and Protest*, pp. 334–35; Dunaway, *How Can I Keep from Singing: Pete Seeger*, pp. 219–43; "Moment of History," *The New Yorker*, Mar. 27, 1965; Gitlin, *The Sixties*, p. 75; Kaiser, *1968 in America*, pp. 40, 41, 147; McAdam, *Freedom Summer*; Cagin and Dray, *We Are Not Afraid*; Sutherland, *Letters from Mississippi*; Belfrage, *Freedom Summer*, p. 55.

Sung after sit-in arrests: Cagin and Dray, pp. 71–72. "The buses all": Ellen Lake letter to her parents, June 20, 1964, quoted in McAdam, p. 71. "We were sitting": Sutherland, p. 117. "Tonight": Sutherland, p. 119. Liuzzo was singing it: Manchester, *The Glory and the Dream*, p. 1061. "I know": Lake letter, quoted in McAdam, p. 112. "Finally we stood": Belfrage, p. 55. "And then": Kay Rawlings journal, June 25, 1964, quoted in McAdam, p. 71. "Rarely in history": "Civil Rights: The Central Point," *Time*, Mar. 19, 1965.

Feelings of civil rights protesters: Richard B. Stolley, "Inside the White House: Pressures Build Up to the Momentous Speech," *Life*, Mar. 26, 1965; *Time*, Mar. 19, 1965; Garrow, *Bearing the Cross*, particularly pp. 381–88; Fager, *Selma 1965*; Williams, *Eyes on the Prize*; *Life*, *Time*, *Newsweek*, *NYT*, *WP*, 1964–65. **Selma figures:** Manchester, p. 1059. **"He was murdered"; "We didn't think":** King, Young, on *Eyes on the Prize: America's Civil Rights Years* television series, Part VI. **Feelings of civil rights leaders about his long record:** Garrow, pp. 381–88. Shaffer (p. 101) says, "Until Selma, the president had no intention of asking Congress to pass another civil rights bill." *NYT*, *WP*, Feb. 1–Mar. 15, 1965.

Had voted against every civil rights bill: "Complete House Voting Record of Congressman Lyndon Johnson, By Subject, From May 13, 1937 to December 31, 1948," pp. 85–92, Box 75, LBJA SF. Evans and Novak, p. 121. **"An effort":** Johnson, quoted in Miller, *Lyndon*, p. 118. In this speech, he called Truman's civil rights program "a farce and a sham—an effort to set up a police state. . . . I am opposed to the anti-lynching bill because the federal government has no more business enacting a law against one kind of murder than another. I am against the FEPC [Federal Employment Practices Commission]. . . ." As Evans and Novak note (p. 120), the speech was "the straight party line of a Southern Democrat." **Maiden speech:** *CCC-T*, Mar. 9, 1949; *FW Press*, Mar. 10; Miller, pp. 143–44. **"We of the South"; Senators lining up:** "Speeches—Filibuster 1," Box 214, Senate papers, LBJL; *Abilene Reporter News*, *CCC-T*, Mar. 9–11, 1948; *San Angelo Standard-Times*, Mar. 10, 1948; *Atlanta Constitution*, Nov. 24, 1963; see also *Kilgore News-Herald*, Mar. 13, 1948, where Russell called Johnson's speech "the best prepared presentation that has been made in the debate." Tex Easley and Walter Jenkins interviews. On the morning of the speech, Russell had "gathered reporters around himself and urged them to hear Johnson's maiden speech that afternoon if they were after a front-page story" (Steinberg, *Sam Johnson's Boy*, p. 291). **"One of the ablest":** Russell, quoted in Doris Kearns, *Lyndon Johnson and the American Dream*, p. 106. **Lafayette Park rally:** *WP*, Mar. 15,

1965; Darden Jorden, Bryce Harlow, and Joseph L. Rauh, Jr., interviews. **"President Johnson's words":** Rev. Channing E. Phillips, quoted in *WP*, Mar. 15, 1965. **"Same old story":** Rauh, quoted in *WP*, Mar. 15, 1965. **Trip in limousine:** Goodwin, *Remembering America*, p. 330; Horace Busby and George Reedy interviews. **"He heard":** Busby interview. **Johnson's speech to Congress:** *NY Herald Tribune*, *NYT*, *WP*, *CCC-T*, *AA-S*, *FWS-T*, Mar. 16, 1965; Shaffer, Chapter 6. **King crying:** Cagin and Dray, p. 427. In a statement issued later that night, Dr. King said: "In his address . . . last night, President Johnson made one of the most eloquent, unequivocal and passionate pleas for human rights ever made by a President of the United States. He revealed great and amazing understanding of the depth and dimension of the problem of racial injustice. . . . His power of persuasion has nowhere been more forcefully set forth" (King, quoted in *NYT*, Mar. 17, 1965). **Pickets were gone:** Stolley, "Inside the White House," *Life*, Mar. 26, 1965; *NYT*, *WP*, Mar. 17, 1965. **Johnson-Celler conversation:** Shaffer, p. 100; *Newsweek*, Mar. 29, 1965; Emmanuel Celler interview. **"Cajoling, threatening":** Farmer, quoted in Miller, p. 434. **Johnson's protection of Selma–Montgomery march:** *Time*, Mar. 26, 1965.

"Greatest accomplishment": Bornet, *The Presidency of Lyndon B. Johnson*, p. 221. **"Thank you, Mr. President":** Marshall, quoted by Lady Bird Johnson, *A White House Diary*, p. 758. **"That horrible song":** Johnson to Doris Kearns, quoted in Kearns, *Lyndon Johnson and the American Dream*, p. 340. **"Some are eager"; "They call upon":** Johnson, speech to American Bar Association, Aug. 12, 1964, quoted in Evans and Novak, p. 531. **"Those who say"; "We are not about":** Johnson, quoted in Evans and Novak, p. 532. **Not a month:** Johnson's inauguration was Jan. 20. The first major air raid of Operation Rolling Thunder was Feb. 7. **Vietnam escalation:** *NYT*, *WP*, Apr.–Dec., 1965. **549,000:** Manchester, p. 1124. **58,000:** *World Almanac and Book of Facts*, 1988. **"The standing":** Eisenhower, unpublished draft of memoirs, quoted in Ewald, p. 120.

Whispers and lies: Berman, pp. 56–57, Halberstam, *The Best and the Brightest*, pp. 569–70, 585–87; Turner, *Lyndon Johnson's Dual War*, pp. 134–46; White, *The Making of the President 1968*, pp. 121–23; *Time, Newsweek, NYT, WP*, Apr. 1–30, 1965. **"The American People"**: Editorial, *NYT*, June 9, 1965. See also June 10 editorial; Berman, pp. 56–57; White, pp. 21–23; Turner. **"American blood"**: Johnson, quoted in Cormier, *LBJ: The Way He Was*, p. 187; Turner, p. 136. **"Was talking to us"; 1500 murdered:** Johnson, quoted in Miller, p. 427. But "Bennett said later that his office had never been attacked and that he had never talked to the President or anyone else from beneath his desk" (Miller, p. 427). Cormier (p. 188), giving a fuller Johnson quote, which shows the vividness of Johnson's descriptive powers, states that the President said: "There has been almost constant firing on our American Embassy. As we talked with Ambassador Bennett, he said to apparently one of the girls who brought him a cable, 'Please get away from the window, that glass is going to cut your hand,' because the glass had been shattered, and we heard the bullets coming through the office where he had been sitting while talking to us. . . .

"Some fifteen hundred innocent people were murdered, and their heads cut off, and . . . as we talked to our Ambassador to confirm the horror and the tragedy and the unbelievable fact that they were firing on Americans and the American Embassy, he was talking to us from under a desk while bullets were going through his windows. . . ."

But Cormier notes that "Bennett later reported that he knew of no bullets being fired into his office, and that he never had cowered under a desk. Nor was it ever established that anyone was beheaded. And the only Americans harmed were two newsmen shot by Marines." **"A band of"**: Johnson, quoted in Turner, p. 136. Evans and Novak were to write that while Johnson's initial decisions in the Dominican Republic were courageous and decisive, his later statements and actions "transformed the crisis of revolution in the Dominican Republic into a crisis of credibility in Lyndon Johnson" (p. 516). Max Frankel of the *NYT* was to say: "Johnson was fundamentally dishonest in presenting the facts about what was happening in the Dominican Republic to the American people. . . .

telling ridiculous stories about 1,500 heads rolling around in the streets and so on. Whatever the credibility gap ultimately became, the combination of opposition to the policy and the horror at the government's handling and explanation of the event is probably where it was born" (Frankel, quoted in Miller, p. 424). For an analysis of the effect on his public image of Johnson's "inconsistent reconstructions of events," see Turner, pp. 134–37. **"Distrust of the President"**: White, p. 102. **"Died at the Alamo"**: Turner, p. 167. **A new phrase:** Turner (p. 167) says "It first hit the newspapers in the *NYHT* of May 23, 1965 over an article by David Wise." **"Ambushed;" buttons:** White, p. 102.

"It is difficult"; "could hardly believe"; "the reverence": Tom Wicker, "Hey, Hey, LBJ . . .", *Esquire*, Dec., 1983. **$20 million:** Caro, *Path to Power*, pp. xxii, xxiii, 788–89.

"87-VOTE 'LANDSLIDE' ": *Life*, Aug. 14, 1964. **"THE STORY OF"**: *USN&WR*, Apr. 6, 1964.

1. Going Back

SOURCES

Much of this chapter is drawn from my first volume of *The Years of Lyndon Johnson, The Path to Power.*

Books and documents:
Dugger, *The Politician*; Miller, *Lyndon*; Montgomery, *Mrs. LBJ*; Steinberg, *Sam Johnson's Boy* and *Sam Rayburn*.

Papers of Franklin D. Roosevelt (FDRL).

Oral Histories:
Helen Gahagan Douglas, Clifford Durr, Virginia Durr, Welly K. Hopkins, W. Ervin ("Red") James.

Interviews:
George R. Brown, Edward A. Clark, Benjamin V. Cohen, Thomas G. Corcoran, Abe Fortas, Arthur ("Tex") Goldschmidt, Elizabeth Wickenden Goldschmidt, Lady Bird Johnson, Alice and Welly K. Hopkins, James H. and Elizabeth Rowe.

NOTES

Johnson's youth, early career through 1941 Senate race: Caro, *Path to Power.* **"I'll never forget":** Mrs. Johnson interview with author, and quoted in Montgomery, p. 27.
McFarlane's exclusion: McFarlane to Roosevelt, July 29, 1939, OF-300-Texas, Box 70, Roosevelt Papers; McFarlane to Roosevelt, May 15, 1939, OF-300, Roosevelt Papers.
Roosevelt's "special feeling" for Johnson: Cohen, Corcoran, Fortas, Goldschmidt, Rowe, Wickenden Goldschmidt interviews; Caro, *Path to Power*, pp. 444-49, 535-36, 555-56, 666-69, and *passim*. **Exceptions in 1941:** Caro, *Path to Power*, pp. 678-80, 724-27. **"In the heat":** Johnson to Roosevelt, July 21, 1941, PPF 6149, Roosevelt Papers. **"Sit":** Rowe, quoted in Miller, p. 88. **"Everything":** Corcoran interview; quoted in Miller, p. 88. **Young Democrats:** Johnson, quoted in Dugger, pp. 237-38; Corcoran interview; Rowe put the suggestion in writing, Rowe to Roosevelt, July 17, 1941, PSF 184, Roosevelt Papers.
"Most remarkable"; "help him": Corcoran interview. **Circle in Washington:** Caro, *Path to Power*, pp. 450-58; Clifford and Virginia Durr, Hopkins, James OHs; Brown, Cohen, Corcoran, Fortas, Goldschmidt, Wickenden Goldschmidt, James and Elizabeth Rowe, Alice and Welly Hopkins interviews. **"I like mules"; "wasn't a man":** Wirtz, quoted in Virginia Durr OH. **Rayburn's birthday party:** Corcoran, quoted in Steinberg, *Sam Rayburn*, p. 97. **"If you had fallen":** Rowe to Johnson, Sept. 16, 1941, Box 32, LBJA SN.
"I would reproach": Virginia Durr OH, and quoted in Miller, p. 73. **"Lyndon would":** Virginia Durr, quoted in *WP*, Nov. 21, 1985. **"Once":** Rowe, quoted in Miller, p. 68. **"Made fun":** Douglas OH.
"He gave": Miller, quoted in Caro, *Path to Power*, p. 273. For Johnson being "in tune" with the conservatives as a congressional secretary, see Chapter 16. **"Basically"; "That was his leadership":** Brown, quoted in Caro, pp. 471, 552. **"Hard to tell":** Douglas OH. **"Protected himself":** Douglas OH. **"Witty":** Douglas, quoted in Caro, p. 550. **"Close-mouthed":** Douglas OH.
Johnson had made Brown rich: Caro, *Path to Power*, pp. 459-75, 577, 583-86,

598. **Brown & Root's role in 1941 campaign:** Caro, pp. 685, 717, 742-53. **Pledge:** Brown, Clark interviews.
Rayburn's loneliness: Caro, *Path to Power*, pp. 317-33. **Relationship with Johnsons:** Caro, pp. 333-34. **"Now, Lyndon":** Rayburn, quoted in Caro, p. 334. **Begging a favor:** Connally to his biographer, Steinberg, quoted in Steinberg, *Sam Johnson's Boy*, p. 94. **Rayburn's help to Johnson:** Caro, *Path to Power*, pp. 452-53, 468. **Johnson's betrayal of Rayburn:** Caro, pp. 557-605. **Rayburn's coldness to Johnson:** Caro, pp. 618-25. **Partial thaw:** Caro, pp. 754-57. **Rayburn's attempts to get Mann a meeting with Roosevelt:** Rayburn to Watson, Sept. 2, 1941, Watson to Rayburn, Sept. 3, 1941, unsigned to Watson, Sept. 11, 1941—all PPF 474, Roosevelt Papers. **"Shook hands":** *Beaumont Enterprise*, Nov. 11, 1941. **"Close enough":** Johnson, quoted in *Beaumont Journal*, Nov. 10, 1941.

2. All Quiet on the Western Front

SOURCES

Books and documents:
Beasley, *Knudsen*; *The Biographical Directory of the American Congress, 1774-1971*; Burns, *Roosevelt: The Lion and the Fox* and *The Soldier of Freedom*; Caidin and Hymoff, *The Mission*; Daniels, *White House Witness*; Dugger, *The Politician*; Miller, *Lyndon*; Mooney, *Lyndon Johnson Story*; Newlon, *L.B.J.: The Man from Johnson City*; Sherwood, *Roosevelt and Hopkins*; Steinberg, *Sam Johnson's Boy*; White, *Queens Die Proudly*.

Papers of Tom C. Clark (HSTL).
Papers of Franklin D. Roosevelt (FDRL).

Oral Histories:
Warren Magnuson.

Interviews:
John B. Connally, Thomas G. Corcoran, Alice Hopkins, Lady Bird Johnson, Sam Houston Johnson, Warren Magnuson, Mary Rather, O. J. Weber, Harold Young, Mary Louise Glass Young, James Van Zandt.

NOTES

"If the day ever comes": For example, in radio address, Abilene, Texas, May 6, 1941. Also *DMN, AA, AA-S,* May 6–June 30, 1941. **Variations**: For example, "I hope as your Senator I shall never have to vote to send your boy to the trenches. I love peace, but I tell you mothers, the day my conscience tells me to vote that way, 32-year-old Lyndon Johnson who registered for the draft will give up his seat and go with your boys" (radio address, Lubbock, Texas, May 7, 1941, "Campaign Speeches," Lyndon Johnson Senate Race—1941," Box 331, JHP). In San Angelo, he said: "If I ever feel it necessary to cast a vote for a declaration of war, I'll offer my services the next day to go up there to the front with the rest of the boys" (requoted on the occasion of his enlistment, *San Angelo Evening Standard,* Dec. 9, 1941). In Elgin, he said: "The day I vote to send your boy to war, that day I will resign and go with him" (requoted, *Elgin Courier,* Dec. 11, 1941). **"Would be in the front line"**: Johnson, quoted in *Fredericksburg Standard,* Oct. 9, 1941. **"If Hitler makes"**: Undated text of Johnson speech, p. 5, Box 331, JHP. He added the "I shall never vote" sentence in hand. **"WE NEED COURAGE LIKE THIS"**: "Postcards," Box 34, JHP. **"I may be scrubbing"**: *Beaumont Enterprise,* Nov. 11, 1941. **"Already in that war"**: *Austin Tribune,* Oct. 9, 1941. In another speech, he said: "When the president said shoot on sight, that meant we were in war!" (*Austin Statesman,* Oct. 7, 1941). **"A number of persons"**: *Fredericksburg Standard,* Oct. 9, 1941. **"Some time ago"**: *San Antonio Light,* quoted in *San Marcos Record,* Oct. 25, 1941.

Had enrolled in the Naval Reserve: "Public Activities—Biographic Information, L. B. Johnson, June 11, 1940, Commission in U.S. Navy," Box 73, LBJA SF. **"When you get back"**: Johnson to Hopkins, Dec. 8, 1941, Personal Papers of Welly K. Hopkins, Box 1, LBJL. **Magnuson appealed to Vinson**: Magnuson interview; *Seattle Post-Intelligencer,* Dec. 20, 1941, May 10, 1942. **Magnuson's combat service**: Magnuson interview; Magnuson OH; *Seattle Post-Intelligencer,* Dec. 21, 1941–May 21, 1942; *HC,* Dec. 12, 1941.

Request for "active duty": Johnson to Roosevelt, Dec. 8, 1941, PPF 6149, Roo-

sevelt Papers. **Pro forma**: Among those aware of the job Johnson wanted were Corcoran and Young. On the same day on which he went to see Roosevelt, he introduced a bill in the House that would create the new agency, which, under his bill, would be headed by a $10,000-a-year director appointed by the President (*Brenham Banner-Press, DMN,* Dec. 10, 1941). During his talk with Roosevelt, it is unclear that any other type of "active duty" was even mentioned; if it was, the type Johnson had in mind may be hinted at by the fact that presidential assistant Marvin McIntyre wrote on Johnson's letter, at the time Johnson was going to Forrestal's office, "File—taken care of," and explained to Grace Tully a few days later that Johnson "is on active duty in the Navy here in Washington" (Tully to Roosevelt, Dec. 17, 1941, PPF 6149, Roosevelt Papers). Johnson himself was to say, "I took my oath as lieutenant commander and went to work as a deputy to Secretary of the Navy, James Forrestal." As will be seen, his lobbying for the directorship continued all during December.

Johnson's previous proposal to merge NYA and CCC: Memo to Roosevelt, Dec. 6, 1941, PPF 6149, Roosevelt Papers. **"Said he understood"**: Johnson, quoted in Dugger, p. 239. **Goes to Forrestal's office**: Barker to Bard, Dec. 16, 1941, Navy Unofficial Personnel File, LBJL. **"How do you want?"**: Forrestal to Johnson, undated, Box 4, LBJA FN. **Dispatched for inspection tour and liaison**: Forrestal to Olds, Dec. 20, 1941; "Memorandum for Commander Gingrich," Dec. 18, 1941, Baker to Beswick, Dec. 16, 1941, Navy Unofficial Personnel File, LBJA SF. **"I am very hopeful"**: Johnson to Roosevelt, undated (acknowledged Dec. 30, 1941), PPF 6149, Roosevelt Papers. **"Will probably get out"**: Johnson to Tom Clark, Jan. 2, 1942, Box 5, "Je-Jo," Clark Papers. **Note from Roosevelt**: Roosevelt to Johnson, Dec. 30, 1941, PPF 6149, Roosevelt Papers. **"Art galleries and all"**: Mrs. Johnson interview with author.

Loathed his work: Mooney, pp. 60–61. **"A paper-shifting job"**: Johnson, quoted in Miller, p. 92.

Encounter with Admiral: Johnson, quoted in Dugger, p. 239.

Not a joking matter; Vinson's relationship with Admirals: Caro, *Path to Power,* p. 537. **"He couldn't stand"**: Caro, p. 229. **"If he couldn't lead"; take his ball**:

Caro, p. 71. **"Settle a personal problem"**: Miller, p. 92; Steinberg, p. 189. **Roosevelt gives him no satisfaction:** Roosevelt to Watson, Jan. 22, 1942, PPF 6149, Roosevelt Papers; Corcoran interview. **Meeting and charming Barker:** Barker to Gingrich, Barker to Bard, Dec. 16, 1941, Navy Unofficial Personnel File, LBJL. **Dispatched as Barker's assistant:** Barker to Pederson, Dec. 16, 1941, Navy Unofficial Personnel File, LBJL.

Restoration of relationship with Rayburn: Caro, *Path to Power*, pp. 754–63. **"We would go"**: Connally interview. **"We had a lot of fun"**: Connally interview. **Faking the photographs:** Otto Crider, quoted in Dugger, p. 240. Dugger does not identify Kellam by name, but Kellam himself often told the story in later years. **Wrestling match; "the next morning"; Weisl's arrangements:** Connally interview.

Alice Glass's biography and relationship with Johnson: Described in Caro, *Path to Power*, pp. 476–92. **"Give Herman the dam"**: Caro, p. 483. **Selling him land:** Caro, p. 488. **Oil deal:** Caro, pp. xiii–xvi. **Told intimates that she and Johnson had discussed marriage:** The intimates to whom she told this include her sister, Mary Louise Glass Young, and Harold Young, who at the time was an aide to Vice President Henry Wallace and an adviser to Charles Marsh. **"A young man"**: Caro, *Path to Power*, p. 482.

"I can write": Alice Glass to Oltorf, Sept. 16, 1967 (copy in author's possession). The letter goes on to tell Oltorf, Brown & Root's lobbyist: "You could certainly write a very interesting chapter on his rise (we must call it from 'rags to riches,' nothing else would pass his approval) in the financial world. I could also add some factual details to your original. This chapter should give hope and ambition to many a young poor Texan—we certainly owe the youth of Texas this. It is our duty. But there you are; nothing but trouble with the Historic Society." When *The Path to Power*—and its description of Lyndon Johnson's long relationship with Mrs. Marsh—was published, a former Johnson aide, Liz Carpenter, for example, said, "I think it is a ridiculous charge made at a time when the man who could answer it can no longer answer." She said she knew nothing "whatsoever" of any romantic involvement between Johnson and Glass (*AA-S*, Oct. 20, 1982). **"She was dis-**

gusted"**: Mary Louise Young interview. **"Lyndon was the love"**: Hopkins interview.

"An interesting time": Connally interview. **Use of "due bills"**: Mary Louise and Harold Young interviews; Dugger, p. 239. Mary Louise, Marsh's secretary at the time, arranged for Johnson to use the bills. **Matsomoto episode:** Connally interview. He showed the author the robe with great pride.

"Placed in line": *HP*, Dec. 11, 1941. **Johnson's location being concealed from Marsh:** On Feb. 21, 1942, Johnson's secretary, Mary Rather, telegraphed Johnson at the Empire Hotel in San Francisco: "MARSH AT BEVERLY WILSHIRE HOTEL, BEVERLY HILLS, CALIFORNIA, TODAY. ANXIOUS TALK TO YOU ON PHONE OR SEE YOU. TOLD GLASS I WOULD ATTEMPT LOCATE YOU" (Rather to Johnson, Feb. 21, 1942, Box 26, LBJA SN). "Glass" is Alice's sister, Mary Louise, who was one of Charles Marsh's secretaries. She told the author that Marsh had instructed her to locate Johnson, a task she was anxious not to carry out, since she knew Johnson was with her sister in California. Mary Louise says that when she called Miss Rather, Miss Rather panicked and not knowing what to do sent the telegram to Johnson. Miss Rather then called her back and said she could not contact Johnson, so Miss Glass was able to tell *her* boss, Marsh, that Johnson could not be located, and the possibility of an embarrassing scene was avoided.

"We were really working": Connally interview. **"Where is that man?"**: Weber quoted Barker's remarks in his letter to Johnson, Feb. 15, 1942 (Box 35, LBJA SN). **"I'm very glad"**: Barker to Johnson, Feb. 16, 1942, LBJ–Navy Unofficial Personnel File, LBJL. **"Crossing each other"**: Johnson to Barker, Feb. 19, 1942, LBJ–Navy Unofficial Personnel File, LBJL. **"I've been wondering"**: Barker to Johnson, Mar. 10, 1942, LBJ–Navy Unofficial Personnel File, LBJL.

The letters from Johnson's congressional office: Weber to Johnson, Johnson to Weber, Feb. 2–Mar. 26, 1942, "O. J. Weber," Box 35, LBJA SN. **Texarkana rentals:** Weber to Johnson, Feb. 16, 1942, "O. J. Weber," Box 35, LBJA SN. **Wrestling with the larger problem:** Connally interview. **Had promised Allred support:** Connally interview. **"Might not ever"**: Connally interview. **Roosevelt's feelings:** See, for example, Roosevelt to

Ickes, Feb. 4, 1942, Box 70 (Texas, 1938–1945, G-J), OF-300-Roosevelt Papers. **Wirtz told him:** His feelings are shown in a letter he wrote to Lady Bird, which Wirtz evidently felt she would pass on to her husband: "If his name were put on the ballot . . . I think it would ruin his future political career because the people would have the idea he is trying to make political capital out of his uniform." Wirtz to Mrs. Johnson, May 14, 1942, Box 37, LBJA SN. **"War fever":** Connally interview. **Plans for draft:** *DMN*, May 13, 14, 1942. **"All over the place":** Johnson to Gingrich, Feb. 27, 1942, LBJ–Navy Unofficial Personnel File, LBJL. **"A very frustrating time"; "a constant stream of letters":** Mrs. Johnson interview. **"Something big":** Corcoran interview. The "something big" was no longer the directorship of a merged NYA-CCC, because by this time, it was already obvious that these two agencies were more likely to be abolished (as, indeed, they were) than merged. **"I can appreciate":** Wirtz to Johnson, Feb. 23, 1942, Box 37, LBJA SN. **Knudsen appointment:** Sherwood, p. 456.
    "Things are very dull": Johnson to Roosevelt, Johnson to Tully, Mar. 7, 1942; Roosevelt to Johnson, Mar. 17, 1942, OF-300-Texas-69(A), Roosevelt Papers. **Requesting transfer to Pearl Harbor:** Johnson to Barker, Feb. 21, 1942, LBJ–Navy Unofficial Personnel File, LBJL. **"I have no address":** Barker to Johnson, Mar. 4, 1942, LBJ–Navy Unofficial Personnel File, LBJL.
    "Get your ass": Marsh to Johnson, Apr. 21, 1942, Papers of Charles E. Marsh, Box 3, LBJL. **"I am doubtful":** Wirtz to Johnson, Feb. 23, 1942, Box 37, LBJA SN. **Lockhart's suggestion:** *AA-S*, Mar. 12, 13, 1942. **"Rendering patriotic and valuable service": "government censorship":** *AA-S*, Mar. 13, 14, 1942. **"Coming to a showdown":** Weber to Johnson, Mar. 16, 1942, Box 35, LBJA SN. **"Have to have an answer":** Weber to Johnson, Mar. 14, 1942, Box 35, LBJA SN. **"I am under orders":** Johnson to Blundell, "Political Correspondence, 1942," Box 37, JHP. **"Getting it":** Magnuson to Parish, from "Somewhere in the Pacific," printed in *Seattle Star*, Jan. 23, 1942. **Magnuson's war service:** Magnuson interview; Magnuson OH; *Seattle Post-*

Intelligencer, Seattle Star, Dec. 23, 1941–May 20, 1942. **Other congressmen's service:** Maas—*Biographical Directory*; Van Zandt interview; Osmers—*NYT*, Jan. 17, 1942. **Unable to decide:** Connally interview. **Wirtz had let him know:** Wirtz to Johnson, Feb. 23, 1942, Box 37, LBJA SN. And see Magnuson OH. There may even have been pressure from the Navy. According to a memo written for his files by Johnson, he met in San Francisco on April 9 with Admiral J. W. Greenslade. Greenslade "discussed briefly the kind of work Ensign Connally and I have been doing since entering active service." Then, Johnson wrote, they "discussed . . . the desirability of extending our present work," and Greenslade suggested an addition to their orders that would permit him to "assign additional duty such as submarine duty, bomber patrols, convoy commands." If there was such pressure—the wording of the memo is ambiguous—Johnson evaded it. "I told the Admiral a request for this addition to the orders would be made on my return" to Washington, he wrote. But when he got back to Washington, he made no such request.
    "For the sake of political future": Daniels, p. 28. **Tells McIntyre:** Johnson to McIntyre, Apr. 7, 1942, PPF 6149, Roosevelt Papers. **Meeting with Roosevelt:** Apr. 26, 1942, memo, PPF 6149, Roosevelt Papers. **Nudge from Forrestal:** Johnson, quoted in Kintner to Fehr, Oct. 17, 1966, p. 2, "Public Activities–Biographic Information–Naval Career," Box 1A, LBJA SF. **Roosevelt assigns him:** "Chief of Bureau of Navigation, Navy Department, to Lt. Cmdr. Lyndon B. Johnson," Apr. 30, 1942, LBJ–Navy Unofficial Personnel File, LBJL. **Signs two petitions:** Connally interview. **Seals photographs in envelope:** The envelope and the photographs of Alice Glass are in Box 10, PPCF, at the Lyndon B. Johnson Library in Austin. One of these photographs is reproduced in Caro, *Path to Power*, in the photo section following p. 582, Plate 2, bottom right. **Flight across Pacific:** Newlon, pp. 87–88.
    "MUCH TALK DRAFTING YOU": Telegram, McIntyre to Johnson, May 19, 1942, OF-300-Democratic National Committee, 1933–45, Roosevelt Papers. A further indication of the importance the White House attached to keeping Johnson out of the race is the fact that four days later, McIntyre had the telegram

traced to make sure Johnson had received it. McCrea to McIntyre, May 23, 1942, OF-300-Democratic National Committee, 1933–45, Roosevelt Papers. Telegram from Alice: "Public Activities–Biographic Information–Naval Career," Box 74, LBJA SF. **Telephone call to Connally:** Connally interview.

3. In the Pacific

SOURCES

Books, articles, brochures and documents:
The Biographical Directory of the American Congress, 1774–1971; Burns, *Roosevelt: The Soldier of Freedom*; Caidin and Hymoff, *The Mission*; Daniels, *White House Witness*; Dugger, *The Politician*; Manchester, *American Caesar*; Miller, *Lyndon*; Mooney, *The Lyndon Johnson Story*; Newlon, *L.B.J.: The Man from Johnson City*; Steinberg, *Sam Johnson's Boy*; White, *Queens Die Proudly*.
Harry G. Baren, "My Combat Mission with Lyndon Johnson," *Saga*, July, 1964; Robert Buckhorn, "S. Pacific Tale: How Johnson Got His Silver Star," *DT-H*, Mar. 16, 1964; Caidin and Hymoff, "How Lyndon Johnson Won the Silver Star," *Saga*, Apr., 1964; Hal Drake, "Saburo Sakai—He Almost Changed History," *Veterans of Foreign Wars Magazine*, Oct., 1966.
Lyndon B. Johnson, "Diary" (81 pages of handwritten notes in small notebook written during his time in Pacific).

Oral Histories:
Marshall McNeil.

Interviews:
George R. Brown, Horace Busby, Edward A. Clark, Benjamin V. Cohen, Thomas G. Corcoran, Stella Gliddon, Walter Jenkins, Joe M. Kilgore, James H. Rowe, Jr., E. Babe Smith, Harold Young.

NOTES

Meeting with MacArthur: *NYT*, May 29, 1942; Anderson, quoted in Newlon, p. 89. See also Steinberg, p. 191. **Tour:** Newlon, pp. 90–91; Caidin and Hymoff, pp. 60–65. **Flying north on airliner:** Johnson, "Diary," p. 9.
Description of Garbutt Field: Caidin

and Hymoff, pp. 66–80. **Johnson's physical timidity as a youth:** Caro, *Path to Power*, for example, p. 174. **"If you hit me":** Caro, p. 156.
Lae was a tough mission: Caidin and Hymoff, pp. 75–76, 82–87, 95–97, 143. Their book, published in 1964, is the best available source for Johnson's adventures in the Pacific. Except where otherwise indicated, the following quotations from men on the mission, and much of the information about it, come from that book. Also, Baren, quoted in Dugger, p. 245; Sakai interview with Saito, and Sakai with Caidin and Saito, *Samurai!*, quoted in Caidin and Hymoff, p. 83.
Johnson's decision to go: Caidin and Hymoff, pp. 78–80; Baren, quoted in Dugger, pp. 244–45; Anderson, quoted in Newlon, p. 92.
Stevens taking Johnson's seat: Marquat to Whom It May Concern, June 17, 1942. The General wrote this letter to support Johnson's claim for $130 reimbursement from the Navy for his motion-picture camera and rolls of film that were left on the *Wabash Cannonball*. "Claim for Reimbursement for Personal Property Lost in a Marine or Aircraft Disaster," "Public Activities–Biographic Information–Naval Career (1 of 2)," Box 7, LBJA SF; Dugger, p. 244.
Raid on Lae: Johnson, "Diary," pp. 9, 10; UP dispatch from "Somewhere in Australia," in *AA-S*, June 12, 1942; AP dispatch from "An Allied Operational Base in the Southwest Pacific," in *HP*, June 12, 1942; Drake, "Saburo Sakai"; Baren, quoted in Dugger, pp. 246–47; Caidin and Hymoff, pp. 111–83; Newlon, pp. 93–95, 97. All quotations are from Caidin and Hymoff. **"It was the kind":** McCredie, quoted in Caidin and Hymoff, pp. 165–66. **"It was rough"; "very interesting":** Walker and McCredie, quoted in Caidin and Hymoff, pp. 166–68.
Wabash Cannonball: *DT-H*, July 23, 1942. **Stevens' death:** Drake, "Saburo Sakai."
Adventure on flight back to Melbourne: Johnson, "Diary," pp. 10–11; *WP*, June 14, 1942; *Washington Times-Herald*, June 15, 1942; White, pp. 263–67; Newlon, pp. 97–100. **"Right away":** "Red" Varner, quoted in White, pp. 266–67.
"Many of the airmen knew": Anderson, quoted in Dugger, p. 248. **"We don't have":** Newlon, pp. 101–102; See also Anderson interview and "reference notes," quoted in Caidin and Hymoff, pp. 190–91. Johnson, in his "Diary" (p.

12), described the incident: "Saw MacArthur at 11:45 a.m. Very sad. Head down. Low voice, 'Glad to see you two fellows here where three were last. It was a mistake of the head to go on combat mission but it did justice to your heart.' It was just what I would have done. I'm giving you the Silver Star. Gave Stevens DSC because he was your leader and gave his life—such is war." The citation that Johnson later received states that "in order to obtain personal knowledge of the combat conditions, [he] volunteered as an observer on a hazardous aerial combat mission over hostile positions in New Guinea. As our planes neared the target area, they were intercepted by eight hostile fighters. When, at this time, the plane in which Lt. Cmdr. Johnson was an observer developed mechanical trouble and was forced to turn back alone, presenting a favorable target to the enemy fighters, he evidenced marked coolness in spite of the hazards involved. His gallant action enabled him to obtain and return with valuable information."

Flight home: Johnson, "Diary," pp. 13–14; Newlon, p. 103; Steinberg, p. 194. **"Terrible"; "got insulted":** Johnson, "Diary," p. 13. **"Lyndon Johnson [was] back":** Daniels, pp. 33–34. **Roosevelt's directive; congressmen's reaction:** Steinberg, p. 195; Dugger, p. 445; *Biographical Directory*. **"I had been ordered":** *AA*, Nov. 6, 1942. **"Distinguished himself":** Winchell, *AA-S*, July 30, 1942. **"Home from the wars":** *AA-S*, July 27, 1942. **"Fresh from the battlefields":** *Brenham Banner-Press*, July 28, 1942. **"Suicide mission":** Text of Johnson talk to newspapermen, Oct., 1966, quoted on p. 3, Kintner to Fehr, Oct. 17, 1966, "Public Activities–Biographic Information–Naval Career (1 of 2)," Box 74, LBJA SN. **"Harrowing flight":** *Washington Evening Star*, WP, July 27, 1942; *AA-S*, July 26, 1942. **"Incompetents"; "tail of a box kite":** For example, *Marble Falls Messenger*, July 23, 1942; *HP*, Oct. 24, 1942. **Pictures:** *Washington Times Herald*, WP, July 2, 1942. **"A changed Lyndon Johnson":** Unidentified clipping, Aug. 7, 1942, Scrapbook, 1, Book 7, JHP. **Weakness during speeches:** For example, *Burnet Bulletin*, Aug. 13, 1942; *Taylor Daily Press*, Aug. 6, 1942; unidentified clippings, JHP; Gliddon, Smith interviews. **Barely make himself heard:** *Taylor Daily Press*, Aug. 6, 1942. **Georgetown speech:** *Williamson County Sun*, Aug. 7, 1942. **"Impressed**

and inspired": *Spectator*, Aug. 28, 1942. **"I have just returned":** Johnson, quoted in *Elgin Courier*, Aug. 20, 1942. **"No non-believers at 12,000 feet":** Johnson, quoted in *Taylor Daily Press*, Aug. 6, 1942. **Pneumonia becoming dengue fever:** *HC*, July 18, 1942. Johnson's Certificate of Discharge from the hospital (June 26, 1942) gives "pneumonia" as his illness and *Time*, July 27, 1942, describes his illness as pneumonia, but by 1943 he is saying he had dengue fever (*Philadelphia Inquirer*, Apr. 4, 1943). Dugger (p. 445) says, "He told me it was some kind of fever." **25 pounds becomes 40:** *AA-S*, July 26, 1942; Caidin and Hymoff, p. 194; *Marble Falls Messenger*, July 23, 1942; Corcoran, Young interviews. **Mission becomes missions:** *AA-S*, quoted in Dugger, p. 251. **25,000 miles becomes 60,000:** For example, *Oregon Journal*, Dec. 8, 1942. **Time he had spent:** By July, he was telling the *HC* (July 18) he had spent "nearly three months" in the Pacific. **"Yes I was":** Johnson, quoted in *Portland Oregonian*, Dec. 8, 1942. **"Months of exciting active duty":** Johnson, quoted in Dec. 8, 1942 unidentified article by Louise Aaron, Scrapbook, JHP. **"I lived with the men":** *A Report to You* by Lyndon B. Johnson, 1944, p. 4. **Parachute:** Johnson, quoted in *AA-S*, June 12, 1942; *Hays County Herald*, Aug. 7, 1942. **Engine was "knocked out"; several of crew wounded:** Waco article, quoted in Steinberg, p. 192. **"I saw fourteen of 'em":** Johnson speech, Nov., 1959, quoted in Dugger, p. 252. **Gave himself a nickname:** *DT-H*, June 12, 1942; "Public Activities–Biographic Information–Naval Career (1 of 2)," Box 74, LBJA SF.

The "home movies": The scene during the showings at the Johnson home was described to the author by Cohen, Corcoran, Rowe and Young. **"Lyndon, now why?":** Cohen, quoted in Dugger, p. 253.

Showing the movies in the White House: The quotes are in Kintner to Fehr, Oct. 17, 1966, p. 3, "Public Activities–Biographic Information–Naval Career (1 of 2)," Box 74, LBJA SF. **Dugger interview:** Described in Dugger, pp. 252–53.

"Bull" Johnson; To his face; "The biggest liar on campus"; Some psychological element impelled him; "A man who just could not tell the truth": Caro, *Path to Power*, pp. 154–56, 160, 197, 198.

Making clear to the same men: Who include Cohen, Corcoran and Young. **Told McNeil:** McNeil OH I. **"I believed":** Johnson, quoted in *Taylor Daily Press*, Aug. 6, 1942. **Drafted letter of refusal; filed it away:** Several drafts, including one with Johnson's handwritten corrections, and a final, formally typed, but unsigned version are in "Public Activities–Biographic Information–Navy, Australia Material" and "Public Activities . . . Award of Silver Star," Boxes 73, 74, LBJA SF. **No other member of crew received a medal:** Dugger, p. 248. **Accepted it in public:** *Marble Falls Messenger*, Feb. 17, 1944. **Waving lapel:** Busby and Smith interviews.

Johnson's conversations with Kilgore: Kilgore interview; overheard and confirmed by Jenkins. **"Convince himself of anything":** Kilgore interview; also Brown and Clark interviews.

4. Lady Bird

SOURCES

The primary source of information for this chapter is the author's ten interviews with Mrs. Johnson. All the quotations from Mrs. Johnson in this chapter are from those interviews unless otherwise indicated.

A number of people saw a great deal of Mrs. Johnson during the period covered in this chapter, and the author's interviews with them were also helpful. They are Edward A. Clark, Ida Nell Connally, John B. Connally, Willard Deason, Alice Hopkins, Welly K. Hopkins, Walter Jenkins, Sam Houston Johnson, Luther E. Jones, Edward Joseph, Gene Latimer, Wingate Lucas, Dale Miller, Mary Rather, James H. Rowe, Jr., Harold Young, Mary Louise Glass Young.

Particularly helpful were the author's interviews with Mrs. Connally. Not only was she closer than anyone else to Mrs. Johnson for quite a long period of years (while their husbands were away together during World War II, the two women shared a small apartment), but once she overcame her hesitancy to talk about the relationship between Lyndon and Lady Bird Johnson, she contributed thoughtful insights about that relationship.

Books and articles:
Lady Bird Johnson, *A White House Diary*. Two biographies—Montgomery, *Mrs. L.B.J.*, and Smith, *The President's Lady*, present an idealized picture of her life, at variance with that given by other sources. Gould, *Lady Bird Johnson and the Environment*. Crawford and Keever, *John B. Connally: Portrait in Power*.

Helpful is the script of "A National Tribute to Lady Bird Johnson, on the Occasion of Her Sixty-fifth Birthday," presented at the LBJ Library, Dec. 11, 1977.

Among scores of magazine articles on Lady Bird Johnson, the most revealing are Blake Clark, "Lyndon Johnson's Lady Bird," *Reader's Digest*, Nov., 1963; Elizabeth Janeway, "The First Lady: A Professional at Getting Things Done," *Ladies' Home Journal*, Apr., 1964; Barbara Klaw, "Lady Bird Remembers," *American Heritage*, 1980; Flora Rheta Schreiber, "Lady Bird Johnson's First Years of Marriage," *Woman's Day*, Dec., 1967; "The New First Lady," *Time*, Nov. 29, 1963; "The First Lady Bird," *Time*, Aug. 28, 1964.

Oral Histories:
Sherman Birdwell, Russell Brown, Ellen Taylor Cooper, Virginia Durr, Daniel J. Quill.

Other interviews:
David Benjamin, Mary Elliott Botsford, Ashton Gonella, D. B. Hardeman, Rebekah Johnson, Ann Durrum Robinson, Emmett Shelton, O. J. Weber.

NOTES

Girlhood and early married life of Lady Bird Johnson: Caro, *Path to Power*, pp. 294–305. **Nellie Connally at the University:** Crawford and Keever, p. 25. **"That's a pretty dress, Nellie":** Mrs. Connally interview. **"I don't know how she stands it":** A number of Texans who had been in Washington at the time made this remark, but asked not to be quoted by name. Virginia Durr said, "I don't know how she lived through it" (Durr OH I).

An obstacle to Alice's happiness: Mary Louise Glass Young, Harold Young, Hopkins interviews. **"My eyes":** Mrs. Johnson interview.

"I thought I was the leader"; "one of the most determined": Solomon and

Benefield, quoted in Schreiber, "Lady Bird's First Years of Marriage." **Despite his avowals:** Caro, *Path to Power*, p. 303. **Visiting Mount Vernon; "I early learned":** Mrs. Johnson interview. **Hints at Longlea:** Caro, pp. 489-92. **Mein Kampf:** Mrs. Johnson interview. "I still remember his chapter on propaganda, which is worth rereading," she said. **No connection with politics:** Caro, *Path to Power*, pp. 489-90. "I went around"; "this little speech"; "didn't want to be a party": Mrs. Johnson interview. **Desire for a home:** Mrs. Johnson interview. **Operation:** Mrs. Johnson interview. "A sadness"; "If I had a son": Schreiber, "Lady Bird's First Years of Marriage." "Like a sightseeing bus": Mrs. Connally interview. "Dull, drab": Mrs. Johnson interview. "The women liked her": Mrs. Connally interview. **Trip to West Coast:** Mrs. Johnson interview. **Decision to have her take over office:** Mrs. Johnson, Connally, Deason, Rather, Jenkins interviews. **No vote of confidence:** Rather interview. And see Weber to Johnson, and Johnson to Weber, Box 35, LBJA SN. **Her first days in office:** Mrs. Johnson, Rather interviews. "Lady Bird is very industrious": Weber to Johnson, Feb. 6, 1942, Box 35, LBJA SN. **That changed:** Mrs. Johnson, Rather interviews. "Some people were already hollering": Weber to Johnson, Mar. 25, 1942, Box 35, LBJA SN. "Looking as if": Rather interview. **Ickes revoking the order:** Mrs. Johnson interview. And see Weber to Johnson, Mar. 25, 1942, Box 35, LBJA SN. "Since she doesn't get pay": Johnson note on Weber to Johnson, Feb. 26, 1942, Box 35, LBJA SN. And Connally wrote Weber: "The only gripe he [Johnson] has had in several days is about Mrs. Johnson not writing for 3 or 4 days at a time. You might mention it to her. . . ." (Connally to Weber, Feb. 28, 1942, Box 35, LBJA SN). "Splendid": Johnson to Mrs. Johnson, Feb. 17, 1942, quoted in "A National Tribute to Lady Bird Johnson," p. 14. "Invincible": Johnson to Mrs. Johnson, undated, quoted in *Ibid.*, p. 15. **Letter of "instruction":** Weber to Johnson, Mar. 2, 1952, Box 35, LBJA SN. On Mar. 6, Weber wrote Johnson that "there seems to be a better esprit de corps in the office."

Telephone calls: Mrs. Montgomery, quoted in Schreiber, "Lady Bird's First Years of Marriage." "She was wonderful": Clark interview. "I was more prepared": Montgomery, p. 30. "I think she changed": Mrs. Connally interview. "We'll see you later, Bird": Corcoran interview. "Kidding, you know": Clark interview. "I'd call": *Goldthwaite Eagle*, undated, but with clippings from March, 1942, Scrapbook 7, Series 1, JHP. Mayor Tom Miller said, "I personally feel that the Tenth District is fortunate in having two such valuable servants as Congressman and Mrs. Johnson," a remark which also irritated the Congressman (*AA-S*, Apr. 18, 1942). He may also have heard that, as Alvin Wirtz wrote to Lady Bird, "Dr. Ross [a prominent Austin physician] says he thinks you would make a better congressman than Lyndon" (Wirtz to Mrs. Johnson, Mar. 10, 1942, Box 37, LBJA SN). "Talk my problems over": Joseph, Jenkins interviews. In later years, Johnson would express a far higher opinion of his wife's political judgment. But for many of those years—until, in fact, he was President—he also expressed the opinion of her judgment that he had expressed in that remark. Shortly after he became President, for example, he gave an interview to reporter Bela Kornitzer of the *Dallas Herald*. Kornitzer wrote: "I asked him if, like other husbands, he ever discussed his problems with his wife. 'Certainly,' he replied. 'I talk everything over with her. She is a most astute person, very wise, an excellent politician.' . . . Then Lyndon Johnson added: 'Of course, I talk my problems over with anyone I think will give me an intelligent ear—including my chauffeur' " (*Dallas Herald Magazine*, Jan. 5, 1964). In earlier years, he would often use the phrase: "nigger chauffeur," as in "I talk my problems over with my nigger chauffeur, too." "Birthday party": Alice Marsh to Johnson, Aug. 19, 1942, "Marsh, Charles E.," Box 26, LBJA SN. **Weekends started again:** Mary Louise Glass Young, Harold Young, Hopkins interviews. **Buying the house:** Mrs. Johnson interview; Schreiber, "Lady Bird's First Years of Marriage."

5. Marking Time

SOURCES

Books:
Burns, *Soldier of Fortune*; Crawford and Keever, *John B. Connally: Portrait in Power*; Daniels, *White House Witness*; Donovan, *Conflict and Crisis*, Vol. I; Henderson, *Maury Maverick*; Ickes, *Secret Diary*, Vol. III; Mann, *La Guardia Comes to Power*; Schlesinger, *The Politics of Upheaval*; Steinberg, *Sam Rayburn*.

Oral Histories:
Helen Gahagan Douglas, Warren Magnuson, W. Robert Poage.

Interviews:
Alan Barth, Richard Bolling, Emanuel Celler, W. Sterling Cole, Thomas G. Corcoran, Helen Gahagan Douglas, Lewis T. Easley, O. C. Fisher, D. B. Hardeman, Charles Herring, Welly K. Hopkins, Edouard V. M. Izac, Eugene J. Keogh, Wingate Lucas, George H. Mahon, W. D. McFarlane, James H. Rowe, Jr., O. J. Weber, Harold Young, James Van Zandt.

NOTES

Lobbying to become Secretary of the Navy: *Washington Daily News*, Oct. 14, 1942; *AA*, Oct. 16, 21, 1942; Pearson in *Abilene Reporter-News*, Nov. 3, 1942; Stimpson in *Abilene Reporter-News*, Oct. 22, and Nov. 3, 1942. **"Secret government mission":** *HP*, Oct. 24, 1942. For other leaks designed to inflate his importance in the war, see, for example, "The Mirrors of Austin" in *AA*, Nov. 23, 1942. **"He regarded"; "carrot juice":** Weber interview. **"Well, I just can't spare":** Johnson quoted by Weber. **Connally's war service:** Crawford and Keever, pp. 46–47. **"Hell, I'll cancel":** Herring interview.

Johnson's fund-raising in 1940; taste of national power: Caro, *Path to Power*, pp. 606–64. **Pauley's rise:** Ickes, p. 392, 524–25; Donovan, pp. 178–83. Among many articles, especially valuable are George Creel, "Big Tooth and Nail Man," *Collier's*, July 20, 1946; Raymond Moley, "Perspective: Dark Democratic December," and "Pauley and Peanuts," *Newsweek*, Dec. 22, 1947; *Time*, May 7, 1945; *Current Biography, 1945*. **"The great hot spell":** Creel, "Big Tooth and

Nail Man." **Flynn's antagonism to Johnson:** Caro, *Path to Power*, pp. 610, 620–21, 625–26. Johnson noted to Thomas R. Amlie, Director of the Washington Bureau of the Union for Democratic Action: "There is much truth in what you have to say concerning the lack of work being done to re-elect Democratic members of the House," but added, "There is little likelihood of my having any connection with either the Democratic Committee or the Congressional Committee" (Johnson to Amlie, Aug. 27, 1942, "Political Correspondence–1942," Box 37, JHP). **Flynn's 1940 failure to circumvent Johnson:** Caro, *Path to Power*, p. 636; Corcoran, Young interviews. And see Roeser to FDR, Oct. 18, OF-300-Texas, 1938–45, Roosevelt Papers, and Roeser to Johnson, Oct. 29, "General–Unarranged," Box 7, JHP. **Flynn's 1942 success in circumventing Johnson:** For example, oilman G. L. Rowsey of Taylor, Texas, at first replied to a Flynn plea for funds by saying he wanted to make his contribution through Johnson, but on October 27, he said that he would nonetheless make it directly to the Democratic National Committee instead (Rowsey to Flynn, Oct. 23, 27, Flynn to Rowsey, Oct. 26, 1942, "Political Correspondence–1942," Box 37, JHP). And see *Philadelphia Inquirer*, Sept. 22, 1943, for Johnson's attempt to regain his DCCC role.

"Haven't waked up": Burns, p. 273. **October 14 incident:** Daniels, pp. 54–55. **Another appointment:** Rowe interview; and see Daniels, p. 77. **"These $200 droplets":** Johnson to Rayburn, Oct. 10, 1942, Box 52, LBJA CF. **Dallas Democratic dinner:** *Wichita Falls Record-News*, Feb. 24, 1944; *DT-H*, *Dallas News*, Feb. 27, 1944. **Vinson as chairman:** Caro, *Path to Power*, pp. 537–39. **"Is the gentleman":** Caro, p. 554.

Johnson's legislative record: *CR*, 1937–48; *AA*, *AA-S*, 1937–48. "Lyndon B. Johnson's Congressional Activities" (compilation by OH staff), WHCF, LBJL; "Complete House Voting Record of Congressman Lyndon Johnson, By Subject, From May 13, 1937 to December 31, 1948," Box 75, LBJA SF; Douglas OH; Douglas, Izac, McFarlane, Fisher, Cole, Lucas interviews; Caro, *Path to Power*, pp. 546–51.

Congressmen and national causes: See, for example, Schlesinger, pp. 142–46; Mann, Henderson, Steinberg, *passim*.

"If we disagreed": Cole interview. Interviews with other congressmen, including Bolling, Celler, Douglas, Fisher, Izac, Keogh, Lucas, Mahon, Mcfarlane, Van Zandt. Interviews with Barth, Easley, Hardeman, Hopkins, Rowe. And Douglas, Magnuson, Poage OHs. **Fiasco over absenteeism bill**: US 78th Cong., House Naval Affairs Committee, J 74 A 23, pp. 253–614; Norton, in *CR*, Mar. 15, 1943, p. 2,139; *NYT*, Feb. 17, 1943; *Washington Star*, Mar. 17, 1943; *Washington News*, WP, Mar. 18, 1943; *Washington Star*, Apr. 8, 1943; Kellam to Johnson, Apr. 1, 1943, "Kellam (1 of 2)," Box 22, LBJA SN.

6. Buying and Selling

SOURCES

Books, articles, and documents:
Barnouw, *The Golden Web: A History of Broadcasting in the United States*; Daniels, *White House Witness*; Dugger, *The Politician*; Gould, *Lady Bird Johnson and the Environment*; Halberstam, *The Powers That Be*; Kohlmeier, *The Regulators*; Krasnow and Longley, *The Politics of Broadcast Regulation*; Miller, *Lyndon*; Montgomery, *Mrs. L.B.J.*; Pearson and Anderson, *The Case Against Congress*; Smith, *The President's Lady*; Steinberg, *Sam Rayburn's Boy*; Wilson, *Congress: Corruption and Compromise*.

A number of contemporaneous newspaper and magazine articles provide details on the genesis and growth of the Johnson fortune, although their conclusions differ in many ways from mine. The most valuable of these are "The Man Who Is the President—How LBJ's Family Amassed Its Fortune," by Keith Wheeler and William Lambert, *Life*, August 21, 1964; John Barron, "Special Report—The Johnson Monday—Presidential Family Holdings Estimated at $9 Million," *Washington Evening Star*, June 9, 1964; "The Story of the Johnson Family Fortune," *USN&WR*, May 4, 1964; Louis Kohlmeier, "The Johnson Wealth," *WSJ*, March 23, 24, August 11, November 23, 1964; Thomas Collins, "LBJ, KTBC—and the FCC," *Newsday*, May 27–29, 1964; Alva Johnson, "The Saga of 'Tommy the Cork,' " *Saturday Evening Post*, Oct. 13, 20, 27, 1945. Federal Communications Commission, "Public Service Responsibility of Broadcast Licensees," March 7, 1946, FCC;

Louis L. Jaffe, "The Scandal in TV Licensing," *Harper's* magazine, September, 1957; Robert D. Leigh, "Politicians vs. Bureaucrats," *Harper's* magazine, January, 1945; Henry F. Pringle, "The Controversial Mr. Fly," *Saturday Evening Post*, July 22, 1944; T.R.B., *New Republic*, May 31, 1943.
Paul Bolton, "History of Radio Station KTBC."
Harfield Weedin, "Anybody Can Write a Book" (unpublished ms.)

Papers of Thomas G. Corcoran (NA).
Papers of Louis M. Kohlmeier.
Papers of William Lambert.

Oral Histories:
Paul Bolton, George R. Brown, Willard Deason, Clifford Durr, Virginia Durr, Arthur Goldschmidt, Elizabeth Wickenden Goldschmidt, Welly K. Hopkins, W. Ervin ("Red") James, Edward Joseph, J. J. (Jake) Pickle, Mary Rather, James H. Rowe, Jr., Harfield Weedin, Edwin L. Weisl, Jr., J. Jerry Voorhis.

Interviews:
James E. Barr, Robert T. Bartley, David Benjamin, Paul Bolton, Ernest Boyett, George R. Brown, Edward A. Clark, Thomas G. Corcoran, Jack Cowden, Willard Deason, Jim Dodd, Albert A. Evangelista, Arthur Goldschmidt, Elizabeth Wickenden Goldschmidt, Harold Graves, Jr., Jack Gwyn, John Hicks, Regina Hicks, Welly K. Hopkins, W. Ervin ("Red") James, Walter Jenkins, Edward Joseph, Edward F. Kenehan, John Kingsbery, Louis Kohlmeier, William Lambert, Eugene Latimer, William J. Lawson, Frank C. (Posh) Oltorf, Max Paglin, Ann Durrum Robinson, James H. Rowe, Jr., Emmett Shelton, Peter Shuebruk, E. Babe Smith, Arthur Stehling, George E. Sterling, Coke Stevenson, Jr., O. J. Weber, Harfield Weedin, Edwin L. Weisl, Jr., Tom Whitehead, Wilton Woods, Harold Young.

NOTES

Marsh's real estate offer: Caro, *Path to Power*, pp. 487–88. **Asking for the "finder's fee"**: Caro, pp. xv, xvi. **Brown felt certain**: Brown interview.
Greenbrier scene: Caro, *Path to Power*, pp. xiii–xv; 787–88.
"Waked up": Johnson to Weber, Feb. 16, 1942. See also Weber to Johnson, undated, "O. J. Weber," Box 35, LBJA

SN. **Purchasing small oil leases:** Brown, Jenkins interviews. Some of the leases are referred to in Weber to Johnson, Feb. 17, 18, 1942, and Weber to Jenkins, Feb. 19, 1942, "O. J. Weber," Box 35, LBJA SN.
Role of government over radio stations: Pringle, "The Controversial Mr. Fly"; Kohlmeier; Pearson and Anderson, pp. 161–82.
History of KTBC: Steinberg, pp. 201–2; Bolton, "History"; Bolton OH, interview; Brown OH, interview; Benjamin, Joseph, Weedin, Hicks interviews; *WSJ*, Mar. 23, 1964; *Washington Evening Star*, June 9, 1964.
In 1942, the FCC was informed that station executives "have on occasions been worried about whether such station would be on the air the next day. The staff has been in constant turmoil because of a definite lack of direction and real leadership" (Exhibit III-20 b, attached to "Consent to Transfer of Control of Corporation Holding Construction Permit or License," Feb. 16, 1943, File No. B3-TC-316, FCC Records, Record Group 173, National Archives, Washington, D.C.). **Permit application; original license:** "In the matter of State Capital Broadcasting Association (R. B. Anderson, President), Austin, Texas, [SCBA] for Construction Permit, . . . Before the Federal Communications Commission, Washington, D.C.," Docket 3846, July 6, 1937, FCC Records, RG 173, NA. **Lack of evening hours an insuperable obstacle:** Walker, quoted in *WSJ*, Mar. 23, 1964; Weedin interview. **Too high on the dial:** In his "History of Radio Station KTBC," Paul Bolton wrote (p. 2): "Austin radio was dominated by KNOW at 1490 on the dial and nearby was the clear channel powerful WOAI at 1200." Weedin wrote that KTSA of San Antonio could also "be heard clearly in Austin" (Weedin ms, p. 205). **Arrangement with Austin School of Business:** "Agreement made and entered into by and between C. R. Belman . . . and the State Capital Broadcasting Association, a co-partnership . . .," Sept. 6, 1939, attached to "West Option" (see below), Dec. 14, 1939. **So amateurishly produced:** Bolton, "History"; Weedin OH.
KTBC's finances: "Profit and Loss Statement," SCBA, July 24, 1939, to Dec. 6, 1939, attached to "West Option" (see below). **Losses in 1942:** *WSJ*, Mar. 23, 1964. **$5,000 in loans:** "State Capital Broadcasting Co.—All Other Liabili-

ties," attached to Exhibit I-14-C, "West Option" (see below). **Last of his capital:** Walker to Fly, April 10, 1942. **1942 revenue and expenses:** "Income Statement, SCBA, Jan. 1, 1942–Dec. 31, 1942" (Exhibit I-12-B), attached to "Consent to Transfer"; Bolton, "History" and OH I.
Delays for Walker, Stuart and Anderson: Haley, p. 62; Steinberg, p. 202; Joseph, Lawson, Jenkins interviews; *Washington Evening Star*, June 9, 1964.
Option to West: "Application for Consent to Transfer of Control of Corporation Holding Radio Broadcast Station Construction Permit or License," File Number B3-TC-207, "Call Letters KTBC," Dec. 6, 1939 (with attached exhibits); "Resolution of the Board of Directors of the State Capital Broadcasting Association, Inc.," Dec. 13, 1939; "Agreement made and entered into this 6th day of December, 1939, by and between R. B. Anderson. . . , R. A. Stuart, . . . and A. W. Walker . . . , hereinafter called 'Sellers,' and J. M. West, J. Marion West, and P. M. Stevenson . . . hereinafter called 'Buyers,' " FCC Records, RG 173, NA.
Revocation of license: "In re: Revocation of License of SCBA, Austin, Tx., To Operate Broadcast Station KTBC," File Number 39012, Feb. 8, 1940, "Before the Federal Communications Commission," FCC Records, RG 173, NA.
Hidden ownership: George Henry Payne, "Before the Federal Communications Commission, In re: Revocation of Licenses of . . . State Capital Broadcasting Association, Inc.," Docket No. 5835, April 10, 1940. **"Eliminate any profit"; agreement to sell for $20,000:** Affidavit ("The following facts obtain . . .") signed by Stuart, Walker, Anderson, J. M. West, J. Marion West, and Stevenson, April 15, 1940, p. 6. According to J. Evetts Haley, *A Texan Looks at Lyndon* (p. 65), "When the revocation order came and his associates thought the Commission was after him, he had, in March, 1940, given a quit-claim deed to them in hopes that this adverse action of the Commission might not affect the West [option]." **Plus $12,000 to cover debts:** KTBC's debts at the time were $12,000, but they were mounting, and would be $19,336 by 1942. **Ask FCC to permit change; Fifteen months of delays:** Walker to Fly, April 10, 1942. Temporary licenses were issued April 2, 1941. **Regular license:** FCC Report No. B-102, Docket No. 5835—Public Notice, June

28, 1941; Haley, p. 63. But the FCC still did not pass on the application to allow the sale of the station to the Wests (Application File No. B3-TC-207), and a month later further consideration of that application was deferred "pending determination of the matters to be considered under the Commission's Order No. 79" (Walker to Fly, April 10, 1942). **No approval because of "Order 79":** Slowie to State Capital Broadcasting Assn., Inc., July 17, 1941. **Petition by West's sons and Kingsbery:** Stevenson to Slowie, Aug. 11, 1941. **Incorrect form:** Slowie to Stevenson, Aug. 20, 1941. All from FCC Records, RG 173, NA.

$4,000 loan: Stevenson to Wroe, Jan. 14, 1943, attached to Exhibit I-14-C (see below).

Frantic to sell: Walker to Fly, April 10, 1942. **FCC's "refusal":** Fly to Walker, April 23, 1942; File Number B3-TC-207, FCC Records, RG 173, NA.

Ulmer frantic: Haley, pp. 62, 65. Haley's book is an anti-Johnson polemic which could not be confirmed on many points, but unlike the rest of the book his description of the negotiations between Ulmer and West at this time is firsthand, since he was J. M. West's general range manager, and represented West in many business affairs—including West's attempt to purchase KTBC. Beginning in August, 1939, he dealt with Ulmer on West's behalf. **Ulmer retaining Wirtz:** Haley, pp. 60–65. Tommy Corcoran recalls Wirtz suddenly arriving in Washington in this month "in a big hurry" to arrange the transfer of KTBC's license to Mrs. Johnson. Bolton, Boyett, Joseph and Lawson either were told by Ulmer that he thought he had retained Wirtz, or were told about the episode by others. Jenkins said, "I heard about it" when he later became active in KTBC's affairs. Also, see Dugger, p. 267.

Kingsbery visit: Dugger, pp. 268–69; Steinberg, 202–3; *Washington Star*, June 9, 1964. **"He knew"; "I understood"; felt an "obligation":** Kingsbery, quoted in Dugger, pp. 268, 270. **"I'll recommend":** Kingsbery, quoted by son, John Kingsbery.

"I told him": Brown interview. **"I didn't like":** West, quoted in Dugger, p. 269.

Details of Mrs. Johnson's purchase: Her note to Wirtz reads: "Dear Senator Wirtz: I am enclosing a check payable to your order for $17,500 to cover my deposit under the contract with the owners of the radio station KTBC, and authorize you to execute contract in my name and make the deposit in my behalf." Mrs. Johnson to Wirtz, Jan. 2, 1943, attached to Exhibit I-14-C. "Application for Consent to Transfer of Control. . . ," January 23, 1943, File No. B3-TC-316, FCC Records, RG 173, NA. Exhibit III-18b states that "transferee . . . has deposited the sum of $7,500 to her account." **$938:** On the basis of a financial statement Mrs. Johnson filed with the FCC showing her assets as of December 31, 1942, she listed her total net worth as $89,412. Since $36,200 of that amount is shown as the value of real estate—apparently the property Marsh had sold them, and their equity in the Johnsons' new home in Washington—and $21,090 is a "secured note," her available liquid assets would be $32,000. She puts her "cash" at $25,044, which is approximately the amount she paid for KTBC or deposited to be applied against the station's debts. According to her statement, "other current assets" are $938 and "securities" total $6,000. ("Balance Sheet, As of Dec. 31, 1942, executed by or on behalf of Claudia T. Johnson," Exhibit III-142a, attached to "Application for Consent to Transfer of Control.") **Consent granted:** "Consent to Transfer of Control of Corporation," File No. B3-TC-316, License No. 1007, Feb. 16, 1943, FCC Records, RG 173, NA.

"I don't have any interest": Johnson press conference, April 16, 1964. At this press conference, the President gave his explanation of the beginning and growth of the Johnson broadcasting business: "Mrs. Johnson inherited some property, invested that property in the profession of her choice, and worked at it with pleasure and satisfaction until I forced her to leave it when I assumed the presidency. . . ." **"I am unfamiliar":** In a press conference on April 11, 1964, Johnson said: "I have no interest in any television anyplace. . . . I am unfamiliar with it [the operation of the company], I am not keeping up with it, and I am not concerned about it. . . ." Public Papers of the Presidents of the United States, Lyndon B. Johnson, 1963–1964, Book I, pp. 471, 458. **"All that is owned by Mrs. Johnson"; "I have never":** Johnson, quoted in Dugger, p. 273. **"It was her station":** Marks, quoted in Miller, p. 108. **"As you know":** Reedy, "Text of Interview," *Washington Star*, June 10, 1964. **"I remember":** Goldschmidt interview. "**This is a success**": *USN&WR*, May 4, 1964. "**The FCC leans**": Wheeler and Lambert, "The Man Who." "**FCC public records**": Kohlmeier, *WSJ*, March 23, 1964. "**Very close-knit**"; "**great intertwining**": Virginia Durr OH. **Corcoran and the FCC**: Pringle, "The Controversial Mr. Fly"; Johnson, "The Saga," Oct. 13, 20, 27, 1945; Daniels, p. 168. "**Greatest wirepuller**": Johnson, "The Saga," Oct. 27, 1945. "**Antennae**": Pearson and Anderson, p. 162; "**Different**": Evangelista interview. "**What you were afraid of**": Barr interview. **Cox affair**: Wilson, pp. 48–68; Leigh, "Politicians vs. Bureaucrats"; *WP, Washington Star, NYT, HT,* Jan. 7–Oct. 1, 1943; T.R.B., *New Republic,* May 31, 1943. "**Nastiest nest**"; "**Guilty**"; "**Gestapo**": Cox, quoted in Leigh, "Politicians vs. Bureaucrats," and in Wilson, pp. 50, 53. "**Judicial wig**"; "**indecent**": T.R.B., *New Republic,* May 31, 1943. "**Perverted and distorted**": *WP,* quoted in Wilson, p. 64. "**All around Washington**": Leigh (who was director of the FCC's Foreign Broadcast Intelligence Service), "Politicians vs. Bureaucrats." "**In effect abolishing it**": Voorhis. "**I wrote the law**": Rayburn, quoted in Caro, *Path to Power,* p. 328. In return Roosevelt had allowed Rayburn to name one of the FCC's commissioners. **Selective Service Act**: Caro, pp. 595–96. "**Lyndon sort of**": Clifford Durr OH. **Late-night calls to James**: James, Durr OHs. **Fly's purported affair and Johnson's taking it up with Rayburn**: James OH. "**Unusual and bold**": Leigh, "Politicians vs. Bureaucrats." For Durr's appeals to Rayburn, see also Wilson, pp. 58, 61, 63; and Leigh. "**This voice says**": Johnson, quoted in James OH. **The price Rayburn paid**: Wilson, pp. 65–68; Leigh, "Politicians vs. Bureaucrats." **Championing FCC's cause in White House**: Daniels, p. 168.

Johnson seeing Durr and James socially: See Chapter 1. **Bringing Wirtz to see James**: James OH. "**Government between friends**": Johnson, "The Saga of 'Tommy the Cork,' " Oct. 13, 1945. Harvard Law School Professor Louis L. Jaffe was to put it in different words in 1957: "what begins in amiability can end in corruption," he said. "In our administrative life . . ., compromise, camaraderie and trafficking are eating away at the fabric of the legal structure" (Jaffe, "The Scan-

dal in TV Licensing," *Harper's* magazine, Sept., 1957). "**Lyndon never had a thing to do with it**": Durr, quoted by Dugger, p. 267. "**Bird came to me**": Durr OH. "**Wasn't any skullduggery**": Durr OH. "**A perfect right**": James OH. "**He wanted to get**": Barr interview. "**I helped him out**"; "**I told you**": Corcoran interview. This statement cannot be verified, but on everything Corcoran said about Johnson's early career that could be checked, he proved to be reliable. "**Bill Drake . . . made an offer**": Joseph OH.

Lawson and KBWD in Brownwood: "Annual Financial Report, KBWD, Brownwood, Texas," 1940, 1941, "F.C.C. Financial Reports," Box 7, FCC Records, RG 173, NA; *Brownwood Bulletin,* Aug. 17, 1941; Lawson interview. **Lawson in Austin**: Lawson died before he could furnish further details about his attempt to purchase KTBC, but his interest in the station (and that of Drake) is confirmed by other businessmen from Austin and nearby communities, to at least two of whom Lawson showed the "odd" letter (Boyett, Jenkins, Joseph, Lawson interviews).

Application to operate at night: File No. B3-ML-1168, FCC Records, RG 173, NA. The crucial importance of this change to KTBC's fortunes is shown by details furnished on the application. The "estimated monthly revenue" was still only $3,500, and, Mrs. Johnson stated, since her purchase of the station, "there has been no substantial change in KTBC's 'financial condition' " (p. 5). **Granting of permission**: File No. B3-ML-1168, Official No. 1007, "Radio Broadcasting Station License, Modified as of July 20, 1943, KTBC," FCC Records, RG 173, NA. **New frequency**: Weedin, in his OH (p. 16), says that the change "makes the thousand watts actually at least five thousand or more." **38 counties**: Reproduced from an advertisement, *AA-S,* Feb. 14, 1945, FCC Records, Accession #162, A55, Box 61. "**Where the dominant station was WOW**": James OH. "**They looked at the thing**": James OH. James also says in his Oral History: "I can truthfully say . . . that I never observed Lyndon B. Johnson get anything that he wasn't entitled to in every way, on the merits of the case, apart from any politics."

Marks reported: If Lawson was philosophical about his loss of KTBC to Lyndon Johnson, Ulmer was not. On Marks' return from the radio convention, he telephoned Walter Jenkins to report on an incident that occurred there. Jenkins relayed Marks' message to Johnson: "While there he [Marks] ran into Dr. Ulmer, who was formerly connected with KTBC. Dr. Ulmer told him a fellow in Texas had recently asked him to 'document' the story of the Johnson entry into the radio business. Ulmer went on to say that he had completed all the engineering on 590 and that you came in and stole it from him" (Jenkins to Johnson, May 20, 1948, "Memos to Johnson," Box 329, JHP). **Also angry was Elliott Roosevelt:** Connally to Johnson, Aug. 31, 1943, "LBJ Family Financial Records," Box 12, PPCF.

Knew in advance: Weedin interview, OH. Confirmed by Hicks, who says that when Weedin asked him, in April, 1943, to join him in Austin, he demurred because of the nighttime restrictions; Weedin, Hicks says, responded, "Don't worry, we're going twenty-four hours." **Increase to 5,000 watts:** File Number B3-L-1977, Official Number 1007, "Radio Broadcasting License, modified as of July 29, 1946," FCC Records, RG 173, NA. **"Took one look":** Kellam, quoted in Steinberg, p. 204. **"The staff":** Mrs. Johnson, quoted in Miller, p. 108. For other accounts portraying Mrs. Johnson as the moving force in KTBC's success, see, for example, Montgomery and Smith. **Johnson's visit to Paley; "announced that":** Halberstam, pp. 439–40. **"This is life and death":** Johnson to Latimer, Aug. 11, 1943, "Latimer, Gene," Box 2, PPCF. **CBS affiliation:** "Agreement between Columbia Broadcasting System and State Capital Broadcasting Assn., Inc., Aug. 27, 1943," FCC Records, RG 173, NA.

Paley's relationship with FCC and Congress: Pringle, "The Controversial Mr. Fly"; Leigh, "Politicians vs. Bureaucrats." For Johnson's later, long relationship with Stanton, who became the chief lobbyist for CBS, see, for example, Halberstam, pp. 326–27, 431, 438–42. **KNOW's attempts to get CBS affiliation:** Weedin interview; Weedin also wrote that KNOW "had tried for years to get CBS, but KTSA had always been successful in defeating an Austin affiliation" (Weedin ms. p. 205). In his OH he says that when he worked for KNOW, "we had tried to get it [the CBS affiliation] in those days unsuccessfully. KTSA was al-

ways able to circumvent it and make it impossible for us." **"We twisted"; Interstate Theater Chain:** Brown interview. In his OH and manuscript, Weedin understandably attempts to argue that his own energy and initiative (which were, of course, considerable) were the key elements in obtaining the advertisers: "National advertisers claimed they were already covering Austin with KTSA. Why should they spend more money to buy something they already owned? There was only one answer. I had to make a trip to Chicago and New York and personally sell these advertisers. . . ." (ms., p. 206). He says that "I think that he [Johnson] and Bird were very reluctant to try to sell the station to any of their friends or advertise it or anything. If they did, I was not that aware of it." In the Oral History taken by the Lyndon Baines Johnson Library, Weedin was asked if Johnson "used his position as a Congressman in order to sell ads for the station." Weedin replied, "I heard rumors later from people that I talked to that he did after I left. He did not do it while I was there. Other than, as I say, to give me a prospect to talk to. Now what he said to those people before I got there, I don't know. Usually I didn't talk to the person. I'm sure that he had mentioned and set up the appointment. But he was not blatant in any way with it." To some extent Weedin was unaware of what was going on, a fact that caused Clark some amusement. After the GE advertising contract came through, Clark wrote Johnson that Weedin apparently felt he deserved credit, but actually, "I am sure that he [Weedin] was quite surprised when [a GE official] advised him that KTBC was being added" (Clark to Johnson, Oct. 27, 1943, "Clark, Edward [1 of 4]," Box 14, LBJA SN). But in his interviews, Weedin was more frank, and indeed even in his OH reveals more awareness than he claims for himself. Immediately after he says in his OH that "he and Bird were very reluctant to sell the station to any of their friends or advertise it," he adds: "But it was awfully easy for me to sell Paramount, because he was Karl Hoblitzelle up in Dallas, and Bill O'Donnell knew what Lyndon was doing for the theater industry in Washington, and they were very anxious to help him any way they could. So Louis Novy, who was the head of the interstate circuit in Austin, had never bought radio before. He didn't like it at all. But I found it very easy to sell it" (p. 25). Weisl, key and longtime fund-raiser for Johnson in the northeast, was, of course, counsel for Paramount. Although it is very important to him that his own contributions to the sale of airtime be recognized, he noted that "A lot of people like to advertise on a radio station that a congressman owned. It's the easiest way in the world to make a contribution."

Weedin also says in his OH that his efforts in collecting letters from listeners were a key factor in persuading CBS to make KTBC a part of its network. But he also adds, in the same OH: "To get back to the CBS thing, where you were asking me how did they get it, I don't really know. I'd like to say that I got it, but I didn't, because either Bird or Lyndon made the deal and I presume right directly with Bill Paley. . . ." Poignantly, in his OH, Weedin also says, when asked about his salary, "I also had 10 percent of the profits, too."

Clark's relationship with Johnson: Bolton, Clark, Oltorf interviews; Caro, *Path to Power*, pp. 362–63. **"I knew":** Clark interview. So, Clark says, "I got Mr. Butt to advertise. . . . That was their [KTBC's] first real account." **"I am today writing":** Clark to Johnson, Oct. 27, 1943, "Clark, Edward [1 of 4]," Box 14, LBJA SN. **"I was happy":** Clark to Johnson, Feb. 3, 1944, "Clark, Edward [2 of 4]," Box 15, LBJA SN. In the same folder is an undated transcript of a telephone conversation between Johnson and an OPA official. In it, the official tells Johnson, "This will make him [Butt] 150,000 extra that we have granted," and later Johnson says: "We gave him 150." On the memo is written: "File Clark, Ed." In 1945, an official of the H. E. Butt Grocery Company, writing to Clark about the OPA's rejection of "our application for a quota" and hoping for "changes" in the situation, said "I know that Congressman Johnson has worked hard on this. . . ." (Clapp to Clark, July 13, 1945), all from "Clark, Edward [2 of 4]," Box 15, LBJA SN. The Butt-Johnson relationship would remain close, and Clark would continue to be an intermediary. In 1960, for example, after Johnson's vice-presidential campaign, he wrote Butt: "You've been so fine—so helpful to Ed Clark and especially to me—I want you to know you are in my mind and in my heart. I am deeply grateful to you for everything you've done" (Johnson to

Butt, Nov. 19, 1960, "Bus-Bz, 1960," Senate Master File, Box 29, LBJL). **General Electric:** Clark to Johnson, Oct. 27, 1943. **"Thanks":** Johnson to Clark, Oct. 30, 1943, both from "Clark, Edward [1 of 4]," Box 14, LBJA SN. **The Gulf program:** On March 29, 1944, Clark wrote Johnson: "The Gulf program came through and will begin April 3," "Clark, Edward [2 of 4]," Box 15, LBJA SN. Clark says that the Gulf Company itself was not his client, "but I had friends there. I spoke to them about it, and they understood." Asked how they knew that advertising on KTBC might help them with government agencies in Washington, Clark said: "This wasn't a Sunday School proposition. This was business" (Clark interview). **Humble:** *AA-S*, Nov. 8, 1986; Jenkins, Bolton interviews.

"Everybody knew": Unidentified person quoted in memo to Lambert, June 10, 1964, Lambert Papers. **Jaques advertising:** "KTBC–590 on Your Dial," Feb. 18, 1945–Mar. 3, 1945, Accession No. 162, A55, Box 61, FCC Records, NA. **Little business:** Former associate of J. C. Jaques, Lambert Papers. **$1,250,000 RFC loan:** Jenkins to Johnson, May 20, 1948, "Memos to Johnson," Box 329, JHP; Jenkins interview. **Other businessmen observed:** Bolton, Jenkins interviews. Among the businessmen, Joseph, Lawson interviews. Those who failed to observe were prodded by Johnson associates. For example, in his Oct. 27, 1943, letter to Johnson in which he told the Congressman that he had advised Butt about advertising on KTBC, Clark added: "I am wondering if anyone is asking Theo Davis and other wholesale grocers here to do likewise." Eventually, Clark himself did the asking. Clark, Jenkins interviews.

"Mrs. Johnson knew": Benjamin interview. **"Over the years":** Marks, quoted in Miller, p. 108. **"I believe he came to trust":** Jenkins interview. **"He trusted":** Clark interview. **"I'm not sure":** Kingsbery, quoted in Dugger, p. 269.

$2,600 per month; "A little over $3,000"; "but in December": The monthly incomes for the last three months before the CBS affiliation began to be felt were September, $3,194; October, $3,183; November, $3,180. Then, in December, the income jumped to $5,645. "KTBC Files, 1940–1950," "Financial Reports of Broadcast Stations—KTBC," FCC Records, RG 173, NA.

By the end of the war: The financial figures for KTBC for the years Mrs. Johnson owned it come from the annual financial reports the station submitted to the FCC: "Financial Reports—FCC General Correspondence (KTBC)," FCC Records, RG 173, NA.

With rare exceptions: The most notable is Kohlmeier, who wrote that the law "is complex in its application, according to the state's legal scholars, but they say that unless Mr. Johnson has signed away his rights, he almost certainly retains a legal as well as sentimental share in the broadcasting fortune." Under Texas law, as Kohlmeier pointed out, the spouse of a person who purchases a property with her own "separate" funds—a spouse such as Lyndon Johnson, the spouse of Lady Bird Johnson, who bought KTBC with her own inheritance—has indeed no interest in that property. But, as Kohlmeier wrote, he has a "half-interest in the income" from that property, and unless he signs away that half-interest (and Johnson never claimed that he had), he owns half of that income (*WSJ*, Nov. 23, 1964). **Didn't sign away rights:** Clark, Jenkins interviews.

"One day": Rowe interview. **Showing to many friends:** Among those who recall him doing it are Corcoran, Rowe, Young.

"Now, Bill": Johnson to Deason, undated, "Deason, Willard–KTBC," Box 21, LBJA SN.

Relationship with staff: Interviews with Benjamin, Clark, Joseph, Weedin, Hicks, Durrum Robinson, Gwyn, Jenkins, Dodd, Latimer.

No contract: Mrs. Johnson to FCC, Apr. 4, 1946, Kohlmeier Papers. **"An oral one"; "station ownership":** Kellam to FCC, Nov. 15, 1949, Kohlmeier Papers.

Relationship with Kellam: Latimer, Shelton, Clark, Gwyn interviews. For the revealing correspondence between the two men, see "Kellam, J. C.," Box 22, LBJA SN. **Man on airplane:** Shelton interview.

7. One of a Crowd

SOURCES

Books, articles and documents:
Brinkley, *Washington Goes to War*; Burns, *Roosevelt: Soldier of Freedom*; Daniels, *Frontier on the Potomac* and

White House Witness; Donovan, *Conflict and Crisis* and *Tumultuous Years*; Douglas, *A Full Life*; Dugger, *The Politician*; Goldman, *The Crucial Decade—And After*; Goulden, *The Best Years*; Hassett, *Off the Record with FDR*; Ickes, *Secret Diary*, Vols. II and III; Sam Houston Johnson, *My Brother Lyndon*; Kearns, *Lyndon Johnson and the American Dream*; Manchester, *The Glory and the Dream*; Mann, *La Guardia: A Fighter Against His Times*; McKay, *Texas and the Fair Deal, 1945–1952*; Miller, *Lyndon*; Montgomery, *Mrs. L.B.J.*; Mooney, *The Politicians*; O'Neill, *American High*; Phillips, *The Truman Presidency* and *The 1940s: Decade of Triumph and Trouble*; Steinberg, *Sam Johnson's Boy* and *Sam Rayburn*; *Texas Almanac*, 1947–48; Truman, *Harry S. Truman* and *Bess W. Truman*; Tully, *My Boss FDR*.

Kai Bird and Max Holland, "The Tapping of 'Tommy the Cork,' " *The Nation*, Feb. 8, 1946; Kenneth G. Crawford, "Everyman in the White House," *American Mercury*, Feb., 1946; Walter Davenport, "The New White House Boys," *Collier's*, Nov. 17, 1945; Arthur Krock, "The President: A New Portrait," *NYT* magazine, Apr. 7, 1946; Allan J. Lichtman, "Tommy the Cork: The Secret World of Washington's First Modern Lobbyist," *The Washington Monthly*, Feb., 1987; Milton MacKaye, "Things Are Different in the White House," *Saturday Evening Post*, Apr. 20, 1946; Cabell Phillips, "How the President Does His Job," *NYT Magazine*, Jan. 4, 1948; Richard H. Rovere, "President Harry," *Harper's*, July, 1948.

CBS interview of LBJ by Walter Cronkite, "An Assessment of Harry S. Truman, the Man," recorded May 7, 1971, LBJL.

Papers of Harry S. Truman (HSTL).
Papers of Tom C. Clark (HSTL).
Papers of Alvin J. Wirtz (LBJL).

Oral Histories:
Sherman Birdwell, Richard Bolling, Paul Bolton, George R. Brown, H. S. ("Hank") Brown, Emanuel Celler, Oscar L. Chapman, Tom C. Clark, Clark Clifford, W. Sterling Cole, John B. Connally, Ernest Cuneo, Jonathan Daniels, Willard Deason, Helen Gahagan Douglas, Clifford Durr, Clifford and Virginia Durr, Virginia Wilke English, O. C. Fisher, Gordon Fulcher, Arthur ("Tex") and Elizabeth Wickenden Goldsmith,

Elizabeth Wickenden Goldschmidt, D. B. Hardeman, Charles Herring, John Holton, Welly K. Hopkins, Welly K. and Alice Hopkins, W. Ervin ("Red") James, Walter Jenkins, Sam Houston Johnson, Edward Joseph, Jesse Kellam, David E. Lilienthal, R. J. ("Bob") Long, John E. Lyle, Jr., Warren Magnuson, George H. Mahon, Dale and Virginia Miller, Dorothy J. Nichols, Frank C. ("Posh") Oltorf, Wright Patman, Edwin W. Pauley, J. J. ("Jake") Pickle, W. Robert Poage, Mary Rather, Ray Roberts, Elizabeth Rowe, James H. Rowe, Jr., Emmett Shelton, Polk and Nell Shelton, George Smathers, Stuart Symington, Grace Tully, Carl Vinson, Warren G. Woodward.

Interviews:
Alan Barth, Rebekah Johnson Bobbitt, Richard Bolling, George R. Brown, Horace Busby, Emanuel Celler, Edward A. Clark, Benjamin V. Cohen, W. Sterling Cole, John B. Connally, Nellie Connally, Thomas G. Corcoran, Ava Johnson Cox, Willard Deason, Helen Gahagan Douglas, Lewis T. ("Tex") Easley, O. C. Fisher, Sim Gideon, Arthur ("Tex") Goldschmidt, Elizabeth Wickenden Goldschmidt, Ashton Gonella, Estelle Harbin, D. B. Hardeman, Bryce Harlow, Mary Henderson, Charles Herring, Hardy Hollers, John W. Holton, Alice and Welly K. Hopkins, Edouard V. M. Izac, Eliot Janeway, Walter Jenkins, Lady Bird Johnson, Sam Houston Johnson, Edward Joseph, Eugene J. Keogh, Eugene Latimer, William J. Lawson, Wingate Lucas, Warren Magnuson, George H. Mahon, Margaret Mayer, W. D. McFarlane, Dale Miller, Frank C. ("Posh") Oltorf, J. J. ("Jake") Pickle, Mary Rather, Elizabeth and James H. Rowe, Lacey Sharp, Emmett Shelton, E. Babe Smith, Margaret Truman, James Van Zandt, Tom Whitehead, Harold Young, Mary Louise Glass Young.

NOTES

"You had to ask": Caro, *Path to Power*, p. 193. **Coming to realize:** Brown, Clark, Corcoran, Hopkins interviews. **Speculation over 1946 gubernatorial race:** Steinberg, *Sam Johnson's Boy*, pp. 226–27; Connally, Jenkins interviews. **"What do you want":** Connally interview. **"By God":** Hopkins interview. **"I was just looking up":** William S.

White article in *NYT*, Apr. 13, 1945. **"From the Master":** Dugger, p. 255. **"Where's everybody?":** Deschler, quoted in Steinberg, *Sam Rayburn*, p. 226. **"Honey, we've got Truman":** Nichols OH II.
Truman-Rayburn relationship: Steinberg, *Sam Rayburn*, pp. 227–35; Donovan, *Tumultuous Years*, pp. 19–20.
Mayflower Hotel luncheon: CBS Johnson–Cronkite interview, p. 23. **Once a dinner guest:** "1945 Chronology," Reference File, Jan. 22, 1945, LBJL. **"Those of us who":** Johnson to Truman, Apr. 16, 1945, PPF 723, HSTL. **Truman's reply:** Truman to Johnson, May 5, 1945, PPF 723, HSTL.
FCC: Houston Harte to Clark, Dec. 14, 1944, Jan. 23, 1945; Clark to Harte, Dec. 19, 1944, Jan. 24, Feb. 1, 1945, Box 4; Albert Jackson to Clark, Aug. 18, 1945, Box 47, Tom Clark Papers, HSTL. **Lobbyist for Safeway; "tremendous and startling":** Quoted in *Current Biography, 1945*, p. 108. Testimony before the Texas Senate Committee showed that after William McGraw, Clark's partner in a Dallas law firm, became Attorney General in 1934, the earnings of the law practice, now carried on by Clark alone, increased from $12,000 in 1934 to $60,000 in 1935 and to $70,000 in 1936, and, as the *Saturday Evening Post* put it, "that Clark had done some lobbying at Austin against a chain-store-tax on behalf of a chain-store system." Clark was to respond that the Senate investigation was an attempt by McGraw's political enemies to smear the Attorney General by attacking his ex-partner (Jack Alexander, "The President's New Lawyer," *Saturday Evening Post*, Sept. 29, 1945). **Persuaded Safeway to advertise on KTBC:** Edward Clark to Johnson, Aug. 25, 1944, folder 2 of 4, Box 15, LBJA SN; Clark, Jenkins interviews. Because KTBC's records have not been opened, the extent of Safeway's advertising has not been determined, but during two periods—one in 1945 and one in 1953—for which records are available, the chain sponsored the same fifteen-minute show five days a week ("Advertising schedules—KTBC," Feb. 18–Mar. 3, 1945, Apr., 1953, RG 173, FCC Records, NA, Washington, D.C.). **Johnson lobbying for Clark:** Tom Clark to Johnson, Nov. 14, 1941, Rowe to Clark, Dec. 1, 1941, Box 9, Clark Papers, HSTL; Johnson to Rowe, May 11, 1944, Box 32, LBJA SN. On June 16, 1945, Rowe wrote Johnson

about Clark's appointment: "I think I detect your fine Italian hand in it" (Box 32, LBJA SN). *DT-H*, Feb. 28, Mar. 14, 1944; Corcoran, James Rowe, Harold Young interviews. **"It is a different town"**: Johnson to Rowe, July 10, 1945, Box 32, LBJA SN. **A far reach**: Johnson to Matt Connelly, Nov. 6, 1945, PPF Box 150, File 66, "A-W," HSTL. **"Because of your friendship"**: Johnson to Truman, Dec. 15, 1945, PPF Box 67, "G to J," HSTL. **Inscriptions**: Connelly to Johnson, folder PPF 66-A(J), Box 1232, GF, HSTL. **Thanks**: Truman to Johnson, Dec. 19, 1945, PPF Box 67, File 9, HSTL. **In Oval Office only once**: Appointment index; Files of Matthew J. Connelly, Presidential Appointments, Box 7, 8; Social Office Card File, Card 8, HSTL; "Contacts with President Truman," Box 8, WHFN, LBJL. **"You've got to have a reason"**: Rowe interview. **Roosevelt's "spy"**: Caro, *Path to Power*, pp. 571–74.
   A *"professional son"*: Caro, *Path to Power*, pp. 145, 150–51, 153, 271, 294, 445, 477, 486–88. **As a professional son with Rayburn**: Caro, pp. 33–34, 452–53, 757–62. **"But Truman had** *watched* **him"**: Bolling interview. **"A pretty sharp judge"**: Symington interview. **"Never quite trusted him"**: Margaret Truman interview.
   Ickes' resignation: See, for example, Donovan, *Conflict*, pp. 181–84. **Truman tapping Corcoran's telephone**: Bird and Holland, "The Tapping of 'Tommy the Cork' "; *The Nation*, Feb. 8, 1946; Lichtman, "Tommy the Cork." For a description of the changed atmosphere in Washington, see, for example, Phillips, "Where Are They Now?" *NYT Magazine*, Sept. 26, 1946.
   "First Mother of the Land": Johnson to "Librarian, Grandview Public Library," Aug. 2, 1947, PPF Box 276, HSTL. **"I regret"**: Truman to Johnson, Aug. 6, 1947, PPF Box 276, HSTL. **"A slowly developing"**: Clifford OH. **Symington relationship**: Symington interview; Symington OH.
   A **"farce and a sham"**: *AA-S*, May 23, 1948. **Johnson's votes on Taft-Hartley Act**: "Complete House Voting Record of Congressman Lyndon Johnson, By Subject, from May 13, 1937 to December 31, 1948," pp. 233–34, Box 75, LBJA SF. **"Gutted us"**: Brown, quoted in Miller, p. 114. **Easley interview**: *AA*, Apr. 23, 1947. **Starting to believe**: Clark interview.

"He was for the Niggers": Brown interview. And Dale Miller, Washington representative of the Dallas Chamber of Commerce, said in an interview: "He gave the impression of being much, much more liberal than he actually was—his manner personified the New Deal—he looked the part: he was young, dynamic, outgoing. But . . . he gave a lot more impression of being with the New Deal than he actually was."
   On one cruise: Guest Book, *USS Potomac* and *USS Williamsburg*, HSTL; CBS Johnson–Cronkite interview, p. 27. **Poker games**: CBS Johnson–Cronkite interview, p. 27. But Symington says, "Johnson was just never part of Truman's inner circle at all." Busby interview. **"The first thing he did"**: Johnson to Truman, Mar. 20, 1948, Johnson to Truman, Apr. 5, 1948, GF, Box 124, HSTL; Truman to Johnson, Mar. 22, 1948, PSF, Box 288, HSTL; *Chicago Tribune*, Apr. 6, 1948; Busby interview.
   Appointed to two new committees: *AA*, Mar. 30, 1944; *Georgetown Sun*, Mar. 31, 1944. **"An able young man"**: Quoted in Steinberg, *Sam Johnson's Boy*, p. 231.
   Johnson's legislative record in House: Caro, *Path to Power*, pp. 544–51, 658–59.
   He and Magnuson had talked: Magnuson interview; Steinberg, *Sam Johnson's Boy*, p. 140. **Resentment among other congressmen**: Van Zandt, Izac, Lucas, Mahon, Fisher, Keogh, McFarlane, Cole interviews. See also Ray Roberts, quoted in Miller, p. 76. For his standing on Capitol Hill over this period, including the time when he had been able to funnel contributions to other congressmen, interviews with the above congressmen and with Douglas, Celler. Also Douglas, Magnuson, Poage OHs. Also congressional staff members, such as Lucas (later a congressman), Sharp, Jenkins, S. H. Johnson. Also persons who observed Congress, including Barth, Easley, Corcoran, Holton, Brown. The gratitude of other congressmen in 1940 is described in Caro, *Path to Power*, pp. 655–59. **Smathers not "aware"**: Quoted in Steinberg, *Sam Johnson's Boy*, p. 235. **"Just could not** *stand* **it"**: Harbin interview. **"He never spoke"**: Douglas OH, interview. **Take me to the Johnson School**: Harlow, Jenkins interviews. For a different description of Harlow's second run-in with Johnson, see Evans and Novak, p. 20. **"Don't wait"**: Robert B.

Semple, Jr., "Nixon's Inner Circle Meets," *NYT* Magazine, Aug. 3, 1989. **"Respected to the point"; "It takes courage"**: Lynne Cheney, "A Quality of Judgment," *Washingtonian* Magazine, Apr., 1985. **"Lyndon would maneuver"**: Harlow interview. **"After Abe got"**: Douglas interview.
Humiliation over office space: Taylor to John L. Nagle, Deputy Commissioner for Real Estate Management, Public Buildings Administration, May 6, 1947; Tom Clark to Steven Heffington, Travis County Tax Collector, Aug. 15, 1947, Box 48, Tom Clark Papers, HSTL; Jenkins, Shelton, Joseph interviews.
Hollers campaign: Clark, Connally, Gideon, Hollers, Joseph, Pickle, Shelton, Smith interviews; Steinberg, *Sam Johnson's Boy*, pp. 227–28; Dugger, pp. 298–302. **Vote Total:** *Texas Almanac, 1947–1948*, p. 403. **"A crusade"**: Hollers, typed transcript of Hollers' public statement, "Hardy Hollers—24 July," Box 55, JHP. **"Enriched"; "an errand boy"**: Hollers, quoted in Dugger, pp. 300–301. **"If"**: Hollers, quoted in Steinberg, *Sam Johnson's Boy*, p. 227. **"A watershed"**: Mrs. Johnson interview with author. **"That's simple"**: Clark interview. **"He simply"**: Steinberg, *Sam Johnson's Boy*, p. 228. **"Never again"**: Dugger, p. 300.
Johnson's belief that he would die young: Caro, *Path to Power*, p. 544; S. H. Johnson, Mrs. Johnson, Jenkins, Rowe, Young, Mary Louise Young interviews. **Uncle George's death:** *AA*, Mar. 12, 1940. **Uncle Tom's heart attacks:** Cox interview. **"Too slow"**: Johnson used this phrase to numerous people, including McFarlane and Young. **Consequences of one mistake:** S. H. Johnson interview. **"When a man reached forty"**: Busby interview. **Telephoning Rayburn and Vinson:** Steinberg, *Sam Johnson's Boy*, p. 210; Dugger, p. 255.
Doctor suggested: Miller, p. 113. **"She insisted"**: Johnson, quoted in Montgomery, p. 35. **Instructions to Mrs. English:** English OH. **105 degrees, blood transfusion, operation:** *AA-S*, June 15, 16, 1945. **"It's cheaper"**: Johnson, quoted in Montgomery, p. 36. **"FDR-LBJ"**: Busby interview. **His moods:** Among many who describe them: S. H. Johnson, Jenkins, Busby, Rowe interviews. **"He lost some of his drive"**: S. H. Johnson interview. **"Driving himself late

at night": Latimer interview. **"Really sucking it in"**: Jones interview.
1946 illnesses: *AA-S*, Jan. 1–Dec. 31, 1946; see also Chronology, Jan. 12, 19, 26; Feb. 2, 4, 7, 12; Mar. 2; Oct. 13, 15, 21, 30; Nov. 5, 1946; S. H. Johnson, Mrs. Johnson, Bolton, Jenkins, Shelton interviews.
"Hopes to return": Jenkins to Bellows, Jan. 19, 1946, "Bellows, W. S.," Box 141, JHP.
Wrote his cousin: Johnson to Oriole Bailey, Feb. 7, 1946, "Bailey, Mrs. Oriole, Stonewall, Texas," Box 140, JHP.
"Could not bear the thought": Johnson, quoted in Kearns, p. 100.
Pose of indecision: Connally, Pickle, Oltorf, Brown, Clark interviews.
O'Daniel's unpopularity: McKay, pp. 171–73.

8. The Story of Coke Stevenson

SOURCES

Books and articles:
Allen, ed., *Our Sovereign State*; Banks, *Money, Marbles and Chalk*; Fehrenbach, *Lone Star*; Gantt, *The Chief Executive in Texas*; Green, *The Establishment in Texas Politics, 1945–1957*; Heard and Strong, *Southern Primaries and Elections, 1920–1949*; Jenkins and Frost, *"I'm Frank Hamer"*; Lynch, *The Duke of Duval*; McKay, *W. Lee O'Daniel and Texas Politics* and *Texas Politics, 1906–1944*; Mooney, *Mr. Texas*; Tolbert, *Tolbert's Texas*; Webb and Carroll, *Handbook of Texas*; Wyatt and Shelton, *Coke R. Stevenson: A Texas Legend*.
Paul Bolton, "Profile—Sheep Rancher," *State Observer*, July 28, 1941; George Carmack, "Calculatin' Coke Stevenson: Horatio Alger of the Llano," *SAE*, 1974 (otherwise undated), Barker Collection; Mitchell McLendon, "Coke R. Stevenson, of Kimble County," *West Texas Today*, Sept., 1941; Walter Moore, "Stevenson Practiced Economy," *DMN*, July 18, 1963; Lewis Nordyke, "Calculatin' Coke," *Saturday Evening Post*, Oct. 28, 1944; Ed Rider, "Hon. Coke R. Stevenson Becomes Governor," *Frontier Times*, Aug., 1941; Charles E. Simons, "Log Cabin Statesman," *Texas Parade*, Mar., 1942; Byron C. Utrecht, "Coke Stevenson, Ranch-

man Candidate," *Sheep and Goat Raiser*, July, 1948.
Austin American-Statesman, Dallas Morning News, Dallas Times-Herald, State Observer, 1941–1944.

Barker Texas History Center.

Oral Histories:
Charles K. Boatner, Eugene B. Germany, Callan Graham, Josh H. Groce, Robert W. Murphey, Coke R. Stevenson.

Interviews:
About the more intimate, personal portions of his life, interviews with a number of persons close to him were helpful. These include his son, Coke Stevenson, Jr., and Coke's wife, Edith Wills Scott Stevenson; his nephew, Robert W. Murphey, and Murphey's wife, Nada; his executive assistant, Ernest J. Boyett; Congressmen O. C. Fisher and Wingate Lucas.

Among the state officials, newspapermen and political observers who were in Austin during the 1940s and dealt with Stevenson during his lieutenant governorship and governorship, the most helpful in interviews were Paul Bolton, Edward A. Clark, Ann Fears Crawford, William J. Lawson (O'Daniel's Secretary of State), R. J. ("Bob") Long, Gerald C. Mann, Margaret Mayer, Frank C. ("Posh") Oltorf, Emmett Shelton, Arthur Stehling, E. Babe Smith, Ralph Yarborough.

NOTES

Coke Stevenson's youth, his self-education and early political career are drawn from Wyatt and Shelton; Mooney; Nordyke, "Calculatin' Coke"; Simons, "Log Cabin Statesman"; McLendon, "Coke R. Stevenson"; Bolton, "Profile"; and from Stevenson's Oral History. Among hundreds of newspaper articles, the most valuable include *DT-H*, July 3, 1941; *Amarillo Sunday News*, Aug. 3, 1941; *DMN*, July 2, 1941; Carmack, "Calculatin' Coke Stevenson." Also valuable are interviews with Coke Stevenson, Jr., Ernest J. Boyett and Robert W. Murphey, and Murphey's Oral History.

Only twenty-two months: Simons, "Log Cabin Statesman"; *DT-H*, July 3, 1941. **Work as youth:** Wyatt and Shelton, p. 17. **"Never any doubt":** Carmack,

"Calculatin' Coke Stevenson." **His experiences running the freight line:** Simons, "Log Cabin Statesman"; Wyatt and Shelton, pp. 23–24; McLendon, "Coke R. Stevenson." **"The task":** Simons, "Log Cabin Statesman." **"I saw opportunity":** *DMN*, July 3, 1941. **Riding the lead horse:** Stevenson, Jr., interview; *DT-H*, July 3, 1941. **"Seldom traveled trails":** McLendon, "Coke R. Stevenson."

"Rare"; "anything": Simons, "Log Cabin Statesman." **"Evenings of loneliness":** McLendon, "Coke R. Stevenson." **"The president laughed"; "work up to something":** Stevenson, quoted in *DT-H*, July 3, 1941. **Finding the ranch; "as pretty":** Stevenson, Jr., Murphey, Boyett interviews; Carmack, "Calculatin' Coke Stevenson."

"The Southwestern stare": Fehrenbach, p. 561. **"Sense of humor"; "slow to speak":** Bolton, Murphey, Boyett, Lawson interviews. **"That shone through":** Lucas interview.
Capturing the rustlers: Mooney, p. 10; Wyatt and Shelton, p. 35; Simons, "Log Cabin Statesman"; *DMN*, July 3, 1941; Stevenson, Jr., Boyett interviews.
Had never considered: Stevenson was to say that as a young man he had become interested in politics, but he thought of politics as political philosophy and issues; he was to say that he "felt an urge to get into politics" because of "wonderfully eloquent speeches" he had heard during the debates that were then a feature of political campaigns. But, he was to say, while he was to be active in sparsely settled Kimble County in the campaigns of various candidates, he had never wanted to run for political office (Stevenson OH, a recollection confirmed by his son and other interviews).
Repairing the trail; building the roads: Simons, "Log Cabin Statesman"; Mooney, pp. 11–13. **Taught himself engineering; "testimony":** McLendon, "Coke R. Stevenson."
"My public life": Simons, "Log Cabin Statesman"; see also Stevenson OH.
During the next eight years: During these eight years, his only connection with politics was in the campaigns in Kimble County of various gubernatorial candidates. And, he was to say, "about running for the Legislature in the first place I got into all these races by accident." In another place in his Oral History, he explains that he would not have

run for the Legislature had not other potential conservative candidates refused: "I tried to get Claude Glimer" to run, "but he refused" (Stevenson OH). **Would never defend**: Nordyke, "Calculatin' Coke." Once, when an accused sheep stealer asked Stevenson to represent him, Stevenson replied: "I won't defend you, but I'll help prosecute you" (Bolton, "Profile"). **Docket for a single term**: *Amarillo Sunday News*, Aug. 3, 1941. **"One of the greatest"**: Wyatt and Shelton, p. 37; *DT-H*, July 3, 1941. **"Best all-round"**: Martin, quoted in Wyatt and Shelton, p. 37. **Try more lawsuits**: Wyatt and Shelton, p. 37.

"A sincere tribute": Simons, "Log Cabin Statesman"; Mooney, p. 9. **"Treats his books like friends"**: Simons, "Log Cabin Statesman."

Building the ranch house; "baronial"; "unbelievable": Tolbert, "Tolbert's Texas"; Carmack, "Calculatin' Coke Stevenson"; Wyatt and Shelton, pp. 47–48; Stevenson, Jr., Murphey, Boyett interviews. **"A Dream Ranch"**: Carmack, "Calculatin' Coke Stevenson." **"I don't suppose"**: Stevenson, quoted in *DMN*, July 2, 1941. **Driving down the river**: Rider, "Hon. Coke Stevenson Becomes Governor."

"Mother believed": Stevenson, Jr., interview. **"The most beloved"**: *State Observer*, July 28, 1941.

"He buried himself": Simons, "Log Cabin Statesman." And see Mooney, p. 8. **"An anti-government instrument"**: Fehrenbach, pp. 434–36. **"Everything possible"**: Gantt, p. 32. **"An ingrained hatred"**: Simons, "Log Cabin Statesman." **Sheltering the Bowie cabin**: Stevenson, Jr., interview; Wyatt and Shelton, p. 96. **Raising the flag**: Kathryn Duff, *HP*, Jan. 19, 1964. **"Ranch people need"**: Stevenson, quoted in *DT-H*, July 3, 1941. **"I did not approve"**: *Amarillo Sunday News*, Aug. 3, 1941. **Trying to persuade others to run**: Simons, "Log Cabin Statesman"; Boyett interview; Stevenson OH.

"A marked man": Simons, "Log Cabin Statesman." **Coke as a legislator**: Nordyke, "Calculatin' Coke"; Simons, "Log Cabin Statesman"; *Amarillo Sunday News*, Aug. 3, 1941. **Shooting the horse**: *Amarillo Sunday News*, Aug. 3, 1941. **"You just instinctively knew"**: Clark interview. **"Truly hated it"**: Lucas interview.

Auditing, bookkeeping bills: Moore, "Stevenson Practiced Economy";

Mooney, pp. 18–19; Stevenson OH. **"Glaringly simple"**: Mooney, p. 18. **Highway bond fight**: Bolton, "Profile"; Mooney, pp. 18–20. **"Gradually"**: Simons, "Log Cabin Statesman." **Prison reforms**: *Amarillo Sunday News*, Aug. 3, 1941; Stevenson OH. **"The darn thing"**: Stevenson, quoted in Murphey interview.

Coke as Speaker: Nordyke, "Calculatin' Coke"; Simons, "Log Cabin Statesman"; Mooney, pp. 20–22. **"As long as"**: Stevenson, Jr., Clark interviews. **"Hot and heavy"**: Mooney, pp. 25–26. **"On your own"**: *Amarillo Sunday News*, Aug. 3, 1941. **"They have never"**: *DMN*, July 2, 1941. **"Whenever"**: Murphey interview. **"Hardly a man"**: *Amarillo Sunday News*, Aug. 3, 1941. **"That worked"**: Lawson interview. **"It's a country of laws"**: Murphey interview. **"His legion"**: *DT-H*, July 2, 1941. **"Borders on genius"**: Simons, "Log Cabin Statesman." **Fight for second term**: Gantt, pp. 240–42; Murphey, Stevenson, Jr., interviews; Stevenson OH. **Only Speaker to succeed himself**: Webb and Carroll, *Handbook of Texas*, p. 930. **"A landmark period"**: Wyatt and Shelton, p. 51. **Decision to run for Lt. Governor**: Stevenson OH. **"Not easy"**: Murphey interview. **Pappy O'Daniel as campaigner**: Caro, *Path to Power*, pp. 695–703. **"I've got a record"**: Boyett, Lawson, Stevenson, Jr., interviews.

Stevenson's style of campaigning: Bolton, Boyett, Lawson, Lucas, Murphey, Stevenson, Jr., interviews; *AA-S*, *DMN*, *DT-H*, 1942–1944. A typical article on a Stevenson public appearance describes it this way: "There was no wooing, no waving, no shouting, but 'Howdy, Coke,' or 'Hello, Governor.' No ostentation. But plenty of love. Texas is in love with Coke Stevenson. From the humblest to the highest, Texans feel that Coke is 'my Governor' " (*DMN*, Apr. 3, 1942).

No loudspeakers, no bumper stickers: Murphey, Boyett interviews. **"Who *is* that man?"** Bolton interview. **"Here's The Man"**: Murphey interview. **"A quiet dignity"**: Lawson interview. **"Say, can I butt in?"**: *AA-S*, July 18. **"He was them"**: Murphey interview; and see Mooney, p. 30. In fact, Stevenson would occasionally—very occasionally—go so far as to say "I'd sure appreciate your vote." **"You knew he meant"**: Lawson

interview. "Coke Stevenson's here":
Lawson, Lucas interviews.
O'Daniel inauguration: McKay, *W. Lee
O'Daniel*, pp. 133–34.
O'Daniel as governor: Caro, *Path to
Power*, pp. 702–3; McKay, *W. Lee
O'Daniel*, pp. 127–215, 331–406; Bolton,
Lawson, Clark interviews. **"Why do
thinking people":** Stevenson speech on
Mar. 2, 1940, quoted in Simons, "Log
Cabin Statesman."
   Coke's speech: Simons, "Log Cabin
Statesman"; and see also Bolton,
"Profile."
   No "radio sex appeal": Bolton, "Pro-
file." **O'Daniel's elevation to Senate:**
Caro, *Path to Power*, pp. 733–36. **Fay at
inauguration:** Stevenson, Jr., interview;
McLendon, "Coke R. Stevenson."
   "A divine inspiration": Stevenson in-
augural address, quoted in *West Texas
Today*, Sept., 1941. **Stevenson's governorship:** Mooney, pp. 34–51; Green, pp.
77–88; McKay, *Texas Politics*, pp. 391–
96; *AA-S, DMN, DT-H, State Observer*,
1941–47; Stevenson OH; Simons, "Log
Cabin Statesman"; Nordyke, "Calculatin' Coke." **Stevenson and Mexican-
Americans:** Gantt, pp. 148–49; Green,
pp. 80–81; Stevenson OH. **Stevenson
and Negroes:** Green, pp. 79–80. **Stevenson and labor:** Green, p. 81. **Rainey controversy:** Green, pp. 84–88; Stevenson
OH. **Near bottom in social welfare:** Allen, pp. 322–23; pp. 317–19 discusses the
tax situation. **"The biggest tax bill":** *State
Observer*, July 28, 1941. **38th to 24th:** Allen, pp. 322–23. **Tripling of old-age pensions; subdued style of government:**
Mooney, p. 43; Gantt, pp. 187, 213, 226.
   "No program"; "I had a program":
Moore, "Stevenson Practiced Economy." **Deficit into surplus:** Mooney, pp.
47–48. The deficit situation was so serious when Stevenson took office, state
employees were being paid in so-called
hot checks—warrants that had to be discounted at stores. **"As liberal as the people":** *Amarillo Sunday News*, undated
clipping, Barker Collection. For an example of this attitude, see *AA-S*, Jan. 19,
1947, which says: "For a man tagged by
critics a do-nothing governor, Coke Stevenson . . . brought the State through
some trying years without losing a single
rock out of the capitol. . . . He got some
vigorous handling, in this newspaper
among other places, [but] he sincerely
wanted to leave the State better off than
it was when he came here, and he probably will."

"A man who": *DMN*, July 2, 1941. **"A
product of the frontier":** Unidentified
clipping in Barker Collection. **"Abraham
Lincoln of Texas":** Among many places
this comparison was used is the *State
Observer*, July 28, 1941; Nordyke, "Calculatin' Coke." **"In the section":** Mc-
Lendon, "Coke R. Stevenson." **"Seldom
traveled trails":** McLendon, "Coke R.
Stevenson." **"HORATIO ALGER OF THE
LLANO":** Carmack, "Calculatin' Coke
Stevenson." **"He started out":** Bolton,
"Profile." **"LOG CABIN STATESMAN":** Simons, "Log Cabin Statesman." **"Coke
Stevenson makes":** *State Observer*, July
28, 1941. **"Statuesque":** Simons, "Log
Cabin Statesman." **Lumbermen's Meeting:** Boyett interview; Wyatt and Shelton, p. 96. **Great hunter:** For example,
DMN, Sept. 21, 1941. **Shearing and
branding:** Bolton, "Profile"; Bolton,
Murphey interviews; he once told *DMN*
"with rancher's pride": "I don't suppose
there's been a calf on my ranch in twenty
years that I haven't branded myself,"
July 2, 1941. **Life style as Governor:** Stevenson, Jr., Edith Stevenson, Boyett interviews; Mooney, p. 46; Simons, "Log
Cabin Statesman." **"We'll just let that
cup":** For example, Mooney, p. 55.
   "Almost everybody": Bolton, "Profile." **"Well, folks":** Gladys Carroll,
identified as a "San Antonio Newspaper
Writer Visiting in Dallas," in *DMN*,
Apr. 3, 1942. **"In fancy":** McLendon,
"Coke R. Stevenson." **"The most important thing":** Murphey interview.
   1942 election: McKay, *Texas Politics*,
pp. 367–89, 393–94. Nordyke, "Calculatin' Coke." **"Out on the squares":** Nordyke, "Calculatin' Coke." **"No danged
music":** Stevenson, quoted in Nordyke,
"Calculatin' Coke"; Boyett interview. **No
platform or promises, only record:**
Mooney, p. 44. **"I have never made":**
Mooney, p. 54. **68.5 percent:** *Texas Almanac*, 1945–46.
   1944 election: Mann's attacks and Stevenson's responses are discussed in Nordyke, "Calculatin' Coke"; and in
Mooney, p. 54. See also McKay, *Texas
Politics*, pp. 394–95, and *Amarillo
Globe*, Feb. 28, 1944. **"Mr. Texas":** In
fact, Booth Mooney's biography of him
takes that as its title. Liberal commen-
tators knew they had miscalculated. See,
for example, *AA-S*, Jan. 19, 1947.
   84 percent, all 254 counties: *Texas Almanac*, 1945–46. **To this day:** *Texas Almanacs*, 1910–89; Heard and Strong, pp.
132–88. **"Perhaps no other product":**

Gantt, p. 292. **Entire career unique:**
Gantt, p. 9. Later Governors, including
Allan Shivers, would serve longer. In
fact, Stevenson may also have been the
only candidate for *Lieutenant* Governor
who had ever carried all 254 counties. He
did so in his 1940 race for that post. The
author could find no other candidate in a
contested Democratic primary who had
done so, but state records are incomplete, and missing for some years, so it
was impossible to compile a definitive
record of Lieutenant Governor races.
    1946 polls: For example, *DMN*, Oct.
19, 1946. And Stevenson's popularity did
not wane after his retirement. In 1947, a
Belden Poll showed that if he ran, he
would defeat Pappy O'Daniel 74 percent
to 26 percent (*AA-S*, Apr. 8, 1947). A
1948 Belden Poll would find that "Stevenson commanded a vast majority of
the votes no matter what candidate was
pitted against him" (*DMN*, May 16,
1948). **"Seems to believe"; "sincerely
wanted":** *AA-S*, Jan. 19, 1947. **Refusing
to consider:** Boyett, Murphey interviews.
    "Now he was alone": Murphey, Boy-
ett, Stevenson, Jr., Edith Stevenson interviews. **The mail, and description of life
on ranch:** Murphey interview; Mooney,
p. 65. A reporter who visited Stevenson
in retirement reported: "Coke Stevenson
doesn't count mail. He measures it—by
the gallon" (*DMN*, Jan. 10, 1948).
Changing the tire: Murphey interview;
DMN, July 23, 1941. **"We hope":** Mooney, p. 65; Boyett interview.

9. Head Start

SOURCES

Books, articles and documents:
    Allen, ed., *Our Sovereign State*; An-
ders, *Boss Rule in South Texas*; Dugger,
The Politician; Green, *The Establishment
in Texas Politics, 1945–1957*; Gunther,
Inside U.S.A.; Heard and Strong, *Southern Primaries and Elections, 1920–1949*;
Henderson, *Maury Maverick*; Kahl, *Ballot Box 13*; Key, *Southern Politics in State
and Nation*; Kinch and Long, *Allan Shivers*; Lynch, *The Duke of Duval*; McKay,
Texas Politics, 1906–1944 and *Texas and
the Fair Deal, 1945–1952*; Miller, *Lyndon*; Mooney, *Mr. Texas*; *Texas Almanac*, 1941–42; WPA, *Texas: A Guide to
the Lone Star State*.
    James M. Rowe, "The Mesquite Pen-
dergast: George B. Parr—Second Duke

of Duval" (unpublished manuscript), Ingleside, Tex., 1959–60; Edgar G. Shelton, "Political Conditions Among Texas
Mexicans Along the Rio Grande" (master's thesis), Austin, Tex., 1946.
    Ralph Maitland, "San Antonio: The
Shame of Texas," *Forum*, Aug., 1939;
Gordon Schendel, "Something Is Rotten
in the State of Texas," *Collier's*, June 9,
1951; Douglas O. Weeks, "The Texas-
Mexicans and the Politics of South
Texas," *American Political Science Review*, Aug., 1930; Owen P. White, "Machine Made," *Collier's*, Sept. 18, 1957;
Roland Young, "Lone Star Razzle Daz-
zle," *The Nation*, June 21, 1941.

Papers of Tom C. Clark (HSTL).
Papers of George E. B. Peddy (Barker
Texas History Center).

Oral Histories:
    Malcolm Bardwell, George R. Brown,
Cecil E. Burney, Tom C. Clark, John B.
Connally, Mrs. Sam Fore, Reynaldo G.
Garza, Callan Graham, D. B. Harde-
man, Luther E. Jones, Joe Kilgore, John
E. Lyle, Jr., Clarence C. Martens, Booth
Mooney, Robert W. Murphey, Frank C.
Oltorf, Daniel J. Quill, Mary Rather,
Emmett Shelton, Polk Shelton, Adrian
A. Spears, Claude C. Wild, Sr., Wilton
Woods.

Interviews:
    Paul Bolton, Ernest Boyett, George
R. Brown, Edward A. Clark, John B.
Connally, Thomas G. Corcoran, Willard
Deason, Anne Edwards, D. B. Harde-
man, L. E. Jones, Joe M. Kilgore, Wil-
liam J. Lawson, Beverly Lloyd, Frank B.
Lloyd, Maury Maverick, Jr., Frank C.
("Posh") Oltorf, Dan Quill, James H.
Rowe, Jr., James M. Rowe, Luis Salas,
Emmett Shelton, Coke Stevenson, Jr.,
Gerald Weatherly, Wilton Woods, Ralph
Yarborough, Harold Young.

NOTES

    **Peddy biography and significance of his
candidacy:** McKay, *Texas and the Fair
Deal*, pp. 168–69; McKay, *Texas Politics*, pp. 124–27; Boyett, Clark, Oltorf,
Stevenson Jr., interviews. The admiration of conservatives for him is expressed
by the extremely conservative *DMN* columnist Lynn Landrum in his columns of
January 12 and March 8, 1948.
    Polls: *DMN*, May 16, 1948. **"That**

strong, silent man": *DMN*, Jan. 27, 1947.
Stevenson's financing: Boyett, Brown, Clark, Hardeman, Stevenson, Jr., interviews. Between $75,000 and $100,000: This estimate was given to the author by, among others, Boyett, Hardeman, Young.
Johnson's first campaign: Caro, *Path to Power*, pp. 405–9. In that campaign, Johnson spent, in a single congressional district, between $75,000 and $100,000, about the amount other candidates spent on a respectable statewide campaign.
Checks or envelopes stuffed with cash: For example, cash raised in Washington and in New York City's garment district by Corcoran and Rowe was sent to Johnson or his aides by trusted couriers; on June 20, 1941, Walter Jenkins arrived in Texas with, he recalls, "bills stuffed into every pocket": between $10,000 and $15,000. Jenkins gave it to Marsh, who gave it to his personal secretary, Mary Louise Glass, to hold, "and I put it in a white mesh purse. It just bulged with money" (Caro, *Path to Power*, pp. 716–17). For other descriptions of checks, or envelopes stuffed with cash, going to Johnson, see Caro, pp. 683–87, and Note, p. 840. Brown & Root alone gave Johnson about $200,000 for the 1941 campaign (Caro, pp. 717–18; 743–53).
Herman Brown's pledges: Brown, Clark, Corcoran interviews.
"The way to play": Gunther, p. 834.
Politics in San Antonio on the West Side: Caro, *Path to Power*, pp. 718–20; Gunther, pp. 832–35; Henderson, p. 177, 180, 181, 185; White, "Machine Made." Johnson buying votes for $5: Caro, p. 277; Connally, Quill, Hardeman, Maverick, Jr., interviews. Johnson buying votes wholesale: Caro, pp. 719–20. His failure to personally oversee the voting there in 1941, however, meant that West Side politicians "got Johnson's money—but Johnson didn't get the votes," at least not as many as he had been promised. His overall edge over O'Daniel in the Mexican slum was 3,058 to 1,110 in the 1941 election, but he had been promised many more than 3,000 votes (Caro, pp. 736–37).
Towns along the river: WPA, pp. 460–66, 509–12. Literacy rates: Schendel, "Something Is Rotten." In *Sam Johnson's Boy* (p. 259), Steinberg says that Duval ranked 253rd among the 254 Texas counties in literacy. "Only": Key, p. 272. "From time immemorial":

Weeks, "The Texas-Mexicans," p. 609. "Lords protector": Weeks, p. 610. "As hard-bitten": *Philadelphia Record*, Nov. 2, 1939.
"The Valley": The overall picture of politics in the Valley comes from Key, pp. 271–74; Lynch; Rowe, "Mesquite Pendergast"; Shelton, "Political Conditions"; Weeks, "The Texas-Mexicans"; Green, pp. 4–5; *Philadelphia Record*, Nov. 2, 1939; interviews with three of George Parr's lawyers—L. E. Jones, Emmett Shelton, and Gerald Weatherly; with Frank B. Lloyd, District Attorney in Alice in the 1940s and with Luis Salas. Interviews with Boyett, Clark, Connally, Kilgore, Lawson, Rowe, Stevenson, Yarborough, Young.
(In his thesis, as was shown in *The Path to Power*, Shelton says that much of the material comes from "personal interviews with men who know politics," including "ex-Governors, candidates for high state offices, campaign managers, local politicians. . . . For obvious reasons, these men could not be quoted directly. Their identity must remain a secret." This thesis is valuable nonetheless because of the identity of the author. Edgar Shelton, Jr., was the son of Edgar Shelton, Sr., one of three Shelton brothers—the other two were Polk and Emmett—who were three of George Parr's attorneys, as well as attorneys for other financial and political interests in the Valley. Through them, Edgar, Jr., had entrée to the politicians in the state, and the Valley, most familiar with its political machinations. And the only survivor among the three elder Sheltons, Emmett, not only confirms the statements in the thesis, but gives further details of many of the incidents involved. In some of them, he was himself a principal; he knew of others through discussions with his brothers, and with Valley political figures.)
Keeping receipts in safes: Shelton, "Political Conditions," p. 107. "Insure discipline": Key, p. 273. "The Mexican voter": Lynch, p. 23. Description of voting procedures: Jones, Hardeman interviews; the herding image is used by Weeks, "The Texas-Mexicans," p. 611. "Poll list": For example, Rowe, "Mesquite Pendergast," pp. 36–37.
Checked only irregularly: *Philadelphia Record*. "The 'machine' votes the dead men": Shelton, "Political Conditions," p. 7. "An excellent location": Shelton, "Political Conditions," p. 74. Dolores:

Philadelphia Record. **Ten to one:** For example, Table 27, in Key, p. 275, shows that in Duval County, "over a 20-year period . . . almost invariably the leading candidate received over 90% of the vote."

Between 20,000 and 25,000 votes: This estimate was given to the author by Quill, Lawson. Salas' own estimates range as high as 35,000 votes.

A decisive consideration: "In negotiating with some *jefes*, an ample supply of campaign funds is no handicap," Key, p. 273; Lynch, pp. 30, 41, 53. **The State candidates:** Shelton, "Political Conditions," p. 113. **"To withstand":** Schendel, "Something Is Rotten."

"A siege"; "bodyguards"; "practiced charm": Schendel, "Something Is Rotten."

"In counties like": Connally interview. **"Denies"; "the facts":** Schendel, "Something Is Rotten." **Murders are not uncommon:** For example, Rowe, p. 180, quotes a longtime resident of Duval County, Dr. John Sutherland, as saying that during his lifetime "I personally have counted 103 murders." Lynch, pp. 69 ff., chronicles a number of murders that began in 1952. **"It is not easy":** Rowe, "Mesquite Pendergast," p. 75.

Beer license: Schendel, "Something Is Rotten." **Extra nickel:** Lawson interview. **Oil wells:** Schendel said he had an interest in "no fewer than 200 wells." **Erasing clauses:** Steinberg, p. 260; Lynch, p. 45. **$25,000 in cash:** Lynch, pp. 39–41; Rowe, "Mesquite Pendergast," p. 14. **Formed own construction company:** Dugger, p. 324; Schendel, "Something Is Rotten." **$406,000 income:** Schendel, "Something Is Rotten." **"Despite"; race track; $15,000 bets:** Schendel, "Something Is Rotten."

Two $25,000 "loans": Lynch, pp. 52–53, 89. **"Therefore":** Rowe, "Mesquite Pendergast," p. 21. See also Schendel, "Something Is Rotten"; Dugger, pp. 324–25.

Divorce: In the actual settlement, she was awarded not only oil wells and other property but $425,000 in cash (Schendel, "Something Is Rotten").

"Little is known": Shelton, "Political Conditions," p. 44.

Revolt in Jim Wells County: Lynch, pp. 60–62; Rowe, "Mesquite Pendergast," p. 33; Ben Kaplan, "Inside the Parr Empire: Opposition to Duval's Emperor Develops in Jim Wells County," *HP,* Sept. 9, 1948. Rowe interview. Sa-

las' biography: Salas, "Box 13"; Salas interview. **"Stop! Don't you know?":** Salas, "Box 13," p. 44. **"He used to tell me":** *Ibid.*, p. 38. **"Spend this money";** **"Through my hands":** *Ibid.*, pp. 44, 36. **"We never said no":** *Ibid.*, pp. 34, 38. For accounts that tally with Salas', see, for example, Shelton, "Political Conditions," p. 107; Key, p. 273; Lynch, p. 23 and *passim*; and Rowe, "Mesquite Pendergast," pp. 56 ff.

" 'Indio, I want his place closed' ": Parr, quoted in Salas, "Box 13," p. 37. **80 percent:** *Ibid.*, p. 44. **"The right hand":** *Ibid.*, pp. 32, 33. **"Stood there like a king":** *Ibid.*, p. 37.

Wirtz negotiating with Archie Parr: Lynch, p. 37. And Steinberg, p. 172, says: "Along the Rio Grande, Wirtz was competing with friends of O'Daniel to buy off county political dictators." **Wurzbach charged fraud:** Steinberg, p. 60. He would never: Lloyd interview. **In 1941, Johnson himself had telephoned:** Caro, *Path to Power,* p. 739. **95 percent to 5 percent:** *Texas Almanac,* 1941–42, p. 385; Heard and Strong, pp. 177–79. **"It was nauseous":** unidentified source quoted in Shelton, "Political Conditions," p. 72. **"Worse than Pendergast":** Quoted in *Ibid.*, p. 25.

Stevenson had been the exception: Boyett, Hardeman, Lawson, Quill, Shelton interviews. **"Straight behind":** Quoted in Shelton, "Political Conditions," p. 45. **"Why shouldn't":** Boyett interview.

Stevenson's refusal to appoint Kazen: Lynch, p. 56; Boyett, Stevenson, Jr., interviews; Callan Graham, quoted in Miller, pp. 125–26, says he was present when Parr and other border dictators told Stevenson, "Coke, we've liked you . . . but we cannot tolerate a Governor" refusing an "important patronage request." Parr himself was to tell reporters flatly: "I have nothing against Coke personally. We went to him and asked him to appoint Jim Kazen. [He refused.] This election is the first time we have had an opportunity since then to vote against him" (*CCC-T,* Sept. 14, 1948). Also see *AA-S,* Aug. 30, 1977.

"For years"; "double the meat": "A source completely inside Parr's circle," quoted in Dugger, p. 323. **"Everybody knew":** Lloyd interview. **Others say:** Quill, Shelton interviews. Moreover, on Feb. 16, 1948, Johnson wrote Parr, "John Lyle and I tried to reach you by telephone the other afternoon. He came by my office, and we got to talking about our friends and just decided to call you. We got as far as Dallas, but they said the lines to San Diego were busy, and we never did get to talk before we had to leave. I still haven't made any definite decision. Expect to be back in Texas the later part of the month, and hope to talk to you then. . . . Take care of yourself and if there is anything I can do at any time, let me know."

Parr himself was to say, in a tape-recorded interview for a projected documentary on the campaign, when asked why he had supported Johnson in the election, "Oh, yes, I had met Lyndon himself and talked to him, and I was for him" (Parr, quoted in *AA-S*, Aug. 30, 1977). **"Very close":** Lloyd interview. **"Style and guts":** Lynch, p. 56. **"Good friends, dear friends":** Jones interview. **Johnson helping Parr obtain pardon:** On Aug. 7, 1943, Parr applied for a presidential pardon for his 1932 income tax conviction. On Aug. 31, 1943, John Connally wrote Johnson: "I talked to [White House Administrative Assistant] Jim Rowe about George Parr. He tried to do what he could before he left. All the papers are in order—they are down with Dan Lyons of the Pardon Board now. On the face of things there is no reason why his civil liberties should not be restored. Jim left last night after talking with the President about an hour" (Connally to Johnson, "LBJ Family Financial Records," Box 12, PPCF). Parr's application was denied on Jan. 22, 1944. On Feb. 28, 1945, Parr requested the U.S. Board of Pardons and Paroles to reactivate his application for a pardon. In Tom Clark's papers is an undated letter from Parr to Lyons, apparently written about this time, stating that Parr had asked Johnson about his earlier application, and Johnson had given him information about the reason it had been denied (Parr to Lyons, undated, Box 8, Tom Clark Papers, HSTL). President Truman granted Parr a full and unconditional pardon on Feb. 20, 1946. Although various accounts have credited newly elected congressman John Lyle of Corpus Christi with obtaining the pardon, Parr himself felt differently.

"We helped him": Brown interview. **"Listen, Indio":** Salas, "Box 13," p. 53. **Polling:** Clark, Connally, Hardeman interviews. **"We didn't care":** Whiteside, quoted in Caro, *Path to Power*, p. 177.

Johnson's new plans for radio: Bolton, Hardeman interviews. **"Have to say**

something over and over": Connally interview. **"The dawn of a whole new era":** Connally interview. **Bright young men felt:** This feeling was described to the author by many of the bright young men, including Bolton, Kilgore, and Oltorf. **" 'He can win!' ":** Kilgore interview.

10. *"Will!"*

SOURCES

The description of Lyndon Johnson's illness, and his struggle against it, is based on the author's interviews with Paul Bolton and Warren G. Woodward, and on their oral histories. They are the source of all quotations unless otherwise indicated.

The scenes in which Bolton was absent, and Woodward and Stuart Symington present, are based on the author's interviews with Woodward and Symington, and on their oral histories.

Books:
Cochran and Brinley, *Jackie Cochran*; Kearns, *Lyndon Johnson and the American Dream*; McKay, *Texas and the Fair Deal, 1945–1952*; Miller, *Lyndon*.

Oral Histories:
Paul Bolton, James Cain, Jacqueline Cochran, Stuart Symington, Warren G. Woodward.

Interviews:
Paul Bolton, John B. Connally, Walter Jenkins, Stuart Symington, Warren G. Woodward.

NOTES

Illness in first campaign for Congress: Caro, *Path to Power*, pp. 433–36. **"Surging blood-red tide," etc.:** *AA-S*, *DMN*, *HP*, May 23, 1948. **"Several shots":** Dr. Morgan, quoted in Woodward OH. **Arrangements with Symington:** Symington, Jenkins interviews. **Campaigning in Panhandle:** *AA-S*, May 24, 25, 1948. **Reports of his hospitalization:** *DMN*, *HP*, May 27, 1948; Connally, quoted in Miller, p. 119; Jenkins interview; Busby to Jenkins, June 6, 1948, "Austin–Miscellaneous, 1948," Box 1, PPMF, LBJL. **Flight to Mayo Clinic:** Woodward, Symington; *AA-S*, May 28, 30, 1948. In her autobiography, *Jackie Cochran*, Miss Cochran, on pp. 252–59, gives an account of this incident in which her role in the decision to go to Mayo's is portrayed somewhat more prominently than by the others involved.

At Mayo Clinic: Cain OH; Woodward interview; *AA-S, HP*, May 28, 1948; *AA-S, DMN*, May 31, June 1, 1948.

"No clippings"; "Again": Wade to Johnson, June 1, 2, 1948, "Austin–Miscellaneous, 1948," Box 1, PPMF, LBJL.

Stevenson's campaigning: McKay, pp. 188–90; *HP*, May 28, 1948; Murphey interview. **"Could give no account":** McKay, p. 190. **"Candidate Stevenson":** *HP*, June 6, 1948.

Stevenson's speech; *DMN*, June 1, 1948.

"I know you didn't send that": Busby to Jenkins, June 6, 1948, "Austin–Miscellaneous, 1948," Box 1, PPMF, LBJL.

"I just could not bear": Johnson, quoted in Kearns, p. 100.

11. The Flying Windmill

SOURCES

More than seventy boxes of documents at the Lyndon Baines Johnson Library contain about 56,000 pages of material on Lyndon Johnson's 1948 senatorial campaign. These include letters and memoranda from campaign headquarters in Austin to district leaders and campaign aides in the field; confidential intraoffice memoranda; communications between the Austin headquarters and Johnson's congressional office in Washington, and reports from local campaign managers on Johnson's activities and behavior in their districts. These boxes also contain memoranda sent back to Austin from Horace Busby, who traveled with Johnson during part of the campaign. Some of these memoranda describe Johnson's behavior. Also in these boxes are Busby's "suggested releases" and speech drafts, including releases to be issued and speeches to be given by others. These boxes also contain poll tax lists, lists of the candidate's supporters, "contacts" and potential financial contributors (with notes about them), briefing papers for the candidate, newspaper clippings, schedules, and expense accounts. They include scribbled notes from one head-

quarters worker to another. These papers provide part of the basis for the description of Lyndon Johnson on the campaign trail. Other collections at the Library that include relevant material are Box 1 of the Pre-Presidential Memo File and the Mildred Stegall Files.

The description of Johnson during the campaign is based also on the author's interviews with men and women who accompanied him. The author interviewed at length his two helicopter pilots, James E. Chudars and Joe Mashman, the helicopter's chief mechanic, Harry Nachlin, and members of the campaign entourage such as Paul Bolton, Horace Busby, J. J. ("Jake") Pickle, Mary Rather, and Warren G. Woodward. I also interviewed campaign aides and strategists who remained back in Austin at either the Hancock House or the Brown Building headquarters, but who received telephone reports on the candidate's behavior from the field. These aides include Edward A. Clark, John B. Connally, Charles Herring, Walter Jenkins, and Joe M. Kilgore. Also interviewed were reporters who covered the Johnson campaign, most importantly Margaret Mayer.

Many newspaper articles give details of Johnson the campaigner, and this chapter is also based on the daily accounts in the *Austin American-Statesman*, the *Dallas Morning News* and the *Houston Post* and, when relevant, on other newspapers such as the *Fort Worth Star-Telegram*, *Corpus Christi Caller-Times*, *State Observer*, *Houston Chronicle*.

While the sources of specific quotations or incidents are individually identified below, the general description of Johnson's behavior is based on all these sources.

The following list of sources includes all interviews and oral histories relating to the campaign, including those above.

Books, articles and documents:

Dugger, *The Politician*; Gantt, *The Chief Executive in Texas*; Green, *The Establishment in Texas Politics, 1945–1957*; Kahl, *Ballot Box 13*; McKay, *Texas and the Fair Deal, 1945–1952*; Miller, *Lyndon*; Steinberg, *Sam Johnson's Boy*; *Texas Almanac, 1949–50*; WPA, *Texas: A Guide to the Lone Star State*.

Joe Phipps, "Tell 'Em About Me, Joe," "Charlie [June–July]," Box 99; JHP.

Papers of Charles Marsh (LBJL). Governor Coke Stevenson (Records), RG 301, Archives Division, Texas State Library.

Oral Histories:
Malcolm Bardwell, James H. Blundell, Charles K. Boatner, Paul Bolton, H. S. ("Hank") Brown, Raymond E. Buck, Horace Busby, Bo Byers, James Cain, Robert Calvert, Leslie Carpenter, Margaret Carter, James E. Chudars, Tom C. Clark, Ann Fears Crawford, Price Daniel, Sr., Willard Deason, Charles W. Duke, Lewis T. ("Tex") Easley, James Elkins, O. C. Fisher, Mrs. Sam Fore, Reynaldo Garza, E. B. Germany, Callan Graham, Walter G. Hall, Mack Hannah, Jr., Charles Herring, Welly K. Hopkins, W. Ervin James, Walter Jenkins, Sam Houston Johnson, Luther E. Jones, Carroll Keach, Vann M. Kennedy, Sam Kinch, Sr., Fred Korth, Stuart Long, J. C. Looney, Sam D. W. Low, George Mahon, Clarence C. Martens, Crawford Martin, Joe Mashman, Margaret Mayer, William Hunt McLean, Sarah McClendon, Marshall McNeil, Booth Mooney, Robert W. Murphey, Dorothy J. Nichols, Robert Oliver, Frank C. ("Posh") Oltorf, J. R. Parten, Wright Patman, Harvey O. Payne, Drew Pearson, Carl Phinney, J. J. ("Jake") Pickle, Sam Plyler, W. R. Poage, Paul A. Porter, Ben H. Powell, Jr., C. W. Price, Harry Provence, Daniel J. Quill, Mary Rather, Joseph L. Rauh, Jr., Juanita Roberts, Ray Roberts, Fenner Roth, James H. Rowe, Jr., James M. Rowe, Emmett Shelton, Polk Shelton, Bailey Sheppard, Allan Shivers, John V. Singleton, Sr., Byron Skelton, Adrian A. Spears, Max Starcke, Arthur Stehling, Stuart Symington, Antonio J. Taylor, Homer Thornberry, Bascom Timmons, Edwin Weisl, Sr., Claude Wild, Sr., A. M. Willis, Mrs. Alvin J. Wirtz, Wilton Woods, Warren C. Woodward, Eugene Worley.

Interviews:
Ray Arledge, Paul Bolton, Ernest Boyett, George R. Brown, Horace Busby, James E. Chudars, Edward A. Clark, John B. Connally, Thomas G. Corcoran, Ann Fears Crawford, Charles W. Duke, Lewis T. ("Tex") Easley, Tom Ferguson, Mrs. Sam Fore, D. B. Hardeman, Charles Herring, Welly K. Hopkins, Walter Jenkins, Sam Houston Johnson, Edward Joseph, Vann M. Kennedy, Joe M. Kilgore, William J. Lawson, R. J. ("Bob") Long, Wingate Lucas, Gerald C. Mann, Joe Mashman, Margaret Mayer, Ernest Morgan, Robert W. Murphey, Harry Nachlin, Frank C. ("Posh") Oltorf, J. J. ("Jake") Pickle, Mary Rather, James H. Rowe, Jr., Luis Salas, E. Babe Smith, Arthur Stehling, Coke Stevenson, Jr., Stuart Symington, Tom Whitehead, Claude C. Wild, Sr., Warren G. Woodward, Harold Young, Mary Louise Glass Young.

NOTES

(All dates 1948 unless otherwise noted)

"Because he had been": Woodward OH; Brown interview.
"While I was sick": *AA-S*, June 6.
Advisers appalled: For example, one Johnson district chairman, Lloyd Croslin of Lubbock, wrote Wild: "Everyone is against Johnson insulting Stevenson," and another, J. Ed Johnson of Brownwood, wrote, "A great many people that I have talked with think that Lyndon is hurting himself by jumping on Coke." Typical of Wild's assurances is his reply to Croslin: "We agree with you . . . that we should lay off Coke Stevenson." Croslin to Wild, June 9; Wild to Croslin, June 12, "District 19 Chairman–Lloyd Croslin (Lubbock)," Box 107, JHP. J. Ed Johnson to Wild, June 9 ("District 21 Chairman–J. Ed Johnson [Brownwood])," Box 107, JHP. **"A very tricky thing":** Pickle, quoted in Miller, p. 117. **"A man ought to have":** Johnson, quoted in *AA-S*, June 17. **Sales of pardons:** For a typical charge, and Stevenson's reply see *DMN*, Aug. 22; *HP*, Aug. 17; *HP*, *AA-S*, Aug. 23, quoted in McKay, p. 233. Stevenson said that in every state, convicts were released through a generous pardon policy so that they might serve in the armed forces. Hectored by pro-Johnson reporters, Stevenson would say at a press conference: "A lot of people have the whole thing mixed up. There is such a thing as a five-day clemency, when a prisoner is permitted a few days to visit his sick mother" ("Full Text of Les Carpenter's Story," "Austin–Miscellaneous, 1948," Box 1, PPMF). Bolton, Brown, Boyett, Stevenson, Jr., interviews. When Johnson attempted to resurrect this charge shortly before the close of the campaign (*HP*, Aug. 18; *AA-S*, Aug. 20), T. N. Whitehurst of Beaumont, a member of the State Prison

Board, repeated that the figure given by Johnson's campaign was false and released figures to prove it, said even the smaller figure included clemencies, and added that if Stevenson had freed as many prisoners as Johnson charged, "the prisons would have been emptied, and we would have had to lock it up" (*DMN*, Aug. 25). **Charges on Magnolia lease:** Bolton, Boyett, Busby, Stevenson, Jr., interviews. **"As my private life":** Stevenson, quoted in *DMN*, June 16. **"I was sure wrong":** Busby interview; confirmed by Bolton, Boyett interviews.

Problems in using the helicopter; decision to use it despite the risks: Interviews with Woodward, with Wingate Lucas, the Congressman from Fort Worth who accompanied Johnson to the Bell Helicopter demonstration, with the two pilots who flew it during the campaign, Joe Mashman and Jim Chudars, and with the chief mechanic responsible for its servicing, Harry Nachlin. **Special train:** The candidate who chartered it, in 1938, was Attorney General William McCraw (Gantt, p. 291). **Chudars noticed:** Chudars interview.

Previous week bad: *AA-S*, June 10; *HP*, June 12, 13; Brown, Clark interviews. **Stevenson shrugging off:** *DMN*, June 16. **"A withering lack":** *AA-S*, June 13.

"The first candidate . . . in history": *AA-S*, June 13. **Defusing the cost issue:** For example, *AA-S*, June 10; *HP*, June 13; *State Observer*, June 14; *DMN*, June 15. **Misgivings from staff:** For example, Croslin to Wild, "District 19 Chairman–Lloyd Croslin (Lubbock)," Box 107, JHP. But on June 12, Wild wrote Croslin, "He [Johnson] insists on trying the helicopter idea."

"JOHNSON TO GIVE 'EM": *HP*, June 16. **"LOOKEE, MAW"; "No comment":** *HP*, June 13. **"I hope":** Peddy, quoted in *HP*, June 13.

"First day in the helicopter: Busby, Chudars interviews; *AA-S*, *DMN*, *HP*, June 16. **"Flitting around"; Campaigning by helicopter in East Texas:** *AA-S*, *DMN*, *HP*, June 16, 17.

Naming the "Windmill": The first use of that nickname that I could find is *AA-S*, June 16. **Third day of campaigning:** *AA-S*, *DMN*, *HP*, June 18. **Wild's news:** Jenkins interview.

Campaigning by helicopter: Busby, Chudars, Mayer, Nachlin, Pickle, Rather, Woodward interviews; Nichols OH; Phipps, "Tell 'Em About Me, Joe";

articles in *AA-S*, *DMN*, *FWS-T*, *HP*, *State Observer*, other newspapers, June 16–July 26. **"Can't wipe your ass"; "He meant every":** Caro, *Path to Power*, p. 404; Morgan interview. **"Coming down":** Mayer interview, which supplements her articles in *AA-S*. **Flinging the hat:** *DMN*, July 4; Pickle interview. Although he threw the Stetson into the crowd, Johnson wanted it back. One of his aides would be assigned to retrieve it from the person—usually a small boy—who had received it. On July 4, the *DMN* could report that though he "flung his hat out of the craft at every stop, [he] hasn't lost his hat yet." **"Come meet Congressman Johnson":** Phipps, "Tell 'Em About Me, Joe." **"They all wanted"; "the blades":** Nachlin interview. **Johnson's speech and reaction:** Chudars, Woodward, Mayer, Busby, Mashman interviews.

Cotton-choppers' terror: *Time*, June 28. **"Two people and a big dog":** Chudars OH. Among many instances of Johnson landing to talk to two or three people, see *HP*, July 9. **"The chickens thought":** Busby interview. **"Hello, down there":** Chudars interview; Dugger, p. 318.

"Hovering": *HP*, July 14. **"Johnson brought people":** *DMN*, July 7. **Headlines:** *AA-S*, June 25; *HP*, July 7; *DMN*, July 9; *FWS-T*, July 19. **"Long Lyndon Johnson":** *Time*, June 28. **"Campaign of the Flying Windmill":** *DMN*, July 2. **Appearances in Bangs, Coleman:** *AA-S*, July 1.

Johnson's view from helicopter: Chudars, Mashman interviews. **Touring the Hill Country:** *AA-S*, June 25; *AA-S*, *DMN*, *HP*, June 27. **"It gives me confidence"; "Happy tired"; "That thing":** *HP*, June 27.

AFL endorsement: *AA-S*, *DMN*, *HP*, June 23–27; McKay, pp. 200–1. **Labor's feelings about Johnson:** *DMN*, *HC*, *HP*, June 25; *AA-S*, Aug. 10. Hopkins, Corcoran interviews. The AFL said that Johnson "by his own actions, vote and continued support of the Taft-Hartley and Case bills has disqualified himself in the eyes of the working people of Texas," *HP*, June 25. **Anti-union sentiment in Texas:** Green, pp. 103–7. **"He just seemingly":** Boatner OH. **Stevenson's reasoning:** Boyett, Murphey interviews; Boatner OH. Boatner was with Stevenson "the day he got word that labor had endorsed him."

Johnson's instinct for the jugular: Graham, quoted in Caro, *Path to Power*, p. 154. **A "secret deal":** Johnson, quoted in

Steinberg, p. 248. Johnson's attack, like his earlier attacks on Stevenson's reputation, came in the face of advice of more timid campaign aides, who advised him to try to put as good a face as possible on the endorsement. For example, Claude Wild told him: "You should be cheerful about it—say that the actual laborers are for you; the political leaders are not. . . . I would not use the expression 'stabbed in the back.' It sounds like the outsider like you are crying over losing your former friends. At least, it is defensive" (Wild to Johnson, June 24, "Austin–Miscellaneous, 1948," Box 1, PPMF). **Johnson "has disqualified himself":** Reilley, quoted in *HC, HP,* June 25. **"Deliberate lie"; "INFURIATED":** *DMN,* June 25.

Johnson's charges of "secret deal": For example, *DMN,* June 24. In this statement, Johnson also attacked Stevenson for his actions on the Manford Bill, which Johnson called "the state's vicious anti-labor law," a rather cynical statement, since it was two of the men who were advising Johnson on this statement—Alvin Wirtz and Edward Clark—who had drafted that law. **"Labor dictators":** *CCC,* Aug. 11.

Johnson's charge untrue: Stevenson's advisers—Boyett, Murphey, Stevenson, Jr.—say this unanimously in interviews. And so do Johnson's advisers including Bolton and Jenkins. **"We knew it wasn't true":** Bolton interview. **Not Stevenson but Johnson was receiving secret labor support:** Corcoran, Hopkins, Rowe, Harold Young interviews. **"He was saying":** Hopkins interview.

Abilene press conference: *HP,* July 3. **"My policy is":** *Abilene Reporter-News,* July 3. Quoted in *DMN,* Aug. 13. **"Repeatedly":** Stevenson, quoted in McKay, pp. 227–28. **Refusing to listen to advisers:** Boyett, Murphey, Stevenson, Jr., interviews.

Johnson's continuing attacks: *AA-S, CCC-T, DMN, HP,* June 24–Aug. 11. **"Anyone who knew":** Murphey interview. **Leach demand:** *AA-S,* June 24. **Stevenson's refusal to reply:** *DMN,* July 18, 30. **Not "be drawn":** *DMN,* June 27. **"Wasn't like other candidates":** Boyett interview. **"Mr. Leach's letter":** *DMN,* June 27.

"He's moving out!": Woodward interview. **Silver Star bar:** And Johnson of course displayed it. If, because of the heat, he removed his suit jacket, on which his Silver Star bar was pinned, he,

as the *DMN* reported on one occasion, "held aloft his coat" to display the emblem, and "got a big hand when he shouted 'I didn't sit and puff my pipe when our country was at war,' " and then "told about his military service in the Pacific" (*DMN,* July 3). This was one of the speeches at which he was introduced by an amputee. See also, for example, "July 1," Box 91, JHP. His attempts to make capital of his wartime experiences grew ever more intensive. Before the end of the campaign, he was telling audiences that the reason he had not run for the senatorial seat in 1942 was that he had been "in the jungles of New Guinea" (*HC,* Aug. 22). **"Congressman Johnson":** For example, *AA-S,* Aug. 17. **"Seven heroes":** *AA-S,* June 29. **"But when the election":** *HC,* Aug. 22.

Johnson's small-town speeches: No complete transcript of Johnson's basic impromptu speech can be found. To reconstruct the speech, the author took paragraphs and phrases from descriptions of this speech that were printed in daily or weekly newspapers. Then he asked members of Johnson's staff who heard the speech repeatedly—most notably Warren G. Woodward, Joe Mashman, Mary Rather and Horace Busby—to give their recollection of what he said and to try to recall the phrases Johnson used. In an attempt to capture the Hill Country intonations that Johnson used, he had relatives and boyhood friends from Johnson City, including Johnson's brother, Sam Houston Johnson, and his cousin, Ava Johnson Cox, try to recall the phrases he used. **"My boy died":** *DMN,* July 18. **An old man's tears:** *HP,* Aug. 15. **"Flying in B-29s, helping bomb one Japanese island after another":** *Port Arthur News,* July 15.

Imitating Coke: Among newspaper accounts of his imitation, the most evocative is Margaret Mayer's in the *AA-S,* June 27; Busby, Woodward interviews. **"Gone berserk":** Busby to Wade, June 24, "Intra-Office Memoranda," Box 98, JHP; Busby interview.

Johnson's emotions: Busby, Mayer, Rather, Woodward interviews. **"Son, they're people!":** Busby interview. **Racing the train:** *CCC-T,* July 7. **Waving his hat:** For example, *DMN,* July 7. **"Hello, Port Arthur!"** *Port Arthur News,* July 15. **"Whipped his Stetson":** *AA-S,* June 25.

Following him by auto: Chudars, Oltorf, Bolton, Woodward, Nachlin interviews; Boatner, Plyler OHs. **"That mad dash"**: Knight to Johnson, "Fort Worth–IJK," Box 87, JHP. **"Three hours"**: Nichols OH. **Johnson's hard work**: Busby, Chudars, Jenkins, Rather, Woodward, Bolton, Clark interviews. **"Worry yourself"**: Wild to Johnson, June 19, "Austin–Miscellaneous, 1948," Box 1, PPMF. **Awake when Woody came to wake him**: Woodward interview. **"I never saw anyone"**; **"harder"**: Caro, *Path to Power*, p. 425; Clark interview.

Visit to Alice Glass's mother: Oltorf, Mary Louise Glass Young interviews. **"Just too nervous"**: Quoted in Steinberg, p. 256. **Stevenson's speech**: *DMN*, July 16. **Coverage of Stevenson campaign**: For example, *AA-S*, July 18; *DMN*, July 8, 17, 18, 21; *HP*, July 16, 18. **"Five towns"**: *AA-S*, June 28.

"Coffee, doughnuts": Steinberg, p. 256. **Raging at clerks; "nudity"**: Busby interview.

"See the [face]": Boatner OH. **Treatment of Cheavens**: Mayer interview. **Switching HP reporters**: Oltorf interview. **Obscenities to Rather**: Mayer interview and OH; Rather interview.

"Umbrage": Busby interview. **Predicting no runoff**: Phipps, "Tell 'Em About Me, Joe." "Having heard it a lot myself, I almost believed it," Phipps wrote. *FWS-T*, June 25, *AA-S*, June 27.

The older men knew: Brown, Clark interviews.

Cowboy Reunion: Interviews with Murphey, Boyett and Ray Arledge, former Reunion president; *HP*, *DMN*, July 3. **"Thinning ranks"**: WPA, pp. 467–70. **"I didn't sit,"** etc.: For example, *DMN*, July 3. **"One constant"**: *HP*, July 3. **Johnson's excuse**: *DMN*, *CCC-T*, July 3. **Poll results**: *DMN*, July 11.

Changing helicopters: Mashman, Chudars interviews; Mashman OH. **"My good pilot Joe"**: Mashman interview.

One of the hottest summers: *Texas Almanac*, p. 168. **"Flying in a greenhouse"**: Chudars interview. **"Just dripping"**: Mashman interview. **Thirty-one speeches**: *CCC-T*, July 8. **Circling thunderstorm**: *DMN*, July 10; Mashman interview.

Stump speeches: See Note, Johnson's small-town speeches above. See also *AA-S*, *DMN*, *HP*, *CCC-T*, June 20–July 21. **"A goatherder"**: *DMN*, July 9. **"Twenty bombs"**: *HP*, July 8. **Germ warfare**: *HP*, July 4. **"Pray"; "the best atomic bomb"**: For example, *DMN*, July 4. For another example of his rhetoric on this subject,

see *DMN*, July 24: " 'The atom bomb we dropped on Hiroshima is just a T-Model compared with the bomb we have ready right now, wrapped up and tied with a blue ribbon.' " **"I wish"**: *FWS-T*, July 20. **"Day is over"**: *AA-S*, July 11. **Oil depletion should be increased**: For example, *DMN*, July 9, 15. **"Big-bellied,"** etc.: For example, *DMN*, July 7. **"Isolationist"**; **"appeaser"**; **"umbrella man"**; **"Munich"**: For example, *DMN*, July 17; *HP*, July 18; *CCC-T*, July 18; *DMN*, July 21. During the Berlin crisis in July, Johnson's attacks on Stevenson as "appeaser" intensified, as did his warnings of imminent war. "The Russian bear is moving!" Johnson "shouted" in speech after speech. "No one knows what the next day or hour will bring!" And his attacks on Stevenson intensified. "Other persons," he said, in a thinly veiled reference to Stevenson, "want to cut the throat of the free country we have always known." He said America must not retreat "one inch. . . . We are willing to draw the quarantine line, and we would rather have it on the Mediterranean than on the shores of the Gulf of Mexico. . . . The people realize the issue in this race is preparedness and peace versus isolationism and appeasement." Stevenson's own statement on the crisis pointed out that he had consistently favored a strong military. "None of us running for office now will be in Washington before January [and] I will not attempt to fool the people of Texas by pretending that, as a candidate, I can do anything effective about this urgent problem. Certainly a matter as serious as this has no place as a political issue. But I would call for a showdown with Russia if I were there." He felt that Russia did not want war at the present time, because "her forces aren't strong enough." So, he said, "I would call for a showdown with Russia if I were there. Make Russia toe the mark, and if we do, too, I don't believe we will have war." **"STOOGE"**: For example, *HP*, July 8. **"Slick tongue"**: For example, *AA-S*, July 11. **Woodward getting caught up**: Woodward interview. **Semicircle edging closer**: Busby interview.

The meeting and greeting: Johnson's phrases in these unwritten speeches are re-created from the recollections of a dozen persons who heard him give them. Some of the phrases are the same as or similar to phrases he used in unrehearsed stump speeches during his 1937 campaign for Congress—because he would use the

same phrases. **"Mighty hard schedule"**: Meredith to Wild, July 17; Wild to Meredith, July, "District 4 Chairman–Fred Meredith," Box 100, JHP. **In the helicopter**: Mashman interview. **Johnson's lack of concern for own safety**: Mashman, Chudars, Woodward interviews. **Rosenberg landing**: Woodward interview. **"Concentrate"**: Parr, quoted in Salas, "Box 13," p. 53. **Conditions in Precinct 13**: Lloyd, Salas, Rowe interviews. **"Inside we had a table"**: Salas interview; Salas, "Box 13," p. 56. **"I tell you once more"**; **"told them, Absolutely"**: Salas, "Box 13," pp. 53, 51. **"I just ordered"**; Holmgreen's arrest: Salas, Holmgreen, quoted in Kahl, p. 93. **"Up many times"**; **"just ignored same"**: Salas, "Box 13," p. 54. **Voting results**: *AA-S*, *DMN*, *HP*, *CCC-T*, July 26; *Texas Almanac*, pp. 462–64.
DMN editorial: On front page, July 23. **Echoed by**: The *DMN* said that "on his [Stevenson's] great record he can hardly fail to appeal to a substantial majority of the 265,000 Texans who in August will make their second choice," *DMN*, July 27. **"Ninety percent"**: Roberts, quoted in *HP*, July 29. Indeed, a Belden Poll published on August 1 provided figures to support the optimism of the Stevenson camp. It showed that of voters who favored Peddy in the first primary, 49.5 percent would favor Stevenson in the second, to 39.7 for Johnson, with 10.8 percent undecided (*AA-S*, Aug. 1). **"So imposing"**: Pickle OH. **"Making up"**: Kilgore interview. As for Johnson's own feelings, he related them at the time to Busby, Clark, Connally, Kilgore and Pickle, among others. He was to recall to Ronnie Dugger: "I thought I'd lead into the run-off by 100,000 votes. . . . I nearly had to get seventy or eighty percent of the votes that went to George Peddy." Johnson interview with Dugger, Dec. 14, 1967, quoted in Dugger, p. 319. **"People do not"**: Busby interview. **"Pulled his weight"**: *FWS-T*, July 26.

12. All or Nothing

SOURCES

See also Sources for Chapter 11.
Books, articles, and documents:
McKay, *Texas and the Fair Deal, 1945–1952*; Montgomery, *Mrs. LBJ*; Smith, *The President's Lady*; Steinberg,

Sam Johnson's Boy; *Texas Almanac*, 1949–1950.

Papers of Welly K. Hopkins (LBJL).

Oral Histories:
Leslie Carpenter, E. B. Germany, Marshall McNeil, Dorothy J. Nichols, Robert Oliver, Drew Pearson, J. J. ("Jake") Pickle.

Interviews:
Paul Bolton, Ernest J. Boyett, George R. Brown, Horace Busby, Edward A. Clark, John B. Connally, Thomas G. Corcoran, Lewis T. ("Tex") Easley, Charles Herring, Welly K. Hopkins, Walter Jenkins, Lady Bird Johnson, Edward Joseph, Sarah McClendon, Robert W. Murphey, Frank C. ("Posh") Oltorf, J. J. ("Jake") Pickle, Daniel Quill, Mary Rather, James H. Rowe, Jr., Emmett Shelton, E. Babe Smith, Coke Stevenson, Jr., Wilton Woods, Ralph Yarborough, Harold Young.

NOTES

(All dates 1948 unless otherwise indicated)
Change in Johnson: Busby, Connally interviews.
The Washington press conference: Articles on it in *AA-S*, July 30, Aug. 8, 9; *DMN*, *FWS-T*, *HP*, July 30; Easley, McClendon, Murphey interviews; "Re: Stevenson's Press Conference 6:00 p.m. July 29, 1948," Files of Mildred Stegall, Box 59, LBJL; "Full Text of Les Carpenter's Story Thursday noon Stevenson Press Conference," "Austin–Miscellaneous, 1948," Box 1, PPMF, LBJL. The description of how the trap was set comes from the oral histories of Pickle, McNeil, Pearson, supplemented by interviews with Pickle, Connally, McClendon, Easley, Murphey, Corcoran and Rowe. The words "and then riding him" can no longer be found in the transcript of the Pickle Oral History in the Lyndon Johnson Library. Pickle has deleted them from the text, but they are in the original text, a copy of which is in the author's possession. Leslie Carpenter's description of the incident does not mention being prepared in advance for the Stevenson visit. In his OH, Drew Pearson said: "When Coke Stevenson came up here, Lyndon tipped me off and I arranged a press conference for Coke Stevenson and had a question asked of him

by one of my assistants about the Taft-Hartley Act. That put Coke on record publicly, where he stood. That supposedly turned a certain number of votes against Coke and maybe made the difference of the eighty-seven vote margin, by which Lyndon won. At any rate he was very grateful." When the OH interviewer then said, "You weren't particularly trying to help Congressman Johnson in his race for the Senate so much as you were just trying to get Stevenson's true stand on the issue," Pearson corrected him. "A little bit of both," the columnist said. "I wanted to 'hep' Lyndon, as he would say."

"We encouraged": Connally interview. **Johnson's "briefing" of the press corps:** Interviews with Corcoran and Rowe, who did most of the briefing. **"Not only primed":** Pickle OH.

Questions on pardons: "Full Text of Les Carpenter's Story Thursday noon Stevenson Press Conference," "Austin–Miscellaneous, 1948," Box 1, PPMF, LBJL. **Abilene statement:** *Abilene Reporter-News*, July 3. **"Unethical":** Timmons, quoted in "night press collect—Beaumont Journal," July 29 (signed "Elizabeth Carpenter"), "Austin–Miscellaneous, 1948," Box 1, PPMF, LBJL. **"Lousy":** McClendon interview.

"Dodged": "Full Text of Les Carpenter's Story" (see above). **"A dozen":** *AA-S*, July 30.

"Why don't you get": Les Carpenter to Johnson, Aug. 2, "Memos: Inter-Office, Prior to 1952, 1948 [2 of 2]," Box 1, PPMF, LBJL. **McNeil drafting:** McNeil OH; Jenkins interview. **"He's got to":** Woods interview. **"If I lost":** Clark interview. **"All on the line":** Brown interview. **Had narrowly escaped indictment:** Caro, *Path to Power*, pp. 742–53. **"In a thousand ways":** Clark interview.

Collecting the cash: This discussion of the financing of the Johnson campaign is based on interviews with Brown, Clark, Connally, Corcoran, Herring, Jenkins, Joseph, Quill, Rowe, Woods, Yarborough, Young. **Reprinting of Liz Carpenter's article:** Busby says that when he saw Liz Carpenter's article, "I said to myself: 'This is our chance!' " **Pearson column:** "Washington Merry-Go-Round," *AA-S*, Aug. 8, 9.

"A damned lie": Bolton interview. **Estes speech:** *AA-S*, Aug. 7; Bolton interview. **A reporter wrote it:** In his OH, Marshall McNeil states: "Stevenson had

issued some kind of a statement. . . . Lyndon wanted to answer it, and he wanted me to write it. Well, I did." **Missionaries:** The description of their use in the Johnson campaign comes from Johnson strategists such as Bolton, Clark, Connally, Herring, Oltorf and Smith and from Stevenson aides such as Boyett, Murphey and Stevenson, Jr.; and from neutral observers such as Shelton and Yarborough. **"I saw him":** Herring interview. **Between fifty and a hundred:** Estimate from Connally. **"He'd just circulate":** Connally interview. **Spread by federal employees:** Analyses of the use of these employees from Boyett, Clark, Oltorf, Smith and Yarborough. **"It was working":** Boyett interview.

Johnson camp knew the truth: Bolton interview. **"Lift either leg":** Johnson, quoted in *AA-S*, *CCC-T*, Aug. 11. **"It would be":** Johnson, quoted in *DMN*, Aug. 3. **"LIKE A BRANDED STEER":** *HP*, Aug. 6. **"You watched":** Bolton interview. **"At the point":** Busby interview. **"All we needed":** Connally interview.

Stevenson's image hurt with businessmen: Busby, Connally interviews; Germany OH. **Schreiner's call:** Boyett interview. He couldn't hear Schreiner's end of the conversation, but Stevenson related it to him as soon as he had hung up, and others knew because Schreiner later spoke to them. **Trying—and failing—to persuade Coke:** Boyett, Murphey, Stevenson, Jr., interviews.

Financing of Stevenson's campaign: Boyett interview. **Letter to Braswell:** *AA-S*, *DMN*, Aug. 12. **"A straw man":** *DMN* editorial, Aug. 14. **"Nothing new":** Stevenson, quoted in *HP*, Aug. 13.

Planting doubts: *HP*, Aug. 13. And see the articles on the letter in *AA-S*, *CCC-T*, *FWS-T*, *HC*. On the day on which a prominent article on Stevenson's letter should have been printed, Aug. 12, the *HP*, for example, ran only two paragraphs on the letter—in a separate story at the end of the day's major campaign story. **"Noncommittal":** Johnson, quoted in *HP*, Aug. 13.

Johnson's use of radio; Stevenson's use of radio: Analyses of radio listings, advertisements, articles in *AA-S*, *HP*, *DMN*, Aug. 13–24; Bolton, Busby, Boyett, Connally interviews. **"With utterly unfounded allegation":** *DMN* editorial, Aug. 26. **"Have to say something over and over":** Connally interview.

Four unions: *AA-S*, Aug. 10; Corcoran, Young interviews. **"No surprise":**

Stevenson, quoted in *DMN*, Aug. 10. **Oliver lining up:** Oliver OH. **Hopkins' activities:** Hopkins has given a number of conflicting statements on his activities in this campaign. In a memo written for his personal papers, he relates one incident that occurred after the *Dallas News* discovered he was in Texas. He says that as he arrived at the little airport in Gonzales that August, he was met by John Connally, who said Wirtz had dictated a statement on Lyndon's behalf for Hopkins to approve. The statement would have had the UMW counsel saying that "I am an old friend of Coke Stevenson and judging by the official record and platforms of the two men, I have no hesitancy in saying that if John L. Lewis and the UMW were taking any interest in Texas politics, they would support Coke Stevenson." Hopkins refused to make the statement, because, he says, "it did not [word unclear] the truth, was an untruth." Hopkins wrote in this memo: "I told him [Connally] further that I had heard Lyndon's radio broadcasts . . . at 12:30 PM, and that Lyndon had made misstatements of fact in reference to Mr. Lewis and the Mine Workers and I was disappointed and ashamed of Lyndon for so doing. Connally apologized for these speeches, saying Lyndon was forced to make them. . . . Connally said the race was very close and urged me to sign the proposed statement and to issue it or to revise it and then issue—All of this I flatly refused to do." In this handwritten memo, Hopkins also said, "I had previously refrained from taking any interest in the campaign." However, in an interview, he said that he "had written a few hundred letters on UMW stationery that had fallen into someone's hands" and that he went back and forth to Texas with the material from and to Rowe and Corcoran (Personal Papers of Welly K. Hopkins). **Funding from Dubinsky, etc.:** Corcoran, Rowe, Jenkins, Young interviews.

Johnson in Peddy territory: *AA-S, DMN, HP, HC,* Aug. 7–8; Boyett, Brown, Clark, Stevenson, Jr., interviews. **"His bid":** *HP,* Aug. 7. **"Have not":** *DMN,* Aug. 7; "Lyndon B. Johnson Speech, Friday, Aug. 6, 1948," Papers of Charles E. Marsh, Box 1, "Lyndon Johnson 1948," LBJL. **"He had to turn it around":** Yarborough interview.
Stevenson's not organizing: His men—Boyett, Murphey, Stevenson, Jr., say

so—and so do Johnson's men: Clark and Connally, for example. **To Canada:** *AA-S,* Aug. 18. **Kinney and Hansford:** *Texas Almanac,* pp. 463, 474; Boyett, Stevenson, Jr., interviews. **"Lyndon Johnson voted":** Johnson, quoted in *DMN,* Aug. 18. **"Birds of a feather":** Johnson, quoted in *DMN,* Aug. 18. **"Does it mean":** Johnson, quoted in *HP,* Aug. 20. **"My first impression":** Connally; *DMN* editorials, Aug. 25, 26. **"COMMUNISTS FAVOR COKE":** *Johnson Journal,* quoted in Dugger, p. 320. See also *DMN,* Aug. 22. An angered Stevenson read the headlines to audiences (*DMN,* Aug. 26).
"Pappy's Speech": Caro, *Path to Power,* pp. 695–703. **Had had speech recorded in 1941:** Corcoran, Rowe, Hopkins interviews. **"The great prize":** Busby interview. **Johnson's decision to give speech:** Busby interview. Although he was the only person present when the decision was made, Bolton was following the developments, and confirms the story. **"Particularly when":** Connally interview.
Stevenson's change of mind: Boyett, Murphey, Stevenson, Jr., interviews. **Meeting at Center:** Murphey interview. **Coke's two speeches:** Stevenson, quoted in *DMN, HP,* Aug. 15; *HP,* Aug. 17; *AA-S, DMN,* Aug. 18.
"It is no secret": *DMN, HP,* Aug. 20. **"Repetition":** Bolton interview. **No funds for repetition:** Boyett, Murphey, Bolton, Brown interviews; author's analysis of newspapers, Aug. 19–28. **"If you have":** One of the places this ad *did* appear is *FWS-T,* Aug. 19. **"So what?":** Connally interview. **Johnson's on the air three times a day:** For example, Pickle to O'Brien, Aug. 16, "District 2 Chairman–Chilton O'Brien," Box 106, JHP. **Transcribed recordings:** For example, *DMN,* Aug. 14. **Mailboxes filled:** A complete picture of the immensity of the Johnson mail campaign, in its various forms, emerges from Boxes 63–127, JHP.
"Strange coincidence": Peddy, quoted in *CCC-T,* July 7. **Same phrases:** *AA-S,* Aug. 19, 20. **"Curiously":** McKay, p. 231. **Stevenson's schedule known:** Boyett, Murphey, Stevenson, Jr., interviews. **"We didn't do":** Connally interview. **Wallace charges:** *AA-S, DMN, HP, HC, CCC-T,* Aug. 19, 20, 21.
"Coke can't do that"; "She'll fly": Bolton, Jenkins interviews. **"I really believe":** Nichols OH. **Fear of flying:** Mrs. Johnson interview with author. **Five gal-**

lons; "You ask them": Steinberg, p. 225; Smith, p. 139. "We need": Johnson, quoted by Busby. **Told Marietta Brooks:** Mrs. Brooks, quoted in *FWS-T*, Aug. 25; see also Montgomery, p. 37. "Overwhelmingly, vastly, horribly": Mrs. Johnson, quoted in Montgomery, p. 37; Smith, p. 139. "Fanning out": Rather, quoted in Smith, p. 138. **Corpus Christi interview:** *CCC-T*, Aug. 3. "Just like me": Mrs. Johnson, quoted in Montgomery, p. 38. "I just pack and unpack": Mrs. Johnson, quoted in *FWS-T*, Aug. 25. "A great asset": Clark interview. "I couldn't possibly": Mrs. Johnson, quoted in *CCC-T*, Aug. 3. **Adjusting the light:** *HP*, Aug. 7. **Car overturning:** *AA-S*, Aug. 29; Smith, p. 140. **Flood of mail:** Smith, p. 140; Clark interview. "Wonderful": Taylor to Johnson, Aug. 28, "District 18 Chairman–Jay Taylor (Abilene)," Box 107, JHP. "Sweet voice": Mrs. W. S. Harris to Johnson, Nov. 4, "10—Hays County," Box 80, JHP. "Hot, muggy": Smith to Johnson, Nov. 4, "Houston–S," Box 79, JHP. "Told her": Montgomery, p. 37; Smith, p. 140. **Telephoning:** Montgomery, p. 38; Rather interview.

13. The Stealing

SOURCES

Books and documents:
    Dugger, *The Politician*; Green, *The Establishment in Texas Politics, 1945–1957*; McKay, *Texas and the Fair Deal, 1945–1952*; *Texas Almanac*, 1949–50.
    Leslie Velie, "Do You Know Your State's Secret Boss," *Reader's Digest*, Feb. 1953.

Oral Histories:
    Malcolm Bardwell.

Interviews:
    Paul Bolton, Ernest J. Boyett, George R. Brown, Walter Buckner, Horace Busby, Edward A. Clark, John B. Connally, Kellis Dibrell, Charles W. Duke, D. B. Hardeman, Charles Herring, Walter Jenkins, Barney Knispel, Henry Kyle, William J. Lawson, Frank B. Lloyd, Ernest Morgan, Frank C. ("Posh") Oltorf, Daniel Quill, Mary Rather, Luis Salas, Emmett Shelton, E. Babe Smith, Coke Stevenson, Jr., Warren G. Woodward, Ralph Yarborough.

NOTES

(All dates 1948 unless otherwise indicated)
    Contrast between Hancock House and Brown Building: Author's analysis of interviews with Bolton, Brown, Busby, Clark, Connally, Jenkins, Woodward, Herring, Rather and Quill. **Polls:** *AA-S*, Aug. 22, 27, 28. The day before the second primary, Hobby's *Houston Post* ran a story—conceived by Charles Marsh—in which his own newspapers and other aggressively pro-Johnson papers "reported a shift in sentiment toward" Johnson. But this "newspaper survey" was not taken seriously by informed Texas political opinion (*HP*, Aug. 27). "We needed blocs"; trips to the Valley: Clark interview. **Secret Boss:** Velie, "Do You Know Your State's Secret Boss." **Using Brown & Root plane:** Brown, Clark interviews. "Knew how": Yarborough interview. "Our people": Salas, "Box 13," p. 55. **Quill's importance to Johnson:** Caro, *Path to Power*, pp. 282, 441, 719–20. "Need some money": Quill to Johnson, Monday p.m., "San Antonio–PQ," Box 67, JHP. "The man with the muscle": Connally interview. **Johnson wanted the Kilday organization:** Johnson to Quill, July 28, "San Antonio–PQ," Box 67, JHP; Bardwell OH; Connally, Hardeman, Duke, Quill interviews. See also Johnson to Owen Kilday, June 29, July 23; Johnson to Paul Kilday, Dec. 2, "San Antonio–IJK," Box 66, JHP. Johnson's reply assures Quill, "We will find some financial help someway," but is notable mostly because of the inspirational tone he adopts to the tough, Tammany-type postmaster who idolized him. "We slept through the last one, but we can easily win this one," Johnson wrote. "Won't you take hold for me as you know I would take hold for you if you had a crisis on your hands." Quill replied: "In a crisis you will not find me wanting." (Quill to Johnson, July 31, all in "San Antonio–PQ," Box 67, JHP.) See also *HP*, Aug. 28; Dugger, p. 3.
    "Of course, there was Valmo Bellinger": Connally interview; Johnson to Quill, July 28; Quill to Johnson, July 31 and undated, "San Antonio–PQ," Box 66, JHP.
    Final week: *AA-S, CCC-T, DMN, DT-H, FWS-T, San Antonio Express-News, San Antonio Light, HP, HC*, Aug.

24–28; McKay, pp. 233–40; *Valley Evening Monitor.*
A thousand dollars: Knight, quoted in Dugger, p. 321. **San Antonio, Johnson on Election Day:** Bardwell OH; Connally interview; *SAE, AA-S, DMN,* Aug. 29. **"This time had no trouble"; scene at Precinct 13:** Salas, "Box 13," p. 56; Lloyd, Rowe, Salas interviews. **Holmgreen felt:** Holmgreen, quoted in the *San Antonio Express-News* on July 31, 1977, said: "I saw more votes stolen for Lyndon Johnson than Johnson won the election by." **Young men were sure:** *HP,* Aug. 29.
Stevenson didn't know: The scene on the banks of the Llano at the Stevenson Ranch was described to the author by Boyett, Dibrell and Stevenson, Jr. It is also described in *DMN,* Aug. 28; *HP,* Aug. 28, 29. **10,000 votes from West Side:** Quill interview; Bardwell OH.
Election returns: All the following returns were reported in various editions of the *AA-S, CCC-T, DMN, HP,* Aug. 29–Sept. 5. They were not official returns—there would be no official returns until the Democratic State Executive Committee certified the returns on September 14—but were the returns announced by the Texas Election Bureau. The Bureau was an unofficial, cooperative organization whose expenses were paid by participating newspapers. Its returns had previously been accepted as official because during the thirty-two years of its existence, the Bureau had always been correct in predicting election results. *AA-S,* Aug. 30.
Wild confusion: The atmosphere of vote counting in Texas during the 1940s is derived from the author's interviews with Texas politicians active at that time, including Smith, Bolton, Clark, Boyett, Quill, Hardeman, Oltorf, Lawson, Jenkins and Shelton. Also *DMN,* Aug. 30, Sept. 1, 7. **"In counting":** *State Observer,* Sept. 13. **Perhaps the only instance:** Caro, *Path to Power,* pp. 733–35. **"Duval always votes":** *DMN,* Aug. 31. On August 30, Duckworth wrote: "The county [Duval] usually reports its vote complete before time for poll closing (*DMN,* Aug. 30).
10,000 Johnson votes in San Antonio: Malcolm Bardwell, a longtime aide to former San Antonio Mayor Maury Maverick and, in the 1948 election, the man who "handled the arrangement of the money and so forth for the organization," said in his oral history interview,

"People have always likened Lyndon to winning by—it was 83 votes and claimed it [was] Duval County. The truth of the matter, the 83 votes were won in Bexar County. Bexar County went about 10,000 votes in the [first] primary against Lyndon Johnson, and in the run-off, we changed it over and it was about 83 votes or 100 votes, something like that, for Lyndon Johnson. So really Bexar County is the guilty one and not Duval County. . . . Bexar County votes were the ones that were changed over." At a later point in the interview, he said, "Over 10,000 votes had changed here. They never questioned Bexar County." (When asked, "You don't have any idea where those 10,000 votes came from?," Bardwell replied, "People just changed their minds.") Bardwell's "10,000" figure is an approximation, of course, but that figure is also used, in interviews with the author, by other figures—from both the Johnson and the Stevenson camp—familiar with the 1948 voting in San Antonio. Postmaster Dan Quill, who in the same interview explained how Mexican votes were bought in San Antonio, and how "they'd just stuff the ballots in there—as many as you wanted," says of the August primary, "We got him 10,000 votes." Quill says the Mexican-American vote amounted to "half the vote" in San Antonio. Stevenson aide Ernest Boyett says that "everyone knew Johnson bought 10,000 votes in the Mexican areas. His people boasted about it for years." Because of the manner in which votes were falsified in San Antonio—the locking of doors and simply pulling levers after the polls were locked for the night, for example—and because, in contrast to some other counties, no testimony was ever taken under oath from any San Antonio election official—it has been impossible, forty years after the election, to determine the number of votes illegally cast for Lyndon Johnson in San Antonio, or to determine if the 10,000 figure is correct. But that figure does not appear to be greatly exaggerated. The votes cast for Stevenson may be assumed—both because of his popularity among Mexican-Americans and because no one from either camp contends that any substantial number of votes for him were cast illegally in either Mexican-American or black precincts—to have been valid votes. (He may, in fact, have received more votes in the second primary than were reported for him; there were reports, unconfirmed [perhaps because no investigation was ever made in San Antonio] of misreported figures.) In the July primary, in the twenty-five San Antonio precincts in which Mexican-Americans comprised 50 percent or more of the population, Stevenson, so popular among Mexican-Americans, had received 4,593 votes to 2,580 votes for Johnson—and, according to San Antonio observers, a substantial portion of even those Johnson votes were, in one way or another, illegal votes. In the August primary, Stevenson received 3,062 votes in those precincts, Johnson 4,396 votes. This represented a net gain for Johnson of 3,347. In fifteen precincts with a population between 30 and 50 percent Mexican, Stevenson's total fell from 4,281 in July to 2,853 in August—a net Johnson gain of 2,266. In eleven precincts in which blacks combined with Mexicans made up 50 percent or more of the population, Stevenson led in July, 2,815 to 1,678, and Johnson led in August, 2,345 to 1,678—a net gain for Johnson of 1,802. In those fifty-one heavily Mexican-American or black precincts, therefore, Johnson's total vote in August—9,594 votes—represented a net gain of 7,395 votes over Stevenson. But San Antonio's twenty-three other precincts also included some with substantial pockets of Mexican-Americans, of course, and dramatic shifts to Johnson, amounting to well over 1,000 votes, occurred in some of them, too. (Author's analysis of "1948 Bexar County Democratic Primary, Precinct-by-Precinct Official Returns" and "1948 Bexar County Democratic Primary Run-Off Precinct-by-Precinct Returns," *Record of Democratic Primary Elections, 1944–1952,* Bexar County Administrator, San Antonio, Tx.) (Bexar County precincts 1–70 and 118–121 were in San Antonio.)

Johnson's night: Jenkins, Rather interviews; *DMN,* Aug. 30. **Brown Building telephone calls:** Clark interview. **Call to Huntress:** Huntress, quoted in *SAE,* June 29, 1975. Also *San Antonio Express-News,* Aug. 7, 1977. **Call to San Marcos:** Buckner, Knispel, Kyle interviews. Kyle, from whom Johnson stole a college election while they were classmates at San Marcos, says that when he heard about the 1948 call, "I thought: it's college all over again."

Calls to Parr: Dugger, pp. 326–27, includes a quote from Homer Dean, a Parr lieutenant who was Johnson's campaign manager in Jim Wells County, that "Loo-

ney and Ed Lloyd [Parr's chief lieutenant and Dean's boss] were in constant communication after the runoffs"; Salas interview; confidential source. **"It was Lyndon Johnson's office":** "Confidential source," quoted in Dugger, p. 326. **Duval County announced:** *DMN,* Aug. 30.

"That was how": Boyett interview. **Stevenson understood:** Boyett, Stevenson, Jr., interviews; *DMN,* Aug. 29, 30; *HP,* Aug. 29; *AA-S,* Aug. 30. **"The thing that brought protest":** *DMN,* Aug. 31. **"All of those":** Green, p. 115. **Jumping into his car:** *DMN,* Aug. 30. **"The news came":** *DMN,* Aug. 30. **"In the closest":** *FWS-T,* Aug. 30. **4,662 out of 4,679:** *DMN* editorial, Sept. 1; *Texas Almanac,* pp. 458, 474. **"The most exciting":** *DMN,* Aug. 31. **Election Bureau announced "complete" returns:** *HC,* Sept. 1; *FWS-T,* Sept. 2. **"Little doubt":** Bob Johnson, quoted in *HP,* Aug. 30. **"Consistently accurate":** *HC,* Sept. 1. **"Should Johnson lose":** *DMN,* Sept. 1. **"STEVENSON LEADS":** *CCC-T, DMN,* Sept. 1. **"STEVENSON'S MARGIN FIRM":** *DMN,* Sept. 2.

351: At 7 p.m., an altered return, apparently due to election night confusion, arrived from Yoakum County in West Texas which showed Stevenson losing 126 votes, and his lead was cut to 255 votes, but a telephone call from Chambers County had already informed the Election Bureau that when the county's official returns arrived the next day, they would show Johnson losing 96 votes, restoring Stevenson's lead to 351. **"STEVENSON HOLDS":** *Brownsville Herald,* Sept. 2. **"Good Senator":** *DMN* editorial, Sept. 2. **Stevenson's statement:** *DMN, HP,* Sept. 2, 3. **Election seemed over:** *FWS-T, DMN,* Sept. 2. **Precinct 13 change:** See following chapters. **Final tabulation:** *Texas Almanac, 1949–1950,* p. 474.

14. Lists of Names

SOURCES

Books, articles and documents:
  Banks, *Money, Marbles, and Chalk;* Calvert, *Here Comes the Judge;* Dugger, *The Politician;* Jenkins and Frost, *"I'm Frank Hamer";* Kahl, *Ballot Box 13;* Lynch, *Duke of Duval;* Matthews, *San Antonio Lawyer;* McKay and Faulk,

Texas After Spindletop; Miller, *Lyndon*; *Texas Almanac*, 1949–50; Steinberg, *Sam Johnson's Boy*; Webb, *The Texas Rangers*.
    James M. Rowe, "The Mesquite Pendergast: George B. Parr—Second Duke of Duval" (unpublished manuscript), Ingleside, Tex., 1959–60; Edgar G. Shelton, "Political Conditions Among Texas Mexicans Along the Rio Grande" (master's thesis), Austin, Tex., 1946.
    Clyde Wantland, "The Story of George Parr's Ballot Box 13," *Texas Argus*, Apr., 1962 and Spring, 1964.
    Stevenson v. Tyson, Johnson et al., Civil No. 1640, United States District Court, Northern District, Texas, Fort Worth, Sept. 21–22, 1948 (Davidson, District Judge). Referred to hereafter as "DC Hearing transcript."

Oral Histories:
    Robert Calvert, Josh H. Groce, Callan Graham, Vann M. Kennedy, J. J. Pickle.

Interviews:
    Paul Bolton, Ernest J. Boyett, George R. Brown, Horace Busby, Robert Calvert, Edward A. Clark, John B. Connally, Kellis Dibrell, O. C. Fisher, D. B. Hardeman, Walter Jenkins, Sam Houston Johnson, Herman Jones, Luther E. Jones, Vann M. Kennedy, Joe M. Kilgore, William J. Lawson, Frank B. Lloyd, Wingate Lucas, George Mahon, Gerald C. Mann, Ernest Morgan, Robert W. Murphey, Frank C. ("Posh") Oltorf, Daniel Quill, James M. Rowe, Luis Salas, Emmett Shelton, E. Babe Smith, Arthur Stehling, Coke Stevenson, Jr., Gerald L. Weatherly, Ralph Yarborough, Harold Young.

NOTES

(All dates 1948 unless otherwise indicated)
    "A concentrated effort"; "The corrected votes": Stevenson, Johnson quoted in *AA-S*, Sept. 4. **DMN comment:** Editorial, Sept. 8. **Johnson's broadcast:** *AA-S*, *DMN*, Sept. 7.
    Restated by Rather, Jenkins, Herring: *NYT*, Aug. 2, 1977.
    Late returns in Johnson's 1941 election: Caro, *Path to Power*, pp. 736–40. **No countywide totals anywhere:** *Texas Almanac*, p. 474.
    "The first instance": Stevenson, press release, Nov. 12; In a statement on Sept. 11 (*DMN*, Sept. 12), Stevenson stated:

"Much has been said by my opponent . . . about certain of those bloc voting counties having cast their votes for me in former elections. . . . This is the first time, however, that the returns have been amended several days after the polls had closed, to the point of trying to control the election of a state official."
    More than a score: Among them, Hardeman, Young, Mahon, Yarborough, L. E. Jones, Herman Jones, Lloyd, Smith, Lawson, Kilgore, Lucas, Fisher, Mann, Stehling, Morgan, Shelton, Rowe, Stevenson, Jr., Kennedy, Johnson, Quill, Weatherly interviews. **"Never":** Connally interview. **"I never did know":** Clark interview. Typical of the opinion of informed observers is that of Gerald Weatherly. Weatherly, a Fort Worth attorney, was considered so expert on election contests in Texas that for twenty years he represented both George Parr and various members of the Guerra family in court battles over elections. "From my knowledge of these contests, and in all the counties from Laredo to Corpus Christi, I would say that Johnson was not correct in saying this was par for the course. It was not usual." The difference, he says, was in the "grossness" of the 1948 results in Box 13, "the two hundred names in different ink," for example. A well-informed outside observer of Valley politics, reporter James M. Rowe of the *Corpus Christi Caller-Times*, who covered the Valley for more than twenty years, wrote in his manuscript, "The Mesquite Pendergast" (p. 40), that "it was customary for the count in Duval County to be complete in almost any election, no matter how many candidates were listed on the ballot, within two or three hours after the polls closed." **"The possible dangers":** Shelton, "Political Conditions," pp. 125–26. **"Lyndon, I've been":** Caro, *Path to Power*, p. 739.
    Stevenson's feelings: Boyett, Murphey, Stevenson, Jr., interviews; Graham OH.
    "Made us spread-eagle": Tijerina, quoted in *San Antonio Express-News*, Aug. 7, 1977.
    Graham's youth in Junction; idolizing Stevenson: Graham OH. **Stevenson's faith in FBI; "no badge or gun":** Dibrell, quoted in Miller, p. 127. **"A little uptight":** Graham OH; Graham, quoted in Miller, p. 127.
    "Very clearly stated in the law"; "we cited": Graham OH. **"About 200 tallies from the end":** Brownlee, DC Hearing transcript, p. 15. **Adams had "snuck in":**

Graham OH. **He had noticed:** Adams, DC Hearing transcript, Sept. 21, p. 10. Also see Adams quoted in Dugger, p. 331. **"Intimidated":** Graham OH. **"Well, I'll just go":** Stevenson, quoted in Dugger, p. 330; Boyett, Stevenson, Jr., interviews. **Hamer biography:** Jenkins and Frost, *I'm Frank Hamer*, p. 42; Kahl, *Ballot Box 13*, pp. 118–28; Webb, *The Texas Rangers*, pp. 519–46. **"Stern and unremitting":** Kahl, p. 119. **"Yes, sir!":** Jenkins and Frost, p. 42; Webb, p. 527. **"Calmly observed":** The description of this incident is from Kahl, p. 119. **"Most fearless":** Webb, quoted in Jenkins and Frost, p. 281. **"It's embarrassing":** Jenkins and Frost, p. 79. **"Hate to bust a cap":** Rowe, "Mesquite Pendergast," p. 29. **Dock strike:** Jenkins and Frost, p. 262; Kahl, p. 120.

Scene in Alice: Described in Jenkins and Frost, p. 277; article in *San Antonio Express-News*, Aug. 7, 1977, based on interviews with, among others, Dibrell and Gardner; and in detail by Clyde Wantland, a writer close to Stevenson and his aides, in *Texas Argus*, Spring, 1964. Also see Dugger, pp. 330, 457, and Rowe, "Mesquite Pendergast," pp. 29, 30. Dibrell, quoted in Miller, p. 128; Dibrell, Lloyd, Rowe, Salas, Stevenson, Jr., interviews. Some of these descriptions differ from each other in some details. **"He appeared to be":** Dibrell, quoted in Miller, p. 128. **"I was being deprived":** Stevenson, quoted in Kahl, p. 131. **"Like a glacier":** Rowe interview. **Scene at bank:** Brownlee, DC Hearing transcript, pp. 14–16; Gardner, DC Hearing transcript, pp. 41–45; Dibrell, quoted in Rowe, "Mesquite Pendergast," pp. 29–30; Dibrell, Rowe interviews. **Same ink; same handwriting; alphabetical order:** Adams, DC Hearing transcript, p. 10; Brownlee, DC Hearing transcript, pp. 15–16; Gardner, DC Hearing transcript, pp. 32–33; Groce, DC Hearing transcript, p. 45; Dibrell, Rowe, Salas interviews; Graham OH; Dibrell, quoted in Rowe, "Mesquite Pendergast," pp. 29–31. In a speech later on, Groce, Stevenson's attorney, said: "According to the sworn testimony of witnesses, the names of the first 841 voters on the list were written in black ink, but the remainder were written in blue ink. . . ." He also said, "Most of the names on the poll list . . . run in alphabetical order after voter 841." Dibrell told Rowe he, too, had seen the poll list

at the bank, and had seen that "the last 200 names" were in alphabetical order. "Also, the last 200 names were made with the same colored ink and in the same handwriting, whereas the earlier names in the poll list which had been kept on election day were written by different individuals and in different colored ink." **Changing the 7 to a 9:** Gardner, DC Hearing transcript, pp. 42, 43, 44. **"People live longer":** Dibrell, quoted in *San Antonio Express-News*. Soliz affidavit: DC Hearing transcript, p. 34. **Cerda not in Jim Wells County:** Cerda, DC Hearing transcript, pp. 27–30. **Three "voters" dead:** Lynch, p. 57; Kahl, p. 174. An article in the *San Antonio Express-News*, Aug. 7, 1977, based on interviews with, among others, Dibrell and Gardner, states that the two attorneys "also discovered the names of three people on the list who had been permanent residents in a city cemetery for many years." Dibrell, in an interview, confirms that three "dead" voters were found on the list at the time of that first, hurried inspection.

"A small army"; Stevenson's affidavit: *CCC-T*, Sept. 11. **Meeting of the Jim Wells Democratic Executive Committee; "I am confident":** *DMN*, Sept. 12. **Committee's resolution:** Copy signed by H. L. Poole and Adams, Sept. 9, to Vann M. Kennedy; *HC*, Sept. 9; *CCC*, Sept. 11. **It is "expected":** *AA-S*, Sept. 11.

"With proof": Stevenson, quoted in *CCC-T*, Sept. 13. **"SENATE RACE":** *HP*, Sept. 10. **"SPOTLIGHT TURNS":** *CCC-T*, Sept. 14. **"Voting Precinct 13":** *CCC-T*, Sept. 11. **"All of a sudden":** Rowe interview. **"The Duke Delivers":** *Time*, Sept. 27. **"200 VOTES GIVEN":** *HC*, Sept. 9. **Democratic Convention; Influence of national politics:** Stuart Long, quoted in Miller, p. 130. Dugger, pp. 332–33; Banks, pp. 92–93; Calvert, pp. 120–29; Kahl, pp. 137–56; Miller, pp. 129–30; *AA-S, FWS-T, DMN, DT-H, HP, HC*, Sept. 12–16; *State Observer*, Sept.–Oct.; Clark, Connally, Boyett, Kennedy, Jenkins, Oltorf, Brown interviews; Groce, Calvert, Kennedy, Pickle OHs.

"Johnson was interested": Eckhardt, quoted in Dugger, p. 333. **"Connived":** Eckhardt, quoted in Robert Sherrill, "Texan vs. Big Oil," *NYT Magazine*, Oct. 12, 1980.

"Strangely silent": Johnson, quoted in *DMN*, Sept. 7. **Dallas changes:** *DMN*, Aug. 29–Sept. 5, Sept. 14; Kahl, p. 108. **"Corrected that error":** *DMN*, Sept. 5.

And see Dugger, p. 459. **Voting patterns in three big cities:** *DMN, FWS-T, HP, HC*, Aug. 29–30; *State Observer*, Sept. 13. **River Oaks Box:** *State Observer*, Sept. 13. **Brown County contest:** *DMN*, Sept. 2; Kahl, p. 108. **Kenedy County vote; No comparison:** *Texas Almanac*, p. 474. **"Home turf"; "Loyal supporter":** Lynch, p. 63. **Johnson's affidavit:** *AA-S, DMN, CCC-T*, Sept. 12. **Archer's order:** Telegram, Helen Sellers, Clerk of the District Court of Travis County, to M. L. Adams, undated, in author's possession. **"Amazed and angered":** Kahl, pp. 130–31. **An "obvious attempt":** Stevenson, quoted in *DMN*, Sept. 12. And see Small, quoted in *CCC-T*, Sept. 15. **"Even if it was stolen":** Adams, quoted in Dugger, p. 331. **"Of course":** Poole, quoted in *DMN*, Sept. 12. Poole also said that he was convinced the returns from Box 13 were fraudulent. Poole expressed his outrage at Archer's order, however, likening political conditions in the Valley to those in Russia, asking "help from the citizens of Texas who live outside the Iron Curtain to give us back our franchise." He said, "I am confident there are more than 200 people shown as voting who did not vote. I helped gather the evidence and obtain affidavits from more than 200 such people." Other members of the committee felt that if they were prevented from investigating the results themselves, they should ask the United States Senate to do so (*CCC-T, HP*, Sept. 13). **Not until Monday morning:** Broeter, quoted in *DMN*, Sept. 12. **"By custom":** *DMN*, Sept. 14. **Poll of executive committee; "We were behind":** Clark, Connally interviews. **Confident front:** *FWS-T, State Observer*, Sept. 13. **"Comfortable majority":** *State Observer*, Sept. 13. **"Just one vote":** Clark interview. **"Wild":** Brown interview. **"Frantic, but orderly":** Connally interview. **Clark and Ramsey; "Herman Brown":** Oltorf interview. **Sending plane for three members:** Groce OH. **"The longest night":** Clark interview.

Sneed's proxy: *FWS-T, HC*, Sept. 13; *DMN*, Sept. 14. **Johnson and Stevenson in ballroom:** *FWS-T*, Sept. 13. **"Canvassing subcommittee":** For descriptions of the meetings and votes of the canvassing subcommittee, the full executive committee and the full convention, see note above, "Democratic Convention." **Hearing in Alice:** Matthews, pp. 101–8; Rowe, Jones, Weatherly interviews.

CCC-T, Brownsville Herald, Sept. 14. **Tarleton stalling:** Matthews, p. 106. Weatherly says, "You could tell Dudley was just stalling for time, and was waiting for something." **"Of which courts":** *Texas Jurisprudence*, quoted in Matthews, p. 105. **"No parallel":** Matthews, quoted in Kahl, p. 138; *FWS-T*, Sept. 13. **Parr's arrival in court:** *CCC-T*, Sept. 14; Matthews, p. 104; Rowe interview. **"Stopped short":** *CCC-T*, Sept. 14. **"Too late":** Matthews, quoted in *HP*, Sept. 14. **"I am not saying"; wouldn't interfere:** Broeter, quoted in *CCC-T*, Sept. 14. **"In the face of the power":** Matthews, p. 106.

Canvassing subcommittee; Executive committee meetings: See note above, "Democratic Convention." **"Question of the correct":** Albert Sidney Johnston, quoted in *DMN*, Sept. 14. **"Would be violating":** Francis, quoted in *DMN*, Sept. 14. **"A tie":** Clark interview. **"The whole atmosphere":** Calvert. **"The issue":** Small, quoted in *DMN, HP*, Sept. 14. **Cofer, Francis arguments:** *FWS-T*, Sept. 14.

"I believed"; "Announce the results now": Mrs. Darbrandt; Johnson, quoted in *FWS-T*, Sept. 14. **Finding Gibson:** Connally interview. And see *FWS-T, HP*, Sept. 14. **Deal consummated:** *AA-S*, Sept. 12–13; *CCC-T, FWS-T*, Sept. 14, 15; *State Observer*, Sept. 20; Long, quoted in Miller, p. 130; Dugger, pp. 332–33. **"AS TARRANT GOES":** *HP*, Sept. 15. **"Helped us":** Eckhardt, quoted in Sherrill, "Texan vs. Big Oil," *NYT Magazine*, Oct. 12, 1980. **"A merry"; "It's stacked":** Small, quoted in *AA-S*, Sept. 15. **"Under the table":** *DMN*, Sept. 15; Kahl, p. 154. **"This is the moment":** The description of Johnson's moment of triumph is from *AA-S, DMN, FWS-T, HP*, Sept. 15. **"To look on":** Johnson aides, quoted in *FWS-T*, Sept. 16. **"A field day":** *HP*, Sept. 15.

15. Qualities of Leadership

SOURCES

There are some 1,040 pages of court testimony, and I read them first. I supplemented this by interviews. Not many of the lawyers for the two sides are alive, but I talked to those who were—Gerald Weatherly, Thomas G. Corcoran, Luther E. Jones, Frank B. Lloyd, James H.

Rowe, Jr., Abe Fortas. I also spoke to the law partners of two of the lawyers most intimately involved. Edward A. Clark, partner of Everett Looney, was a key strategist in the Johnson campaign; although he did not appear in court, he participated in the meetings, some of them in his home, on the court strategy. Emmett Shelton was not only the partner but the brother of Polk Shelton, Judge Raymond's lawyer, and was himself intimately familiar with the cases. Clark and Shelton were also helpful to me in understanding the legal strategies involved. I also interviewed the only two Johnson aides to sit in—as notetakers—on these sessions: Mary Rather and Walter Jenkins. I interviewed the single most important witness in the case, Luis Salas, and also relied on his manuscript, "Box 13."

Although most of the oral histories taken by the Johnson Library from persons involved are self-serving, the oral history of William Robert Smith, the court-appointed Master in Chancery who presided over the hearing in Alice, Texas, is extremely valuable, because it provides his opinion of the case—an opinion he never wrote.

Among other sources were articles in the various newspapers that covered the hearings, not only the *AA-S*, *DMN*, *HP* and *HC*, but the *CCC-T*, the *Brownsville Herald* and the *Valley Evening Monitor*.

Books, articles and documents:
Dugger, *The Politician*; Evans and Novak, *Lyndon B. Johnson: The Exercise of Power*; Kahl, *Ballot Box 13*; Lynch, *The Duke of Duval*; Matthews, *San Antonio Lawyer*; Miller, *Lyndon*; Murphey, *Fortas*; Sherrill, *A Question of Judgment*; Steinberg, *Sam Johnson's Boy*.

Ronnie Dugger, "Two Cheers for the FBI—Up and at 'Em on Box 13," *Texas Observer*, Sept. 23, 1977. Abe Fortas, "The President, the Congress, and the Public: The Lyndon B. Johnson Presidency," in Kenneth Thompson, ed., *The Virginia Papers on the Presidency*, Vol. X, Lanham, Md., 1982; Marshall McNeil, "How Fortas Gave LBJ His Senatorial Start," *Washington Daily News*, Aug. 3, 1965.

James M. Rowe, "The Mesquite Pendergast: George B. Parr—Second Duke of Duval" (unpublished manuscript), Ingleside, Tex., 1959–60.

Papers of Luther E. Jones.
Papers of Hugo Black.

Oral Histories:
Abe Fortas, Callan Graham, Josh H. Groce, Luther E. Jones, Stanley Marcus, Paul A. Porter, James H. Rowe, Jr., William Robert Smith.

Interviews:
Ernest Boyett, Kellis Dibrell, Lewis T. ("Tex") Easley, Abe Fortas, Walter Jenkins, L. E. Jones, Robert W. Murphey, Mary Rather, James M. Rowe, Luis Salas, Coke Stevenson, Jr., Gerald L. Weatherly.

NOTES

(All dates 1948 unless otherwise indicated)

Stevenson's feelings: Boyett, Murphey, Stevenson, Jr., interviews; Graham OH. **"That whole week":** Graham OH. **Attorneys told him:** Boyett, Weatherly interviews; Stevenson, quoted in Dugger, p. 334; Kahl, p. 156. **"Just couldn't":** Murphey interview. **"Fight right on":** Bolton interview. **Decision to ask for injunction:** Graham, Groce OHs; Boyett interview. **Picking a judge:** Groce OH.

Renfro's trip: *CCC-T*, *DMN*, Sept. 16; Groce OH.

Judge Davidson's hearing: The basis for my description of this hearing is the transcript of it: Stevenson v. Tyson, Johnson et al., Civil No. 1640, United States District Court, Northern District, Texas, Fort Worth, Sept. 21–22, 1948 (Davidson, District Judge). This will be referred to hereafter as "DC Hearing transcript." (Tom Tyson was chairman of the State Democratic Convention; Stevenson's attorneys had named him and other Democratic officials as co-defendants, to prevent them from certifying Johnson as the party's nominee.) Also *AA-S*, *Brownsville Herald*, *CCC-T*, *DMN*, *FWS-T*, *HP*, *HC*, Sept. 21–24; Jones, Weatherly interviews. **"Now, gentlemen":** Davidson, DC Hearing transcript, Sept. 21, p. 3. **Fraud in Zapata and Duval as well:** Moody, DC Hearing transcript, Sept. 21, pp. 5, 10, 11. **"Stuffed":** Moody, DC Hearing transcript, Sept. 21, p. 4. **Crooker's arguments:** DC Hearing transcript, Sept. 21, pp. 17–38. **"Fatally defective":** Crooker, DC Hearing transcript, Sept. 21, p. 32. **"All of the irregularities":** Crooker, DC Hearing transcript, Sept. 21, pp. 32, 33.

But not in this court: Crooker, DC Hearing transcript, Sept. 21, pp. 25, 26. "They now seek": Crooker, DC Hearing transcript, Sept. 21, p. 26. "Solely": Crooker, DC Hearing transcript, Sept. 21, p. 17. "No jurisdiction": Crooker, DC Hearing transcript, Sept. 21, pp. 18, 27. "Under cover": Moody, DC Hearing transcript, Sept. 21, p. 13. "The Constitution provides": Moody, DC Hearing transcript, pp. 13, 14. For a slightly different version of Moody's statement, see *AA-S* and *CCC-T*, Sept. 22. "The court wants to say": Davidson, DC Hearing transcript, Sept. 21, p. 40. "Public sentiment": Davidson, quoted in *AA-S*, *CCC-T*, Sept. 22. "Sure I'm for it": Stevenson, quoted in *CCC-T*, Sept. 22. "No comment": Johnson, quoted in *HC*, Sept. 21; *AA-S*, Sept. 22. Johnson's conference with his attorneys: Jones interview. "I received": Johnson statement, quoted in *CCC-T*, Sept. 22. "Fight to the political death": Steinberg, p. 267. "They would rather": Cofer, quoted in *HC*, Sept. 22; *DMN*, Sept. 23. "It was the defendant Johnson": Moody, quoted in Kahl, p. 171. Concealment of poll list: Adams, DC Hearing transcript, Sept. 22, pp. 6-8; Brownlee, DC Hearing transcript, Sept. 22, pp. 14-15. "Mr. Adams, did you notice": Groce, DC Hearing transcript, Sept. 22, p. 10. "I call to Your Honor's attention": Groce, DC Hearing transcript, Sept. 22, p. 45. 7 changed to a 9: Gardner, DC Hearing transcript, Sept. 22, p. 44. Cerda testimony: DC Hearing transcript, Sept. 22, pp. 27-30. Salinas testimony: DC Hearing transcript, Sept. 22, p. 26. Martinez testimony: DC Hearing transcript, Sept. 22, pp. 23-25. Herrera affidavit: DC Hearing transcript, Sept. 22, pp. 39-40. Soliz affidavit: DC Hearing transcript, Sept. 22, pp. 33-37. Gardner's testimony about Soliz affidavit: DC Hearing transcript, Sept. 22, pp. 38-39. "Luis Salas brought the returns in": Price, DC Hearing transcript, Sept. 22, pp. 30-31. For more detail, see Price testimony in Master's Hearing, Alice, transcript, pp. 212, 228-49. Witnesses from Zapata: Natividad Porras, Luvovico E. Vela, and there was also testimony from Truman Phelps, who had begun an investigation of the Zapata returns at Stevenson's request. Their testimony is in DC Hearing transcript, Sept.

22, pp. 45-57. Fraud "upon their face": Moody, DC Hearing transcript, Sept. 21, p. 5. "Sufficient illegal votes"; "loaded": Moody, DC Hearing transcript, Sept. 22, p. 62. "Even glummer than": Steinberg, p. 268. Encounter in the corridor: Dugger, p. 334. If the "allegations be true": "Court's Pronouncement on Motion to Dismiss," DC Hearing transcript, Sept. 22, pp. 2-6. "Text of Judge Davidson's Opinion Denying Johnson's Dismissal Plea," *FWS-T*, Sept. 23; Steinberg, p. 268. Davidson's ruling also throws some light on Johnson's later contention, made over many years, that Davidson was biased against him. While preparing to make his ruling, the judge commented (p. 2), after noting that Johnson attorney John Cofer was a longtime friend, "along the same lines, of close ties and friendships, the respondent's [Johnson's] father-in-law in this case was one of the first clients to enter my office when I opened my door and for 20 years he remained a continuous client. So if this case is to be decided on friendship, we don't think the complainant would have very much standing in court, but . . . real justice is blind, she neither sees her enemies or hears her friends." Not "one word of evidence": Davidson, quoted in Banks, p. 93. "It was the right and privilege": Davidson, DC Hearing transcript, Sept. 22, pp. 72-73. "Throws such a cloud": Davidson, DC Hearing transcript, Sept. 22, p. 73. "A sound principle": *CCC-T*, Sept. 23. "Whenever I steal": Davidson, DC Hearing transcript, Sept. 22, pp. 72-74. Davidson, quoted in *CCC-T*, Sept. 24. Appointing Masters in Chancery: Stevenson v. Tyson, Johnson et al., Civil No. 1640, United States District Court, Northern District, Texas, Fort Worth, Exhibit A, Sept. 25. "A preparation for trial": Davidson, quoted in *CCC-T*, Sept. 24. "Unwilling"; "Be glad": *CCC*, Sept. 24. See also *DMN*, Sept. 23, 24. "Not in a position": *CCC*, *DMN*, Sept. 24. "Will proceed": Davidson, DC Hearing transcript, Sept. 22, p. 77. "Unique": *AA-S*, Sept. 19. Analysis of Johnson's situation: Boyett, Jones, Weatherly interviews; *AA-S*, Sept. 19, 20; *DMN*, Sept. 20; *HP*, Sept. 19, 20. "We thought": Boyett interview. "The greatest": *AA-S*, Sept. 20. "In the midst": *AA-S*, Sept. 19. "No parallel": Kahl, p. 161. Crisis facing Johnson:

Innumerable analyses of the situation and accounts of the conference of the roomful of attorneys exist, but almost all are based on interviews with lower-level Johnson aides not privy to the actual events, or on other secondhand sources. The account in this book relies on the oral histories of, and my interviews with, the only two attorneys present at the conference still alive when I began my research: Abe Fortas and Luther ("L. E.") Jones. Their accounts concur on all major points. Mary Rather, present at part of the conference, added some details. Fortas' pre-1948 relationship with Johnson is described in Caro, *Path to Power*, pp. 453–65. For a description of Jones' relationship with Johnson, see Caro, pp. 207–11, 227–40. He was known as the "finest appellate lawyer" in Texas, "the man with probably the finest technical legal knowledge in the state." See also Miller, pp. 132–33; Murphey, pp. 90–93; Steinberg, p. 271. Fortas briefly discussed the conference in "The President, the Congress, and the Public," p. 13. Also Porter, Rowe OHs.

"**Grounds for 'black marking' **": *FWS-T*, Sept. 16. "**Rules were perhaps**"; "**Allred wrote one**"; "**Where's Abe?**": Jones interview. "**Do you know?**": Marcus, quoted in Miller, p. 132. Fortas was to say that he received a call from Wirtz, but all other accounts agree Johnson called himself. "**Acres of lawyers**": Fortas OH. "**I said**": Fortas interview. **Immense gamble**: Jones interview. **Unrealistic**: Jones interview. "**Confident**": Fortas interview. "**This was**": Fortas OH. **Fortas' reasoning**: Fortas, Jones interviews. "**Problem was**": Fortas OH. "**Courage**"; "**Everyone was delighted**": Fortas interview. "**Let's do what Abe says**": Fortas, Jones interviews.

"**A thing of beauty**": Jones interview. **Corcoran group analysis**: Biddle, Arnold and Rowe to Wirtz, Sept. 18, 1948, Jones Papers. The crucial sentences in this letter are: "In another case . . . asking for a stay, Judge Hutchinson [*sic*] informed him that in his circuit it required three judges. If this be so, you might have difficulty getting them together." **Hutcheson hearing**: "Defendant Lyndon B. Johnson's Notice of Appeal, Filed Sept. 22, 1948: Johnson, Streigler, Shelley et al. v. Stevenson et al., No. 12,529, United States Court of Appeals for the Fifth Circuit, Appeal from the District Court of the U.S. for the Northern District,

Texas. **Consternation**: Jenkins interview. **Hutcheson's decision**: Hutcheson, quoted in *CCC-T*, Sept. 25. **Telephoning Black**: *CCC-T*, Sept. 26.
"**The most dramatic**": Daniels, quoted in Miller, pp. 134–35. **Truman campaign trip**: *AAS, Brownsville Herald, SAE-N, CCC-T, DMN, FWS-T*, Sept. 25–28. "Texas—September, 25, 26, 27, 28," President's Secretary's File, Box 11, HSTL; Evans and Novak, p. 25. "**My advice**": Truman, quoted in Kahl, p. 193. "**A defeated**": Carter, quoted in Dugger, p. 335.
Masters-in-Chancery Hearings: The basis for my description of these three hearings is the transcripts. They are:
1. Stevenson v. Tyson, Johnson et al., C.A. 1640, United States District Court, Northern District, Texas, Daily Transcript of Proceedings Had on Hearing Before Hon. J. M. Burnett, Special Master, San Diego, Duval County, Texas, Sept. 28, 1948. This will be referred to hereafter as "Master's Hearing, SD, transcript."
2. Stevenson v. Tyson et al., C.A. 1640, Transcript of Proceedings Had Before the Master W. R. Smith, Jr., Alice, Texas, Jim Wells County, Texas, Sept. 27, 1948. This will be referred to hereafter as "Master's Hearing, A, transcript."
3. Stevenson v. Tyson et al., C.A. 1640, Daily Transcript of Proceedings Had on Hearing Before Honorable J. B. Burnett, Special Master, Zapata, Zapata County, Texas, Sept. 29, 1948. This will be referred to hereafter as "Master's Hearing, Z, transcript."
In describing them, I have also relied on interviews with persons who were present, including Stevenson attorney Gerald L. Weatherly; Emmett Shelton, brother and law partner of Judge Raymond's attorney Polk Shelton; Alice District Attorney Frank B. Lloyd; the oral histories of Josh Groce and W. R. Smith, Jr., and my interview with Luis Salas, and his unpublished manuscript, "Box 13."
Expeditiously: Master's Hearing, A, transcript, pp. ii–xiv. **Unable to serve subpoenas**: The opening sentences of the Master's Hearing, A, transcript, p. xv, set the tone: "The Master: Come to order. Mr. Marshal, were you able to locate any of the witnesses? The Marshal: I wasn't, your Honor. The Master: You haven't found them in the county? The Marshal: I haven't found them at all.

. . . The Master: Did you find out anything about their present whereabouts? The Marshal: I wasn't able to get anything on it at all" (Master's Hearing, A, transcript, p. xv). **Only eight of fifty:** *CCC-T*, Sept. 29. **"On vacation":** Master's Hearing, SD, transcript, p. 4; Master's Hearing, A, transcript, pp. 43–44. **Donald's whereabouts:** Master's Hearing, A, transcript, pp. 37–45. **"Lay . . . hands on those records":** Smith, Master's Hearing, A, transcript, p. 40. **No hint:** Master's Hearing, A, transcript, pp. 45–48.

Unaware of judges' names: Tobin, Master's Hearing, SD, transcript, pp. 14, 16. "I can't recall the names, but I am sure I know them when I see them," Tobin said. **Salas' demeanor:** Salas, Master's Hearing, A, transcript, pp. 212 ff; Salas interview and "Box 13," p. 66; Dibrell, Rowe interviews; Kahl, pp. 199–200; *CCC-T*, Sept. 29. **"It is lost":** Salas, Master's Hearing, A, transcript, p. 145. **"So much talk"; "the election was level":** Salas, Master's Hearing, A, transcript, p. 150. **Visit to Alice News:** Master's Hearing, A, transcript, pp. 151–52. **"Viva, Luis Salas!":** Salas, "Box 13," p. 66.

Benavides testimony: *DMN*, Sept. 29; Master's Hearing, SD, transcript, pp. 99–112.

Stevenson's lawyers have affidavits: Dibrell, Stevenson, Jr., interviews; Graham OH; DC Hearing transcript, p. 4. **"Gone"; "missing":** Master's Hearing, Z, transcript, pp. 180, 188, 189. **Four envelopes become three:** Gutirez, Master's Hearing, Z, transcript, pp. 177–82. **Bravo didn't know:** Bravo, Master's Hearing, Z, transcript, pp. 184–89.

Groce's request: Master's Hearing, A, transcript, p. xvi. **Only "An express order":** Looney, Master's Hearing, A, transcript, p. xix. **"The evil days":** Tarleton, Master's Hearing, A, transcript, pp. xxv–xxvii. **"I have the power":** Smith, Master's Hearing, A, transcript, p. xxxii. **The mere fact:** Smith OH.

Black's hearing: Fortas OH and interview; Porter OH; Easley interview; McNeil, "How Fortas"; *Washington Daily News*, Aug. 3, 1965. **Civil rights issue never raised:** Weatherly interview. McNeil says it was, but others say it wasn't, or was raised only tangentially. **"To prevent the reaping":** Moody, quoted in Kahl, p. 194. **"Irrevocably":** Fortas, quoted in *AA*, Sept. 28.

Sowing confusion: Master's Hearing, A, transcript, pp. 136–70; Salas, "Box 13," pp. 224–27. **Not among the twenty:** Salas, Master's Hearing. A, transcript, p. 137. **Not one but two:** Salas, Master's Hearing, A, transcript, p. 140. **Salas' conversation with Lloyd:** Salas, "Box 13," p. 63, handwritten p. 1; Salas interview; Kahl, p. 203.

Black's verdict: McNeil, "How Fortas;" *CCC-T*, *NYT*, Sept. 29; *Harvard Law Review*, Dec. 1948, pp. 311–313; Black to Mrs. O. C. Phelan, Oct. 8, 1964, "General Correspondence, Johnson, Lyndon B.," Box 35, Papers of Hugo Black. **Smith telephoning Davidson:** Smith, Master's Hearing, A, transcript, pp. 171–72. **"The court":** Smith, Master's Hearing, A, transcript, p. 175. **Exchanges between Smith and Johnson attorneys:** Smith, Tarleton and Looney, Master's Hearing, A, transcript, pp. 175–79. **"We will open":** Smith, Master's Hearing, A, transcript, pp. 178, 185; *DMN*, Sept. 29.

Opening the boxes: Master's Hearing, A, transcript, pp. 179–85. **"The most potent":** Smith OH. **Salas' resolution had hardened:** Salas, quoted in Kahl, p. 203. **New Motion:** Master's Hearing, A, transcript, pp. 186–90.

"We object to": Tarleton, Master's Hearing, A, transcript, p. 195. **"To a lot of other things, too":** Smith, Master's Hearing, A, transcript, p. 195. **"Examining":** Looney, Master's Hearing, A, transcript, p. 198. **"A violation":** Tarleton, Master's Hearing, A, transcript, p. 200. **Opening the remaining boxes:** Master's Hearing, A, transcript, pp. 202–11. **"Let's pass [them] up":** Smith, Master's Hearing, A, transcript, pp. 249–52.

Black's order: It read "ORDERED that the temporary injunction issued by the United States District Court, for the Northern District of Texas, Fort Worth Division, on September 23rd, 1948, in the case entitled *Coke R. Stevenson vs. Lyndon B. Johnson, et al.*, Civil No. 1640, be and the same is hereby stayed, and that the temporary injunction is and shall be of no force and effect, until further order of the Supreme Court" (Johnson, Striegler et al. v. Stevenson, No. 466, Supreme Court of the United States, October term, 1948, Hugo L. Black, Sept. 29, 1948). **Scene in court:** Master's Hearing, A, transcript, pp. 253–55; *CCC-T*, Sept. 29; Rowe, Salas interviews. **"Judge Davidson has":** Smith, Master's Hearing, A, transcript, p. 253. **"I hardly see"; "I am so full":** Smith,

Groce, Master's Hearing, A, transcript, p. 267. **"It will be"**: Master's Hearing, A, transcript, p. 268.

Evidence about dead "voters": Dibrell, in an interview, confirms that three "dead" voters were found on the list at that first inspection. He says that at the time of the Master's Hearing, Stevenson's attorneys were prepared to present conclusive evidence that one of the three was dead; as for the other two, Dibrell says, "We had evidence, but not the kind of evidence we were ready to present in court" because there had not been time to obtain it. That evidence would have been ready by the time of a full trial, he says. Similarly, the attorney who represented Stevenson in the State District Court hearing in Alice—Wilbur Matthews—wrote in his memoirs that at the time of that hearing, the earliest legal proceeding in the case, the names that had been added to the Box 13 poll list "included at least one person who had died prior to the primary election" (Matthews, p. 102). Dibrell and other leaders of the Stevenson camp such as Boyett and Stevenson, Jr. feel a fuller investigation—which would have been carried out had Black not ended the legal proceedings—would have revealed the presence of "many more" votes cast in the names of dead persons.

Supreme Court refuses to reconsider stay: Journal of Proceedings of the Supreme Court, Oct. 5, 1948. **Supreme Court rejects Stevenson petition for trial**: Stevenson v. Johnson et al., Petition for Writ of Certiorari to the Court of Appeal for the Fifth Circuit and Supporting Brief (Supreme Court of the United States, October term, 1948). *DMN*, Feb. 1, 1949.

"A notable lack"; "a fancy dance": Dugger, "Two Cheers for the FBI." **"Without a trace"**: Kahl, p. 242.

Senate investigation: *HP*, Jan. 4, 1949, said that when the committee was "Republican controlled," "the rumor that Johnson would be denied his seat was widely circulated on Capitol Hill. When the Democrats won control, the rumor died immediately as to the election contest. No one in authority would speak for publication, but no one seemed to have any idea that Johnson may be unseated." See *FWS-T*, Jan. 6, 1949. See also *DMN*, Jan. 14, Feb. 1, July 28, 1949.

16. The Making of a Legend

SOURCES

Books and documents:
Baker, *The Good Times*; Dugger, *The Politician*; Evans and Novak, *Lyndon B. Johnson*; Miller, *Lyndon*; Steinberg, *Sam Johnson's Boy*.

Luis Salas, "Box 13" (unpublished manuscript).

Stevenson v. Tyson, Johnson et al., C.A. 1640, United States District Court, Northern District, Texas, Transcript of Proceedings Had Before the Master W. R. Smith, Jr., Alice, Texas, Jim Wells County (referred to hereafter as Master's Hearing, Alice, transcript).

Oral Histories:
William R. Smith.

Interviews:
Thomas G. Corcoran, Luis Salas, Harold Young.

NOTES

Smithwick letter: Smithwick to Stevenson, Mar. 23, 1952, reprinted in *DMN*, May 24, 1952. **Told him not to bother**: Stevenson, quoted in Dugger, p. 340. **"Some guards"; "somewhere"**: *FWS-T*, May 26, 1952. **Cartoon**: "The Ghost Returns," *DMN*, May 27, 1952. **"A continuation"**: Johnson, quoted in *DMN*, May 26, 1952. **"Historical Markers"**: *Texas Monthly*, Jan., 1976.

"Exactly 87 votes": Eliot Janeway, "Johnson of the 'Watchdog Committee,'" *NYT Magazine*, June 17, 1951. **"A fabulous"**: Leslie Carpenter, "The Whip from Texas," *Collier's*, Feb. 17, 1951. **"Johnson's attorneys"**: Paul F. Healy, "The Frantic Gentleman from Texas," *Saturday Evening Post*, May 19, 1951. **"His power reaches"**: Gordon Schendel, "Something Is Rotten in the State of Texas," *Collier's*, June 9, 1951.

"Likely to arise": Bill Davidson, "Lyndon Johnson: Can a Southerner Be Elected President?," *Look*, Aug. 18, 1959. **"Suspicious 87 votes"**: "Sense and Sensitivity," *Time*, Mar. 17, 1958.

"THE STORY OF 87 VOTES": *U.S. News & World Report*, Apr. 6, 1964. Many magazines ran major biographical articles on Johnson in 1964 to introduce the new President to the American people, and most recounted the story of the 1948 campaign. A two-part article in *Life* magazine, "The Man Who Is the President," examined it in detail, mentioned his ironic nickname, "Landslide Johnson," under the headline "AN 87-VOTE 'LANDSLIDE' PUT HIM IN SENATE" (Wheeler and Lambert, *Life*, Aug. 14, 21, 1964). **"It seems":** Richard Rovere, Letter From Washington, *The New Yorker*, Sept. 23, 1967. **"After Lyndon Johnson":** Tom Wicker, "Hey, Hey, LBJ . . . ," *Esquire*, Dec. 1983. **Salas interview with Mangan:** It ran in newspapers across the country on July 31, 1977. Its complete version can be found in the *San Antonio Express-News*: James W. Mangan, "Vote Fraud Put LBJ into Office." Among the scores of newspapers in which the Salas interview was displayed under banner front-page headlines were the *Boston Herald American* ("LBJ RACE CALLED 'STOLEN' "), the *Chicago Tribune* (" 'I STOLE '48 ELECTION FOR LBJ' "), the *Rocky Mountain News* ("LBJ'S ELECTION TO SENATE 'STOLEN' "), the *Sacramento Union* ("LBJ'S ELECTION FIXER TALKS"), and the *Worcester Sunday Telegram* ("POLLING OFFICIAL: PHONY VOTES STOLE '48 RUNOFF FOR LBJ"). **"Suspicions have persisted":** *Newsweek*, Aug. 8, 1977. **"I know":** Middleton, quoted in Miller, p. 137. **"I am without knowledge":** *WP*, Aug. 6, 1977. Jenkins, Rather, Herring press conference: *NYT*, *AA-S*, Aug. 2, 1977. Typical of the tone with which the documents were treated was the story in the *WP* under the headline, "LBJ MEMO CONTRADICTS FRAUD CHARGES," which stated: "Discovery of the Johnson statement came today, as 16 reporters and a bevy of television news crews examined some 5,000 documents contained in eight boxes in the archives of the LBJ Library" (*WP*, Aug. 4, 1977). In the aftermath of the Salas interview, other stories appeared detailing interviews with Parr before his death on the subject of the election, filled with inaccuracies (for example, *AA-S*, Aug. 30, 1977).

"Reader, I don't know": Luis Salas, "Box 13," p. 6. **Salas' description of his youth:** *Ibid.*, pp. 1–24. **"My life changed"; "Wearing a gun"; "I never forget this man":** *Ibid.*, pp. 32, 33, 44. **"Any vote"** . . . [smile]: Salas interview. **"Now is the year":** Salas, "Box 13," p. 25. **"We put LB Johnson":** *Ibid.*, p. 68. **"Exactly the way":** *Ibid.*, p. 6. **"How an Indian boy":** *Ibid.*, p. 70.

"Many people": *Ibid.*, p. 50. **"A good reason"; "I lied under oath":** *Ibid.*, unnumbered page following handwritten, p. 5. **"Go to the Lyndon Johnson Library":** *Ibid.*, p. 65. **"May be I":** *Ibid.*, p. 1. **"Having trouble":** *Ibid.*, unnumbered page following handwritten, p. 5. **"I gave George":** *Ibid.*, p. 50. **"I looked at Coke Stevenson"; "Asking forgivings"; "I don't blame him":** *Ibid.*, p. 66. **Description of adding the 200 votes:** *Ibid.*, pp. 57–58. **"I told Cliff":** *Ibid.*, pp. 56, 64. **"Everyone is dead":** Salas interview. **Salas recognized Johnson:** Salas interview. **DuBose testified to 765:** DuBose, Master's Hearing, Alice, transcript, pp. 30, 31. **Price testified to 765:** Price, Master's Hearing, Alice, transcript, pp. 230–31. **"I told Cliff . . . 765":** Salas interview; Salas, "Box 13," pp. 56, 64. Also, on an unnumbered page of his manuscript, an Salas wrote: "I lied under oath, that Johnson had received 967 instead of 765 votes. After closing the election voting place, I went to the *Alice News*, and gave Cliff Dubose the amount of votes received by Johnson, and they were 765, later on our party changed the amounts to reach 967, enough for Johnson to defeat Stevenson." **Holmgreen:** "I saw more votes stolen for Lyndon Johnson than Johnson won the election by," he told the *San Antonio Express-News* (July 31, 1977), quoted in Kahl, p. 93. "A ballot would be pulled from the box marked for Stevenson, but would be called out for Johnson. I know because I watched and I saw it." **Poole:** Quoted in Kahl, p. 118. **"If they were not":** Salas interview. Also see Salas, "Box 13," p. 64: "Charles Wesley Price was right, so there you are."

Smith statement: Smith OH.

Johnson in campus politics: Caro, *Path to Power*, pp. 174–201. **Johnson and the "Little Congress":** Caro, pp. 261–68. **Johnson telling the joke:** For example, Steinberg, p. 272, Baker, pp. 284–85. In 1953, when *Time* magazine ran its first cover story on Johnson, the joke was included in it (*Time*, June 22, 1953). **Johnson imitating Parr:** Hugh Sidey, *Time*, Aug. 15, 1977. **"From the start":** Steinberg, who began covering Capitol Hill for several publications, p. 276. **Johnson popularizing nickname:** In April, 1949, when the

House had passed by a 176–174 margin legislation he wanted favoring natural gas producers, Johnson, according to the *Fort Worth Star-Telegram*, "rushed to the phone and reported to his chief ally, Senator Bob Kerr of Oklahoma: 'We won by two votes—"Landslide" Johnson rides again.' " It was even in the headlines: " 'LANDSLIDE' LYNDON JOHNSON WINS AGAIN—BY TWO VOTES" (*FWS-T*, Apr. 8, 1949). Evans and Novak wrote (p. 40) that when Senate Majority Leader Scott Lucas introduced Johnson to the Democratic caucus on January 3, "he good-naturedly referred to Johnson as 'Landslide Lyndon.' To Johnson's dismay, the term stuck."

No longer wanted "Landslide" nickname used: Russell Baker, who arrived in Washington in 1954, would later write: "Duval County was a sensitive subject with Johnson. . . . If you wanted to stay on his good side, you didn't call him 'Landslide Lyndon' or otherwise joke about that election" (Baker, pp. 284–85). **By 1964:** Steinberg, p. 686. **Interview with Dugger:** Dugger, p. 341. The photograph is reproduced in this book, in photograph section III. It appeared in print: *WP*, Aug. 8, 1954.

17. A Love Story

SOURCES

Coke Stevenson's later years were described to me by Ernest Boyett, Nada and Robert W. Murphey, Coke Stevenson, Jr., Marguerite King Stevenson and Jane Stevenson Murr. Unless otherwise noted, my description of those years comes from these interviews and from my visits to the Stevenson ranch.

Among the newspaper articles written by reporters after visits to the ex-Governor during his retirement, partic-

ularly helpful were Dawson Duncan, *DMN*, Aug. 8, 1951; Frank X. Tolbert, *DMN*, Aug. 16, 1959, July 7, 1960, and undated; *HP*, Jan 19, 1964; *HC*, Apr. 6, 1969, June 29, 1975.

Also, Wyatt and Shelton, *Coke R. Stevenson: A Texas Legend.*

NOTES

"After that": Horace Busby interview.
"Fees . . . that I could write on a blackboard": Stevenson, quoted in *DMN*, Aug. 5, 1951. **Asked him to run:** *DMN*, Aug. 5, 1951; *HC*, Sept. 14, 1952. **"I would not want":** Stevenson, quoted in *DMN*, April 22, 1952. **Stacks of mail:** *DMN*, Aug. 5, 1951; *HC*, Sept. 14, 1952. **A "gifted speaker":** Marguerite Stevenson, quoted in Wyatt and Shelton, p. 167.
"Took a bride": *Junction Eagle*, quoted in Wyatt and Shelton, p. 100.
Telephone installed: For example, Frank X. Tolbert, "After 40 Years, Ex-Governor Finally Puts in a Telephone," *DMN*, undated clipping. **"At 71":** Tolbert, *DMN*, Aug. 16, 1959. **Building the garage:** Wyatt and Shelton, p. 102.
"Well, of course": *San Angelo Standard-Times*, 1964.
"After spending": *DMN*, Aug. 16, 1959. **"You sense":** The reporter's description of his day with Coke, Teeney and Jane, printed in *HC*, Apr. 6, 1969, is the basis for this scene.

18. Three Rings

NOTES

Swearing-in: *AA-S, DMN, El Paso Herald-Post, HC*, Jan. 4, 1949. **Winked; three rings:** *AA-S*, Jan. 12, 1949 (by Margaret Mayer).

Index